The Gaia Effect

The Remarkable System of Collaboration between Gaia and Humanity

KRYON

Monika Muranyi

www.ariane-books.com

Published by: Ariane Books

1217, av. Bernard O., suite 101, Outremont, Quebec, Canada H2V 1V7

Phone: (1) 514-276-2949, Fax: (1) 514-276-4121

info@editions-ariane.com – www.editions-ariane.com

© 2013 Ariane Éditions Inc

www.ariane-books.com – www.editions-ariane.com

The moral rights of the author have been asserted.

Cover design: Carl Lemyre

Interior design: Kesse Soumahoro

All rights reserved. No part of this book may be reproduced by any
mechanical, photographic or electronic process, or in the form of a
phonographic recording; nor may it be stored in a retrieval system,
transmitted or otherwise be copied for public or private use, other than for
'fair use' as brief quotations embodied in articles and reviews,
without prior written permission of the publisher.
The information given in this book should not be treated as a substitute for
professional medical advice; always consult a medical practitioner.
Any use of information in this book is at the reader's discretion and risk.
Neither the author nor the publisher can be held responsible for any loss,
claim or damage arising out of the use, or misuse, of the suggestions made,
the failure to take medical advice or for any material on third party websites.

Reprint, April 2015

ISBN: 978-2-89626-132-1 (pbk)

ISBN: 978-2-89626-231-1 (Pdf)

ISBN: 978-2-89626-150-5 (ebook)

We acknowledge the financial support of the Government of Canada through the Canada
Book Fund (CBF) for our publishing activities.

Distributed by: New Leaf

401 Thornton Rd. Lithia Springs, GA 30122-1557

Phone: 770.948.7845 – Fax: 770.944.2313

domestic@newleaf-dist.com – foreign@newleaf-dist.com.

Printed in USA

This book
is dedicated to
all Lightworkers
across the planet Earth.
It was written
in honor of
Gaia and our ancestors.

CONTENTS

ACKNOWLEDGEMENTS... ix

FOREWORD BY LEE CARROLL xi

PREFACE xiii

Chapter One: The History of the Earth 1

What does Science say? 15

Lemuria. 18

The Indigenous 31

Chapter Two: Science of the Future 43

Designer Magnetics. 49

The Missing Laws of Physics 59

What does Science say? 69

Here's what Science is saying about the rotation of our galaxy... . . . 72

Here's what Science is saying about the laws throughout
the Universe.... 73

Chapter Three: The Energy Grids of the Earth 77

The Magnetic Grid 79

The Gaia Grid. 83

The Crystalline Grid 94

Whales and Dolphins 117

The Ley Lines of Gaia 121

A Summary of the Grids 132

Chapter Four: The Kundalini of the Earth 135

Kundalini (The Letter K in Kundalini) 142

Unity (The Letter U in Kundalini) 148

Notifying Gaia of Your Conscious Actions
(The Letter N in Kundalini) 153

Don't Think Like a Human (The Letter D in Kundalini) 158

Ascension (The Letter A in Kundalini) 164

Love (The Letter L in Kundalini) 168

Intuition (The Letter I in Kundalini) 171

New Human (The Second Letter N in Kundalini) 178

Illumination (The Second Letter I in Kundalini) 183

The Eagle and the Condor 187

The Awakening of the Puma 191

A Summary of the Movement of the Kundalini 194

Chapter Five: Gaia and the Universe **203**

What does Science say? 207

Gamma Energy and Gaia 210

The Magnetics of the Solar System 212

The Solar System and Astrology 216

The Pleiadians 230

Ascended Land of Gaia 248

**Chapter Six: Unsolved Mysteries of Gaia or Part
of a System?** **253**

Hauntings – Multi-dimensional Information or Trapped Souls? . . . 255

Animals 265

Extinction of Species 270

In Closing 281

ABOUT THE AUTHOR 283

ACKNOWLEDGEMENTS

Firstly, I would like to thank Lee Carroll for all of the Kryon messages he has been giving to humanity for over 23 years. While there are many different channellers throughout the world, it is the messages from Kryon, through Lee Carroll, that resonate with me the most. Everything that Kryon talks about makes so much spiritual logic. I want to feel the love of God and at the same time I crave the information and knowledge of how the Universe works. So for my process, Kryon and Lee deliver the full package of spiritual enlightenment that I can apply in my daily life. Otherwise, what is the point? How are you helping anyone if you don't apply what you know? Thank you, Lee, for giving me encouragement and support to write this book. Thank you for also granting me permission to include the Kryon channellings and contributing the answers to the questions for Kryon that have been asked throughout this book.

I have been blessed to have several people contribute their wisdom and knowledge to the writing of this book. I would like to express my deep gratitude to Michelle Karen for sharing her immense knowledge on astrology; Laurie Reyon for sharing her story and gift as an interspecies communicator; Jorge Bianchi for inspiration to keep thinking out of the box and his knowledge about the 33 Miners Rescue in Chile; Kahuna Kalei'iliahi for sharing her wisdom and knowledge on behalf of the ancients; Intai Aguirre Farias for providing information about *Raices de la Tierra*; Bethi Black for her in-depth knowledge of The Human Design System; Peggy Phoenix Dubro for creating new energy tools that have helped accelerate my evolution; and Janusz

Grabowski for providing valuable information and knowledge about quantum physics. Thank you for all the work that you do. An extra thank you to Lourana Howard for editing the entire manuscript!

I would like to thank my publishers, Ariane Editions. Thank you for sharing my vision to help others find their spiritual truth. Thank you for turning that vision into a reality.

A big thank you to everyone who has supported me along the way. While writing this book many Lightworkers from across the planet gave me encouragement by telling me "they are really looking forward to reading it!" You know who you are and I'm deeply honored by your thoughts, words and loving support. Yes, it did make a difference.

Finally, I'd like to thank you, dear reader, for choosing to read this book. By doing so it is obvious that you are seeking spiritual knowledge and looking for things that feed your soul. Your presence on the planet makes a bigger difference than you could ever Dream. I love what we are doing, and that collectively we are all raising the vibration of the planet!

FOREWORD

BY LEE CARROLL

For a moment we all stood motionless in awe. The air was unusually still for a mountaintop, but soon the intense chilled breath of Mt. Aconcagua in the South American Andes was slowly turning our way. We silently stared at the majestic sight before us. It was the highest mountain in the Andes, and it seemed that we could almost touch the surreal snow-covered summit that shimmered in sunlight before us. Then the cool breeze touched our faces with sweetness, like a gentle sacred message being delivered specifically to our small group.

I sat down on a boulder ... there was a pause, and I began...
"Greetings, Dear Ones, I am Kryon of Magnetic Service."

The Kryon message that day is in the pages of this book, as well as many other unique Kryon messages that have never been transcribed until now. Many of them were given in some of the most sacred areas of the planet. The common denominator for all of these is that Monika Muranyi was there in person for all of them.

Monika has spent her entire professional life immersed with nature as a Ranger for the government in Australia. As she awakened to spirituality and more esoteric subjects, her passion turned to finding out more about Gaia, the consciousness of the planet. When she discovered Kryon, the light turned on. Monika wanted to do something that had never been done before: to create a compiled book with everything Kryon has ever channelled about Gaia, and more. She wanted answers to questions that might expose the beautiful workings of the Gaia energy, with which she was so in touch.

What is The Crystalline Grid and how did it get here? What is our creation story, and when was Gaia consciousness aware of humanity? What does Spirit think about the extinction of species? What are portals, nodes, nulls, vortices, vortals and "ascended land"? Her questions were profound and numerous. Within this book there are dozens of questions put to Kryon with answers that nobody has ever seen. I was happy to work on them, for they were questions that had never been asked.

There is a major shift going on within our planet, and the 2012 indigenous prophesies have told us that South America is one of the most profound areas where this shift can be felt. So in preparation for this book, Monika moved from Australia to Chile, learned enough Spanish to live alone in Santiago for a full year, and started compiling the book that is now in your hands. She wanted to be right in the middle of the energy of the GAIA shift!

She plowed through hundreds of Kryon audio channellings, most of which have never been transcribed. She read every Kryon book that might have Gaia information, and attended most Kryon events in South America. The culmination of her work coordinated with the Kryon Kundalini Tour in late 2012. This 19-day tour found our group in sacred energetic places like Mt. Aconcagua, Machu Picchu, and The Island of the Sun in Lake Titicaca.

Within the 23 years of my Kryon channelling, nowhere is there a compilation of what Kryon has channelled about a singular subject. With 15 Kryon books in 23 languages, I have never compiled a summary that was subject-driven like this one.

Now you have in your hands the kind of book I was never able to do.

Thank you, Monika, for this very complete information about our beautiful planet.

Lee Carroll

PREFACE

A s a child growing up, I loved nature. Despite living in a suburban house with a small backyard in Canberra, Australia, I had a large variety of pets that came and went from my life. These included ducks, geese, guinea pigs, a rabbit, a turtle, cats and dogs. My love of dogs meant that I would often come home with a stray dog, much to my mother's dismay. The strays would never stay long, but long enough until they could find another home. I also loved horses and all the other farm animals. What kid doesn't want a pony? As a young adult I was able to fulfill my fantasy. I had the most amazing experiences riding horses, mustering cattle, milking dairy cows and enjoying the taste of rural farming life in between my university studies.

I went to University to undertake a Bachelor of Applied Science with a focus on Conservation Technology. The University was located in Lismore, New South Wales, which meant that our field trips were often in spectacular rainforests or magnificent coastal beaches and environs. My favorite subject was Techniques in Animal Conservation, which greatly influenced my decision to do an Honors Thesis. The purpose of my thesis was to investigate the population dynamics of a rodent native to Australia. Yes, I actually went out every three weeks to trap and release native rats known as the Pale Field Rat (*Rattus tunneyi*). Pale Field Rats are so much friendlier than your common Bush Rat and I truly believe that some rats that were caught more than once remembered me.

After graduating from University with my Honors degree, I did several different jobs in the environmental field before returning back

to my hometown of Canberra, where I eventually became a park ranger with the ACT Parks and Conservation Service. It was more than just a job, as anyone working in that industry will tell you. I was doing something that I felt passionate about and I have been blessed in the many experiences I've had over the years. I also was able to experience working as a Ranger with the Department of Conservation in New Zealand and Parks Victoria in Victoria, Australia.

Many of the programs I was involved in related to endangered species, and developing recovery programs to save these species from extinction. All across the world you will find government agencies, volunteer groups and private industry focused on trying to save endangered species. There is also a greater awareness of the importance of ensuring that wild plants and animals are sustainably harvested. I have often wondered why there is such an imbalance between humans and the natural ecosystem.

Being passionate about nature, and working in the environmental field, results in an awareness of the many environmental problems and challenges that face our Earth today because of what humans do. Pollution, deforestation, unsustainable harvesting practices, extinction of species and worst of all – over population of humans!

I was absolutely convinced that humans were the root of all evil in regards to our planet Earth, and if we weren't careful, we were going to destroy the planet and eventually ourselves. Imagine my surprise to discover that I couldn't be further from the truth.

I now have a much deeper understanding of our planet Earth – GAIA – that goes way beyond my academic qualifications and years spent working as a Ranger. In order to unlock the secrets of Gaia, however, it is necessary to go beyond the veil. But what does that mean "to go beyond the veil"? What does that phrase mean to you? And more importantly, how does one get across to the other side of the veil? The answers are likely to vary depending on who you talk to. For me, it is something you achieve when you drop the 3D logic of your brain. Notice I said 3D. You still need spiritual intelligence. Next, you allow all of your other senses to activate. You open your heart. Let yourself feel and sense the emotions. Listen to your intuition and your innermost thoughts. Allow your own "knowingness" to talk to you. That's the best way I can describe it, but it may not make sense if you can't get out of 3D thinking and logic. I guess it comes down to you wanting to know more. Having pure intent to find the divinity that is inside you.

Everyone has their own story about how they started their awakening process, and experienced the other side of the veil. I guess because I am so stubborn, and have an extremely logical brain and scientific mind, I needed something a little dramatic to get my attention. When my marriage ended, it was an incredibly powerful personal trauma that brought me to my knees. Seemingly overnight my world as I knew it had collapsed, and I felt so alone, abandoned and unloved. I realized that I didn't really know or understand anything. I was in a very dark place. It was only then I was open to receiving help from the Universe.

The darkness that I was in started to shift when I had three sessions from a very gifted Lightworker. Actually, as further evidence of my resistance and stubbornness, my logical brain nearly stopped me from this experience. I only agreed to one session because my work colleague and friend Rod kept telling me, in a very gentle and loving way, to see his wife Lynda for a spiritual healing. Every time Rod saw me he would gently say, *"You should go see Lynda."* He could obviously see how distressed and miserable I was. It got to the point where the next time I saw Rod, and he repeated his advice, I screamed in my mind, *"Okay, I will go see her and get it over and done with so you can stop telling me to see her!"* After all, I thought, *"nothing will happen!"* My situation couldn't get any worse. I had nothing to lose.

The day of my session arrived and I remember thinking, *"Here we go. Let's get it over."* But as I walked through the door, my whole reality started to shift. Before I knew it, a floodgate of tears was pouring out of my being. What triggered this outburst? It was looking into Lynda's eyes and seeing within her so much love and compassion. I had met someone with great spiritual knowledge and second sight. Before leaving that day, I booked some more sessions with Lynda that opened up the door for me to start learning and understanding esoteric things. I was ready for Spirit to enter my life and show me more.

As I kept surrendering myself and suspending my previous ideas of what I thought about life and God, I became more and more aware of spiritual truths. I discovered these spiritual truths coexist with science, something that I had always seen as being separate. Eventually, I wasn't

just learning the wisdom and knowledge, I was remembering it. I had discovered that inside of me is a divine spark of God. Within each and every single Human Being there is divinity. All of us are a piece of God, which is found within our DNA.

And what if I hadn't found this spiritual truth? Well, I would still be looking at the planet Earth with my three-dimensional filter, and only seeing and observing parts of the puzzle. I would not have been able to understand the elegant design and system that exists between Gaia and humanity. I would have been stuck in a world where I only understood pieces and parts of a system, never understanding the role I have in creating the life I want.

This book is essentially for those people who are on their spiritual path. Whether you have just begun, or been walking this path for decades, there is something here for you. The information presented is an esoteric study of Gaia, our planet Earth, and the intricate relationship that is shared with humanity and the Universe. The writings have been driven by the channelled messages from Kryon, as given by Lee Carroll. Kryon can be described as a loving, angelic entity that gives messages of peace and empowerment for humanity. Lee Carroll is the original Kryon channel and has been giving the messages from Kryon for over 23 years. Lee is the author of twelve Kryon books and the co-author of *The Indigo Children*, *An Indigo Celebration* and *The Indigo Children Ten Years Later*. These books have been translated into over 24 languages.

If you are a fan of Kryon, and read many of the books written by Lee Carroll, you may already be familiar with most of the information presented here. What this book does, however, is to synthesize all of the information relating to Gaia into a concise form in order to reveal the profound truths about humanity and the planet Earth. In addition, Kryon has provided some profound answers to over 40 questions relating to the topics within this book. The Kryon channels that have been used as excerpts in the book are available as audio files from Lee Carroll's website: *www.kryon.com*

If you are new to the Kryon work, or perhaps you have never heard of Kryon but you have an open mind or heart, be prepared to read about things that may seem unbelievable. There are a lot of subjects covered within the book. The name of each chapter is a guide to the type of information presented. Although the book is intended to be read in its entirety from start to finish, some readers may prefer to consult only those chapters that are of interest to them.

The information contained within this book is a blend of scientific and esoteric (spiritual) information. This is deliberate and intentional because it is the way things work. The quicker we can dispel the notion that God and science are two separate things, the quicker we can forge ahead with new discoveries and enlightenment. You cannot have higher science without enlightenment. The very fact that you have chosen to read this book is a good indication that you are already on your path to enlightenment and, therefore, potentially higher scientific consciousness! The Universe resounds with joy and celebration that you will read these words and hear the messages that come from the other side of the veil.

But what about the skeptical reader who has decided to look at this book out of mild curiosity? Maybe it has been given to you by a friend who is very insistent you read it! Perhaps you are a physicist or astronomer who is not interested in any of the esoteric information? You just want to get to the hard facts and science that may assist you in your next scientific breakthrough. I would like to ask you something. How do you describe love? Do you use science? Or is there something else going on? What if you could suspend your beliefs and what you think you know for just a few moments while you read some of the channels from Kryon? It may even be worth listening to one of the many free audios of the Kryon channels found on Lee's website. What have you got to lose? Words are just words, aren't they? What if they're not?

Let me explain. How would you feel if a stranger walking in the street suddenly turned to you, looked you in the eyes and said, *"I love you."* Would you feel anything or are these simply words? Now, compare that to being with someone whom you have developed a bond with. Someone you trust completely. Someone who opens your heart. What is it that you feel when they look you in the eyes and speak from their heart to say, *"I love you."* Does it feel any different than when the stranger said it? Words are just words, aren't they?

And so the real purpose behind all the topics in this book is to provide you with information to spark the remembrance of wisdom and knowledge that already exists within you. To let you know that there is a loving God, a benevolent Universe, and we are all part of a beautiful system.

You could ask yourself, is this book about Gaia or is it about humanity? Is it about the Universe or is it about God? When you realize that all of these things are interwoven together like a soup of energies, that they are entangled, you will find that you can't separate and compartmentalize them into different categories. It is my hope that you, dear reader, are able to synthesize all of this information and realize the personal message that is here just for you. You are a magnificent piece of God and EVERYTHING you do affects Gaia and humanity.

As Kryon says, *"Blessed is the Human Being who takes his spiritual life seriously. It's not an addition to your biology. Instead, your biology is an addition to that which is your spiritual core."*

Finally, it has not been possible to include everything about Gaia in this book. Additional chapters are on my website: *www.monikamuranyi.com* under the "Extras" tab.

Love and blessings,

Monika Muranyi

Chapter One

The History of the Earth

If you decide to do a bit of research, and find out about the history of the Earth and how it was created, you will find information from various natural science fields that will describe things mostly in geological and biological terms. In fact, a very good summary can be found on the BBC website: Nature – Prehistoric Life.

The Earth is a little over 4.5 billion years old, its oldest materials being 4.3 billion-year-old zircon crystals. Its earliest times were geologically violent, and it suffered constant bombardment from meteorites. When this ended, the Earth cooled and its surface solidified to a crust – the first solid rocks. There were no continents as yet, just a global ocean peppered with small islands. Erosion, sedimentation and volcanic activity – possibly assisted by more meteor impacts – eventually created small proto-continents which grew until they reached roughly their current size 2.5 billion years ago. The continents have since repeatedly collided and been torn apart, so maps of Earth in the distant past are quite different to today's.

The history of life on Earth began about 3.8 billion years ago, initially with single-celled prokaryotic cells, such as bacteria. Multicellular life evolved over a billion years later and it's

only in the last 570 million years that the kind of life forms we are familiar with began to evolve, starting with arthropods, followed by fish 530 million years ago (Ma), land plants 475Ma and forests 385Ma. Mammals didn't evolve until 200Ma and our own species, Homo sapiens, only 200,000 years ago. So humans have been around for a mere 0.004% of the Earth's history.

Source: http://www.bbc.co.uk/nature/history_of_the_earth

The above summary gives a reasonable account of what I would call scientific observation. However, what is lacking is how does humanity fit into all of this? Why have we come into being on the planet at the last possible minute? Billions of years of the planet evolving and humans have only been here for 0.004 percent of it! How do you explain that? The explanation requires you to look beyond the scientific observation and beyond our three-dimensional bias. The history of the Earth needs to be understood in conjunction with the history of humanity, because the consciousness of the Earth, known as Gaia, is all about humanity.

For billions of years, the development of life on Earth was all in preparation for humanity, and Gaia was the one regulating the timing of when she was ready for humanity to show. Humanity as defined by divinity, not evolution. There were at least four attempts to start life on Earth, and the final one succeeded only when there was photosynthesis. Humanity was delayed on purpose, and there were two reasons for the delay. The first reason was to let the solar system settle down so that all the rocks, asteroids and comets would find their orbits and not hit the Earth. The second reason was to ensure that humans would be in alignment for when the Pleiadians were ready to seed us with their divinity.

So the Earth is very old – while humanity is not. Enlightened Human Beings began when the planet was touched by sacred design. Kryon describes it in the following way:

With sacred design, this planet was visited in a quantum way by enlightened creatures who were not angels. It's hard to describe how such a thing would be, but it was. Listen, there is life abundant in this Universe, and some of it is in lessons like you and some of it is not. There are biological creatures living on planets like yours, with atmospheres like yours, but where there is no war. They live in a quantum state, where there is agreement of what they're there for. They represent societies twice as old as Earth. Humanity and such an enlightened group existed back then and it still does to this day. It is located light years away from you, yet you were visited by them easily. They came to this planet to plant the seeds of sacredness within your DNA. They came with permission, by design, and within the agreement of all the angelic beings in the Universe. It wasn't an accident, and it wasn't part of a conquering plan. It was their loving job...

...What they gave this planet is difficult to describe to you in a three-dimensional discourse. For, using the gifts of being in a quantum state with everything, they gave humanity on the planet two extra layers of DNA. And it happened all at once to only one of the 26 kinds of humans, the kind you have now. Only one kind was ready to receive this gift.

Kryon live channelling "The History of Humanity" given in the western Mediterranean Sea. 8th Annual Kryon Cruise – August/September 2007

According to Kryon, the divine Human Being was created through sacred design, and humanity's parents are the Pleiadians, who came from the Seven Sisters Constellation. Over the years, Kryon has given information about the timeline of when the Pleiadians seeded the planet, and sometimes the dates seem confusing. During a recent channel, however, while on a cruise ship docked in a Hawaiian port, Kryon gave clarification on the timing of creation.

Greetings, dear ones, I am Kryon of Magnetic Service. There should be no reason for any anxiety that my partner would feel in a channel such as this. In the hundreds of times he has sat in the chair and used the portal through which his Higher-Self comes in, a clean and clear message from a messenger he is very familiar with comes through. Yet there is anxiety – there always is when he is in the shadow of the mountain of Lemuria [Hawaii]. For this is an energy which he recognizes, but he does not recognize the things that are hidden from him, which are in his Akash.

Therefore, the energy of where you sit now is ripe for information that I wish to bring and that my partner is nervous about, only because he's home and has his most profound Akashic remembrance here. For the listener and reader, we shall tell where we are sitting so that you will understand. First of all, we are upon the water. But in this particular situation [the ship is docked], we are not moving. The past channels on board these vessels have been easier for my partner because he and the others were moving [the ship was under way]. That is to say, there was no grounding element at all [totally separated from the land]. But here and now, although you are floating and although you are anchored, it is dichotomy, you might say, that you are indeed grounded by being in the "static" [not moving] presence of The Crystalline Grid. This is a combination that produces an energy that is unique, for the water is reflective and so the energy is indeed similar.

Today it's a reflective energy of the past, reflective of history, and reflective of you and the part you might have played in this place where you literally sit "in the shadow of the mountains of Lemuria." If I could take you back in time, there would be no harbor here. As we have indicated before, the peaks of these mountains were far, far higher than they are now. For a geological anomaly involving the hot spot [the attribute of the Hawaiian mountain chain] took place, which created a bulge in the crust of the Earth that pushed this mountain higher – not quite all the way out of the water, but enough so that the peaks that you now call the Hawaii Islands were always covered with snow and ice. Even glaciers formed here in Lemuria (up to 30,000 ft. high) and the peaks of these mountains were where the work was done that is considered sacred, and today it gives an entirely different feeling to the tropics that you now experience. Back then it was COLD![1]

---

1   There is credibility for this possibility that the hot spot of the Hawaiian chain of mountains could have been greatly elevated at one time. Another hot spot called Yellowstone on the mainland of the USA has recently been discovered to also have a "bulge" in its geologic history. It raised the elevation of the mountains high enough for glaciers to form. The elevated single mountain of Hawaii has been Kryon's reported history of Lemuria for more than 15 years, and only recently are we seeing some geologic precedence that this "bulge" premise also could have happened in Hawaii.

So now my partner gets information about himself that he does not know. Perhaps that is why he is apprehensive. He doesn't like the cold, even to this day. He has selected those areas of his life, literally for hundreds of lifetimes, that would never again put him in a situation where he would experience frozen winters. He knows the lifetimes that have been showed him by the readers (past life readers) of where he's been and what he has done, even to the next lifetime of where he is going! None of them have frozen winters because of what happened right here (Lemuria). For my partner, the one who sits in the chair, the Human Being who is the Lemurian you are looking at was a messenger. The job of the messenger in Lemuria was to run up and down these hills from those areas which were not so cold to the areas that needed communication up high, for there was no other way to communicate efficiently. So he was constantly cold. There are places that he has not visited on this island today for that very reason. The pathways bring up too much of a memory for him of being uncomfortable, and it carries through to his Akash from the time he was Lemurian to this day. So now you know why he is a "warm weather man."

The Times of Lemuria

This shifting energy is now ready to reveal many things about the Earth, about Lemuria, and about how things transpired here. Each year that goes by seems to clear the communication on The Crystalline Grid, allowing for something to be given that is more succinct for you, so you will have a better understanding of the plan that took place on this planet and when it occurred.

This sacred plan was in place in other areas for a very long time. It's a galactic plan, and it graduated to an energy which then included you. It, therefore, started something in this very place that was different from any other place on the planet. This sacred plan was brought to Earth, and it was implemented all at once and was "planetary wide." But here is where it was *sequestered* and matured at a rate that created a civilization that could not occur any other place. It was confined to this mountain, and the humans here couldn't leave. And so literally thousands of years went by when this particular mountain was pushed up out of the water

and the civilization lived upon it, which literally helped create what we will call the *soul seeds of the Cave of Creation*.

There are a lot of Lemurians awakening as old souls on this planet who had a turn taken [had a lifetime] on this mountain, and the ones who sit in the chairs today are among them. You [the ones in the group in front of Lee] will feel it at some level; you feel it. There are some things that are hiding in the scheme of this planet, including the real consciousness of Gaia itself, that have to do with you. Now, I've just shown my partner what we are going to do and now he's even more anxious. For when we get into the history and the dates and the concepts that he has not seen before, he gets nervous. He wants it to be correct, accurate, and true to the information given him. So I say to him, *"Just stay clear. The words will come out perfectly. They will come out logically, for this is the promise and always has been, that the synthesis of a multi-dimensional being-energy called Kryon will meld in a confluence of thought and energy that creates a three-dimensional structured conversation"*. This is his gift – accurate and grounded translation of Spirit.

The Timeline

I wish to again give you the timeframe of the seeding of this planet and honor your spiritual parents, those who you would call the Pleiadians. It has been confusing in the past, so not only do I give you the timeframe that will help unscramble the puzzle from previous channels, but also I'm going to give you a fact that we have never spoken of, which starts to explain something on the planet – a question that never was asked. It's one of my specialties, bringing up things no one thinks of, due to a 3D bias of "the way things are." We have said recently that 200,000 years ago was the approximate timeframe of the seeding of the planet Earth with enlightenment. But a few years ago, we also told you that Lemuria was only 50,000 years old and that the seeds of it were here in Hawaii. We've also given you information about what happened 100,000 years ago (actually more like 90,000 years ago). These things would seem to be contradictory to each other if you felt that the descriptions were of the same attribute, but they are not. So we start slowly. The question that is never asked is this: *"Why is there only one kind of Human Being on the planet, when there are dozens of kinds of other mammals? What changed in the evolution of humans that would cause this?"*

The Pleiadian Involvement

About 200,000 years ago, when the Pleiadians first came to Earth, humanity was a group, a variety like all the other evolution on the planet. The mammal called Human Being had many varieties of forms. Like other mammals today, variety insured survival. Up to 26 kinds of humans were present, but were eventually reduced to 17 kinds before the Pleiadians got here (through normal evolutionary processes). This was the puzzle for the Pleiadians, for in the seeding of the planet back then, the DNA had to change to allow for the spiritual, Pleiadian DNA complement. Humanity needed to end up with one kind of Human Being, the kind that you have today, but also to have the "DNA of the cosmos." That kind of Human has no variety like the other mammals of Earth, as you may have noticed or not. It's the way you are today.

So you are unique in an evolutionary way to everything you see around you. This process created a 23-chromosome Human Being, when all around you there were the 24 of conventional mammals. So the fusing of portions of your DNA to create the 23 was the element of the Pleiadians who came in and gave you their DNA. In the process, many things happened simultaneously.

When a farmer looks at his field and decides to grow corn, he surveys it in a different way than those who would eventually eat the corn. For the eater of the corn would ask, *"When does the corn exist for consumption?"* He would then be told, *"It exists when the stalks are high and it is then collected, cooked, and provided on the table."* That would be the *story of corn* for the consumer. It starts with the collection of grown corn. But the farmer looks at it differently. He looks at the raw land that has to be plowed and fertilized, and perhaps turned over a few times with other crops to allow nitrogen in the soil until the dirt is ready. Perhaps he would plant it and then take the seedlings as they came up and turn them into the ground again; you know the story. So the farmer would have an entirely different idea of *the story of corn.*

So you have at least two questions and scenarios, don't you? When did corn begin? The eater gives you one answer and the farmer another. So which is which? It depends who's asking – the consumer of the corn or the grower of the corn. Now, there's a third question: What about the conceiver (creator) of the corn? Who made corn? When? I give you this as an example as to why the dates are different, and I'm going to give you all of them. Then I'm going to tell you what happened. I'm going to be succinct and I'm not going to draw it out.

The First Look

About 200,000 years ago is when it literally began. The concept of the "divine seeding" of planet Earth happened at that point, and the fields metaphorically started to be plowed. There is an issue and we're going to call it the *way species work with Gaia*. This is something that happened simultaneously with the *grid creation* of Gaia. For now we give you something that no one has thought about. When we speak of the *grids of the planet*, you make an assumption that these grids always existed on the planet. For the planet is old and you might say, *"Well the grids have always been there."* But I'm here to tell you that only one was always there, and that's the magnetic grid. But it was spiritually void. That is to say, it only had that which was created from the Earth's core movement. Today, when we talk about the grids of the planet, our conversation involves the consciousness of humanity, which is imbued upon the magnetic grid. We also tell you about The Crystalline Grid and about the *Grid of Gaia Consciousness*. Both of these react to Human compassion.

Now, here is the puzzle: If you don't have divine Human consciousness, then what about the grids? Do they exist without the Human Being? The answer is that they needed to be created simultaneously with the seeding of divine DNA. So what the Pleiadians did was not only to start the seeds of humanity's change into divine DNA, but they created the *conscious grids of Gaia* as well. They had to, for the conscious grids of Gaia are a confluence of humanity's decisions brought to Gaia's energy. The consciousness that we are talking about is the spiritually sanctioned Human Being that exists with a piece of God inside him, and with DNA that has 23 chromosomes instead of the common 24 that all the others have through biological evolution.

Let us back up and say it again and make it simpler, my partner [admonition to Lee to speak more plainly]. The triad of grids on this planet that we have spoken of over and over are the consciousness grids of Gaia, and were created at the same time as the seeding of humanity with Pleiadian DNA. For all the teachings we've been giving, especially about The Crystalline Grid, these grids have been reacting to Human consciousness and compassion. Therefore, the very essence of the current Gaia energy is also related to the creation of humanity.

These are the attributes of the Pleiadians' work 200,000 years ago, and it was done quantumly in ways that you have no conscious awareness of at the moment. For these things are beyond your ability to understand right now, since you are still in a single-digit dimensionality. But the result back then was "a conscious Gaia." So you might say Gaia itself was actually created quantumly from the Seven Sisters energy, just like you.

The Gaia that existed before then was still Gaia, but not as it is now. It was a Gaia that was creating the dirt on the Earth and the energy of biological life of the Earth. It was the mother of all life on the planet, but not a Gaia that responded to Human consciousness. That's very different. So Gaia greatly expanded when the Pleiadians came, and that was by design.

It took 110,000 years for this to settle itself, and for the ground to be ready for more than 16 species of Human Beings to leave so that only one was left. When that occurred at approximately 90,000 years ago is when you can start calibrating who humans were and who they became.

The Others

Now, what about all of those other types of humans, and how did they leave? I'm going to give you an attribute of something that exists even today. This is difficult for my partner, for he has not heard this before. This information has not been brought in this fashion before. Go slowly, my partner.

The variety of species on this planet comes and goes accordingly as they are needed for the energy they create. So one of the tasks of Gaia is to create and eliminate species. When they are no longer needed for the purpose of Gaia's development, they cease to exist and they die out. If new life is necessary, if new concepts of life are needed, Gaia is cooperative and they are then created. The actual creation of species is something that environmentalists have not clearly seen. That is to say, the mechanics of how it works is not fully recognized as something that is strongly coordinated with your weather. But you have already seen the mechanics of some of this in your long-term studies, for you have already noted the coming and going of many species through the ages. It's ongoing.

The Appropriateness of the Elimination of Species

Now, along come humans and they see all this coming and going of living things, but they want to save them all – all the species that exist. For in their linear mind, all species should remain and exist, since they are here. The attribute of Gaia, however, is to eliminate them, cull them out, to bring in new ones. I just gave you the mechanics of the reasons species come and go. It's appropriate and is a natural building process for new species.

When the Pleiadians started to create the grids of the planet, Gaia *cooperated* in what was to come, knew the purpose, and what was needed for survival of this new spiritual Human. Gaia knew this, since the energy of Gaia had seen it before [reason given below]. So the old attribute, which needed many kinds of Human Beings, slowly died out. It was natural. There was not a war. There were no horrible plagues. There were no volcanoes or tsunamis that consumed them. Through attrition, appropriateness, and 110,000 years, they disappeared.

So approximately 110,000 years ago, there was only one kind left, and this is science, for everything that you study will bear this out, and anthropologists have already seen it and have asked, *"What happened back then at this time that would have eliminated these other kinds of Human variety?"* It's a puzzle in science that I have just answered, for science looks only for physical events as triggers.

But instead, it's the marriage of Gaia consciousness that you call "Mother Nature," which facilitated this. It's the same today when you see a variety of species diminish as humans take over a greater portion of the Earth. I'll call this "the appropriate elimination of unique life forms, which allow for the growth of global awareness and quantum evolution." Some species only exist to allow others to climb the ladder of nature, then they disappear. Gaia knows what the ladder looks like. You don't.

The Spiritual Link

So historically, this "creation of one kind of Human" also started the esoteric engine of the pattern of spiritual life on the planet, where you could then start to measure the soul energy, a quantum energy of spirituality that is allied to Gaia. It's the very work that you're attempting today as you try to track the history of spirituality and what the intuition was of the creator of that system. Human consciousness is quantum energy, and it is the *sum of all souls*.

Now we're at 90,000 years ago. We are looking at the Human Being who has 23 chromosomes ... the ones of the Seven Sisters. It then took another 50,000 years for this Human to develop into a quantum, sentient Human Being who could put together a civilization without any previous organizational model. It takes generations of trial and error for this, even though it seems normal to you today. All cooks know that it takes a very long time to cook a quality meal. Without a recipe or any training, how long would it take a Human who had never seen a kitchen or food ingredients to create a truly gourmet 7-course meal through trial and error only. It's similar, and things did not move as quickly as they do today. This was the very beginning of humanity trying to figure out how to make things work for groups of humans together.

Wisdom is learned this way, and time is the stove of the wisdom meal. The attributes of consciousness that the Pleiadians put in place through a 23-chromosome Human Being created growth, and every single generation got wiser with time. Eventually, far beyond Lemuria, Human DNA would develop an efficiency that would allow for what you see today – the divinity inside a Human

Being that is recognized and sensed almost at birth and a population of almost 7 billion people, where more than 80 percent believe in the same God and even the afterlife [today's civilization].

Lemuria's History

Now we're at 50,000 years ago. It took another 20,000 years to build the Temples of Rejuvenation and have the old souls begin to appear, the kind that you were part of.

Now we're at 30,000 years ago. This truly is the timeframe of the Lemuria we speak of now when we say, "The civilization of Lemuria." For that's a mature Lemuria, and one that had developed spiritually far more than any civilization on the planet at that time. The island has created a pure group of spiritually seeded humans. We've told you the rest of the story. When the bubble of the Earth's crust began to subside (which had lifted up the land), the mountain of Lemuria slowly started to sink. Lemurians scattered and took to boats, not knowing if there would be any land left.

While Lemuria was in its prime, there were thousands of years where this mountain contained an unchanging Lemuria, and it was like a pressure cooker of information, lineage, training, and experience. It never changed, and that which was learned here was different from the other places of the planet. In other areas, humans could go forth and do whatever they wanted. All they had to do was pick up and leave! But not here (Lemuria). So, here, they were forced to find ways to deal with the common problems of living together.

So this became the place where the Akash of humanity chose to train old souls. Humans would come in only one time, then go back and incarnate to another place on the planet. Therefore, there were a lot of souls who came through Lemuria within the last 20,000 years, who lived at the base of these very mountains where you are currently floating. It also explains why there are so many Lemurians on the planet now – think of it as a Pleiadian school.

The Lemurian Awakening

There is an awakening going on, dear ones, and the awakening right now on this planet involves your brothers and sisters who spent time running up and down these hills. Many of the old souls today spent time here, and they are all over the planet.

There was a special group of Lemurians who were able to use the Temple of Rejuvenation (at the tops of the mountain) on a regular basis. It greatly extended their lives. I have discussed this for years. They were the royalty and the "keeper of secrets." They outlived most of the other Lemurians by up to three times, but they needed to, since they were the ones with the original knowledge. This was the way of preserving the ancient ways in Lemuria and keeping the sacred information pure.

As I told you, my partner gets cold easily. He was in the Temple of Rejuvenation many times, and this is his association with Yawee (Dr. Todd Ovokaitys), and some of you know who this is. For as a messenger, he was the one who carried sacred information – the secrets – back and forth to the Temples. The Lemurians of the day did not want to share those secrets with many. Therefore, my partner had a very, very long life. He continued to be rejuvenated in the temples as many times as even those of royalty. This messenger lived a very long time and he spent lifetimes as one soul here, and the whole time he was here, he was cold. Now, for the first time, I've given my partner the reason he comes here, and why he feels so connected to this land – and doesn't like being cold!

Gaia is Part of You

Gaia and the consciousness grids of this planet were all created at the same time you were, through the same energies you were, from the same source you were. Today, if you could go to a special existing planet in the constellation of what you would call the Seven Sisters, a constellation which to this day is celebrated on this island [Hawaii], and talk to them, you would see something you recognize. They have a name for the energy of their planet. It's not the word "Gaia," but it's close. They also have a Crystalline Grid and, of course, a magnetic grid. They have a Gaia-like grid. They had to, for all of that was quantumly transported here! The very

grids of this planet, the ones that we are calling *the consciousness grids*, are also Pleiadian! Now you know, and perhaps this is news you didn't expect, given to you in an energy that can only be given as we sit here in the shadow of the mountain that used to be cold.

That's enough for today. It's your history, Lemurian. So here's the invitation for those who sit in front of me: I want to challenge you right now to feel what is here. This is for only one reason – so that you will be spiritually rejuvenated and so your Akash can be activated as it remembers. Let your body emotionally validate what you already suspected: You're an old soul and there's a reason why you're awakening now and why you're on this particular journey [the cruise].

Oh there's more, but that's enough for now, that's enough for now.

And so it is.

Kryon live channelling "The Timing of Creation"
given in Hawaii. 11th Kryon Cruise – August 12, 2012

As Kryon describes above, slowly, over 50,000 years, humans began to become spiritual, and the Lemurian society started. 40,000 years ago, the Earth was rotating at 28 degrees on its axis, different from what it rotates on today. It was the end of an ice age, and one third of all the water on the planet was ice. The average temperature was 8 degrees lower than what it is today. The temperature of the planet is dependent on how much water is on it. The water cycle of the planet is what controls the temperature and the wind.

The average water level of the oceans was 133 meters (400 feet) lower than what it is today. Fifteen thousand years ago, the ice started melting. It melted slowly over 5,000 years. The water balance of the Earth changed and poured into valleys. The new weight distribution of the water had a significant effect on the movement of the Earth's crust, and many earthquakes took place. 10,000 years ago, the water stopped rising, and the water level became similar to what exists today.

The water cycle of the Earth is what makes the planet warm and cold. It is dynamic – always in motion. This planet has experienced many temperature changes that are all part of normal cycles. There have been several small ice cycles recently. These cycles are evident when you study the advance and retreat of the many glaciers that are found around the planet. One thing that all of these small ice events have in common is that the temperature rises at the beginning of a water cycle, and then, eventually, the temperature gets lower. This warming at the beginning is typical, cyclical and normal.

The interesting thing is that recorded civilization started approximately 4,000 years ago. There is never any reference to the Lemurian society. This had been part of the plan, but there is now a shift going on, and the old Lemurian souls on the planet are starting to awaken and discover the truth that is being communicated to them through their DNA.

What does Science say?

I would like to address some of the information that Kryon has given. Kryon states that there were up to 26 kinds of Human Beings that were reduced to 17 when the Pleiadians arrived to give us the seeds of enlightenment. That was 200,000 years ago. 110,000 years ago we ended up with only one kind of Human. 90,000 years ago was really when humans were able to put together a civilization, and 50,000 years ago was the beginning of Lemuria (in Hawaii).

How many times have you seen or read information about the different kinds of humans that existed on the planet? When I went to university I don't remember ever learning about this. This seems quite odd, don't you think? If you are a Kryon fan, and have read all of Lee Carroll's books, then you probably remember Lee getting very excited when he spotted the cover of the January 2000 issue of *Scientific American* in an airport. You will even find the magazine cover presented in Kryon Book Eight, *Passing the Marker,* on page 369. So what was all the excitement about? I think the title speaks for itself:

> *"We Were Not Alone. Our species had at least 15 cousins. Only we remain. Why?"*

It is truly worth reading the article if you ever get your hands on a copy. In the meantime, here are a few excerpts from the article, written by Ian Tattersall, so that you get an idea of what science has been discovering about our evolution.

"*Homo sapiens* has had the Earth to itself for the past 25,000 years or so, free and clear of competition from other members of the hominid family. This period has evidently been long enough for us to have developed a profound feeling that being alone in the world is an entirely natural and appropriate state of affairs...

...The "single-species hypothesis" was never very convincing – even in terms of the rather sparse hominid fossil record of 35 years ago...

...Although the minimalist tendency persists, recent discoveries and fossil reappraisals make clear that the biological history of hominids resembles that of most other successful animal families. It is marked by diversity rather than by linear progression. Despite this rich history – during which hominid species developed and lived together and competed and rose and fell – H. *Sapiens* ultimately emerged as the sole hominid. The reasons for this are generally unknowable... "

What do you think? Is it unknowable? Or, do you think Kryon has given us the answer and it lies within our sacred DNA (smile).

So there is evidence that there was more than one kind of Human. What evidence is there, however, that humans were on the planet 200,000 years ago? New dating techniques have indicated that Human fossils found in Africa are 195,000 years old. In an article called "Oldest Human Fossils Identified" by Hillary Mayell for National Geographic News, we discover that:

"The new date also widens the gap between when anatomically modern humans emerged and when 'cultural' traits – such as the creation of art and music, religious practices, and sophisticated tool-making techniques – seem to have appeared. Evidence of culture is not extensively documented in the archaeological record until around 50,000 years ago."

Source: http://news.nationalgeographic.com/news/2005/02/0216_050216_omo.html

Isn't it interesting that scientists are making the distinction between modern Human anatomy and modern Human behavior! By the way, if you are wondering why the Human fossil remains found on Hawaii are not very old, I'll give you a hint. Nearly all of the land that the Lemurians lived on is now mostly under water. The islands of Hawaii are actually all part of one large mountain. The mountain known as Mauna Loa on the island of Hawaii (otherwise known as the Big Island) is the world's biggest mountain as measured from its true base, at the bottom of the ocean.

Finally, is there any evidence about this so-called fusing of chromosomes, in which we went from having 24 pairs of chromosomes to 23? Renowned author Gregg Braden, who wrote *"Deep Truth,"* states that:

> Counter intuitive to all the evolution around us, Human chromosome 2 seems to be fused, or combined into a single large piece of DNA (giving us 23 instead of the common 24 pairs that apes have).

> The conclusion against main stream science is that "Only a rare process could have given rise to such a genetic phenomenon." We are, therefore, a unique species on the planet, and did not evolve from anything "here."

Question for Kryon: Is the history of our planet Earth similar to the history of the other planets that have ascended within our galaxy?

Kryon: It's interesting, is it not, that no Human has ever asked this question of me? Yet it now begs to be asked! The new energy is beginning to show you a larger truth that has always been there, but has not been at the tip of the Human's curiosity. The reason is that with the new energy, new intuition is being released to you that has always been within you, but not at a survival level. It's instead buried deep in the Akashic level of "galactic inherited information." This, like other things, is being slowly released as Gaia postures itself to further help humanity through new magnetics coming in through your solar system's travels around the center, and the release of ancient information.

So the simple answer to your question is yes. It's very similar, just like basic evolution is similar. One might think that each planet that has gone through this might have a very specific evolved path, due to the vast differences in planetary variety. The truth is

that evolution, both physical and consciousness, has a well-worn path of sameness throughout the galaxy. This is because some very basic laws, and not what you would call "chance," are at work. These laws, yet un-named, are the same everywhere, and always help "point" evolving life in the same direction.

The bigger answer, however, that I just revealed is that GAIA is very involved in the "pointing" process! So here is still something else that will eventually be revealed that is part of the partnership of humanity and GAIA.

Lemuria

I wish to talk about Lemuria. I first heard this name when I read my first Kryon book that was given to me in 2006. Kryon would often refer to Lemurians, the old souls of the planet. For a long time during my awakening process I would often wonder if I was, in fact, a Lemurian. Now, of course, I realize that I was definitely in Lemuria, and I have received confirmation many times, including being present during a Kryon channel where Kryon acknowledged every single person in the room as Lemurian. I am always overcome with emotion every time I am fortunate enough to visit Hawaii. My cells tingle with remembrance, and there is a blanket of such sweet, loving, Mother Earth energy, especially when I'm on Kauai.

So what about you? Are you a Lemurian? I can almost hear the ones who respond yes to this question, and then I can feel or sense that some of you are not really sure. I want to assure you that regardless of whether or not you are Lemurian, the very essence of your DNA resounds with the divinity that you have inside. You are a piece of God and eternal. You always were and always will be. So please don't get too fixated on trying to work out if you are Lemurian.

The birth place of Lemurians took place on the world's biggest mountain that is now a chain of islands known as Hawaii. Back then, 80 percent of this mountain was above the water and the peaks were at much higher altitudes than they are today. This mountain was created over a hot spot. There was a bulge in the crust of the Earth that was pushed up. Much of the island was cold. The highest peaks were covered in snow and ice and there were glaciers that formed. Eventually, geologists will find evidence of this.

The Lemurians represented the relationship between Gaia and humanity. In a spiritual way, they were preparing and building the Akashic Record of the planet. This was the population center of divinity. Every soul that came to Lemuria received a pure imprint, others elsewhere did not. The DNA of the Lemurians was, therefore, the purest on the planet. With a few exceptions, each Lemurian had only one life. This was designed on purpose so that there was an old soul experience. The Lemurians established the energy on The Crystalline Grid. They also imprinted their energy in the Cave of Creation while waiting for the civilization to be complete. Once a soul had passed through Lemuria, it would wait or reincarnate to another place. Therefore, the Lemurians carry the oldest Akash for an old soul, and part of the system of spiritual seeding back then was that it was an avenue for only new souls to come in. Only a few of the Lemurian priests had a past-life in Lemuria, and most were women. Almost all the Lemurians were new to the planet. Kryon has given an estimate that approximately 350 million old souls passed through the Lemurian experience. We can estimate, therefore, that this is approximately the number of old souls on the planet today, many of whom are awakening.

Humanity, in the Lemurian energy, was the one seed-group that was totally isolated. Lemuria was a mountain island (Hawaii), and the group survived in a form that was purer than others. Even the most remote groups on Earth had room to spread out (land), and that created a diversity of thought. But Lemuria was the same for thousands of years, making it one of the longest-lived civilizations in history, and almost totally lost to science because the places where the Lemurians lived are now covered by water.

For thousands of years, Lemurians had DNA that was directly affected by spending time with the Pleiadians who carried the wisdom and knowledge in an isolated and closed environment, and consequently this wisdom and knowledge was not diluted. Lemuria was a one-time experience in order to build the Akashic Record of the planet.

At a certain point in time two things occurred that were very frightening to Lemurians. The mountain started to sink into the ocean, and magma started to come out of the volcanoes. This was the signal to leave the island, heralding the end of Lemuria and the beginning of humanity's work on the planet. The Lemurians became

a sea-faring race, and started to voyage out to find other places to live. Some Lemurians made it and some did not. Many went south and others did not.

The Lemurians that left their mountain island known as Hawaii established populations on Easter Island and New Zealand, among other places. This is why the energy of the old soul Lemurian is felt so strongly when on these lands. Kryon gave a lot of information about the Lemurian civilization during a cruise in the Mediterranean:

It was the grandest society the planet had ever seen – not huge in numbers, but in consciousness. It was not something that you would be emulating later, for it was part of the set-up of humanity. It was the Lemurian civilization. I've never identified how long they lasted, so I will now. What would you think of one society that lasted more than 20,000 years? They lived in peace. It would dwarf, would it not, anything that has ever happened in recorded society on the Earth? Nothing you know of comes close to that...

...I have much more to tell you about the Lemurians. So let us move now to the spiritual part. There were a total of 350 million Lemurian souls who passed through the planet during their culture of 20,000 years. That's not many considering they went through 800 generations. Let me explain why.

Now, this is different, my partner, and this is specific. So translate it correctly. [Kryon speaking to Lee out loud for all to hear] Lemurians didn't reincarnate back as Lemurian. So what I'm saying spiritually is that there were almost 350 million individual, unique souls – not just Human souls, but 350 million angels took their turns going through the Lemurian culture as humans, and didn't reincarnate. They came one time only. The Lemurian birth rate was not typical to what yours is today, not nearly what yours is today. It wasn't even a geometric progression like you have today. This is complicated. Biologically, there was a reason why the Lemurians did not have many children. It had to do with the temperature of the planet and their culture. Men were not as fertile as they are now. It also facilitated the spiritual aspects of what was needed. So all you must know is that of the Lemurian spiritual culture, 350 million souls is all there were, representing the longest-lasting society the Earth has ever known. More on that in a moment...

...The following is scientifically controversial, for what I'm going to tell you is that small meteor strikes were more common than believed, in these times. As little as 13,000 years ago and then 5,000 years ago, there were strikes. The last one of 5,000 years ago was bigger. It did two things for the planet. The first is that it created such a shift of the mantel of the planet that the Earth moved from 28 degrees tilt to 23 and 1/3. It was quite an impact! That was only 5,000 years ago. The second is that it affected civilization. Much dust was thrown into the atmosphere up into what you call the stratosphere and the result mainly was rain. The rain terminated much of humanity. Many animals and many humans died. It was needed, necessary, and we have spoken of it before. It was part of the plan. The main purpose was to erase all of the Lemurian knowledge and create many lakes for humanity to use. Science can see it in the strata, and it has even been associated with the mythology of a great worldwide flood and an ark...

...The Lemurian civilization basically existed from 35,000 years to 15,000 years ago – the longest single-governed civilization on Earth. It was different from any society you will ever have, for we will review with you what happened. The whole reason for Lemuria and for all of the attributes of their DNA was to set a stage for what was to come. When the cook prepares the meal, quite often they will grease the pan, get all of the attributes ready for the actual food, and then proceed with much preparation that will enhance the food, but that does not include the actual food yet.

The Lemurians represented that relationship to Earth and you. In a spiritual way, the meal was being prepared. Therefore, we again tell you that they had a different Akashic attribute than you do. Three hundred and fifty million Lemurians existed for the lifetime of their culture. They were unique Lemurians, and with a few exceptions, each one had one life. You might say they were building the Akashic Record of the planet. Imagine the Cave of Creation with all of the crystals we have described as the souls on the planet. Each time an angel would come in and be a Lemurian for a little while. The essence of their energy would then be placed into the planet. The crystal with their name on it would go into the cave. Some of these things will not make sense to those of you who have not heard this story before about the Cave of Creation.

The entire Lemurian civilization was to build the Cave of Creation and to implant it with the energy of 350 million souls. And in all of their history, there were only a few thousand that had past lives that would come again as a Lemurian – most being their scientists. The rest of them would live a life and then back away and wait for the civilization to be complete [speaking of the angels who represent the different souls of humanity]. This was on purpose, and was in order to seed the planet spiritually with what was to come, and increase the crystalline value of the Cave of Creation.

The Lemurians saw what was happening. As we told you, about 15,000 years ago, the ice began to melt, and it did so slowly for at least another 5,000 years. You might say they had plenty of time to prepare, and so they did. What they did first was to become a sea-faring nation building ships. Slowly, many of them left the valley that they were in, which was already slowly flooding, as the ice melted and the waters rose on the planet. So you might say that there is part of Lemurian society that populated the edges of other land masses via ship. Look for them in New Zealand, Easter Island – not much left there – and the large continent of what you call the Americas. They were on the West Coast areas you call Alaska and the bridge to the other continent. They were there. Many of them went to the mountain called Shasta and they existed there in their Human form long before they put themselves into the mountain as multi-dimensional beings.

Some of them started other societies in combination with other humans who had travelled far from the core, and had forgotten their lineage completely. One of the cultures was called Sumerian, and was in the Middle East. This eventually led to the Egyptian culture many years later. It's odd that this is where you think history actually started!

Now here is something we have not told you before. All evidence of old Lemuria has been erased. The ocean currents under the seas are very strong; almost like rivers they surge, washing with sand and silt for eons. So there are those who say, *"That means we'll never find the artifacts of Lemuria."* Not only *will* you find some, you have already, and many are hiding them. Because when these collectors show them to science, they'll be laughed at. For there will be an oxymoron … a contradiction within the actual artifact.

It will be too old to be what it is! At least according to modern thinking, that is. What would happen if you found an automobile part that carbon dated to 3,000 years ago? It would be an artifact that "couldn't exist." That's what the artifacts of Lemuria will be like. For they will be charts of the stars and biological information that "couldn't have been known."

And why would anyone be able to have an artifact of Lemuria? I just told you that Lemuria is washed away. It's because of the ships! Many of them went down in storms carrying everyday Lemurian objects – artifacts. Some are waiting to be found, and some have already been found and sequestered by collectors who cannot get anyone to look at them because they don't make sense...

...So now you know about the Lemurians. You also know that they are not what you have today in the way of consciousness. They're part of the set-up of the test, and you have lost a piece and a part of the activation of the DNA that they had through the energy you have selected for your duality. And that is free choice, to see if you can realize it and get it back. And that is the quantum part of DNA. It is what we have called the Lemurian and Pleiadian layers and one of them is the Akashic Record. Now, if you're putting this together, you'll also realize that Lemurians were responsible for the creation of the cosmic Akashic Record of Earth...

...Now let me tell you something that you may love to hear. Between 1987 and 2007, something amazing happened. Due to the new energy, the crystals awakened in the Cave of Creation that had Lemurian names. They whispered, *"Time to come back!"* Three hundred and fifty million of them. Listen to this, listen – all of the Lemurians who ever lived on this planet are alive again in Human bodies right now and are back! They are spread all over the globe. Listen, I've got a roomful of them right here. I'm looking at them. And that's why you're here, dear one. That's why you're reading this. And you wonder why you resound with these things? You wonder why you're vibrating higher? You wonder why there's an alliance with your cellular structure and the Kryon? It's because you're Lemurian, an old soul in a new energy.

"Kryon, does that mean my soul hasn't been here before 1900?" Now that answer is complicated. Pieces and parts were here, but not

the full Lemurian core energy. You think of yourself as one entity, one soul, one name, and one face. But you're not. You're a combination of many energies. It's difficult to explain, if not impossible. Each time you arrive, you're like the soup that gets made and comes to the planet. There is a Higher-Self, which is the same core energy every time. But what surrounds it has great spiritual variety. But now some of you are back with the Lemurians' core energy surrounding you, something that hasn't happened for 50,000 years. Those pieces of DNA are being re-activated.

Listen to what I've been telling you for years: Less than one-half of one percent of this planet has to awaken to make a difference in the vibration for all. You will move into 2012 with a new vibration. Less than one-half of one percent of seven billion people has to awaken. It's not that many. In fact, it's only 10 percent of the 350 million Lemurians who are alive today – a very reasonable percentage.

Kryon live channelling "The History of Humanity" given in the western Mediterranean Sea. 8th Annual Kryon Cruise – August/September 2007

The main difference between the Lemurian old souls, and other old souls, is that you lived this pure DNA experience once. It stays in your Akash. Kryon has indicated that the task of the old soul Lemurian is to reawaken the DNA that you used to have.

There is something else that I would like to share with you about Lemuria. It will explain why Kryon is always referring to the wisdom of the ancients, our ancestors, and that would be you, old soul. Why were these Lemurians so special? The answer lies in their DNA. I'll let Kryon explain:

Slowly, the first civilization on the planet was born, and it was called Lemuria. Know this: It was not an advanced civilization in the way you think about "advanced." But they had something you should know about. Their quantum DNA was at 90 percent, not 30 percent as yours is today. All the quantumness of their DNA was activated, for that is what the Pleiadians passed on to them. Lemuria was the oldest civilization on the planet, the one that was the most long lasting, which never saw war.

It was eventually broken up only because the oceans and seas rose. As I have described to you before, they became a sea-faring people and scattered to the many parts of the Earth. Ironically, some made it to far away continents and science sees them as actually starting there, instead of traveling from somewhere else.

Lemurians were the original Human society on the planet, and they were located where the Pleiadians originally landed, on the top of the highest mountain on Earth, as measured from the bottom to its top ... currently the largest island of Hawaii, where the Lemurian "canoes" are buried. Hawaiian elders will tell you today that this is the lineage of Hawaii, that the Pleiadians came there, for it is what they teach as how humanity began.

Lemurians had a quantum understanding of life, and they knew in their DNA all about the solar system. A quantum DNA, working at 90 percent, creates a consciousness that is *one with the Universe*. One of the most ancient of your spiritual beliefs on the planet asks you to be one with everything. It's not an accident...

...Here is some historical advice: Do not place so much attention on Atlantis. Atlantis was much, much later, and there were actually three of them, and much confusion around what was there, and what happened there. Which one do you want to talk about? Atlantis did not play near the role that those in metaphysics and esoteric teachings wish to assign upon it. Oh, it was important, but one of them is not ancient at all! It was so recent, off the Greek Isles, and was even reported within the history that you see today from the Greeks. Humans have a dramatic interest in civilizations that get destroyed quickly. It creates further mythology, creating ideas that Atlantis was one of the most advanced civilizations. It wasn't. Lemuria was, but in consciousness only.

Lemuria was not an advanced technical society, for it had no technical abilities at all. Yet they knew how to heal with magnetics. It was in their DNA, you see? It was intuitive information. Quantum DNA produces quality intuitive information. Being one with the Universe, they knew all about DNA. Doesn't everyone? [Kryon smile] They even knew the shape of it ... all without a microscope. That's what quantum DNA does.

The ancients knew!

Lemurians knew much due to the quantum DNA they carried, thanks to the Pleiadians. They knew all about the solar system, and about the galaxy in general. They looked at the stars and understood what was there. This created a seemingly advanced society, but without any technical advancement as you now have.

Kryon live channelling "The History of DNA and the Human Race"
given in Portland, Oregon – August 29, 2009

Lemurian society was less technical than our society today; however, Kryon has said they were incredibly advanced. How did this advanced society function? Lemurian society functioned in ways that would appear to us like "out of the box" thinking. This is exactly what is needed today to develop solutions to our current problems. Perhaps if we started to adopt the Lemurian way of thinking and living, many problems would be resolved. Kryon gave two examples of how things worked in Lemuria. I'm sure you will agree that the way they did things demonstrates just how quantum they were. Can you see how their approach might work in today's consciousness? I think this is why Kryon often tells us about ancient wisdom and knowledge:

The Schools of Lemuria

Let me tell you a little more about Lemuria and some attributes of their society. You might say, *"Why would you do such a thing?"* The reason is so you can start to "connect the dots" as to what else is happening on the planet. I now speak of the Lemurians way back then, in a land that was beautiful before the ocean covered it. Let me tell you about their children.

Schooling was very, very different in major Lemuria. This was before Atlantis, and it went like this: The teachers were called *elders*. They were greatly respected, for they dispensed the knowledge of the culture. They were all seniors, and represented some of the highest attributes in society. Yet they didn't run the schools as your teachers do, or have anything to do with day-to-day business. There were no administrators or administration buildings in the schools either, and the buildings were all small, isolated, and unconnected classrooms.

There was no linear system either! Instead, the elders would get together and decide what the children should learn and know by a certain time. The parents would send their children to the local classrooms at a certain age. In a typical classroom, the children and the elder [teacher] would all decide together what had to be learned. The children would then take over and collectively decide how fast they could learn it, and report this to the elder. The teacher would be flexible and go along with the children's plans. Then the children would often choose a leader among them, or a rotation schedule of student leaders, to help with the tasks of maintenance and administration of what their goal was.

So the elder was there to dispense the knowledge and make certain the children got the appropriate knowledge. But the children had high conceptual ideas and could often conceive of the entire project of the year's learning in one day. So even without the actual knowledge, they would lay out what they felt was the best way to learn it, the quickest method, and how to best "plug it in" to their schedule in class. When they felt they'd learned it, they would request to be tested. If the class passed, they would all earn the end of the term. Then the vacation would begin (the real goal of the children at that age).

So instead of a common term of duration, they'd start at the same time, but there were no set ending points. So the children would determine the term's duration by how fast they'd learn. This was conceptual, and reflected their ability to understand what had to be learned without actually knowing the information. There was no school year or grades – only the goal of certain degree of knowledge, and the goal to get it done so they could play! The children were in charge, but they absolutely understood that they had to learn what was required

Now many might exclaim, *"No, this is too unusual and odd. It couldn't work. Human nature wouldn't allow for it!"* My reply is this: Perhaps 4D Human nature would never allow for it, but a conceptual, multi-dimensional child could do it easily. The reason I'm telling you this is that this is the beginning attribute of the Indigo Child that we

channelled many years ago. It's very Lemurian! Even some of the "labels" of the Indigo Children were listed as multi-dimensional.

Back to Lemuria: If there were slow learners in the class, the children would see the situation immediately and tutor them! What you now call homework was instead an assignment for each student to tutor another so that they could all keep up with the class. But the only things they took home were other students! The faster they learned, the quicker the vacation. It made sense to the kids. You might say, *"Well, what about those who were trouble-makers? Were there any of those in this great land of Lemuria?"* Of course. Make no judgments as I reveal how this was handled.

The children would handle the discipline themselves – oh, not by the bully system, for that's not in the consciousness of a con-ceptually-minded child. Remember, in this type of consciousness, the overview is the goal of the group, not individual power. The children would handle it logically. If there was another student getting in the way of their vacation, they would tutor them in the best way they could. If some didn't respond, or were troublemak-ers, eventually the students would cast them out. Anyone who was cast out of school by a consensus of the class could never rejoin that class. Instead, they had to go to other classes that were not in major Lemuria. This (of course) created another complete society, one which was dishonored and often didn't live long, since they didn't earn the right to go to the Temple of Rejuvenation, which was a huge part of the health system of Lemuria.

Harsh, you might say? Indeed. Within the evolved standards of today, perhaps it was. But this is how the schools worked. Your society has progressed in ways that they did not, because you've worked on other parts of your enlightenment.

These explanations may help you understand why school is so difficult for the current Indigo, for the Crystal, and for all children of the new Earth energy. For within them is a layer of DNA that's activated and ready to work. And it *remembers*. I'm going to tell you about that in just a moment.

Lemurian Health Care

I'd like to tell you about the Lemurian health-care system. You know, Lemurians didn't have tremendously high science. They didn't have the computers you do. Instead, they had highly developed multi-dimensional intuition. Those of you who know what a medical intuitive is will understand this. All of them had this kind of intuitive knowledge. The body is smart. Lemurian bodies, depending on how far back you go, were far larger than yours. But as we said, they devolved ... became smaller and shorter. They were aware that this was happening. That also might give you information that Pleiadians are larger than you are. They still are.

Here is what the Lemurian society decided to do about health care. Most of the resources of Lemuria were spent making sure that all were as healthy as they could be. There were no health-care payments, since they were a conceptual culture. They had a far better evolved intuition about the entire picture, rather than an individual Human one. The Lemurian society intuitively realized that the healthier the population, the more it helped the economy. There was land ownership, but of a very different kind. It was group ownership. Therefore, it always involved group decision.

If you had one who was sick all the time, then they weren't able to share their load. This hurt the whole, so they found out very quickly that if everyone was healthy, they had a far better economy.

Now, again, I'll discuss the reason I take you to Lemurian history. It's because this very thing is about to happen once more on your planet. Suddenly, the realization that Human Beings who aren't sick can buy land and pay taxes will create a revolutionary idea ... if a government can heal its population, it can have an abundant society. What an idea! Watch for a shift of funds, resources, and focus regarding this. How can we cure the most for the least amount of money? How can we take from one financial focus and apply it to another? Did you ever wonder how you're going to cure the diseases of the planet? Many have complained: *"Humanity will never reach the point of enlightenment where they'll dedicate enough funds to heal the masses."* You're right! So another method, which makes far more sense to your current Human nature, will!

Do not make any judgments about this, but be aware that you're about to face a new idea that's all about "economic healing." How else would the Earth provide something so needed at this time? The answer: Find a way to fit this into the agendas of those with the biggest amount of money to invest. Healing will become an investment in global health. How will the investors get their return? They'll take a portion of the GNP of the governments they work with, as measured by the "cure rate" of the country. Watch for this. It's inevitable, and under way at this moment.

Kryon live channelling "The Lemurian Connection"
given in Mt. Shasta, California – June 20, 2004

Do you see how the Lemurians were conceptual thinkers? Do you see why Kryon says "thinking out of the box" will create the solutions we seek? Can you see how the old soul Lemurian that awakens on the planet will make such a huge impact? Once again, if you are confused as to whether or not you are Lemurian, please remember that it is not that important for you to study this in great detail. This is because the energy of the planet is beginning to open up to the Lemurian energy. The spiritual seeds that were planted back then are becoming "watered" so to speak, so that it can blossom and become available to all the souls on the planet. Later on I will talk about the grids of the planet Earth and how they are being recalibrated, and providing help and support for each and every Lightworker. What's a Lightworker, you ask? I guess, dear reader, if your eyes are on this page and you have managed to read this far without throwing away the book, then you should assume you are a Lightworker (smile). Thank you for shining your light!

Q.: Can you further explain about how the planet is beginning to open up more to the Lemurian energy?

Kryon: This isn't that difficult, since this was always the potential of humanity, if it would pass the 2012 marker. Other planets had their own markers, based on the energetics of time and their own fractals of history. But yours was linked to the 26,000-year wobble of the planet, and was kind of a "deadline" to get to a certain place in conscious evolution. As little as fifty years ago, it was undetermined if you would again destroy yourselves (this time with technology), or if you would instead move forward. You indeed passed this marker, and now have "opened the time capsule" of Lemurian energy and knowledge.

All this means is that a new page is being turned, where the original Pleiadian teachings, which were well developed by the Lemurians, are now more available than ever. The next step is in how quickly you allow these new ideas and evolved principles to be applied to your society. Each planet has a different scenario politically, so this is your next big step.

The Indigenous

If you take a look at the ancient indigenous cultures, they all have something in common. They honor their ancestors! They all intuitively know that their ancestors are still with them. The indigenous know how to mine the Akash and they realize the circle of life contains accessible information. They know this information is inside them. They also know Gaia and consider the Earth as a life force partner. A partner in their soul life. We are now in the middle of a great shift on Earth, and the knowledge and wisdom of the ancestors are ours to inherit if we choose.

During my work as a park ranger, I was required to attend cross-cultural awareness sessions in relation to the local indigenous Aborigines. In addition, we would often consult the Elders on matters relating to Indigenous Culture. The recognition and inclusion of local Aborigines regarding national park management within Australia is gradually improving. In fact, many important events and meetings include a "Welcome to Country" invitation from an Elder. The Elders always pay their respects to their ancestors and to the land, Mother Earth, and there is now an acknowledgement that the local Aborigines are the Traditional Owners of the land.

When I was working at Tidbinbilla Nature Reserve I started a project that involved updating and replacing all of the interpretation signs that were featured along a popular walking track. The track was called the Birrigai Time Trail and it was a fantastic place to take international visitors, as you would always see mobs of kangaroos grazing and emu's foraging along the open grassland. The track also had interesting sites

31

from European settlers who had come to the valley, and a significant Aboriginal Rock Shelter that has revealed startling information about Aboriginal occupation in the South East part of Australia. Prior to excavations done at Birrigai Rock Shelter it was believed that occupation in the area existed for only 8,000 years. Artifacts that were carbon dated indicated the area was occupied 21,000 years ago. I should point out that the record of Aboriginal occupation in Australia dates back 61,000 years ago, from evidence found in Arnhem Land, north Australia.

The former signs on the track had been done without consulting the local indigenous groups. My job was to redo the signs and ensure the local indigenous groups were consulted and had an opportunity to contribute their knowledge. As a part of this process, one of the interpretation signs mentioned the custom of banging two clap-sticks together and calling out your name before continuing your journey or entering a site. The sign also invites you to do the same, and I was also told the reason this is done is to ward off any bad spirits. I never really understood much about this custom, and I even remember yelling out my name once when I was alone on the track, and I felt extremely foolish and laughed about such a silly custom and wondered how anyone could have been so superstitious.

I guess the cosmic joke was on me because it wasn't until I participated in a sacred ceremony in Hawaii at the edge of the Kilauea Volcano, given by a Hawaiian High Priestess Kahuna Kalei'iliahi in August 2012, that I truly got a sense of just how profound this custom can be. It was like opening a hidden door that only your own spiritual key could unlock.

Kahuna Ali'i Wahine Kalei'iliahi is a Kanaka Maoli (aboriginal) of Hawai'i. She was born and raised in the lush Kalihi Valley on the island of O'ahu. Her ancestral roots trace all the way back to the stars, to the Makali'i (the Pleiades), to Papa (Earth Mother) and Wakea (Sky Father) and down a long line of Kahuna Ali'i Wahine and Kahuna Ali'i Kane (Royal High Chief Priests and Royal High Chiefess Priestesses). Kahuna Kalei'iliahi's family God is Lono, God of Peace (also of Fertility, Abundance and Agriculture). Lono is uncle to Goddess Pele, of whom she is a descendent. Whenever you are in the presence of Kalei'iliahi you can feel the love and compassion that radiates from her core.

Kalei'iliahi started the ceremony by letting us know that the ancestors had communicated with her, and that it was now appropriate for her to do an ancient ceremony because the people that were in our group were now ready to receive this special anointment. She explained that the ancients knew about places where there were bad spirits or bad energies, and so they would stand firm and call out in a loud voice, "E Ku Mau Mau" which means "I am here," and then wait for their ancestors and the Universe to respond before proceeding. Kalei'iliahi explained that the very act of saying "E Ku Mau Mau" would activate the energetic field around you. She explained to us that we know this field by the name Merkabah. The ancients had a different name, but it is the same thing. By activating your Merkabah, you send a signal to the Universe that you are aware of your divine magnificence and the Universe and Gaia "know" you and embrace you.

The real magic of how this works was later described to me by Kalei'iliahi. She said that the profound moments happen when "entering the silence" after you have spoken the words "E Ku Mau Mau." In her own words she told me...

"After you spoke those words you then enter into the silence, into the stillness ... get quiet and listen ... for this is when you will hear the whole Universe and Gaia respond to you with 'We see you!' It is a profound moment and if one does not go into that stillness *they will have missed it*. In fact it was at that exact moment at the Kilauea crater that the winds picked up strong around each of you precious ones ... did you hear it, or feel it? It was powerful! Winds of the ancients responding to you."

Absolutely I felt it! And I'm pretty sure that everyone else who was there could feel it as well. It was like Gaia and the ancestors were making sure we were being touched physically and spiritually in a very strong and powerful way. The other aspect to this teaching is that the dark energies that are our tests hear these words and see us standing tall (the meaning of the word Ku is to stand tall) and these energies then retreat. They smile and bow before us, for they see our Light. We have passed the fear test and they know it. So beautiful – and in complete alignment with the Kryon teaching that fear is a love test

in disguise, and when faced, disappears like a smile in the night just before the dawn.

Once we all understood the significance of what we would be doing, we individually stood in front of Kalei'iliahi and called out "E Ku Mau Mau" while looking into her eyes. One by one, as we stood in front of Kalei'iliahi, we could feel our magnificent selves and the love of our ancestors. During the ceremony we all took turns calling out the sacred words while the entire group was reverent and holding energy, tuning into something that was very profound and sacred and at the same time was very personal and unique for each of us present. The ground was thick with energy, and our cellular structure within our bodies responded with remembrance.

I remember asking for a sign from spirit so that I would remember this overwhelming love wash. Most of us saw the physical sign which was a white bird flying high above (and later during a Kryon channel we were told that we were visited at the ceremony by a Pleiadian in the form of a white bird). However, the most significant thing, that will stay in my heart forever, was when the last person in the group knelt down to "wash the feet" of Kalei'iliahi. This act of compassionate action resulted in most of us weeping uncontrollably because of all the love that we could feel embrace us in that moment. It was like getting a glimpse of just how loved we are by God, Gaia and the ancestors.

It took me several days to assimilate the profound energy I experienced during this ceremony. Every single time I thought back on the ceremony, and the heart energy when Kalei'iliahi was being honored in that way, I would weep an avalanche of tears. If I tried to recount what happened I would just choke up and cry. The experience was very sacred and profound. So what had changed between the time when I thought a custom practiced by the ancients silly and foolish, to the time that I actually participated in an ancient ceremony and experienced a deep spiritual experience? The answer is that I had changed. I had given myself permission to open my heart, and with pure intent I wanted to connect with Gaia, our ancestors, the Universe and God.

One of the most amazing things about this experience is that six months later, when I attended the Lemurian Reunion event held by Dr. Todd Ovokaitys to sing the pineal tones in Maui, Hawaii, I was retelling what happened at the ceremony to my Australian girlfriend Wendy, and once again I became so choked up with emotion that the tears slid down my face and my words came out in sobbing gasps! When I was talking to Kalei'iliahi about this, she told me that when we weep with love and joy in this way, we honor the ancestors.

Kalei'iliahi has said that so much of what Kryon speaks of is indigenous wisdom in current language – the third language of the Gods. Here is a prayer given to us by Kalei'iliahi that is traditionally chanted three times. The energy of three acts as a catalyst for change. It is also the energy of compassion and the ancients knew this.

Mai ke Akua

Mai ke Kukui

Mai Kalani

Mai ka Maluhia

Mai Kalani

Mai ka Hau'oli

Mai Kalani

Mai ke Ola

Mai ke Akua

Mai ina me Apau

The translation of this prayer is:

From the Gods

From the Light

From the Heaven

From the Stillness

From the Heaven

From the Happiness

From the Heaven

From the Life

From the Gods

From the Giver of All Things

If you are ever fortunate enough to visit Hawaii you may wish to seek out the beautiful and loving energy of Kahuna Kalei'iliahi. Her website is: *www.kaleiiliahi.com*

I used to think that the ancient early civilizations were superstitious, primitive and ignorant about how the world operated. I knew that they certainly lived in much more harmony with nature than we do today, but I was biased against thinking they possessed wisdom and knowledge by my perception that modern humans, in comparison, have such advanced technology and scientific discoveries. I never fully understood just how aligned the ancients were with Gaia and the Creator because I, myself, was ignorant. Yes, we have much more technology and inventions than the ancients did, but the ancients had a much clearer understanding of the divinity within. And they were masters in their own right, with systems for astronomy and navigation, and advanced calendars. Modern society certainly has more technology, but the ancient indigenous had something far more precious – spiritual knowledge of who they were, and a constant communication with Gaia and the Creator.

We are now entering a period on Earth, in which many of the old souls who lived in Lemuria are on the planet now, and awakening to the truth of who they really are. We have the opportunity to rediscover the wisdom and knowledge of the ancients. Traditionally, this wisdom and knowledge was only given to the chosen few. In case you haven't noticed, there is a shift going on and more and more of the wise indigenous Elders that are on the planet are starting to open up and share their teachings with those that are outside of their culture, as well as with each other. Against all odds, the indigenous tribes are coming together and sharing their knowledge, recognizing that we are all one.

There is something else that the ancients did that we can learn from. They intuitively recognized three energies: male energy, female energy and Gaia. It was because of this recognition that the ancients had ceremonies that were exclusively for women or men. In fact, some of the indigenous cultures today still retain this tradition. In many places I have visited in Australia, the local indigenous Aborigines have identified areas that are sacred, and only allowed to be visited exclusively by women or men, depending on the location. They honor and recognize that male and female energies are unique and distinct, each with a special purpose. I think it is important to realize that one is not better than the other. What is important is to unite the two energies to create equilibrium and balance. This is what is happening now on Earth, and has resulted in a shift which is recalibrating everything: Gaia, the Human Being, the Universe. At this point I would like to express my gratitude and thanks to the indigenous of this Earth for holding their light for all of this time, but especially now, when the rest of humanity has begun to awaken.

One of the things that I love about the messages from Kryon is the honor that is given to the ancients, our beloved ancestors. I would like to share some information Kryon gave during the Kryon Kundalini Tour of 2012:

Let's talk about the ancients. Why were they so interested in this time? How is it that you could go back thousands of years and find the prediction that you have happening today? The indigenous of Earth were more concerned with the dirt of the Earth than anyone who has ever existed. What is your reality today? What is your survival plan for life? For you today, it has to do with your job, your family, and perhaps the economic consciousness of your government. However, what was the reality of the indigenous? It was two things: Food and water. All of it. It all revolved around these two and was driven by what they considered a third consciousness, which to them was Gaia.

The indigenous actually had a triad of sacred importance; they did not see humanity together. In those days, they would split it to include men, women, and Gaia. This was the energetic triad that they existed in. If you go back and look at their traditions, you had to separate the traditions from men and women, for they put a different honoring on each gender, but they came together with Gaia. If they did ceremonies, it was to create rain or to create the food representing the crops in the ground. This was their total reality and all very Gaia-related. All of the worship that they knew how to do was about the Earth, so the relationship with the planet was their science and they had a lot of information about it.

Slowly they began to understand the circle of time. Eventually they understood the cycles of the weather, but for a while they did not. So they prayed to the Gods of the south, east, north, and

west. All of this tells you something about them. The prophecies of the indigenous were all wrapped around the consciousness of Gaia. So what does this tell you? It tells you about *today*. From the north and from the south, they all knew something, somehow. They didn't know each other at all. The tribes in the north had no idea about the tribes in the south. They had never met each other. Hundreds of tribes had never even seen each other and yet they prophesied what's happening today! So I want you to think of this. Does it appear that perhaps they knew about the entanglement of consciousness and Gaia?

Indeed, they did, so today you listen to their truth, and here it is: There is an alignment of the planet's wobble based upon the 26,000-year cycle of the Earth. It has a potential opportunity for the movement and the creation of energy that you see today. The closer you get to this, the more the potentials grow. So even as recently as 600 years ago, it looked to them as though these predictions were a fact and not just a potential. They started including the information in their calendars and you could see it in the glyphs on the walls of their pyramids. Ask an indigenous. What's happening now? Is it what they expected? The answer is yes, right on schedule.

Kryon live channelling "The Letter K (in the word Kundalini)"
given in Mendoza, Argentina — October 17, 2012

I sincerely hope that one day all of humanity will be able to honor and recognize the wisdom and knowledge of the indigenous across the planet, and perhaps our attitudes will change and we'll start seeing compassionate action being demonstrated towards those who have inherited the Earth, and honor their ancestors. In the meantime, what a beautiful and precious gift that we have many Ambassadors for the indigenous such as Kalei'iliahi, who are able to open up and share their wisdom and knowledge with their Lemurian brothers and sisters who are now awakening all across the planet.

Question for Kahuna Kalei'iliahi: Are there any messages from our ancestors that you would like to share with us?

Kahuna Kalei'iliahi actually gave two channelled messages. The first one was given on January 9, 2013, while the second message came through on January 14, 2013. I have to smile when I look at the numerology of these two messages. The first date adds up to a number 7. In numerology, 7 represents "Divine Purpose." It is also a representation of the Seven Sisters, the Pleiadians. The second date adds up to 3 – a catalytic number – and I feel that this message is a catalyst for us to remember our Ancestors.

The Ancients from the Distant Past

"The Ancient Voices speak softly and quietly from the night, from the distant past … from Lemuria. They speak in a language all of its own and they share secrets. They speak of the power within, the power of Divine Light from the vast cosmos and how that grand power is held within our cells. They speak of things also not yet written, things about the light and color that holds a vibration too high for the average Human, but now being held in the new Human, the Awakening Ones and the New Children. They speak of silent colors and sounds, so soft and barely audible or visible to the Human eyes and ears and yet known intimately by every Human Heart. They speak of how we are all Gods and Goddesses that carry knowledge of life on other planets that we communicate with in our sleep. They whisper the most loving and gentle and kind words, always filled with Divine Love. They say this is the language of the Gods, the third language, and that every Human is capable of it … but we must enter into the silence, into the void … and dare to go where no man has gone. They are the 'Aumakua i ka Po' … The Ancestors from the Distant Past."

A Message from the Ancients going all the way back to the Stars

"We come from the Stars, and so do you. It is where you will return when you have fulfilled your contracts on Earth.

You are our Family and we are yours. Be still, and know, we are real…

We come to speak to the hearts of our Family who are open to receiving our love and our message for you. We come in humility, for Dear Ones, you are the exalted humans. You are the ones who make the sacrifice over and over again to come into a body and leave your Spirit Home for the planet called Earth. You have done this over and over and over. Why? Love … you are in love with Gaia. She is Family too.

Now we are here with a message that for some of you will have immediate impact and for others it will sink in a little later. But all of you reading this will eventually get this message at a deep level, and it will change you.

Your cells have recorded things that your conscious mind does not remember. Your cells have recorded things that were created in your biology that you are not aware of … an energy that is real that creates miracles. The power behind miracles is the energy that is the engine that drives them to where they need to be … manifested in your world. This energy is a field all of its own, and it is powerful. It has a color and it has a sound and your cells have it recorded. The color is pinkish blue … a very pale shade of blue mixed with pink or rather swirling around the pink. It is a color with Spiritual overtones so it looks different to the Human eye than it does to ours. It is the color none-the-less. And the sound it has is: Maaaaaaaaaaaaa Naaaaaaaaaaaaa.

Now we wish to share with you that the Hawaiian word 'mana' in its original pronunciation was exactly as we described. It was shortened over time but it never changed its original meaning: Divine Power. When you say this word, this very sacred word, in the method we have described above, drawing out the vowels, you will create an energy field with the colors we also described. This, Dear Ones, is the energy that drives the engine that creates the miracles and brings them into your reality.

So we say to you, when you are envisioning those things you wish to manifest in your lives, with your pure intent

and that which is for your highest good, include the sound: 'Maaaaaaaaaaaa Naaaaaaaaaaaa'

...the color will be included on its own because it accompanies the sound. They are the two creating the energy of the three ... where miracles are born. There are 12 counts of the sound 'a.'

Precious Ones, you are empowered to create anything you wish. YOU are God. Be brave enough to transcend your limiting fears and take your powers and use it to create grand Miracles on your planet. Start with you. Heal the bodies you came in with. Heal the planet at the same time, for there is no separation between your biology and the dirt of the land. We are the Ancients going all the way back to the Stars. We know you each by name and you are missed by those of us who have chosen to remain here and assist you while you do your work on that beautiful water planet. We are sending you profound Light and Love..."

Q.: Many of the indigenous cultures have an animal totem or a special animal that they consider as part of their ancestry. Can you tell us a bit more about this connection? Is it part of a system?

Kryon: The system is based on original survival in the days of beginning humanity. Everything was tied to "other life" on GAIA. The animals were seen as mysterious, life-giving, and even mythological. Their meat kept you alive, and their fur kept you warm. You built things using parts of their bodies, and the medicine men and women used other parts to heal. So they were associated with life force. This, in combination with the plants, was the "system of all things." So in those days, having an "animal totem" was actually a claim to the ancestry of the alliance with nature. It was a statement of how your energy was allied to the system of GAIA, and the energy of all that is. It was a statement of your personality type.

Naturally this is not the case today, but it was for far longer than anything you currently have now. So this energy is still imbued into The Crystalline Grid, and to this day many of the Indigenous still claim the importance of the alliance.

Q.: Is there anything else about the ancient indigenous that we should know?

Kryon: They had to survive with only what GAIA gave them. There are still plants and herbs in the forests that hold the key to health. Even today's "modern" diseases, such as cancers, could be helped with some of the natural medicines which the indigenous knew about. Today's humanity depends too much on design-er-chemistry, instead of GAIA balance. When you ingest certain kinds of plants and herbs, you also ingest all that went into their growth, including the very "system of the Earth." So doesn't it make sense to use what GAIA has produced, in order to then balance your body? You get so much more this way. Chemistry is cold, and has no consciousness. At best, it is a temporary fix to a much larger issue ... staying alive.

Chapter Two

Science of the Future

The ancients intuitively knew that the world was round. They understood astronomy, and even developed highly detailed calendars. How is it that all of this wisdom and knowledge was lost, and the "civilized" world for years believed that the world was flat? The answer has to do with Human consciousness. The vibration of the planet is like a big door that opens and closes with the vibration of an enlightened or non-enlightened humanity. Kryon states that:

> When these insights [of discoveries or inventions] are received by humanity, they normally *land* as inspiration on the planet in more than one place at a time. That is to say, epiphanies of discovery happen all at once, usually three to four places in order to assure that they will not be lost. It's like this: The vibration of the planet is like a big door that opens and closes with the vibration of an enlightened or non-enlightened humanity. If you [humanity] choose to close this door by creating a low vibration of the planet, then information, invention, and discovery are lost. They actually go away, since humanity doesn't even care to look! However, when the vibration becomes higher, the door opens and discovery and invention just "lay there" ready to be seen. So Spirit does not dole out inventions, but rather the system you have created allows for

it. For high science is always there no matter what, but the Human Beings on the planet temper how much of it becomes available by how high the planet vibrates with human consciousness.

Kryon live channelling "Needed Science for the Times"
given in Albuquerque, New Mexico – February 14, 2010

Have you ever wondered where invention and discovery comes from? How long did it take to create fire? How long did it take to create the wheel? And did you notice the length of time between discovering fire and creating the wheel? Now compare that with the length of time between discovering electricity and creating the radio. And what about our current age of technology? It seems that every time you update your computer or mobile phone, the next generation is already on the shelf and it's a great improvement on the one you just bought!

So why was there such a big gap in time originally between our early inventions and discoveries? Kryon states that there is a direct correlation to how in touch humans are with the divinity inside. The more we know about the divinity within us, the more we are able to open up to what we already know, which is how things really work.

What I describe next will make more sense if you have read Lee Carroll's Kryon Book 12, *The Twelve Layers of DNA*. If you haven't read the book, don't worry. Just be open to the idea of your DNA containing 12 layers and three of them are Pleiadian.

The Pleiadians knew all about quantum energy, how entanglement works, and all of the laws of physics, and they used this knowledge to get here. Three of our twelve DNA layers are Pleiadian. Inside these three layers exists everything we wish to know. All of the inventions and discoveries to come for the next 4,000-8,000 years are already there. The ability to access this information is directly correlated to the coherence of compassion on this planet. Pretty amazing, to say the least!

Ideas and inventions are given to the planet when our consciousness is ready for them, and not before. Have you ever wondered why? The consciousness of humanity has been to separate, conquer and war with one another. Can you see how this consciousness would like to take new inventions and use them as weapons in war?

The ideas and inventions have also been imbued within The Crystalline Grid of the Earth. Who put them there? Well, the Pleiadians, of course. I'll let Kryon explain:

Here is what happened: Within that which you call Gaia, there is The Crystalline Grid. This is the memory of all things placed there by the Pleiadians. The Crystalline Grid was created for this purpose by the Pleiadians. When it's proper and when humanity's consciousness has reached a certain point, these ideas are released. It is a time capsule of invention and more. This does not happen from the great central sun; it does not happen from outside the Earth, but rather, it happens from within.

In the beginning of the 2000s, we sat in a place called Mount Shasta [California] and we told you of the Lemurians in the mountain. We told you of the time capsules there, and now you have the explanation. Those in the mountain are not going to come out and present themselves and shake hands. A time capsule is about information and ideas. The capsules are about quantum attributes of science and life that you're going to discover. It is about ideas you need to have to move into a new energy...

Tesla the Man

There was a point in time when humanity almost stumbled, by the way. You were having a hard time with electricity. So a man came along who was way ahead of his time and was available and his name was Nikola Tesla. He gave you a principle that today you call *alternating current*. Dear ones, I challenge you to understand this principle. Most of you can't, because it is not in 3D. The attributes are still considered "genius-level thinking" to this day. The whole idea of the kind of electricity you use today comes from this man's quantum mind.

That was all he was *allowed* to do. Tesla himself was a kind of time capsule, delivered at the right time. He had more, but alternating current was all that was allowed to be given to the planet at that time. Oh, he tried to give you more. He knew there were other things, but nothing was able to be developed. If I told you what else he had discovered, you might not be aware of it at all, since it was never allowed to get out of the box. Earth was not ready for it.

Tesla discovered massless objects. He could alter the mass of atomic structure using designer magnetics, but he never could control it. He had objects fly off his workbench and hit the ceiling, but he couldn't duplicate or control it. It just wasn't time yet. Do you know what else he was known for? It was seemingly the failure of the transmission of electricity. However, he didn't fail at all.

There are pictures of his tower, but every time a Human Being sees a tower, there is a biased assumption that something is going to be *broadcast through the air*. But in the case of Tesla, he had figured out how to broadcast *electricity through the ground*. You need towers for that, because they have to pick up the magnetics within the ground in a certain way to broadcast them and then collect them again from the nodes of the planet's magnetic grid system. We talked about this before. He was utilizing the grid of the planet that is in the Earth itself! He was on the edge of showing that you could use the whole grid of the planet magnetically to broadcast electricity and pick it up where you need it, safely, with no wires. But the Earth was not ready for it.

Tesla died a broken man, filled with ideas that would have brought peace to planet Earth, but he was simply not allowed to give any of them to you.

Now I'll tell you why he was stopped, dear ones, and it's the first time we have ever told you – *because these inventions were too easy to weaponize*. Humanity just isn't ready for it. You're not ready for massless objects, either, for the principles are too easy to weaponize.

"*So,*" you might say, "*when will we be ready for it?*" I think you already know the answer, don't you? At the time when Human consciousness reaches a point where that which is most important is *unification* and not *separation*, it will happen. A point where conquering and power are not desirable ideas or assets. A point where humanity will measure the strength of its population by how healthy they are and not by economic growth. A point where coming together with your neighbor is the main objective to social consciousness, and not conquering them or eliminating them. That's coming, dear ones. It's a ways away, but it's coming. Look around the planet at the moment. The old energy leaders are obvious, are they not? It's like they are relics in a world of thinking that is passing them by.

The Opening of the Time Capsules

There is a storehouse of future knowledge and ideas in these time capsules you call Gaia, placed there a long time ago by those who you would call the Pleiadians, and these time capsules will open with new ideas about unity and peace first before they open with inventions. Humanity must soften before the inventions will come your way, and you will see what I mean over the next period of 18 years. These are the time capsules beneath your feet in the form of the nodes of the Crystalline Grid, and how fast these things are released to you will depend completely and totally on what you do next...

...Do you realize what you've got inside? You're going to need this entire engine of knowledge and the quantumness that is in you to start developing the divinity inside. It must become real to you, old soul, in order to go to the next step.

The Personal Time Capsule

Now, this is *your* personal time capsule, and it's what we really wanted to talk about. There are three kinds of time capsules. There's one kind that we won't speak of yet. There is another kind in the Earth and there's still another kind in your DNA. It's the spiritual inheritance that you came in with that's ready to open up like a lotus. When it does, there will be new awareness. There will be peace in a countenance that is not necessarily peaceful. There will be patience in a countenance that is not necessarily patient. That's when *you* get to change *you*, for it releases ideas, emotions and a consciousness that has been within you always, but only now is beginning to show itself in this new energy...

...We've been waiting a very long time to give you these messages. Now is when the work begins. It must begin with you in ways that perhaps you're not really prepared for. It's not about doing, but rather about *being*.

Kryon live channelling "The Time Capsule of Gaia"
given in Salt Lake City, Utah — February 9, 2013

Earlier I mentioned that new ideas and discoveries are within our DNA – specifically, the three Pleiadian layers. This is the time capsule that Kryon speaks about. What exactly do the Pleiadian layers represent? Is there more to them than what we think? The answer is yes.

Those who seeded you have DNA, and the ones who seeded them have DNA. Interesting, is it not, that this sameness of life you will discover some day in the smallest of the small, in far away places. You will realize that it did not come from your planet, and then you will start to understand that perhaps there is a "common galactic life system," and it's beautiful.

There's a time capsule within you: the three Pleiadian layers of your DNA are not all that unique to the galaxy, and they carry the seeds of the Pleiadians, their parents, and the parents of their parents. Why I am telling you this? It's because the time capsule that is in you is longer lived even than your planet's life history. It represents those in the galaxy far, far older than you, even the Human race itself ... and it's in you. We have told you for years that there is more here than you can imagine...

Kryon live channelling "The DNA Time Capsule"
given in Sacramento, California – February 10, 2013

Can you see how this applies to you personally? You don't have to be a scientific genius and create an amazing invention to make a significant contribution to the planet. Your compassionate actions and love of the divine self are changing the planet in a most profound way. Do you see how the actions of one change and affect the actions of all? The actions of all change the collective Human consciousness. A change in Human consciousness either opens or closes the door to new inventions and discoveries.

For over 23 years, Kryon has given us loving messages that are often blended with high science. We have passed the marker of 2012. On numerous occasions, the controversial information given by Kryon has become validated by science. Watch for this trend to continue. As humanity becomes more compassionate, new discoveries are made. Now, prepare yourself for some high science.

Designer Magnetics

What is designer magnetics? What is the difference between normal magnetics and designer magnetics? Well, magnetics is to designer magnetics like a crayon picture done by a child is to the Mona Lisa. The child is aware of the colors, but doesn't have any concept about what really can be created. It is the true artist that knows how to take all the colors and create a masterpiece. So when it comes to designer magnetics, we have to learn how to design energy. If this design can be presented to an object in the right way, the object can become massless. This is something we have not seen yet in a controllable way. We don't know how to design a magnetic field in the way that Kryon talks about it. Not yet, anyway, but eventually we will. This is part of the new discoveries waiting to be found.

This type of designer magnetics can be found naturally occurring on the planet. Have you ever heard about the healing waters in Lourdes, France? Every year, people from all over the world travel to bathe in the legendary healing waters that bubble up from a spring in the grotto. Kryon has said that the healing attributes of the water in this grotto are a direct result of the magnetics, and the anomalies in the rocks through which the water flows, and it has a quantum energy.

Before we launch into what Kryon has to say about designer magnetics, I want to tell you about entanglement, which Kryon often speaks about. In physics, entanglement is described as the relationship between two or more parts of a quantum system governed by one probability wave function. The term entanglement is used in quantum theory to describe the way that particles of energy/matter can be correlated to predictably interact with each other, regardless of how far apart they are.

Do you know what Einstein called entanglement? He called it "Spooky action at a distance." The phenomenon of entanglement is real and has been demonstrated repeatedly through experimentation. In 1997, Nicholas Gisin and colleagues at the University of Geneva, used entangled photons to enable simple – but instantaneous – communication over a distance of seven miles. This explains why distance healing sessions work. Science has not yet discovered the mechanism behind entanglement, nor can it be fully explained by any theory, yet. Kryon has said that quantum entanglement is locking together atomic

structure, whether matter or energy, in its own time and space in a unique pattern of quantum symmetry.

To help you visualize entanglement, let's look at some research and experiments that are currently happening. This will also prepare you for the next Kryon channel (smile).

A group of researchers has established a superconductivity group in Tel-Aviv University, Israel. They have been able to demonstrate "Quantum Levitation" and "Quantum Locking." They explain the process in the following manner:

> We start with a single crystal sapphire wafer and coat it with a thin (~1μm thick) ceramic material called yttrium barium copper oxide (YBa2Cu3O7-x). The ceramic layer has no interesting magnetic or electrical properties at room temperature. However, when cooled below -185°C (-301°F), the material becomes a superconductor. It conducts electricity without resistance, with no energy loss. Zero.
>
> Superconductivity and magnetic fields do not like each other. When possible, the superconductor will expel all magnetic fields from inside. This is the Meissner effect. In our case, since the superconductor is extremely thin, the magnetic field DOES penetrate. However, it does that in discrete quantities (this is quantum physics after all!) called flux tubes (or fluxons).
>
> Inside each magnetic flux tube, superconductivity is locally destroyed. The superconductor will try to keep the magnetic tubes pinned in weak areas (e.g., grain boundaries). Any spatial movement of the superconductor will cause the flux tubes to move. In order to prevent that, the superconductor remains "locked" in mid-air.
>
> *Source: http://www.quantumlevitation.com/thephysics.html*

If you visit the above website, you will also be able to see a video, in which the researchers demonstrate something that they call "quantum levitation" and how their supercooled "puck" is "quantumly locked" with a magnetic track. The "puck" then floats around the magnetic track and will even stay locked at any angle. It will even travel around the magnetic track upside down. What they have created opens the door to helping us further understand entanglement. While the experiment is not what you could call 100 percent entanglement (it is probably about 0.5 percent entanglement), they have shown that by supercooling an object, you can change its mass. This is the same video footage that Lee Carroll has shown in many seminars.

During an event held by Dr. Todd Ovokaitys, Kryon gave some very profound information to indicate that density is a variable attribute, not an absolute Newtonian law. Therefore, the density of any object can be changed. If you have not heard of Dr. Todd Ovokaitys, he has been featured in Kryon Book Six, *Partnering with God,* and Kryon Book 12, *The Twelve Layers of DNA*. Dr. Todd is a researcher who is on the leading edge of discovering the reality of what Kryon has spoken of – magnetic DNA healing and rejuvenation. He has developed some astounding theories that are now being proven – just as Kryon said would be the case. Although his research is directed toward DNA rejuvenation using new physics (with remarkable results), he is also working on discoveries that everyone can use right now. In addition, Dr. Todd has also been teaching the Pineal Toning Technique^{TM}, which uses 24 multi-dimensional tones that activate the pineal gland, and create profoundly expansive experiences.

Here is an excerpt from the transcript of the Kryon channel that gave us information about designer magnetics. The channel included a conversation with Dr. Todd, whom Kryon always refers to as Yawee.

Kryon: Now, back to physics. I want to talk about mass.

Yawee, is it possible to have something the size of a small boulder, and have two of those objects next to one other, the same size, yet one might weigh 40 kilo and the other one 400 kilo? Is this possible?

Dr. Todd: *Yes.*

Kryon: At the atomic level, would you explain why, please?

Dr. Todd: *Well, there would be a variety of ways that you could have such a differential density of the same size. You could have a boulder of lithium, which has a low density, and a boulder of gold, which has a high density. That would be one explanation but I suspect you are looking for another?*

Kryon: No. That's good. Density is the answer. However, the density of what?

Dr. Todd: *Density, by definition, is the unit of mass, by the unit of volume. So it would suggest that it would ultimately be the number of nuclear particles which contain the mass per said volume.*

Kryon: Aha! So it's the measure of 3D parts in a specific space. Earlier, my partner [Lee] showed the seminar group a video of a macro object [piece of iron] quantumly locked and partially entangled with a magnetic field. There were two processes that helped create this: One was magnetism and the other was supercooling. Together, this created the locking that you saw. That process did something to the atomic structure of the mass of the object, which was then locked with the magnetic field in the video. It changed the atomic structure of the mass of the object, and locked it to the magnetic field. The object appeared to float, but it actually just had the same quantum symmetry as the magnetic field, so it was entangled with it.

Now, here is the hint that I want to give yet again. Mass is a designed attribute and not a law of Newton. Weight and mass does not have anything to do with size. It has to do with density. Now, density is an attribute of atomic structure that has entanglement at its center. The density **conforms** to the 3D space it is in. What if you could change that specific atomic structure density? There is a way, and it doesn't necessarily change what the substance is. [Gold would still be gold.]

If you were to cool a specific atomic structure so that the atomic particles would stop vibrating the way they were originally vibrating, then you could re-design them the way you wanted, using designed magnetics. This also changes what we call the quantum symmetry of the locking. You could make a pebble weigh a ton. You could make a car weigh nothing. That is one of the attributes of quantum entanglement and locking, which science has not yet discovered. It allows for **designer mass**.

We have told you before that there is no such thing as anti-gravity. Instead, it is simply the creation of a massless object. Mass can be designed and manipulated. This is one of the first of many lessons we gave twenty years ago, and it is related to entanglement as you know it. But there is a side effect ... energy (I'll get to that).

Supercooling, **designer magnetic fields**, and one other element that you will discover, can come together to actually manipulate an attribute of atomic structure which you now call density. You see it all the time with natural substances. What is the difference between that heavy metal you mentioned and the light one? If you could go in and look at the atoms, could you observe it? The answer is yes. If you could change some attributes of the patterning of the atoms and the symmetry of their quantum relationship, it would change the mass. Would they all come together again in a way that is coherent because they are entangled to keep the object, the same object, but change its mass? The answer is yes.

So, although it's difficult for my partner to explain an attribute that's never be seen, it explains why an object hangs together as an object. The answer is entanglement. It is entangled, or locked with itself in a specific time and space. Do most of you recognize that an object is mostly space? Then what makes it hang together as an object? The answer is that it is quantumly locked with itself.

So you can see that every object has its own "time and space," and the density is by default, conformed. [A natural conforming density that tends to return to its conformed state as is commensurate with the area of the Universe it's in]. But that density can be adjusted. That is one thing. Here is another.

Yawee, we sat together and discussed something personally. It's not confidential. In one of my communications to you, I asked you to put on the shelf the experiments in free energy. Do you remember that?

Dr. Todd: *Yes.*

Kryon: I told you there were two reasons: One is that you have more work to do in other areas first, and I gave you some homework. [The Lemurian Choir Pineal Tones] The second reason is that it would not come to fruition as you would suspect it might. In your own vernacular, I told you that you would *spin your wheels.*

Now I reveal the second part of free energy. There is no such thing as free energy. It is simply *redirected conforming physics.* Now, go slow, my partner [an admonition to Lee to be careful and slow down if needed]. If you're going to have energy created, it's going to have to come from atomic structure somehow. What holds atomic structure together is its *conforming energy source.* If you can change the attributes of that atomic structure, does it make sense to you that you might be able to release energy by reconforming an

object? When you alter the attributes of the entangled or locked state, can you see that there might be an adjustment of energy?

Dr. Todd: *Yes.*

Kryon: That is one of the secrets. Here is another attribute, a hint: Human Beings, listen to this: Physicists, try some experiments with energy that are new, within a very special place ... that would be in orbit. For if you do that, you will be able to have the coldness you need without the additional energy you need to create it. I'll leave that alone and you can decide why. It's part of the secret. Energy used to create a state, often affects the state.

The releasing of the attributes of entanglement or locking within a conforming object, will release great energy. The unconforming of an object must absolutely release energy in a way that you have not seen yet. This is quantum, reflecting two new unrecognized laws of the strong and weak force of multi-dimensionality. This is not the same as the release of nuclear energy as you know it now. This is the release of locked energy within the structure of an object as it changes its attributes of density. It does not reach a critical mass, and it will not explode. It simply channels the energy to another place, which is not seen well in 3D. Multi-dimensional energy is very real. You have even called it "dark energy." It holds the galaxy together.

At the moment, it's going to take supercooling to unlock this. The oxymoron here is that it takes a great deal of energy to supercool anything, but not in space. At another time, I'll give you hints on how to create the temperature you need without space. [See Kryon's answers to the questions below in this section]

Eventually, can you see how you might be able to create a circle of energy from this process? If you can set up a constantly changing density-mass scenario, it will release energy each time the object changes conformity. So remember: Mass wants to always return to a "conformed state." If you change it by unlocking the quantum symmetry, it will return to its natural density when you release the "engine" of unlocking. This is then a push-pull energy. That energy can be harnessed and some of it can be re-used to keep the supercooling active. Then you have an engine that runs itself, and at the same time releases more energy than it uses. It's not free energy. It's redirected energy. The release of this energy is far greater than any of the 3D formulas. You have to guess what it might be. For it is the very core of keeping matter together, and there are simply no known formulas to measure it. It's far greater than you think.

You are used to seeing energy as heat. Redirected energy is quantum, and invisible. So you are going to need a quantum invention to capture it.

Kryon live channelling "Science" given in Sedona, Arizona — June 11, 2012

In summary, Kryon has said that, after you supercool an object, you can redesign the attributes of its atomic structure using designer magnetics. The only problem is we don't even really know what that is yet. If you look into matter, there is a big mystery regarding the atomic structure. For example, if you look inside a rock there is a quantum patterning that makes it a rock, but one of the attributes is its density (how far apart the atoms are). Part of the quantum patterning: is (1) the density of the matter (mass), and (2) what holds it all together to make it a rock. In our gravity, mass equals weight, so designer magnetics could potentially reprogram the density of an object to even make it almost weightless. Can you imagine the practical applications that can be achieved using this technology?

Q.: If entanglement can occur with any object to any other object, then theoretically it would be possible to create a laboratory that is entangled with outer space that could then allow for supercooling of objects where you wouldn't have to use a lot of energy. Is there any information that you can provide about this?

Kryon: A laboratory is not an object. Entanglement requires "designer rearranging" of atomic structure within a substance. Energy and mass can be entangled, but complex mixtures of objects as a package, cannot easily be.

Gaia as a consciousness is entangled with the center of the galaxy. Gaia as rock, water, and air ... is not. But a single rock could be. Entanglement requires a confluence of symmetry within each side of the equation. Don't expect to understand this just yet. But you will.

You don't have to use a lot of energy to create supercooling. This is also something you will discover when supercooling is something you wish to do with more efficiency.

Q.: Can supercooling be achieved on Earth without huge expenditures of energy, for example, using ceramics?

Kryon: The answer is yes, but not by using ceramics only. There is some chemistry that you have not developed yet which will help supercool objects if you can get them to a certain cold (resting) temperature to start with. This is why the mountaintops were especially nice for the technology of the Lemurians. For it was a great starting point, without any energy at all, except that required to travel there (-35°C).

Chemistry is not normally thought of as an answer for temperature control, or something that might create zero point energy, but it can be the answer in this situation in order to take something that is already frozen, into a supercooled state with a little more energy involved. So the extra 240 degree drop needed for absolute zero would be significant, but you don't really need zero point for simple quantum locking (see next question).

You already have seen this chemical process in the lab, but not on a large developed scale. So develop it!

Look for chemistry formulation that attracts heat and "sucks" heat out of almost anything. Like osmosis works through a semi-permeable membrane, heat can also be "sucked" from a more concentrated area to a less concentrated area in ways you have not really seen yet. It will be the eventual basis for portable field refrigerators, and ways of keeping food fresh while off the grid. A battery will be able to keep the chemistry "active."

So the answer is that through a combination of: (1) starting cold, (2) using new chemistry, and (3) new exotic materials, it will give you the ability to supercool without tremendous energy involved.

Q.: Is physical entanglement an entanglement via consciousness of quantum physical objects? Is it the same for love? Kryon states that the space between the nucleus and the electron haze in atoms is filled with consciousness and love. How does this relate to physics?

Kryon: Last question first: We told you that one of the first quantum mysteries you will have when you finally have a "quantum field measurement device" will be the discovery of another kind of life ... quantum life. The instrument will reveal life everywhere! But it will be quantum life. This life will have consciousness without death or reproduction. So the definition of life will have to be re-written, and quantum life will then be included in your reality. But you will be able to see it and interface with it in 3D, making it especially interesting.

Therefore, consciousness and love (something that is created from structured consciousness) will have to be considered a quantum life force, for it will be seen as multi-dimensional life by this new instrument. A building has 3D structure, but life force that varies from moment to moment has potential-based structure ... quantum structure.

A strong and weak multi-dimensional force are the two missing laws of physics. When they are realized, then it will make sense that the space between the nucleus and the electron haze is not space at all, but filled with potential-based reality and structure. It will have energy that explains the space, just like it will explain the puzzle of dark matter in the galaxy (which isn't a variation of a Newtonian function). So the new understandings can now include love and consciousness as structural players in physics. It will also "allow" your logic to see them both as players in entanglement.

Therefore, having consciousness and love in that mysterious atomic space will be a possibility and will make far more sense than it does at the moment. It is the "glue" of God, and the reason why atomic structure has "attitude" and "intelligent design."

First part of the question: Physical entanglement is an illusion. You are only seeing the physical part in 3D. The invisible strings of the missing laws of physics are the real players here, and they

come in many forms and colors. So, entanglement is really a bag of many attributes, and many variables, and therefore, many forms of it exist: elementary to complex.

Quantum locking is only partial entanglement, and an elementary form. You can see it in 3D, and it is created by designer magnetics and designer atomic structure alteration (supercooling). This is beginning entanglement, and involves energy and an object, but distance is still an issue, so it's not full entanglement.

Consciousness is energy, and it can be "locked" to an object. Love (patterned consciousness) is energy and can be locked to either other energy or an object. Objects are harnessed energy, and can be locked together ... many of them. But in both these cases, there is far more involved than magnetics and supercooling. There is a missing quantum engine that hasn't yet been discovered, that "throws" the strings and creates a confluence of coherent atomic structure. Then the two are truly locked into one reality together, and they share the same space atomically. This would be complex entanglement.

There is a lot of energy needed for complex entanglement ... more than you will want to know about, even more than the chemistry we discussed in the former question. For, real entanglement takes lots of energy. Quantum locking doesn't. This is why the complete and complex entanglement that you see in atomic structure (at the very small level), and also in galactic motion (macro level) is possible. Both of these have very strong quantum energy resources to pull from. In the case of atomic structure, it's the energy of the atom itself, which could be seen as very small wormholes connected quantumly to infinite energy. In the case of galactic motion (Vera Rubin's discovery), it pulls upon the center of the galaxy for power.

But in the "middle ground 3D reality" it isn't seen as much, so it's difficult to figure out how to really work with it or make it happen in the lab without a tremendous power source. This will happen when you get cold fusion. Then it will be more viable to work with and much more fun.

The Missing Laws of Physics

Physics, by its very definition, is the science of energy and matter, and the interactions between them. Everything around us, including us, is made up of energy and matter. The science of physics helps us to better understand the world around us, the world inside us and the world beyond us. It is the most basic and fundamental science we have. Here is what the American Physical Society says about physics:

> Physics challenges our imaginations with concepts like relativity and string theory, and it leads to great discoveries, like computers and lasers, that lead to technologies which change our lives – from healing joints, to curing cancer, to developing sustainable energy solutions.
>
> Physics encompasses the study of the Universe from the largest galaxies to the smallest subatomic particles. Moreover, it's the basis of many other sciences, including chemistry, oceanography, seismology, and astronomy (and can be applied to biology or medical science).
>
> *Source: http://www.aps.org/programs/education/whystudy.cfm*

Physics is also considered a general analysis of nature through its study of fundamental natural phenomenon, and the interaction of natural forces. There are currently four known fundamental forces: Gravity, the Electro-magnetic Force, the Strong Force and the Weak Force. The study of gravity and electromagnetism is called Classical Physics, while the study of the last two is mainly comprised of Quantum Physics. To date, Quantum Physics has mostly been studied at the extremely small scale, such as subatomic particles like electrons.

The science of physics, however, is facing a conundrum. Observations are being made that do not fit within the known fundamental forces. Could it be that there are other fundamental forces that haven't been discovered yet? The answer is YES! Kryon has indicated that there are two more laws of physics yet to be discovered. There have been various channelled messages providing information about the missing laws of physics. The following extract helps us to understand what Kryon is trying to tell us:

The New Laws of Physics

Now we speak of physics. Let me give you some history about a conundrum. Let me tell you what science has done with the conundrum. Then let me tell you some things that we have never said before.

It's a beautiful law, it is, and the scientist Newton designed it. It is a law that is responsible for all of the orbital mechanics in your solar system. It explains them all, it does, and it's the *second law of Newton*. It is a description. Careful, my partner, go slowly. [This is Kryon's admonition to Lee to be extra clear.] It is a description in its fundamental formulation of force, matter and acceleration. And these fundamentals explain the movements of the planets – the movement and inertia of motion everywhere. It does it so well that this formula is responsible for the calculations you use to send satellites up, and your space probes throughout the solar system. All of the math, so centered around Newton's second law, works.

If you've noticed, in your own solar system and if you're into astronomy, you'll see what Newton saw – that the planets [items with constant mass] that are closer to the gravitational influence of the sun travel at a different speed than the ones that are further away. This became the formula of the second law of Newton, and holds true today and has held true ... until recently your science discovered some challenges.

The first thing that raised interest was when the particles became too small, and then the law broke down. It didn't follow the rules anymore. When you got into atomic structure, the formula was different. This was actually the reason for the birth of quantum physics – the explanation of the small and the very small and the theories that would go with it, including multi-dimensional ones. And it was OK with science. New theories said that when matter gets super-small, there has to be a difference in the interaction between mass objects. Some say it was due to the fact that smaller particles didn't have the *constant mass* that the planets and moon did ... not too hard to deal with in the mind of the scientist. Also, Human Beings have the ability to experiment with the super-small with atomic accelerators – protons and anti-protons colliding at almost the speed of light to see what happens. So

humans could verify the new laws within the super-small world. Then something happened.

With the advent of the new "eyes" of the Earth through computer-controlled mirrors in telescopic arrays, you began to study distant galaxies and *see* them clearly. Much to the surprise of astronomers, they could see the stars rotating around the center of the galaxy, much like your solar system rotates around the sun, but with a big difference. It didn't follow Newton's law!

To the astronomers' surprise, they discovered that the stars rotating around the center of a galaxy were in what is called a "flat rotation mode." Let me explain this to you – go slowly, my partner [more Kryon admonition to Lee]. If you were to take a disc and put some pebbles on the disc close and far from the fulcrum [center], then gently rotate the disc, you would notice that all of the particles you put on the disc rotate in tandem together, keeping their influence with each other in the same perspective. In other words, one does not go faster or slower due to the distance from the center. That is called flat rotation and that is what galaxies do.

However, suddenly, Newton's second law doesn't work! Stars would have large constant mass, yet they were not following the rules of orbital mechanics. Newton's law seemed to work for solar systems, but not for galaxies. This makes no sense, and is at the heart of controversy, and eventual discovery of something astronomy is starting to see.

In the mathematics of energy measuring of the Universe, science says that something is creating an energy you cannot see that is pushing on the matter in a way that is affecting Newton's law. They say they don't know what it is and cannot see it. It is unseen energy creating a new kind of orbital system, which they are now realizing is in all galaxies. So they call it dark matter, mystery matter that has influence on everything.

Dark matter isn't really dark. It is simply the scientific expression for missing energy. That's all it is. Something is pushing and pulling in ways that do not follow the orbital mechanics of the classic Newton's law. How can that be? Now the conundrum is there. The very small doesn't work well. The very big doesn't work well. Your solar system seems to be fine. Somebody's working on this issue right now, and I have to mention it. So put on your

esoteric hat for just a moment. Newton had an assistant who was very involved in his work. This assistant is alive today and he's an astronomer, of course. He has reincarnated with the passion in his cellular structure to continue the work, and he is! And he's very close to figuring this out.

I'm going to tell you why this conundrum exists. I'm going to do my best to give this to my partner in a succinct way so that you will understand the physics. This has never been revealed in this fashion. You're close to discovery, and it's in the ethers. So I am not giving you anything that Human free choice wouldn't discover on its own. The solution is floating in *the system,* ready to be found.

Adding to the Known Forces in the Universe

When it's seen, the new theory is going to run up against lots of scientific resistance, and I'll tell you why – because you're going to have to rewrite and add onto the four forces of the Universe. [Gasp! Change the known forces? Lee is breathing hard now.] As known by physics, I will give you the names of the four forces of the Universe, and what they're called. I will not explain them, for this is not the venue for that today. Listen to what the scientists have said are the *only* four forces that control everything. The first is *gravity*, and is known as the *weak force*. The second is *electro-magnetics*, and is known as the *strong force*. They're a pair. And the next two are another pair; number three is known as the *weak nuclear force*, the fourth is known as the *strong nuclear force*. Those four supposedly are responsible for everything that happens, but now suddenly there is a conundrum. There's missing energy! Does that not tell you perhaps those four forces might be six? And they are as follows.

I want you to take a look at nature. On your planet, take a look at nature. Almost everything comes up in the factors of 12. Mathematician, you know what the factors of 12 are. [There are six.] The most common factors of 12 that you see in nature are three, four and six. When you crystallize water on its own, it comes up with a six-arm pattern [a snowflake]. The crystallization formations are base-12 with the factors of 12 clearly showing, mostly with six. We have told you for many, many years that the elegant science of physics should be base-12. It is a multi-dimensional math that includes a zero that doesn't mean *nothing* or *infinity*. A zero in universal base-12 math means *the potentials of all the answers probable.* It's not an empirical math as in 3D, yet this math will bring you some realizations when you begin to use it. For instance, does it make sense to you that one of the most profound equations that you have, being that of the circle – called pi [π] – is an *irrational* number? [An irrational number in math is one having an infinite and nonrecurring expansion when expressed as a decimal.] It goes forever! Does that make sense for one of the most profound formulas of the Universe? We happen to know that on one of your spacecrafts to communicate with anybody who might find it, you put that number pi right on the plaque on the spacecraft. It's like a communication in math, in case any intelligent life force should find it, they would then say, *"Oh, humans have pi! Therefore, they must be intelligent."* Let me tell you what an intelligent society will know when they see that. They will look at it and say, *"These creatures are flying in space, and they don't even have base-12! Look what they think pi is! They must still be in base-10."* It's like finding an advanced society with black and white TV. π as expressed in base-12 is not an irrational number.

There are *six* forces of nature. Although four is a factor of 12, six and 12 are the ones that appear the most, and are most naturelike. Look at the chemistry of DNA and behold the factors of 12 in the chemistry. It's everywhere. Before I tell you what the other two forces are, let me tell you about naming things. I will give them attributes, not names, because they will be named according to what science wishes to name them later, and they will then explain dark matter.

There's a difference between the galaxy and the solar system – a big difference. Newtonians, listen up. At the middle of a solar system is ordinary mass. No matter how big or how small the sun is in any solar system, it represents ordinary, consistent mass. When you get into the giant systems such as galaxies, that's where the magic is, and that's where the discoveries are. Years ago, we told you what was in the middle of each galaxy that would cause the rotation, even before it was notated in science. We said there

is something in the middle that is multi-dimensional – a black hole. Some years ago, we then gave you the rest of the story; we said there are twins in the middle of each galaxy. There are two quantum attributes. One that you call a black hole, and one you cannot see that is its twin. They are a push/pull system of multi-dimensional energy. They represent the *missing piece* of the named forces of the Universe and the energy that surges back and forth.

Now, stay with me, [mainly said for Lee]. I'm going to give you some pictures in your mind for this. Let me tell you what happens when you have this kind of multi-dimensional energy in the center of anything. Newton's law no longer applies, since the center is not ordinary mass. This multi-dimensional energy has a cohesion to it. It creates a flat, rotating galaxy because of this cohesion. There's a whole set of laws that must be developed for a *strong and a weak multi-dimensional force*. These are the last two, and now you have the six. You have gravity, you have electromagnetics, you have strong and weak nuclear, and now you have number five and number six, which are strong and weak multi-dimensional force.

New Information about the center of the galaxies

Every galaxy has a push/pull system at its center. This is a twin energy system, but you only *are aware of* one. You're convinced it's invisible, and it's a black hole. No light escapes, but you think it's singular – one thing. How 3D of you! [Laughter] It is not one thing. Instead, it's a beautiful, double eye of a needle. Now listen. When you start mapping the Universe and you see how the galaxies are really laid out, you already know they're not random. Isn't that interesting? Wasn't what you called *The Big Bang* supposed to be something that randomly distributed everything from almost nothing? So why is there a pattern? This is the beautiful part, dear Human Being. There is a pattern in the seeming chaos of the multi-dimensional event that the Big Bang was. As we have told you before, your Big Bang was really a big, multi-dimensional collision with another multi-dimensional force. Multi-dimensionality seems to be *chaos with a hidden pattern*.

Picture with me for a moment a giant needle and thread, two of them. One goes into the black hole and one comes out of it.

These threads are multi-dimensional strings of force that connect themselves to the other galaxies, weaving in and out of their centers, which are all double-eyed black holes. A push and a pull – a multi-dimensional force of which you are not aware of yet, threading the galaxies one to another and to another. Now, picture in your mind that quilt work having a symmetry and a purpose. If you could look down the middle of it, into the middle of the Universe from a certain angle, you would even have the symmetry of a mandala. The galaxies are shaped beautifully together in an elegant dance. The symmetry makes sense, and it's base-12. We challenge you to find this. And those seeming threads that go in and out of those galaxies' centers with this new force I have just described are a lattice. It's a lattice with symmetry and purpose ... *the cosmic lattice* [as originally defined by Kryon many years ago]. It has beauty. And it's the missing energy of the Universe, as seen by those who are looking for it. The dark matter that everyone looks for is not in the empty spaces between things. It's in the strings of the multi-dimensional force between galaxies, purposely put there. Oh, it's a wonderful system. You want the dark matter to make 3D sense, but it can't. It deals with the two multi-dimensional forces of the Universe that are quantum, and therefore out of time and out of the purview of your 3D formulas.

The next big discovery – quantum sight

OK, there is one more. I want to give you this hint. Again, this information is in the ethers. That is to say, that it is available for discovery, and imminent. Humans must discover these things on their own, but we give hints. When the discoveries happen, you'll know you heard it here first. [Kryon smile]

This is technical. Don't worry, my partner. I'll give you the picture. For years, astronomers have been putting special lenses on telescopes in order to give them different kinds of views of the Universe beyond normal light. The collection of ordinary light is passé for real astronomy. They now wish to collect radiation. They wish to have the spectrometry so that they can have an analysis of what things are made of. They like to measure the coming and the going of the speed of objects, so they will have red shift or

blue shift to know if objects are advancing or retreating from the observer. For years, they have been putting special lenses on their telescopes so they can analyze what common light cannot show them. Most of you are not even aware that many of the telescopes of the planet don't even let you look through them anymore! It's all about computer-controlled collection of what is hidden in the light, or what is available through other measuring methods. They know how hot things are, what they are made of, where they are going and their trajectory anomalies.

Wouldn't it be wonderful if someone on Earth came up with a multi-dimensional astronomical lens? And if they did, what would they see? They would see exactly what I've described. First, they would be able to see the twin black holes that appear to be one. A multi-dimensional lens is looking at gravity and time, and the warping of them into patterns.

If you were *looking* at the Universe with this lens, you'd see how the twins relate to each other, the pulse of them, and you'd see the strands connecting the galaxies very clearly. Wouldn't that be wonderful? It would explain the missing energy, wouldn't it? It would give the scientists the reason to increase the four forces to six! And, *it's doable.*

Now I'm going to tell you what it looks like, *almost.* (Kryon smile) Number one hint: You cannot put it on the lens. It must go as close as it can to the receiving device. In the case of an optical telescope, that is the mirror. In the case of a digital telescope, that is its *digital eyeball.* That is to say, that this lens cannot go anywhere but the focal plane. That will be meaningful to those who build telescopes. It must go there where the focus is collected. Hint two: This lens is not physical. This lens is plasma. The plasma is held together by incredibly strong magnetics. Oh, and it's very cold. And those are the hints.

And when you develop it and when you turn it on and work out the adjustments to the magnetics that allow the plasma coherence, you will have the next step in astronomy – a revolution and a revelation. Physics will change; your reality will change; and I will tell you why. This is the last point I make in science before I close. I'll tell you why. When you look at multi-dimensional things, one of the unexpected things you're going to see is life! Life sticks out,

because of life force. You can look into a galaxy and the *stars* that glow [using the filter] will have life around them! How about that one? And everybody can get scared. [Laughter] It's inevitable, you know? That is our science channel.

Kryon live channelling "Physics and Science" given in Mt. Shasta, California. Kryon Summer Light Conference — June 17, 2007

In summary, there are currently four laws of physics, and in very basic and simple terms they are:

1. Strong gravitational force

2. Weak gravitational force

3. Strong electro-magnetic force

4. Weak electro-magnetic force

Kryon has indicated that there are two more laws of physics that have yet to be discovered. This brings the laws to six — which is then more aligned with a "base 12" math for all things. The two missing laws, according to Kryon, that explain dark matter are:

5. Strong quantum force

6. Weak quantum force

The missing laws have multi-dimensional attributes. They are quantum, and explain things that we have not been able to understand. During a channel in Philadelphia in 2012, Kryon further explained the missing pieces of the puzzle and gave us two new things:

Number One. In astronomy, those who look at the galaxies, including this one, don't understand why the stars move around the middle the way they do. All the stars seem to all be moving at the same speed around the center. That's not Newtonian, if you noticed. It doesn't have anything to do with mass or gravity, if you noticed. Every spiral galaxy like the one you live in, has this attribute. The reason is because it's *entangled* with the center. That is to say, that the middle of the galaxy contains something you have called the *potential of a singularity*. It is not a *black hole* per se, but rather, it is a quantum event. It is a push-pull energy. You call it a

black hole, but we call it *the twins*. There is a push-pull quantum energy there, a strong and weak quantum force.

Physicists, listen to this channel. Perhaps things here will lead to discovery of ideas. This galaxy is entangled. Entanglement has many levels, but the largest you can see is that all the stars are quantumly locked at the same speed, no matter how far away they are from the center. There is an "event" which is happening in the middle that is so strong that you rotate with it. You are locked with what happens there. Every spiral galaxy has this attribute, for this is the undiscovered physics of what happens at the center. So what is it that could be in the middle? There's an event there, dear ones, and that's as far as we're going describe it for now. It's not where you meet God. It's something even grander than that. Perhaps there is even a communication with something else?

Number Two. Regarding number one [above]: Isn't it interesting that astronomers and physicists have decided that the only simulation that makes any sense to solve the stars moving at the same speed around the center, is to add in an enormous amount of invisible energy that is not understood, called dark matter? Well, it isn't matter at all, dear ones. It's a quantum law of physics that creates entanglement. Quantum energy is not definable using three-dimensional attributes. So we will just say that it's quantum laws that push and pull on the three-dimensional parts. There's no such thing as dark matter as presented by those who have envisioned it.

Physicists and astronomers, when you start understanding the push-pull energy that has created the Universe, and which is part of the center of this galaxy, you will see the strong and the weak multi-dimensional force that is everywhere, and explains it all. It will solve the puzzle without dark matter, and the formulas will work. Then you will see the truth of it, in almost everything you're looking at. For it will be quantum laws that are at work. Then I beg you, biologists, to start looking inside the Human. For as it is in the small and the large, it is in the Human Being. You will start to see the miracle of quantum DNA.

Kryon live channelling "All about the Grids" given in Philadelphia — April 14, 2012

What does Science say?

In the lectures I attended at university, the creation of the Universe was explained by the Big Bang Theory. One of the objections that I have to the Big Bang Theory is this: How could everything have come from nothing, and then, at a speed greater than the speed of light, instantly expand, thus violating every law of current physics, to create the current mass of the Universe in a nano-moment? Don't get me wrong. I believe that the Big Bang occurred, but I don't believe it came from nothing!

If we look at the information that Kryon has given, then the "Big Bang" is actually a quantum event. This means it is still happening. This is because there is no timeline in a quantum state. It explains the energy of the universal expansion. Science, however, has yet to discover the two missing laws of physics, and scientists try to fit what they see into the three-dimensional Newtonian laws. I believe it is only a matter of time before the missing pieces from the Big Bang puzzle will be discovered. When they do you can just smile and say *"I know that! Kryon told us years ago!"*

There are already renegade cosmologists who think they have the answer in what they call a "cyclic Universe." Paul Steinhardt and Neil Turok have a radical idea that our three-dimensional Universe is but a very tiny part of a "multi-verse." They claim the Big Bang is the result of a collision of membranes between our reality with another. They also say the Big Bang is just the latest in a cycle of cosmic collisions stretching infinitely into the past and into the future. Each collision creates a new Universe. Thus, time and space are both infinite.

So what's stopping cosmologists from accepting this new model? One reason is that at the moment of collision, the extra dimension goes from vanishingly small to literally zero. This creates what physicists call a singularity, a point at which the laws of physics break down, which has created a problem for the cosmologists. Despite this problem, David Spergel, a Princeton astrophysicist, says that the model presented by Steinhardt and Turok "...has the best chance of being right." Kryon has already given the answer by saying there is no such thing as a singularity.

I interrupt this scientific discussion to bring you a Kryon channel that tells us how Universes are created.

Greetings, dear ones, I am Kryon of Magnetic Service. Why would an angelic entity from the other side of the veil choose that name? The very name, Kryon, is an odd name. That's not my name. It's the vibration in the air that I wanted you to hear when you pronounce it, so that your perception would be a certain way. We didn't want the perception to be too fluffy, you see? [Kryon humor] For then we would be accepted or rejected immediately by a certain strata of those who like, or don't like, *fluffy*.

You must understand that we constantly deal with that which is perceived by those in three dimensions. You perceive with a bias of your dimension and your life experience. So a three-dimensional world is still only a piece of reality, even for those who are the highest-minded thinkers on the planet. They are in a perception box. It cannot be helped, and it is honored, but it makes it harder for us to communicate with you. It makes it harder for you, too, for you are constantly trying to perceive a multi-dimensional Universe using linear three-dimensional rules. The 3D perceptions then control the very concepts that you question. It drives your belief. You can't know what you don't know, so you can't even ask the right questions about what you don't know. You are biased in three dimensions and you can't help it, for it is your reality. We understand all of that.

The Universe is expanding. It's expanding because of unseen energy, of course, but it's simply energy you cannot see in 3D. It's expanding at a faster rate than the equations in 3D say it should, when you look at all the mass. So that ought to tell you something which is happening. It ought to tell you something is happening which is out of the realm of what you would expect ... perhaps even out of 3D? Perhaps, it's not even explainable by what you know. So I will discuss it again, for this is old information that I have carried around for a long time.

There are those who would project the possibilities of dark energy, for they are starting to ask the question about energy in the Universe, which you can't see. If you try to fit it into a Newtonian system, then there has to be incredible amounts of some kind of energy you can't see, but which is pushing everything around. However, could it be, that whatever "it" is, is coming from

somewhere else? Then you get into conjecture, so I will tell you this: That which creates what you consider to be the Big Bang, if you wish to call it that, is at work within your expanding Universe ... making it expand.

Your Universe co-exists with other dimensional realities ... other Universes. Postured and sitting in what you think is 3D, is a whole scheme of other dimensions which overlap. They don't interfere, but occasionally an attribute of another dimension gets close enough to yours to affect it energetically, and it pulls upon yours and creates energy that is odd, and doesn't add up in 3D rules of physics. You are expanding at a greater rate because there is a dimensional overlap that's pulling it that way. Eventually, it will get to the place where it will pull it faster and faster. Your science is looking at this, by the way. Over billions of years, another Universe will be created from the *dimensional membrane* of a different dimension scenario, that comes too close to the vibratory rate of yours. In another realm of reality, you will then have another *Big Bang*.

Of course, as your science has described it, there is no such thing as the Big Bang. You don't get something from nothing, yet that's still the prevailing attitude. In the beginning, at least, there had to be energy. So, rather than just saying there was energy which all of a sudden went from nothing to everything, doesn't it make more sense, even in 3D, to think that just maybe ... perhaps ... there was something already there? It's a beautiful system, and an elegant one, that creates Universes. Yours exploded into existence in this way. It had its beginning due to a dimensional shift. Then you have to say to yourself, *"Well, what was the beginning of that?"* And we say, "Oh how Human of you!" There was no beginning. All is in a circle.

Guess what else is in a circle? You won't understand it. You can't. It won't make sense. It's out of linearity. It's *time*. I'll tell you what's going to happen. In your future, what remains to you as a potential, will change what happens right now, for it tends then to become a reality. It pulls upon you, and that is why we are so safe to say that the future potential of your civilization on the planet is positive. The future, which you think has not happened yet, exists as a potential in a multidimensional state, and you are

pulling toward it. So we see it as existing now, and you see it as something that is mysterious. Does energy exist? Does a quantum state exist? Physicists will say yes. Therefore, dear ones, potentials are reality.

If that's the case, is it also possible that your present energy is pulling on past energy? Are there potentials in both directions? There are physicists who are starting to experiment with that very thing. Time is in a circle, and it tells you something. It tells you that potentials are actually catalysts. There are now physicists starting to ask the question, "Is it possible time goes in both directions?" Indeed it does.

Kryon live channelling "Hard Science" given in Sedona, Arizona – July 21, 2010

Kryon often talks about time being in a circle. This is such a difficult concept for us to understand, but it really is important to understanding universal truth. Slowly, science is beginning to see the truth of Kryon's statement about time being in a circle. On November 17, 2010, physicist Yakir Aharonov received the National Medal of Science, the highest science honor bestowed by the United States government, in recognition for his work in quantum mechanics. Aharonov appeared to show that actions in the future can alter measurements made in the past. The full article can be found at:

http://usatoday30.usatoday.com/tech/science/columnist/vergano/2010-11-21-physics-future_N.htm

Here's what Science is saying about the rotation of our galaxy...

Kryon gave specific information about the way that our galaxy rotates and mentioned that it is also the way that all spiral galaxies rotate. The very first astronomer to observe this was Dr. Vera Rubin who has been star gazing since the age of ten. She pioneered work on galaxy rotation rates, and is famous for uncovering the discrepancy between the predicted angular motion of galaxies and the observed motion, through the study of galactic rotation curves.

Dr. Rubin's discoveries seem to present some challenges to the existing Newtonian laws. An alternative scientific theory has been proposed by Moti Milgrom, and is called Modified Newtonian Dynamics (MOND), as a solution to explain the galaxy rotation problem. The theory has little support from the scientific community. However, Dr. Rubin supports the MOND theory stating that:

> *If I could have my pick, I would like to learn that Newton's laws must be modified in order to correctly describe gravitational interactions at large distances. That's more appealing than a Universe filled with a new kind of sub-nuclear particle.*
>
> *Source: http://www.newscientist.com/article/mg18524911.600-13-things-that-do-not-make-sense.html?page=2#.Ul7_9oLNiM8*

Eventually, science will discover that Newton's laws do not need to be modified. Instead, the two missing laws relating to the strong and weak quantum force that push and pull will shed some light on an otherwise dark subject!

Here's what Science is saying about the laws throughout the Universe...

An amazing discovery has been made by a team of astrophysicists based in Australia and England uncovering evidence that the laws of physics are different in different parts of the Universe. The findings have been published in the October 31, 2011 issue of Physical Letters Review, a scientific journal for the American Physical Society.

The report asserts that observations of over 300 distant celestial bodies show that the strength of electromagnetism may change at different places in the Universe.

"A change in alpha generates a very unique fingerprint in the pattern of absorption lines," said John Webb at the University of New South Wales, and lead author of the recently published paper.

Weirdly, the differences in the spectral lines weren't consistent. Quasars in the northern hemisphere seemed to have a slightly smaller value for alpha, while those in the southern hemisphere tended to have a slightly higher value.

"We found that it looks as if one of the laws of physics seems to vary throughout the Universe," Webb said.

The claim is dramatic, and could potentially have far reaching impacts. In their conclusion, the researchers say that this could be evidence for multiple universes, because these results could *"infer a very large or infinite Universe, within which our 'local' Hubble volume represents a tiny fraction, with correspondingly small variations in the physical constants."* Members of the team have also said it might hint at why the laws of the Universe seems so perfectly tuned to support life.

Source: http://physicsbuzz.physicscentral.com/2011/11/
another-law-of-physics-broken.html

These results fly in the face of the long established equivalence principle, which holds that the laws of physics are constant at all points in the Universe.

I think we are living in very exciting times! The shift in Human consciousness has created a new awareness on the planet. Old souls are reawakening and creating a more enlightened society. An enlightened society, in turn leads to higher science, and new discoveries, inventions and technologies. Do you see how everything is "related?"

Q.: What changes can we expect once the two missing laws of physics are discovered and accepted by the scientific community?

Kryon: The very acceptance of the last two laws (bringing them to 6), will be full acknowledgement that Newton's laws are limited to single-digit dimensionality. The entire physics world will split into Newtonian and non-Newtonian, as the new realities begin to settle into provable scenarios. Even with the new laws, there will be the old guard who simply wish to alter the old laws into improbable models, rather than accept the new quantum laws that are potential-based.

Humans love structure, and single-digit dimensionality gives that. It's when you begin to deal with the probability curves of energy in a chaotic state, that scientists shy away. They want formulas to work the same each time, and for math to always equal what charts say it should. But the idea that solutions can change with outside altered attributes is foreign to the linear thinker.

74

Linear: If a chicken will cross the road at 2 kilometers per hour, and the road is 16 meters (52 feet) wide, you can calculate exactly how long it will take for the chicken to cross. In the linear world, this solution is forever.

Quantum: The chicken is crossing the road at 2 kilometers per hour, and sees a rooster coming. Now the solution is variable, since the chicken may or may not change speed. So there has to be a "rooster" rule in the equation. See what I mean? Potentials are important in the solutions of complex problems involving a constantly shifting quantum soup of energy and mass, which you call atomic structure.

You have only observed atoms in 3D, where the space within them is filled with nothing. What if you could see the space as volatile? It would then give a potential to atomic structure that might change ... or not. Welcome to a world where things move around. You allow it in your own consciousness. So why not allow it in physics?

There is a "rooster" effect in ever atom, depending on some variables that you can control.

Chapter Three

The Energy Grids of the Earth

The subject of the Energy Grids of the Earth is what prompted me to write this book. For several years I looked for published information that was specifically about the energy grids of Gaia that Kryon talked about during the channels. The more I searched for this information, the more frustrated I became. The majority of information was about the work done by Bill Becker and Bethe Hagens on the "Planetary Grid"; the Curry Lines, discovered by Dr. Manfred Curry and Dr. Wittman; the Hartmann Net or Hartmann Lines, named after Dr. Ernst Hartmann; and the various descriptions about ley lines and portals on the Earth (none of which corroborated what Kryon said). I couldn't find information anywhere about the Gaia grids that directly relate to humans. Because of my life-long passion about the environment, and my subsequent discovery of the esoteric (spiritual) aspects in all life, I felt an overwhelming desire to make this information available in published form. I also feel that the old souls that are awakening on the planet should have access to all of the information relating to the Gaia system in one place, so that they don't have to search through

many different channels and piece together all the information Kryon has been giving us for the last 23 years.

It is my hope and desire that others will feel differently about the planet once they have the knowledge that everything Gaia does is for humanity. I especially hope that any environmentalists and people that think like I used to (that humans are the root of all evil on Earth) will get a glimpse of the bigger picture, and how every soul that awakens on the planet and demonstrates compassionate action in their daily life is changing the Earth in an incredibly grand way.

The planet Earth has many energy grids, but there are three main ones and they are all here for the divine Human Being. This is because the three energy grids were created at the same time as the seeding of humanity with Pleiadian DNA. The three grids are the Magnetic Grid, the Gaia Grid (or Gaia consciousness) and The Crystalline Grid. In numerology, three is a catalytic number. The three grids are interactive. They are entangled. The three grids exist as one; therefore, things that affect one grid affects all the grids. Human consciousness changes the grids. The changes in the grids create changes within the humans. It is part of a beautiful system that involves our galaxy and the rest of the Universe. (see Chapter Five – Gaia and the Universe).

Each grid has a specific purpose. Kryon explains the three grids in the following way:

The grid system of the Earth is specific in its purpose. It is fine-tuned, and it exists for only one reason: Human setup. Although you might think it is a geological attribute of the physics of the planet, it is more than that. It is a DNA delivery engine! That is what the grid system does. It talks to humanity, Human-by-Human, and it is part of who you are personally. It helps to both separate you and also unite you. It gives you setups, challenges, solutions, and love. It is what some of you relate to even when you think about God! Some would say, *"Kryon, I don't like that idea of physics entering the realm of spirituality. I don't like the grid[s] of the Earth being part spiritual."* I will say to you ... it is the way of it! For as creators that you are, you have created everything that you have before you, including the test, the duality, the contracts, and the engine [of reality] that administers them to your cellular structure. You cannot separate Spirit from your reality. You might wish to believe that it is somehow above that which is physical, but the truth is, that it is the center of all that is physical. You can't leave God out of anything!

Kryon live channelling "The Grid and DNA" given in Breckenridge, Colorado
Kryon Annual Summer Light Conference — July 14, 2001

The Magnetic Grid

The magnetic field of the Earth has been described in an article by NASA Science: Science News, titled "Earth's Inconstant Magnetic Field," in this way:

> To understand what's happening, says Glatzmaier, we have to take a trip … to the center of the Earth where the magnetic field is produced.
>
> At the heart of our planet lies a solid iron ball, about as hot as the surface of the sun. Researchers call it "the inner core." It's really a world within a world. The inner core is 70% as wide as the moon. It spins at its own rate, as much as 0.2° of longitude per year faster than the Earth above it, and it has its own ocean: a very deep layer of liquid iron known as "the outer core."
>
> Earth's magnetic field comes from this ocean of iron, which is an electrically conducting fluid in constant motion. Sitting atop the hot inner core, the liquid outer core seethes and roils like water in a pan on a hot stove. The outer core also has "hurricanes" – whirlpools powered by the Coriolis forces of Earth's rotation. These complex motions generate our planet's magnetism through a process called the dynamo effect.
>
> *Source: http://science.nasa.gov/science-news/*
> *science-at-nasa/2003/29dec_magneticfield*

The researchers say that our planet's magnetic field is in a constant state of change, and that they are now beginning to understand how it behaves and why. The changes they have detected on the planet's surface are driven by what takes place inside the Earth. Their observations

have led them to believe that there is chaos down there. Perhaps, if they were to understand the interactions between the Earth's three grids and Human consciousness, they would realize that this is all part of a system, and that instead of chaos, there is intelligent design, or as Kryon likes to call it "benevolent design."

Kryon is often referred to as the Magnetic Master. Kryon first started to deliver messages to the planet in 1989, and arrived as part of a grid-changing entourage. The reason Kryon arrived was because Human consciousness changed. One of the messages given by Kryon was that the magnetic grid of the planet would move more in the next 10 years than it had in the previous 100 years. By 2002 that is exactly what happened, and it is measurable even with a simple compass. The changing of the Magnetic Grid was a direct result of humanity's intent to create a new reality. The collective consciousness of humans raised the vibration of the planet and the magnetics changed.

The actual changing of the grid is, therefore, more than just a change in magnetics as measured by a compass. The Magnetic Grid interfaces with The Crystalline Grid and the Gaia Grid, and so they have also been changed. Instead of termination, humanity has created a new setup and a new Earth potential.

Kryon has described the Magnetic Grid as the grid of communication. It can even be described as the engine of cellular communication. The Magnetic Grid of the planet is complicated, but in simple terms, it is a delivery system to humanity. For many years, the Magnetic Grid remained the same, because humanity never gave the intent to claim the power of what lies within our DNA. That is, until recently, when humanity decided that it wanted to change its reality.

You might wonder how the Magnetic Grid communicates, and the answer lies in our DNA. Our DNA has quantum attributes, and through the quantum communication (magnetics) we can make changes in our DNA that also affect The Crystalline Grid. One shapes the other, and the biggest thing that is going to take place within The Crystalline Grid is the rewriting of the past. Such a concept is difficult to understand, because Human Beings are biased towards linear thinking. We think that time is on a track. There is a past, a present and a future. Time, however, is actually in a circle, which is why you can change the past and the future. Even the physicists are beginning to understand this.

When you begin to understand the communication flow between our DNA and the planet's magnetic field, it starts to explain what scientists are beginning to observe. There are scientists that measure the magnetics of the Earth on an hourly basis. They have found that the Earth's magnetic field becomes stronger and weaker with the profound events of humanity. During the Boxing Day Tsunami in December 2004, the magnetics peaked. During the event called 9/11, the magnetics of the Earth changed dramatically. The very hour the airplanes hit the towers, the magnetics of the planet changed (as measured by two National Oceanic Atmospheric Administration space weather satellites). During the rescue of the 33 miners in Chile, the magnetics changed. Human consciousness is allied with Gaia.

I think this is incredibly profound. Compassionate events by humans actually raise the vibration of the planet. Here is a statement from Princeton University:

> The Global Consciousness Project is an international, multidisciplinary collaboration of scientists and engineers. We collect data continuously from a global network of physical random number generators located in up to 70 host sites around the world...
>
> When human consciousness becomes coherent (and synchronized), the behavior of random systems may change...
>
> When a great event synchronizes the feelings of a million people, our network (of sensors) becomes subtly structured. *We calculate one in a trillion odds that the effect is due to chance.*
>
> Source: *http://noosphere.princeton.edu*

Magnetics help Human consciousness. There are places on the planet that are neutral; where there is no polarity, such as the equator. In these places, it is more difficult for the Human Being to find the divinity that lies within them. Specifically, it is harder to eliminate fear and negativity. The equator is a difficult place to live. All around the globe on the equator there is war, fear and inhumanity. These places and peoples are the last to awaken. Those few who live on the equator who have already started to awaken, quantumly awaken all others who live on the equator. I would like to honor these souls for holding their light in such difficult circumstances. I have been very fortunate to

have met a group of Lightworkers in Ecuador, and want to encourage you and thank you all for being here and helping to raise the vibration of the planet.

The Magnetic Grid is also like the planet's antenna to the Universe. It communicates with the magnetics of the Solar System. In order for entanglement to occur, you have to have magnetics. Entanglement is quantum energy, and so the magnetic field becomes part of the engine of entanglement between us and the center of the Universe (see Chapter Five – Gaia and the Universe).

> The Earth's magnetic field reverses itself every 250,000 years or so. The North Magnetic Pole becomes the South Pole, and vice versa. Scientists have no clear theory about why the reversals happen. [Many scientists believe] that we're long overdue for a reversal.

Source: http://www.Universetoday.com/27005/earths-magnetic-field

Q.: What can you tell us about the magnetic field reversal cycle and why the poles reverse?

Kryon: Geomagnetic reversals are common and occur every half million to one million years to GAIA. They are slow and sometimes take thousands of years to actual do the reversing process.

The cause of this is not a mystery. You have the magnetic poles of the planet generated by a molten core within the planet, going at a different speed than the rotation of the planet. This causes the generation of the electric, or magnetic field of Earth. It's like an electric engine that then creates a giant field. But a molten core is volatile, and is also prone to anomalies and distress (such as constantly interfacing with the sun's magnetic field). The result is an occasional "magnetic chaos" and flip of polarity.

You are thousands of years away from another full flip, but the process has begun, the last one being almost three-quarters of a million years ago. This very process is why I arrived, for the beginning of the flip helps to recalibrate consciousness. All this is controlled by GAIA, so it is right on schedule and is in cooperation with the 26,000-year wobble of the Earth.

By the way, nothing physical happens to the planet when the magnetic poles reverse. It's the electric polarity that changes. Some have misunderstood this and believe that somehow the actual globe turns upside down. This, of course, would terminate all humanity, and is not the way of Spirit. (Kryon smile).

The Gaia Grid

During my many years working as a park ranger, I was able to experience some remote and pristine places in nature that very few humans have visited. Often, these places would have spectacular views of wild rugged beauty, magnificent mountain ranges, beaches that would stretch for miles or a forest that would blanket you with peace and tranquility. Have you had your own experiences of visiting such places? I sure hope so, and if not, perhaps it's time to find such a place.

While I was working for Parks Victoria, one of the key messages of the organization was Healthy Parks, Healthy People. Most environmental organizations that are directly involved in the conservation and protection of national parks and reserves are starting to rethink and re-evaluate the connection between parks and people. This shift in thinking has been influenced by Richard Louv's book, called *Last Child in the Woods,* in which he coined the term "nature deficit disorder." Nature deficit disorder is not a medical condition; it is simply a description of society's lack of a relationship to the environment. My own personal view is, that it also refers to humanity's disconnect with Gaia, a connection that the ancients understood really well, and one that many of the indigenous still have today. In a follow-up book by Louv, called *The Nature Principle,* seven basic concepts are identified that can help us to reshape our lives.

> *"By tapping into the restorative powers of nature, we can boost mental acuity and creativity, promote health and wellness; build smarter and more sustainable businesses, communities, and economies; and ultimately strengthen human bonds...*
>
> *...we are entering the most creative period in history, that in fact, the twenty-first century will be the era of human restoration in the natural world."*

Isn't it interesting, that this potential "restoration" talks about the reconnection of humans with the natural world. And what does Louv mean by the restorative power of nature? Could he be talking about a special type of energy that exists within nature? Is this Gaia consciousness? Doesn't it make sense that humans who visit areas where Gaia is purely herself, feel a tremendous amount of sweet, loving energy. We experience a sense of peace and re-connect with our divine selves.

The ancients intuitively knew that Gaia, often referred to as Mother Earth, had a consciousness. They understood and recognized the alliance that they shared with Gaia. If you study the many indigenous cultures that are still alive and being practiced to this day, you will see that they are aware of their connection and alliance with Gaia and communicate with the planet every day. They see the Earth as a part of them, not something that is separate. During my time working as a Ranger, it was important to have an appropriate Aboriginal representative at key events. They would always acknowledge their ancestors and the traditional owners of the land, and would include a "Welcome to Country" message.

The Gaia Grid is about life on the planet. The actual consciousness of Gaia is all about humanity. Gaia is, therefore, the grid of life. For over 15 years, the primary voice for Gaia (Mother Earth) has been channelled by Pepper Lewis. Pepper is a world-renowned author and teacher and has carried Gaia's unique wisdom and guidance to many corners of the globe. If you are interested in learning more about what Gaia has to say, you might like to visit Pepper's website: *www.pepperlewis. com*

Gaia holds the Akash inside her. Life holds the Akash inside of it. So any life on Gaia holds its own Akashic Record. Humanity holds its Akash in two places; within its DNA and in the Cave of Creation, which is within Gaia.

Kryon has given very succinct information about Gaia and how she interacts with our Akash:

Let us speak of *Gaia* and the *Akash*. You might have heard that Gaia is an energy, which is of the planet Earth. Gaia is sentient [conscious]; Gaia has innate intelligence; Gaia, therefore, has an intelligent consciousness that "knows" about you. Gaia is able to converse and speak, much like Kryon does. If you have heard that, you'd be right.

Gaia's energy speaks in so many ways, and one of them is seen by looking at the Akash. If you asked Gaia what this is, it would be defined as the "life force of the planet." This takes into consideration everything that is alive, including those things you don't even think are alive. So the concept of the *Akash* of Gaia is huge and is very grand. But tonight, I wish to speak specifically of Gaia's system of the *Akash of the Human Being* in relationship to the Earth. We speak of Gaia's cooperation in the Human spiritual experience, and that, essentially, everything revolves around the Human, even the planet's purpose.

If we start at the beginning and give simple definitions, we will say that there is a system to keep track of *who* is on the Earth. Now you may not think Spirit would need a system at all, and you'd be right. But Gaia does, and there is a reason. For, every single Human soul that comes to this place called Earth makes a difference as a unique energy that actually modifies the life force of Gaia. So when that soul arrives, Gaia creates a record, and more. So, here come the specifics.

The Cave of Creation

Many times I have reviewed a concept with you that I again present. Deep within the Earth, there is a multi-dimensional cavern that will never be found. It has 3D properties that connect it with Earth reality, but it is also multi-dimensional. This is difficult to explain to you, since you only perceive reality in a single-digit dimensionality. So I can explain all I want, but my explanations fall short of your understanding. It would be like I spoke to you in your language and suddenly changed to one you had never heard, where the words were jumbled, backwards, and all rearranged in a nonlinear way. Not only would you not understand the message, but the very strange language itself would be disturbing for you to hear. This is how multi-dimensional things appear to you – chaotic. But I will at least give the information as best I can, so you will know the "what," if not the "how."

The Cave of Creation is one of the only physical objects on the planet that is a dimensional hybrid. That is to say, it has three-dimensional properties that absolutely you would see and understand if it were visible, which it is not – for it can never be found or detected, and it won't be. Within this multi-dimensional place is the record of who you are. Again, it's called the Cave of Creation.

When you come to the planet, this is the first place you visit, even before the birth canal. When you leave the planet, it's the last place you visit before you come home. It, therefore, is the depository of the record of humanity – all of the lives that humanity have lived and the very core soul essence of who each of you are. Here is more information on how it works. It is the Akashic Record.

Each soul in the Cave of Creation is unique. Let us take yours, for instance. What is your spiritual name? It's not a name you can pronounce, dear one, but rather an energy. That energetic name is partly the name of God and is recorded in the Cave of Creation metaphorically, as a stripe on a crystalline structure. The crystalline structure, you might say, is that which remembers the vibration of who you were. So when you come into the planet for the first time, there is a crystalline structure waiting for you (since the potential of your arrival is known). As you live on planet Earth, Gaia and the entire system "knows" you are here. Then you pass over to the other side of the veil. When you leave, you visit the cave again and enhance that crystalline structure with an energy of everything you have done. Then you leave the Earth, but the crystalline structure with your *information* remains.

Now, let us say you come back to Earth, and you're going to have another life and another Earthly name. Before you arrive within the birth canal, another stripe is added to the crystalline structure. Note: *It is the same soul*, but now has stripe number two. As it develops on the planet, the cave knows you will return and activate or awaken the stripe every time you return. So, therefore, you have a crystalline structure for every soul, not every lifetime. Some of the souls represented have a thousand stripes! So perhaps you might understand that there are far fewer of these crystalline soul records than you thought. One for every soul, not every life.

Now I want to tell you something: There are old souls in this room and reading this. That's who you are. Even the one or the two here that have come to this place not necessarily for the program, but to be with somebody else, are old souls as well. You don't have to know about spiritual things to be an old soul. Many walk this Earth and never awaken to who they are, for this is their free choice. But the fact is that the humans who often come to meetings of this kind are the ones feeling the calling to be part of a shift of the planet, the end of one age and the beginning of another. These are the ones whose eyes are on the page now.

The Mysterious Functions of the Cave

So the Cave of Creation becomes the Gaia record of who is here and who has been here. This, then, is the physical part. What I tell you next is the multi-dimensional part that is confusing to the Human Being. Listen: The cave is static in 3D and yet dynamic in multi-D; that is to say, there are never any crystals added or taken away in 3D. That means that there's a crystalline structure for every potential Human Being who will ever live on planet Earth. Now you might say, *"Oh, no, that doesn't make sense. It sounds like predestination. Spirit knows everyone who is coming?"* No, we don't, but this is not predestination. Instead, the cave is predisposed in a quantum way to be complete every moment. A quantum energy deals with potentials, and not empirical [absolute] attributes. Therefore, as things change on the planet, the cave changes quantumly, but not physically. The crystalline structure counts do not change. I can't explain that to you, except to say, this is a quantum event. The cave is always complete. It always has all of humanity in it. It is connected to the past, present and future.

The very confusing thing for you is that this means you are actually *interacting with those who are not here yet*. Again, I can't explain it any better than that, and your three-dimensional mind is not ready to go on that journey. But know this:

The cave is complete.

It's sacred.

It's sealed forever.

The soul crystals remember your lives and the energy of your lives.

The soul energies within the crystals interact with each other.

The lifetimes you live modify the energy of the cave and, therefore, Gaia.

Gaia is there, since the cave resides multi-dimensionally within Gaia.

So, in summary, this cave becomes the record of souls, of their many lifetimes and the energy that they create. Now listen to me, for this is the focus of this message. Whatever you do on the planet, whatever vibrational energy you create on the planet, is imbued into these crystalline substances. The record of that life energy remains on the planet with the accompanying vibration within that crystal – forever.

Mary and George

Let's say you are Mary tonight. I'll talk to you. Mary, when you cross over, the cave is where you're going. It's a three-day Earth journey. Mary, old soul, you've been there before. Oh, Mary, you've been there before – and because of that, you go there in joy. You remember it! You know where you're going, and you remember what it means. You're going home. There is no sting in death, for although there might be a temporary fog of multi-dimensional reconnection, you remember the feeling of joy! This is the promise to you, Mary, that we all take your hand and you feel it. Death of the Human Being is a transitional energy, not a terminal one. There is no "end," but rather a journey to an energy that you remember the moment you take your last breath.

Let us say Mary is a healer. Let us say Mary has increased the vibration of this planet by her very presence of walking on the Earth. Let us say that the Earth remembers Mary's footsteps, because Gaia knows who she is. Let us say that Mary is in touch with her Higher-Self. Let us say Mary has created a mini-portal wherever she goes because of this, and now she passes over.

There is a gathering of humans ... much sorrow. They are so sorry to see her go, because she was a marvelous presence, a wonderful mother and loving Human Being. They cry and there are tears and there is grieving. Well, here's the metaphysical truth: Mary goes to the Cave of Creation and everything she ever was, and the portal she created as a Human, is imbued into her soul crystalline structure. That portal then remains, because Mary was here! The marvelous presence, the wonderful mother and the loving Human is not wasted! It's imbued into Gaia itself, through the process of the Cave of Creation, and that energy of remembrance never goes away. It never goes away! It becomes part of the Earth life force consciousness from then on.

Then she comes again as George.

[Laughter]

Don't just laugh, because here's the real process and the beauty of the system. Ready? When *George* comes in, he picks up Mary's record! Then both George and Mary go to the next area of Akashic teaching, the second of the four parts we are teaching today. The system continues.

The Akash Within your DNA

Everything that is represented in the crystalline of the Cave of Creation regarding your core soul crystal is transferred to your DNA at birth. You transfer it in the Cave of Creation. That's why you go there. It becomes your personal Akashic Record, every lifetime you've been, everything you've ever done is all in your DNA. As we have mentioned before, this Akashic Record resides in every double helix in a multi-dimensional way, and is represented by the billions of chemicals in the 90 percent of DNA that science sees as junk! Science is looking at it with 3D eyes and it seems vastly complex with no symmetry or order. It is, indeed, multi-dimensional to the max! But it's all there in a beautiful system. We have told you that before. But perhaps you didn't get the full implications of what it means?

Think. George, you now have George *and* Mary in your DNA, but only George's body is there. So, what is George going to do with Mary's lifetime in his DNA? I'll give you the answer. Everything that Mary learned is now available to George. Remember

that Mary and George are the same soul, just taking a different form on Gaia at the moment. The beauty of the system is this: The Higher-Self is also the same, since it represents core soul energy. Therefore, George doesn't have to learn again what Mary learned! It's in his DNA. Even the compassionate mother is there. Mary's spiritual journey is there, and at a level that couldn't care less about gender, the love of God is there, created by the journey of a Human soul on planet Earth.

Listen to me. You came into this life and you sit in the chair hearing and reading this – and you're learning spiritual things today. Maybe you think there is a steep learning curve and so much to know? Maybe all this is new, and you are overwhelmed with all this information and the feelings that go with it? Let me tell you, old soul, that you are simply awakening something you already knew. If you give intent, old soul, you will *remember* it!

What if you are a very old soul on this planet? That means you're going to have the wisdom of the ancients in your DNA right now. It means that every page you read in a Kryon book, you can say, *"I remember this. It's right. There's nothing new here. But it's nice to see it in writing."*

[Kryon smile]

Let us now look at the first two attributes of the Akash of humanity. (1) The Cave of Creation is a record of who comes and goes. The energy thereof stays with the Earth and helps the vibration of the planet to change. Therefore, human lifetimes modify the vibration of the planet. (2) The DNA of each Human contains the individual record of the one soul and helps the next incarnation [Human expression on Earth] to become more aware, if this is their choice.

Look at the first attribute in this lesson: It's Gaia related. The cave is in Gaia. It is deep in the Earth and it represents many crystalline structures. "Known by the Earth," you are. Loved by the Earth, you are. Those of you who deal with Earth-like things – nature, animals, even the study of the rocks and land – can feel it. When you walk in certain places, you can feel it! The intelligence, which is Gaia, speaks to you. There is a confluence of energy that wraps around you that says, *"I know you. You belong here. It is appropriate that you step upon the planet.*" Oh, Human Being, for what you do here will change the Universe eventually. Can't you feel it? How many of you have ever walked into a forest alone and felt the company of the trees? That's real!

Kryon live channelling "The Akashic System"
given in Syracuse, New York – September 11, 2010

If you have managed to feel the energy of Kryon in the above channel, and absorbed the messages, you can now see how entangled Gaia is with humanity. Many of us, however, especially those of us who live in cities, often forget to give honor and thanks to Gaia. As often as I can, I mentally say two sentences. *"Thank you, Gaia, for being here. Thank you, Gaia, for loving us."* We so often get caught up in the business of our day, or our own self-awakening process, that we forget to acknowledge our relationship with Gaia. Gaia, our Mother Earth, is loving and giving and ready to renew her relationship with you, should you choose. During a channel given at Mt. Shasta in 2010, Kryon has given us an invitation to reconnect with Gaia:

So the message this night is all about your relationship to Gaia, what is happening on the planet that you understand, some things perhaps you don't understand, a review of some of the things many of you have not heard, and then the discussion of new things you might not have heard. We start with the energy of a remembrance.

The indigenous of the Earth, the ancients, revered the planet they were on. It was like a mother/father to them, and they considered it a source of all good things. It supplied the food, both from the forest and from the ground [hunting and planting]. It supplied water, and gave them shelter, even when it seemed angry. Mythology developed around it and many stories prevailed. Many of the gods of old became depictions of the energy of Gaia. And rather than put it into one scenario of singularity, often the divinity was split into many, god-like energies of the sea, of the air, of the land, of the crops, of the sun, of warmth, and of the cold. But this was always in respect. This has been the longest held view of the planet, and has existed with the indigenous even up to a few hundred years ago ... always in respect.

The Lemurians saw it and were some of the first to establish a protocol with Gaia, seeing Gaia as an energy of consciousness that you then labeled as Mother Nature. And it's this consciousness that we wish to speak of today.

The Lemurians discovered that there was a balance that could be accomplished through the give and take of nature. It was almost like you would go to visit a friend. You'd bring a gift, and so Gaia always was given gifts in return for requests. These offerings always created a balance for those who considered nature to have consciousness. If you took something from the land, you gave something back ... something simple, but something you owned or possessed and that had your energy upon it.

Now, in the process of modern civilization, dear ones, even among Lightworkers, this has not been sustained – for you do not get up in the morning and make an offering to Gaia. You may do all of the other things – talk to your cells and have visions that intertwine with your Higher-Self – but somehow that entity which is Gaia is left behind.

So here is a channelling that invites you to re-establish your connection to the energy of the Earth. This will rebuild a bridge of consciousness of the Human Being with Gaia. For Gaia is in service to humanity and changes itself as your consciousness changes. Remember the premise we gave to you long ago? *The consciousness of humanity on Earth actually goes into the ground [The Crystalline Grid]. This is stored and the Earth responds. Dirt does not respond, but Gaia does. So you might say that humans are actually in charge and responsible for Earth's changes and shifts.*

If you can realize this, then you are going to have substantial control over what is going on Earth-wise. But you must again start by having a relationship. Right now, humans only look at it in fear and say, *"What is happening? I'm afraid of these changes that are outside of the normal I am used to."* The Human is not understanding that much of what is happening, he has caused! It isn't a causation through anything humanity has done in an environmental way, but as humanity in an awakening, consciousness way.

Kryon live channelling "The Relationship to Gaia"
given at Mt. Shasta, California – April 24, 2010

There are some other profound things about Gaia that you should become aware of, but I'm not going to tell you about them just yet. I'd like you to know about The Crystalline Grid first, and then, get ready to learn about something you never would have expected about the system. Which also might explain why you are in love with the whales and dolphins of the planet (smile), and why you are so drawn to certain places like Mt. Shasta and Machu Picchu (bigger smile).

Q.: Gaia has so many wonderful ways of dealing with pollution. For example, the recovery of the ocean and its inhabitants was much faster than predicted following the oil spill in the Gulf of Mexico during 2010. However, how will Gaia cope with all the non-biodegradable waste that is being buried in landfills and filling the oceans? Every year hundreds of marine animals die as a direct result of the rubbish that is polluting the oceans because of plastic products and drifting fishing nets. How can we help Gaia combat this problem?

Kryon: This is easy, for GAIA is at the mercy of humans and their ways. Remember when you stopped producing certain kinds of bags, because your children were smothering with them? How long did that take? Well now it's GAIA's turn.

Look into biodegradable nets that dissolve when submerged in water for more than 30 days; waste that must pass the GAIA test, before being buried; plastic that also dissolves in contact with salt water over time ... etc., etc. Your technology can do these things, and a higher consciousness on the planet will see the sense in it, even at the costs of development. There will come a day when altruistic thinking is applied to the Earth in a much larger measure. It will be "known" at the intuitive level ... a return to the indigenous ways of seeing Earth as "mother of all life."

At the moment, there is the old energy profit motive. Eventually, there will come motives that truly honor environmental issues as much as Human safety. This is what we mean by consciousness shift. If you pollute your planet, you won't live as long.

Q.: The ancient indigenous would regularly make offerings to Gaia and they had a very strong connection with Gaia's consciousness. Should we do as the indigenous do or is our intent to connect with Gaia enough?

Kryon: Intent is enough, for in this newly developing energy, you are becoming allied with the planet in ways that you can't imagine. So, physical offerings are a nice ceremonial remembrance, but a true offering to GAIA is to ponder the love of God daily, and know that mother GAIA is your connection to a greater source. Return to the "knowing" which the indigenous had, where GAIA had a face, and where there was a beautiful system that enhanced each Human who saw it. This is the offering that GAIA wants from an advanced Human race.

The Crystalline Grid

The Crystalline Grid is the most difficult to explain. Before we get into the specifics of The Crystalline Grid, let's take a look at how society interacts with The Crystalline Grid. Many of us are fascinated by ancient sites. Millions of people visit the pyramids of Egypt and the ruins in Italy and Greece. Many archaeologists, anthropologists and scholars seek answers to the questions they have about the civilizations that lived there. Then there are the ancient sites that draw millions of visitors because of the mystical and spiritual qualities that are associated with the site – places such as Stonehenge and Glastonbury in England, Lourdes in France and Machu Picchu in Peru. But what does this mean – a place that is mystical and spiritual? Why do people go there? What is it that they feel there and why do they feel it? The answers are different for each person because we all feel things differently based on what is happening with our spiritual core, our connection with Gaia and our Akashic maturity.

I would like to relate what I have felt at certain places to help explain The Crystalline Grid. When camping in the Australian Alps, where I was flown in by helicopter, I felt really good to be in that spot. It was nice and peaceful, and the energy there was mostly just Gaia as, nothing else has really happened there. Very few humans have been in that area. The first time, however, when I visited the site where the 33 miners were rescued from 700 meters (2,300 feet) below the ground in northern Chile, I felt a profound compassionate energy. This energy was coming directly from The Crystalline Grid. In contrast, when I visited the historic jail known as Port Arthur in Tasmania, Australia, I felt a heavy darkness there, and indeed, it was a place that held many horrors for the prisoners who had been there, as well as the tragedy of a mass shooting where many tourists and staff of Port Arthur were killed by a crazed gunman. This event greatly shocked Australian society, and lead to gun reform laws. This dark energy that I felt at Port Arthur was coming directly from The Crystalline Grid.

So what exactly is this Crystalline Grid which creates this energy that we can feel? The Crystalline Grid is best explained by Kryon, who, during the last ten years, has given us detailed information. The following information has been taken from two Kryon channellings that have been combined to explain all the attributes of The Crystalline Grid:

The Crystalline Grid is a metaphor. You cannot see it, but you can feel it. Crystals hold vibration, and are the only rock on the planet that do. Therefore The Crystalline Grid is a metaphor and the attribute of holding a vibration should give you an inkling of what it does. Not only does it "hold" vibration, it remembers and stores *information*.

...It is an esoteric grid, which means it is spiritual in nature and you cannot see it...

...So let's refine the definition from the above for clarity. The Crystalline Grid of Gaia [the planet] is a grid of the Earth that is esoteric [spiritual] and that stores the life force energy of humanity, the energy of you. Now, this is different than the Cave of Creation. The cave is a record of who you are and what you've done. The energy of your contribution to Earth [whatever it is] goes into the cave, becomes part of the Earth, and stays there. The Crystalline Grid, however, is above the Earth; imagine it laying upon the Earth. This grid is on the exterior. You can't see it, but it's there.

Now, this Crystalline Grid also contains imprints of your energy, but is location specific. The best example I can give you is this. When you go to parts of Europe, you might feel what has happened there. There are layers and layers of war. Some of you have

a hard time meditating there. It's difficult to clear the land, isn't it, because of what's happened on the land? The Crystalline Grid contains everything that ever happened and where it happened. You see? So it is a location-specific Human energy storage grid. Is it part of Gaia? Absolutely. It lays upon Gaia like a blanket of energy of Human consciousness.

Did you ever notice that when you go to certain parts of the planet where almost nothing happened significant in Human history, it's clear and clean and you meditate better? I want to ask you something. Do you think this has an effect on where the spiritualists in this new energy come from? Take a look at where all of the channellers have come from in the last 25 to 30 years. They have come from the pristine lands that never had major wars [many from the western portion of the USA]. Did you think of that? Take a look. This is because it's easier for a Human Being to relate to a pristine essence of Gaia. It creates a far stronger spiritual connection. Again, here it is. The connection with Gaia is there – the connection with the Earth. Why the Earth? Because Gaia is part of a measuring system, a vibrational measuring system. There'll come a day when the Earth is measured for its vibrational attributes – attributes created by what the humans did. Collectively, the entire Human experience lays upon and within this planet, and creates a vibratory rate that is measurable by Spirit. That's The Crystalline Grid.

Everything you do, old soul, is recorded on The Crystalline Grid. It remembers your life. Every footstep is recorded. Just recently in another continent, we told you that The Crystalline Grid is beginning to change the way it "remembers." There are certain things it remembers with certain kinds of strengths. For instance, there are battlefields close by and you can go stand in them and sense things. Some of you who feel things will say, *"This was a place of death and much happened here."* So, how do you sense this? Is something "talking" to you about the past?

It's The Crystalline Grid, giving you a multi-dimensional picture through your emotions and actions. Up to this point in your Human existence, The Crystalline Grid has remembered things in a very linear way: That which was war, that which was healing, and that which was compassion, was remembered and imprinted on the grid in fairly equal ways.

If you go to Europe, you can stand where there were battles and past death in the millions. Many civilizations are represented in one place by layers in the ground. It's hard to channel there, dear ones, just ask my partner. This is because the energy there is not commensurate with a clear portal that needs to open as fully as it can, for channelling. This is The Crystalline Grid at its best. What humans did, it remembers.

Now, I would like to tell you some things about The Crystalline Grid that we have not talked about much. If The Crystalline Grid remembers things that humans did, that would mean that most of the remembrance and "imprinting" is on the land. Water is always being exchanged, so it can't be "imprinted" like the land. Some things that took place on land were later covered by water, so these covered areas do not fully give you the remembrance, due to this. So, even though profound things took place in the past in a certain area, if it's now covered by water, you won't feel it much. Most of all crystalline remembrances are therefore on dry land, so that's where you are going to feel most of the Human action.

Now, you may wonder about such things as the *Bermuda Triangle*, which is water. But it has nothing to do with The Crystalline Grid. We haven't gotten there yet in this discussion, but that's about magnetics. Right now we're talking about what you feel when you stand in certain places, dear ones, where the old soul resounds with the land and feels what happened there. That's The Crystalline Grid, which Human consciousness is resounding with.

We have told you that The Crystalline Grid is responsible for what you perceive as ghosts. This is not what you have been taught, so it's difficult for you to grasp this new idea.

The Crystalline Grid is the ultimate *energy recorder and player.* It will play the event, and play the event, and play it. Where there were profundities of Human drama, it will play it stronger. Sometimes it is so strong that you can actually measure what you are feeling with magnetics and even with temperature variance. That's because it's still *real* in a quantum way. This odd energy does not represent entities from the other side or entities who are trapped.

It is simply a recording of past energy. Sometimes humans can see it happen repeatedly, over and over in these areas. This is The Crystalline Grid at its best, broadcasting what happened there. So understand that ghosts are real, but not what you think. They are a multi-dimensional coherence of past energy, as captured on the grid. This also explains why so much of what is felt is always in the same place, and often repeats and repeats.

Now let me tell you what's happening regarding the grid: As the Earth shifts its energy, The Crystalline Grid is being realigned for compassion. Therefore the way it *records and plays* the energy is changing. Where there is compassion, there will be energy that everyone can feel. Where there was darkness and war and death, there will be less energy than ever before. This realignment means that you'll be able to walk over places that used to disturb you before, and The Crystalline Grid will now be quiet. You'll go to places where there was healing, and now the energy will soar! Where there is appreciation for God and love, there will be portals of gratitude. Even the smallest healing will be noticed grandly.

The realignment of the grid is a refocus to the mother energy. We call it Mother Earth, and it's about time it responded accordingly. So the *remembrance factor* of the physics of the crystalline is changing. What this means is that there will be less energy radiated as the remembrance of hatred and drama, which often fuels the fires of those who sit within certain older historic areas of the planet. In certain places on this Earth, humans are simply not going to feel it, and they're not going to co-operate anymore with hate and war.

Religious belief systems of the planet are going to soften. You're going to see a realignment of what you call Catholicism, one of the largest. Within one to two generations this church will change, and the love of the Christ will be paramount, as it should be, but the rules around the old energy will start to crumble. The church is not going away, dear ones. It doesn't have to go away. Do not judge what you think is correct or not correct for any other Human Being. For, some need the organization, where they should go, and who to report to in a linear fashion. They feel the love of God the same way you do, but they need structure. Some sing the songs and have the healings that you also have here [within the

New Age belief system], and they are comfortable with this. Some are *joiners*, and there is nothing wrong with that. How you decide to love the Creator is up to you. We feel this love no matter what.

So if you can visualize something for this grand church, visualize purity, appropriateness, and integrity change. They will have a chance to do this because The Crystalline Grid remembrance method is starting to change. As Human Beings live on The Crystalline Grid, certain areas *feed* them energy every day with what has taken place there. Can you see what that might do? If the grid starts to remember things more profoundly that are beautiful, then that's the energy that will be felt. This is a recalibration of the grid.

There is no symmetry on The Crystalline Grid. Humans like to work in symmetrical ways, so they look for symmetry in all things. If you start drawing lines between these places, you should know that you're not going to find that they spell something, or solve a hidden mystery. There is no puzzle from one to the other, that will reveal more information. Instead, it's what Human action did in certain places that creates the patterning of the grid, and the patterning is not a symmetrical one.

Kryon live channelling "The Akashic System" given in Syracuse, New York
— September 11, 2010; Kryon live channelling "All about the Grids"
given in Philadelphia — April 14, 2012

Earlier I mentioned feeling a profound compassionate energy at the site where 33 miners were rescued in northern Chile. This event also changed the magnetics of the planet. Do you know that the number of people who watched the rescue of the 33 miners, was as many as watched the Apollo landing on the moon? That's almost a billion people. Were you one of those who watched this event? I was actually in Chile at the time of the rescue, and I remember cheering and crying as the drama of the rescue unfolded. It wasn't until later that I truly appreciated the enormous significance of this event. If you take a look at every other compassionate event on the planet, they all have one thing in common. They involve tragedy. The rescue of the 33 miners, however, was the first planetary compassionate event caused by celebration and joy instead of sorrow and death.

A very good friend of mine, Jorge Bianchi, was paying close attention to the numerology and various facts that surrounded this event. Jorge is from Chile and has presented the profound truths about the rescue of the 33 miners at various Kryon seminars, including Australia, New Zealand, Bulgaria, Russia, Kazakhstan, Ukraine, Portugal, Spain, USA, Colombia, Argentina, Brazil, Peru and of course Chile. Here are Jorge's words regarding the 33 miners:

. . . .

A Compassionate Event that Changed the World

It was the year 2010 and the world was about to witness a first of a kind event. This event signaled the beginning of new times. A completely new cycle in human history. The event took place in the country with the southernmost lands in the world: Chile. The sequence of events and the startling coincidences that surround the accident and entrapment of the 33 miners and their amazing rescue clearly show the infinite benign power of the Human Spirit. The words that follow cover the main highlights around this event, but there is so much more to discover. Enjoy!

Chili or Chile?

Let's begin where we should. First of all, there is no link whatsoever between Chili and Chile. Believe me, there is none! In fact, Chileans do not even eat spicy food all that much … Chili is a Mexican thing! Chile, on the other hand, is a long, skinny country, ranging almost 5,000 kilometers (over 3,000 miles) from north to south. Its width? Not much, just an average of 170 kilometers (about 100 miles). Very high mountain tops on the east: The Andes, and a vast ocean on the west: The Pacific Ocean. Population: a mere 17 million people, with about 40 percent living in the Capital's metropolitan area, named Santiago. Chile, a 200-year old republic, has Spanish as its main language.

A main aspect I would like to highlight is Chile's economic and business performance. The country has adopted and steadily applied the western recipe. One of the most opened economies in the world, in recent years Chile has ranked among the top 10 economies in the Index of Economic Freedom, usually an indicator of economic opportunity and prosperity. The country's economy has doubled in just 10 years and is considered to be the most stable and solid economy in the Latin American region.

Nonetheless, Chilean people do not seem all that content about all of the country's economic achievements. Cheerfulness is not necessarily one of the Chilean culture's main attributes as it compares to other Latin American countries. However, it almost seems as if there is an intrinsic level of restlessness that no economic or material achievement would ever satisfy. As a Chilean I am allowed to say all of this!

2008: A Message of Great Profundity and a Warning

Throughout the years, I have always felt very blessed about being part of events and retreats with Lee Carroll and the messages from Kryon, both as an organizer and as a speaker and teacher. The Kryon information has consistently been very encouraging and eye opening, which explains why crowds gather from hundreds to thousands to share with one another and to hear each new message. However, one particular event marked me deeply. It was the first Kryon Discovery Retreat to take place outside of the United Sates. The retreat was in October 2008, at the beautiful Valle Nevado Resort, located at an altitude close to 3,000 meters (about 10,000 feet) high up in the Chilean Andes.

There were many amazing details and synchronicities that surrounded that retreat. Unfortunately, there are too many to relate. Instead, I would like to focus on two major messages from Kryon. In general, Lee Carroll never records the messages from Kryon at Discovery Retreats. Following this protocol, the messages at this particular retreat were not recorded, either. However, Eduardo Borrello, a wonderful Argentinian film director and a good friend of ours, asked for permission to film some portions of the retreat. He was putting together footage for a documentary he was creating. Little did we know that this footage would capture a most profound and prophetic recording of a message from Kryon. I had completely forgotten about this recording until Eduardo contacted us almost two years later, sometime in March or April 2010. He said that we should look at a

particular segment from one of the messages from Kryon during the 2008 retreat. I transcribe it here:

"What is happening in Chile?

Some of you don't know, do you?

The ancients have foretold us.

Go find it.

So you know that Kryon didn't somehow give you something that is not so.

For within the Gaia structure, there are spiritual lines of influence that move down the planet's landmasses.

And there is a great shift occurring on Earth.

And there is something called the Kundalini of the planet.

A spiritual term, go find it, go see what it means, because you will be impressed.

Kundalini is an energy that vibrates and then moves.

Whoever is in the Kundalini of the planet cannot sit still.

The greatest masters of the planet often come from the countries where the Kundalini is residing.

Since your grandfathers were born, the Kundalini has resided in India.

It is now moving and will end up in Chile.

Now, this comes with a price!

When you have this kind of action, the Earth moves a little more than normal.

Most of it will be south of here.

But get ready for shift!

I did not give this to you first, it has been written and it is so.

The Indigenous of the planet, the ones who track these things spiritually, have seen it coming.

It is written, go find it.

In Chile."

The implications of the shift of the Kundalini energy of the planet from the northern hemisphere to the southern hemisphere are enormous, so much so, that the subject deserves an entire book of its own at some other moment (soon!). For now, I would like to emphasize some key phrases from above:

"Kundalini is an energy that vibrates."
"The Earth moves a little more than normal."
"Most of it will be south of here."
"Get ready for shift!"

February 27ᵗʰ, 2010

It was originally reported to have started at 3:33 am and later adjusted to have been at 3:34 am. February 27th, 2010 was the date when a three-minute long, 8.8 Richter-scale magnitude earthquake hit Chile. This was one of the ten strongest earthquakes in the world's recorded history. It was roughly 1,000 times stronger than the one that hit Haiti at the beginning of that same year.

The most destructive forces were the consecutive tsunamis that followed after the earthquake, impacting hundreds of kilometers of the Chilean coast. Tsunamis of much lesser magnitude hit different places from Japan to New Zealand.

Several research reports using GPS revealed that the 2010 earthquake shifted Chile's capital city, Santiago, almost 30 centimeters (11 to 12 inches) to the southwest and moved Chile's second largest city, Concepción, at least 3 meters (10 feet) to the west. Some cities south of Concepcion were raised by up to 3 meters (10 feet).

Although the large majority of modern buildings and construction resisted the earthquake well, Chile was still devastated. The earthquakes and tsunamis had been so vast, that the overall level of damage was enormous; there was chaos everywhere. The percentage of population whose homes were either destroyed or severely damaged was as high as 20 percent in the two most affected provinces. In terms of casualties, over 500 people lost their lives, a very small number when compared with the Haiti earthquake earlier that year, or with the 2011 earthquake and tsunamis in Japan. Nonetheless, the suffering of so many families, with losses of loved ones and their homes, struck Chileans very deeply and the entire country was deeply moved into action and helping those in critical need.

I was fortunate. My family was not hurt and our homes were not badly impacted. We were very thankful. We focused on fixing some minor damages to our homes — my house's roof had a hole in it — and

helping as we saw fit. I did not recall the 2008 message from Kryon, in which I believe we were given an advance notice. In fact, Kryon seems to have even hinted to us about where the epicenter would be "... Most of it will be south of here." Our friend from Argentina, Eduardo Borrello, contacted us several weeks later to let us know about that particular message from Kryon. The message seemed so oddly related to the recent earthquake. That significantly increased my level of attention to what was happening. Could there be a deeper meaning to all of this?

Chile recovered fast. Main infrastructure was repaired or replaced with temporary solutions after only three months. Building all the new houses to replace temporary, emergency housing required many more months. However, Chileans were not necessarily proud about this amazing recovery. They remained introspective, emotionally moved inside. I now believe, that this major natural disaster was key in creating the profound level of connectedness and emotional intensity that gave rise to the very unique series of events later that year.

33 Miners

Less than six months after the earthquake, on Thursday, August 5th of that same year, Chileans were struck by the news of a major mining accident in northern Chile involving dozens of miners. A century-old mining operation, called Mina San Jose (Saint Joseph mine) had collapsed, leaving 33 miners trapped inside. The San Jose gold-copper mine is located deep in the Atacama Desert. This region is one of the harshest and driest on Earth. The mine is 45 kilometers (28 miles) from the city of Copiapo. This particular mine operation had a long record of safety violations and previous geological instability.

It was not known whether the men were alive or not. No communication with them was possible, since all communication lines and vent pipes were severed, as rocks weighing thousands of tons collapsed inside the mine.

Initial rescue attempts met with failure. Rocks continued collapsing and geotechnical instruments confirmed that the earth was still moving. It became clear that the 33 men, alive or not, would be trapped for a long time, or perhaps even forever. Trapped at about 700 meters (2,300 feet) deep inside the ground, in a dangerously unstable century-old mine, meant that chances of ever getting back to the surface were really slim. Given the mine's past history, it was originally thought that the miners probably did not survive the collapse, or if they did, they would most likely starve to death before they were found, if ever!

However, Chile was different. The suffering of so many families because of the earthquake earlier that year meant that Chileans were not willing to so easily accept further suffering from more families. You could say that Chileans were a bit emotional, touched in their hearts a few months earlier, and not very rational. And in this case, that made a big difference.

Think about it for a minute. What would you "rationally" do about this situation? 33 miners, of whom you have no idea of whether they are alive or not, are trapped 700 meters (2,300 feet) deep – almost 2 times the height of the Empire State Building, but going underground. There is no possibility of communicating, in an almost completely collapsing mining operation. I will tell you what most places in the world have done (including Chile in earlier instances): they wait to see if there is any communication, while some experts assess how a rescue team could eventually go down there, and if not much happens after two or three weeks, you just prepare families and people in general to withdraw any efforts and pray for the souls of those who were lost to the depth of the ground. In China alone, more than 2,000 miners are killed each year in mining accidents similar to this one.

But this situation was different. The emotional state of so many Chileans, including many top government officials, was closer to that of a heartbroken mother. What would a mother, not a country, do for her children if they were trapped deep in the ground? Easy answer: she would do whatever she could, regardless of whether it made sense or not. This was Chile's behavior. The country undertook what many could call desperate actions to reach the miners, hoping that they would be alive, at least most of them. The Chilean government, led by President Sebastián Piñera, who had just taken office some ten days after the earthquake, got involved and took control of the rescue efforts, understanding that the mining company would lack the resources to do it effectively. Chileans' public opinion did not hesitate to support all government-led actions. There were not even discussions on popular TV programs about whether this level of involvement and expenditure

made any sense at all. At times, I felt as if the Chilean people were hypnotized, but hypnotized by their active hearts, which were so deeply connected with the hearts of the miners and their families.

The first rescue strategy was abandoned. A second plan began to develop. There had to be another way to get the men out of the mine, without using the main tunnel. Chile is a mining country that has mastered the technique of getting precious metals out from deep inside the ground. A decision was made. Chile would drill to reach the miners.

August 22ⁿᵈ

Chile searched for the best experts in drilling operations with specific, long-range targets. The country also gathered and opened the doors to the best rescue intelligence possible, with teams from many different countries and international organizations, including NASA. The heart of the country began to fuel the best brain and skill sets available. And so the adventure of rescuing 33 men from the ground began.

Following the global appeal for help, there were more than 25 companies from at least seven different countries that offered assistance. In the end, there were nine drills nearby that were available to assist. There was no real plan behind the drilling and 15 holes were created with an urgency to reach the miners. Many of the drills encountered problems along the way. If the miners were alive, they would likely be down at the refuge, as that was the place where the miners knew they could potentially find some very basic and limited supplies. This was the target toward which the drillers were headed.

A camp was established on the surface. Its name was Campamento Esperanza (Camp Hope), which began with just family members and mining experts, and then grew larger and larger as teams from more and more news broadcasters joined in to learn and report about what was taking place. As the days turned into weeks, the families were filled with despair, but continued to hope for the miracle that would reunite them with their loved ones. 33 small white structures, resembling small shrines, were put in place up on a small hill next to the camp, one for each of the men trapped. Prayers could be heard day and night.

The drilling continued. Some probes reached the right depth but seemed to have missed the refuge altogether. Emotions of everyone involved continued to soar between hope and despair. Seventeen days after the accident one of the drills hit an opening. The drill was turned off and lowered into the hole. When the drill was retrieved onto the surface, rescuers were amazed by a message taped on to it. It was August 22, 2010, the 33rd week of that year. Furthermore, if we apply conventional esoteric numerological systems to this particular date, when we add up the digits (numbers) in the full date – day, month, year – we get a 33. In numerology, numbers 11, 22 and 33 are considered to be Master Numbers. The digits in these particular numbers are never added up together. So, a 22 does not become a 4 (2+2) but instead it remains as a 22. August 22nd 2010 then becomes 8+22+2+0+1+0 = 33.

That message on a small piece of paper written in red color would soon become a symbol of human determination and endurance. More importantly, it represents the enormous power that we humans have when our motives come from our heart.

The message read:

"Estamos bien en el refugio los 33"
("All 33 of us are fine in the shelter")

Against all odds, all of the 33 men were alive. Their message was not, "Get us out of here! And please send some food!" It was a different message, one written in heart-red color, speaking of family love. Their message was directed to their families, to give them peace and calm. Their message was to dispel the anguish that they knew their families were experiencing.

The men had survived on rations found within the refuge. Waves of great excitement could be seen throughout the entire country. There were people celebrating on the streets everywhere. The 33 miners are alive! Sure, they were still trapped down there and it was not evident that they could be safely rescued at all. However, the inner feeling of having done the right thing, of having decided to drill and search for them, gave the Chilean people an almost euphoric mood that lasted for weeks. Kindness and smiles could be seen everywhere in the streets of Chile's busy cities. No economic or material achievement of any kind had created that kind of effect before – not even the national team winning soccer matches at the World Cup!

The ordeal was far from over. The big questions were: How would they continue to stay alive and how would they get out?

The original message, written by the miners in Spanish, contained a total of 33 characters, counting the spaces in between words. It became evident that something of historical importance was taking place. I was completely engaged and paying close attention to all of the details day by day.

33 Days of Drilling

Once the miners were reached with the probe on August 22nd, everything got set in motion to get them out. The rescuers had decided that they would need three drills working in parallel 24 hours a day. The three parallel drilling efforts to rescue the miners were called Plan A, Plan B, and Plan C. The three drilling boreholes to be utilized were baptized and called "Hope," "Perseverance" and "The Hand of God." Walter Herrera, one of the managers of a drilling firm involved, was even reported to say "It was almost impossible to get to the point where we are, we had many problems with (drill holes – probes) deviating. It was God's will that guided us." Basically, in one way or another, all three plans were meant to drill a hole wide enough to be able to send a rescue capsule down and bring the miners, one by one, back to the surface.

During the entire time of the preparation and drilling of the 3 plans, the miners were fed, sent clothes and medicines, and taken care of, both emotionally and mentally, through a very long and thin pipeline, put in place in one of the boreholes drilled by the mining probes. It is said that reality exceeds science fiction. It was the case here. To me, this whole situation resembled so well the nurturing of a baby through the umbilical cord that connects her with her mother. It would seem as if Mother Earth was having 33 men in her womb, being nurtured by father humanity, until the time would come to be born onto the surface as new men.

While the three drills carried on with the drilling, the Chilean Navy was busy manufacturing three metal rescue capsules. What a coincidence – three plans and three rescue capsules – another 33! In the end, Plan B reached the miners first. It took Plan B a total of 33 days of drilling to do it. Here we see that mysterious number once again.

This event was filled with the number 33. It is just everywhere. My background is in engineering and business. In my early career, I studied and applied statistics and probabilities quite a bit. You may consider the numerous appearances of number 33 as just a coincidence, if you wish. However, I have to tell you that the probabilities of something like that happening is 1 in billions … Is there anything more realistic to believe than just coincidence? Is there enough space in our minds and hearts for the extraordinary?

The Rescue

October 13th, 2010 turned out to be the day of the rescue. The miners had been trapped for 69 days already. This is longest time anyone survived underground after a mining accident. Rescue leaders did not want to wait a single day longer. The capsule specifically designed and built for this rescue was tested through the rescue shaft. This capsule was given the name Phoenix, as the miners were about to be re-born from an almost certain death path. The test went well and five rescuers were sent down to the refuge to assist the miners in the process of getting securely into the Phoenix.

Miners were brought to the surface one at a time. Every half hour or so, another new Human Being would get out of the Phoenix and set foot on the surface. A previously chosen family member would be there to greet and hug them. It is estimated that over 1.3 billion people all over the world watched the rescue. Only four events in history have had that level of attention. Some even argue that this has been the one with the largest audience of them all. The rescue of the 33 miners was profoundly different from any other event on Earth. The key attribute is, that it was all about good news and about the great capacity of humans to do good. It was about love and family, celebration and joy, not tragedy.

For me, that October Wednesday is a date I will never forget. Throughout the entire time from the earthquake in February to the events of the 33 miners, my personal life had being filled with intense synchronicities and profound events. In June of that same year, my father-in-law had fallen ill, diagnosed with terminal cancer in his brain. He came to live with us right when the miners got trapped in early August. He passed away on the very day they were being rescued,

shortly after the third miner had been brought to the surface. In addition, on that same date, Lee Carroll, Doctors Sid and Amber Wolf, Peggy Dubro, Robert Coxon and the author of this book, Monika Muranyi, were all gathering together in Chile to join in the second Kryon Discovery Retreat high up in the Chilean Andes.

On that October 13th, the rescue operation lasted for almost 24 hours. The last person to be brought back to the surface was one of the rescuers. He set his foot out of the Phoenix and on to the surface at exactly 33 minutes past midnight on October 14th.

A Present for a Mother

Mina San Jose, where the miners had been trapped, is located in northern Chile. It is deep within the Atacama Desert, famous for being the driest in the world. Every few years a beautiful phenomenon takes place in Atacama. The desert blooms alive with amazing flowers. 2010 was one of those years. The week of the rescue, flowers exploded with bright colors and incredible life force, making 2010 one of the most magnificent blooms of all.

Mother Earth had just given birth to 33 men. They were born anew in this same lifetime without dying. What is one of the most traditional gifts usually given to a mother when she gives birth to a baby? You got it! Flowers.

Number 33

So, what is it about this number 33? What does it mean? Why did the number 33 appear so many times throughout this event? Of course, there are biblical implications, such as the age of Christ when he was crucified and many other links to historical or biblical information.

My research showed that many consider 33 as the number of the avatar – incredible humans such as Jesus Christ, Buddha or Mahomet. Others consider 33 as the number that represents the Master Healer. Some say it is related to the strengthening of the energies of love in the presence of higher Human consciousness. What is it in this case? Many have suggested that this event may be signaling the second coming of Jesus Christ, in the form of a new consciousness emerging in common men and women. What is it?

I decided to ask Lee Carroll if we could get a message from Kryon about it. He accepted and the message was, that this particular number 33 symbolizes "Compassionate Action." Right on, I thought! I couldn't agree more. This event certainly illustrated a very high level of compassion, expressed in the determination of Chileans to search for and rescue the miners. At the same time, lots of intelligent and skillful action was required to actually do it, to find and rescue them.

Another number that sticks out is number 7. The miners were trapped at approximately 700 meters deep (a 7) for about 70 days (another 7). When linked to a specific event, several numerology systems regard number 7 as an indicator of "Divine Purpose." Could it be?

My inner self, Higher-Self, my consciousness, or whatever you would like to call that part of ourselves, tells me even more. I believe that this event signals the beginning of new times: the cycle of the New Kundalini of the Earth. According to many indigenous prophecies – Mayans included – and other sources, including Kryon, this new spiritual cycle will last for about 13,000 years. Some of those sources explain that the core of the New Kundalini is centering itself in the area of the Andes Mountains shared by northern Chile, northern Argentina, Bolivia and southern Perú. That is exactly where the Atacama Desert falls and where the miners were trapped! In fact, that entire area of the Andes is where Condors are most often spotted, thus hinting links between these events and other prophecies of similar content but with other names, such as the coming together of the Eagle and the Condor.

I will say even more. I believe that the events of the 33 miners are not only a marker signaling the definite beginning of the cycle of the New Kundalini of the Earth. I believe that these events also show that this new cycle involves the choice to be born anew as a new kind of Human Being, a next step in evolution – a process that is similar to the transformation of the caterpillar into the butterfly. This is the beginning of the era of the New Human, who emerges from the old human, without dying – a New Human who acknowledges and honors a very profound link to Mother Earth.

Welcome to the era of the New Humans, those able to create a New Earth through Compassionate Action. Are you becoming one of them?

If you would like to connect with Jorge or attend one of the many seminars or events you can find more information on his websites:

www.jorgebianchi.com

www.NewHumanNewEarth.com

. . . .

I hope that one day, the rest of humanity will be able to recognize the significance of this event. I was fortunate to have actually visited the site of the 33 Miners Rescue during the Kryon Kundalini Tour in 2012. We all felt incredibly special to be the first spiritual group to visit this place. I hope that many more will visit and that those in Chile will see the potential of this site and create opportunities for many more visitors to go there. While we were on-site at the San Jose Mine near Copiapo, Kryon said the following:

A compassionate event occurred here. Compassionate events on the planet have almost always been through tragedy. It's difficult to talk about, because it is not understandable by humans. The idea here is that you know before you come in, the potentials of what you might participate in. It's not predestination, but rather a setup of appropriateness that has a potential to be fulfilled.

A hammer is not predestined to pound a nail, but it is predisposed for the task. If the hammer never is near a nail, then there will never be the pounding. Karma steers you into predisposed plans, but if you drop it, then you are your own life's map. This has been the teaching of Kryon for years. But those who are hearing this message are mostly the one percent of the Earth's population who are wise old souls, and know what this actually means.

Compassionate events raise the planet's vibration. Therefore, those who participate have then been a catalyst to help Gaia in those times where these things needed to happen. This is currently the only way that the planet has to create large vibrational shifts where over one billion people at a time can see and participate in the feelings of one event. Your science has now proven that compassionate events create a coherent energy that affects geomagnetic energy.

Another compassionate event on the planet occurred in what you call 9/11 [referring to the terrorist attack in the USA of September 11, 2001]. Do you think that those three thousand people agreed to what took place? The answer is, Yes. You have the *mind of God* before you arrive here. Creating a compassionate action for the planet is one of the finest things you could do, and many went right into it.

Two hundred eighty-three thousand Human Beings perished in the tsunami [referring to the Tsunami of December 26, 2004]. Many of them were children and the compassion was great throughout the planet. Do you think each soul knew of the potential of what they might go through at that moment? And the answer is, Yes. Even the death of one or two creates compassion, if many know of it. The death of Princess Diana [August 31, 1997] was celebrated and honored by many. The celebration was of her life and yet one billion people knew about it.

Now, I want you to take a deep breath for a moment. What other compassionate action event on this planet have you seen in your lifetime, which was not a tragedy? What other compassionate event was seen by the entire world, that wasn't about death and sorrow? The answer is none.

Pause

Oh, there have been things that a billion people have watched together, but nothing that created the feelings that were created right here in the dirt, where you are [San Jose Mine, site of 33 miners' rescue]. Think about this, and what this area then represents to the planet.

What you are seeing here, dear ones, is a change of paradigm. For the first time, compassionate action was created through the saving of lives, and it was against all odds that it could happen. It was not a tsunami and not a terrorist attack, but the energy and compassion of mother. As Gaia birthed 33 men in this desert, let it not be lost on you all of the symbology of what took place here. For it symbolizes the very birth of a new paradigm of compassionate joy and thankfulness ... right in South America.

113

Each of these men knew of this potential before they arrived. It was the first time that a compassionate action event took place in this way on your planet ... first time. This is important, for it changes the very idea of how Spirit works with humanity. It's the beginning of a new paradigm ... even of a new Gaia. Think on these things, for it is the reason why you are here on the Kundalini Tour. Celebrate the changes, and look at the land where it is happening. Feel the Pachamama! For it is here now.

And so it is.

Kryon live channelling "33 Miners"
given at San Jose Mine, Copiapo, Chile – October 24, 2012

There are a few other things you should know about The Crystalline Grid that Kryon has talked about:

Gaia takes its cue from Human consciousness for the *energy to create* on the planet. We have told you that for 22 years. It also goes the other way, for your DNA as a whole responds to something called *The Crystalline Grid* of the planet. It's an esoteric "memory grid" and is the stored energy and events of humanity. We've given you teachings about The Crystalline Grid before, but you might say, it is a shell around the dirt of the Earth that is not seen, but that holds all of the energies and history of anyone who has ever lived on the planet. When you are born, and at your first breath, the quantum field of your humanness looks at The Crystalline Grid and adjusts its efficiency for the energy of the planet. This energy is what humanity has been created, in the time it has been here.

Right now, the energy on this planet is filled with millenniums of war, old energy fighting, machismo, and intolerance. This, then, is what the DNA adjusts to at your birth. Whereas you are designed for 100 percent DNA efficiency, right now it's at 30 percent. And that, dear ones, is what is changing, for the DNA is now starting to operate at a higher efficiency, because there's a consciousness shift going on. You're seeing it first, of course, with the ones who are currently being born. At their first breath, they're now at 35 percent, and this translates into a Human Being that is far more aware and more conceptual at a far earlier age. It's almost as though they have an instinctual awareness of overall Humanism, instead of having to learn it all over again, as you did.

We have told you about these new children, and that is why your children are so unusual, and you know they are. Many in the audience who have grandchildren are really seeing it; the kids are different. So you might say, *"Well it's too bad that we can't do that ourselves, raise our DNA efficiency."* Well, you can! For the energy of the planet is alert and ready to send the signal to the old soul who starts to understand that they can change their own fields through the templates that float in them, through consciousness, pure intent, and through that which is compassion. You can change the quantum "print" of DNA with compassion! We have said that from the beginning, so let me summarize this in simple words that are not scientific. Go slow, my partner. Make this succinct. [Kryon talking to Lee]

New DNA Adjustment to New Gaia Energy

Your DNA adjusts itself for what has happened on the Earth when you're born. It has created a reality for you that you call *Human Nature.* The Earth changes, The Crystalline Grid is actually lifting the veil slightly, and your DNA is starting to respond. The first response will be seen within your children, and they are already coming in with a different conceptual Human attribute. They don't think in the same linear fashion you do. Have you noticed?

This is going to change more and more as time goes by. Eventually, there will be a much more efficient DNA that creates the missing bridge between the Innate and the normal Human brain. That means that you will have more intuitive thoughts about what is wrong and right within your own cellular structure. Some of you will discover different eating habits for the first time, and you'll be tuned in to a cellular structure that says, *"If I will change this and that, I'm going to live longer."* The result will be instinctive eating changes that have no explanation. Innate is starting to communicate.

Habits that you've had for years will start to drop, away because your cellular structure will start to help you eliminate them, knowing they don't suit you. Don't be surprised if one of

them is overeating and metabolic adjustments to bring your body weight into line without the discomfort of extreme diets. Others are the dropping of substances that you are addicted to, and within that process, an allowance that lets you live much longer.

You will see regeneration of cellular structure that will surprise you. You'll heal faster and you'll know it. You'll start to see a situation where you're less sick than you've ever been in your life. The prevailing 3D wisdom will tell you, *"Well, you're older now, so you're going to get sick more."* But you won't, and you'll know that something is changing. So what we're saying to you, dear ones, is that you can have the same things that the youngsters have. You will now slowly awaken to a new energy on this planet, which will allow you to live longer. Your DNA is going to start cooperating in a more efficient way. 35 percent? Perhaps even 40 percent, old soul? It's on its way to something far higher.

Kryon live channelling "The Recalibration of Gaia" given in Melbourne, Australia
— March 18, 2012

Do you understand now how important you are? How everything you do affects the planet? That Gaia knows you, and that every step you take, Gaia blesses you and you bless Gaia. What will you do with this information? Does it change anything for you? How would you like The Crystalline Grid to remember your life? Dear old soul, if you are reading this, what you do is "seen" by Gaia and The Crystalline Grid, and has so much more "impact" than a new soul on the planet. Your awakening and compassionate actions are changing the planet! Whatever you decide to do is your own free choice. No matter what you choose, you are deeply and dearly loved by God and Gaia.

By the way, remember that I mentioned Machu Picchu as one of the sacred and mystical sites that is visited by millions of people every year? Well, guess what? The energy you feel there has absolutely nothing to do with The Crystalline Grid! *"What?"* – I hear you ask. *"How can that be?"* To find out, you'll have to make sure you keep reading (smile). Hint: Don't miss what Kryon says about the ley lines of Gaia later in this chapter.

Q.: If time is in a circle and each time fractal comes back magnified, does this mean that the time fractals when there was a low consciousness will come back, or are we able to change the potentials of this occurring and, if so, does that information go into The Crystalline Grid?

Kryon: The fractals of time are in a quantum soup of potentials. So if the consciousness of the planet never changed, then the cycles would be linear, predictable, and would return on schedule. This is what has been the case for thousands of years, and gave the engine for prediction to the calendars that worked with it. But now add "The Shift of Human Consciousness," and the fractals suddenly are altered, just as we described in the last [Kryon] question in Chapter Two, with the metaphor about the chicken crossing the road.

Moving through this shift will change the fractals of predictions of time. It will recalibrate itself to cycles of high and higher, instead of high and low. As this happens, indeed, The Crystalline Grid also recalibrates to allow for higher level activity and thinking. The bias of the grid is changing, and is becoming non-linear. This has been explained already. So, yes. New fractals will be generated in part by a new crystalline grid energy, created by a new Human Being.

Whales and Dolphins

Humans have always had an association with whales and dolphins. In the past, hundreds, if not thousands, of whales and dolphins were harvested, from the oceans and seas as a resource. In some instances, they are still being harvested but not to the same extent that they were. In December 1946, an international body called the International Whaling Commission was established, with 14 member states, and an aim to conserve whale stocks. Today, the Commission comprises 89 countries, including countries that are without oceans! The Commission has taken some encouraging steps towards the conservation and protection of whales that includes the establishment of the global moratorium on commercial whaling in 1986. Currently, there are a

number of countries that oppose the moratorium, including Japan, Norway and Iceland.

The collective consciousness of humanity wants to protect the whales and keep them safe. This includes dolphins as well, for they belong to the same family known as Cetacea. The family Cetacea includes whales, dolphins and porpoises, so the dolphins are like cousins to the whale and part of a support group. The dolphins play a role in the whales' development. Even more than just protecting whales, thousands of people have had life-changing experiences after a whale watching tour or a swim with the dolphins. The reason we are so affected is because of the cellular information that is within our DNA. There is an intuitive level of understanding within all humanity that knows that whales cannot be eliminated without changing the life force balance of Earth.

The three grids of Gaia have already been explained in detail. The Human DNA is also part of the Gaia system, as it represents a biological evolvement of humanity on the planet. The whales and dolphins are the living portions of the grid system. They contain the "history of Earth" and they are sacred for that reason. They coordinate and cooperate with The Crystalline Grid.

Kryon describes it as a type of "backup" system. Not a linear one, in case you lose the first one, but a system that assists the others all the time. The information of the three combined Akashic systems is stored in the whales and dolphins. This is the final layer, and it connects humanity with Gaia, as well as the rest of life on Earth, in a most profound way.

The whales are in Gaia. They are under the water and they are mammals, just like humans. They contain the information. The Akashic cycle is complete. The oceans and seas of the Earth glow with everything that we have done, who we are and who we might be.

The whales and dolphins have many things to teach us, and can even help heal our corporeal body. Laurie Reyon Anderson is an internationally known Interspecies Communicator and Soul Healer. Her gift allows her to speak to the animals and translate their messages to humanity. She recognizes the cetaceans as the Ancient Beings on this planet. Her work involves communication and healing with the dolphins and whales of Earth. Laurie Reyon has been named "Standing

Whale Mother" by the Native Americans and she brings the wisdom and healing energies of the whales and dolphins to humanity. Here is a beautiful message from the whales given to humanity and communicated through Laurie:

. . . .

We are the ancient of the ancients. We are the Soul of the Souls. We are your past and we are your Memories. We are your present and we are here with you in the Now Time. We are your link, joined with you to create the future for the Healing and Ascension of Mother Gaia. We are a Group Consciousness, stewarding this planet as an example of the Good of the Many.

The whales are the molecular librarians of Earth's evolution. What we call the Akashic Records lives in the oceans of planet Earth. The information is stored in the water molecules. Since water is never destroyed, only recycled, Earth's entire history remains safe in our ocean archives. The whales can access the information, circulate it and contribute to it, communicating by connecting to the intelligence in the water molecules. They tell me that the information in the water will teach us that in the future, the body fluid of the Human will eventually be used to provide flawless individualized treatment for people's health maladies.

The whales would like to assist us in remembering who we truly are. Knowing and honoring who we are is an important aspect of our personal growth toward love of self and our Earth. They tell us that it is important for the Human to reach a point in our evolution where we truly become the seeker of ourselves. It is important to reach for the knowledge that is held in the Akash that tells us who we truly are, and where we are from and what we are made of and why we are here today.

In our quest for this knowledge of self-awareness, we are identifying ourselves as beings who value Love above all else and we are confirming our belief in Love by changing our lifestyles accordingly. We are coming to know ourselves as vibrations of Love, and in doing so, are coming to remember our world and our beautiful Mother Gaia in a new light.

In our remembrance, we are drawn to gather with like-minded people, and start to take back the conscious control of our environment. We are remembering that what we think and feel affects our environment and the others living around us. Once we take control of our emotions and thoughts, we see that we do truly create our own realities and that we do have control over our own environments and that we are not the victims. The whales call this intentional evolution.

And finally, the last piece of remembrance of self is to recognize and develop our connection to the cosmos and to life beyond the third dimension. We are not alone in the Universe and never have been. There are billions of other life forms that are not visible from our 3D perspective. We can connect with these other planetarians, who are our brothers and sisters of Light. We can benefit from their wisdom and knowledge and join with them as we move through our fears back to the truth of who we are and why we are here. The dolphins and whales are masters of cosmic travel and masters of multi-dimensionality. They are here to teach us, assist us in healing our minds and bodies and they are here now, inviting us to open our belief systems to multiple realities of Love.

Laurie Reyon has other messages for humanity from the dolphins and other animals. If you would like to find out more, you can visit her website: *www.lauriereyon.com*

. . . .

Q.: Is there anything else that you can tell us about the whales and dolphins?

Kryon: The Cetaceans of the ocean (mainly the whales and dolphins) are holding energy for humanity that we will not discuss at this time. Eventually, when the planet is ready, this will be explained.

But you must know this, don't you? These mammals are all protected world-wide, with treaties from countries even without oceans! Humans intuitively know that these animals are special, and they need to be undisturbed and allowed to thrive. Continue this endeavor.

The Ley Lines of Gaia

Although a substantial amount of people have heard about ley lines, very few people truly understand them fully, and I think it would be fair to say, that they remain largely unexplained. Even those that claim to understand them fully have often misinterpreted the true nature of what they are. When I first heard about ley lines, I started to investigate and ended up becoming very frustrated by the wide variety of definitions of what ley lines are. The ancient indigenous were very in tune with Gaia and were very aware of when they came across the ley lines of Gaia. The indigenous had another name for them, however, referring to them as Spirit Lines or Dragon Lines.

The term "leys" was coined by Alfred Watkins in the 1920s, based on what he considered to be a network of landscape alignments that joined sacred sites such as churches, megaliths, springs and hilltops. In the 1960s, John Michell expanded on Watkins' work and named the St. Michael ley line, which links many places in Great Britain that are dedicated to St. Michael such as: St. Michael's Mount in Cornwall, Avebury Henge and Glastonbury Tor.

While I was in Hungary, I also learned about the St. George ley line and discovered that there is a place called St. George Energy Park in Lenti, which is in the southwest corner of Hungary very close to the borders of Austria, Slovenia and Croatia. According to the park: *You can walk along the stone pavements that show the directions of the St. George lines, while the "posts" along the way mark the intercept of these lines, where the energy waves are the most powerful.* The park also has a variety of thermal spas.

None of these examples, however, was able to tell me exactly what a ley line is. When you look at some of the attempts that have been made to show a ley line on a map, they are always a straight line that starts and stops abruptly. This didn't make sense to me, especially when I was then reading that ley lines were all across the globe and found at places like the pyramids of Egypt and Machu Picchu in Peru. The desire and fixation with drawing a straight line on a map is a classic example of how we are biased in our linear thinking and try to interpret everything in a three-dimensional way.

So why is there so much confusion, and exactly what is a ley line? I suspect that there is a lot of confusion and misinformation because we are only seeing pieces and parts of a puzzle. Add to that that the

puzzle is multi-dimensional, and it starts to explain why ley lines have not been defined until recently, at the 2012 Summer Light Conference in Sedona, when Kryon gave this information:

Ley lines are energy lines based in Human conscious action. There are many ley lines in the northern hemisphere, as this is where eighty-five percent of the population has lived. The ley lines re-form when there is compassion there, when there is heart (energy) there. Where there is great compassion or past compassion, there are portals. Portals are connected by ley lines and the patterning is not symmetrical. They are constantly in motion, especially today as the Earth energy reshapes itself. The Kundalini of the planet is moving. A recalibration of where the center of wisdom should be is being accomplished. Don't be surprised if you go to former places of power and there's nothing there. Or perhaps you may go to another place where there was formerly nothing there, and now you are overwhelmed by energy. Gaia reacts to you, and Gaia has recalibrated in response, a shift from war to compassion. So the grids will begin to be biased towards compassionate love. Ley lines shift and respond.

Kryon live channelling "Gaia & Kryon" given in Sedona, Arizona.
Kryon Summer Light Conference – June 9, 2012

There is now a clear definition of what a ley line is. Ley lines are energy lines based in Human conscious action. The characteristics of a ley line is that they shift and respond to what humans do, and as a result, they are not symmetrical and not necessarily in a straight line. That also means that it is not something you can draw on a map and then say "here are the ley lines." And the places where ley lines historically occurred are not necessarily where they are found now.

During the Kryon Kundalini Tour in 2012, Kryon gave additional information about the ley lines of Gaia. The channels were profound and gave us new insight to the bigger picture. Kryon first revealed the information about ley lines when the tour group sat high up in the Valley of the Moon, which is found in San Pedro de Atacama, Chile. The overwhelming love of Gaia in this spot was enhanced by the magnificent sunset that followed the channelling. If you go to Lee's website you'll see some of the photo's I took of our tour (smile). Here is what Kryon had to say:

We would like to start to explain a little of how the energy of Gaia proportions itself on the surface of the planet. There are those in this assemblage, those who are on the mountain top with my partner, who have gone to many sacred places. Perhaps you felt the energy of each one, and you feel that no place is the same? You are correct. There are seemingly different things to feel, depending upon where you are. This becomes a complex subject, but all of it has to do with what we have described to you as The Crystalline Grid.

In review, The Crystalline Grid is an esoteric grid. This is the one that the Pleiadians originally placed upon the planet, which allows for full communication from Human consciousness into the dirt of the Earth, which is called Gaia. This is the grid that *remembers* what humans do on the planet. This is the grid that is responsible for a Human feeling something when he walks into a battlefield, or when he walks into the place where the heroes came out of the ground, the 33 (speaking of the 33 Miners that were rescued from a mine in Northern Chile during 2010).

So let us describe this subject of The Crystalline Grid, and Gaia. My partner now stands in what is called a "null" point (referring to the Valley of the Moon in San Pedro de Atacama in Chile). Let me explain some things. The grid that is crystalline has a field around it. It is not the magnetic field, but rather it is a field which is multi-dimensional and interacts with the Human consciousness field. That is why you feel what you feel in different places on Earth. Let me tell you some things about fields. Nature actually does create straight lines. It does it through crystallization. That is in 3D. Every time you have a multi-dimensional field, however, there are no straight lines. Let us talk about that for a moment, for what I'm about to tell you will dismiss some of the traditions of the past.

Human Beings love to talk about ley lines. Indeed, there is such a thing as a ley line; however, Spirit hasn't really called it that. It's a 3D perception of humans, who draw straight lines between things they believe are important, spiritually. These Human lines are the

kinds of lines that you find architects have built – between pyramids, between churches, between sacred areas ... very straight lines following the shadows sometimes created by the sun. These are not ley lines. These are lines that Human Beings have drawn. I can tell you that they are not ley lines because they are straight!

Now let me give you something that is complex. Some of you have actually seen portrayals of what appears to be magnetic lines of influence around a magnet. You will notice that they are curved from the north to the south pole of the magnet ... curved lines. Now, if you are very, very small and microscopic, you could stand on one of those magnets, and the lines would appear to be straight, even though you know they are not. If you were able only to see one and a half lines, you would not be aware of what we would call the symmetry of the field. So this gives an example of how straight things are not really straight at all. But there is more.

Let us talk about the crystalline field. Sometimes it appears to be straight, although it is not. The lines are complex. Unlike the lines of a magnetic field, they don't go from one pole to another. They go to and from what we will call "nodes." Nodes are records of overlapping Human consciousness. To add to this complexity, Gaia also has a kind of field apart from the crystalline. When the crystalline overlaps with Gaia's grid in certain ways, you get the attributes of "nodes." This is a build-up of energy. In some cases when you have the overlap, they cancel each other in energy. When they cancel each other, you have a null, where there is absolutely no energy of the crystalline, and it becomes pure Gaia only.

Let me ask you the question again: "What are you feeling when you have a null?" The answer is, "the absence of The Crystalline Grid." This is an energy which talks to you directly from Gaia. You feel the purity and the love of the planet being given to you directly, since there is no interference at all from The Crystalline Grid. You sit in a null right now [speaking to the group seated before Kryon]. There are many of them on the planet, and the energy or lack of it, feels just like this one.

Now, the complex part comes next. Let's speak of nodes. There are three kinds. For instance, let me tell you about Machu Picchu. Machu Picchu is a node that overlaps and amplifies that of the

Pachamama, and also the wisdom of the South and divine feminine energy. This is a profound energy, which some have called a *portal*. A portal is a kind of node. A *vortex* is also a kind of node. A vortex is when energies collide, and the energy is constantly moving, or circulating. To some, it feels good for a while, but it's hard to live in a true vortex. A third kind of node would be a *vortal*. It's half and half between portal and vortex. It's complex.

Now what creates all of these? The Crystalline Grid does. What creates The Crystalline Grid? Human consciousness. Now, I made a statement awhile back and now I'm going to emphasize it – it's very difficult to draw a map that would have this crystalline grid. When we say to you that it has no symmetry, it means that it has no overall pattern as a grid, as seen together on a 2D surface. You look for symmetry in all things – but don't do it with this one. Let's add to the puzzle that the grid lines are beneath the Earth as well as on the Earth, so it becomes even more complex than you think. Is that too technical for you? Why do I tell you these things?

It's part of the wisdom that we are now collecting and giving to you that you never had before, which is this specific. You're going to need to know these things. Humans like to go to certain places and feel energy, and make up stories as to why those energies are there. It's time to close the door on that kind of foolishness, old soul, and start understanding the processes and mechanics of the real energy of the planet, and the complexities of them.

The sun is going down. While we've been talking, it set. It's almost like a wink from Gaia. So now I'll give a message from Gaia directly, from this spot, because it's a null. *"The Earth honors the Human! There is a direct connection with the compassion of the Human and the compassion of the planet. These are the places which allow you to feel this directly without interference. When you feel this energy again, stop and give us love, for it makes a difference and it amplifies what the planet is and what it can do for you, and all those who follow."* That's enough for today.

And so it is.

Kryon live channelling "The Ley Lines of Gaia Part I"
given in the Valley of the Moon, San Pedro de Atacama, Chile – October 26, 2012

Kryon then continued to give us the rest of the story when we arrived at the Island of the Sun in Lake Titicaca, Bolivia. It was certainly a test of endurance for everyone to climb to the top of the mountain where we sat at 4,000 meters above sea level. I'm not sure if you have ever been at that altitude but if you have, (and, like me, you prefer being at sea level) it was very difficult to breathe, let alone climb to the top! The reward, though, was to sit and feel the love of Gaia, and the love of our ancestors, and at the end of the channelling, we looked across the Lake towards the snow-capped mountains and found that in one place the snow had melted into the shape of a gigantic love heart. Thinking this was part of a natural phenomenon, we asked the locals how often it happened and they responded by saying they had never seen it before. A mere coincidence? Or was it a wink from Gaia and spirit? I'll let you decide which one. In the meantime here is the rest of the story about ley lines:

There is much we wish to discuss, but in order to make it succinct, we are going to continue a discussion that we just had with you when we sat in nature the last time. At that point in time, we sat in what is called a crystalline grid null, and the lesson was about ley lines, nulls and nodes. This lesson was an attempt to try to explain how The Crystalline Grid of the planet works, and why you feel the things you feel. It would also try to explain why on Planet Earth there would be places which might feel more sacred than others.

So, in review we speak again of nodes. Nodes are overlapping energies, which are esoteric, representing The Crystalline Grid. They overlap because of the quantum symmetry of the nodes on the planet. Each node has its own specific symmetry, and it is not necessarily linear. When you put them all together in a complex way, the overlaps create nodes. Some nodes are more powerful than others. Sometimes when The Crystalline Grid intersects in a certain way, you have nodes that you will not feel much. However, if the overlapping is profound, you have nodes that you will feel, and we discussed some of them before.

Now, there is actually an energetic accounting system on the planet. All of this I am telling you now tries to explain where you sit and why you feel what you do [referring to the group sitting before Kryon at the Island of the Sun, Lake Titicaca]. So let us tell you something about nodes and how complex they can be. But first, let us review. The Crystalline Grid of the planet is an esoteric grid, which remembers Human consciousness, and all that has happened. Every single Human who has ever lived, is part of it. It explains a lot, and why you can walk into a former battlefield and feel the negative energy there, or sit in other places where you might feel elation and thankfulness. This is all driven, or caused, by that which we call The Crystalline Grid. This Crystalline Grid, therefore, is like a quantum time capsule, which reflects Human consciousness and Human action.

Lately, we started to explain this process and we said that, up until now, it was a linear process. If something negative happened at a certain place, it had the same weight as something positive. We also asked you to look at your Human history and realize that there was a lot more negative than positive. The consciousness of the planet itself, therefore, was lower than you might think. Then we told you that all of these things had begun to change, and when Kryon came in 23 years ago, I told you that the planet was in a process of change. You had begun the precession of the equinoxes, which would then fulfil the prophecy of the ancients. The ancients told you that, potentially the Earth could rebalance itself with regard to masculine and feminine, and that this new balance would be complete in 2012. It would recalibrate almost every process that was esoteric and energetic on the planet.

Now, back to The Crystalline Grid. We continued to tell you that even the grid itself would start to recalibrate, and that it would no longer be linear. That is to say, that compassionate events would now hold far more energy than negative events. We also told you that Gaia would respond, and that Human consciousness would change through generations. Humans would actually start to think differently. Spiritual logic would start to become evident. All through this, we mentioned that the wisdom which was being recalibrated was the wisdom that belonged to the indigenous, for they knew how to communicate with Gaia. They understood the relationship between the Creator, which included all life on the planet, and the relationship to the Earth, which is Gaia. If you can

communicate with those things, you can set the Earth on another path.

Again, back to The Crystalline Grid. What happens when you have complex overlap of nodes? Sometimes you get attributes of the land that are very confusing. A vortex is an example. A vortex is a collision of energies that may feel good, but they are always moving. So, after a while, they don't feel good anymore. Sometimes you have overlapping energies which create a node which makes you feel good all the time. This would be called "a power spot" by some. Others call it a portal. So, is that what is here [referring to the Island of the Sun]? No. There is something else here.

Let me give you an explanation of a very confusing overlap of crystal grid intersections. There's a place on the planet that is so confusing, it even affects how the magnetic grid functions, and it's called the Bermuda Triangle. It's all caused by nodes on The Crystalline Grid. Now, I want you to back up with me (in your mind) a long time ago. It's difficult to explain this, but if you understand that there's a plan of the Creator, it makes sense. When the Creator put this Earth together, the potential was, that always there would be the spiritual seeds eventually coming from another place in the galaxy to begin Human spiritual evolvement. In this particular case [Planet Earth] it would be the Pleiadians. They would potentially plant the seeds of the Creator, which is to say, "The knowledge of dark and light." We even told you that they came prior to this to set up The Crystalline Grid. Part of this also was to create the Cave of Creation, preparing for the Akashic Record of humanity to begin.

Now, this is very difficult to understand. There have to be places on the planet, nodes on the planet, almost like the magnetic poles, where there is greater and lesser wisdom. Depending on what Human Beings did, it would then shape future Human consciousness, and those places would also change. Most of humanity, for obvious reasons, settled in the northern hemisphere, for this is the land hemisphere. In that process the *wisdom node* that was accepted and needed was in Tibet and India. Spirit does not see borders of countries, but I just gave them to you so you would know where these wisdom nodes were. They were profound.

Take a look at the wisdom of those areas and you will see that they served the northern hemisphere for a long time. There were several prophecies for this planet, and there were actually several re-starts of Human consciousness, all bringing you to this point today. You are on a tour called the *Kundalini Tour*, and this is all a metaphor for what is taking place on this planet. The northern hemisphere wisdom is starting, then, to surrender to the southern hemisphere wisdom, and the node that you now sit on, which you would call Bolivia and Peru, is the stored wisdom that the planet now needs.

The metaphor of the Eagle and the Condor is a unification of understanding of the transfer and acceptance of this protocol. The prophecy is that a new node on the planet would start to appear in 2012, and the wisdom that *was always here* would then replace the wisdom of the other node in Tibet and India, representing the premier balance of the planet. That's what's happening, but it's slow. It's here, but the slowness is in the realization that it's here, and what it all means. Small groups of people will start to see it, and they already have. The unification of indigenous tribes is no longer saying, "It's coming." They're saying, "It's here."

There will be many more visitors who don't know why they're visiting, but they'll feel it profoundly. A rebalance from the North to the South is only part of the change. The wisdom has always been here, so it's literally a reassignment of the importance of the nodes. The Incas [followers of King Inca] walked here, and you give them a lot of credit as the ancestors of the land, but you really don't know who came before them. That's where all the energy and wisdom here really started. These things will be discovered, but if you take a look at your history, it was all interrupted by the northern hemisphere conquering the southern, and from then to now the land that you're sitting on was sleeping. It took all this time to awaken it to the prophecy.

Even the calendars of the Mayan spoke of the potential for the rise in Human consciousness for this moment. That's a North American prediction about a South American prediction. All over the planet they knew it, and the Eagle and Condor, therefore, had the same prediction. This has been sleeping for a long time. The

puma awakes, wisdom awakes and it does so slowly, so that it is gentle. But you are going to feel it.

Kryon live channelling "The Ley Lines of Gaia Part II"
given on the Island of the Sun, Lake Titicaca, Bolivia – October 29, 2012

In summary, ley lines shift and respond to Human consciousness and so they don't stay the same. The lines are complex and go from one node to another. Nodes are overlapping energies that interface between The Crystalline Grid and Human consciousness. Gaia also has a field apart from the crystalline, and when the crystalline overlaps with Gaia, in certain attributes you get either a build-up of energy that creates nodes or the overlap of energies will cancel each other out, resulting in a null. A null is, therefore, a place where there is an absence of The Crystalline Grid, and so what you get is pure Gaia energy only.

There are three kinds of nodes: portal, vortex and vortal. A portal is a node that overlaps and amplifies Gaia. A vortex is where energies collide and the energy is constantly moving. To some, being in a vortex may feel good for a while, but it's hard to live there. A vortal is half portal and half vortex. There is no symmetry with these lines and they occur beneath the Earth as well as on the Earth, so it becomes more complex than we think. All of these lines are created by The Crystalline Grid, and The Crystalline Grid is created by Human consciousness.

Furthermore, there are nodes on the planet where there is greater and lesser wisdom, depending upon what Human Beings did with it, that then shaped Human consciousness. Most of humanity has been residing in the northern hemisphere and in the process, the wisdom that was accepted was from the node which resides in Tibet and India. With the current shift in Human consciousness (the movement of the Kundalini of the Earth), there is a new node on the planet, which resides in Bolivia and Peru, that is starting to surface and the wisdom that was always there is starting to replace the wisdom of the other node in Tibet and India. The metaphor of the Eagle and the Condor is a unification of understanding the transfer and acceptance of this protocol (see Chapter Four – The Kundalini of the Earth).

Q.: Can you tell us more about the places on Earth that have an overlapping of nodes, such as the Bermuda Triangle, and also can you tell us about other null points?

You have mentioned before, that portals are where there has been great compassion and that some areas of the Earth are being removed from their role as portals, such as Stonehenge, while others are being enhanced, such as Glastonbury (both in England). Can you tell us more about this?

Kryon: Sometimes synchronicity will create a situation in which answers to one question will help with the answers to another. In this case, I point you to the question about the reversing polarity of the planet.

Since the magnetics of the Earth are always in constant shift, it means that the magnetic grid is always changing, too. When I came here in 1989, I told you that the magnetic grid would shift more in the ten years than it had in over 100. Indeed it did, and this shows that the grids are on the move, and that the polarity shift has again begun.

All this allows for the many grids of the planet, besides the magnetic one, to also recalibrate themselves. Nodes, nulls, portals, and vortices are all a result of overlapping grid energies. This also means that as the Earth changes and compassion changes, you should expect the nulls and portals to change, too.

So, seemingly sacred places that have been a certain energy for decades may suddenly feel odd to you, and ones that never had any energy may suddenly start changing into areas you can actually "feel." So don't expect known sites to be the only ones to change, but also sites that are not known.

A Summary of the Grids

In summary, there are three places where the energy of humans exists, all at the same time.

1. The Cave of Creation. It keeps a record of who you are as you come and go, and imbues your lifetime of experience into the vibration of the planet even after you have gone. It is the multi-dimensional system that captures the Human experience for Gaia and it stays with Gaia. It is therefore, the Akashic Record of all humanity.

2. Human DNA. The DNA in the Human body helps you while you are alive in each lifetime, for all that you ever were is information and energy that is stored multi-dimensionally in the double helix. If you live a thousand lifetimes, they are all there and accessible. You never have to relearn anything spiritually, since it's cumulative. It stays with you from lifetime to lifetime. You are your own ancestors.

3. The Crystalline Grid. It is a spiritual grid that lays over the planet's surface that remembers everything that humans do and where they do it. The energy of humanity is affecting the vibrational level of the planet in actual time. This means that, instead of waiting to receive energy after you pass to the Cave of Creation, you can receive it now. This creates a feeling of time going faster for you. Finally, The Crystalline Grid is being aligned for compassion. It is an alignment to the mother energy. So the remembrance factor of The Crystalline Grid is changing. There will be less remembrance of hatred and a greater remembrance of love and compassion.

The Magnetic Grid is all about communication. The Magnetic Grid made it possible for the Pleiadians to arrive on Earth and give the seeds of enlightenment to Human Beings. It is also the magnetics that enable entanglement. The planet Earth is entangled with the middle of the galaxy.

The whales and dolphins are the living portions of the grid system. They contain the "history of Earth" and they are sacred for that reason. They coordinate and cooperate with The Crystalline Grid. They know who you are. When you spend time with them, you will most likely "feel" the connection.

Ley lines are energy lines based on Human conscious action, and they shift and respond to what humans do. The lines are complex and go from one node to another. Nodes are the result of an overlap of The Crystalline Grid with Gaia. There are three kinds of nodes: portal, vortex and vortal. In some cases, the overlaps in energy will cancel each other out and you get a null, which creates a place where The Crystalline Grid is absent and you get only pure Gaia energy.

Q.: Is there anything else we should know about the grids?

Kryon: There is a great deal more the grids will be doing with you as your planet evolves, for the many grids are a massive time capsule of information, ideas, invention and past knowledge. So the real purpose of the grid systems is to help humanity as it becomes ready – to help posture life on Earth, and even drive evolution. Never underestimate what might be there that you don't expect. Think of the grids as a time capsule, releasing energy and information as humanity needs it.

Chapter Four

The Kundalini of the Earth

Before I started writing this book I moved to Santiago, Chile in February of 2012. I felt drawn to the area because of what I knew was unfolding with the Kundalini energy. This was one of the reasons why I wanted to experience living in Chile. After six months of living there I woke up one morning with a crystal clear message to write a book that pulled together all of the channelled messages from Kryon about Gaia and humanity. I wanted to fill a gap that was so obvious to me so that there was at least one publication that provided a point of reference for all of the esoteric information about the Gaia system. For more than two years I searched for publications and websites that had information about the energy grids of the Earth and all the other things that Kryon was mentioning in the channels given by Lee Carroll. I couldn't find anything. It appeared that no such publication existed. I wanted to change that, hence this book!

I believe I had a few romantic ideas about what it would be like to live in a place toward where I heard the Kundalini energy was moving. For some reason, I expected that it would be much easier to get in touch with my Higher-Self and, therefore, I would also be able to keep myself walking in a constant state of enlightenment. Hmmmm. I know what you're thinking. I was pretty naïve, huh! In fact, I think I had moments in which everything was the opposite of what I expected.

135

Kryon has said that the Kundalini energy is constantly moving and that those that sit in the Kundalini energy can't sit still. From personal experience I found this to be true. When I was in Santiago, I found it difficult to get to sleep. I constantly felt restless and by the end of each day I felt like I would implode! My temporary relief came from walking my dog in the park, and even that was short lived. When I travelled away from Santiago, I started to calm down and feel normal again. I spoke with other Lightworkers and they had similar experiences. It is only since the beginning of 2013 that this restless, uncomfortable feeling has been replaced with a calm peace and tranquility. It almost feels like the Kundalini has done the greatest part of its shift and is now continuing its movement in a gentle way.

During October and November of 2012, I went on the Kryon Kundalini Tour with Lee Carroll. Everything I knew expanded and I was given so much more information to include in this book. I think everyone that went on that tour experienced a profound personal transformation. I now realize that moving to Chile was part of my journey. It helped increase my awareness of the consciousness of Gaia and the infinite connections between all consciousness. Moving to Chile created a space in my life where I could write this book. It allowed me to stop searching for a book that I thought already had been printed with all the esoteric knowledge about Gaia and start creating one myself. One that I felt needed to be done so that you, dear reader, could access the profound information about Gaia and humanity.

But what is Kundalini energy? What does it mean and why is it something that is happening within the planet Earth? Kundalini is a Sanskrit word that means coiled, like a snake. The Kundalini represents the balance of male and female coming together with great energy to create perfection and balance. The Kundalini is therefore associated with procreation. Kundalini energy is not recognized by medical science; however, it is mentioned extensively in the literature of Yoga and Tantra, both Buddhist and Hindu. You have probably seen the Caduceus symbol, which has been used as a symbol for medicine for hundreds of years: a short rod entwined by two snakes and topped by a pair of wings. The irony is that the Caduceus symbol represents the Kundalini rising up the spine or Sushumna Nadi, the main energy channel of the Human body and chakra system. Throughout history, the Caduceus has been used as a symbol of healing in many cultures and in different forms.

The Caduceus Symbol

Kundalini energy found within humans is a dormant energy that lies at the base of the spine, coiled three and a half times around the lingam. Lingam means "pillar of light" and is pure life force energy. The most common practices used to awaken the Kundalini energy within the body are Yoga, Meditation, Reiki and Qi Gong. An awakened Kundalini energy rises up through the spine, travelling through the chakras until it finally reaches the top of the head.

The Kundalini also resides within the planet, and has often been described by many indigenous cultures as the movement of the Feathered Serpent. This movement needs to be considered both metaphorically and physically. Many of the ancient cultures have said that there would come a time of potential, of a magnificent change for planet Earth. It would represent a consciousness shift and would start moving the Feathered Serpent south. Information on the Journey of the Feathered Serpent was presented by Woody Vaspra in Kryon Book Eight, *Passing the Marker.* I found the revelations so compelling that I am re-writing it here.

Over 20 years ago, Gerardo Barrios, Mayan Elder, began a quest to validate and understand the sacred Mayan calendars. He travelled to different villages in Central America, searching for the most traditional Mayan Elders in very remote areas. He wanted to know if they were using the same calendars. Except for some

variation in names and small language differences, most of them matched. As part of this research, in 1988, he and nine other Mayans travelled to a very remote village where the traditional Mayans have dedicated their lives to keeping the temple fire for over a thousand years. The Mayans maintain this fire 24 hours a day as a prayer for peace on Earth. After a five day walk through the deep forest, Gerardo and his team finally reached the village. The Elders had known through their own visions that this group was coming. The ten Mayans were given divinations, and only five were welcomed into the village's sacred temple. Gerardo was one of them.

Once inside the temple, one of the Elders took Gerardo aside to talk to him privately. The Elder began to introduce him to the story of the feathered serpent Kukulkan, a snakelike sacred Earth energy that moves throughout the land. It took two more visits to this village to complete the story. The Mayan Elders of the village explained how this energy rises periodically and showed him on the map he had brought with him, where and when it had appeared. Later, when Gerardo tracked through history, he found along its path events such as the great spiritual awakening of Tibet in the 1950s, the anti-Vietnam War movement of the '60s, and leaders such as Martin Luther King.

The Elders said this that this *feathered serpent* has the intention to move down the Americas via the spine of Mother Earth to Lake Titicaca in the Andes, to be there in 2012. If one were to open a map of the Western Hemisphere and track the mountain ranges from Alaska in North America to Chile in South America, you would see them extend in a continuous line from North to South. This was described as the spine of Mother Earth.

It is important to understand why this is happening and what it represents. The northern hemisphere of the planet has contained masculine energy while the southern hemisphere carries a more feminine energy. This is the polarity of the planet. It could also be called the planet's duality. As Human Beings start to change, all of the grids in the planet change, which in turn creates the movement of the Kundalini.

In reviewing history, most of the major wars and all of the world wars have occurred in the northern hemisphere. That has been the balance of the planet, with the masculine "war" imbalance being very strong in the north. Most of the wars in the southern hemisphere have been caused by those from the north.

As the planet starts to rebalance itself in consciousness, it means that the consciousness of male and female is rebalanced. Humanity becomes more balanced and so the Kundalini must move. The Kundalini has been in place for a very long time in the northern hemisphere – India and Tibet. Many call it the center of spiritual wisdom. This helped to balance the heavy male energy, but it was also male-heavy. You do not really see female leaders in the ranks of the monks and other orders in those areas. The southern hemisphere represents the female energy of the planet. The Kundalini is moving in response to humanity and it is moving south – to South America.

It is important to understand that the movement of the Kundalini has nothing to do with a shift of wisdom.

If you study the ancients from South America, you will find the wise divine feminine. In fact, Kryon has said that you could call Machu Picchu the capital of the wise, divine feminine on the planet. So to clarify this even further, the movement of the Kundalini is NOT about the wisdom of Tibet moving to Peru. Peru has always contained wisdom.

The Kundalini is the heart chakra of the Earth and it is now beginning to seek another wisdom center that is more balanced. It is moving to a place of softer wisdom and seeks the wisdom of the divine feminine. The Earth is ready to glean this wisdom and pull upon the portals in the area and in the process, the consciousness of the planet will change. The Earth has been waiting for this and it has been prophesized by the ancients.

If you have ever been to Machu Picchu, then you may have felt that the energy there is very sweet. It has the feeling of being in the mother's womb – safe and protected. Kryon has said that it is time for the wisdom that has always been here to be placed on The Crystalline Grid and shared with all. The capital of the wise, divine feminine has secrets that may never be revealed. There are those who represent the Seven Sisters there that have not yet shown themselves. There is an awakening there and some of the shamanic humans of the area are aware of it.

During a channel given in Lima, Kryon told Peruvians to celebrate, as this is what the old souls there have been waiting for. The
old energy does not want to accept this and there is resistance. The
old energy has come from the northern hemisphere long ago and it's
out of balance. It does not honor the land, the air or the water. (Kryon
live channelling "The Recalibration of Wisdom" given in Lima, Peru
– November 27, 2011).

During the Kryon Patagonia Cruise at the start of 2012, some
esoteric (spiritual) information about the Kundalini was given.

The Kundalini is coiled at the bottom of the spine of the body.
It only uncoils when the male and the female are balanced. It
wraps around three energies of the body three and a half times,
and it wraps around what is called the lingam. Three wraps represent easy-unwrapping parts of energy, but the final half wrap represents the most difficult part, which is the divine enlightenment
of balance. When the Kundalini unwraps and stays that way, you
have a balanced Human Being, if not even enlightened. This is the
metaphor of the planet and this is beginning to happen.

The unwrapping process has already begun to happen, and the
large earthquake in Chile during 2010 was the physical movement of
the planet's response to the Kundalini energy. This means that as the
unwrapping process continues, the Earth is going to move more in
South America, and perhaps in places where there has not been movement before.

Kryon has identified the timeframe of the movement of the Kundalini energy:

The 26,000-year alignment of the equinoxes of your planet is
a grand alignment, and it has been known in astronomy as the
Galactic Alignment. It is called that because the start and stop
point of the wobble of your Earth on its axis aligns through your
sun to the center of the galaxy. This alignment only happens
every 26,000 years.

In order for the equinoxes to proceed through the equatorial
plane of your galaxy [the Milky Way strip in the sky] and work
themselves through the end of this cycle and the beginning of the
next one, it will take 36 years. This final stage began approximately

18 years ago, and 2012 is now the center, or beginning of the last half of the last cycle. You have 18 years left of this energetic event, which actually represents the end of one thing and the beginning of another.

This 36-year window is the timeframe for the potential unwrapping of the entire Kundalini. Do you not find it interesting that it wraps around the lingam three and a half times? Each of the three represents a decade of time in this metaphoric code. Three and a half would be 35 years, very close to the 36-year astronomical event you are in. So this Kundalini prophecy has always been the metaphor of the promise of the Earth and what actually started 18 years ago and that is now centered [2012]. That is where the ceremony should be – at the center of the 36 years, the midpoint of the unwrapping.

If all this sounds confusing, let me simplify it. Even the ancients who watched the stars knew of this alignment. It corresponded to the potentials of consciousness shift, since it also represented a decision point or time fractal in the pattern of potentials that has been the core of ancient astronomical prophecy for eons. So all this was expected and is not a surprise. But it carries with it profound change, and this is what we all saw more than 20 years ago when I arrived to begin my messages. Humanity has these opportunities about every half cycle of the 26,000-year alignment. The last one was 13,000 years ago and humanity was not ready. Now you are.

Dear Human Being, you're sitting in a very, very special place [speaking of the group before Kryon]. You are the first Human group ever to celebrate this movement at the bottom of the South American tip, where the shifts really begin. Oh, there have been those who have chosen to come to the bottom on land and celebrate the coming of it. However, let this go on record that this group now, on the open ocean, at the bottom of the Earth, is where this celebration starts in 2012. [The date during this channelling is January 2012.]

Kryon live channelling "The Movement of the Kundalini"
given during the Patagonia Kryon Cruise – January 28, 2012

To conclude, the unwrapping of the Kundalini has begun. It is a very slow process. The unwrapping is not a linear process any more than Human consciousness is, but the potential is that it will be unwrapped and in place within 18 years from 2012.

Earlier I mentioned that I went on the Kryon Kundalini Tour in 2012 with Lee Carroll. This was organized and put together by a close friend, Jorge Bianchi. The tour started in Mendoza, Argentina and continued to visit many profound energetic places in Chile, Bolivia and Peru. A total of 12 Kryon channellings were done during the tour and Kryon gave nine specific channels that related to the nine letters of the word Kundalini. In numerology, nine means completion. All of the audio channellings from the Kryon Kundalini 2012 Tour can be heard from the Kryon website, but in summary, the theme of the channellings related to each letter of the word Kundalini is listed below.

Kundalini
Unity
Notify Gaia of Your Conscious Actions
Don't Think Like a Human
Ascension
Love
Intuition
New Human
Illumination

The information given throughout the Kryon Kundalini Tour in 2012 gave a new awareness and perception about just how significant the current shift in Human consciousness is and the connection this shift has with the Kundalini energy of the Earth. The key messages from these channels are provided here. The complete audios are available on Lee's website.

Kundalini (The Letter K in Kundalini)

Let's talk about the ancients. Why is there a prophecy about the movement of the Kundalini? What is actually going on? This particular channelling will be called the *Channelling of the Letter 'K'* and through the twelve events you have scheduled, there will be nine channels specifically involved in the letters of the name KUN-DALINI. Today's subject will add information about the Kundalini [representing the 'K'], but we are not going to repeat core information that has already been given. Go back and study the other channellings if you want to know what the Kundalini is all about...

...The results of the shift are multifaceted. If you want to look at the grand result, it's going to eventually push humanity into a new reality, but that's the future. However, immediately you are going to start seeing some changes. Let us review what this means within the context of the Kundalini shift.

The planet has been polarized emotionally for some time, and it's based mostly upon where most of the humans live on the Earth. This has come together over time to create a masculine Earth. If 80 percent of the population of the planet live in the north, and if the north has a certain consciousness, then the whole planet assumes that consciousness. Yet, that is not the consciousness that began in the south. If you take a look at the indigenous of the south before conquerors came, and you take a look at what they believed and what they taught, it was far more feminine (soft). So really, you have a masculine north and a feminine south, but because there were so many more humans in the north, the consciousness of the planet was more masculine in general, and history has reflected this. Suddenly, however, we have a shift. And this is where it gets complicated.

In your reality, you feel everything is linear. Perhaps you really haven't seen a shift of consciousness in the north? But it's there. The majority of it comes from old soul awakening, but it's not how many humans have awakened, but rather, the amount of energy within the ones who have awakened. They're the ones in the room here, and many of them are listening and reading here. There's a shift even in the way the accounting of energy is working on the planet. It's shifting from a linear way to a nonlinear way and Gaia, who is entangled with all this, is starting to move and shift the very Kundalini, or center heart chakra, of the planet. So let's look at who is doing what.

The Movement is Not Linear

Number one: Gaia is a conscious, sentient, proper and appropriate energy that is linked to you. Because of the quantum shift that has been predicted due to what has happened, humanity has started to think differently and this different thinking is more profound within the old souls. This has been seen by Gaia, who is now doing the shifting. So Gaia is involved and that is the mechanics of how the energy is being moved. You, however, look at all this in a linear fashion. So you ask the question, *"Well, where is the Kundalini now? It's moving from north to south, so where is it now?"* So, I'm going to answer that in a moment, and that answer will be different than what you imagined. But right now, let's speak about what this movement really means.

What happens if the Earth becomes balanced in masculine and feminine energy for the first time? What would it mean? It means there is going to be an increase in what we call *compassionate action*. Do you know what the results of non-compassionate actions are? War. That is a non-compassionate action – also, separation, judgment, and a non-caring population. Do you know what the results of compassionate actions are? Working together, unification, peace building, non-judgment, tolerance, understanding, and the beginning of universal unconditional love. Do you see the kind of shift we are speaking of? It's going to change how you think – inside and out.

Increase in Compassion

When you meet someone for the first time, what are your first thoughts? That's a good exercise for psychologists to suggest. How many of you look at another person and say to yourself, *"This is a creator of God energy, just like me. They are family, just like me. They have been here on the Earth, just like me. So I will greet the God in them and I will take them in my arms and have a heart to heart hug."* What if everyone did that? But that's not how you greet one another, is it? Oh, some of you do, but this is the difference between a masculine and a feminine Earth. Mother energy allows for these things and this is what is taking place on the planet – an increase in mother energy. It is growing here, in this place called South America.

The wisdom in The Crystalline Grid that has been placed here for eons is being placed upon the north through a process that has yet to be explained. That's an inward explanation. Outwardly, you're going to see many Human changes. You're going to see the beginning of tolerance and integrity. If things do not have integrity, then you are not going to be interested in them. Can you imagine humans with that attribute? Can you imagine what that will do to your politics? [Laughter]. That's a Kryon joke. But this is worldwide, not just the politics in this country. Can you imagine compassionate action not only in government, but perhaps in institutions, corporations, and even from the health industry? It would vastly change the kinds of products that are offered. Can you see how this would change everything? It would. You've already started. There are things you've already began to change, over the last 18 years, slowly. They happen so slow you don't even notice!

What about your continent? [speaking to the South Americans] If you go back 100 years, what do you see? What did your governments look like compared to what they look like today? Did you have free choice in voting back then? You did, but it didn't seem to make a difference. Your lives are way too short, and after 70 or 80 years, you turn around and come back. You don't remember anything when you get back, but if you could talk to your ancestors, they would remember. You went from a conquered continent with borders that changed and dictators that controlled everything to what you have today. Do you realize the amazing difference? Do you realize that this is against what some would call Human nature? If you asked somebody about the role of Human nature, they might tell you that you'd always been warring. The cynics would say humans kill humans and they always will. There will always be dictators, they would say. So if that's true, then how do you explain South America? Slowly, it has changed as much as any other continent on the planet – slowly preparing itself for *now*.

The fields have been plowed and they are ready to receive the seeds. Your bodies will change. Do you know what happens with compassionate action? Cellular structure changes. We've given you channels about that and even the new changes at birth regarding intuition that a Human Being is born with.

The Crystalline Grid is Recalibrating

Let's talk about Gaia, since there are numbers of things that are changing. One we have told you about, but not in your language [Spanish]. So let us review: There is something called *The Crystalline Grid*. It's an esoteric [invisible] multi-dimensional grid. Calling it crystalline is a metaphor for *a grid that holds memory*. It remembers vibration. It remembers you! Now, this is complex and difficult to understand in 3D. As you live your life, you put energy that is YOU onto this Crystalline Grid. Light that you create through working with spiritual energies creates an imprint on the grid. Things that are dark also create energy on the grid. Wars will create energy on the grid and so will compassionate actions. So again, it is a grid that remembers Human action and it has been a linear imprint up till now – that is, that all energies were imprinted equally.

Suddenly, this grid is giving a bigger weight to that which old souls do than to that which humans do in general. So it's no longer a linear energy grid, but one that is now being biased in the direction of the Lightworker. So the things that will be remembered the most are starting to be the things that generate compassion, and not the darker things that generate sorrow and death. This is part of the new way things are going to work in the future.

There are many things that we could say about this grid which is crystalline. We could tell you how it responds or how it works. But much of this has already been channelled and more of it will be. So instead, I would like to tell you something that hasn't been given before and this is for the curious. When I talk about Gaia, what do you think, and what do you visualize? The energy of the Earth? What is in your mind when you hear the word *Earth*? Well, many of you will visualize the globe floating in space. You're right, for this is the consciousness of Gaia; it is the globe. Gaia does not surround the globe with energy, but rather it *is* the globe – the whole thing. Perhaps you feel that the "Gaia" part is only the surface or the crust? And if it is, what about the rest? What about the mantle of the planet? What about the core? Do you realize how much matter is in the Earth that is not on the surface? What is the relationship between the mantle and the core and the crust? And does this relationship have consciousness? It does, and it's called Gaia.

Dear ones, I am not giving you these things to complicate your perception, but rather to give you a feeling of how Gaia moves with energy. If you had a burner on the stove and you decided to warm it up, you are moving energy into the iron in order to create heat. Would any of you ask, *"Where is the heat located on the burner?"* The answer is no. The burner heats up *all at once* and it cools down all at once. It's similar with energy movement of the planet. The movement of the Kundalini is coming *through* the Earth, not just *on the surface*. Does this make sense to you? What is happening on the planet is happening all at once.

So as you think of the movement of the Kundalini, don't ask, *"Where it is now? What country is it going through?"* The energy of the Kundalini involves the whole of the planet and not a trek on the surface from one point to another. This is a quantum shift, and it does not happen in a linear fashion. However, for all of these years, the movement has been discussed as though it were a linear change coming from India and Tibet and landing in South America. You can have an energetic rebalance from one area to another without it travelling on the surface.

So all of these past years, the shift has been happening all at once, for the whole of the planet. It's a shift from one consciousness to another, not one place to another. There is more feminine starting to be felt, creating a balance of the two hemispheres and involving even the core of the Earth. It's not happening on the surface; it's happening for the whole planet. But we tell you the center of the new balance can be felt most in Bolivia and Peru. But it didn't arrive that way by travelling down an imaginary road.

Now, some years ago, I sat in a place in Chile and I spoke of the movement of the Kundalini (Valle Nevado, 2008). When you look at the metaphor of the Kundalini, you have movement of the Human Kundalini, as mapped by the Human body. Some of it moves back and forth. In this case, it's a metaphor for oscillation and for vibrational shift into higher consciousness. But Gaia is involved this time – the crust, the mantle, the core. You're entangled with Gaia and at that time in 2008, we told you that the

Earth had a potential to move soon. We told you that it would be south of the position we were channelling, and it was! [talking about the earthquake in Chile, February 27, 2010]. There is more coming for Chile and again it's going to be in the south.

All this movement is needed, and sometimes it's physical. Gaia knows you, and it's going to move and adjust. But as it must adjust, it's going to do most of its adjusting where no one lives. Dear ones, when you see this happen, do not go into fear. When you see volcanic activity, don't go into fear. Instead, you have the courage to raise your hand and say, *"Thank you, Gaia,"* for where you did it! You have to know that the area you are in, even now, is volatile [speaking of the place the channelling is being given]. However, old souls can even change the attributes of plate tectonics. The Earth will move in places you didn't think it would, and when you see it, *"Thank you, Gaia!"* You'll know I'm right, and that you are forever linked in consciousness, dear ones, to your Earth.

The planet is changing and the indigenous were right. They lifted the dirt in their hands and said, *"This is life."* It represents more than they knew and more than you knew. It represented the consciousness of Gaia and the partnership with humanity. All of these things are happening in a way to honor humanity.

Kryon live channelling "The Letter K in the word Kundalini"
given in Mendoza, Argentina — October 17, 2012

Unity (The Letter U in Kundalini)

Today's channel will be about the letter 'U'. This is the second letter in the word KUNDALINI. Two is its number, for it is the second letter. Numerologically, the two is about *structure*. We're going to make it stand for a word that also starts with 'U', and that would be *unity*. The energy of the Kundalini movement starts to express itself in some of the spiritual attributes of the teaching of the day, and unity is one of the greatest ones. So we will define unity as the *putting together of difficult and unequal energies*.

Last night, we spoke of the coming together of the north and the south. This is not in a linear way, but as a nonlinear event. It's not when energy is taken from one place and delivered to another.

Instead, it's a melding of energy to create a balance so there is unification. Unification is what we would call the melding of the masculine and feminine. This particular unification creates the attribute of increased compassion for the planet, and compassion is the key word.

There are many kinds of unity, but in this particular unity, you will hear over and over "the increase of the feminine attribute on Earth." In many ways, you should look at this as mother energy, for the mother has attributes that the male will never feel. The Kundalini has been associated with procreation, so let us look at the mother and the child. Is there a union there? The child is growing in the womb, connected to the mother's bloodstream, and even her consciousness. When the mother sings, the Human fetus knows it. Did you know that a baby comes out of the mother already knowing who she is? Being on Earth might be a shock, but the baby knows mother and even when the umbilical is cut, the first thing the child wants to do is to find mother. So this is instinct and belongs to the mother and child, but it's the kind of unity we speak of. It is one of the reasons the indigenous assigned to Earth the feminine energy called *Mother Earth*. Therefore, the rebalance of the planet is not about becoming more feminine, but instead, it is about becoming more compassionate.

The Human race has been out of balance for some time. The consciousness of humanity has been what we would call male-heavy for eons. The unity we speak of in this letter is putting together the energies of the male and the female to create an equal balance for Gaia. This is not so it will become feminine, but rather to create a balance. But it will appear that you will have more feminine energy than you have ever had before, to make the energy of masculine and feminine equal. When it's more equal, it creates the desire for unity.

There is a new attribute on the planet that shows this in action. If you look at Europe, there is an interesting thing that has just occurred within the new association called the European Union. It just received an award for peace (2012). Why is it that an economic union would ever receive an award for peace? The answer is that the putting together of former enemies has created a union

of compassion that now keeps Europe from warring. It's the first time in Human history where so many former enemies have decided to unify in ways that are permanent.

I will remind you where you sit today, that 12 years ago, you had the opportunity for still another war. This war would have happened if the consciousness on the planet had stayed the same as it had been for the last 100 years. This war would have been the final war and would have been called the Armageddon. This event was prophesied by many, including the man you call Nostradamus. You will also find it in your holy scriptures, yet the war didn't happen.

In order for such a major scheduled event to change, Human nature also had to have changed. Within the last 18 years, there has been a concentrated effort to put things together on the planet instead of tearing them apart. The ancients predicted this as well, for their predictions were for a balancing of the planet by 2012 and for the beginning of a shift in Human nature. If you, as humanity, would make it past the year 2000 without destroying yourselves, the potential was that the galactic alignment of 2012 would then be an energy where Human consciousness could change forever. It has begun.

Spirit has always given you messages of unity, and from many sources in many areas. It has come from every single master who started every single religion, on purpose or not. If you look at the Jewish master Abraham and his sons, you have the theme of unity. If you look at the prophet Muhammad and the message that he was given in the cave, it was to *unify the tribes of Arabia*. It was all about unity. If you look at the master Christ, it was profound. Look into the eyes of Jesus and ask Him one question: What is this all about? He would say, *"It is the unity of God and man. It is the ascension of Humankind. It is the compassion of the mother."* Isn't it interesting that the first and largest Christian religion on the planet emphasized the mother of Christ almost to the same degree as the Christ himself? This is because compassion is at the center of the search for God.

We have said this before: There is a saying that, *if mothers ran the Earth, there would be no war, for the mothers would never send their children into the battlefield.* This is the kind of energy that is now being presented to the whole of the planet. This, dear ones, is the change that you are seeing.

There is still the potential of another small battle in the Middle East. It will come within the next two years. That particular battle will create something you have never seen. It will create the start of a unification of countries that you would never have seen unified before. It could have the opposite effect of one that is expected. It could start unification.

Now, South America, we have given a prophecy. We have no clock. We cannot tell you when something is going to happen, but instead, we see potentials. We see the potential of a unified South America – all countries involved in something similar to what the European Union has done. Look at the European Union for the moment, and you will see that they appear to be in trouble. You cannot take unequal economies and force them together and give them the same currency and expect it to work smoothly. You can't take different consciousness of government, then force them together and expect everything to work. Dear ones, this is one of the most difficult things you have ever done on the planet!

Intuitively, over the last 40 years, you have realized that this will save you and is needed, and it will eventually work. It is the secret to keep you out of war. So you will face the same issues here (South America), for there are economies here that are strong and weak, just as in Europe. There is government consciousness, many governments that wish to unify, but others are not so certain. There are attributes where the small ones are afraid of the big ones. Some say it can never happen here, and we will say to you: oh yes, it will!

Imagine something with me for the moment. Imagine the continent of South America being so unified that it can trade as one unit with any other continent or country in the world. What kind of economic power will be the result of that? What would the quality of life be as a result? It is the answer to getting rid of the poor in South America, for the very unification will raise the poor out of that which they have been in for years. There will come a time when the favelas of Brazil will be bulldozed over, for there will be

no more people there. They will have moved on to things that they have deserved for a long time. The same goes for Bolivia and other places that suffer from poverty, for those living under the bridges will no longer have to live in that way. This is the potential we see.

It will happen slowly and in South America, there is a potential of partial unification first. And over a period of years, the countries that reject it will shift and change and eventually join. There will be controversy and difficulty, and yet you will do it, because it will put together something that has always been needed to be put together. The union of South American states will eventually occur. There will come a time on this planet when there may only be five currencies total, and a unification will be created of continents and countries who will never go to war again.

This is the U of Kundalini. This is the promise for you and it's not going to happen tomorrow. In 18 years, many of you will awaken and remember this moment (speaking of the attendees in the room). Something inside you will bring you to a point where you remember this, being in this city, and you'll look around you at what has happened to South America and you will know it has begun.

Finally, there is a unity within yourself that has also begun. There are so many of you who struggle with the duality! You can define duality any way you wish, but we say, *it's the existence of dark and light within the same corporeal Human Being.* What is it that you struggle with within this duality? I'll tell you: You struggle with a difficult energy that has always been here, against that which you know is divine and a part of you. This is the struggle. It is the light and the dark within yourselves: fear vs. the light of God. Now, imagine what's going to happen, old soul, as Gaia helps to increase the light on Earth. The planet begins to balance, and the duality will diminish. The battle will be less, and you will start to unify this dark and light to a place where it no longer appears to represent opposing forces that cannot exist together. It then becomes the unification of self.

There is a time when the three-dimensional Human Being will actually be able to meld with that which is the multi-dimensional Higher-Self. That's the final unity!

How are you feeling right now as you hear this? Are you at peace with yourself? I didn't ask you if there were problems in your life. I asked you if you were at peace. For those who can say yes, then you're beginning to understand this unification of self. It's like it stands alone, outside of you and yet it is inside you. No matter what is taking place around you, it can relax even your cellular structure. It can relax you to the point where you can say, *"All is well with my soul."* It is beyond comprehension; this is the unity of self.

There are some of you listening to my voice and who are reading who can do this and feel this. You're starting to see the true self. You are seeing the piece of God in you and who you are, and the three-dimensional things around you simply become things that you have to solve instead of things that define your life. What defines your life is the compassion of God, and that is the unity we speak of.

So I will say it one more time and then we will close. The movement of the Kundalini of this planet is about the individual Human Being and what is going to happen to them at the cellular level. The ancestors are smiling, for they expected it.

Kryon live channelling "The Letter U in the word Kundalini"
given in Uspallata, Argentina — October 18, 2012

Notifying Gaia of Your Conscious Actions (The Letter N in Kundalini)

In the word KUNDALINI, what do you think the first 'N' means? Today, for this lesson, the 'N' means *notifying Gaia that you are part of the shift.* Some will say, *"Kryon what do you mean? If we are having a shift, I'll be a part of it. So why do we have to have a notification?"* Oh how linear of you. [Kryon smile]

There are paradigms of spiritual action which are changing. You naturally feel that a shift of this magnitude would simply have all of humanity involved in it. Oh, indeed, some will be, but the ones who really need to come along and change things are *old souls*, and that's you. This is a change in spiritual attributes within yourself, for you can no longer just sit there and participate in a passive way. It's no longer enough to simply hold light. Oh, that's

153

honored and it makes a difference to the planet, but it always has. No. This is different. There is a shift going on, a kind of re-birth of humanity, and the old soul must either join it or not. There's no penalty for not joining, and there's no judgment. But it really is the reason you are here.

Old systems and old ways are very interesting, for many of you see these things as static. That is to say, that you feel they are set and they never change. Have you heard the words, *"God is the same yesterday, today and tomorrow?"* If this is so, and it is, many feel that there is nothing different to do regarding God. But what if the relationship between humans and God is changing? If it is true that your DNA is changing and that your spiritual awareness is changing, then the old paradigms of how you work with Spirit and Gaia must also change.

Sometimes, those who are esoteric [New Age] believe it is enough to sit on the ground and absorb energy. With their hands in the air, they say *"Thank you, God, for loving me!"* Then they get up and do what they have always done. There is nothing wrong with this, for what they have always done is to hold light for the planet. This has been the Lightworker's job for centuries. However, this is now starting to change. It is moving from passive to active, and the old soul is the catalyst.

Compassionate action is a term we are using that means you do something besides what you are used to as a Lightworker. It is action, and not something that is passive like holding light in your area. What this action is about, is what we want to discuss. For as you alter what you do in your reality, Gaia then *sees* that as action and this is *your notification* that you are part of the shift.

There are things in every one of your lives that are ready for shifting to compassionate action. That's why you are here. Before I even move forward here, let me tell you once again that there is no judgment of you if you choose to remain the same. An old soul spending time having light shine through them on the planet is a good thing. Many will decide this is what they will continue to do, and they will be the anchors to help the ones who then move to compassionate action. So there is a balance within the old soul group.

An old soul, who feels the rejuvenation of the birth of humanity, cannot sit still. For them, this entire shift is like a miracle. It
is what they came for, and they are ready to go to the next step.
What they will do in that next step will automatically notify Gaia
to continue that shift. Remember, Gaia is linked to the consciousness of humanity. So, if humanity simply does nothing different,
the shift will stall. So, the old soul understands that what they do
in these next 18 years will affect their children and their children's
children.

Compassionate action: What kind of action is it? It's what we
have been talking about for years. How are you going to change
your life? What can you do that is different to create more light
on the planet? I don't mean you must change in an unusual way; I
mean change in a way that will create a more peaceful life. So let's
list a few of the areas of creating compassionate action.

Number one: How do you perceive other Human Beings? When
you come to a meeting like this [speaking of the large seminar in
Santiago] and you meet those you have not met before, what is
your perception? A big smile, perhaps? You may even hug them
and recognize another old soul, a Lightworker perhaps? You'll
have compassion in your heart and see them as ones of like mind
with you. You may even love them, for the connection to God is
there, and it's beautiful. Then, seemingly in a very short time, you
leave the room and get into your vehicle and go out on the road.
While driving, some person in another vehicle, who obviously
is not enlightened, cuts you off! You stamp on the brakes and
almost have an accident. Now, what do you think about them?
Well, of course ... naturally, you will love them ... right? [Laughter]

So I'm speaking about how you see humans in general, and I'm
talking about initial reactions to who you meet, no matter what
the situations are in life. I'm not speaking about Lightworkers in a
love-based meeting, but other Human Beings in what you would
call normal life. How do you see humanity? Can you see every single corporeal person as part of the family of God? Perhaps some
are in drama and some are sick; perhaps some are in fear and
therefore, they are not very nice to you, or good to be around.

How do you see them initially? So this is one of the best compassionate Human exercises. See all humans as part of God.

When the masters walked the Earth, how did they perceive those they met? Oh, you know the answer. They saw everyone with the eyes of God. Now, some will say, *"Wait a minute, Kryon. Those were the masters of the planet! They were not like us."* Yes, dear ones, they were masters. So we are telling you that as masters, they showed you how to do this. Now, there is a shift happening on the planet that begs you to practice this compassionate action more than ever. The more you practice your new perception of humanity, the more that the cellular structure in your body will agree with what you are doing. Then your patience will increase; your tolerance levels will increase; your anger will diminish; and no matter how anyone treats you, you will see them with *the eyes of God.*

Now, I want you to get ready for some reactions. Because as you practice this, it's going to make some angry. They won't like it. They will want you to react and get angry; they expect and want drama, and some of you know exactly what I'm talking about. Some humans thrive on this very thing! Even as you leave here, you are going to have to go home and practice this immediately.

What happens if you do not engage in drama? What if you refuse to participate with others in something they expect? No matter what they do to you, no matter what they say, there is peace in your eyes. There are no words given back to them in anger. Can you do this? If you can, you then join the ranks of those who are practicing mastery. If you can do that, you've just informed Gaia! You've just told Spirit that you are a part of this shift!

The rebirth of humanity will create a different paradigm of consciousness. Oh, believe me, you're going to be noticed! Oh, dear ones, there may be friends who leave you because of this. But before they leave, they may say to you, *"You know, I don't like being with you anymore. You're no fun. You won't join into our conversation like you used to. I liked the 'old you' better."* They're right! Because their conversations were usually ones that pulled down other people in value, or they wallowed in victimization, or complained about others all the time using the same verbiage over and over. You know exactly what I'm talking about, don't you? You see, I know who's here. I know who is listening and reading.

Number two. This is an easier one: Where are you in the scheme of the judgment of others? *"What, Kryon? We do not judge others."* Perhaps you think this is so, but you all do it in subtle ways. It's part of what Human Beings do. You *size up* those around you. How much do they know? How smart are they? You can instantly see where they are in the social status structure, and what they do for a living. How much money do they have? You all do it, but you don't do it on purpose. You do it because that's what your parents did, and their parents before them. You do it because, in the past, it used to help with your very survival. When you have *figured them out*, then you know what to say and what not to say, and whether to trust them or not to trust them. It was part of an automatic old energy system.

What if you surrounded yourself with a bubble like the masters did, and there is no judgment or pre-judgment at all? All are within the family of God, and there is nothing that anyone can do that would affect your spirituality, which is now your survival. There's no one on this planet who can make you sick, not if you are holding that beautiful light that's active around you. Your light voids any dark energy that comes your way. This includes how your emotional body reacts to what people have to say about you.

Suddenly, many start to feel the compassion of the masters coming from you. Did you ever read about the masters? Did you know that animals used to follow them around? Animals used to sit at their feet, because animals are instinctive. They can sense peaceful consciousness. You'll have the same thing happen to you. Where are you in that scheme of things?

Number three. Fear. It's time to dissolve the energy of the things that you are afraid of, including other humans. Who are you afraid of? Who is it that you don't wish to meet face to face? Who is it that you have thrown out of your life and don't want to see again? I know who's here, and I know who's listening. This is an old consciousness shift. Forgiveness does not change the past. Forgiveness changes the future. It is a wise, courageous old soul who can stand in the bubble of their truth and say, *"I forgive you because I recognize that you are a piece of God like I am."* You might say to them that *"the reflection of God is in us both."*

Number four: Lastly, we again bring up the issue of duality. There are those who will tell you that duality will never change. This is the balance of dark and light, which is in your corporeal nature. Well, it just changed. I want to tell you that you have so much power over the dark! Begin to exercise the light in your life. Do it for your own personality, not for others around you, and not for your workplace, but for you. Most of you don't do this. You turn your light outward. But if you start focusing it on yourself, the darkest parts of you begin to disappear. You will have a more peaceful life. That's duality.

If the balance between dark and light is starting to shift on the planet, then let it start first in you. In that process, you're going to be more peaceful and you're going to live longer. You're not going to age as much. Disease will run the other way when it sees the divinity in your cellular structure. Stop getting sick. I'm telling you that all of these things are real. Your light quotient affects the very biology of your existence. That is compassionate action. It is the 'N' in Kundalini. Notify Spirit that you are going to be a part of everything that is going on!

Kryon live channelling "The Letter N in the word Kundalini"
given in Santiago, Chile – October 20, 2012

Don't Think Like a Human (The Letter D in Kundalini)

The 'D' in KUNDALINI stands for *Don't Think Like a Human.* It means "Don't think like the *old Human,*" who thinks as they were trained. Instead, think like the *New Human,* who is starting to develop a multi-dimensional sense of reality.

My partner mentioned something about South America [in the seminar] and he's right. There are more young people awakening in South America than in any other continent on Earth. Spiritualists and sociologists will give you information about who gets interested in spirituality. They will tell you that it is mostly those over forty. For, they are in a place in life after they have achieved their education, they are more settled and are no longer busy. So they turn to the things of God. They prove their point by then doing research on the age groups of people who attend spiritual meetings. However, what we see here in South America is not that way at all.

So, what is it that is taking place in South America that is different? It's a new paradigm of humanism. The youth are interested in their spirituality, because the youth are beginning to look at something called *spiritual awareness*, and the *logic of God*. They are not suddenly becoming religious, but rather, their curiosity of life is bigger than yours was at their age. Their spiritual interest includes things that are out of 3D, and they are starting to ask some of the most profound questions that humans have ever asked. They are using the wisdom of their ancestors to solve these spiritual puzzles, instead of the wisdom of the adults who are in their culture. There is a difference.

I'm going to invite you to join them, speaking to anyone listening to my voice or reading these words. I'll give you some examples in the following discussion: Do not take these things as criticisms. Instead, take them as a new path of spiritual logic and an invitation to look at some things differently than you have in the past. Don't think like a Human.

In this room there are many Lightworkers and old souls. The message that I give tonight is more for those listening to my voice in another time, than for those in the room. But, there are those in the room who also need to hear it, as well. Some of you have already gone in this direction and it lets you sit here and enjoy this energy called channelling.

There is a tradition of spirituality, which is taught from birth: God is the Creator of the Earth and the Universe is big. Human Beings are small. In fact, there are those who will tell you that humans do not even deserve to be here. There are those who will tell you that humans are even bad for the Earth. It would have been better if humans were never here. There are elders who wear the costumes of the church, who will tell you that you are born dirty and nothing you can do will satisfy God, except a very few things ... and they know what these things are. They'll tell you that, if you don't do these things, this loving God of yours is going to take you to places after you die, and punish you every day.

There are some who will say that you've done such a bad job here on Earth that you will burn every day after you leave this

planet in death, as punishment. Dear ones, this is not the way of God! Right now, I want you to suspend everything you have ever learned about what you think you know about God, and clear your mind. Today I want you to start using spiritual logic, and use the piece of the Creator inside to check this out. Is what you have been told, valid or not?

You are part of this creative energy family. You are the essence of what created the planets, all of them ... the ones that you know about and the ones you don't. They all have your energy. You might even say God is the very parent of your energy. We are a piece of you and you are a piece of us. There is a light, which is God, and this light is in each of you. It doesn't matter what you do, you can never lose it. Indeed, you come into the planet with a test at hand, because you don't know you are part of God. The test is whether you can discover it while you are here, and change the Earth or not.

There has never been a judgment of you. There's no system of punishment from God, and even some of your scriptures say this, yet you still don't believe it. In the newer scriptures [New Testament], there is a parable. It is *The Parable of the Prodigal Son*. It describes two sons who were sent into the world by the one father. One son does everything correctly for his culture, and the father is pleased. The other son does everything incorrectly, and the father is worried about him. But when both sons return home, they get the same party and the identical welcome. For the children are the same before the father and are loved the same. This is in your scripture. It's an example of how God works with humanity. In the parable, God is the father, and the sons represent the choices of humanity. There is never a judgment of your behavior. How much do you think you are loved by God? You have no idea. God's love surpasses any kind of Human love you have experienced. It surpasses even the love of the Mother for a child.

Parents, how much do you love your children? Imagine for a moment setting up a test for your children ... a profound test of wisdom. You then send them into the world to see how they will do. Then let's say one of them does something that shows poor wisdom. So now you are going to torture their soul forever? How does that sound, mom? It's absurd! Absurd! These "judgmental rules of God" are the creations of men, not God, and created only recently for political reasons.

I want you to go back with me and look at the beliefs of the original spiritual organizations on the planet. When humans began to put together belief systems, which you now call organized religion, look at the very first ones. They represented full intuition and wisdom of Human Beings about God. Do you find judgment in their doctrines? No. What do you find instead? Take a look: You find belief systems that describe the ability to ascend while you are on the planet. Almost all of them believed in the circle of lives, and that Human souls come and go from this planet, each time learning something different. They believed in the love of God and it did not include being "born dirty." Instead, you were an appropriate part of the life system.

This is spiritual logic that we ask you for. I want you to start comparing it to the things you've been told by your culture. Do not weigh it by the history of humanity or what you've been told is the history. Instead, weigh it with that which is your own intuition about God and God's love. *Don't think like a Human.* Don't cling to what you were told about God from an ancient book. God is in you! If you want good information, you can get it right from the source! Do you understand what I'm saying? That's spiritual logic.

There's a shift going on within this planet. You want me to prove it? Go take a look at the young people, because some of them have figured it out. They're talking to the source! They are getting current information. Adults don't like this, because sometimes the young people suddenly gain more wisdom than their elders!

Here's the second one: The Human Being sets goals and then works toward them. This, then, is linear thinking and planning. Even ones who are spiritual set goals, and puts themselves into a future box. That box then becomes the target of their actions.

Let me ask you this: What if that potential box is one you don't know about? What if it's bigger, or more profound and beautiful than the box you designed with your goal? Then, perhaps you spend all your life trying to get into your Human small box, and you never get to the big one, because you've got "your Human

161

goal" all figured out. Do you understand? It's time to stop thinking like a Human!

Make a goal that is one your neighbor won't understand: *"My
goal is to be where I belong with those who belong with me, and it may take
me many unusual places. My goal is to be at peace in my heart with all of it. I
am not worried about my future, because I am not alone. I believe that there
is spiritual logic in this, for it has to do with potentials I cannot know about
now, but instead, I trust that they are there and that, therefore, my pathway
is illuminated with lights that I am not seeing yet. But I can see one ahead of
me, and it is called spiritual logic, intuition, and the love of God. After I pass
the one light, another one will show itself; I don't have to see them all. I don't
have to know where I'm going. I am relaxed in the arms of Spirit."* That's the
parable of the missing bridge that I gave you earlier, dear ones. In
that parable, you have no idea that the bridge has even been built,
but you proceed at full speed toward the canyon as if it were there.
Don't think like a Human.

Let me give you one more, the most esoteric of them all: Many
will tell you that you have arrived on this planet with all you're ever
going to have. Your body, your brain, your intellect, your intelligence, these are all you have. They will say that if you're fortunate,
you'll learn and grow, but you'll always be using the same tools,
the ones you were born with. Now, if you believe that, you're sol-
idly in this linear pattern, and you've created a prison for yourself
that says you'll never be able to get out of *the box that you are in.* You
can grow in the box, but the box is permanent.

That's the way humans have taught you. However, there is
an energy that is being developed on this planet which starts to
release the protocols of what you were taught, which is that box.
Imagine, for a moment, a box that expands, which is you. The
expansion is the current you, and that which used to be you, in the
form of what you would call past lives. What if I told you, that you
come into the Earth with the wisdom and the knowledge and the
talents of every single lifetime you have ever lived? In linearity, the
only one you are aware of is your current box. So you never even
attempt to open the door to the storehouse of wisdom, knowledge, and talent that represents what you have learned in past
lives.

Humanity will tell you that this is ridiculous and silly. Yet the proof is all around you in the form of observable Akashic inheritance ... the child prodigies, and other kinds of profound attributes of birth that are unexplainable, unless you apply this new idea. You cannot think on these things, unless you use a little multi-dimensional intelligence that understands that time is in a circle. It is not linear, in many cases, it doesn't conform at all to the model you have been taught. Welcome to the now! The New Human starts to think out of the box of linear time, which must start to include the idea that the Human soul is eternal in both directions.

This, dear Human, is the awakening of past wisdom. I would like to give you a secret about the indigenous. There is very little written down about what they do in ceremony. Instead, they pass their history to their children via verbal stories. There are some things that they know, but which they cannot pass to you because the information is not linear. Your culture has become modern and, therefore, throws away the multi-dimensional secrets of God. Many times when the indigenous circle around to start ceremony, the very first thing they do is to honor the ancestors of their culture. You might say, *"Well, that's really nice. They really like their elders and it gives credibility for the wisdom of the dead."* That's not what they're doing! That's what your linear mind in modern day makes it look like. They're smarter than that, but you don't give them credit.

Let me tell you what they are doing: They know about the circle of life. They know they're not born dirty, and they understand they are a part of Gaia, and are part of the whole system. They have always honored the Pachamama. Therefore, as they honor the elders and the ancestors, there is an acknowledgement that they are also honoring themselves. *For they are aware that they are their own fathers and grandfathers.* No wonder there is so much honor! They are in the now, and their box has expanded to include themselves in a past life. They look at their past as the same as their now. The wisdom of their ancestors is the wisdom of *them*. Did you know that?

So how about it? What are you going to do with this? The invitation is to expand your box and understand who you are, old soul, and understand you have the ability to take all of the things

that you used to be and bring them to the present. This will create the wisdom necessary in order to move into what we would call an *ascended Earth*.

The difference between an ascended planet and a non-ascended planet is not that one has more angels or fairies than the other. Instead, it's if they have become multi-dimensional in their realization of self, and recognize that they are no longer singular. It's a return to original wisdom, an acknowledgement that you are your own ancestors; an acknowledgement that you have more wisdom than you thought you did, and that your *box* is bigger than you thought.

Get ready to break some rules, for almost everything you were taught is only a piece of the whole truth. Use spiritual wisdom right now. How does this feel? Does this information feel silly, or does it give you chills of truth? What's this going to do for you? I'll tell you: First, you're going to start changing the very cellular structure that you call DNA. You're going to live longer and be more peaceful with everything. You're going to start seeing things on the planet which make more sense to you.

Eventually, humans are going to start doing things you never thought they would do, and you'll know I'm right. You will start to see common sense in politics, even though as I say that, you don't believe me. [Laughter]. Watch and observe. The young people of today will eventually end up in those government offices, and they're going to be smarter than the ones who are there now.

Common sense and spiritual logic are starting to imbue themselves into humanism ... the very attributes of a multi-dimensional God.

Kryon live channelling "The Letter D in the word Kundalini"
given in Santiago, Chile – October 21, 2012

Ascension (The Letter A in Kundalini)

The guardians are the ones who have always been here and the indigenous would call them their own, but they were here even before that. They guard the vibration of the area, which they instituted and established originally. This brief channelling is going to reveal the meaning of the letter 'A' in the word KUNDALINI.

'A' is the first letter of the English and Spanish alphabet, so it represents the first, or the number one. It is the fifth letter of the name KUNDALINI as we have been exposing each letter in order, and telling about each. Once again the numerological aspects of these things tell a story. The one (A in the alphabet) represents *new beginning* and the five (fifth letter) represents *change*. So here is the theme of the KUNDALINI: The Beginning of Change!

The meaning of *change* doesn't simply mean old things that change, but sometimes it means a start-over. This is a recalibration of the planet, for all things will change over a long period of time. Already you are starting to see Gaia actuate itself with the weather shift. The drought that you have here (Elqui Valley) is temporary and it will be followed by rain – too much. But this is the cycle of Gaia which must run through extremes before it settles. For this is a new calibration for a virgin area. The 'A' is going to stand for *Ascension*. Let us define ascension for you and we're going to do it in three stages.

First, we're going to tell you what you think *ascension* means, and then we will tell you how we define it. In the past, you have used the word ascension to describe something which moves away from the planet and goes into a spiritual land. So, an ascending Human Being would disappear from their body and go someplace that is not familiar to you ... the beyond. This is how you've seen ascension. The very word ascension means, *to go up*. In a 3D world, *up* to you, means sky. So let's recalibrate your thinking.

Ascension, to us, refers only to dimensional attributes. Ascension is, therefore, to *ascend dimensionally to a higher vibratory rate* ... some would say, a quantum state. But this only means a multi-dimensional state, and one that is out of 3D [4D]. You are simply moving through the dimensional scale, but let me remind you again, that this scale is not linear. For once you get past four dimensions, you are no longer linear and that means there can be no more counting [because counting is a very linear attribute]. Therefore, you cannot call the next step after 4D, *dimension five*. You can agree that it's higher than four, but the truth is, that the

step after four is into a multi-dimensionality, which encompasses *all* the rest. Changing dimensional attributes means that you are changing the very fabric of time, and the way you think about all things. You must now change the way you think about the way things work, so let us start with Human consciousness.

You will be ascending in (1) consciousness, in (2) body, and in (3) the relationship with Gaia. Once again, there are *three attributes* as part of the shift, so we will speak of them briefly.

The ascension of Human consciousness: This is what we've been telling you for years: It's where you start thinking differently, and a bigger picture of wisdom begins to be yours. The very attributes of your normal life start to shift, which includes more than just what you thought was real. You start to see that consciousness is also aligned with other things that have life, realized and not. The trees are included, of course, and all the plants that give you oxygen, of course. Things in the air that you do not think are alive are also included. There is multi-dimensional life everywhere. Even the dirt of the Earth has multi-dimensional energy. Gaia itself, Pachamama [Gaia consciousness], has attributes of intelligence and life.

The expanding consciousness of humanity will start to include these things and you'll notice that you are going backwards to what the indigenous of the planet believed. For, again we tell you, that what they saw, in their wisdom, was an alliance with all things around them, even the clouds in the sky. This is an ascended consciousness ... a larger awareness of Human divinity. That awareness then triggers the next item, and that is an ascension at a cellular level of biology.

Now, there's a crossover point, a bridge between consciousness and biology at the base of the brain, in what you have called the pineal. As you stimulate the pineal, it passes this consciousness as a signal to the cells of the body. This starts to activate your DNA.

Body: So let us define DNA activation: DNA activation is helping all of the 3D parts of DNA to work with the quantum instructions in the ninety percent of DNA, which is not protein-encoding [non-gene producing]. It starts to create a DNA which is more efficient than you currently have. It helps to re-write the instructions and information within the ninety percent. This will create a Human Being who is different, and a biology that works better.

Let me give you some examples that you haven't thought of: Some of you are concerned about the things around you environmentally, as you should be. There is pollution in your air. But it's not just air, for there is also what you would call electro-magnetic pollution. This changes the atomic structure of everything around you, rearranging the polarity slightly. Electro-magnetic pollution is real, and it's there. Does it affect Human cellular structure? Yes. What are you going to do about it? Well, in a linear way, you try to correct it. So you stop the polluting as best you can, and also get protection from the fields of energy which you are exposed to. So, are you stuck with this? Something may surprise you, which is coming.

If your DNA starts to work better at a biological level, then the children who are starting to be born now will have built-in protection to that which their parents have created as pollution in the environment. Call this spiritual evolution if you wish. Watch for an overall increase in size of human livers. Children will have bigger livers to process biological pollutants. They will also not be affected by the electro-magnetic field pollution nearly to the degree that you are, because their DNA has rearranged things with an intelligence of what has happened in the past.

Watch for the possibility for intuitive thought to be greater at birth. The children will be more in touch with their Akash [past life history]. Children will start learning to speak earlier, and will begin remembering things intuitively, much like the animals do in what you call instinct. Walking, language, and the wisdom of life will come much faster with an increased efficiency of DNA.

Finally, Human consciousness and the relationship to Gaia: Gaia mirrors Human consciousness. It reflects the consciousness that humanity gives it. If you give Gaia the consciousness of war, Gaia's vibration will lower to meet what you give it. If you give it the consciousness of love or compassionate action, Gaia will respond accordingly.

Now, certainly you know the complexities here are great, and the Earth does not have one vibration everywhere on the globe.

Even The Crystalline Grid creates pockets of what you would call low and high vibrations, based on what has happened with humanity in certain areas. But let me tell you something: There are places on this planet where the Pleiadians visited early, and they purified the grid in those areas, so that nothing that ever would happen there, would change the purity of the dirt of the Earth. We have mentioned it before.

Kryon live channelling "The Letter A in the word Kundalini"
given in Elqui Valley, Chile – October 23, 2012

Love (The Letter L in Kundalini)

We continue spelling the word KUNDALINI, and the letter that is next is 'L'.

Do we have to tell you what 'L' stands for? We spoke of it all day, and it is *love*. So today's message will be a little more about love ... just when you thought this subject had been completely explained!

The day began with an indigenous ceremony giving honor to Gaia, and many of you participated. So I'm going to ask some questions, and then ask you to answer them in your mind as I discuss them.

In the process of honoring the planet today in ceremony, was there love? Is it the kind of love that you expected? Could you even call it love? Did you feel anything in response? All of these things start to ask questions about how you would define the very word **love**. We have spoken of the love of God and we will again. We have spoken of it being very similar to the love between a mother and a child. It is unconditional in all ways.

What about Gaia? Does the Earth love humanity, or is that different? So I will tell you this, dear ones, indeed it does. Indeed, the planet knows who you are. Gaia has been imbued with The Crystalline Grid, and therefore, the consciousness of Gaia is aligned with the consciousness of humanity. It loves you. Gaia is not God, but it has in itself a consciousness. It responds to the same Creator as you do. It is in service to humanity, and is here for you. When you honor Gaia, it responds. There are many things happening on the planet now, which involve this love of Gaia. Gaia is honoring back what has been reflected to it lately, from Human consciousness.

Many of you are embarking on a journey [speaking of the start of the tour]. Physically, you are going to new places on the tour of the KUNDALINI. You are about to go to the center of ancient wisdom and there will be many feelings there. But these shifts that you are feeling are what the indigenous would say is *The Awakening of the Puma*. This is the awakening of the wisdom of the region, and you're going to hear this expression and you'll know what it means. It is the increase in the intelligence of that relationship between Human consciousness and Gaia, making this relationship even closer than it has been. It is a form of love.

The 'L' in KUNDALINI is Gaia's love for humanity. It's interesting, this relationship that you have with the Earth, for you look at the globe as one object. You also look at God as one energy or even an entity. You're not aware of the total aspect. Anything that is multi-dimensional has an infinite number of consciousnesses, but that are aligned as one. They present themselves as one in your perception, but they are many.

If you have ever felt Gaia speaking to you, this was the part of Gaia who knows you, and that follows the footsteps that you create within The Crystalline Grid. Yesterday, you found yourself in the null place where there was no crystalline energy [The Valley of the Moon, Chile], and where Gaia can reach out and touch your heart. There was some weeping there, and that is love. So, it is time to recalibrate your feelings for the Earth. This might mean that you literally walk out of this space and view what you would call nature, differently. There is love there, and it's unconditional.

Let me tell you a little bit more about the love of God, and explain it in a way I have not before. When you think of unconditional love, you think of the relationship between a mother and a child. It goes beyond that, way beyond that. Humans have free choice. They come into this planet with an intuitive sense of creation. What they do next in their search for God is quite linear. They set doctrines and rules and defined *truth* in many ways. They do this, since it helps them to organize themselves into a system

169

that is comfortable for a linear reality. So, immediately in this discussion, you might ask, *"What is truth? Who has it right and who has it wrong?"*

So let me give you something to consider: Let us say, that a Human awakens spiritually and realizes through intuition that there must be a Creator. Let us say, that the Human Being sees a situation in front of him involving an animal, which they consider a sign from God ... and in their mind they then assign the Creator energy to that animal. Now let me ask you *"What is truth? Do they have it right or do they have it wrong?"* Is that action of assigning the Creator to an animal, honored by God, or not?

The answer? Whatever the Human Being does that draws them closer to the love of God, is truth. Anything that creates an alignment of the Human Being with Gaia is accepted by God as appropriate and is honored. If the Human Being spends his entire life in front of an animal, and he believes that it represents the Creator energy God, it may not be the entire truth, but it is a part of truth and is appropriate. Are you understanding this? In your best moments, do you think you have the entire truth? As your spirituality grew with age, did you discover a greater truth along the way? So, at what point could you say, *"I have the truth?"*

As you approach the Creator and the wisdom thereof, you begin to understand that God's truth is bigger than anything that humans can visualize. You are free to discover the love of God in any way you wish. There will be those who point at you and will say, *"We are sorry for you, because you don't have it right."* Perhaps they will say, *"You are doing something foolish."* I want to tell you something, dear one: God is there with you and Spirit is going to enhance the love that you feel, no matter how you do it. The only fool is the one who believes that he has the entire truth and can stop looking and learning.

Yes, there's appropriateness and inappropriateness in the Human's search for God. Anytime you doubt the love of God, it's inappropriate. Any time you accept it in any form, it's appropriate. So the only thing that God asks of you is to use the spiritual logic of your intelligence and intuition to know *what is God, and what is not*. But know that you will find God in everything, if you look. It will be in the smallest of the small, and the largest of the large. Let this start to redefine the paradigm of unconditional love. God doesn't care where you find that love, since it is everywhere.

Kryon live channelling "The Letter L in the word Kundalini"
given in San Pedro de Atacama, Chile – October 27, 2012

Intuition (The Letter I in Kundalini)

We wish to expand the teaching. The letter in the word KUN-DALINI for today is 'I', the seventh letter. The meaning of this will be *intuition*. You may have had definitions of intuition before, but almost none of them would have been correct. For this particular attribute is beginning to increase in power within your lives.

Let us look for a moment at what those who study the brain say about intuition. It's extremely hard to define. Some have said that it's *random thoughts created by the brain at random times*. It presents itself randomly through the intellect and the logic. That's about as good as it gets.

Main Human consciousness has four attributes: Intellect, logic, emotion, and intuition. These represent the full gambit of Human thought and action. Psychologists love to trace your thought groups and put them in these boxes. An intellectual person will make certain types of decisions based on intellectual thought, and an emotional person will make certain kinds of decisions that are entirely driven by feelings. The ultra-logical person will only do things that are filled with solutions based only on logic. So where does intuition fit in? The answer is that it really doesn't fit much, until now. You'll have to look at what intuition is, and where it comes from, and how you feel about it. When I'm finished, you'll understand more.

Intuition is becoming something that you're going to have to deal with, and it will be as strong as any of the other attributes. Intuition is not something that comes and goes randomly that you just dismiss as a brain hiccup. Up till now, intuition has often been treated by psychologists as a small dream while a Human is awake. It carries no more weight than that, and it's something

that quickly comes and goes. However, intuition is not something that pops up randomly between logical thoughts. It is far more powerful than that. There is a shift going on within the planet, and a recalibration of some of the most basic attributes of Gaia. You're sitting in a classic wisdom center [referring to Cusco, Peru] that is awakening and becoming powerful, because the consciousness of humanity is starting to honor wisdom a bit more.

If you take a look at the tourist numbers in this city, it's almost like there has been an exponential increase in recent years. This was not caused by an emotional reaction, and there has been no logic or intellectual promotion. It has been almost exclusively intuitive. Here, dear ones, lies the difference between intuition and the other Human attributes, for intuition is quantum consciousness, and the only one that you can measure through observing mass action. Millions of visitors have all been brought here because something is happening in the area, and they intuitively feel it. So you might say, intuition, therefore, is a quantum part of the brain, and this particular quantum part is far bigger than anyone thought. It has reached the masses with one idea, occurring to many.

Now, in the past, the other attributes have been responsible for what you would call three-dimensional survival. War is not an intellectual thing, it's emotional. There are intellectuals who would argue for or against war, but there is no one sitting on the sidelines arguing with intuition. What I'm saying is that up to now, the three-dimensional parts of your brain have been in control. But now, with the kind of recalibration happening on this planet, the quantum part of your brain is starting to show itself, and intuition is multi-dimensional. This is why we have included it in the Kundalini meanings.

Let us just stop for a moment and look at intuition. What is it supposed to do? How is it manufactured in your body? Why don't you believe in it when it happens? Let us start looking at where it comes from. This will not be a shock to some of you, for intuitive thought is a product of the pineal gland. The pineal gland, which represents the third eye to many cultures, is that part of your consciousness portal that responds to your Higher-Self.

The small little thoughts that you might receive, which some of you might dismiss, are intuitive action. These thoughts may come and go so fast you're not even certain what they were about. They arrive through the pineal portal, through your Higher-Self.

As the Human Beings begin to recalibrate the cellular structure that we talked about, the very DNA of their bodies responds to the new instructions from an evolving consciousness. Those who seek truth, and those who are awakening to light, start to have an increased portal size in the pineal. The communication to the Higher-Self widens, and intuitive thought starts to take precedence over logic and emotion. This, dear ones, starts to draw the line between you and others around you. For intuitive thought does not look like it makes sense, when examined by logic.

If you decide to change your life's path because you had a momentary intuitive thought, those around you may say, *"Wait a minute! This doesn't make any sense. Have you studied it? Is it logical? What does the intellectual mind say about it?"* Your answer is that it doesn't matter, because *"My intuitive thoughts come from that place where I am God."* Now you start understanding why the puzzle widens for the Lightworker. You're starting to get messages from your God-self. Now listen, dear Human Being, this is not a judgment. But you have a tremendous tendency to ignore your intuition, or even to admit you have it. So let us look at how it works.

If intuition is mostly multi-dimensional, it is not going to be linear in communication to you. Let me take you into the mind of an artist who is writing a piece of music. Now, here's what that artist can never explain to you: The composition that he is writing happened all at once in his brain. All of the phrases, the melody, and those things that bridge from one part to another is not happening as the ear will eventually hear it. Instead, it's all happening in a split second, presented all at once to the brain. Then the artist proceeds to translate all this by writing this elusive intuitive idea down as structured musical notation.

What music composition touches your soul? Perhaps it even brings a tear to your eye and touches your heart? I'll tell you something, this amazing music may be profound when you hear it in linear time, but it all came as a flash to the composer, yet it has the power to touch you inside. This is channelling!

An artist knows about quantum intuition. The one who puts the colors on the canvas is not experimenting and erasing as they go. The master's artwork you see in the galleries were not a result of them experimenting with color. They knew exactly what to do. They got it all in less than a second, as intuition. The painting, in all of its beauty, was in their mind long before they started with a brush. We've said it before, that the sculptor takes a rock and removes what doesn't belong there in order to create what he already knew was there. It was all created in a split second.

Now, carry this into your life. There is a new process, a new paradigm where intuitive thought has to be felt, known, and recognized. The more you do this, the better you get. However, why is it that you don't believe your own intuitive thoughts? It's interesting, is it not, how emotions and intellect respond to authority? But intuition is not even a player in that scenario. Instead, you have to get out of the 3D world and start letting intuition be a player that is equal to the others. If you can do that, both the intellect and the emotion will line up and unify and will make sense.

Let us say, you have some intuitive Human Beings guided by quantum intuition. If you start asking them how it feels, they will give you very balanced answers about their intuitive thought. The intellect, which manufactures the logic, will now make sense, because it has become subservient to the intuition. Emotionally, they also feel balanced, not fearful.

The purest indigenous on the planet are the ones who have used their intuition to the highest degree. Imagine, thousands of years ago, Human Beings so intuitive, that they saw the cycle of life in themselves and nature. A modern world looks at this and says it's mythology and foolishness. What if they were more quantum than any of us in the room?

Let's do a test. Intuition comes and goes so quickly that you don't believe it. So here is the test. I'm going to ask you to dismiss everything that you've ever learned, and intuit answers. When I give you a question, I want you to feel the intuitive thought that happens around it. First impressions are the way of this. Use the first intuitive thought that you have, and when you do this, it is a revelation to your own mind. Intuition is not hooked to your

3D thoughts, so when you start to recognize it, it starts to reveal what you really think. The portal to the Higher-Self does not lie to you. It's going to give you the truth every time. It's how you accept it that is the puzzle. If it fights with what you've been trained to believe, then the three-dimensional part of you has won.

So let's sit for a moment. Some of these questions are easy, and some may not be. I'll ask a question and I want you to grab the first intuitive thought you have, not what you've been told, and not what your parents told you, or that society has pressed upon you. You're totally alone in this, with your own thoughts. What are your answers to these questions?

Question: Is God real?

Feel it. Did you feel it? Oh, that's an easy one. You wouldn't be here otherwise; you wouldn't be in this group otherwise, would you? So you know the answer to that. It was your first intuitive flash: *"Of course, absolutely."* But your intellect and logic knows there is no proof. So why were you so certain? Because your life experience with an invisible God has supplied you with all you need to say yes. It was, therefore, your first intuitive thought, and you recognized it.

Now, watch what happens if we start asking you to define God. For the intuition starts to fight with the intellect and the emotion.

Now it gets harder.

Question: Is it possible to talk to God?

First intuitive flash. Go with it! Can you have a conversation with the Creator? Yes or no? Now, this starts to interfere with your training, doesn't it. Do you feel the slight conflict?

Question: Is God inside you?

You're getting pretty good at this. I know who's here, and I am purposely giving you intuitive lessons on things you already know. This is to exercise the *intuitive muscle,* so that you know what it feels like. No question I'm asking is provable, however, so the intellect cannot authoritatively give you good information about it. It can only give an opinion based on your training ... that you're a fool, or that it's not logical, or that you're being too emotional. Those are not proofs or dis-proofs. Those are judgments! This, dear ones,

starts to identify the duality of the Human Being. Is God inside you? Use your intuition. Don't get an opinion from your brain.

My partner gave an answer earlier today that was from me, and not him. Some of you picked it up and even he was uncertain as to why he said it. He told you that Human Beings have a tendency to judge themselves. This is the fight between divine intuitive thought and emotion and intellect. The intellect will say, *"Well, you got an intuitive thought and it didn't last very long, did it? Therefore, it was just a mini-dream and didn't mean anything. It wasn't even logical. You can't even figure out what your intuition said, so stop thinking about invisible stuff and come back to Earth."* Your own consciousness has made a judgment based on opinion, not a conclusion.

Is God real? Does God talk to you? Yes. If you can strengthen the intuitive muscle in the brain, you can make intuitive thought clearer and last longer.

Answer this question: Picture yourself in the forest or the jungle, or perhaps in the wilderness. You're completely and totally alone, and there is no other Human for hundreds of kilometers, and there you stand.

Now, answer the question: Does nature know you're there? Are you just an observer, or are you participating in nature by being there? Almost everyone here knows the answer, and it is that you sit and bathe in *being known* and that you're not alone. The very leaves on the trees greet you. The air that you take into your lungs knows who you are, and the dirt of the Earth knows the size of your shoe. There is tremendous communication! Now, prove it.

Where is the intellect and the emotional body when you need to prove it? It can't be proven, yet the Lightworker doesn't hesitate with intuitive truth. So, you have placed the emphasis and power on intuitive thought, and you don't have to use the other to verify anything. You "Know" at the intuitive level, and you let the intellect and the emotion come along later. In this case, you know truth with intuitive thought first. These are examples to help you see what good intuitive answers feel like, so you can start using intuition for the hard questions of life.

One more question, and we close. There's a man sitting in a chair on a stage in Cusco. He says he is channelling Kryon. Is this message real?

The intellect, logic and the emotion will yell at you, *"No! God does not talk to humans this way."* All the training and bias of your past will be there, represented by the intellect. Although there is no proof one way or the other, it still represents itself as the authority, based on nothing but what you were told. That's an opinion.

However, what if God is more than you think? Maybe there is a tremendous creative energy that writes the songs that you love to hear and paints the pictures that you love to see. But you can't deny one part of an energy while you say the other part exists. Do you see what I'm saying? You can't draw a line and decide which invisible thing is real and which one is not. This is a creative event you're seeing, just as the artist paints and the musician writes, and it's called channelling. Is it real?

It's a good exercise today, for there are those in the room who say, no. I will tell you this, dear ones: These things can change tomorrow, if you'll give your intuition a chance to give you messages. This is so basic. *"Where is this going, Kryon? Why are you talking about this?"* Because it is the intuitive mind that is going to guide the future of the planet. It's the intuition that is going to say, "No more war." It's the intellect and the emotion that is going to be in the back seat now.

It's the intuition that's going to unify things that haven't unified well in the past, and it's the intuition that's going to create new paradigms of life. It's intuition that's going to drive biologists to find life in the dirt and in the rocks, that live in a semi-quantum state. These are future things that can't happen, if humanity is only driven by the intellect, logic and emotion.

Watch for this. There'll come a day when the scientific method will give credibility to intuitive thought, and then you'll know it's real. But they're not going to be able to find it quickly like you can. There is a loving, caring God that is inside you, and part of you. This God knows all about you and wants to talk clearer to you, expanding cellular structure and communication, so you'll be able to determine real truth.

One more question, without an answer: Human Being, with all that you are, does it really make sense that you're only supposed to live about 80 years and then you're gone? What kind of a plan is that? Think about it and let your intuition answer it completely.

Kryon live channelling "The Letter I in the word Kundalini"
given in Cusco, Peru — October 31, 2012

New Human (The Second Letter N in Kundalini)

I want you to look at what is happening on stage. There is a bigger picture here; there is a metaphor here; there is an honoring here on several levels. This is a quantum event. Take a look at what has just occurred. There are North Americans here [referring to Lee Carroll and Peggy Phoenix Dubro] on the stage, firmly planted in South America. They are grounded here, channelling the Wise Divine Feminine energy, which is pouring from this place. When you think about the Eagle meeting the Condor, it's happening here; it's happening now.

Why else would these North Americans be here? They don't come bringing wisdom for you, for you have your own! They come honoring the wisdom that is coming out of the ground here. Some of you are your own ancestors! Did you realize this? This is an honoring of the ancients, that's what it is. Look at the metaphor from the very beginning of this tour [Kundalini Tour 2012]. The theme has been *the changing balance of the north and the south*. Now, here it is in front of you, on the stage. This is part of the prophecy fulfilled.

Some of you may wonder about channelling. You have two before you who sit in the chair today, but they channel as one. It's not one Human Being with one source and another Human Being with another source. Instead, the one source flows into the other. The source is the one source from the other side of the veil. Some of you call this God, but we call it *family*. For you are part of us, and there is no separation. But I want you to look at the other thing that has occurred. I'm about to give you a channelling on another letter of the word KUNDALINI. The next to the last letter is the eighth letter. Eight, in numerology, is manifestation. The letter is 'N' and I do not have to tell you what it means, because it's already been given. The wise divine feminine just gave it to you. We come as one and the message is of the *New Human*. I didn't give it, she did [referring to Peggy Phoenix Dubro who is channelling next to Lee]. You see, we are one.

So, what does it mean, the movement of this Kundalini energy? Is it some Earth attribute that's interesting? Is it a shamanic thing? Is it just Peruvian? No. It is about all of humanity, and this area of the world is playing a major part in the shift.

It has been mentioned that new seeds of consciousness are being planted. Let them now be seeds of understanding. The events that happen on the planet because of this new balance, have a direct effect on humans everywhere. Everything that is happening is not just about the Earth, but rather, it is about humans. The predictions were not about the Earth. The predictions were about an Earth balance that will affect humans. It's about Human consciousness that changes, and in the process of the consciousness changing, a New Human is created. The very paradigm of humanism starts to change, even what you call Human Nature.

We have covered several subjects in the last weeks, as we have talked about this new balance of the north and the south. The melding of the Eagle and the Condor has been the theme. The coming together of them is the new balance. They meld in a way that creates a Human consciousness potential, which then starts to balance the male and the female aspects for all humans, not just the ones here.

We then went on to talk about unity, and we discussed the unity that is now starting to occur, which is new for the planet. We've given you predictions of the unification of South America. You're starting to see it in the north, where former enemies came together and now trade as peaceful parties. Things that could never have happened within an old energy are now becoming common. New ideas that never would have worked in an old energy are actually starting to work. This is the New Human, a Human who comes and looks at life differently than you or your parents did, or your parent's parents.

This is a shift in the paradigm of Human thought, and in the process, it creates other things that begin to accelerate the New

179

Human. The last channelling of a letter in the Kundalini word had to do with intuition ... taking that which is a quantum energy, which is created from the pineal, and bringing it forward as a major player with intellect, logic and emotion. That's a New Human paradox and paradigm, and it voids out the *survival at any cost* instinct.

A paradox is created, however, where, at the moment, you really can't define the *new* part of the Human, yet you are beginning to use it as much as you use any other part of your brain. Welcome to the quantum puzzle! You are moving out of logic-only based thinking and giving things credibility and reality that heretofore have not even been definable. There's more: I would like to talk to you about the potentials of what it is that's going to happen, not just about New Human thought, but also what happens on a planet that starts to become more quantum. What can you look forward to?

There are those who will forecast the future based upon past thinking. They will base their predictions upon things that humanity has done naturally over time, yet very few of those things are going to happen. What if the Human changes the way they actually think or process thought? What if the very core of the Human brain starts to move in a way that connects itself quantumly to the planet?

Let me discuss some things and paint a picture for you that you may not have thought about. I want to talk about Human invention. Now, some of these things I have spoken of before, but not in your language [Spanish]. So, it may seem a review to many, but it needs to be new for you. Have you noticed that the major inventions that you have called *global technological advances* have occurred almost simultaneously around your planet? When humans flew for the first time, it was in North America. But it was also being developed simultaneously on the other side of the globe. In fact, the North Americans only beat the Europeans by one week! At the same time the Wright Brothers were developing their aircraft, so were the French. Do you think that was a coincidence? Why did these ideas clump together like that, with so many doing the same thing at the same time? Think of what that brought you? The ability to fly.

Doesn't it strike you odd, that humanity had been watching birds for thousands of years, and the Chinese even had kites? Yet, this obvious invention of manned flight had never been developed, and when it was, the very ideas happened globally all at once.

The development of the radio was literally finished and revealed weeks apart, also. Those working on the same invention did not even know each other, or that the other was working on it. There still is controversy of who was first. Have you ever looked at the odds of this? How can these things occur in this fashion? Well, let me give you a little information: It has to do with what the Earth is ready for. When humanity has the Consciousness for it, then Gaia brings it forward, and allows the invention. Everything moves in a system, and as humans begin to think differently, Gaia responds. The very Earth that you walk on gives back to you what you give to it. The ancients knew this when they grew food. They honored the Earth, and it honored them back. It's a system.

Did you ever consider, that humanity would be delivered ideas when it was ready, which would then promote more technical invention? Well, despite the intellectuals who believe that humanity can think its way through anything, anytime it wants to, I can tell you that this is not the case. Otherwise the major inventions of your era would have occurred long, long ago. Humans didn't suddenly become super smart in the last 100 years.

It's going to happen again. Get ready for major inventions that will change everything, for you are now planting the seeds for a quantum civilization. This is a different reality than what you are used to. What's going to happen when you can see quantum energy? It's going to be a catalyst for major new awareness. Did you see what happened when you began to develop the electronic age? Did you see how one thing led to another so quickly? It seems like only a few years ago that you learned how to send messages without wires. Now look where that has led you. Look at the computing powers on your desk! This is what happens when you have a major invention breakthrough, and one thing leads to another quickly.

What will happen when you can see quantum energy? When the instruments are built and they figure out how to peek at

quantumness, you have no idea what they're going to see. This is going to open a door, and that door is going to be complex, unexplainable, and it will take the breath away of all humanity. For, when they turn the knob that allows them to see quantum energy around them, it will rewrite all of the science books on Earth. This is just one thing of many, and it will lead to astonishing new awareness. It's going to happen in the next 18 years.

It's happened on other planets, so that's how I can tell you about it. But let me give you some hints: When the new humanity has this invention and they start looking around them with the eyes of a quantum seer, they are going to see things they never expected. When they look at a Human Being, a *quantum energy bubble* will be seen around each one ... with amazing colors that change. It will be eight meters wide.

When they turn the quantum seeing instrument and look into the forest, they will see the quantum life and the multidimensional energy that is there. They will be shocked when they look at the rocks and find life in them! It won't be three-dimensional, as you are used to, but quantum life. It will start to explain that which was so mysterious in the forests and the trees. Earth science will have to redefine what life is, for it will respond when it is being looked at, and meet many of the current requirements of the definition of life.

There are certain discoveries which humans must make on their own. Can you imagine dialogue with a tree? Can you imagine dialogue with a rock? What about the air you breathe? Dialogue! It speaks to you, and you speak to it. It won't be through Human language, or even the kind of conversation that you have, but rather *quantum talk*. It's coming. I can't explain it, but it's going to redefine everything, everywhere they look. Wait till they look at the stars! That's just one of several things that you will see. It's coming. The New Human creates a new energy into Gaia which responds with new energy to you.

Ah, now let me tell you about the last one, and it has to do with DNA. I said it before, and you need to hear it in your language: The DNA of Human Beings is starting to become more efficient, so part of the paradigm that you have gotten used to will

182

change greatly. We've spoken of this before, but again, it's odd to us: When you look at the animals on Earth, you think nothing of some very interesting things. When a calf is born in the wild from a buffalo, within hours of its birth, the calf is running with the herd. The calf is born knowing what's poison, and what isn't poison. He knows who is his enemy!

However, when Human babies are born, they are helpless! Some have said, they are even useless. It takes years for them to walk and learn language. And you think that's normal, don't you? Here you are, the highest evolved creature on Earth, and you can't even do what the animals do. There is no instinct passed to the baby. Every Human birth is almost like starting over. That's going to change. Imagine having a child that has already been taught not to put their fingers on the stove? Did you see the video that played today? [Speaking of the video in the seminar of the 4-year old playing the piano like a virtuoso] Did you see the child on the keyboard? That's the future! Eventually, the Human will be born with far more instinct, remembrance, and wisdom. It's already happening.

Human DNA is going to evolve and old souls will come into this planet knowing they're old souls. You'll know it the next time around by the time you are five or six. By then, you will be doing what ten or eleven-year-olds are doing now. Watch for this. For the first time on the planet, your DNA will begin to be balanced, and balance creates that which is manifestation. That's the New Human, and it starts now. You'll see.

Kryon live channelling "The Second Letter N in the word Kundalini"
given in Lima, Peru — November 3, 2012

Illumination (The Second Letter I in Kundalini)

Let's identify the last letter in KUNDALINI. The ninth letter is a completion letter. It is an 'I' and in a moment I will give it a name, but I'm going to tell you some things I've not said before: What has happened in these last years has been fully predicted. As in all predictions, they are only measures of potentials. But in 1987, things began to move, and the predictions that have been

based on old energy were starting to move away and diminish in potential. The predictions in the old energy had humanity ending, a final war, and the end of what you would call "normal civilization." Those predictions were accurate for their time, and again, it didn't look like Earth was going to make it. This is the attribute of fair free choice, and if that had happened, there would be no judgment.

The test is the test, and the puzzle would not have been solved. But then everything changed. In 1987, something happened. You have called it the Harmonic Convergence. It was just before 1994 when the precession of the equinox time period began, but in 1987, we saw it coming. The potentials begin to shift. There was a collection of old souls, who, over a period of time, began to imprint The Crystalline Grid. This started to change Gaia, which then responded to consciousness again, and the Harmonic Convergence became known as the 11:11. This became the number that many of you continued to see in a nonlinear way, almost everywhere. Twenty-five years would go by, and Lightworkers would speak of it and wonder what it meant. Then my partner awakened, and started to find out what he was supposed to do.

Two years after that is when I came in. Kryon has been here since the beginning and there have been those who have channelled me here before, but in 1989, I came to my partner and asked him if he was ready to take on the entire mantle of Kryon, and do what he came on Earth to do. In typical fashion, he said no. It took four more years to convince him I was real, within his own free choice to find out. But that was still in time for the beginning of the shift. By 1994, he was ready and the shift began. Part of the shift was moving the predictions from the ones you had been used to in the old energy, to the ones that you began hearing about in the new.

There's a paradox here, for the old predications aren't really that old. They've come from recent scripture and those like Nostradamus. Those Humans are all new. Those are new predictions about old energy. The predictions that began the shift in the change you are seeing now, are the ones from the indigenous ... the ones who have been here for over ten thousand years. These are the ones who began to figure out what the stars were saying.

These were the ones who talked to Gaia. They saw the potential shift over the 500-year periods of time. They kept quiet during the other predictions, but then after the millennium shift, they knew the predictions of their ancestors were correct. Twelve years ago, when it became obvious that the old energy predictions were not happening, the potentials of the original predictions became apparent.

The tribes of the indigenous that were still left on the planet became aware, and together they began meeting, and the shift and recalibration became real to them. The indigenous of the Northern hemisphere and Southern hemisphere came together, and they discovered that their predictions were the same. The modern Lakota, Hopi, Navaho, and the Maya began to realize that they were all one, and that the prophesies were the same from the ancients of all the tribes.

You're going to see the beginning of a new unity of Earth. There will be many names given to it – the Journey of the Feathered Serpent; the Awakening of the Puma; the meeting of the Eagle and the Condor. But those many names represent the shift, and are all the same. What do you think about that? The shift is here. The 11:11 is real! What do you think the 'I' stands for? *Illumination.*

When I started with my partner and he began channelling, I gave him many metaphors. In the very beginning we spoke of a very simple one: Illumination. This started the very concept of being a Lightworker, so a Lightworker is one who illuminates. I gave him the simple metaphor that we have given every year since: There is a dark room where many humans are living, but they can't see each other very well. They would bump into one another all the time. They couldn't see each other's faces, so there was mystery and always fear. They would separate themselves into small groups for protection and huddle in fear. This created misunderstanding and no trust. They would sequester their cultures and then judge the other cultures because they were in the dark.

Then, as the metaphor continues, along comes one who lights a match and suddenly the room is no longer dark. It's not lighted yet either, but suddenly, many can see dimly. But they don't go looking for the match-bearer, or where the light came from.

Instead, they are able to see their neighbor! Suddenly there is no more fear. They can see their neighbor's face and it is just like their own. They get excited by the light, for it has created something they have never seen ... an awareness of other things. It's an awareness of one another, and a reduction of fear. So now they are interested, and they go looking for other matches and they find them. Someone else lights one, and another, and another. Suddenly there is more light than there ever was, and they realize they are all family, because they can see.

There are so many metaphors, but this is the shift and this is what was predicted by some of the oldest of the old. The ones who were in touch with the Earth long before the Incas, were right here. The Incas were a special civilization. They were master builders, but the wisdom of the land was already here by the time they arrived.

Now, I want to tell you what is next, and I also want to tell you that what is next is going to go slow. Where were you in 1987? Some of you in the audience will say, *"I wasn't here yet."* Others of you will say, *"I was half the age I am now,"* and still others will say, *"I was just growing up."* Where are you going to be in 18 years? It goes slow, dear ones, but you already know that. These things are not happening instantly like you'd like them to. So, as I explain some of the next steps, I will say again that we have no clock. I see these coming things as potentials in a quantum soup. These are the potentials of the moment and it has to do with awakening. Right now, in your time, is the midpoint of the awakening. This is the midpoint of the shift and many things are going to start happening slowly.

The consciousness shift that we have talked about is in progress. Slowly, you will see this all over the world. You will watch it, and you will be aware of it. More and more countries will discover their integrity and they will not be happy with the status quo that has been there for hundreds of years. This very year, you saw it with three countries, ones who had been stable for hundreds of years, but who decided that they would change. Some did it softly and some didn't, because the old energy is not going to die easily, but it will be replaced. We've told you the potentials that the consciousness will bring in the Middle East. We've told you to watch for startling things. Things that no one had predicted. Just like no one had predicted the fall of the Soviet Union back at the very beginning of the precession of the equinoxes, no one has predicted the revolution in Iran that I tell you will take place. This is the potential at hand.

The beginning of peace in the Middle East will happen in a way that no one has considered, and it won't be easy, and it won't be fast. But within 18 years you'll see it happen and it all has to do with something you have never seen before. It will be a complete shift in the paradigm of how they have worked with each other for centuries. Suddenly, there will be the emergence of compassionate action. You know what compassionate action is? It's where one country looks at another, and it says, *"I don't care what happened in the past. Why don't we start over? Why don't we sit down and start over, so we don't worry about each other ... so we can trade, share resources, and relax that the other is not coming to get us. Let's spend our resources on schools and hospitals. Why don't we start over and forget what the past pushes us toward?"* That, dear ones, is not what Human nature used to be.

Kryon live channelling "The Second Letter I in the word Kundalini"
given in Lima, Peru — November 4, 2012

The Eagle and the Condor

The prophecy of the Eagle and the Condor is thousands of years old. It is known by many of the indigenous cultures all over the world, including the Amazon, the Andes, Central America, South America and North America. The prophecy states that Human societies would divide and take different paths. The path of the condor represents the heart, intuitive and mystical energy. The path of the eagle represents the brain, rational and material world. From a personal view, I can also see that the condor represents the wise divine feminine, while the eagle represents the masculine.

The prophecy indicated that, during the 1500s, the two paths would converge, and the eagle would drive the condor to the verge of

extinction. If you take a look at history, you will find that the Aztecs, Mayans and Incas were all invaded by the Spanish conquistadors during the 1500s.

The prophecy then states that in the next 500 years, the condor and the eagle would have the opportunity to reunite and fly together in the same sky, along the same path. It is said, that if the condor and the eagle accept this opportunity, the world will come into balance and create peace on the planet.

The prophecy foretells the sharing of indigenous knowledge with the technologies of science and the balancing of yin and yang. The timing of the prophecy also corresponds with the shift of Human consciousness that we are currently experiencing, as old souls awaken. This prophecy is another expression for the movement of the Kundalini.

Something amazing has been happening on the planet regarding the fulfillment of this prophecy. A profound indigenous gathering of tribes known as *Raices de la Tierra*, translated as Roots of the Earth, has provided an opportunity for the indigenous to share their wisdom, knowledge and prophecies with thousands of non-indigenous participants.

Raices de la Tierra was the vision of a man named Raymundo North "Tigre" Perez. Raymundo grew up in Texas, where he was involved since childhood in the native spirituality of the Diné (Navajo) of the Reserve Montaña Grande (Big Mountain) and Lakotas in the region of South Dakota. Tigre Perez dedicated his life to spreading the essence of spirituality among the American Indians, indigenous and mestizos. Throughout his entire life, he organized and held many *temazcales* throughout Mexico and the United States. A *Temazcal* is a therapeutic ritual to purify the mind, body and spirit, using fire (sometimes volcanic rocks and herbs are placed on the fire).

During a special ceremony known as Hanblecheyapi (vision quest), Tigre Perez received a vision, in which he was given a mission to bring together the grandmothers and grandfathers across all of America, to pray for Mother Earth and humanity in their own language, and for him to surrender and offer his teachings to others.

For over 35 years, Tigre Perez dedicated his life to fulfilling this vision. In 1989, for the first time, he brought together an inter-tribal alliance of many indigenous and mestizos of the Americas in the

Kalpulli Teopantli community in San Isidro, Mazatepec, Jalisco, Mexico.

In 1995, Raymundo "Tigre" Perez was recognized as a Leader of Intertribal Council of Elders and a member of 7 distinct tribes. During the recognition ceremony, a plume of feathers of condors and eagles was presented to him in respect and recognition of his years of working with intertribal gatherings. This was the last day of a Kiva ceremony in Texas. Two days later, Raymundo entered the spirit world.

Raices de la Tierra is a result of Tigre Perez's legacy. It is the mission of the community group known as *Raices del Sur* (translated as Roots of the South) to bring cultural and spiritual traditions of indigenous peoples to "mixed people," enabling social and cultural exchange between peoples, including sharing and expanding forms of respectful and harmonious relationship with the environment. They are dedicated to promoting the cultural and ancestral knowledge of the Americas to all the inhabitants of planet Earth.

Raices del Sur is composed of 45 active volunteer members, including students and professionals from different areas and ages. The guiding principle of their work and volunteer services is to treat and recognize everyone as an equal, regardless of social, cultural, economic, ethnic, creed or sexual orientation, in order to contribute to building a multicultural society in harmony and respect.

The ceremony of *Raices de la Tierra* is part of the fulfillment of the ancient prophecy of the eagle and the condor, in which there is a spiritual union between the people of the north with the people of the south. The first event was held in Zapoteca, Mexico in 2005. It was held in this area for four consecutive years, and the reason this particular site was chosen was because it represented the North – the Eagle. Mexico is part of the Eagle's natural habitat. Following the ceremonies in Mexico, the location was moved to Casablanca, Chile, where the ceremonies were held in November from 2009 to 2012. This location was chosen because it represented the South – the Condor. Chile is part of the Condor's natural habitat. In December of 2012, the ceremony was then held in Bogota, Colombia, which represents the Center – both the Eagle and the Condor. This location has been chosen because it sits in the Sierra Nevada de Santa Marta in Colombia, where the Eagle and the Condor co-exist. It is one of the few places in the world where their natural habitat overlaps.

Raices del Sur invites others to participate in their sacred fire ceremony, inherited from Raymundo "Tigre" Perez. For more information, visit their website: *www.raicesdelatierra.org*

Other profound ceremonies related to this prophecy have also been held. During the spring equinox in March of 2006, a group of Hopi Indians from Arizona, North America, gathered water from sacred springs from all over the world, which was carried in traditional gourds. Hopi runners ran 2,000 miles on foot to the World Water Forum in Mexico City.

The Hopi Nation took part in a long-awaited ceremony at Teotihuacan, Mexico, where they were welcomed by a gathering of tribes that included Navajo, Aztec, Mayans and others. For the first time in 500 years, they performed the Eagle dance. The event was blessed by the appearance of an Eagle above the ceremony. The Eagle circled in six odd, figure-eight patterns.

One year later, the tribes that welcomed the Hopi decided to do a return trip. They gathered the four elements; water that was brought by the Hopi in the previous year, fire that was lit by a Mayan elder, earth and air. Members of these tribes ran the 2,000 miles back to Hopi land. For the first time ever, the Hopi allowed an outside group to dance in their sacred courtyard. A wonderful recording of these events can be found on You Tube under the title "Eagle and Condor – Film Trailer."

The prophecy of the Eagle and the Condor is all related to the movement of the Kundalini and the current shift of consciousness that we are experiencing on planet Earth. Further validation that this has been a prophecy foretold by the ancients comes from a channel given by the Hawaiian Kahuna Kalei'iliahi during 2007:

> *The Eagle meets the Condor … The Eagle meets the Condor … The Eagle meets the Condor…*
>
> *It is time for the Eagle to take flight. It has sent its White Spirit. It will travel around in a clockwise direction. The Eagle meets the Condor … It's about prophecies being fulfilled … The indigenous of all the Earth spoke of this occurrence. The Eagle has taken flight … to meet the Condor.*
>
> *(Kalei is now being told to take this message to her Apache niece Maria Yraceburu). The time is right to build the strong foundation for*

the New Earth. The time is right (4:48 was the time of the message being received). Things have sped up, time has sped up ... for the Eagle meets the Condor. The Human race will shift in its conscious more rapidly now. Trust. All is well.

Fly on the wings of the Eagle, Brave Warrior of the Light (referring to Reynolds) ... Look for the Earth changes in the north-east direction. Send Light there. Many will choose to leave the Earth Mother. But fear not! They will return as little doves of Peace. They circle the heads of the Anointed Ones. All is connected in the web of life.

The Great White Sky Chief speaks to all who will listen, to those of pure and loving hearts. It is time for all 4 races to come together and to celebrate your unity, your oneness. Forgive – forgive the past and release it. Forgive ... brothers and sisters, we beseech you ... FORGIVE. Forgive now.

The Eagle has taken flight. The White Eagle Spirit soars in sacred journey, to meet the condor. The Spirit journeys to fulfill the prophecy.

The one known to us as Brother of the Light (referring to Reynolds) is feeling the "pressure" as the vibration of the Earth increases. (He is just a boy, riding the Great White Eagle). A boy from a long ago promise ... promise at the Lake (referring to the channel Reynolds received at Lake Tahoe).

Balance. Balance the Earth and balance yourselves. Merge the feminine and the masculine. Others come to fill in the pieces of this message. (Have a) Safe Journey into the New Earth.

Channel given by Kahuna Kalei'iliahi at Hilo,
Hawaii – August 26, 2007

The Awakening of the Puma

I first heard about the Awakening of the Puma when I visited Cusco in Peru. It was in Cusco that I met a shaman by the name of Mallku Aribalo. One of the things that I immediately liked about Mallku was that he wasn't afraid to speak out about his knowledge, wisdom and intuition, even when it went against some of the old traditions of the past. Mallku believes that holding on to traditions, especially when they are based in mythology, will stop us from learning truths and moving forward. I have to agree, and even Kryon talks about the

importance for humans to use spiritual logic. So let me tell you a few things about Mallku.

Mallku is a gifted Visionary and Spiritual Leader. He is deeply passionate and devoted to promoting awareness, accuracy and clarity about the Andean Culture. Mallku is an intuitive expert in the understanding and translation of esoteric knowledge within the Andean Archaeo-astronomy, which he first revealed in his book "*Camino Iniciático Inka, el Despertar del Puma*" (translated as Inka Initiation Path – the Awakening of the Puma). In his own way, Mallku brings to life the knowledge of the ancients that Kryon talks about. Mallku's website is: *mallku.me*. Here is a summary of what his book is about, taken from the Mondial Association of Andean Writers (AMEA) website.

> Mallku in "The Awakening of the Puma" brings us convincing messages of a time in Andean history when the masters in the Andes lived and celebrated with an intense conscious connection and interdependency with Pachamama – Mother Earth. With their foresight and respect to nature, these sages have left a tangible path clearly traceable for future generations.
>
> Mallku guides our soul on an enlightening pilgrimage from power places and dimensional doorways, to healing springs, magic nature and celestial mountains. The physical journey through these highly power sites is a fascinating second step in this exploration to show us beauty and wisdom.
>
> The land and people of this magical mountains of the Andes are indeed tremendously awe-inspiring, and combined with the addition of Mallku's detailed research and clarity of explanation, we can witness the beauty of the past and present coming together, alive with the exciting promise of future continuity.
>
> For the ones acquainted with shamanic experiences and practices of master cultures, some parts of these messages will motivate the recognition of their cosmic path and the need of uniting their voices for a better world. The initiate assimilates the secrets of nature, giving him intuition, dexterity, vision, and the ability to create and transform energy for the purpose of peace in Human kind. One of the most interesting aspects of Mallku's teachings is that the doors to these new

dimensions of awareness have recently been opened for us as a result of the beginning of a new time named "Pachakuti," or Cosmic Cycle. Andean history is divided into segments of one thousand years, with a transformational era after every five hundred years. In June solstice of 1992 we recently passed one of these historical transitions.

The visionary master Inka Pachakuti was responsible for designing the Andean city of Cusco in the physical shape of a Puma as bringing this celestial animal to Earth to extent illumination and strength to all inhabitants and pilgrims of all times. This Puma, center of the Inkan society, is progressively illuminated by each sunrise, symbolizing the gradual awakening of the transcendent development of awareness in Human Beings. Andean history was written by the invaders of a land which, after 500 years of domination, is now returning to a new epoch of balance and independence. Spiritual and psychic doors closed for centuries are now been opened, inviting and propelling us to new heights of responsibility and re-connection with our planet.

There is much more for us to rediscover about the foresight and vision of our ancestors. We are now in a new time, and the mission of this new epoch is related to, but different from that of the last cycle. Tolerance and respect between cultures, combined with the capacity to agree and disagree, is a major evolutionary step destined for the new Pachakuti. The ongoing and constant destructive fight for domination occurring between people of limited vision, who cling to and worship one manifestation of Divinity at the expense of another, will be replaced by recognition of the many aspects of the divine.

Mallku announces that other secrets of the Andean wisdom will be explored in subsequent books. Subjects are the healing practices and magic connections of the coastal areas and jungles. The ceremonial use of power plants, and the interaction with sacred sites in cosmic time and the guidance to the amazing world of the Andean masters with the intention to awake our own Solar Puma and make peace come true on Earth.

Source: http://www.andes007.com/MALLKU.html

193

The Awakening of the Puma is therefore all about the current shift in Human consciousness that we are in the middle of. Kryon has even said that some of the indigenous on the planet who can feel the shift refer to it as the Awakening of the Puma. Kryon describes this as:

...the awakening of the wisdom of the region, and you're going to hear this expression and you'll know what it means. It is the increase in the intelligence of that relationship between Human consciousness and Gaia, making this relationship even closer than it has been. It is a form of love...

...Be aware of what the indigenous call *The Awakening of the Puma*. Watch for this, and study it. See what the ancients have said about it, and you will find that the Kundalini experience is not anything modern, for it was expected.

Dear Human Beings, this journey of yours is to learn more about the shift. It is greatly honored by Spirit. Why don't you just take a moment and feel this, for the love you feel goes both ways. There is great energy here of appropriateness and wisdom. It represents a great shift of the Earth.

Kryon live channelling "The Letter L in the word Kundalini"
given at San Pedro de Atacama, Chile – October 27, 2012

A Summary of the Movement of the Kundalini

Regardless of the name of the prophecy, the movement of the Kundalini is now upon us, bringing the balance of the masculine and feminine. Lemuria was one of the only civilizations that had a society with a balance of both male and female energy. The Lemurians lived in harmony for 20,000 years. They were on an island, and the pure spiritual core of the Pleiadians and all their teachings was passed from generation to generation undiluted. The Pleiadians visited other areas outside of Lemuria (Hawaii), but if you look at those civilizations, the prevailing trend was to separate and become a tribe that then focused their efforts on their own tribal survival. In Australia, we can find evidence that within the indigenous Aboriginals, there were at least 700 different tribes, each with their own language.

When you look historically at the pattern of past civilizations, the trend has been to separate and become a tribe. The European continent has a history of many countries at war with each other, including World War I and II. Nearly everyone expected that there would be World War III that would end our world. But something different happened. One of the first things to shift was the fall of the Iron Curtain in Eastern Europe, followed by the birth of the European Union. Who would have predicted that the countries within Europe would have trade agreements, and a common currency? The European Union is not without its problems, but the point is that, instead of war and separation, the countries are trying to work together.

Could it be that this is evidence of the movement of the Kundalini? Is this evidence that there is a shift in Human consciousness? I believe that it is. Kryon has also given us potentials that the model of the European Union is being looked at by other countries. Kryon has said that within two generations, the countries of South America will want to create something similar to what has been done in Europe. Putting things together instead of keeping them apart. Can you imagine visiting South America and crossing the borders without the hassle of immigration and customs, and having just one currency? One of the potentials Kryon has talked about is that eventually, there will be only five or so currencies on the planet.

What other evidence is there that the balance of energy on the planet is changing? That the wise divine feminine is starting to merge with the masculine? Take a look at what has been happening to the institutions that have a "macho" energy, and where there is a lack of integrity. These institutions are starting to fall over. Take a look at the countries where the women are not honored and you will start to see changes.

Kryon has said that the young ones coming to the planet are going to arrive with a much stronger balance of male and female energy, because of a more balanced planet. They are going to pick up their relationship with Gaia and will be supported by The Crystalline Grid that is being recalibrated for compassion. The younger generation will have concepts that are going to help create a more balanced society. All that we do now, especially within the next 18 years (from 2012) is going to help create a more balanced planet, planting the seeds for peace on Earth.

And what about you? What is it that you would like to do in the next 18 years? Everything you do is recorded on The Crystalline Grid. The grid is being recalibrated towards compassion, and the old souls on the planet are the ones who will make a difference. Dear reader, the fact that you are reading this book at all has sent Gaia and the Creator a signal of your intent that you are a part of the shift. Your thoughts, words and especially your compassionate actions to those around you make all the difference. I would like to congratulate you and honor the magnificent divine Human Being that you are. Well done!

Before I close, I would like to address some of the concerns that people will be seeing and feeling in the next 18 years (from 2012). Kryon has said on many occasions that things will appear to get worse before they get better. We should not see this as something to fear, but rather, as something that happens when you recalibrate from one thing to another. In a profound channel, the first given in 2013, Kryon told us to expect many new things. Here are three that I'd like you to know:

The Darkness

Because you have changed the actual Gaia grid system and have given intent to move past this 2012 marker into 2013, the rules by which dark and light battle one another have changed. Now the light is going to have a bigger impact – a far more powerful one. The definition of *dark* is the absence of light. So the dark is the void that is not filled by light, but it still has energy, although it is weaker than ever before. So let's define something else – the "Consciousness of Darkness."

Darkness and light are measures, not entities. They represent the way humans think and the waves of consciousness that influence others and create paradigms on Earth. So when we say, "the darkness wants this or that," we are describing groups of humans who have no light. This is the opposite of Lightworkers, who are groups of humans who have awakened to a realization that God is inside. This realization, by the way, is available for all humanity, since God is inside of every soul on the planet. But for a very long time, there simply has been no Human understanding that there is an actual personal choice of being anything but what they are told they are.

So the battle has always been between consciousness and how much light could be given to those who might see it or wish to see it. But as you know, most of humanity has wallowed in a very dim light that hasn't changed much for centuries – until now. This is not about goodness or evil. This is about a confluence or natural consensus of how humans think about themselves and what is appropriate behavior for humanity. Some may even call it Human nature.

Well, this old energy thinking wants to remain and remain. It won't believe there has been a change, but it will flail in unbalance for a little while, as it starts to realize it isn't as powerful anymore. This is going to be uncomfortable for you.

Some of you are saying, *"Well, 2013 ought to bring a release, a breath of fresh air. Ah, we made it! We did it!"* Well, I'll tell you, like a child that didn't get its way, the old ways of the dark will invade every cranny of life it can. It will battle for its life and its survival, and it will feel the fact that things are not the same. So in this release period, I want you to take a step back. When you see these things rear their ugly heads, don't make a decision that 2013 is not what you thought. When you see more unbalance on the planet, even some things that you didn't expect – and indeed, they will be there – don't throw up your hands and say, *"Here it is again. We didn't make a difference."* Because you did. These kinds of things work slowly.

The Beginning of Modern History

Energy is shifting and we have given you this information before. The very balance of the protocol of the battle is realigning itself. That's what this time is about. If you ask those in other solar systems who have gone through this before, it was the beginning, literally, of their written history. They don't even look at anything before it. Everything begins *now*. So as we've said before, if you look in the future of humanity, they will point to this day and mark it as the beginning of modern Human history. They will look at everything before it and say, *"Those were the days of barbarianism. Those were the days of modern mythology. Those were the days we didn't know better, and now we see the face of God in ourselves."* That is what you're stepping into. But it's tough, and it's slow.

The Planting of the Seeds

I have used the metaphor of *planting seeds* many times, so we will examine that just a little more and give you some more information. The metaphor, of course, is the farmer, and we use it so that you will see all of the attributes that the farmer looks at, which are common to you all.

While you were battling the old energy, you weren't plowing the fields, getting ready for the seeds. Instead, you were surviving. Now it is time to prepare the fields for planting, and in the process of release, you turn inward. *Preparing the fields* is a metaphor for discovering the Higher-Self, the quantumness in you, and moving to a place, personally, where things start to make more sense in your everyday life.

There are those in this room and reading right now who I'm hearing from: *"Help me, help me."* You don't think I know who's here? So I'm going to say to you: You know who you are, dear ones, and I want you to relax for a moment. You are loved beyond what you think you're loved. You are known by God beyond what you think you're known by God, and this you are feeling now is temporary. Ok? This is temporary. If you're pleading for help, you're in unbalance. It's time to relax in God and know you're loved. There is time. You will survive. You're going to make it.

There is wisdom in the plan of the seeding metaphor. First, you plow the fields; then you add the fertilizer and nutrients. Finally, you get ready for the seed planting. The fields aren't ready now, so you must pause and get them ready. So all this talk is a farming metaphor. This may not all make sense to you, but what it says is that the demarcation point from old to new is now, and only now may you begin what you came for. You have not planted the seeds yet. The fields must be prepared. In the process of this preparation, you will find that the dark energy is easier to battle, allowing you to do the planting.

New scenarios will pop up to show you that this is true. You won't believe that you got through some of the challenges so easily. Because now the energy supports you and it didn't a year ago. The year 2013 really is a demarcation of intent, and affects manifestation. You start to *prepare the fields* for new energy and begin to plant the seeds, using that which the old soul has: the wisdom of the past. These seeds of wisdom are planted into the economy, into the government, into the household and families. These are seeds of integrity and will speak of the wisdom of coming together instead of tearing apart.

Kryon live channelling "2013 – Now What? The Transition Begins"
given in Phoenix, Arizona – January 6, 2013

I hope that you really understand the message that Kryon is giving us: *You are needed on the planet to continue to hold your light. The next 18 years (from 2012) are extremely important.* Like many of you, there are times when I've thought I've had enough of this world. The challenges are always there. I'm tired and would love to check out. It is natural that a lot of us feel this way. It is part of the test. When you self-balance again, you see the test. When I'm balanced, I realize how it's actually in my own best interest to stay! That way, I get to create an incredibly powerful foundation for when I come back. I don't have to repeat any test or challenge I overcome this time around. I'll be able to awaken much earlier than I did this lifetime.

I like to look at it as delayed gratification. Let me present you with two choices. Choice one: You can get your world travel ticket right now in this moment, but it's only valid for one trip. Choice two: You can get your world travel ticket in five years' time, BUT if you wait five years, your world travel ticket gives you unlimited travel for the rest of your life! Because the rewards are so great, I'm going for choice two! What about you? I would love you to overcome your personal tests and challenges. I would love you to have peace in your life, no matter what is happening around you. I'd love for you to help raise the vibration of Gaia for all of us to enjoy next time around. After all, isn't that what we are here for (smile)?

Q.: There is great concern by some indigenous groups that the creation of the Panama Canal has created a barrier for the movement of the Kundalini energy. What can you tell us about this?

Kryon: We have channelled to you that your perspective of the movement of the Kundalini is limited to only what you can see. So

think for a moment of the profound example of the Kundalini of the Human body. When you have personal Kundalini movement, your entire body is involved. If you had a cut on your chest, it wouldn't stop anything from happening regarding Kundalini shift and movement in your body.

The Earth is this way also, in that it is a "whole earth" energy movement, and is within the planet. So really, the Kundalini movement from north to south is actually THROUGH the Earth, and not riding along on the surface. All GAIA is involved, so the canal is simply a small groove in the surface.

The Panama canal has no effect on this movement of planetary energy.

Q.: For many years the Kundalini has resided in the northern hemisphere. There have been many spiritual leaders emerge from places like India and Tibet, such as the Dalai Lama and Mahatma Gandhi. With the Kundalini moving to South America, will we see any spiritual leaders emerge from this continent?

Kryon: Yes you will. It's a very profound thought to think that the storehouse of spiritual wisdom has been in the north, but indeed it is true. There are libraries filled with wisdom in Tibet that have been as yet undiscovered, and filled with the very prophesies that you are now experiencing.

It was not an error that the north captured this attribute, for most of humanity resides there in what is called "The land hemisphere." But now, as the Earth becomes more allied in a quantum (multi-dimensional) way with total Human consciousness, it doesn't matter how many humans are living in the north or south. So the Earth can balance itself, and help recalibrate Human consciousness to the level it must go to in order to continue to the next step.

The great shift that has been predicted is now underway, and those in Tibet and India who are wise, will feel it. It will not subtract from their wise storehouse, but instead, it will enhance it with the beautiful soft energy of the south, which has always had this. There is a storehouse of wisdom and emotional "mother" balance in the southern hemisphere that has been there all along, and like a time capsule, it now is releasing its beauty.

It is time for mother energy to be part of the wisdom of the planet, for the macho-heavy spiritualism of the past will no longer serve an ascended Earth.

Q.: Can you explain more about what you mean when you say those that sit in the energy of the Kundalini cannot sit still?

Kryon: The Kundalini is a moving energy. As it unwraps itself (as we discussed in a former channelling on the water – three and a half times around the lingam), it unravels and creates male and female energy, so that it can be recalibrated and reassembled. This is difficult to tell you about, since it is a process that is not seen, but felt. The recalibration of male and female energy is a rebalance.

As this happens, there are those who are more tuned to it than others. Those who are totally oblivious to any of this motion may feel nothing at all. Those who are invested in heavy male energy attributes of the planet will be stressed, for they are losing their comfort zone. Those who are tuned into this and have expected it may actually feel vibration which keeps them awake and uncomfortable.

So, depending on the spiritual path of each Human Being, and their Akashic age (old soul or not), they will feel it at different levels. Some will simply be anxious and impatient and have no idea why. This will be frustrating, for it's uncomfortable to be irritable all the time, and many will not know why they are feeling this way.

Most old souls will feel it and know that something is happening. As they understand more about what "recalibration" really means, they will relax with it, welcome it, and be more tolerant of the shift that is occurring. But at some level, everyone is involved.

Chapter Five

Gaia and the Universe

S cientists have estimated that our solar system formed about 4.5 billion years ago, and that the Universe continues to expand. Our solar system is located in the outer reaches of the Milky Way Galaxy, which is a spiral galaxy. The Milky Way Galaxy is just one galaxy in a group of galaxies called the Local Group. The largest galaxy within this group is the Andromeda Galaxy. Looking out into the Universe, many have wondered what lies beyond. Who else might be out there? What discoveries are waiting for us? How did it all begin and what is the end goal of a Universe that continues expanding?

As scientists, including astronomers and physicists, look to the stars for answers to these questions, they are starting to see an attribute that they didn't expect. What they are seeing has given rise to the theory of "intelligent design."

The theory of intelligent design holds that certain features of the Universe and of living things are best explained by an intelligent cause, not an undirected process such as natural selection.

Source: www.intelligentdesign.org

Kryon has explained that, against all odds, the Universe was created for life. The Universe is biased towards life and is benevolent. This attribute goes against what we have come to expect. Kryon provides information about how it all works:

...Did you know that light and other matter regularly changes from waves to particles? Did you know that light changes to a particle when it is being observed by a Human Being? Now, how can a mathematical system "sense" that it is being observed? Already you know that quantum energy might just be very different than anything you thought. What if it isn't physics at all? What if quantum energy is "the Creator's fingerprint?" It would be physics and also have a consciousness. But then, perhaps that's just too strange?

The Large Quantum Energy of the Galaxy

I'm going to give you information to think about. The quantum energy you see in the very small also occurs in the very large. In fact, we'll even go so far as to tell you that physics is actually different in different parts of the Universe, depending on what is at the center of each galaxy. Let's start with that premise – that physics is not a set standard of universal rules. It varies, depending on the quantum stamp of the Creator energy of each one. Some of them are very similar, but all of them are slightly different. And if you could know the differences, you'd wonder why, and I just told you – it's what's in the middle.

Because your physics is mainly 3D, you have difficulty with how things really work. And quantum physics is the only clue you have to a multi-verse and the possibility that some laws of mass and gravity are determined by what happens in the middle of each galaxy. The creation energy is in the middle. That bipolar energy, that push/pull that we have called "the twins" are in the middle of your galaxy. You see it in 3D as a singularity – which, by the way, is impossible – but it's really a double event. Science doesn't know that yet. So we give this to you, so that when they discover it, you can say you heard it here. It will then give credibility to everything else I'm going to say. By the way, how is it, when everything in your physics comes in pairs, even your current laws of physics, that you create a singularity in the middle of the galaxy? Did anyone consider that it could be another pair?

Let us start with the astronomer and ask, *"Dear Astronomer, do you believe in God?"* The astronomer will think for a moment and might then say, *"I am not one to define divinity. It's not my science. I might believe in God, but that's not my study, for I deal in the scientific method."* So you might ask him instead, *"All right, what do you see that is scientifically interesting to you about our galaxy?"* This is where the astronomer may get a bit excited and say, *"All right, I will tell you what is interesting to all of us. We've discovered something we don't understand. There are physical principles in large things that do not apply to orbital mechanics as you have learned them within Newtonian and Euclidian physics. It's odd to us that the galaxy moves as one plate, almost like the stars were pebbles glued upon it. It all rotates together. There has to be some kind of energy that holds that form. For, orbital mechanics as we know them have to do with gravity and mass and orbiting objects around a fulcrum, such as our sun, and it creates orbits that are all different. All objects around a gravitational center seek their orbits based upon mass and speed. That's why all the planets have different orbits. It's the physics that we expect. That's what our solar system does. But not a galaxy. Galaxies have something in the middle that must be gravity based, yet everything moves around the center as one. There is some kind of gravitational or attractive unity there. We don't understand it."*

The Incredible Design – Against All Odds

But that's not all. Then, they will tell you something that you cannot believe. It has to do with what you call random chance. So we're going to call this channelling, *"The Quantum Factor."* There is something you didn't expect that is happening all around you. In your three-dimensional reality, everything that happens on the Earth seems to be in a random state. That is to say, reality responds in an expected bell-shaped curve. Common things happen more often than uncommon things. The odds take a shape of expected randomness. If you were to roll a dice over and over thousands of times, you would see a consistency of randomness that is what you call the way things work. That's what you expect. There's no bias to it.

Back to the astronomer – the astronomer is saying, *"Everywhere we look, examining what you would call 'the creating energy of the Universe,' is incredibly mathematically improbable. It would be as if you rolled the dice and you got six and then six and then six, a thousand times. It is beyond the realm of randomness. It shows there had to be intelligent design."* Now, I'm not talking about a metaphysical person. I'm talking about an astronomer. Everywhere they look, against all odds, the Universe is benevolently designed for life. They've used the term "intelligent design." I use the term "benevolent design." And I will tell you that the energy that glues the solar systems of your galaxy together, more than 100 billion stars, is a giant quantum hand that sits upon all the galaxies of your Universe like the hand of God. It's a quantum, benevolent hand.

How can this be? It is the first of many examples we are going to give you, for this is the quantum factor, the very Creator fingerprint of the Universe. It is biased in love, biased for life, biased in benevolence. Here you are, sitting on an Earth that shouldn't actually exist, for the only thing that allows it to exist is *intelligent design*.

How long did it take for science to realize this? For them, it's a puzzle, not a divine statement. It's out of statistical probability and seems to only have been possible by design – a benevolence that is the Creator energy of the Universe. Think of that. What does this mean to you? If there is a benevolence in the overall creation of the Universe allowing for life, allowing for this Earth to exist, it means that other Earths exist. There's life everywhere! We told you that many times. However, we sit on a very special Earth – the planet that is the only planet of free choice anywhere. There's only one in every Universe, and there have been other planets of free choice before. There are also *graduate planets of free choice*, providing the seeds of life to other planets, which then become new planets of divine free choice.

So here you are, the creative energy in you has the wisdom of the ages. It is the wisdom of the ages of your galaxy, not of your Earth. Others before you in the billions of years that this galaxy has existed have participated in other tests of consciousness. They have graduated to new levels of benevolence, passing it on to the next planet. It is a long-term event, and eventually you will do the same. In this way, you populate the galaxy with your own seeds and the seeds of those before you – seeds of divine purpose.

As you pass this benevolence, it actually shapes the next Universe and how intelligent the design will be. It has been around a long time to get to this place where physics can be shown to have an attitude. It is an attitude of benevolence. That's the big picture.

Kryon live channelling "The Quantum Factor"
given in Edmonton, Alberta, Canada – April 10, 2011

In summary, at the center of every galaxy there are "the twins" that have two energies: one pushes and one pulls. Our perception is of one giant Black Hole and the assumption is that the gravity of the Black Hole is somehow gripping the spiral galaxy and making it spin together in an unusual fashion which violates all the laws of Newton. This is not the case. What is happening at the center of our galaxy is a multi-dimensional force (strong and weak quantum energy) which spreads throughout the entire region of our entire galaxy.

Multi-dimensional physics has something that we didn't expect. It has consciousness: physics with an attitude. The multi-dimensionality of our galactic center has consciousness, and anything that is multi-dimensional is aligned with creation.

So, dear reader, if you have made it this far and believe that all of what Kryon has said is possible, then prepare yourself for something that is going to sound esoterically unbelievable.

The Universe is cooperating with the current shift we are going through – it was expected – for this is why we are here.

What does Science say?

An article in *Scientific American,* titled "How Black Holes Shape the Galaxies, Stars and Planets around Them," states that the *"matter-eating beast at the center of the Milky Way may actually account for the Earth's existence and habitability."* Some of the other things mentioned in this article include:

...The connection between black holes and life is complex, but our galaxy's central black hole seems to have made

numerous contributions to our ability to exist at this place and time…

…One of the questions we are now asking is how deeply our specific circumstances are connected to this majestic universal scheme of stars, galaxies and black holes…

Source: http://www.scientificamerican.com/article.
cfm?id=how-black-holes-shape-galaxies-stars-planets-around-them

Q.: During a channel, you said that the "system's goal is to raise the vibration of the galaxy and be surrounded by planets that have ascended and passed the energy to one another." Can you tell us anything more about this?

Kryon: We have given a number of channelling referring to this, and it is fairly new information. For the purpose of this book, and this space, let us just say that there is a system within the galaxy which is about pure love, and is what many will call "the Creator energy," or God.

The system is one which promotes free choice among those who have agreed to have their biology enhanced with spiritual DNA. DNA is common to all life all through the galaxy. When you someday are able to find and measure the first kinds of life you encounter outside of the Earth, you will find the structure of DNA. The potential right now, is that you will be able to see this on the moon called Europa, within the oceans under the ice (in your own solar system). This may be the first real extra-terrestrial life you find, which will then show you that the potential of life is everywhere.

When you find it, the structure will be similar to much that you have seen on Earth, and will give you an idea that DNA may very well be a consistent way that "evolution energy" works everywhere. It is, and this is on purpose.

One at a time, planets are "seeded" with spiritual potential. Evolution on that planet is then altered, but free choice is not. Each planet is able to develop to ascension status or not, and time limits are given to each one. The time limits are fair and long enough to allow them to make mistakes, to start over if needed, even several times. This is the way this system works. It requires an unbiased discovery of God, in order to create high vibrational shift.

Many planets do not make it, and others are then seeded instead. When one crosses the barrier into a multi-dimensional understanding of the Creator energy, then the truth of God is known, and they begin to awaken within. Billions of life forms on a planet, all working together in a peaceful way, create a bigger quantum energy that is felt by the galaxy and actually changes the center in ways we cannot explain to you here.

As one planet reaches a certain level of enlightenment, it is entangled with all other life in the galaxy. This, then, is the time when it can seed another planet. This has happened over and over, and your seeds are the Pleiadians. Their seeds and the seeds of their seeds are also known to you in the form of Orion, and Arcturian.

The profundity of all this is that every Human has Akashic inheritance, and carries within them the seeds of all the parent seeds. So, an Earth Human carries the wisdom of galactic creation and spiritual purpose, even more than your spiritual seed parents. Think about it.

Someday this will be known, but not now. You have a great deal of work to do, old soul, before any of this is presented to you in a meaningful form.

Author's note:

Astronomers have identified one of the stars within the Pleiades cluster. The star has many properties similar to our sun. They have named this star HD 23514. If we look at the numerology, we can see that 2 represents duality, 3 – catalyst, 5 – change, 1 – new beginnings and 4 – structure and Gaia. When we combine these meanings into a sentence we can say:

Understanding the duality is the catalyst for change for new beginnings on our planet.

If we add all the numbers up we get the number 6, which represents the Higher-Self in Kryon's DNA layer discussions.

Gamma Energy and Gaia

There's a lot of energy hitting the Earth — a tremendous amount, in the form of gamma energy. This is yet to be understood by science, but Kryon has said that it makes up a part of the *instructions* to Gaia.

...Science wonders where it's coming from, but it remains elusive. They realize that it's cosmic and coming from space. The truth is that it's coming from the center of the galaxy, but it appears to be coming from everywhere. That's because the main attribute of this kind of energy is that it is not 3D. Therefore, it has quantum [multi-dimensional] attributes that do not carry a "location" or place of origin with it. This is difficult to explain, but things in a true quantum state are everywhere, entangled in a universal soup of being "one" with everything. Therefore, you can't say *"it comes from there."* There is precedent in science for this, so it is not all that strange to a physicist reading this.

An example: Did you know that very low, deep audio sounds have no discernible, directional source? In other words, the Human ear can't tell where they are coming from. High sounds are very directional. Testing this is easy. Place a deep sound [very low vibrations per second] speaker, hidden in a room, and you can't identify where the sound is coming from. Place a normal speaker in a room [with higher sounds] and you can target where the sound is coming from instantly. The reason is that the vibrations are so far apart in the lower sounds that the ear can't distinguish "location." It's the same principle with things that are in a quantum state. They are not perceptually in any "place" and no 3D instrument is going to locate "where" they are coming from. In fact, the very idea of "where" is very funny, for "where" is just for 3D creatures. That's why *"God, where are you?"* is a very cute and simple-minded question. The answer is, "Yes."

There is what your science has called a *singularity* at the center of the galaxy. They also call it a black hole. Now, we have told you there is no such thing as singularity, and even your science knows it is an oxymoron in physics. It's also only a black space called a hole, since you can't see any light there. Because you have no multi-dimensional physics laws yet, and because you have absolutely no instruments that can "see" multi-dimensional energies, you still don't really know what's actually there. Long after my partner is gone, you can read these words and know the truth, as you eventually develop these things. When you turn them upon the center of the galaxy, you will see two very clear sources.

Instead of one singularity, there is instead a polarity. This polarity is a push and pull attribute of a multi-dimensional law you have not yet discovered, or at least not yet recognized. Once you do, you will have the missing two laws of physics, for there are six, not four. This push-pull polarity blasts out its own multi-dimensional message to the entire galaxy, and your sun receives it, as well. These polarities at the center of your galaxy have a connection with all the other galaxies, too – something for another channelling. You might say that matter has a message, or *matter that cannot be seen* has a message and it hits the Earth constantly and powerfully in ways that "talk" to Gaia.

So here you sit, Human Being, feeling that you are a victim of what happens with Mother Nature. But we are telling you this: the message of today is to reawaken the relationship with Mother Nature, the Gaia source. Once you are able to do that, you will understand that you are in control of all of it. No matter what the instruction sets for the water cycle, for the seasons, for that which you think is uncontrollable, you are more powerful than you can imagine. The intensity and locations of volcanic activity and earthquakes are alterable with this relationship to Gaia, and the indigenous knew it! They could make rain when none was in the forecast. You called it ignorance! They could grow crops in places where they shouldn't grow. You called it lucky. They honored the land and gave gifts to it, and they received from it. This is absolutely real and is everywhere in your history.

Kryon live channelling "The Relationship to Gaia"
given in Mt. Shasta, California – April 24, 2010

The Magnetics of the Solar System

In 1989, Kryon's message was that the magnetic field of the Earth was critical to our consciousness. Magnetics is a quantum energy. So is gravity, and so is light. We are surrounded by a quantum field, and that is the magnetic field of the Earth. The potential was that, if Human consciousness changed, then the magnetics would change. It did. The magnetics have moved greatly since 1989. However, there has to be more. Our solar system is the engine of magnetic change for the planet. If the magnets on Earth have changed, what is happening with our solar system?

The sun is the core of our solar system. It sends out solar winds, which are almost entirely magnetic. It's a magnetic energy that literally blasts out from the sun and contains what was generated from the sun. This magnetic energy is called the heliosphere and it "blows" its magnetic wind against the magnetics of the Earth, and that changes the planet.

If the energy on Earth is always the same, then very little will change. Two interacting magnetic fields create what is called inductance. It allows for energy exchange of information and amplification without a power source. It is used regularly throughout the world, but the attributes are seen as mysterious. If you have ever seen the Aurora Borealis, then you have witnessed the "inductance" of the Earth's magnetic field with that of the sun.

Get ready to see changes in the sun. Scientists call these changes solar storms, but Kryon has said that they are just a recalibration for humanity. These solar storms cause concern and worry because we have many sensitive electronics and instruments that react to magnetics. We have counted on the magnetic field of the planet to remain the same, but it can't when a giant solar storm is happening. Certain kinds of communications get disrupted. Perhaps even the power grid could be interrupted.

Kryon has said to watch the sun, for it is in the process of shift. It is happening through intelligent design, the love of God and Creator, changing things for our consciousness. It is a new way of thinking that is developing, literally touching the very DNA field of each Human. This changes the information within the DNA and allows us to capture and enhance attributes of a new reality we have never had before.

The information is also for Gaia. It tells Gaia when to do what she does. It is all related.

There is another thing that is related and still yet to be understood by science. There are other sets of instructions to Gaia that come from the center of the galaxy. With all these changes, there is an invitation to reawaken our relationship with Mother Nature, the Gaia source. If we are able to do that, we will understand that we are in control of all of it. No matter what the instruction sets for the water cycle, the seasons, for things we think uncontrollable – we are more powerful than can be imagined. The intensity and locations of volcanic activity and earthquakes are alterable with this relationship to Gaia. The ancient indigenous knew it. They could make rain when none was in the forecast. They could grow crops in places where they shouldn't grow. They honored the land and gave gifts and received from it.

What about the rest of the solar system? Kryon has talked about something having been *on the way* for a very long time:

...The magnetics of your solar system itself is changing. So here's the challenge: Go find that fact. You'll see it, literally, as your solar system moves through space. It intersects certain attributes of space and this is changing some of the magnetics, which then become different from the way they ever were before. This, then, changes the sun. Do you see the cycle? One enhances the other in a fractal of circular reality. Your movement around the center changes your solar system. The solar system's new position changes the sun's attributes. The sun's attributes are sent to the planet via the heliosphere, and this affects your DNA...

...You are changing the past by changing the future. You are rearranging the energy of your solar system and also something else...

...The change of consciousness on this planet has changed the center of the galaxy. This is because what happens here, dear ones, is "known" by the center...

Let me tell you something about physics. Yet again, I'll make it simple. Everything your scientists have seen in physics happens in pairs. At the moment, there are four laws of physics in your three-dimensional paradigm. They represent two pairs of energy types. Eventually, there will be six. At the center of your galaxy

is what you call a black hole, but it is not a single thing. It is a duality. There is no such thing as "singularity." You might say, it's one energy with two parts – a weak and a strong quantum force. And the strangest thing is it knows who you are. It is the Creator engine. It's different in other galaxies than this one. It's unique.

The very physics of your galaxy is postured by what you do here. The astronomers can look into the cosmos and they will discover different physics in different galaxies. Could it be that there's something going on in the other galaxies like this one?

Kryon live channelling "The Recalibration of the Universe"
given during Kryon Patagonia Cruise – January 27, 2012

Q.: Can you tell us more about how we are rearranging the energy within our solar system?

Kryon: Your solar system, along with all the others in the galaxy, rotate around the center. You are all going at the same speed, so you encounter certain attributes equally. The attribute that your solar system is having now is increased magnetic activity. You are moving through an area of the galaxy that has a greater effect on your sun, which will in turn create a difference in magnetic energy for the Earth. The whole of your solar system is affected, of course, but this is something that is not frightening, but expected.

We told you years ago that the magnetic grid of the planet was "postured" like a couch that your consciousness sits in. When that changes, so do the potentials of consciousness of those on the planet. It's like an enhancement of the couch, and it creates differences in synapse and logic, and even how the DNA "sees" what it must do. So you might say that the magnetics of the planet is highly involved in Human life and advancement ... and you would be correct.

Q.: Can you explain more about why other planets with life have two suns and yet our solar system only has one?

Kryon: Many, if not most, of the planets selected to be seeded, have more than one sun. This is not your reality, so you don't know what it means or why it should be. But it enhances evolution, and speeds up any planet's life cycle and the variety potentials. So you might say that, if you were looking around in the Galaxy to find a planet that had evolved life, you would first be looking for solar systems with two suns, which revolve around each other. These are "binary stars."

The Earth had this for a while, but you lost one of them, which became small and inert after burning out. It was small and couldn't sustain the process inside itself which makes a qualified "sun." The remains of it were spun out of orbit, because it changed mass, and long ago it left the influence of your sun and all the bodies in the solar system that you can see and track. It's dark, small, and long gone.

What this has done, however, is to further "hide" you from those in the galaxy who are "looking" for life. There are many, and most are not advanced spiritual entities. Many are just "smart" animals with no spiritual complement within their DNA. But they are looking for binary star systems instead of what you have ... one sun.

Some of those have found you, but cannot exist within your Merkabah field. They come and go, while never understanding the odd power you each have that can vaporize them if they are not careful. We have told you before, that these who visit you, who are not appropriate, cannot stay. If they generate fear within you, they can manipulate you ... but only for a while. Then they have to leave.

This validates the situation you have where UFO's have been sighted for half a century, yet there has never been an organized mass landing or official contact. They can't, and humanity is simply too powerful for them to ever have you focus on them as a group. They are in the dark as to who you are, and have no impact on your evolution.

However ... you should also know that, if any of these ever became an "event" of any magnitude, there are those all ready to keep you protected, and have the ability to make them uncomfortable enough to leave you alone. I will not list these, but they are the parents of the Pleiadians.

Yes, you are known by the other ascended planets, and you are looked after, dear ones.

The Solar System and Astrology

What is it that you know about astrology? Most people know about the 12 signs of the zodiac that include: Aries, Taurus, Gemini, Cancer, Leo, Virgo, Libra, Scorpio, Sagittarius, Capricorn, Aquarius and Pisces. You often hear people ask the question, "What star sign are you?" There are literally hundreds of books and websites that can tell you all about your personality, love life, career and relationships, based on the interpretation of your zodiacal sign. There are some people who take astrology very seriously, and almost won't leave the house without consulting their horoscope, while others seem to look at the whole subject of astrology as a bit of a joke. Something that is just made up by weird people from a fantasy realm, and it has no scientific basis. Nothing could be further from the truth.

I have to be honest and admit that, before I experienced my awakening process, I was often quite skeptical about astrology. While some of the horoscope readings appeared accurate, other readings had information that was so general it could literally apply to anyone. Because I really didn't understand astrology and was ignorant of how it all worked, I had great fun in laughing at some of what I thought were ridiculous statements. Once again, I discovered how wrong my assumptions had been.

Astrology is something that has been practiced by many of the ancient cultures, some of which continues today. I was very surprised to find that there are numerous types of astrology. Some of the different types include: Western astrology, Hindu astrology, Chinese astrology and Tibetan astrology. Furthermore, there are many branches, such as horary astrology (a method of answering questions based on the date, time and place it was first asked), medical astrology (for medical diagnosis), mundane astrology (that predicts the future of states and countries), financial astrology (that studies the fluctuations of the market) and election astrology (used to determine the best day and moment to start any given project). The study of astrology is vast and it is beyond the scope of this book to give a comprehensive account of astrology. What I would like to emphasize is that astrology has a vast wealth of knowledge to give to humanity, if we could just set aside our Human bias of what we think we know about astrology, and start looking at astrology as an important and valuable science.

Unfortunately, astrology is still considered to be something that is mystical and esoteric. Kryon has said that astrology is one of the most misunderstood of all of the sciences. Someday future students of astrology will marvel at how humanity could ever have believed differently! So, if astrology is a science, then how does it work? Astrology literally means "the language of the stars." Astrology studies the influence that distant cosmic objects, usually planets, sun, moon and stars have on Human lives. It is based on the position of the luminaries (Sun and Moon), the planets and stars at the exact time of the birth of any person or project, and its exact date and its location in terms of latitude and longitude.

In Chapter Three, Kryon told us that the magnetic grid is the grid of communication. You should then realize that the solar system talks to you through the magnetic grid. You are literally patterned through the sun, and it talks to you through your DNA. Still having trouble believing this? Perhaps you may have been someone that rejected the idea that humans have a spiritual core and are a piece of God? No judgment if that's you, because for a long time, that was me (smile). But let me give you an example, so that you might begin to think about it differently. Have you ever noticed how full moons affect Human consciousness? Just ask a policeman, doctor, nurse, paramedic or a mental health professional. Most of them will tell you how incredibly busy they are during a full moon, and that often, extra staff are working during the night of a full moon. Some studies have even found that murder rates increase during a full moon. In fact, in England in the 18th Century, a person who committed murder during a full moon could plead "lunacy" and get a lighter sentence. The phases of the moon also affect things like our biological clock and the menstrual cycle of women, and that's because we are made of 80 percent water, and the Moon traditionally rules big bodies of water, such as the oceans.

If you can think for a moment that the phases of the moon are like a quantum cycle, then this cycle has a quantum influence on you

through gravity and magnetics. So, your DNA is being directly affected by the moon. However, as Kryon often says, we are not simply humans walking around being victims. We have the ability to communicate with our DNA, and the potential to rewrite the instruction sets. The moon is only one of the various astrological influences. Can you see now how astrology is a major influence on Human behavior? It is science and involves DNA and Human thought. Imagine what this might do to help humanity, when it is finally acknowledged. You are susceptible to the movement of the planets. You are alive with Gaia and a part of the system.

Kryon has given a wonderful summary of the way astrology works:

The sun is the fulcrum of the solar system and the center of energy for life for you. There is a physical mechanism for the sending of information from the sun to the other planets and it's called the solar wind. This energy stream carries with it whatever pattern of multi-dimensional energy the sun has at that moment, and delivers it to whatever is in reach of the sun's magnetic field. It's always there, but it has cycles of intensity. Although science sees the solar wind as an energy player in the solar system, they have yet to see the multi-dimensional patterns it carries to the planets as this wind blasts out from the sun.

These patterns reflect the posturing of the sun as the other planets exhibit their tugs and pulls on it via gravity and magnetics (both are multi-dimensional energies). Therefore, these sun patterns change continuously, as the planets provide new gravitational and magnetic situations to the sun.

When the solar wind, carrying this sun pattern, hits the Earth, it deposits the pattern upon the magnetic grid. The magnetic grid is dynamic (changes all the time), and is responsive to being constantly re-patterned. The grid lines of the planet alter the pattern slightly, due to the fact that your grids aren't consistent and have greater and lesser areas of influence in different Earth locations.

Human DNA is sensitive to magnetics, since it is a magnetic engine itself. At birth, when the child is separated from the parent, there is a signal sent to the brain of the infant that says, "Your system is now active and on its own, apart from your mother." During that first breath of independent and unique life, the child's

DNA receives the pattern from the magnetics of the Earth's grid, and takes on what you have come to call "astrological attributes."

Different places on the planet will carry the basic pattern, plus or minus what Earth's magnetic field has contributed, due to geographic location. This explains why world-class astrology must take into consideration the location of birth. Astro*cartography is also based on this principle.

Astrology is the oldest science on the planet, and can be proven to be accurate. In addition, "generic" astrology is also a significant influence in Humanism, from the cycles of the female's system, to the profound changes in Human behavior when the moon is full. You can't separate yourself from it, and those who don't believe in it might as well not believe in breathing, because it's that much of an influence on your life.

The new energy on the planet invites you to change your DNA. This is the teaching of Kryon. When you change your DNA, you're working with the very core of the pattern you had at birth, and so you're able to then work on some of the attributes of your astrological blueprint, and actually change it – even neutralize it. We told you all about that in 1989. Masters did this, and you're now coming into a time where your abilities are those of the masters. Look into your life and eliminate the things that are challenges and keep the attributes that support you. This is the true balanced Human Being.

You can change your sensitivity to attributes within your own individual astrology type, but the generic influences of the planets' and moon's movements will always affect you to some degree, since you're not an island apart from others. These would be things such as retrogrades and the moon's influence (as indicated). You might say, *"I'm no longer affected by retrogrades,"* and sit and smile all you want. Meanwhile, you still shouldn't sign contracts during that time, since all those around you are still affected. Think about it...

...By the way, what happens to the solar system when the magnetics shift? Now you start to see where astrology will begin to shift as well. There are those who will start to apply the quantum filter to astrology. It's happening now. What is your quantum sign?

It's different than the three-dimensional sign. Oh, there'll come a day, dear ones, in science, where the scientists will be able to apply what I will call a quantum filter to alter what they see. This will be a filter developed for telescopes that involves a supercooling of the filter itself. Astronomers will be able to look out into the cosmos and, for the first time, see quantum attributes.

The first thing they'll notice is two things in the center of the galaxy, not one. The next thing will be the colors around the Human Being. And science will start a whole new section called "The Study of the Human Auric Energy." All of these are coming.

How long will all this take? That is up to you. Meanwhile, plant the seeds of understanding, of peacefulness, of appreciation and of love. Become slow to anger, slow to create drama. Take on the attributes of the masters, and that is what your abilities are changing to right now. Soften in all things. Look at each other differently.

There'll come a time when there's no war. Those in this room and those listening will know I'm right. Watch for these things in your science. When they happen, remember this day when I told you how it really works.

Blessed is the Human Being who has understood this message as personal for themselves, not about the cosmos. It's about the inner being and the journey of the soul – and the Universe within.

Kryon live channelling "The Recalibration of the Universe"
given in Patagonia (bottom of South America) – January 27, 2012

What is it that you think about astrology now? Perhaps you already knew this and it confirms your own intuition, or perhaps you are beginning to see astrology as something that is different from what you thought. What will you do with this knowledge and information? Speaking personally, I now pay more attention to things that I didn't before. For example, if I know there is a Mercury retrograde occurring, then I realize communications are greatly disrupted. I'm sure you have experienced this yourself – those days where your emails don't get through or you miss your flight or things have gone haywire, and chances are that a Mercury retrograde was happening at the time. I certainly wouldn't want to be signing any legal contracts or the equivalent during a Mercury retrograde.

So how can we learn more? There is a wealth of information available about astrology, but it is important to use discernment. Following my own spiritual logic and discernment, I met a world-class astrologer named Michelle Karen. Kryon has said that Michelle *"reads the Akashic Records directly and is the first one (astrologer) to bring quantum astrology to this planet."* The reading I received from Michelle provided me with a wealth of knowledge and information about myself, and confirmed what felt intuitively correct for me. It also helped me to relax about certain situations, and in a way, prepare me to align with my highest potentials that I wish to achieve in this lifetime. If you would like some more information about Michelle Karen or would like a reading from her, you might like to visit her website: *www.michellekaren.com*

I would also like to mention that, during the reading with Michelle, I received maps based on my own astro*cartography. Astro*cartography maps are based on your birth chart (a picture of the heavens for the date, time and location of your birth). They reveal for any given individual the specific locations in the world which are either neutral, or where he/she receives the push, or experiences the hindrance, of a given planetary energy.

Ever since I can remember, I always felt a desire to move away from Canberra. This feeling didn't really make sense, as logically it's my home town where I was born and grew up, with a wonderful family and many close friends. Despite this, I was always moving away and then returning back. For over 10 years, I had a great job working as a Ranger across the different nature reserves and national parks. Why would I want to leave? Why did I always feel like I needed to "get away?" My chart revealed that Canberra was near my Saturn line and that this is not the best place for me. Michelle explained that on a Saturn line, we feel like life is tough and difficult, and there is a sense of loneliness. There is a sense of responsibility, and nothing comes easily. It is also a place where we can feel as though we are stuck there. All of a sudden, my feelings about Canberra were validated, and it explained why I had always felt this "stuck" energy and that my life was going nowhere while I stayed in Canberra. It was a feeling that kept pushing me to move elsewhere.

When my marriage ended, it felt like my entire world had collapsed. It was very traumatic, but it was also the catalyst for me to

awaken. I believe that my former husband and I arranged this event from the other side of the veil as a potential. When this potential occurred, I was presented with a choice. Would I fall into bitterness and victim mode? Would I see it as a planned life lesson? As it turns out, it was an opportunity for me to awaken. What about you? What are your challenges? Are you a victim? Or can you see the opportunity you have been presented with? Each of us is unique and so our individual challenges are personal. Take courage that you can change and transform your life.

As part of my awakening process (and a need to get away from memories of my formerly married life), I moved to New Zealand, because my intuition told me to go there. At that time, I had no idea that New Zealand had Lemurian origins, or what my astro*cartography line of influence was. I was totally amazed when Michelle said that I had moved to a place that was right on my Chiron line. Chiron is the wounded healer, so by following my intuition, I had moved to a place where I could heal myself and transmute my pain in a very powerful way. Michelle also said that there would definitely have been a shift of consciousness for me there. I have to now smile to myself about how Spirit works.

When I moved to New Zealand, I felt such strong emotions and a feeling of coming home. It was like the land was literally talking to me and saying how happy it was that I was back. Within a week of my arriving at Franz Josef Glacier (South Island), I was given a Kryon book from someone in my Yoga class. As I started to read Kryon Book Seven, *Letters from Home,* every cell within my being shifted and was tingling with remembrance. When I read the chapter on the EMF Balancing Technique™ (EMF), written by Peggy Phoenix Dubro, I felt compelled and drawn like a magnet to learn more about it and do the work. Within a few weeks, I found a teacher and began my training to become an EMF Practitioner. The training and tools I have received from the EMF body of work has greatly assisted the expansion of my consciousness and the ability to radiate more of my own core energy. In both giving and receiving the EMF Balancing Technique™ sessions, I have been able to transform my life in ways that I never thought possible. I am positive that anyone who has experienced a session with a genuine desire for transformation has had a similar experience.

The originator of this work is Peggy Phoenix Dubro. The EMF sessions are the result of 20 years working with quantum energies within the Lattice. All humans have a Lattice. It is a profound matrix of quantum design, a sphere of co-creation that surrounds you and works the Universal Cosmic Lattice. When you are around Peggy, you can feel the wise divine feminine inside her. Peggy's ability to move and transform energy is incredible. Kryon has given the following information regarding Peggy:

For over twenty years, the teacher Peggy Phoenix Dubro has been receiving information on a profound technique called EMF Balancing. Now the teacher actually becomes the process, and her DNA shifts accordingly. She is the only Human on the planet to absorb the full impact of what EMF teaches ... at 100 percent. What this means is that she can now reflect on the compassion of Humanity in a unique way, and create channelling that embodies the full energy of what a true master would have. Her DNA portal opens.

Peggy has a new body of work called Reflections, a tool for quantum reasoning in the new energy. Her new work is highly relevant. The purpose of her Reflections session is to help people evolve their ability to make conscious choices as to how they use their energy. Peggy has stated that:

We are just beginning to express the new levels of consciousness as we open to defining more of who we are as the multi-dimensional Human! My heart's desire is to assist and support you in the development of your unique expressions and how to communicate with distinction and authenticity in the world. That deeply motivates me, for I know we all have the ability to create a life of choice with the talents and abilities we have and that equals more freedom to BE!

If you would like more information about Peggy Phoenix Dubro or would like a Reflections session from her, you might like to visit her website: *www.emfbalancingtechnique.com*

And now for something you probably didn't expect. Kryon has said that you can rewrite your own astrological attributes! Masters can do this and have done so many times on the planet. Astrological

attributes are magnetic and gravitational imprints on the multi-dimensional portions of the DNA, which occur at birth. They are part of the system of personality setups, beginning contracts and potential interactions with other humans. Although you will always have your birth sign and personality attributes, the reactions to the system can now be tempered and changed. Retrogrades will be less of a problem. Your intent can potentially override these imprints, because you're reprogramming the imprints. At this point, I again emphasize that Kryon says we are not humans walking around as victims!

Kryon often gives metaphors to let us know that you don't just walk around the planet being a victim. Imagine being in a boat, seemingly at the mercy of the ocean. Everything is fine when the ocean is calm, but when the waves get bigger and the storms and wind toss you about, you get angry and shake your fist and think that you are simply a victim of what is happening around you. What if you were to look down and see that in your boat is a piece of wood? The wood has always been in your boat. You decide to take the piece of wood between your hands. The moment you do, you discover you are holding the tiller that controls the rudder. You can now steer your own boat! You are still not able to control the waves and the storms, or change what is happening around you, but you can steer the boat. You are not a victim.

Can you see how this might apply to a current challenge you face? The storm represents the challenge that is outside of your control. It could be losing your job, ending a relationship or financial hardship. You can't control what happens, but you can direct and steer the course you take when things do happen. What if you lost your job because a better one is available? What if there are other people you need to meet? What if your challenge is to push you to do something you normally wouldn't?

Having a positive attitude and open mind is a great way to live. Why is it, however, that at certain times, things don't really seem to flow? You have been working on changes within, and yet, nothing really seems to have changed around you. Sometimes, this is because Spirit has no clock. The synchronicity you are looking for isn't ready until it's ready. I am someone who always wants things yesterday! Who wants to wait? I have learned, however, the waiting goes so much faster when you just relax and trust that all is well.

So, having patience is a good strategy. Is there anything else we can do to steer us closer to our true nature and purpose? I believe there is. I want to introduce you to a new system (perhaps you have even heard about it). It will give you a completely new awareness and understanding about yourself. This is because every decision we make either keeps us on our path or takes us on a detour that can be confusing and sometimes painful.

I have also been fortunate to receive a reading from Bethi Black, based on The Human Design System. Bethi is the Assistant Director of the International Human Design School, and the editor of the new book, *The Definitive Book of Human Design: The Science of Differentiation, by Lynda Bunnell and Ra Uru Hu*. We each have a unique design and a specific purpose. This system is new and fundamentally different from anything else that exists in the world. The information was received by Ra Uru Hu in 1987 and is a synthesis of two types of science: The ancient observational systems of Astrology, the Chinese I'Ching, the Hindu-Brahmin Chakra System and The Tree of Life from the Zohar/Kabbalist tradition; and the contemporary disciplines of Quantum Mechanics, Astronomy, Genetics and Biochemistry.

The information given to me in the reading was like receiving an instruction manual for myself. It has given me greater clarity in regard to my decision-making, and really opened up an entire new way of being. It has increased my ability to co-create and manifest a life filled with divinity that resonates with my true authentic self. I have a deeper understanding of my gifts and how I can share them with others. I can also see the important role that others have in order to help and support me, and vice versa. The wonderful thing about The Human Design System is that it is not a belief system. Instead, it is a map of your own unique genetic code that provides great detail about the mechanics of your own nature. By using the map provided by The Human Design System, I can more fully appreciate my journey here on Earth, instead of allowing my "not-self" to try and impose decisions which only result in frustration.

Learning about yourself through the Human Design System opens you up to a whole new way of living. Let me give you an example. My Human Design Chart reveals that I am a Generator. When I am in the flow of my true nature, I feel satisfaction. When I am not in my flow, I

feel frustration! We each have nine centers. The Human Design Chart will show these centers as being defined or undefined (open). I will give you two examples to explain how this aspect of the chart works.

I have an undefined Solar Plexus Center. This is found in approximately 47 percent of the population. When this center is undefined, it absorbs and amplifies the emotions present in the environment. There is a deep conditioning that you potentially become vulnerable to the needs, moods and feelings of other people. It explains why confrontation always makes me feel nervous. Unconsciously, I would avoid confrontation at all costs. Understanding this trait means that I can detach from the emotions I take in from others. I am more aware of what my true emotions are, not the emotions of others. Spending time alone everyday helps to release any emotional conditioning I have taken in. Does this sound like you? If not, chances are, you have a defined Solar Plexus Center. It is not easy to be patient. You are designed to wait until you go through the ups and downs of an emotional wave before you make a decision. When someone with a defined Solar Plexus Center feels good or bad, someone whose center is undefined will feel VERY good or VERY bad. See how it works?

I have a defined Splenic Center. This is found in about 55 percent of the population. This center is responsible for our survival and well-being in the world. In a defined Splenic Center, you receive non-verbal communication in the present moment. It is your intuition, gut instinct or hunch. It always gives you trustworthy information. In the moment to moment awareness, the Spleen never repeats its first alarm. It means you should always listen to your intuition. It can be disastrous if you don't. When the Splenic Center is undefined, the seven primal fears that reside in the Splenic Center become magnified. These people enter the world with a fundamental fear that they are not equipped to survive. They are also sensitive to the lack of well-being in the world and take it personally. They often grow up unconsciously seeking people with a defined Spleen for security and well-being and will cling to these people regardless of the outcome. This means they can hold on to a relationship that is not good for them. A healthy orientation to the undefined Spleen enables the ability to discern the difference between their needs and what is a lack of well-being in their environment. They can sense when someone or something is not good for them. As professional healers, they may also be able to step into a patient's aura and instantly recognize whether the person is healthy or ill, and what might be out of balance.

Can you see how there is no right or wrong in having a defined or undefined center? Our unique design literally draws us into life. It is designed to attract what we desire, if we can learn to surrender our conditioning. One of the aims of the system is to help guide you in your decision-making. I have given just two examples, but the system is designed to tell you a lot more. Imagine how different your life could be if you understood your unique design imprint.

If you would like a reading with Bethi Black, or information about classes, you can contact her at beth@ihdschool.com. For more information about the Human Design System, visit the following website: *www.ihdschool.com*

I hope you can appreciate and understand the influence astrology has on our lives. Humanity has so much to learn and as we discover deeper truths and apply them to our daily life, we not only change and affect our inner self, but also change and affect the Universe.

Q.: Originally, how and from where was astrology brought to this planet? Why does Jupiter have such a strong influence in astrology?

Kryon: Astrology is the oldest science on the planet, right next to numerology. As soon as humans were able to look at the sky and track the planets' movements, there was the intuitive idea that there might be influences on all life on Earth. The influences of the moon were already seen, and especially when the moon was full. So right away, humanity was aware that astral bodies disconnected from the Earth, but allied gravitationally, could change human behavior in what appeared to be cyclical.

This is not mythology, but rather it is based in physics, and we have given you the mechanics of astrology in past channelling. We also told you something you still don't understand. Listen, astrologer, if the magnetics are changing in the solar system (and they are), do you not understand that the influences on Human behavior will also change? You can't just sit there and say, "everything is kind of the same," any more than a person can deny that

it's getting colder on the planet. They can sit there without a coat, but eventually they will be too cold to function.

So, start looking at the potentials of what the altered influences mean, and how they might affect you. Jupiter is one of the most influential for the new energy. One of the reasons is that its size is so influential to the magnetic lines of influence that pull upon the sun. See this pattern as something that changes the way the sun's engine works. The sun's solar engine is very much linked to the magnetics of the gasses involved in the engine. When the magnetics are altered, then the sun's engine creates new solar patterns. The "solar wind" that then blasts out information and messages to the entire solar system, is also changed.

It's the solar wind that interfaces with your magnetic field profoundly, and creates some of the energies you feel that affect your personalities and life force. This is astrology at its best, and it's moving slightly and repatterning. Jupiter, within the charts of this science, is the biggest area of movement.

Q.: At the present time, only 10 planets have been discovered. Cosmic balance would require that 12 signs correspond to 12 planets. Interestingly enough, 2 planets, Venus and Mercury, rule both an Earth and an air sign, respectively: Taurus and Libra for Venus, and Virgo and Gemini for Mercury. Is Venus the true ruler of Libra, and Mercury, the true ruler of Gemini? And if this is so, this would mean that 2 Earth signs have, as of yet, no ruler. Earth is traditionally associated with how we deal with our physicality. Would that mean that Human Beings still haven't evolved into their true bodies?"

Kryon: Everything you have mentioned is part of gravitational and quantum magnetic systems that have an influence on the sun. You already know that Human Beings haven't evolved into their true bodies. That's what the new energy is beginning to create. So, as we said above, expect the system to realign with some new energies, because of new quantum influences. I'm not going to tell you what you must discover and verify for yourself, but intuitively, you have noticed that the system is incomplete. So complete it.

Let me give you a hint: Are you ready for a new ruler for two Earth signs that don't really align in 3D with Earth? If so, will you accept one that is quantum (entangled at a distance)? This would be the beginning of quantum astrology, and might eventually involve a fairly nearby star cluster with nine major stars, seven of them significant, and one of them with multiple planets. Does it make sense that a ruler of Earth signs might be parental, that is, related to Earth but not in the solar system? If you are moving in to quantum realization, perhaps it's time for a new quantum ruler in the system?

Q.: When twins are born, especially when their birth time is very close to each other, their charts are almost identical. Yet things – like their Akashic inheritance – could make them different. There is also the other phenomenon of "astral twins," two individuals born from different parents, but on the exact same day, in the same place, at the exact same minute. Can you explain how in both cases, their astrological charts reflect their unique Akashic Records?

Kryon: In your Human Design systems, you already know that up to 300 to 400 humans, within 7 billion on Earth, can have the same identical life chart for the reasons you have listed. But this does not make them the same, since their "Earth history" is not the same. This is called the domestic (Earth) Akashic Record. So their life design might be identical, but it is altered by their life's path, based on Akashic inheritance, and also their current life experience.

This, then, calls for a new tool within basic astrology that senses, or "plugs in" the quantum energy of an old soul's Akash, into the equation of working a chart. It then becomes a modifier of the 3D astrology chart and further fine-tunes that pattern for that individual person.

There are those who are already working this puzzle, and are doing "quantum astrology." It requires that the reader be part scientist and part intuitively potential aware. Welcome to quantum science.

The Pleiadians

Prior to my awakening, I had never really heard the term "Pleiadian." Sure, I knew about a cluster of stars that was called the Pleiades or the Seven Sisters, but I simply thought of it as something of interest to astronomers, especially since it is one of the closest star clusters to Earth and is visible from both the northern and southern hemisphere. It lies approximately 425 light years away from Earth and is also called Messiers 45 (M45). The Pleiades star cluster is also part of the Taurus constellation, one of the 12 zodiac signs. It wasn't until I started to open up to my spiritual core, however, that I was ready to learn about the Pleiadians, who are our divine parents, from a planetary perspective. Before I start explaining more about our divine parents, I thought I would share a bit of trivia regarding the Pleiades. I guess one of the reasons I wish to include it is that it highlights how our Human bias can adapt and filter spiritual truths to fit what our perceived belief system is.

According to Greek mythology, the seven brightest stars in the Pleiades represent the daughters of Atlas and Pleione. The names of the seven daughters are:

Alcyone – meaning "queen who wards off evil." Alcyone is the central and largest star of the Pleiades constellation. She is often seen as representing the whole cluster of stars.

Asterope – a double star in the Pleiades constellation, literally translates as "lightening."

Merope – the only Pleiad to marry a mortal, her star shines less brightly than those representing her sisters.

Maia – the eldest of the Seven Sisters, Maia was said to be the most beautiful. According to Greek myth, Maia was a lover of Zeus and gave birth to Hermes.

Taygeta – after being defiled by Zeus while unconscious, Taygeta went into hiding. For her protection, she was transformed into a doe.

Celaeno – was married to Poseidon. Translated, her name means "darkness" or "blackness." Sometimes referred to as the Lost Pleiad, as her star is sometimes difficult to see with the naked eye.

Electra – the third brightest star in the constellation, Electra means "amber," "shining" and "bright." Electra was the wife of

Corythus. Seduced by Zeus and gave birth to Dardanus, who became the founder of Troy.

Don't you find it interesting that Greek mythology places these stars in the realms of the Gods? It makes me think that, at an intuitive level, the Greeks had some remembrance of our spiritual parents, but it's almost like their spiritual knowledge was diluted, and the end result was something that made sense to how they perceived their world and Universe.

If you travel back in time, way before the Romans, Greeks, Egyptians and other ancient civilizations, and learn about the ancient indigenous creation stories, you will discover that all over the world, many of them made reference to either the Pleiadians or the Seven Sisters. What are the chances of that? Mere coincidence? I think it must be a pretty amazing coincidence when the Aborigines living at Uluru in the center of Australia have such a similar story to the Hawaiians (who are isolated in the middle of the Pacific Ocean), the Maori's in New Zealand, the indigenous within South America, and indigenous from other countries that are incredibly remote from each other in a geographical sense. And while I was attending a Kryon seminar, we visited a Hindu monastery on Kauai, where I heard the Hindu guide say that we came from the Pleiadians and started in Lemuria, which is why they were building their temple on Kauai, Hawaii. The Hindu religion is one of the oldest religions on the planet. What a coincidence that they are saying the same things as the indigenous are saying all over the planet!

During 2010, I was visiting Uluru with Lee Carroll and some of the Kryon team, when I walked into an art gallery that was displaying the local women's artwork. Every single piece of art in the gallery was showing a story about the Seven Sisters, and after talking to the local Aboriginal man in the store, he gave us a pamphlet that described their creation story as follows:

> The Seven Sisters decided to visit Earth and flew down. They looked for their favorite plateau to land on but found their landing place was covered with little men called Yayarr. They called to them to get out of the way, but they refused. The sisters finally landed upon another hill. The Yayarr men saw where they landed and decided to capture them. The

sisters ran off and eventually the men grew tired of the pursuit, except for one.

He kept on following them and following them. At last, one of the sisters left the group to find water. The man followed her. She found water and was drinking it, when she heard the faint sound of a foot being placed carefully on the ground. She looked up, saw the Yayarr man and raced off. He charged off after her and finally caught her. She yelled and screamed. He picked up a stick to quieten her and swung it. The woman jumped out of the way. He swung the stick again and again and missed and missed. The marks of his stick can still be seen on the side of a hill in that country.

Finally, the woman escaped back to the hill where she and her sisters had landed. They had gone. She looked up into the sky, saw her six sisters there and rose to join them. The Yayarr man followed after and became Orion.

I believe that the ancient indigenous contain a vast deal of knowledge and wisdom of our spiritual lineage and core truths, and I have been fortunate to have met some of the divine beings that represent their indigenous cultures and are willing to share this knowledge with those who are seekers of the truth. Kryon often talks about the ancients during the channels, and often the information that Kryon gives us is exactly what the indigenous teach, but presented in a modern language and context.

But if the Pleiadians really are our spiritual parents and responsible for creating us humans, what is their story? How did they get here? Are they like us? If they seeded us with divinity, are they still here? Why don't they show themselves to us? Kryon has given us lots of information about the Pleiadians, but often we are only given pieces and parts of one subject. I have, therefore, included more than one channel to tell you about the Pleiadians.

I'm guessing that most people don't really like the idea of beings from outer space coming to Earth to "seed" us with enlightenment. I believe, however, that that kind of thinking comes from our Human bias. We get stuck with 3D thinking and end up with people visualizing an alien invasion, complete with big flying saucers. Kryon has said several times that the Pleiadians don't have to have spaceships to get to planet Earth. They're entangled with Human Beings, and always have been, because they are part of the Universe. In fact, in Kryon Book 12, *The Twelve Layers of DNA*, Kryon gave a great example of how we should see it differently:

Think of it this way – you are everywhere at once! Draw a circle in the sand; ants are in the circle. You place your finger in one place and startle an ant. Suddenly, you place your finger in another place almost instantly. The ant thinks you have moved from one place to another at frightening speed! All it sees is the finger. Understand? You are always above the circle, and you didn't "travel anywhere." This is entanglement, and it is a staple of multi-dimensional "travel."

Hopefully, by keeping the above example in mind, the rest of what Kryon has told us is now better understood. By the way, if you haven't already, it is truly worth reading Kryon Book 12. It will most likely answer many of your questions that have come up while reading this book.

If you understand entanglement, dear ones, and what it means to be in an entangled state, then some of what I'm discussing here will be more understandable to you. Multi-dimensional physics is the way of all reality around you, but most of you are not aware of it. When you are, you will begin to understand that *teleportation* is not something that is science fiction. Anything in an entangled state *is part of itself* and therefore, can be in two places at the same time.

Thousands of years ago, the Pleiadians understood this. It's not simply high science, but rather, it's part of spiritual awareness. The more spiritually aware this Earth becomes, the higher scientific knowledge it will be given, and the more it will understand about the creation of true peace.

I want to tell you something: In all appropriateness and love, they are seeing what you're doing. They realize that you made it, and that there's going to be a lot of activity on this planet in the future. They are using part of the magnetic grid, and that's how they come and go and observe. If your Earth did not have the grid that Gaia put here through the molten center of the Earth, which

to this day, still moves and creates the engine of your magnetic grid system, they would never have been able to have come. If you did not have the crystalline that they set up, there would be no "Earth remembrance."

The Earth is changing, consciousness is shifting, and the old souls are awakening.

Kryon live channelling "All about the Grids"
given in Philadelphia – April 14, 2012

During the Patagonia Kryon Cruise in 2012, Kryon gave a lot of information regarding the Pleiadians that allowed us to get a bigger picture of our galactic history. This particular channel mentions some of the things that have been covered earlier in the book. I think you'll agree that our understanding increases when we read things more than once.

Now, let me take you back only a billion years. You are in this galaxy back then, and we admonish you not to look out of this galaxy for any of your history. Each galaxy has its own spiritual plan, and that affects each galaxy's physics. That is why science is able to see different kinds of physics in the Universe and they don't understand why. Stay in your galaxy for this examination. At this point, if I told you that consciousness defines physics, you might not understand. So let's just leave it at that.

Let me take you to a planet that is going through what you're going through. Four billion years ago, yours was simply cooling off. Life hadn't really begun as you know it. Oh, the seeds were there, but that's all. Life as you know it really hadn't begun at all. But other places in the galaxy, there were already sophisticated groups taking hold that were Humanoid - Human types. They look like you, for this is the plan. That was four billion years ago, when life began on their planet, very different than your time line.

A billion years ago, they went through a change and they went through a shift, and they had free choice. Back then, they were the only planet that did in their time, and eventually, they went through a metamorphosis of consciousness.

Exponentially, it seemed they changed, and it took only a thousand years to go from full corporeal to an enlightened form. Only a thousand years and they became mostly quantum thinkers. Life was divine and defined separately and differently for them, for they had discovered the quantum parts of life within them. Everything changed. They didn't die, and according to the plan, at a certain point in time in their futures, they would then "seed" another planet with their evolved DNA. When that planet was ready, they would seed their knowledge of light and dark and divine intuition, and so they did so, on a planet very far from yours. It was a planet in the Seven Sisters constellation that became what you now know as the home of the Pleiadians. This, then, was the beginning of the Pleiadian civilization. That is how the Pleiadians started, from others who seeded them[2] with the DNA of awareness.

Millions of years later, you had Humanoid forms moving into ascension within the Seven Sisters. I'm giving you the history of the galaxy, not the history of life. It's the history of divinity, all being affected by the center, and all in an entangled quantum state. All this was with free choice.

Your Story

Several hundred thousand years ago, humans began to form into the Human that you recognize today. That's just yesterday. Don't confuse this with Human development. You have had that going on for a very long time. But the DNA that is within your body is not the DNA that developed naturally on the planet. Yours is outside of the system of Earth-based evolutionary processes, and the scientists are starting to see this. The "missing link" that they speak of is not Human.

So again, we tell you, that the ones who came to help seed you approximately 100,000 to 200,000 Earth years ago were the Pleiadians, who had gone into graduate status and who had changed consciousness. They had become quantum with free choice, and you have parts of their DNA within you.

---

2   Kryon has told us that not only did the Pleiadians create an ascended planet, but also those from Orion did it, and the Arcturians also did it. These are the parents of the parents of the parents of the planetary systems, and some day humans will be the planetary parents of another civilization within our galaxy. *(Source: Kryon live channelling "The Bridge of Swords" given in Toronto, Canada – September 29, 2012)*

New information for you: the seeding process was not a one-time event. This is why we give you these large sections of time where the Pleiadians worked with you. It was done over time and in many places. It was not all simultaneous, and this was for reasons that will remain unknown to you for now, but will later explain why you will find other Human types that now are extinct. Now you only have one Human type, and that is counterintuitive to all mammal development on the planet. This was a design, and it took more than 100,000 years to create this for humanity as you know it.

It's your Human bias that has the creation story of the knowledge of light and dark being given to humans in one day in a garden involving a talking snake and other mythology. Spiritual logic should tell you that these stories are simply metaphors of a real truth, that indeed there was a major shift of consciousness, but over a longer period of time and not instantly. The same mythology has the Earth created in seven days. However, this only represents a numerological truth [7 is the number of divinity], meaning that there was a divine design in the creation of the planet. It's time to start using spiritual logic within the teachings you have about spiritual history, for the revelations will be wonderful and lead to fuller understanding.

Now, what really is in your DNA? It's the Pleiadians' code, and it's the ones before them, and even the ones before them. You can't remember it, for that is not the set-up. The system is that your Akashic Record is only from Earth, but your "divine remembrance" will take you back to the beginning, where system after system after system created that which you see as the divinity within the galaxy and the Universe.

Who are they? They're your "divine" parents. They're the seed divinity in you and they visit here. They're not all Pleiadians, did you know that? Instead, they're from all over the galaxy. You see, they also represent the seeds of the Pleiadians, and they keep you safe. You wouldn't have it any other way, would you? *"Safe from what?"* you might ask.

The Bubble of Safety

Your Universe is teeming with life. Only a relatively few planets over millions of years have made it to a place where they have "Creator DNA" in their corporeal bodies. Some were seeded and never made it. Some are now dead. Some are technically advanced, but have no spark of divinity at all. So while a planet is "deciding," it is kept safe from other life that might interfere.

You're surrounded by divine beings that keep you safe, and will continue to while this only planet of free choice – the only one at the moment – makes its decision. You're turning the corner of consciousness and they all know it, for they've all been through it and they remember it. Oh, dear ones, consciousness is volatile! You've seen it change so slowly, but it's about to change faster. It's not going to take generations and generations as in the past. Instead, you're going to see real-time changes. Humans won't wait to have children for them to grow up and have children.

Keeping you safe is done quantumly and at a 3D distance. But you have to ask the question, *"With all this life in the galaxy and how old they are* [potential for advanced science and travel], *why don't the ETs just land and announce themselves? They have been here for hundreds of years!"* The answer is proof of what we say. They know that you are "hands off" and they only come and go with marginal disturbance to Earth.

Kryon live channelling "The Big Picture"
given during the Patagonia Cruise – February 3, 2012

Are you starting to see the big picture? Can you feel the divine love that the Pleiadians have for humanity? Maybe all of this seems a little strange to you, or perhaps you are starting to remember the truth and knowledge held within your DNA. If you are like me, you might have moments where every cell of your being tingles with remembrance and knowingness, then the next moment you are telling yourself you are crazy and that none of this is true. If that is you, then perhaps you need to go out and spend some time in nature (smile). In particular, I recommend that you go and visit some mountains. There is nothing like looking at a landscape of beautiful snow-capped mountains. What's so special about mountains? Well, I'll let Kryon explain:

Many of you are aware of the seeds of creation. In your DNA is an attribute that is not from Earth. It is not even from this planet. Inside of you is an attribute that is divine, and at the same time, it has the seeds from others who are Human-like, but not Human. We speak now of what we would call your galactic spiritual parents. The metaphor of the Garden of Eden was more about the Pleiadians than anything else. When the Human Being was implanted with the knowledge of light and dark, is when the Pleiadians visited Earth and started that which you call the *spiritual seeding of humanity*. Now, I have given many channels about that, so I'm not going to review it here, but there are those who would disagree, and they would not want to hear any of this. If they knew the truth, however, they would understand. It's every bit as beautiful as the metaphor of the Garden of Eden, and just as sacred.

Long before you were here, this galaxy of yours teemed with those much like you. We say *teemed*, meaning there were many. The Earth is the only place of its kind right now, with the attributes like this. It's an Earth that is learning how to take a balance of former darkness, to that of light. That is what the shift is all about. But let me tell you about something that I have not said before. When the Pleiadians surveyed the planet before they came, they needed places to prepare for what they were going to do. These places needed to be high in altitude, for, in order to set up what they were going to accomplish, they needed it to be cold. This would explain one of the reasons they chose the Lemuria (Hawaii) that you know today only as tropical islands. They needed a mountain that was in excess of 10,000 meters high, and at that time there was only one. [Hawaii is the largest mountain on Earth, but is now submerged. The tectonic hot-spot pushed it up over 100,000 years ago, so it was over 10,000 meters.]

They also visited some other mountains on the planet, and for many of the same reasons. I'm not going to tell you all the reasons they needed this, not yet, but I tell you this in order for you to understand something. This is one of those mountains, and they are here! [Speaking to the group at the base of Mt. Aconcagua] It's part of what you feel. Ask those who have climbed the highest mountains on Earth. There are similarities in all of them.

I'll tell you this, dear ones – there is no mountain climber on the planet who is an atheist! By the time they visit the summit, they know the truth. Those who seeded you are here. They are still in the mountain, because a multi-dimensional attribute states that where things seem to begin and end don't always mean the same to you. Time is not the same for you as it is for them.

There are those who would say, *"Now Kryon, I don't understand anything that you said! Should we be afraid?"* Don't be afraid of your spiritual parents! Don't be afraid of the sacredness of what Spirit has given. Gaia knows them, and in a profound way, they are part of Gaia. They helped set up part of what Gaia is today. The very consciousness of the Earth which responds to you today, was not here before they arrived. All of this is to say that the Pleiadians not only seeded you, they created the system of *remembered Human consciousness* which you know today as Gaia and The Crystalline Grid, and they needed high mountains to do it.

Kryon live channelling "Mount Aconcagua"
given at Mount Aconcagua, Argentina – October 19, 2012

There is something else that you need to know about the Pleiadians that has to do with The Crystalline Grid that they created. Kryon gave some very profound information during an event organized by Dr. Todd Ovokaitys. The event was held in Maui during the winter solstice, December 21, 2012. The purpose of this event was to create a Lemurian Choir that would sing specific pineal tones (as developed by Dr. Todd). Unfortunately, it is not within the scope of this book to give you all the wonderful information about the pineal tones. If you want to know more you should visit the following websites:

www.lemurianchoir.com
www.pinealtones.com

While the majority of the channel was mainly targeted for the Lemurian Choir attendees, I am including it here, as I feel that it is important for you to read this message.

The information that follows is difficult. It is not complex, but rather, it is simply the first time that it has been given in this fashion.

To set the stage, I will review something that has been given to you in the last weeks. My partner took me to some of the most profound energies in the southern hemisphere (speaking of the Kryon Kundalini Tour of South America in 2012), where the Earth is recalibrating itself. The Eagle is meeting the Condor, where compassion is starting to be seen as a catalyst, changing that which is called The Crystalline Grid. A channel given there gave you the accurate, historic way, in which creation was given to humanity.

The duration of years was given as to how long it took, and when it began. It began with the Pleiadians, and the first thing they did was to set The Crystalline Grid. It was placed upon the Gaia Grid, which is the magnetic grid. You may even call The Crystalline Grid, *The Creation Grid* if you wish. It is an esoteric grid that responds to Human consciousness, but it goes both ways: it receives, and it gives.

Part of what is going on now is the recalibration of The Crystalline Grid via Human consciousness. What do you know about crystals? Crystals are one of the only geologic substances that can retain a vibration and therefore have *memory*. So The Crystalline Grid is really two things: (1) It is an esoteric grid that works with the vibration of Human consciousness, both in retaining and transmitting back to the Human DNA, and (2) It talks to Gaia, and the Gaia part it talks to, is anything crystalline within the Earth's crust.

If you talk to a geologist about how much crystalline there is in the Earth's crust, you would be amazed. So there is a retention of frequency between the quantum crystalline and the Earth crystalline ... the dirt of the Earth. Within this system, therefore, are the things you recognize as responsible for portals and vortexes, and for nulls. But there is more than that. For in the building of The Crystalline Grid, the Pleiadians have built a lens. This lens is something that will focus that which is appropriate, a signal, and send it to the center of the galaxy.

26,000 years ago, you put that possibility in place, dear ones, when you sang the tones here. [Referring to the Pineal Tones that have been taught by Dr. Todd Ovokaitys]. You created what we will call *the lock*. It locked in place this particular grid, and the lens it represents. It is not a rusty lock, but rather, it is a lock that responds and is ready, should you arrive at the right time and place at the end of the precession of the equinoxes. Then you can turn the key with compassion, and lubricate it with the love of the ancestors, and bring the energy to a place where, through the tones being sung again, the key starts to turn the lock. The Crystalline Grid would respond, and the lens would start to focus itself to the center of the galaxy, which intersects your sun during the equinox.

At that point in time, the tones would be the key to unlocking the grid, and it would start to change. It is the grid and the lens which send the signal, based upon the tones you sing to it. Now you know the mechanics, so the next thing to tell you is *who* is listening.

As the lens is activated and the crystalline sends a signal through the orbit of your sun into the center of the galaxy, an esoteric thing happens: The signal immediately arrives in the center of the galaxy and is received by a quantum engine of which you know nothing.

The Center: In three dimensions, and with the limited laws of physics that you have, it appears that there is a singularity at the center (which, by the way, is impossible in 3D physics). You call this a black hole. It is a place that literally has its own lens, for it bends light and bends time. That should give you a hint that there is something going on there which is beyond your known physics. For twenty-three years we have discussed that there is a set of energies, a push-pull set, that is the quantum engine for what you would call *an entangled galaxy.* All of the stars in your galaxy, unlike the workings of your solar system, travel at the exact same speed around the center. This is impossible with Newtonian physics. Newtonian physics requires objects to respond to weaker gravitational forces, the further they are from the center. But your galaxy does not. This in itself, should tell you that something is happening beyond your laws.

All of the stars of your galaxy move at the same speed, and are therefore entangled with the middle. The middle of your galaxy, therefore, becomes more than just an anomaly of physics. It is

the engine of quantum communication. Things in an entangled or locked state, are one with each other, and therefore when one *knows* something, they all know something. In an instant fashion, the entire galaxy and all intelligent life that has the ability, knows that Planet Earth has gotten to a point where compassion counts. It has graduated to a point where the barbaric notions of war and the basic differences between Human Beings are starting to recalibrate themselves.

Planet Earth has graduated to a point where many civilizations also graduated to, so the signal that is sent at the end of this day is one that was expected. This is esoteric and unbelievable to many, yet the ancients told you that this was possible. The end of the long count of the Mayan calendar was simply the beginning of another calendar. In your own home, you tear the old calendar off the wall, since it is no longer appropriate, and you put a new one up that is different.

In the case of your New Earth calendar, it's a different color, a different attitude, and a different consciousness for humanity. For, what I want to tell you now is what you need to hear: If these things are multi-dimensional, they are then quantum. The new calendar is about humanity, not about Gaia. This is what you're not seeing, and you don't recognize how profound this is. I told you 23 years ago that there's something called The Cave of Creation, and it is in the physical Earth and is crystalline.

This Cave of Creation is quantumly aligned with The Crystalline Grid and it contains the record of all of humanity's souls. These are souls who will come, and who have come, both Lemurian and not Lemurian. These souls are all *touched* as the key is turned. So the Cave of Creation represents your ancestors and those who will be your ancestors [a quantum attribute]. All are feeling what happens here today. Let's speak of your direct ancestors, dear ones, as you sit in the room.

How many of you have parents who are no longer here? Well, I want to tell you that, as you sing these tones, those passed parents (the ones who have died) are aware! Although some of them may not have given you what you needed during life, they are now aware and their parents are aware, and all of the souls to come

242

are aware. The Akash of the Earth is being recalibrated and they all know it today. This is why you are here. You're not just sending a signal to those perhaps you'll never meet. But rather, you're sending a signal to those you've loved and lost, and ones you know very well.

The Pleiadians are not far away. Part of the system of the planet, the very essence of creation, is that they would remain here in a quantum state. The ones who seeded you remain in the mountains of the Earth. Some say they even have cities that have names there. All of these things are out of 3D perception. Some of them are in the south and some in the north, in places that you know about.

The Pleiadians don't really need a lens to know what's going on today, for they are here. As the key begins to turn in the lock, they are feeling it now. These are the ones who are rejoicing first, and who carry the essence of your DNA. Where their energy is stored, are the places which will be activated to new levels first. So these are the ones who you are getting the messages from first. The main message is, *"Thank You!"* Beyond that, this is a release for them as well, and in a multi-dimensional state, you have released them to complement the recalibration of the grid that they built.

None of these things happen quickly, dear ones, but in those moments of silence we just had [speaking of what just occurred in the ceremony], there were many messages given to those in the room, and some were from the Pleiadians and some were more personal. Fourteen of you here have lost children. Did you hear them? If you thought it was your imagination, it was not. Others heard from your sisters and your brothers, who are not here. *"Thank you. Thank you."*

A few months ago, I described the timing of this event. For you, it is one day, but for astronomers, it is 36 years! 18 years ago, the seeds were planted for the potential of today. The precession of the equinoxes entered the 36-year window, which you call the dark rift. As the alignment precessed, it passed halfway through that which is the strip in the sky called *The Milky Way*. You are now in the center of this 36-year cycle, and there are 18 more years to go, as the precession continues into another 26,000-year cycle.

Consciousness moves slowly, but there are events along the way which push it faster into a higher vibration. Compassionate events are the catalysts for this. Many events like this have taken place on this planet within the last 18 years, and this, today, is also a compassionate event. The key begins to turn, and light is released on the planet.

The darkness is going to fight you, dear ones. Months ago, we told you to expect yet another small war in the closing months of 2012, and it occurred. We told you to watch for unbalance, and not be distraught when things break your heart, as they did last week [The Sandy Hook School shootings in Connecticut]. When you see this unbalance, try to find a place inside you that says, *"Thank you, Spirit, for we are winning the light-dark balance. These things represent the unbalance of darkness flailing against a consciousness that is being recalibrated on this planet."*

Dear ones, today is more than an event, sending a message that you've *arrived*. For in the process of sending the message, you're also stating that you understand that you're in a battle. However, the battle has just turned. Yes, there will be unbalance, and yes, the wars will still be there for a while, and yes, we will lose more lives before it's over. So let us take a moment to welcome to the room the lives who have been lost in just the last few weeks, and they can look at you and say, *"Thank you,"* as well.

This is more important than you think. It has to start with *you* before it means anything at all to the Great Central Sun. There must be a healing in the hearts within the room before it means anything to a Pleiadian in the Seven Sisters constellation.

You're planting the seeds for the next 18 years, and the energy is ready for that planting. You're doing a good job.

And so it is.

Kryon live channelling "Lemurian Choir A"
given in Maui, Hawaii – December 21, 2012

We are truly living in remarkable times. The original choir master, Yawee (Dr. Todd) recreated the Lemurian Choir in Hawaii during the winter solstice of 2012 with over 900 participants. Kryon stated that

Dr. Todd's memory of the tones sung by Lemurians 26,000 years ago was "shockingly accurate." The 24 Pineal Tones were sung together in pairs in the exact same configuration as previously done. Kryon explained that the original Lemurian choir created a "lock" on The Crystalline Grid when the 12 pairs of tones were sung. The "lock" is a metaphor that represents the "time capsules" within The Crystalline Grid. The information held by this "lock" is something that couldn't be released until the end of the 26,000-year cycle. Therefore, there was a very specific window in which to sing these tones and this window was the winter solstice of December 21, 2012. Kryon described the tones sung by the 2012 Lemurian Choir as an event that *turned the key in the "lock."* This is another metaphor that represents humanity's choice to recalibrate The Crystalline Grid with compassion. Turning the key in the lock is about communicating with the "time capsules" in the grid.

But there is more. The Pleiadians also placed a "lens" within The Crystalline Grid. The "lens" is a metaphor that represents the focus of the tones, should they ever be sung at the right time and place. This means that the Lemurian Choir event of December 21, 2012 was a profound marker in the course of humanity and Gaia, continuing the path of becoming an ascended planet. The "lock" and the "lens" placed on the grid are in a state of entanglement with the center of the galaxy. So the "signal" that was sent was actually an esoteric unlocking of the information, and the transmission happened all at once. If this event had not taken place, the potentials of Gaia and humanity ever reaching ascension status is doubtful. I give great honor and thanks to everyone who participated in the Lemurian Choir event of 2012. We did it! We have made a profound difference, far grander than you can ever imagine.

And so, the significance of all this is that the Human Beings on Earth are going through a shift brought on by a change in consciousness, and the Pleiadians are celebrating that, against all odds, humanity has made it.

If you are interested in what the Pleiadians have to say, you may wish to visit Barbara Marciniak's website. The Pleiadians have been speaking through Barbara since 1988.

For more information, visit Barbara's website: *www.pleiadians.com*

Q.: Can you tell us more about the reasons why the Pleiadians chose the highest mountain peaks, and why they needed it to be cold?

Kryon: In order to create quantum reactions with Earth-based elements, you have to rearrange the atomic structure of some of them to allow for them to "quantumly lock" to other elements. In the case of the Temples of Rejuvenation, there was a lock within the DNA of a living Human fetus, to that of a grown Human Being. This required a tool that helped create that lock. That tool had to be supercooled, so that the electrons almost stopped moving, allowing a superconductivity to occur that then could be directed and manipulated. The result was that life force could re-write DNA in the grown Human, and those who took on that attribute would then have fresh blueprints for their own regenerative process.

Lemurians knew how to do this because the Pleiadians showed it to them. Only the highest peaks, with the coldest atmospheric conditions, could create this process. The remainder of the process (to make a supercooled object) was then created by chemistry (something I discussed in the physics question).

In the case of the Temple, the locking was done between DNA and DNA. This was not that difficult, since both energies have quantum attributes already, and are "designer-ready" for this to occur. It's more difficult to quantum lock unequal things.

Q.: Can you tell us a bit more about what happens on those planets of free choice when they don't pass the marker? Where does their divinity go?

Kryon: Indeed, there are many planets that have been seeded and didn't make it. This is the honor that Spirit gives to free choice ... the ability to fail. Having divinity within the DNA is simply a tool that can be awakened or not. If a planet doesn't achieve a higher vibration, the inhabitants go into dysfunction, and they end up with several scenarios: one is that they might terminate themselves through several methods, and one is GAIA related, and may be of interest to this book. A low consciousness of a planet's population tells the "GAIA" system on that planet to cooperate with that energy. Remember that the energy of any planet of free choice has the same conditions you do – the planet's conscious-ness, which you call "mother nature," tries its best to match the consciousness and will of the divine inhabitants of the planet. This is "GAIA" cooperation, and is the same as you have now.

Cooperation with a very low or stagnant consciousness then allows for pandemic and death. This might seem harsh, but it's truly an evolutionary tool, where a species outlives its usefulness to the whole of life. GAIA cooperates fully and allows this to occur.

Another scenario is that they destroy the planet completely through war. Sometimes they may war until there are few left, and then there is simply a void of desire to ever create anything better. The time is up, and all remains static. God is still with them, but their vibratory level is so low that there is no hope of them ever finding the divinity inside. They repopulate (sometimes), but never achieve the goal of an ascended energy.

You almost did this very thing, and it has only been in the last two generations that you changed your entire future.

Q.: There are a growing number of people all over the world who are starting to acknowledge that we are part of a galactic family. Many individuals have described their experiences of being in contact with these other loving and peaceful humans that visit us. Will the global population on Earth meet our galactic family in 3D, or is this something that will only occur in a quantum state?

Kryon: The last part of the question is funny! A "quantum" state will eventually become your reality. So you will meet them within your reality. Yes. But remember this, a multi-dimensional state includes 3D. So it's like this – you are currently in black and white, and are asking if you will ever meet your galactic family in black and white. No. But later, when you are in color, you will. Does this mean that it's some obscure reality where you float around and things are invisible? No. It means that your reality became more complete ... and includes black and white and all the other colors, too. Remember, color includes black and white.

Yes, you will meet them. First, it will be through non-physical communication, and later it will be as physical as in your current 3D. Your family is corporeal, and also multi-dimensional. Did we never tell you that? Hugs are very appropriate when you meet them. They will insist on it, but you might have to reach up a bit.

Ascended Land of Gaia

The first time I heard the term "ascended land" was during the Kryon Kundalini Tour 2012 with Lee Carroll. At the time we were in the Elqui Valley, and even before the channelling began, many of us were feeling overcome by the energy of the place. Most of us intuitively knew that this particular place was special. I believe that nearly all of us who were there during the channel were deeply affected, especially when Kryon asked the Guardians of the land permission to channel and later invited them to come into the room.

I had never really thought about the possibility of land being ascended, but now it makes complete sense that the Pleiadians would create "pockets" of land that always remains in ascension status. Having now visited the Elqui Valley, I understand why my friend, Jorge Bianchi, kept telling me that I had to go there. The fact that Jorge deliberately chose the Elqui Valley as one of the places to visit on the Kundalini Tour was certainly not a coincidence. To me, it serves as another example of how we are recalibrating our intuition more than ever.

So what is ascended land? I'll let Kryon explain:

Gaia mirrors Human consciousness. It reflects the consciousness that humanity gives it. If you give Gaia the consciousness of war, Gaia's vibration will lower to meet what you give it. If you give it the consciousness of love or compassionate action, Gaia will respond accordingly.

Now, certainly you know the complexities here are great, and the Earth does not have one vibration everywhere on the globe. Even The Crystalline Grid creates pockets of what you would call low and high vibrations, based on what has happened with humanity in certain areas. But let me tell you something: There are places on this planet where the Pleiadians visited early, and they purified the grid in those areas, so that nothing that ever would happen there, would change the purity of the dirt of the Earth. We have mentioned it before.

You are sitting on ascended land [referring to the Elqui Valley in Chile] and you feel it. Nothing that would ever happen here could change it, and the guardians are here to make sure of that. That is why we ask their permission to speak as we do. I'm going to ask the guardians to come into this room, for in just a moment some of you will know that all of what I'm saying is real, and you will feel them. You will recognize them as the seed of your seed.

As those who have kept this area pure and clean, the guardians invite you to know them and greet them in every meditation, every prayer, and every exercise. You sit on ascended land. Ascended land represents places like this all over the planet. Not all of these places are on the mountain tops. Many are in the desert, as well, and these are what the Pleiadians have created here.

Call it spiritual Gaia accounting if you wish, but there had to be part of the planet that always is in ascension status. It's like a time capsule, so that the rest of the planet could go to that state if it ever needed to. It's a place that is pure.

Thank the guardians, and we say goodbye to them for a moment, for this area is theirs.

And so it is.

Kryon live channelling "The Letter A in the word Kundalini"
given in Elqui Valley, Chile – October 23, 2012

Q.: Can you tell us the difference between ascended land and nulls (land where there is an absence of The Crystalline Grid energy, such as the Valley of the Moon in Chile)?

Kryon: This is simple. Ascended land is filled with divine energy, often planted there by the Pleiadians or Lemurians (one and the same in some cases), and the other areas are virgin and void of any energy, including normal Earth energy.

Ascended land allows you to sit and be sustained by the love of those who planted the seeds. These are wonderful places for humans to visit and sometimes, live. A null, or void land may feel wonderful, but it's too overwhelming to be in for long time periods. It represents pure creative energy. It's far harder to live in, and the places on Earth where it exists are often uninhabited for that reason (some are in the ocean as well). It also has odd magnetic field characteristics, making it difficult for life force and balanced brain synapse (which requires a magnetic field balance of what you are used to). Unbalance and confusion is the result.

Q.: What is the difference between ascended land and nodes, such as Mt. Shasta? Is this where all the "time capsules" are?

Kryon: We have already given you the attributes of ascended land (above). It's a great place for humans to "Feel" the sacredness of what has been planted there by those who wanted it to be sacred. Sometimes, where the masters of Earth walked, is ascended land. So, it has attributes of divinity, which could have been given by several kinds of divine sources. Now you ask about the difference between this and nodes.

First, *ascended land* can also be nodes. So, don't put them in separate boxes. There is naturally an overlap of some of these terms and energies, and there is a complexity that goes beyond simply defining them.

Nodes are exactly what has been stated. They are places of immense intensity, where The Crystalline Grid can store the time capsules of the creation template, as placed there by the Pleiadians. So, nodes can also be ascended land, and feel very good. However, nodes are often in places that are less accessible or desirable for normal Human habitation. However, as mentioned before, nodes are often in places that are less accessible or desirable for Human habitation. But humans are very attracted to them anyway, and the indigenous of the Earth often built their temples there.

These time capsules need to be on the planet as a guide or blueprint for the starting creative energy of Gaia. We have told you that, as they are slowly released, they modify The Crystalline

Grid to help Human consciousness shift, and eventually create an ascended planet.

The templates are not just information. They are quantum portals of Pleiadian life. This is difficult to explain, but consider for a moment, that quantum energy can exist in two places at the same time. This is an attribute even of your own quantum physics, so it can't be that odd to you. So, consider for a moment, that even life can have these attributes. Therefore, know that your seed Creators have always been here in a certain quantum way, and are in the time capsules.

When you feel these energies in 3D, you tend to linearize them all. Therefore, those who are sensitive will see "a city," or feel entities that might even talk to you. But the reality is that these feelings are only the residuals of looking at profound quantum energy while in 3D.

Mt. Shasta is one of these time capsules. The mountain is ready for activation, and the release of the time capsule there has already begun. But now, with the passing of 2012, the Pleiadians can take a more active role. You will know what this means in a later time.

Chapter Six

Unsolved Mysteries of Gaia or Part of a System?

During the 1990s, well before I had become consciously aware of our benevolent Universe, one of my favorite TV series was *The X-Files*. This American science fiction drama was a huge hit, and starred two main characters, known as Mulder and Scully. Mulder is a believer in the existence of extra-terrestrials and the paranormal, while Scully is a medical doctor and skeptic assigned to scientifically analyze Mulder's discoveries. Those that assigned Scully to Mulder had a hidden agenda that she would debunk Mulder's work, and return him to the mainstream Federal Bureau of Investigation. Some of the well-remembered slogans from the show included, "The Truth is Out There," "Trust No One," and "I Want to Believe." Like everyone else who was hooked on the show, I reveled in the conspiracy theories, and embraced the search to find answers to the paranormal activity that mysteriously happens around us, but without any explanations. I loved that the show was pushing the boundaries outside of mainstream thinking. I often had a feeling that maybe there was more to things than we knew, but we would never find out, unless we opened our minds to a different way of thinking.

The hype that surrounds the so-called paranormal activity and unsolved mysteries is still very much alive, and is evident in the many types of movies and TV series that are centered around this theme. Perhaps, because there is so much money to be made, there isn't too much interest in finding out that, not only are the mysteries solvable, but they actually are part of a system. A system that is all about you! The Divine Human Being.

I'm sure that a lot of people would be devastated to learn that there is a system, a bigger picture, and that we are part of a galactic family. Many of you know exactly what I mean by that statement. The reason I know is that so many people are held tight within their belief systems that do not allow for such things to exist. Perhaps you're one of the lucky few who have a new age family, and all your friends are aware. I suspect, however, that you may be like me. You probably have family members that are limited by their religious beliefs, or have gone the opposite direction of rejecting anything spiritual. Either way, they don't want to know about what you're into, or to discuss the epiphanies you have had. The truth, however, is the truth, regardless of what people think. It's like gravity. You can believe in it or not, but gravity still exists, despite the fact that you can't see it.

Many people have even been communicating with our galactic family members, such as the Pleiadians, who are here in love and peace, and are celebrating that humanity has chosen to stay and create peace on the planet. The governments and religions are not really interested in admitting to this truth, as that would make it incredibly difficult to hold onto their power. Personally, I don't feel that we need to get rid of governments and religion, because I recognize that some individuals really do need this structure. It serves their needs, and as Kryon says, there are many pathways to God. I think eventually, we will evolve to a point where we no longer need to get in touch with God via a pre-scribed set of rules. In the meantime, I still love and honor people that are in government, and people who strongly believe in their religion. What is important is performing actions of love and compassion, and having integrity, because this helps to raise the vibration of our planet.

For over 23 years, Kryon has given information that has provided explanations for different types of phenomena and paranormal activity that people have experienced. If you would like to start learning about how all these unexplained mysterious things are a part of the system that Kryon talks about, then read on (smile).

Hauntings – Multi-dimensional Information or Trapped Souls?

What is it that you know about ghosts? It is a topic that has fascinated humans for thousands of years. There are a large number of movies about them, and lately, many television series involving humans communicating with ghosts. Various theme parks have their own haunted house theme ride. It is also possible to go on a ghost tour. There are literally hundreds of books for sale about ghosts. I have even discovered that you can buy "A Field Guide to Ghosts and Other Apparitions." I wonder if the task of producing the ghost and apparition images used in the field guide were ghastly? Sorry, bad joke, but I couldn't resist!

Ghosts are often described as something that is supernatural or paranormal. There seems to be so much more media hype and marketing opportunities when something is mysterious, frightening, or unknown. If there is a logical explanation for something, then it no longer has that same fascination and lure of delving into an unexplained mystery (insert dramatic music here).

If you have been diligently reading this book from the first page, then you would have read the section on The Crystalline Grid. You should, therefore, already have a good understanding about what a ghost is. If you haven't read that part, don't worry. The information in this section is similar, as well as much more expanded for the reader.

Apart from all the media hype and mass marketing of ghosts, a greater acceptance that they do exist has resulted in many investigative agencies consulting psychics to provide assistance in helping to solve homicide cases. Can a psychic access a murdered Human and ask what happened? And the answer is yes, but they are only accessing the Human in transition, and therefore, will only get what that Human knew at that point. This all comes together under the category of understanding the multi-dimensional self, because every one of us has our own imprint on the Earth. As difficult as it seems, these imprints can be accessed – a term that Kryon describes as "dipping into the Akash." It's part of the system that's been built to give you peace and not sorrow. It's part of the system that's been built to honor

your divinity and create something that you didn't know was there. There are many, many people who have sought out a psychic or medium to communicate with a loved one who has passed on. For many of these people, this type of communication has helped their grieving process and restored a sense of peace.

During a channel given by Kryon in Berkeley Springs, West Virginia, some very detailed information was presented regarding ghosts. The title of the channel was, "Energetic Consciousness." The section on ghosts is, therefore, repeated here in its entire form to ensure nothing is lost through trying to summarize. I am sure you will agree that it is a fascinating channel.

Humans love things that go bump in the night. They love to be frightened and they love to be scared. They love movies that scare them, and they love haunted places. Have you seen the upsurge in the interest in haunted places lately? Much of your media is creating new shows around them.

Now, let me tell you what they are and why they work the way they do. Now we get into the power of the information of the Human lifetime and the Akash. Human consciousness carries an imprint that affects the planet, and we have told you this from the beginning of our teachings. Human consciousness is what is going to change the planet. Human consciousness is information. It is information, not just random energy, that you develop based upon what you think, and it's powerful. Human consciousness actually goes into what we have called The Crystalline Grid of the planet, which is a multi-dimensional grid. You can't see it, but it holds energy. It holds multi-dimensional information.

When we measure the planet for spiritual vibration, it is The Crystalline Grid that is measured. The Crystalline Grid only has on it what humans have put there. It is a multi-dimensional record of thought, of lifetimes and of happenings. Why is it that certain land seems filled with old, layered energy of war, and other land is clear and clean? The reason is always the same – it's what happened on the land that humans created. Therefore, you already have the concept of Human energy affecting places.

Here's what I'm going to tell you: In certain conditions and in certain ways, a Human life or an interaction of multi-lives together in a profound scenario will create an energetic infor-mational imprint in a place. It's information and energy that will replay itself over and over and over like a recording tape in 3D. You see it as a haunted house! So, here are some of the things that will give you something to think about: Did you notice that in a haunting, you have a scenario that repeats itself over and over? Nothing new ever happens. The man comes down the stairs; the man goes up the stairs. The woman in the kitchen moves from the left to the right, sits in a chair, rocks for a while, moves away. If it involved dramatic things such as murder, the man comes down the stairs with the ax, over and over and over and over. It's a good movie, isn't it? And that's all it is! *"Why does it feel the way it feels, Kryon?"* Because it's the result of a Human consciousness imprint and you've got one, too. When you're there overlapping with it, it gives you chills, because it's real. It happened. It can even interface with you!

Now, science has gotten involved also, as they should. They're noticing something about true "haunted" areas. The imprint (the haunting) carries scientific attributes that are measureable and – ready – they're all multi-dimensional! Guess what changes they have measured in these places? Magnetics, gravitation, light, and even time anomalies, because what it is, is a multi-dimensional event, imprinted onto a place on the planet that plays over and plays over and plays over. Multi-dimensional attributes also often carry temperature change, always to the cold side. We even told you that, if you are going to develop a multi-dimensional lens, you will need to have a super cryogenic attribute. Do you remember? This is an attribute of things "out of 3D."

Can you capture it on your video recording devices? Yes. Because it knows it's being observed. (Just like light knows it's being observed in physics experiments.) Because it's part of an imprint that is multi-dimensional. In a quantum sense, it knows. I can't explain this to you, since your bias is that you assign knowing to specific consciousness. That is to say, you feel something can only know if it's intelligent and Human, or animal. This isn't either of those. It's a knowing that is quantum. Much of your quantum physics lets you see these very unusual attributes of light and mag-netics where there is no distance or time. It's present here, too.

Don't ponder this too much, for you won't like it. You absolutely want and need for there to be an intelligent "soul" where you feel something seemingly intelligent. How can it just be information? The answer is beyond your experience, so you can't understand it. But multi-dimensional information seems to have what you consider to be "life consciousness," yet it isn't. Let me ask you this: When you interface with your artificial intelligence machines (computers), and they talk to you and call you by name, do you then panic and say there is a "ghost in the machine?" No. It's only code ... information. Now, amplify that by a million-fold and you have multi-dimensional imprints.

How to Get Rid of a Ghost or Haunting

Oh, I have more to tell you. There are things that you wouldn't believe that you can do to change this imprint. How would you like to get rid of a haunting? Careful, you better not do it in a commercial area, since the tourists won't like it! [Kryon humor] They depend on the tape playing to sell tickets.

So, let's say it's in your house. You're going to have to present an energy that is stronger than the imprint of the haunting. Got that? You cannot order it away. It's not an entity, dear ones (told you it would be controversial). No amount of huffing and puffing or calling upon God will make it different. The imprint was created by magnificent, powerful beings (called Human), sometimes seeming to do ordinary things. There's a reason for that as well. I digress; you really don't know the profundity of old soul energy. Have you ever wondered why all the indigenous of the planet call upon their ancestors and give them the honor that they do? Because there is a knowing of the power that is there! Sometimes, a person who seems to be ordinary to you, instead is a very old soul and carries much information and energy to the grid. This is all about the Akashic Record that is contained in the Human DNA.

Back to the subject, to rid yourself of an imprint (haunting)? You've got to present an energy that is stronger than the haunting. Now, what could that be? As inappropriate as it is, I will tell you. Why don't you bring lovers into that room? That will do it! That will do it, because that's a much stronger energy than the information in the multi-dimensional "tape" that's playing. There are those who have been in love here in this room. There are beautiful secrets here that I know. Some of you know that I teach that the power and the energy of humans coming together in intimacy, which creates a third energy, is far more powerful than the two creating it. It almost creates the sound of angels singing, far greater than any physical act. And you know it, Human Being. It is sacred. It's beautiful and stronger than any haunting. Maybe you didn't want to hear that today? [Kryon smile] All right, perhaps you want another method? Then present the love of God in that place with celebration and ceremony that will eventually reduce the haunting to nothing, and will instead replace it with strong love energy of creation. It takes the powerful emotion of love! And, you might even call upon the ancestors for help. [bigger Kryon smile]

Even More Controversial

"But what about other things? Kryon, what about demon possession and those kinds of things?" So I will tell you this: It's far different than you think, because there are no demons. Humanity can conjure up the most evil things imaginable, and it can do it very well. But you knew that too, didn't you? Because you're powerful, the pieces of God in you, even in your mythology, are responsible for the devil himself. A fallen angel became the devil? How can that even be? It can't. God does not create evil; humans do. Evil is the metaphor of what a Human can do on the Earth with the energy that they have. Things are not always what they seem, Human Being. Demon possession is the work of Human unbalance and supported by Human mythology. Is it real? Yes. But it's Human created.

You see what you believe, and create what you wish to have there. Creating your own reality is one of the powerful attributes of the Human Being, and you can do it in the negative as well as the positive. You can even create the devil if you wish, with all the trappings of smoke and fire. This is free will. But be aware that it all will disappear when the light is turned on. This is a very difficult subject to convince you of. Humans always want a devil to blame for evil things.

Talking to the Dead: Different Than You Think

"What about talking to the dead? How would that work, Kryon? How could you talk to famous people when, in the scheme of soul incarnation, they've already come back as other people? If they've already left and their soul is back as another, how can you talk to them?"

The answer is this: They haven't left! Oh, the part that you think is the Human soul has left, but the imprint of their lifetime information, and everything they knew – their consciousness, their wisdom, their knowledge – goes right into The Crystalline Grid and stays there. We've talked about this before. Can you contact famous people and get information? Yes. Will it be accurate? Of course! Because you're talking to the source information, which is accurate and represents their life. The imprint remains. *"You mean you're not actually talking to them, you're talking to the imprint?"* Let me give you something to think about. I'm going to ask a question right now. It's going to be a rhetorical one. Who are you? I have old souls in front of me and reading this. There's a woman in the room who won't wear red, and you know who you are. I'll tell you why. Because it got you killed! Because that was the color of the plume on your helmet, warrior. Because you were the captain, and the enemy before you in that battle knew, if they would take you out, your whole regiment would be in disarray, and that's what happened. Wearing red not only killed you, it killed everyone around you! You'll never wear red. You just don't like the color. It's just not for you. You shun it, don't you, old soul? Therefore, as you sit here, who are you? Are you the warrior who got killed, or the woman in 2010 who won't wear red?

Indeed, it is a rhetorical question, because in my reality, you are a piece of God. I see you in all your incarnations. You see? You can't wallow in the singularity of Human bias when you discuss these things. You are more than you think and, metaphysically, this is the way God sees you, and the way you are just barely beginning to see some of those around you.

So, getting back to the question, when you wish to conjure up one who has lived before and ask them questions, who are you talking to? Are you talking to the Akash of a soul? Are you speaking to that which is alive or dead? I will tell you: None of those things are accurate, because it's far more magnificent than that! We have told you before. Can you ask Aunt Martha where the treasure was buried? Yes. And she'll know! Why? Because you're talking to Aunt Martha's informational imprint and the information is the information, preserved in a form that you absolutely feel is Aunt Martha!

However, can you ask Aunt Martha, *"How are things on the other side?"* Go ahead, but the imprint has no idea! It will only give you the platitudes that it was told during the life of the Human it represents.

She'll say, *"Beautiful."*

"What's it like over there?"

"Lovely."

"No, give me some specifics."

"I love you."

She doesn't know! Aunt Martha's imprint knows what Aunt Martha knew, since you are not talking to anything actually on the other side of the veil. You think of it in singularity, but it's not. It's powerful, and it's real, and it can be accessed and even dialogued with. It's multi-dimensional and those with gifts can access the wisdom of the ancients. Go back and ask them what they knew. Go back and ask them how it felt. Go back and ask them where the treasure is buried. You're going to see some of this soon, but be aware – those in the places of power on this planet, wearing the costumes of spirituality, and the heads of state in religion, will call it evil and will call it a cult. They do not understand that you are moving into a multi-dimensional state – appropriate, accurate, true, useable, correct, helpful, and very much seen as something you should do. Asking the ancients what they knew will bring you full circle to what you are now studying.

Kryon live channelling "Energetic Consciousness"
Berkeley Springs, West Virginia – July 17, 2010

Can you see the system here? Ghosts are simply a recording on The Crystalline Grid. Wouldn't it be great if those that currently offer ghost tours could change tactics and invite people to come and see a

recording on The Crystalline Grid! I'm sure if they did, they would probably go out of business. It's not nearly as exciting to see something that is completely explainable as compared with having the living day-lights scared out of you and your friends.

Q.: With the recalibration of The Crystalline Grid, will this affect the tapes that play over and over, particularly those instances where horror took place?

Kryon: This is a wonderful question, for with your conscious intent to graduate into a higher vibration you are now recalibrat-ing the way The Crystalline Grid actually works. I have channelled this, and you can read it more clearly in other places. But the basics are that this grid has remained linear to all Human energy for centuries. This means that dark and light had equal effect on the "recording" process.

You might also note that in Human history, war and death were far more abundant than compassion, celebration and joy. So The Crystalline Grid is packed with darker things, and the tapes play this over and over, like when you step onto former battlefields.

Now, however, these lower energy tapes will begin to diminish with time, and in addition, the way things are recorded and stored on the grid will become non-linear. Compassionate events caused by victory, unification, joy, celebration and honor will be the most impressionable. These things will affect the grid up to twice as much as any kind of lower energy.

Dear ones, this is the Earth responding to what you want. It's needed for you to feel better in general, to have entire societies get out of victimization and gloom, and begin to feel that they can actually create something better for themselves, taking them into balance and health.

This is GAIA at its best, in cooperation with humanity. The old energy tapes will diminish in power, and eventually, will not have the same impact they have had for centuries. So you might even say, that what you are doing right now is actually changing the past.

Q.: People have experienced being visited by a relative seemingly right after they have died in a distant place. Can you explain this, as it is not really clear if the visitation is like a replaying of something that has been recorded on The Crystalline Grid, or it's more like a deliberate visitation to herald their death?

Kryon: There is a time right after death, and a few weeks afterward, where soul communication takes place. This is from the Higher-Self of the individual who has passed, to friends and relatives (and even sometimes enemies). It's quantum, of course, so distance makes no difference. Sometimes it comes in dreams, and other times with blatant visualizations and the feeling of being with them personally somehow. Often you can even smell them.

Slowly, this communication dissipates and eventually, it's gone. The only communication left would be that of the system in which a family member who has passed over becomes part of your guide-set for the rest of your life. This is not the kind of real-time communication that you are talking about, but a gentle and loving "knowing" that you are not alone, and that you have the wisdom and love of family helping you personally. For instance, a part of your deceased parents are always with you, winking and nodding and holding your hand. This, even though their soul may be back on Earth as another Human! It's all part of the complexity of the Akashic system, and souls can be in many places at once (a known quantum attribute).

The imprint they left on The Crystalline Grid is also still there, which means that you can talk to their "memory" if you wish (such as in séances), but this is less satisfactory for those who understand the real energy of the soul.

So the real answer is yes, there is a time right after death when the soul is communicating.

Q.: How do you explain when someone has passed away who was an atheist, that when contacted by a medium, they say that grandma was right and that they were wrong (grandma believed in the afterlife and they didn't)? How can this be possible when

The Crystalline Grid only plays the tapes of what the person's memory left behind?

Kryon: Ah ... it's because part of the "memory they leave behind" is what happens right before their death. The light and the love of God they see and feel during their last dying synapse are the last moments they have of life. This is a gift to the living, so that at death there will be less fear. It's then etched magnificently onto The Crystalline Grid as their last memory of their life on Earth.

Many have experienced this, and then come back (don't die). This is known as a Near Death Experience (NDE) and is all part of the Human dying process, no matter what their spiritual belief is. Look at this for what it is. It's given to you, Human, so you will not be distressed when the time comes to make the crossing again. Do you see the compassion for you in all this?

So the imprint on The Crystalline Grid of their life, then, includes this realization, for it was created clearly in the last moments of their existence.

Q.: Can you explain instances where a new dwelling has been built, and subsequently a ghost repeatedly walks through the back door (the physical evidence is that the locked door is now unlocked and wide open). It is always the same door, but how can this happen when the building is newly constructed?

Kryon: The ghost and all the old building attributes around it, remain. If there is no stairway in the new building, the ghost still walks the old one. If there is now a wall in the new building, the ghost will walk through it. Sometimes new doors will be thrown open. The tape plays with the old *movie set* no matter what, and sometimes enhances it by interfacing with the new set. This creates some confusing scenarios, but basically, you are seeing the memory of the ghost performing similar actions, even in new surroundings. New doors often are where old ones were. If there is no door, the memory doesn't care.

Animals

The diversity of animals on the planet is vast. Each animal has its own niche within its ecosystem. It serves a biological process within the food chain and the web of life. Some animals have characteristics that make it possible to farm them agriculturally, or harvest them from wild populations, for the purpose of Human consumption or the manufacture of products, such as wool. There are also animals which have allowed themselves to be domesticated, and serve as companions or pets. Each of these three characteristics is in accordance with why animals are here on the planet.

Kryon has often talked about the role of animals on the planet, and the information given is repeated here so you can gain a greater understanding.

The harvesting of animals for Human consumption often elicits many different points of view between humans. Whatever your personal point of view, you should understand that collectively, the animals understand that some of them are here to be eaten by humans. For those that have decided to be a vegan and never eat meat, that remains a personal choice. It may be the most perfect choice for their health. However, it is appropriate that the Human race nourishes and sustains itself with the consumption of animals. Humanity doesn't have the ability to grow things fast enough and distribute that food, so again, the consumption of animals is appropriate for those that choose to do so. If you are having trouble understanding this, perhaps Kryon can explain in a way you might understand.

I speak of the precious animals all the time and how they're here to service humanity and how they do it so completely. I've spoken about how some of them are here to be eaten. Many don't like to hear this, but understand that collectively, the animals understand this. They have to be part of the Human food chain, since humanity doesn't have the ability to grow things fast enough and distribute that food. So that's a service, you see? For those of you who are vegan, you might say, "*I never eat them!*" That is a choice for your health. It's appropriate and accurate, but doesn't hold true for the survival of the Human race, for animals are needed for Human nourishment and survival at the moment.

So let's divert for a moment and give you some valuable information about Human consumption of animal life. Many humans need to eat them, but never understanding that the animal knew this when it came in. Is this too spooky for you? This is known by those who know of animal spirits and can see the sacrifice and appropriateness of this. It was also very well known by the ancients. But here is the question, dear Human: How do you treat them? With that kind of purpose on the planet, how do you treat them before they become your food? How did the ancients treat them? Now that's a hard question, isn't it? Let me give you an attribute of truth. Did you know the better they're treated, the more nutritious they'll be within your body? *"Kryon, please don't talk about that. We don't want to think about it."* Dear ones, if not me, then who? Listen, if these animals are willing to come and be so grand a part of the life force of this planet and help it to vibrate higher by keeping you alive so you can make choices, don't they deserve respect and comfort while they are growing up? The end result will be a far better contribution to your health. Let the scientists lead the way and do some comparison studies to show that the nutritional values increase dramatically when an animal is honored during its short lifetime. The ancients knew this and honored each animal before it became part of their life force.

There is no Cave of Creation for the animals. They are here in support of humanity. Some of them are here to love you and you know that. We speak of the ones in your home. They're here to love you – another great service to humans. You look in their eyes and they look back. They see the old soul within you, did you know that? They know the system ...

...So, in a way, many animals have souls, too, but they're not in the Cave of Creation. They don't have the profound system of planetary change that you do, which is a consciousness that can increase itself by free choice. The Human is the only being on Earth who can do this, because the Human has divinity in the DNA.

Kryon live channelling "The Akashic System"
given in Syracuse, New York – September 11, 2010

While understanding that many animals are knowingly on the planet for Human consumption, it is important that these precious animals are treated well and honored for their sacrifice. Those animals that are treated well and honored before they become food provide much more nutrition than those that are not. When animals are not treated well, they will often self-destruct, and diseases such as the Mad Cow disease demonstrate this. These animals deserve respect and comfort while they are growing up, and should be honored for their contribution to the survival of humans. When I consciously think about what I'm eating, I silently give thanks to Gaia. The trouble is, I don't always remember to think consciously about my food. I have asked my DNA to always be thankful every time I consume an animal product for the life force it gave. I asked my DNA, because it's smarter than me (smile).

In relation to pets or animals that humans have bonded with, there are many questions. Do they have past lives? Do they reincarnate? If they reincarnate, what do they reincarnate into? During a channel given in Laguna Hills, California, Kryon gave some specific answers to these questions and more:

First of all, throw away your idea of the linear progression of animal incarnation, if you happen to believe it exists. A mouse does not become a dolphin, and a dolphin does not then graduate to become a Human. You may look into a Human's eyes and say, *"I see dolphin energy in there,"* but it doesn't mean they were a dolphin. So right away, we're going to shatter the idea that there's a graduation process through animal incarnation, somehow into the divine Human soul. But there is indeed, a system for animal incarnation.

Do animals incarnate? Yes, some do. This attribute is difficult to describe, for it is not linear. I will tell you that the only animals that will incarnate are the ones around humans. Those are the only ones. The animals in the forest do not. Animals in the plains, they don't either. In other words, only those who have been influenced by Human consciousness incarnate.

Animals do not have divinity in their DNA, as you do in yours. There's no test of their consciousness on the planet, as there is in yours. However, the ones around you have in their intelligence, the

concept of unconditional love. This is, therefore, their one purpose: Companionship and love.

If love and companionship is generated in an animal, it sets up a system with their essence, and that system can be extended over and over and over. For, most animals don't live long enough to serve a single Human for their lifetime. There is a way to extend the love affair of your animal. After it goes, and the dust is put in the Earth, there is a system to help them come back, for they want to.

Go look for them and they'll be there. That's the system. It's beautiful. Don't wait any longer than 90 days. Don't expect to find the same color or the same breed, or even the same kind of animal. However, you can look in their eyes and you will see them as they hover around you. They are in the places around you if you go look, and synchronicity will guide you to them. They will continue the love affair and you'll know it in what they do, and their old habits. Then there will be no question if it's the same one. Go do it! It is a beautiful system and it is created for you.

The magnificence of the divinity within a Human Being means that whatever it touches, changes that which is around you. You can affect the ones with 24 chromosomes [animals] and they respond. It doesn't matter, dear ones, if it's a mouse or a horse or even an elephant. It won't matter, for they come back. If you love them, they come back. If you don't wish to find them again, there's no negative thing attached to this. It's only an opportunity. They'll go on to love humanity just as much, and help others as they helped you.

Not all animals you find have been here before. Many are coming in for the first time, having volunteered their part to make you feel more loved and peaceful, so that you can be a stronger Lighthouse for the planet.

Kryon live channelling "The Greater Akashic System"
given in Laguna Hills, California — July 15, 2012

I hope the channel you just read gives you a greater understanding of the role of animals on the planet. Many of us have pets, including reptiles, amphibians, fish and mammals, to mention a few. Over the years, I've had many pets. My current dog, Bella, an English

Staffordshire Terrier, gives me much joy and happiness. Our pets are always filled with unconditional love for us. Isn't it wonderful to know that there is a system where our beloved pets can reincarnate again to be with us!

Do you find the idea of our pets coming back again and again and again too esoterically unbelievable? Perhaps you should read about Laurie Reyon Anderson's story. Laurie has given me permission to share with you her own journey with her beloved cat.

Laurie Reyon's story begins with her cat, Puddy, literally saving her life in 1994, when Laurie had a near death experience. If you look through history, you will find many stories of pets saving the lives of their masters. During this experience, Laurie noticed that her telepathy became highly activated. She could actually hear Puddy talking to her, as though Puddy were a Human!

Sadly, Puddy died on August 29, 2001. Sometime after this event, Laurie Reyon was told by Amelia Kinkade, who is a world-renowned animal communicator, that Puddy would be reborn on March 3, 2002 and look exactly the same. The message came true and Puddy reincarnated as Puddah 1 on the exact same date as her previous birth. By the time Puddah 1 was seven weeks old, she was communicating with Laurie Reyon and saying how their lives would change. And change it did!

The relationship between Laurie and Puddah 1 was the catalyst for Laurie to attune to her gift as an interspecies communicator. With the loving help and guidance of Puddah 1, Laurie Reyon began to work with wild dolphins, attuning herself to hear the frequencies of the dolphins. Since then, many wondrous and amazing things have unfolded for Laurie Reyon and her cat companion. Puddah has passed away twice since this time. Guess what? Both Puddah 2 and Puddah 3 continued the birthday tradition by being born again on March 3. Look at the numerology, it's a 33. Three is a catalyst. 33 is a master number with the Christ energy. 33 also signifies compassionate action. There is something else you should know. Laurie Reyon's birthday also adds up to a 33 (smile). What a coincidence?

Puddah 3 will be five years old on March 3, 2013. For more than two decades, Puddah has given her unconditional love to Laurie Reyon and the rest of the planet. I guess there really is truth to the old saying of a cat having nine lives!

In summary, animals are here on Earth for three reasons:

1. The balance of biological life.

2. To be harvested. It is a harmony between Human and animal. Many animals exist for Human sustenance, but there needs to be shift in the way that some cultures treat these precious creatures. When there is an honoring ceremony at the animal's death, humans are nourished better. Ceremonies that honor the animals could benefit all of humanity.

3. To be loved and to love. In many cultures, animals serve as surrogate children, loved and taken care of. This gives humans a chance to show compassion when they need it, and to have unconditional love when they need it. For many humans, this is extremely important, and it provides a mechanism to center and balance them.

Q.: Will the recalibration of all the grids, and the recalibration of humanity, change animal behavior?

Kryon: Yes, it will. The answer provided in the next question relating to extinction of species will help you understand this better. All life on the planet exists for balance, and to assist the Human Being to create an ascended planet. As humans do this, everything will change around them. The way things have worked for centuries are being recalibrated, and the animals of the planet, their cycles and very existence, will bow to the new energy and allow for it. They are part of your support group.

Extinction of Species

For as long as species have existed and evolved, species have also become extinct. It is estimated that over 99.9 percent of all species that ever lived are extinct. The average life-span of most species is 10 million years, although this varies widely between populations of species. A simple definition of an extinct species is: any species that cannot survive or reproduce in its environment, and cannot move to a new environment where it can do so. The species eventually dies out and becomes extinct. The extinction of species may come suddenly, or it may occur gradually over thousands or millions of years.

Just as some species become extinct, others, through evolution, become new species through a process called natural selection and speciation. This is a process whereby new varieties of an organism arise and thrive when they find and exploit an ecological niche. One of the best examples of natural selection and speciation is the English Peppered Moth. Typically, this moth is whitish with black speckles and spots all over its wings. The moths are very well camouflaged when they rest on the speckled lichens on tree trunks. Occasionally, a few moths had a genetic mutation that caused them to be all black. These black moths on the light colored, speckled lichen were not very well camouflaged and became an easy meal for any birds passing. These moths never got a chance to reproduce and pass on their genes for black coloring.

But in the 1800s, many factories and homes in British cities started burning coal, which resulted in a lot of black soot and pollution. Eventually, the tree trunks were covered in soot, enabling the occasional black moth to be well camouflaged. Subsequently, the black moths lived long enough to reproduce, while the "normal" whitish speckled moths were eaten.

Studies done in the early 1900s showed that the predominant moths in the country were the whitish speckled type, but in the cities they were almost non-existent. Nearly all the moths in the cities were the black form. In the cities, black moths were breeding with the other black moths, while in the country the whitish speckled moths were only breeding with other whitish speckled moths. Had this trend continued, the two differently colored moths would have eventually become genetically distinct species. As it turns out, the cities found ways to clean up the pollution, and the tree trunks once again had healthy light colored lichen. It was then that the whitish speckled moths became the predominant type of moth to survive and reproduce and the black ones couldn't.

While I was at university, there was a long list of things that cause extinction: genetic pollution, habitat degradation, predation, competition, disease, overharvesting, climate change and co-extinction (which

happens as a direct result of another species critical to survival of the first becoming extinct). After working directly in many different programs targeting threatened and endangered species, I developed an attitude that humans were directly responsible for a staggeringly large number of extinct species, and felt that this alarming rate of extinction through Human influence was really out of balance, compared to what would happen if we didn't exist on the planet. In fact, I'm pretty sure that a lot of my former work colleagues would still argue strongly that humans are the root of all evil. There are probably a lot of people who think this way. I'm sure they are convinced that, without Human impact, the rate of extinction would not be what it is today. Scientists estimate that up to half of the species that exist today may become extinct by 2100.

The extinction of species is an extremely important research topic for zoologists, botanists and biologists. The threat of extinction has become an area of concern outside of the scientific community. The result is that a number of organizations have been created with the aim of preserving species from extinction. One of the fundamental principles often overlooked is that not all species are meant to be in the cycle of life forever.

The majority of my career in the environmental field was directly related to the protection and conservation of threatened and endangered species. I helped develop education materials, programs and signs about the plight of various endangered species. I worked with several volunteer groups that are dedicated to doing everything possible to increase the breeding success of their 'adopted' endangered species. I assessed wildlife management plans to ensure that commercial harvesting of kangaroos and crocodiles were sustainable, and I spent countless hours controlling pest plants and animals that are considered a threat to native indigenous Australian species.

It seems quite odd that I (and so many others in the world) would dedicate so much energy toward trying to save a species that Gaia is potentially designing, deliberately, to become extinct. I believe that all of these efforts and actions are because many of us feel a moral responsibility towards minimizing our actions and influence on other species. It is an attempt to be in balance with Gaia, something that the ancient indigenous knew how to do intuitively. Perhaps, if we can rekindle our connection with Gaia, we will become better able to discern Gaia's plan and better able to focus our efforts and actions. I also think that modern environmentalists have much to learn from our indigenous brothers and sisters.

Gaia is the one responsible for the coming and going of life on the planet. Gaia also responds to Human consciousness. Kryon has told us how it works:

The variety of species on this planet comes and goes accordingly as they are needed for the energy they create. So, one of the tasks of Gaia is to create and eliminate species. When they are no longer needed for the purpose of Gaia's development, they cease to exist and they die out. If new life is necessary, if new concepts of life are needed, Gaia is cooperative and they are then created. The actual creation of species is something that environmentalists have not clearly seen. That is to say, the mechanics of how it works is not fully recognized as something that is strongly coordinated with your weather. But you have already seen the mechanics of some of this in your long-term studies, for you have already noted the coming and going of many species through the ages. It's ongoing.

The Appropriateness of the Elimination of Species

Now, along come humans and they see all of this coming and going of living things, but they want to save them all – all the species that exist. For in their linear minds, all species should remain and exist, since they are here. The attribute of Gaia, however, is to eliminate them, cull them out, to bring in new ones. I just gave you the mechanics of the reasons species come and go. It's appropriate and is a natural building process for new species.

When the Pleiadians started to create the grids of the planet, Gaia *cooperated in* what was to come, knew the purpose, and what was needed for survival of this new spiritual Human. Gaia knew this, since the energy of Gaia had seen it before [reason given below]. So the old attribute, which needed many kinds of Human Beings, slowly died out. It was natural. There was not a war. There were no horrible plagues. There were no volcanoes or tsunamis

that consumed them. Through attrition, appropriateness, and 110,000 years, they disappeared.

So approximately 110,000 years ago, there was only one kind left, and this is science, for everything that you study will bear this out, and anthropologists have already seen it and have asked, *"What happened back then at this time that would have eliminated these other kinds of Human variety?"* It's a puzzle in science that I have just answered, for science looks only for physical events as triggers. But instead, it's the marriage of Gaia consciousness that you call "Mother Nature," which facilitated this. It's the same today when you see a variety of species diminish, as humans take over a greater portion of the Earth. I'll call this "the appropriate elimination of unique life forms, which allow for the growth of global awareness and quantum evolution." Some species only exist to allow others to climb the ladder of nature, and then they disappear. Gaia knows what the ladder looks like. You don't.

Kryon live channelling "The Timing of Creation"
given in Hawaii 11th Kryon Cruise – August 12, 2012

My deep love and appreciation of nature resulted in my working as a park ranger for over 15 years. I am guilty of wanting to rush out and save everything, just like Kryon says! I'm not sure I like the "do nothing" approach. I have spent a substantial amount of time and energy in actions that help to increase and maintain biodiversity in the natural landscape. But are we just putting off the inevitable? What if the rapid rate of extinction is deliberate and planned by Gaia? What if this is so Gaia can then prepare and create for life yet to come? After all, Gaia has been doing this on the planet for over 4 billion years! Hopefully, Kryon can shed some more light on this ponderous topic by answering the question below.

Q.: There are many cases where it appears that humans have been directly responsible for causing the extinction of a species. For example: by direct overharvesting a species, destroying habitat, or by introducing predators or viruses that then cause extinction. On the other hand, there are many cases where it

appears that humans have been directly responsible for bringing back some species from the brink of extinction through actions such as creating habitat, protecting and conserving existing habitat, banning hunting and controlling introduced predators.

It therefore appears that the actions taken by humans do have an influence on whether or not a species becomes extinct. However, if Gaia is the one that regulates the coming and going of a species, where do humans fit into this scheme? Should we do nothing and just leave it up to Gaia? Or if we are able to make a difference, how can we better use our discernment as to when we should take conservation efforts to help an endangered species?

Kryon: This will be the most difficult answer for many reading this, and some will shut the book, because they are so disturbed by it. But it is time you knew how all of this comes together, and also why humans do what they do. I'll try to be succinct.

FIRST:

As you indicated, and we have told you before: GAIA regulates the coming and going of species on Earth, in order to support the evolution and purpose of responding to Human consciousness. There is no axiom or truth of GAIA that states that a species should remain on the planet. Animals (in particular) come and go as they are needed, then they leave. They are seen as placeholders for Human Evolution.

Human Beings today, especially as they further discover their divinity, cherish life force. In addition, they love all the life they can see around them. They cherish the trees, the plants, the animals and the fish. They can "see" the quantum love that is there in some of these animals, and make them *family* in their homes. They begin to feel the Akash of their ancestors, where all animals were respected as part of the Earth's life force. In short, they have "the bias of love" for all living things. Therefore, they go out of their way to save everything that is alive, never understanding that many things are "scheduled" for extinction, and should be left alone.

There are many issues here, but I'll create just three discussions: (1) The extinction of species, and the GAIA system, (2) Human responsibility, and (3) Human intervention guidelines.

THE EXTINCTION OF SPECIES:

In order for evolution to exist, and to eventually create the Human Being as it is now, much had to happen in a certain order. Biologists who look at this will see a system that is the "survival of the fittest," and create their own ideas of why things evolved the way they did. The anomalies they see, they simply sweep under the carpet and say, "*Nature is sometimes odd.*" Well, GAIA is not odd, and there is a far greater evolutionary process besides the "accidental appearance of evolved Human Consciousness on Planet Earth through chance."

First you must rearrange how you think everything took place. The entire evolution of Planet Earth was designed to create the Human for their chance to create a divine, ascended planet. "Intelligent Design" is the way of the Universe, and is the way of your Earth. So nothing happened by chance. Instead, it was "guided chance."

When you look at the very early beginnings of life itself, there were up to four times when it tried and failed. GAIA had to have a balance for what was to come, so in the scheme of natural processes, GAIA terminated life four times before the "right process" emerged. That was photosynthesis. It was needed to give life to animals that would eventually lead to the existence of humans. Some form of life could have existed and thrived all by itself, but not life that needed oxygen. So GAIA terminated it over and over until the "right" evolved system occurred that had a system of oxygen exchange in a closed system environment.

So you realize a conundrum immediately: Is this a natural process, or not? The answer is both. Call it a "guided process" if you wish. For it's an *aware* process that guides the evolution of species with a specific goal in mind, using natural processes of common galactic evolution cycles, and lots of time.

In order for Earth to develop the way it did, thousands of species came and went. In the process, each one created a platform for the next. Then they were done. The dinosaurs were a great example of this. They needed to be there for the next step in the Earth's evolution, but they also needed to go extinct. Yes, GAIA was involved even in the asteroid strike, for the consciousness of the Creator is part of all attributes of the main purpose of the galaxy ... to vibrate higher. Therefore, there is even an alliance with disaster, you might say. GAIA is the master of evolution, and played a part in getting things ready for the very moment the Pleiadians arrived.

Enter current time: You now have a planet inhabited by humans who have passed the marker and are moving into a place where the very paradigm of existence will change. Quantum energy will be discovered within two generations via the "quantum viewer," and the path of civilization will slowly begin to shift forever. Can you see where this is going?

Humans are the reason for the season, and now life around them must change. One of the greatest civilizations is yet to occur, and now it will begin. Africa will eventually emerge as one of the finest evolved societies Earth has ever seen. The central and northern parts of this continent will be healed, and be ready for development, something that will change the planet forever and will assist greatly in becoming "ascended" within the galaxy. It will evolve in ways that will rival the best political systems that have ever been tried. It's the next step in political evolution of civilization on Earth. They will be able to design and build their cities from the bottom up, and with no existing infrastructure to contend with. This continent will be the most modern on the planet. Now, Africa is also rich in animal life, as you know. So what do you think is going to happen?

There will be those who will tell you that humans have no right to encroach on nature in this manner. They will tell Africans not to do this. There will be those all over the Earth who will cry for the lost species, as the cities are built and slowly the habitat for magnificent animals in the plains of Africa disappears. Eventually, the animals will only be able to be seen in zoos. So who is right here? I told you that you would not like this discussion.

Let me show you something: If you were around to watch the dinosaurs, you would have been alarmed at how they encroached

on their environment. Dozens of medium sized animals simply disappeared from the planet at an alarming rate as the larger carnivores arrived and evolved. The herbivores fared much better, until the larger carnivorous started to eat them! Then they too were endangered! To Human eyes, this would have been an ecological disaster. It might seem to you that they must have had plenty to eat, but you were not there to see the situation. Many were social and territorial, and didn't travel much. Some of their lands had a delicate balance, and you could slowly watch them destroy much of it. So while they were here (millions of years), the animal life force changed greatly and morphed into something completely different because of them. Today's humans could never have watched this without trying to save something or rebalance something or add something to the situation.

To GAIA, it was "the correct time for many species to leave, based on the evolution at hand." In other words, the dinosaurs were the next step in the process, and their impact was appropriate over the time they were here.

You don't like to hear that humans are the reason for the planet, and their existence should trump all other species. However, this is the case; but here is a large admonition: Let GAIA do the culling out, and not the humans. As the cities are built, and the lands are changed, natural process will occur because of this. Many will say that Human development is NOT a natural process. But in the scope of evolutionary energies and force ... it is.

The beaver has a natural process to dam up streams, robbing water from those who need it downstream. So the question is this: Does the beaver get to have a "natural process," or do you see it as "inappropriate behavior" on the part of the beaver? Is he encroaching on other life, or simply existing normally? What do you think about what happens downstream? What if life is terminated due to it? Do you understand the issue?

The truth is that GAIA sees humanity as the next step, and is allowing the extinction of many species to occur slowly and appropriately because it is time. Now ... keep reading.

THE HUMAN RESPONSIBILITY:

Humanity has the responsibility not to impact the life force of the planet in ways that are not in integrity. If whales are eventually going to disappear (they won't, by the way), it should be because there is a natural response from GAIA and the oceans, and not because humans want their blubber. If forests are to be cut down for cities and homes, then new trees should be planted (as they are in many places). So, there are responsibility issues for resources, and they are to be taken with integrity. So, conservation isn't environmental control. It's conserving naturally existing resources and keeping them clean.

The indigenous never took any more than they needed, and then they honored GAIA in the process. This is a lesson for all. Do not hunt for sport. This does not honor GAIA. Fish for what you and others will eat, and no more. Fish with responsibility for other life. If you don't, again, you will pay the price and you will eventually learn this.

Humans have the responsibility not to contaminate the air they breathe due to greed. Shouldn't that be clear to everyone? To do so is to kill yourselves! Humans should be careful not to pollute their oceans or throw away their waste in ways that trap any animals. This is not part of normal evolution. Instead, it's part of a poor consciousness on the part of the Human Being. As you treat GAIA, it will treat you! Is this really that hard to figure out?

HUMAN INTERVENTION:

As humanity grows and continues to populate the planet, let the species go that are affected. Don't force the issue by trying to save or eliminate anything. You will be surprised how resilient GAIA is and how things work when you do not try to "correct" things you see that seem to be out of balance.

This is difficult for so many environmentalists. For instance: Allow certain forest fires to burn, but protect your homes. The forest is self-balancing, and if you keep the fires from happening, the bugs that cause tree disease will flourish, due to a forest that has become too dense. A forest that is too dense will also burn differently, and not the way it was intended. Listen ... trees grow back, and always have!

Never try to control a seeming imbalance that you think you have caused. You can't! The result will always be more imbalance. Let GAIA do it in its own way. It may take longer, and you may not like what it looks like as nature works the issue, but the admonishment is to let GAIA work the issue. Sometimes things have to reach a critical point and get ugly for you to see the kind of natural balance that will take place. But this is the way of GAIA.

Use your science to create new, more efficient ways to grow and protect crops. This is honored. Don't genetically alter the seeds. You will pay the price, dear ones. Help the crops to grow, using natural methods for insect control and soil replenishment. Don't decide you have a better idea of what the genetics should be. You don't.

Understand that GAIA has a system that has worked for eons, getting ready for YOU. Your logic for nature is primitive compared to what the Earth "knows." If there are too many predators for a certain species, or too many animals eating too many plants ... or too many bad plants that have happened because of something humanity did, or that nature did, try to think differently and let them alone. It may be just the way it needs to be.

Allow death, and even forest destruction due to "too many animals," if need be. For these things will reach a natural balance, even if you think it's a disaster. Let GAIA determine what is appropriate within the balance, for GAIA is the master of the life force of the planet, and has done this over and over.

The thing you need to know is that GAIA is in support of HUMAN life, and will adjust everything around it accordingly. Did you know the weather cycle you are going through right now will eventually replenish the ocean with fish? Stop polluting the water, and it will happen faster. But you did NOT kill the reefs of the planet (as you have been told). They die and rejuvenate on a regular basis! It's mostly accomplished over a long time by water temperature variation (using the water cycle). But the reefs all come back, and so do the fish. Help this along by not interfering and not polluting. This is what we ask of you. Honor species and let them go, even some of the ones you cherish as part of your past. They may have served their purpose, and helped hold the land for you.

The plants and animals are part of the support system of this planet of free choice, and have always played their part in support of YOU, Human Being. They come and go in a system to help you to help Earth become an ascended world in our galaxy. This is the focus, and always has been.

In Closing

If you read this book from the beginning, and have finally arrived at this chapter – congratulations! There has been a substantial amount of information, and there is a lot to absorb and assimilate. One thing should be clear. There is a beautiful system that you are a part of as the magnificent divine Human Being. You are bigger than you think! So what is the point of it all, and how does all this apply to you? What are you going to do with all this knowledge and information? My deepest desire is that you can apply it at a personal level. That you can create a deep level of peace within, no matter what is going on around you. I hope that you can then use this new level of peace, wisdom and knowledge in all of your relationships.

How is your relationship with yourself? Do you talk to your DNA? What about asking it to slow down the aging process? How about telling your cells to skip every second day. How about "mining" your Akash? You can access all the wisdom and information that you hold from all your previous lifetimes. What about your relationship with God? What about your relationship with others? The idea is not to surround yourself with others of like mind, but to shine your light with others. Perhaps those in drama will look at you and see some-thing different. They may even ask you, "*Why don't you have drama in your life?*" How will you respond? What will you say? Some will be ready to hear your answer and others will not. It is up to you to use your own spiritual logic and discernment. To have compassion for those around you, especially the ones that choose to remain in the dark.

Finally, what is your relationship like with Gaia? You don't need to be constantly immersed in nature doing ceremony and giving gifts. What about starting with acknowledging Gaia as part of your life? What about saying, "*Thank you, Gaia,*" when you see beautiful flowers in a vase? You may like to give gratitude and appreciation to Gaia for the abundance of food she provides. If you give continual gratitude

and appreciation to Gaia with an open heart, I'm pretty sure you will start hearing Gaia respond. Her response to me is that she is here in loving service to humanity. I now realize why I get so excited when I see plants, animals and landscapes. I'm looking at an entangled piece of myself.

I would like to end this book with some profound words from Kryon about Gaia, and how she relates to us, and the rest of the Universe:

Do you see the profundity of the system? Look at what it is about. It's about you. All of it. Why would the Earth be designed so intelligently to keep track of you, to honor you, to know who you are and the spiritual name you have? Why would that be, unless you were important, unless you were part of the master plan, unless you had something to do with the Universe's future. Think about it. That's the system. I won't be the only one to channel this information to you. There are others who've never heard these words, who will tell you the same thing. If you get a chance, you might even ask Gaia, and she'll tell you the same thing.

Gaia exists for the sacred Human Beings who are on this planet in lesson. I give you this in love today. I want you to think about something. Everywhere you walk, you're known by the Earth. What a system! Why do I give this to you today? It's so that you continue to feel loved and cared for. It's so you know there's a hand-holding going on between Spirit and you and Gaia, if you want it. There are so many things here for you if you want them. Old soul, you sit here for a purpose. Maybe you needed to hear this today. Important you are, precious you are, and a master you are. Now go claim it. Live a long time. Be joyful in the process. Don't make up your mind what's supposed to happen. The worst thing you can do is predispose what God has for you based upon what you think is happening now. Instead, relax, be joyful in all things, and fall in love with yourself.

Leave this place differently than you came.

I am Kryon, lover of humanity – for a good reason.

And so it is.

Kryon live channelling "The Akashic System"
given in Syracuse, New York – September 11, 2011

ABOUT THE AUTHOR

Monika Muranyi has always had a deep affinity and connection with our planet Earth. She has a Bachelor of Applied Science degree with Honors, obtained at Southern Cross University, New South Wales, Australia. Monika has worked in various national parks within Australia and New Zealand for over fifteen years. She is an accredited Electro Magnetic Field (EMF) Balancing Technique™ Practitioner (Phases I to XIII). Her passion also includes photography. Many of her photographs can be seen on Lee Carroll's website, as well as her own:

www.kryon.com and *www.monikamuranyi.com*

Monika has carefully researched the information within this book, and travelled to many places to discover what Gaia and humanity has to say. Some of the places where she has travelled include: Australia, New Zealand, United States, Chile, Argentina, Brazil, Uruguay, Bolivia, Peru, Ecuador, Colombia, Venezuela, Mexico, Hawaii, Russia, Ukraine, Poland, Bulgaria, Hungary, Switzerland, Spain and Portugal. Monika has also participated in several indigenous ceremonies with Shamans in Peru, Chile, Mexico, and with a Kahuna High Priestess in Hawaii.

The inspiration to write and produce this book came when she was living in Santiago, Chile – a place that vibrates strongly with the Kundalini energy of the Earth! Additional material can be found on Monika's website under the "Extras" heading.

Ariane Books, titles of related interest:

The Human Akash
A discovery of the blueprint within
Authors: Monika Muranyi, Kryon
ISBN: 978-2-89626-173-4

Have you ever wondered where your personality comes from? What about your fears and phobias? What creates a child prodigy? Is it possible that you have lived before? The answer to these questions and more is the purpose of this book.

Australian author, Monika Muranyi, has compiled everything that Kryon has ever channelled about the Akash! For over twenty-four years the loving messages of Kryon, as given by Lee Carroll (the original Kryon channel) have become known world-wide. This book, second in the Kryon trilogy series, represents an amazing job of research that covers in detail the elusive information within your Akash and includes material never before been published by Kryon. In addition, she has posed over thirty new questions answered by Kryon. Thanks to her work we now have a greater understanding about the Human Akash, where it is, what it contains and how it can be mined.

See Monika Muranyi interviewed by Lee Carroll on our video section (http://ariane-books.com/videos/)

This title is also available in ebook version.

The Great Human Potential: Walking in One's Own Light
Authors: Wendy Kennedy, Tom Kenyon
Edited by Martine Vallée
ISBN: 978-2-89626-133-8

The information that is shared in this book is what we consider the most appropriate vibrational match for where you are right now. When we give information, we always look at the vibrational level of the majority of whom we think will be reading this. We do this to give you a version of the truth that will best serve you in accessing your highest potential.

We are truly excited for you as you embark on this journey. This window in time is rife with amazing potential that is only limited by your imagination. The greatest challenge for you will be to release the constraints of your past beliefs and judgments and know that all things are possible. *That is what ascension is all about.*

Despite negative aspects, games or manipulation, when you recognize that you are a creator being, you can change your version of reality. And when enough of you decide that you want a different version of reality, then a brand new timeline is created, followed by a change in current events, all leading to a brand new world.

So, there is only one thing left to do: dream your most beautiful dream!

This title is also available in ebook version.

We hope you enjoyed this book.
If you'd like to receive our online catalogue featuring additional information on Ariane Books and products, or if you'd like to find out
more about the Ariane Editions,
please contact:

Ariane Éditions Inc.
1217, avenue Bernard O., office 101, Outremont,
Quebec, Canada H2V 1V7
Tel.: (1) 514-276-2949, Fax.: (1) 514-276-4121
info@editions-ariane.com

www.ariane-books.com

KU-446-043

PROPERTY SERIES

House Buying, Selling and Conveyancing

Joseph Bradshaw

**Revised and updated by
Georgia Bedworth, barrister**

Bromley Libraries

30128 80049 096 6

House Buying, Selling and Conveyancing by Joseph Bradshaw

Revised and updated by Georgia Bedworth, barrister.

Lawpack Publishing Limited
76–89 Alscot Road
London SE1 3AW

www.lawpack.co.uk

First edition 1999
Second edition 2001
Third edition 2003
Fourth edition 2004
Fifth edition 2006
Sixth edition 2010

© 2010 Lawpack Publishing

Land Registry forms, official copy registry and title plan are Crown copyright and are reproduced with the kind permission of Land Registry.

ISBN: 9781906971809
ebook ISBN: 9781906971458

Mixed Sources

Product group from well-managed
forests and other controlled sources
www.fsc.org Cert no. SGS-COC-003985
© 1996 Forest Stewardship Council

FSC

All rights reserved.

This book is for use in England or Wales; it is not suitable for use in Scotland or Northern Ireland. The information it contains has been carefully compiled, but its accuracy is not guaranteed, as laws and regulations may change or be subject to differing interpretations.The law is stated as at 1 October 2010.

Exclusion of Liability and Disclaimer

While every effort has been made to ensure that this Lawpack publication provides accurate and expert guidance, it is impossible to predict all the circumstances in which it may be used. Accordingly, neither the publisher, author, retailer, nor any other suppliers shall be liable to any person or entity with respect to any loss or damage caused or alleged to be caused by the information contained in or omitted from this Lawpack publication.

For convenience (and for no other reason) 'him', 'he' and 'his' have been used throughout and should be read to include 'her', 'she' and 'her'.

Contents

About the author   vi
Introduction   vii

1 Buying   1
   Damp   4
   Electrics   9
   Decorations   9
   Plumbing   10
   Surveys   11
      CML *Handbook*   15
   Seven good questions   16

2 New houses   19
   First-time buyers   21
   Last-time buyers   21
   Part exchange   23

3 Sell first or buy first?   25

4 Estate agency   27
   Estate agents say they...   28
   Now for the facts...   28
      Middlemen   32

5 The moneylenders   33
   Bridging loans   33
   House exchanges   34
   Mortgages   34

6 No agents, please!   37
   Why private vendors win   37

7 Selling   41
   Marketing your house – what you must do first   41
   Fixtures and fittings: what is included?   41

Valuations are easy: use comparisons 43
Window dressing 46
Modernisation 46
Decorations 47
The hall 48
Central heating 48
Gates, fences and paths 48
Gardens 49
The front door 49
Ventilation 50
House names 50
For Sale boards 50
How to put up your own For Sale board 51
Advertising 52
The copy: composing your advertisement 53
The wording: what to put on; what to leave out 55
Photographs 56
Instructions to printers 56
There is a buyer for everything 57
Particulars 59
Photographs 60
Drafting 60
Disclaimers 61
Showing them round 62
How to negotiate 66
The opening from a serious prospect 66
Bargaining points 67
Anglers need patience 68
To sum up 70
What to say when a buyer says 'I will' 70
Never say die 71

8   Contracts 73

9   Gazumping and gazoffing 85
The cure 87
How to prepare the 'legal' side of your sale 89
Not STC, but CST (subject to contract, contract subject to) 90

10 The Registers 93
Possessory title 100

11 Introducing conveyancing for laypeople   109
Selling a registered house   110

**12 Conveyancing: the sale and purchase of a registered
house**   119
Planning for completion   152
    Cash buyers   156
    Builders   158
    Delays   159
**13 Conveyancing: the sale and purchase of an unregistered
house**   161
Overview   161
Looking more closely at the deeds   163

14 Matrimonial homes   185

15 Flats   189
What are the terms of the lease?   190
    Service charges   190
    Consents to assignment/subletting   192
    Breaches of covenant   192
    'Share of freehold'   193

16 Commonhold   195

17 Tricks of the trade for layperson conveyancing   197
Buying at auction   200

Postscript   203
Glossary   205
Appendices   211
Index   259

About the author

Joseph Bradshaw was an estate agent and mortgage broker who came to prominence in the 1980s when, from their garage and kitchen, he and his wife Margaret published a series of his books on DIY conveyancing.

With his unique sense of humour and tub-thumping message to homeowners about doing things themselves, his books gained wide press coverage and sales were phenomenal. Bradshaw's *Guide to House Buying Selling and Conveyancing* made headlines in newspapers and magazines, ranging from the *Financial Times* to *Gardener's Weekly*. Among the many accolades he earned, his favourite was 'the guru of layperson conveyancing' from the Legal Correspondent of *The Times*. This new Lawpack edition is an updated version of Joe Bradshaw's original.

Introduction

It isn't true that only those who have gone through a long, expensive and involved training can possibly understand the intricacies of house buying, selling and conveyancing.

Traditionally, trained and qualified solicitors have done conveyancing. A nineteenth-century government, grateful for their support in collecting some taxes, gave them a legal monopoly of conveyancing for a fee. This can also be done by licensed conveyancers. That leaves doing a conveyance for no fee, which means that you can do a conveyance for yourself or anyone else for whom you wish to do a favour. The principal skills required are reading, writing and an ability to count your money.

People do far more for themselves than ever before. From painting and decorating to car maintenance, people are having a go themselves. And it isn't only practical things that are tackled.

A few years ago, the technicalities for obtaining a divorce were simplified and a little later the government withdrew the provision of legal aid for parties to divorces that were not defended and where there is no ancillary relief or issues with children. The increasing popularity of divorce and the level of solicitors' fees for doing the transaction have between them produced thousands of do-it-yourself divorcees, who have done their own divorces, and saved themselves over £500 by expending a little time and effort. Moreover, during the process of doing their own divorces, people have found that what hitherto they thought was a thoroughly legal process is only judicial in so far as a judge has to give a nod over their papers, and all the rest is an administrative matter.

Often, housing transactions have little to do with the law. Nowadays, transferring a house from one owner to another is done, in most of England and Wales, by filling in simple forms – that is the legal side of it.

The bit that can be complicated is when you are using money from the sale of one house to pay for the purchase of another. But that is not a legal problem; it's a business transaction. You don't hare off to a lawyer when you are trading upmarket from a Bentley to a Rolls; settling the Hire Purchase on one and taking out a new loan on the other. In most straightforward cases, you no more need to know the relevant Acts of Parliament inside out when you buy a house than you need to know the Road Traffic and Consumer Credit Acts when buying or selling a car. Whether it's a house or car that is being dealt with, you need to know about honesty and fair dealing and if you meet up with someone who sells you an unroadworthy car or seriously misrepresents a property to you, the laws are there to punish the offender and obtain compensation; it's then that you really need a lawyer – a good one.

Just because you might have a legal remedy against wrongdoers, this doesn't mean to say you should not be prudent within your competence. If you are considering buying a car that has done a fair mileage, you put it through some stringent tests, and if you are not sure about it, but are still interested, at a price, you get a qualified mechanic to give you a report on it. If you want to make sure there is no Hire Purchase on it, go to the local Citizens Advice Bureau (don't ring, there's a form to fill in) and for little more than the cost of a stamp they will check it out for you. So there you are, the legal owner of a bigger and better car, and you need know no more law at the end of the transaction than at the beginning. But look at what you have accomplished: you have satisfied yourself that the car is what it's cracked up to be and checked that the person offering it for sale owns (has good title to) it. 'Ah!' you say, 'houses are not like cars. Surely it's more complicated, and doesn't the rule *caveat emptor* (let the buyer beware) apply in full force to a housing transaction? Isn't the whole business a splendid opportunity for scoundrels to practise their wicked ways?'

My answer is: certainly houses are not like cars. Cars can be stolen, repainted, engine and number plates swapped. You can't very well shift a whole house. As for 'let the buyer beware', in its application to housing it's, in the main, a reference to the purchaser making sure that the vendor has good title (can prove he owns and has the power to sell) and as you will learn from these pages, you obtain this assurance by sending a simple form (no fee payable) to the Land Registry. Other potential flies in the ointment can also be discovered from the Land Registry entries.

Most Land Registry forms mentioned can be found on the Land Registry website, www.landregistry.gov.uk, where they can be filled out and printed off (but, currently, not saved, so check before printing), others from law stationers, still others from HM Revenue & Customs Stamp Office (www.hmrc.gov.uk/so).

If, when you last bought a house, any precautions were taken to make sure that you did get vacant possession before the money was handed over (and vice versa when you sold), the odds are that it was you who did the legwork. Solicitors rely on the general law, together with the basic honesty of the absolute majority of house owners on these practical points. On the legal point of proving ownership, where the ownership is registered, they rely on the state-backed guarantee provided by Her Majesty's Land Registry. I invite you to do the same.

HM Land Registry was established at the end of the nineteenth century, the Land Transfer Act which set it up having finally made its way through Parliament after centuries of attempts had failed. If you read what the sponsors of the Act had to say in its support, you will see that they intended to make dealing in land as simple as dealing in, to use their nineteenth-century words, 'stock and chattels'. To that end the Land Registry was established, and of course someone has to pay for its upkeep. Who better than those who benefit. The public? Today, the buyer of the average house pays nearly a hundred pounds to the Registry – but who has had the dealing simplified for him? The lawyer.

Since 1984, governments have laboured mightily to bring about competition in the conveyancing business. According to the Council for Licensed Conveyancers there are now approximately 750 licensed conveyancers in the UK (including both fully and limited licensed) to compete with more than 38,000 lawyers. So throughout we will refer to fee-taking conveyancers as solicitors, under the generic surname of Skinner.

I have done my own little survey. I put this question, 'What do you think a solicitor does for you that you could not do for yourself?' Invariably the answer is, 'All those searches'. This answer is usually spoken with such reverential awe, it seems that ordinary trusting people have come to believe that every time they buy a house their solicitor has worked his way through reference after reference, file after file, and book after book in office after office and cellar after cellar, emerging with the scrolls into the light of day, covered in dust and with a cold wet towel round his head.

In reality, the searching consists in sending off a few forms, which have ready-printed questions, to the authorities who answer them for you. If you really find this difficult to believe, at least have a look at the said forms. When you see them, I am sure you will agree that of all the forms you have ever had the misfortune to struggle with, those used in housing transactions suffer least from officialese and gobbledegook. If you have already bought or sold a house, you will have found that the only thing about the whole transaction which struck you as truly professional was the sheer size of the bill at the end of it. It doesn't matter whether your conveyance was done by qualified solicitors or their clerks, you got the same job done and the same bill.

Another thing that really seemed to puzzle the respondents to my survey was: how did one manage to use the money from the sale of Flitsville for the purchase of Newsville, when it's well known that you actually have to flit from Flitsville before you get your money for it? As you will learn, it can be done when you can get all the parties or their representatives together at the same time. But where that is not possible it's done by the simple expedient of taking a bridging loan for a few days. The interest is up to three per cent over base rate, as well as an arrangement fee on the loan. At present the base rate is low but could rise. It may be a practical possibility increasingly in the current difficulties with the housing market. To bridge a day, you can even leave your furniture in the van overnight and get bed and breakfast somewhere. Because those who cut out estate agents can choose their own buyers and control the pace, they seldom need a bridging loan.

The high costs of moving house do deter many people from changing their abode, particularly those people with young growing families. The older end, having seen it all before, cannot face the anxieties generated by the selling and conveyancing system. To them, the opportunity to do their own and cut out the middlemen has proved a godsend.

Over the years I have, as a property owner, conveyed shops, offices, houses and the like for myself – nothing has ever gone wrong. Never have I regretted my choice, and neither have I ever met any other person who does his own conveyancing who has any regrets. Sorting out the problems that house buyers and sellers have has convinced me that it would have been far better for many of them had they tackled the job themselves from the beginning.

Transferring property is nowhere near as difficult as it has been made out to be, but that doesn't mean to say that the technical work can be done by a two-year-old chimpanzee suffering from brain damage. If in a few of the pages that follow it seems rather complicated, take courage and keep going, remembering it's all new to you.

Though it's hoped that this book makes an interesting and useful read in itself, it's intended to be kept at the learner estate agent's and conveyancer's elbow for reference as he picks his way through buying and selling and conveyancing for himself.

On the way he will notice that strategies and tactics are given so that purchasers pay less and vendors get more. This inherent paradox can only make life more interesting all round where both vendor and purchaser have invested in the book. So if you spot from your opposite number's tactics a fellow reader, keep the knowledge to yourself, turn back to the book and check up on how to cope. Why let the professionals have all the fun? Do the job yourself and take a pride in it!

A word about forms

One word of warning regarding form numbers, which this book refers to frequently. These numbers come from a variety of sources. All Land Registry forms and Land Charges Department forms are numbered by the Land Registry and the numbers are used by all law form publishers. The same principle applies to HM Revenue & Customs forms. There are also forms which are produced by commercial firms that use the name and number of the originating party, such as the local search forms.

However, other forms are given their number by the publisher of the form and, frequently, different publishers use different numbers. Plus, over the years solicitors have got used to using general conveyancing expressions. For example, 'preliminary enquiries' and 'Enquiries before Contract' are the questions to be asked in writing before exchange of contracts; the publishers will name and number them according to their own preference. So when asked to answer preliminary enquiries if you are selling, don't be surprised to find that the form has a different name. In the old days, the buyer's solicitors sent these to the seller's lawyers; they still do if they don't accept the Seller's Property Information Forms.

The various Property Information Forms. These were introduced in an attempt by the legal profession to create a seller's property information pack and the idea was that the seller's solicitors would complete and send these to the buyer or his solicitors, along with a local search, draft contract, title information and so on. These forms have generally been replaced by standard Property Information Forms, which are used in most residential conveyancing transactions. These forms are available online.

Don't be surprised to find that when you sell your home you may be asked to volunteer replies to the Property Information Forms, or you may be sent the buyer's solicitors' preferred version of preliminary enquiries. When you buy your new house, don't be surprised if you are sent replies to Property Information Forms, or are invited to send in your preliminary enquiries. This confusion simply represents the distinction between solicitors who prefer the old way and those who prefer the new.

A similar confusion in names and numbers applies to the Requisitions on Title, questions posted by the buyer to the seller's solicitors after contracts have been exchanged.

CHAPTER 1

Buying

First of all, you must find something to view. Answering estate agents' and private vendors' advertisements in local papers is one obvious way, and touring round finding 'For Sale' boards is another. In many gated developments which ban 'For Sale' boards this is not much use! But there are also the not so obvious, such as placing your own advertisements in newspapers or on websites such as www.gumtree.com and even shop windows in the locality you have decided is the one for you. There is also the direct approach of knocking on doors and asking 'Is this house for sale?' to which you might be lucky enough to get the answer, 'No, but that one over there is.' In any case, such an approach can often lead to a useful conversation about the area and its qualities and problems.

The internet is now the buyer's best friend when it comes to searching for property to purchase. Websites such as www.findaproperty.com, www.propertyfinder.com, www.zoopla.co.uk and www.gumtree.com, to name but a few, have made the process of finding a property that you want to buy even easier. These websites contain flexible search engines which allow you to search in your chosen area, even if it's many miles away from where you currently live.

When you have viewed a number of houses within a short period of time it's sometimes, at the end of the day, difficult to remember which had what – the address alone is not always sufficient to bring the memories flooding back. So try to pick on some salient feature – the more ridiculous the better, such as 'the one with the surly butler', 'the one with the circular pink mirrors on the bathroom walls', 'the one to suit mother-in-law', etc., and make a note accordingly on the particulars if you have got some from an agent. Why not take your camera (though the owners might think you are a burglar's agent, or worse a reporter!)? Remember, when viewing property to which you have been introduced by an agent, that he gets his commission from the vendor – he owes very little, if any, duty to a purchaser. The higher the price he gets for the vendor, the more his commission, but he's got to be a bit of a dullard if the only reason he is sticking out for the extra couple of hundred pounds is because it will push his commission from £500 to £505.

Having found a house to view your main consideration is: can I make a home here? I suggest that there are two additional criteria to which you should pay attention. The first is already at the back of your mind: is it structurally sound? The second sounds a bit daft when you haven't yet bought, but old hands who have often been moved up, down and across the country for one reason or another will testify to its importance: will it be easy to sell if ever I need to move? We will look at each in turn.

Whether you can make a home in the house you are about to view is a highly personal question. Nevertheless, there are a few points that are common to many people. For instance, if you are getting on in years you have to consider whether children screaming at all times of the day and night are easily tolerated. Even if you are young, you might well find other people's kids too much to bear. A new, neat and tidy development where there is just a bunch of nice newly married couples but very few children is no guarantee of a quiet life for those who want one. Noisy, late-finishing house-warmings, followed by every conceivable sort of party, followed by slamming of car doors can disturb the sleep just as effectively as the screaming children the newly weds will soon produce!

If you are buying a semi or terrace (town/mews/cottage-style) house, get to know as much as you can about who will be doing what at the other side of that joint and party wall, and if the vendors have the television, radio or CD player going full blast when you call, have it switched off and listen. When there are neighbours' drives that you look out over, try to make sure there will not be a boat or caravan blocking your view.

Vendors who insist on viewing 'strictly by appointment' often do so because they want to manipulate the situation – for example, if they have at one side a neighbour who takes his bagpipe band off every weekend in his caravan, while the young mariner at the other takes his boat and yapping dog away at the same time, who can blame such a vendor for insisting on weekend viewing? And it's a certainty that any vendor, if questioned, will only vouchsafe that the neighbours are quiet people who keep themselves to themselves, but are of sterling worth if called upon in a crisis. And if he thinks you have an inkling that a band next door is trying to perfect its line-up and gets it all together on Mondays, Wednesdays and Thursdays, he will laugh that off with: 'Oh, it's quite lively, we quite enjoy it – keeps us young, you know. Actually, we've heard that they are splitting up – pity, really.'

If vendors don't mention why they want to sell and where they are moving to, ASK! If the answer doesn't have the ring of truth, you have been warned.

If you are a non-gardener or simply can't find the time for Britain's major hobby, don't be persuaded to buy just because the garden looks so well established, so neat and tidy already, and appears to need only a minimum of maintenance. All gardens need constant attention if they are to look as though they need no attention. A shower of rain just after you have viewed can germinate a thousand weeds.

Any objection from any member of your family should be listened to before you finally decide. Teenagers might say of an open-plan house that there is nowhere for them to go. Open-plan houses seem to suit the very young and the very old, but situations near rivers don't suit either. They are too wet for non-swimmers and too damp for the arthritic.

Before you go out viewing, it's a good idea to get into your head what hectares, yards, feet and metres look like. When told a room is 20 feet by 14 feet or 6 metres by 3 metres, can you visualise it in your mind? Is the bath at your present abode of such a size that you can enjoy a long, lazy soak in it? Whether it is or not, measure it, and use the size as a comparison. Will your furniture fit? If it will, fine. If it won't, then you have to choose – furniture or house.

Having made your first visit during the week, make your second at the weekend (or vice versa), so as to get a different perspective of the neighbours and the neighbourhood. Park your car some distance away and walk – you will see a lot more of the district that way.

With a bit of luck, there will be heavy rain before you move in, so while you're around, look for damp, and you never know, there might have been a burst pipe or a fire to ruin the decorations. Even if contracts are signed you may still say, 'You didn't tell me about this lot. To be fair you must put it right', but that very much depends on the contract, as you will see from chapter 8.

You are not really entitled to make these subsequent visits (but why should the sellers object?), and maybe the first thing you must really persuade yourself of is that though you are going to the house to poke around in somebody else's private domain, you must not be embarrassed about it. The vendors knew you and others were likely to do this from the moment they thought about putting the house on the market, and they have had ample time and opportunity to hide any dirty linen and to empty the cupboard of skeletons.

A lot can be learned while walking up the path. A gate that is falling to bits isn't a very good introduction. Is the path itself cracking and subsiding? Is the drive likely to help or hinder when you have a flat battery? Will icing cause problems in the winter? Can you see any cracks in the stucco or brickwork? If there is a lot of zig-zag cracking around the windows and doors, they are signs of old or new subsidence. If the cracks have been filled in some time ago and have not re-appeared, all is no doubt well.

All houses subside a little after being built and it usually expresses itself in no more than cracked plaster. But if the cracks have been filled and parted again, or, worse still, bricks have cracked vertically, there is real trouble, as there is if a wall is starting to lean or taking on the shape of a saucer. You don't need to start digging around the foundations or paying a surveyor to do so to know that this one is not for you – unless it can be bought for the price of the land.

While still walking slowly up the garden path, have your first look at the downpipes, roof and chimney if there is one. Have another look up from the back garden later, and if it's a tall house bring along your binoculars so that you can inspect the chimney stack and pot. A swift look at the TV aerials in the vicinity will tell you about TV reception. If there are a lot of tall fancy ones about, reception is likely to be poor.

Damp

Once again, you are looking to see if the structure is doing the thing that a house is supposed to do: shelter you from the elements. Damp is the indicator of most structural problems in a house. Water tries to get in from the top, ends, sides and bottom. As if that were not enough, we bring it in via pipes, and builders use thousands of gallons of water in the building of a house. Houses are built of such things as bricks, mortar and wood, all of which are porous, and the soil in Britain seldom dries out, so the fabric of a British house is always damp to some extent. It's when that dampness passes an unacceptable level that things begin to rot and owners have to start paying out.

Blocked, overflowing gutters and cracked downpipes can be a source of water which will penetrate in sideways, as also can badly pointed chimney stacks. Driving rain can find its way in through cracks around doors and windows. Otherwise, sideways penetration of water is very rare as modern houses are almost certainly constructed with two outside walls roughly two inches apart and pinned together by metal wires or straps. The two-inch gap, called a cavity, forms an insulation barrier ensuring that water can penetrate only as far as the cavity and no further. However, in the building process careless builders have been known to drop mortar down the cavity and allow it to accumulate on the ties.

In this case the mortar build-up can form a bridge to convey water from the outer to the inner wall. If you are buying a house in the course of construction, take your torch to have a look and tell the foremen if you find his brickies are laying up problems, as well as bricks, for the future. Once a house is completed and there is no internal evidence of damp from this cause you can be pretty sure there is none. If you really want to be sure, there is only one way to find out and this applies to much else – take the house down brick by brick!

In all modern, indeed in nearly all, houses, there will be a damp-proof course. This is needed because the ground in Great Britain is nearly always damp, the brickwork in the foundations will soak it up, and it will quickly spread round the house. A damp-proof course is a water-tight skin of some sort.

The old system was to set slates on the third or fourth brick course above the ground, and below the level of the floor joists. Slate doesn't bend and the slight movements of a house can, over time, fracture parts of the slate course. For many years now, builders have used mineral felt or plastic sheet, both of which are flexible and can cope with anything but a really radical structural movement. What it can't cope with is the owner who piles soil up against the wall to a height above the course.

Count to the third or fourth course of bricks and you will see the slate or black, bituminous material protruding a little somewhere along the line. Once you have found the height follow the line right round the house to see if your vendor has been silly. If he has, pay really particular attention to the plaster, skirting board and any other woodwork on the opposite side of that patch inside the house and give general attention to the whole of the ground floor woodwork if there are wooden floors, because damp does spread. If no real damage has been done, removal of the offending material from the outside wall is imperative. This done, check to make sure that the air bricks are clear and if the damp is only slight it will soon disappear.

What can be done when the damp course is damaged or the house was built without one? You could get a builder to go round the house knocking out a brick at a time and inserting a damp course as he goes. It might work – it will certainly be expensive. There are firms who specialise in various, what can loosely be described as, 'patent systems'. You can find them in the *Yellow Pages* and they will usually give a free estimate. Some of these systems have a good success rate. Most firms will give some sort of long guarantee. And here it's worth making a point about 10-, 20-, 30-year or even lifetime guarantees and it's this: it's easy for the firm to give the guarantee, but who will guarantee that the firm will still be in business if ever you need them?

So that's the base and sides dealt with; what about the roof? The most common form of construction for residential property is a pitched roof, covered with either slates or tiles. It's often difficult to gain access to roof space, but if you have any doubts about the construction, it's best to cope with the difficulty now. In the case of an old house, it's reasonable to assume that any fault in the construction itself will have developed already and your external examination will have told you whether the roof is bowing or not. If it is and has been bowed or buckled for a number of years and there is no internal evidence of damp, it's probably all right. However, if you decide to have a look in the roof space, take a good torch with you but keep switching it off to see if any daylight is coming in because of missing, broken or drifting slates or tiles. While you are up there you can check on insulation of ceiling, tanks and pipes, and if there is none or it isn't done up to modern standards, you have found another bargaining point or two.

Recent decorations can provide internal evidence of damp. Vendors do titivate their houses up ready for sale; and they also, sometimes, do it to cover up evidence. If you suspect this has happened, see if you can borrow a damp meter from your friendly DIY shop, but be careful that you are not tracing the run of a water pipe or drain and mistaking it for damp. The instructions that come with the meter will tell you about all that.

Flat roofs need special attention. If a pitched roof covered in slate or tile goes wrong, the replacement of a few slates or tiles will, more often than not, solve the problem. But the only remedy for a badly damaged flat roof is often the complete replacement of the covering. The most usual coverings are lead, asphalt roofing felt and sometimes zinc, and it's important that roofs be laid to a proper fall so that water doesn't gather in any depressions. If you can see any such pools, then trouble is on its way – sooner or later.

As the covering is exposed to heat in one season and cold in another and sometimes both on the same day, and its expansion and contraction rate is not equal to the boards on which it's laid, you can often see the skeleton impression of the boarding showing through the covering. Now, that boarding should run at right angles to the gutter; if it's parallel to the gutter, water will gather in the depressions, which will have nothing on the depression that will settle over you when you get the builder's quotation (avoid estimates) for the repairs. Felt roofs last about ten years, asphalt up to 30 years. Evidence of downward damp can be seen on ceilings, upstairs walls and chimney breasts. The fault can often be located and dealt with by climbing a ladder and cleaning out the gutter. Where there are stains all round the upper walls, unless you are getting a real bargain, it might be as well to try elsewhere.

It's not always easy to examine floors, particularly when they are covered with lino or carpets. A vendor refusing to let you have a careful look might give grounds for suspecting his: 'Oh, the floors are all right, you can take my word for it.' It's particularly desirable to have a thorough examination made if there are any indications of springiness, such as ornaments rattling, when you walk across the floor, or you suspect that it's rotting joists that are allowing the floor to part company from the skirting board. The floor into a bay window is the favourite place for the rot to set in and by an outside door is runner up. If your vendor tells you that you can have every confidence in it, ask him to jump up and down on it for a while; after all, he knows the way round his cellars better than you do.

Timbers can be affected by dry rot, wet rot, beetle or woodworm. Dry rot is insidious. It's a fungus and it glories in finding a bit of damp wood to set up business in. It gets down between the fibres of wood and dries the wood out. Dry-rotted wood looks as if it has been dehydrated to a brown cracked appearance and crumbles to dust at a touch when in an advanced stage of development. Unfortunately, the damage is well under way before there is any external manifestation of it as mentioned above. But the conditions under which it thrives can be spotted: damp, smelly, unventilated corners.

Wet rot gets going when the wood becomes so saturated that the fibres break apart, weakening the wood. It tends to happen at the end of timbers (hence the attention to skirting board gaps) where water can get in between fibres, but of course, it can occur elsewhere; around sink, bath and WC wastes are likely areas. Depending on how far the wet rot has gone it can be cured, often quite inexpensively, by replacing the rotted timber and rectifying the fault that caused it. Take a strong torch with you into the cellar (if there is one), because the floor joists are more likely than not to be nicely exposed for your inspection. Poke around with a strong penknife – if you can slide it into the wood at right angles to the run of the grain you've found something.

The third ill that can affect timbers is beetles or woodworm. Woodworm is the caterpillar of the beetle. The flying beetle alights and injects her egg into timber and flies away until she is ready for a repeat performance. The egg develops into a worm which, feeding on the life-giving juices of the timber, transforms itself into a beetle in the image of its mother, and burrows out into the light of day leaving behind it a tunnel in the wood and a little pile of sawdust beside it. Which all goes to show that if you simply go round, no matter how meticulously, squirting things into the worm holes, you can't be sure you have got all the little beggars; that is why you need a specialist firm in to say whether the beetle is still active, and if it is, to give you a quote for pressure spraying the timbers.

To find out if the worm has been active enough to cause real danger, the penknife test is used. As with the wet and dry rot, badly affected timber can be replaced and your decision must be based on the amount of repair required; so if you find evidence of wood rot of any kind, call in one of the specialist firms who will give you a quotation and offer a guarantee. If the problems have been discovered early enough the cost need not be ruinous.

There are a lot of solid floors about nowadays, so if such a floor has parted from the skirting board the supporting fill has rearranged itself and that is why settlement has taken place – it can be rectified, but make sure there is no zig-zagging on the outer wall because in that case the foundations might be rearranging themselves too.

Electrics

Another point to cover is the electrical system. A sure sign of wiring that has had its day is the plug with round pins. The whole house needs re-wiring. In older houses during your inspections of the roof space and cellar, look out for any wires that pass across the joists. If you see two element wires twisted together and festooned along you can be pretty sure some re-wiring is necessary to bring the electrical system up to modern standards of efficiency, and, above all, safety.

Some electricity companies will be only too glad to make a visual inspection without charge and they will give a free quotation for any work required. If for any reason the supply is cut off, as it no doubt will be, if there is to be any gap between the time when the vendor leaves and you move in, no re-connection will be made if the whole system is not up to standard.

You should also be aware of recent changes to building regulations which require any recent changes to electrics to have been carried out by a qualified electrician. If you spot any new wiring, this might be something to keep in reserve to ask when it comes to Enquiries before Contract. If the work was done after January 2005, the vendor should have a certificate to prove that it complies with the regulations.

Decorations

Decorations can cover a multitude of sins, and are, of course, like sin, a matter of personal preference. Costs of decorating can be high particularly if you have tall ceilings, with fancy cornices or moulding. The rooms might look immaculate but always take the precaution of lifting a picture off the wall to find out if pale patches will remain when the vendor has gone. Incidentally, whether you redecorate because you dislike the colour scheme or because the place is a dirty tip, the cost will be pretty much the same, although if the wallpaper is already peeling off it might be cheaper!

Plumbing

We've dealt with unwanted water getting into the house and causing damp – now we will have a look at the water that we do want in the house. If you are to get your water from a well, you will need someone to tell you if the well is sufficiently deep to avoid pollution of the water by any drains that might be or become defective. A well must also be situated at a reasonable distance from any possible source of contamination. In fact, before you go any further, a few words with the local authorities would be in order – they might already know the situation and have costly plans for the owner or his successor.

Find the tap at the highest point and try the pressure. Also try the hot water pressure to the bath – you don't want to wait all day for the bath to fill. Neither do you want to spend all day pulling on the WC plunger, so drop a piece of paper into the pan and see if you can send it on its way with one shot, and while you are about it note if the pan or the washbasin is cracked.

When you walk round the garden and find a portion that is squelchy or there is an ominous line of subsidence in the driveway it might be that the vendor is a bit of a stinker and is not levelling with you. However, you can square him up by getting a firm in to test the drains. If they use the water pressure system, they could cause damage so get the vendor's written permission first – as a matter of fact, if the firm has anything about them they will have a standard form intended to indemnify themselves, so have a word with them to make sure it isn't amended to land you in the …

I would like to instruct vendors not to read the next paragraph, but if they can't resist reading I implore them not to draw any guidelines from it to help them with their sales!

Central heating systems need examining. Ask to see last year's receipts for the fuel used. If it's a system such as gas, ask if it has been regularly serviced. Find a radiator at the highest point in the house and as you turn the air-release screw hold a lighted match to it. If you set up a lighted gas jet it isn't because gas has got into the system; it's the product of some corrosion that has started. It might only need some anti-corrosion fluid putting in the system – on the other hand that might not be sufficient. In any case, all the more reason to have a careful look round for leaks particularly at joints. Leaks also tend to make nasty stains on carpets.

If you remember most of the tips given above, a vendor will not notice how much you are noticing. A glance takes in that the electric socket on the skirting board has square holes, and the same glance tells you that the floor is well up to the skirting board, and as you walk over to the bay to admire the view your ears tell you that the presents from Blackpool and Malaga on the sideboard are not doing a clog dance accompanied by castanets. And while you are admiring the view, you might as well test the window to see if it opens.

Surveys

There might seem to be a lot to look at, but houses are big things and cost big money. You can't expect to get satisfaction if you buy one with the same nonchalance as when you buy a new light bulb.

Can you rely on a lender's surveyor's report thinking: 'Well, he will tell me if there is anything wrong with it'? Well, he will and he won't. His job is to tell the building society whether the land and buildings thereon (as the saying goes) is good enough security for the money they are thinking of lending you to assist you in your purchase. He has no obligation to you although he does owe you a duty of care; he will not stick his neck out telling you that the structure is perfectly sound, but you can be sure that he will let the building society know if the foundations or the roof are in danger of collapse, and that whereas they think they are getting a desirable residence as security, there is the distinct probability that in a year's time all that would be left for them to get their money back on would be a plot of land covered in rubble. (Incidentally, it doesn't necessarily work quite like that. When a borrower defaults, the building society does take and sell the property. In the extremely rare case where they don't raise sufficient money to cover the defaulter's indebtedness, and their own and their agents' and solicitors' costs, then the defaulting borrower can still be sued for the balance.)

A vendor of a property less than ten years old is apt to say that it's guaranteed by the National House Building Council (NHBC). Well, not quite! What a builder gets for his purchaser is a ten-year cover. It's sometimes called a 'ten-year structural warranty', but this is inaccurate. It covers more than just the structure, particularly for homes registered for cover since 1 April 1999. Since 1988, the scheme has been known as 'Buildmark'.

You require the balance of the period of cover to be transferred to you, but NHBC and builders don't require it. Add a clause to the contract saying the vendor will assign it to you (using a Form CS12, or HB12).

The protection which NHBC gives is in two sections: first, the builder's obligations and second, NHBC's insurance cover. Under the first section, the builder has to put right at his own expense any defects that arise as a result of his failure to comply with the NHBC minimum standards of workmanship and material and which are notified to him in writing during the first two years of the house's life. Don't think that buying a recently built house means that you will get a repair-bill-free ten years – you won't. A house owner is not relieved of his normal maintenance responsibilities, and the agreement doesn't cover normal wear and tear, or normal shrinkage. Some items such as fences, white goods and lifts are not covered at all.

Under the second section, cover is in three main parts. First, against loss of deposit in the event of the builder's insolvency between exchange of contracts and completion. Second, against the costs of repairs that result from the builder's insolvency or failure to meet an arbitration award or judgment which arise during the period up to two years from the date of the NHBC Certificate. Third, the cost of more serious items which arise during the third to tenth years from the date of the certificate (please note that the 'certificate' is also known as the 'Ten-Year Notice'). There is a fourth element of cover: the NHBC is the building control authority in place of the local council. This covers costs of putting right breaches of the statutory building regulations.

The NHBC cover saves you from the consequences of basic bad building and that's about it. That is to say, broadly, the cover is for such items as subsidence or settlement, and other major structural defects due to non-compliance with standards, such as collapse or serious distortion of joists or roof structure, or chemical failure of material affecting the load-bearing structure.

Since 1 April 1999, the cover has been expanded and includes, among other things, double glazing, defective flooring, defective flues and wet applied plaster. It also includes insurance against the cost of cleaning up contamination of the plot on which the house stands, if a statutory clean-up notice is served on the owner.

Since 1 April 2003, the Council of Mortgage Lenders (CML), the House Builders' Federation (HBF), the new home warranty providers (NHBC, Zurich and Premier Guarantee) and the Law Society of England and Wales have introduced a solution to the problem of home buyers reaching legal completion and moving into the newly built property before the property has been classified as satisfactorily complete, and in some cases before the pre-handover inspection. It has been agreed that lenders will not release the mortgage funds for a new property until the buyer's conveyancer has received confirmation in the form of a cover note that the property has received a satisfactory final inspection and that a new full home warranty will be in place on or before legal completion.

If you are a second or subsequent buyer, you cannot claim on the NHBC for defects that the first purchaser reported to the builder, nor defects that were visible, on reasonable inspection (whatever that is), at the time of purchase.

During its existence, the National House Building Council has done sterling service for the owner-occupier, particularly the original purchaser from a builder, in raising minimum standards of building and finish. If you are thinking of buying a newly built house, see if the builder is on the NHBC Register. If he isn't, it might be that he has been kicked off. If he has, there may be problems with obtaining cover regardless of the fact that he may have hung onto the documents. On the other hand he might be a splendid, upright, entrepreneurial character who knows what he, like his father before him, is about and is determined not to have any 'pen-pushers' telling him what to do. Ask some of his previous buyers. They'll soon tell you how good he is. Mind you, he might be the salt of the earth, but he will never sell his house to anyone wanting to raise a loan on it and a cash buyer will never sell it to anyone wanting to raise money to aid the purchase. Fact is the absence of an NHBC Certificate for a new house renders it unsaleable unless something similar is in place which enjoys market recognition. Generally, this means insurance or the benefit of one of the other schemes recognised by the Council of Mortgage Lenders. See next section.

You will see from the necessarily brief description given above some of the things the NHBC is and isn't. When you are in any deal which involves the ten-year structural warranty, write off to its Council and get just as much information as you can. While we are dealing with newly built houses, it's as well to ask a vendor of a second-hand house whether he intends moving into one. Builders' dates for completion are seldom kept and can often be weeks, or even months, wide of the mark. Also, find out if you are likely to be tagging yourself into a chain and how long it is.

Given the climate in England and Wales, and the rarity of a long summer drought, the NHBC guarantees given in the past three or four years could well have expired before we experience a drying out of sub-soils, thus testing the foundations and possibly starting some nasty movements in many a dream home. So the old hands will prefer to buy a house that is six or seven years old, where any weak spots have had time to show.

All the above might seem like a great song and dance production number, and if you employ a surveyor to make a full inspection of the property that is exactly what the vendor will tell you he did. Surveyors are responsible and can be held for cash damages at law if they put it down in writing that a house is sound, but experience proves otherwise. For example, when you move in together with a grand piano and a host of can-can dancing friends for a house-warming party and the floor is not strong enough to support the revelry, the surveyors could have to pay for new timbers for the floor, and wooden legs for you and your friends. So surveyors have to be very cautious, otherwise they don't get their insurance renewed. The premiums are high in any case and that, and the interminable time surveyors spend looking at property to make sure they are safe, is reflected in their bills. It's also reflected in their reports, which are sometimes splattered with gems of ambiguity.

If you opt for anything less than a **full structural survey** (very costly), all you will get are such masterpieces as 'from a .head-and-shoulders inspection through the loft aperture the roof timbers appeared to be sound', or this page filler: 'the kitchen tiles are of a somewhat dated design'.

However, don't buy the idea that a full structural survey is a kind of insurance. If, after you move in, you spot things that the surveyor missed, don't think that a polite letter saying, 'Dear Mr Tape, please will you send me £2,000 to pay for repairing the wood rot that you didn't warn me about' will take any tricks. It won't. It's not easy to sue for professional negligence, which is not the same as getting it wrong. You (on your own) have to prove that the surveyor (backed by his professional association and his insurance company, even into the Supreme Court) didn't use the level of skill and care that one would normally expect a qualified person to use. Not easy! Also, even if you do succeed, there is no guarantee you will get the costs of putting the problem right. The usual measure of damages is the difference between the amount the surveyor valued the house at and the actual value of the house with the defects.

A house which has been standing 50 years may be ready for a face-lift, but it isn't likely to fall down tomorrow, and though the finish on recently built houses might not be of the best, it's ridiculous to be frightened of what our builders have produced by the hundreds of thousands for private buyers. And there is always the National House Building Council guarantee.

CML *Handbook*

This is perhaps as good a place as any to make one cardinal observation. There are – in the estimation of solicitors and the banks, building societies and other organisations that lend money to aid a purchase – right ways and wrong ways of doing things.

Buying a new house from a builder who is the salt of the earth – as honest as the day is long sort of thing – who cannot offer NHBC or similar protection (see section 6.6 of the *Handbook* noted below) is something you are perfectly at liberty to do if you are not borrowing money, but don't be surprised to find you may have trouble selling later.

There are other issues of a more technical nature, which will be referred to in the coming chapters; if you want to know what they are, have a look on the internet. Much of this 'lore' (not 'law') was first published in 1999 as the Council of Mortgage Lenders' *Handbook for England and Wales*. You can find it at www.cml.org.uk. Check for updates (only available online as hard copies are no longer produced) as it has been changed on several occasions since first published. This is the guidance followed by banks and building societies. If these guidelines aren't followed, it will be difficult to borrow money to buy your property from a mainstream lender and will make selling it on more difficult.

Try to read Part I of the *Handbook*; it tells you what all the solicitors you will deal with ought to be doing. Part II sets out the special requirements of some of the main CML members. If you are buying and your lender is not named in the *Handbook*, ask if it is a member, and what its Part II requirements are. Then follow them to the letter! The CML *Handbook* is not the final word on what to do, but be warned: you can ignore all or any of it if you wish, if you are not borrowing money to aid the purchase, but if you gloss over some of the problems discussed in the *Handbook*, you may find you will have trouble selling later, or will be put to expense that perhaps your seller should have incurred when you bought the house.

Seven good questions

You can usefully look a vendor straight in the eye and ask him a few pertinent questions, the answers to which could determine whether you should spend further time and money on the project.

1. Is the property freehold? If it isn't, what is the ground rent and how long has the lease to run?

2. Does the owner have to pay any maintenance charges to anyone apart from builders, decorators, etc., to whom he himself has given specific orders?

3. Is the road and main drain taken over by the council or do the frontagers have to club up every now and then to have them repaired?

4. If you are in a business or profession, can you put up your brass plate and can your spouse hang out the washing or are there any restrictions?

5. Has anyone got the right to traipse across any part of your property? Ever?

6. If there is any evidence (extra cookers, sinks, etc.) of more than one family living in the property, what guarantee is there that they will all move out, thus ensuring that you get full vacant possession on completion?

7. Has the property ever been flooded or faced serious risk of flooding?

In case you are thinking of making alterations, ask if the vendor happens to know if there are any restrictions in the deeds on this point (this would particularly apply to leases) and if there aren't, whether there are any restrictions imposed by the local authority – such as a preservation order or conservation area. A vendor might not declare all that he knows at this point, but don't worry too much as we have other ways of making him talk as you will learn later.

Think long and carefully about buying a house that will only fit your requirements if you make a number of structural alterations. Such alterations invariably cost more than the number you first thought of. It's the etceteras and extras that are costly. In any case, if you are buying a house on an estate, it will be a property of a certain class (or there may be restrictive covenants preventing this) and by improving it you risk bringing it out of that class and making it difficult to sell, if and when you decide to move again.

This is the third criterion you must have in mind when you go viewing. Put the question: 'Is it a good investment, in so far as I will be able to realise it without too much anguish, if ever I need to?' You might think that, compared with similar properties, the one you are looking at is a snip. It no doubt has to be, to attract a viewer at all! You don't want to be in that vendor's situation ever, so you would be wise to avoid buying a house situated near any of the following: a fish and chip shop, a take-away cafe, a hospital, a public house, a church, a garage or repair shop, a fire station, or a public lavatory. All the foregoing, and a few more besides, can be anything from a nuisance to a serious disadvantage; even if you happen to be deaf and have no sense of smell, others are not so afflicted. Any estate agent who knows anything at all, knows that such badly located properties should only be put on the market at the height of a house-selling boom when, literally, anything will sell.

At the first whiff of any rumour about plans for any kind of non-residential development round about where you live, get together with your previously independent and apathetic neighbours and protest loud and long at any hint of intrusion by such property-price-debasers into what has previously been such a highly respectable area, unless, that is, you stand to make a vast profit because the property under discussion is your very own. In such a case, the protesters are dog-in-the-manger reactionary luddites opposed to all forms of progress which public-spirited individuals (you) are slaving away trying to introduce.

Sometimes it takes ages to find a property that comes up to scratch and suits your requirements; sometimes it's a case of beginner's luck. In either case remember you are not the only bargain-hunter around, and the race goes to the swift. Don't go groggy when the finishing line is in sight – be ready with your own pack of conveyancing forms.

CHAPTER 2

New houses

For young people buying their first home, a brand new one has what can only be called a strong romantic attraction. Here they will make their attempt to create a home. Builders know what attracts – note how they advertise homes for sale, when what they are trying to sell is a plan, and more often than not, a half-finished house or flat. But when the house is finished the starry-eyed home makers move in, secure in the knowledge that no one has been born, lived, loved, divorced or died in it. The aura of the past will not seep out of the brickwork. The dead hand of the past will not push them into outdated ways of living. It will all be new! It's all brave! But as in all romances, beauty is in the eye of the beholder – desire overpowers reason, and faults and blemishes are ignored. Another great attraction of a newly built house is that it promises to be repair-free for a number of years – if anything goes wrong it's likely to be because of a fault in manufacture for which someone else is responsible, and not wear and tear, which falls to the user to put right.

There is also the National House Building Council's Certificate, the benefits and restrictions of which we have already noted. With this protection you have the warranty against ruinous subsidence, but some would say you can do without running the risk of a nightmare experience of subsidence in the first place. If you get subsidence from any other reason than climate it has to be because of bad building and that means solicitors, barristers and courts for you.

From an investment point of view, it's often the case that the last house to be completed on a development is the best buy. The romantic ideas and repair-free attraction of brand new houses militate against the resale of a house on an unfinished development. A vendor can have for sale a house to which he has added a number of refinements, is offering a fair list of extras and be only asking the same price as the builder is for a brand new house, yet the vendor has to search high and low for a buyer while the developer is signing buyers all the while, and he signs them up on a take-it-or-leave-it basis. Builders and their Skinners know how to take advantage of a situation where desire overpowers reason.

The developer appoints a solicitor who acts for him in the sale of each of the houses on the development. Except for the address or plot number, the contract and transfer (there are one or two things you need to know about contracts and transfers – all will be revealed in later chapters) are identical for all. It's almost unheard of for any purchaser's Skinner to persuade the developer's Skinner to change any detail in the contract or transfer and if this does occur, these changes will only cover minor issues. Layperson conveyancers get to see the papers with their own eyes, and if they see anything they don't like they can take it up with the builder face to face – whereas the Skinnerhood is deskbound and at best will only write a letter.

It's a common occurrence that builders and their agents will often try to pressurise buyers into signing a contract when a house has a substantial amount of work to be done on it, or even when the building has not been started. In such a case, you need to ensure that the contract is made subject to the house being completed in accordance with a set of plans and a specification. These would be attached to or referred to in the contract to ensure that the developer is under an obligation to carry out the work to a clearly described set of standards. The less of the house you can see when you sign the contract, the greater the risk. This is because the sale agreement will generally confer on the builder the right to change materials of construction and the design. Not necessarily to any material degree in his estimation, but it may be important from your standpoint!

Also try to tie the developer down to some kind of completion date. Houses are built in the open air, by people who are relying on others for supplies of material to arrive according to the hopes and dreams of a deviser of a critical path analysis, which pleased its creator when he put it on paper. But his Creator might send flood, storm, tempest, lightning and thunderbolt to thwart his plans, and deep down the developer knows about that. So we are introduced to the almost meaningless phrases that abound in house sale and purchase transactions; a proviso for completion will be a slight variant on the well worn 'will use his best endeavours to complete the house with all due expedition'.

Sometimes builders will ask for stage payments. That is to say they will require a proportion of the purchase price to be paid when, say, the footings are in, followed by more money at window sill height, more when the roof is on, and a final payment on completion. This method can be costly, particularly if you are taking a mortgage, because at each stage the building society surveyor has to have a look, and you have to pay him a fee, and as soon as the stage payment is advanced you start paying repayments on the loan, even though you might not move into the house for many a month.

Your deposit money can also be at risk because the developer will usually want to use it to fund the later stages of his development and if the builder were to become insolvent before the completion of your purchase, your deposit could be lost.

First-time buyers

Some builders advertise as though there are some terms, prices, mortgages and services special to buyers of their houses. There are not. It's all put on the price of the house. There is help for first-time buyers in the form of 'HomeBuy Direct' (a government scheme) or 'Rent to HomeBuy'. In addition, until 25 March 2012, provided that the house is the first land the purchaser has owned (whether alone or with anyone else), will be his only or main home and costs less than £250,000, a first-time buyer will not need to pay Stamp Duty Land Tax in any event. So tell the builder you will do your own conveyance, get your own mortgage, pay cash – how much discount for relieving them of all that worry? You could get a pleasant surprise provided you promise not to tell your new neighbours!

Last-time buyers

Now it's your turn. A plethora of advice to those about to retire pours forth from accountants, solicitors, estate agents, travel agents, stockbrokers, banks and building societies, all of whom claim to offer financial services.

Financial services hate stillness. Their motto is: Let's get them churning their money in my churn, and some of it will stick to the sides for me.

The death of a spouse or your retirement are not sufficient reasons to move house. It might be that you would save money on rates and heating in a smaller house, but just look at what the move will cost you. No matter where you live, you will pay some Council Tax and heating bills. It could take you donkey's years to recoup the expense of moving.

If it's the cost of upkeep that bothers you, get down to your Citizens Advice Bureau (CAB) and find out what practical help is on offer from local charity organisations for someone like you who has spent a lifetime fighting and working for the country.

Elderly people sometimes fear a disabling fall and are attracted to living complexes where wardens, either resident or on call, can get an ambulance for them. The same reassurance could be gained by installing in one's present home a radio call signal; speak to the CAB or Age UK about it.

There is also the Department of Social Security. At long last the government is realising that though houses might be *privately* owned, they are part of the *national* stock of housing and wealth, and to those who can't cope financially, help should be given. Though less and less as time goes by.

Don't forget, when doing your sums, to ask yourself a few 'comfort' questions:

- You have a garage of your own. Could you tolerate sharing? Is there a parking place for every resident and his visitors?

- You have, at worst, only had one wall through which noise could seep. Could you tolerate noise from the sides, above, below, and across the landing?

- When the sun shines you can sit in your own garden chair in your own garden, a few feet from your own door. Will you be able to do that?

- You have your own place for your own dustbin. Will the new compare favourably?

- Can you choose your own odd-job man and your own time for the job to be done and, indeed, whether to have it done this year or at all?

Those who have never occupied a home under a lease usually only fully realise what they have committed themselves to when the bills come in. Leases inevitably have service charge provisions to provide for maintenance of the whole block. More about this later.

Part exchange

Find out what's the discount for cash. It can be considerable. If you and the combined high-powered salesmanship of the local estate agency could not find a buyer for your house, neither can the builder … not at the price you were asking. So consider knocking your asking price down by the combined amount of the cash discount and the agent's fees and get the house sold yourself. You can then bargain with anybody anywhere and from then on get your sums right about how much your new house actually cost you and how much profit you made on the last one. No builder will be upset by the tactics recommended here. His advertisement drew you to the site, he has sold a house and that is what he wants … the sooner the quicker!

There are a lot of risks in buying and selling, but in order to get anything done one has to take some risks. The art is in drawing the line between acceptable and unacceptable risks and each person will decide for himself where that line is to be drawn when buying a new house, or for that matter in any of the other transactions outlined in this book.

CHAPTER 3

Sell first or buy first?

If you have never bought a house before, then the question answers itself. But if you are an owner who needs to move to a larger or smaller house, or needs to get away from the neighbours or in-laws, or needs to raise some money by buying a cheaper house, which way round you work is crucial. The decision has to be made in the light of both your personal needs and resources, and the general state of the housing market at the time.

You can, of course, go out viewing properties, and when you see one that suits you, say, 'Yes, I will buy this when I have sold my own.' And you might drag the vendors on for ages while you screw the last penny out of your sale. On the other hand, the vendor of your dream property may have read this book too, and the answer will be, 'I'll give you x number of weeks.' How many times have you heard of 'chains' breaking down? How many times have you seen the silly 'sold subject to contract' slips pasted onto and then taken off For Sale boards? Greed, slipshod estate agents and lawyers' bad timing are the usual causes.

Since the mid-1930s there has been a drift upwards in prices, but the movement goes in fits and starts, so spot the rising market and you can safely buy first, and be pretty sure of selling your own house swiftly and profitably. You can always tell when the housing market has reached its bottom and is about to rise. Similarly, you get a very clear signal that a boom is within six months or so of petering out: the mass media will tell you. When they make headlines out of the fact that young people are being priced out of the market, and when they have stories about people making fortunes in a few years out of houses, the market is at the top. Nevertheless, so as not to miss the bus, new buyers join in, and so keep the pot boiling a little longer. But the bus was just about to pull up at a compulsory stop.

On the other hand, when, on your telly, you see a lugubrious man standing in front of an agency For Sale board, which has obviously taken root, and he tells you that he has not had sight, sound nor smell of a viewer for over 18 months, then the market is about to pick up. Keep an eye on the general economy. At present, we are in the middle of a recession. It is difficult to know when the market will pick up, even though things have been bad for 18 months. The freedom with which the banks will lend is a good indicator. The easier it is to get a mortgage, the more likely it is that there will be competition for your dream home, and on the seller's side, a market that is likely to rise sooner rather than later. Also have a look at local free property magazines – these will often contain a market report.

Houses adjacent to petrol stations, hotel car parks, fire stations and the like should always be sold when the market is on the boil, if they are to get sold at all.

February, March and April are the best months to put your house on the market – May and June are particularly active times for buyers especially of family houses, because parents want to make sure they can get their children settled before the start of the new school year in September. But life goes on 365 days a year. There are always some buyers about. Even Christmas can be good if a couple of your neighbours make you a present of having 'For Sale' boards planted in their gardens. Take advantage of their viewers, who know all about their houses from the agent's particulars, so might drive past them, but if you have your own board – which will only cost you a few pounds, they might knock on your front door, even if it's only to ask your price. Don't keep them on the doorstep in such poor weather – invite them in to discuss it.

CHAPTER 4

Estate agency

Insurance companies, building societies and brokers of all kinds have put together strings of house-selling shops, and distorted the business out of all recognition, but they still trade on the folk-memory of the personal service that independent estate agents took many years to establish in the minds of home owners.

Branch office after branch office has been opened. Every city and town centre is stuffed with them. Their numbers have increased out of all proportion to the increase in owner-occupied houses. Many offices are lucky to sell more than one house per week. Each office is staffed with a couple of receptionists who try to look busy for seven days a week, waiting for victims to give themselves up. The person who knows what estate agency is now about (possibly a chartered surveyor, more likely an insurance man) oversees a number of offices and can be called on the mobile on the golf course or in bed, when required.

If your name is Feather, and not Bold, and you give yourself up to an agent, the receptionist will make an appointment for the representative to call and 'survey' and value your house. It will no doubt happen on the same day as you applied. That's the last time you'll see any greased lightning in this transaction. Agents always have spent more of their own time and money on getting in houses for sale than in selling them, because, as you have already read, houses sell themselves – eventually, if you will let them.

Estate agents say they ...

1. make a survey of the house to be sold;

2. make a valuation;

3. prepare a set of particulars;

4. commission a photograph;

5. circularise the particulars using their computers and network of associated agents;

6. display your property in their own monthly circular and in the press;

7. display a full-colour photo of your house in their shops;

8. negotiate with interested parties;

9. offer you and your purchaser a full range of financial services including using the money from one house to buy another;

10. liaise with your solicitor;

11. advertise your property and their charges;

12. conduct viewings.

Another service which used to be offered by estate agents was the provision of a Home Information Pack or 'HIP'. The use of HIPs was suspended from 21 May 2010 but sellers are still required to produce an Energy Performance Certificate within 28 days of putting a house on the market. There are a number of independent contractors who can provide these certificates – an estate agent isn't needed for that!

Now for the facts ...

1. **Survey:** If it were a written structural survey that you could pass on to the prospective purchaser, that would be OK, but you won't get that. You are selling. What do you want with a survey? You check for subsidence every time you open a door or window. You check the drains every time you pull the plug, and if you haven't fallen through the floorboards into the cellar lately, the woodwork is good enough to

be going on with, and you know without any help from agents. Of course, if counting the number of rooms and jotting down their sizes is a survey, you get that. Big deal.

2. **Valuation:** When you have read chapter 7, you will be entitled to put the letters FBSPV (Fellow of the Bradshaw School of Property Valuers) after your name.

3. **Particulars:** If you can't go through your own house with a notebook and pencil, who can?

4. **Photographs:** Have you seen some of them? You've no doubt got better ones in your own album.

5. **Lists, computers and networks of agents:** Your postman, who sees your For Sale board every day, has more up-to-date news about who's looking for a house such as yours than any agent sitting in front of a computer 50 miles away. Having been a potential buyer, you will know what a fat lot of use the stuff is and it's nearly certain that your buyer will come from within 25 miles. Anyway, you too can use the internet to advertise your property and get that out-of-town buyer. www.houseladder.co.uk in particular provides such a service for private sellers together with advertisements on findaproperty.com. Or try www.gumtree.com or simply try putting 'selling a house privately' into a search engine and see what you can find.

    As far as matching people to houses, what has been your experience when you were looking for a house? New buyers come on the market every day, as they sell their own houses, having decided to get married, divorced or take promotion, all of which can necessitate a move.

    People drop off the lists when they get fixed up. You know how long they keep on sending you particulars after you have found a house. Sometimes they keep coming from an agency through whom you have just bought.

6. **Monthly magazine:** More junk mail. Newspapers: you will read the chapter on advertising and learn how much expenditure of time and expertise that requires. Do you think that what the agent does in this regard amounts to much?

7. **Shop window:** This is about the only thing that agents have that you can't have for yourself, and so 'anything you can do I can do better'

doesn't apply. In this respect, property shops are worth considering because they do the display job at a fraction of the cost. Very few people buy houses they first saw displayed in an agency. The agency has already paid the rent, so putting up your photo costs next to nothing. If this is what works, why do they go in for all that costly advertising in the press, buying boards, paying signwriters to look after them, putting them up and taking them down; why not just use their own shop window (no prizes for even a polite answer)? Shop windows are used as much for attracting new vendors as for anything else. But the pictures are of houses they have not sold. If they can't sell those, how can they sell yours? Nowadays, even the estate agent's biggest shop window is the internet.

8. **Negotiating** with a buyer usually amounts to persuading you to bring your price down and in getting you to wait till the buyer sells his house. You are in as good a position as anyone to negotiate with a buyer.

9. **Financial services:** There are so many agencies at it nowadays that selling commissions are not enough to keep them all going, so they have to look for other sources of revenue. So they try to sell you and your purchaser insurances, mortgages and, if things go badly enough, chain-breaking and bridging loans, so as to grab the commission amounting to thousands of pounds. This is where they come into their own, and yours as well, if you give them half a chance.

    Using the money from one house to buy another: the estate agent to whom you left it leaves it, in turn, to the solicitor, who in turn will often leave you with the problem of a bridging loan or a costly chain-breaking scheme.

10. **Liaison with your solicitor:** This amounts to the agent writing to your solicitor saying 'this is one of ours' and eventually, if ever, 'here is our commission bill'. If you do choose to use a solicitor, it's always better to keep in touch with him yourself, then you are in control, not the sharp-suited agent. The agent may get in contact with other agents in the chain, but there is no reason why you cannot deal with the buyer directly; indeed, this personal approach may well achieve better results.

11. **Advertising:** Historically, estate agents have written the most appallingly ambiguous descriptions when advertising the charming, deceptively spacious family property, in which, in real life, you can't

swing a cat. Nowadays, this can be a criminal offence and so the agents will ask you to validate their claims and that can make you a criminal as well! They do the same when advertising briefly about their charges. 'No sale – no charge' sounds good enough, but it might mean that all you get is a mention of your house to anyone who enquires for a property such as yours. 'Free advertising' might mean: we put a few lines about it in our monthly bulletin, which is given out to callers and distributed to the Skinners' waiting rooms, where it takes its chance among a pile of magazines and other junk.

12. **Viewings:** Estate agents will (sometimes) come and show round potential buyers. This can be convenient. But too often, you have to show round the buyers yourself. Who can do a better job of showing the house than you who lives there?

So after a little run-of-the-mill advertising you will be expected to pay for your share of their full-page adverts, of which anything up to a quarter can be taken up in publicising their own outfit. If you do use an agency, it's worth looking at the contract to check what publicity you are agreeing to pay for and what is extra.

Now here's a little gem of business sense for you: if your name is Feather and you have been persuaded to use an agency and a Skinner, at least gird up your loins to write a letter to Skinner, Hand and Glove incorporating the following: 'Do not pay the agent's commission out of the sale monies, but forward their account to me and I will deal with it.' You will then have some bargaining power if you have come to the conclusion that you have not had value for the money claimed, or charges have been made that you never agreed to. But if you do decide to do this, act very carefully and make sure that you read the contract before you refuse to pay the whole commission. Estate agents will think nothing of suing you for the commission – which could ultimately involve you in paying court costs. The contract will be carefully worded and most of these contracts work. If you want to challenge the commission and it's less than £5,000, you could try pointing out that they will never recover their costs under the small claims track regime and negotiate for a discount.

Agency agreements do need looking at and studying before you sign; see what the agreement says about selling yourself or later through another agent. Don't be afraid to say to the representative, 'Leave it with me for my grandad or grandson, solicitor or nerve specialist to have a look at it.' Then calculate the likely bill, and ponder 1. to 12. above. Looked at in the cold light of day, the list of things agencies claim to do for you doesn't amount to much. Certainly not to the enormous commissions that get spirited away out of the price you get for your house.

If your local branch of Dick, Turpin & Co. only put a board in your garden and a picture in the shop window and then start charging for adverts, you can get that from a property shop at a fraction of the price.

Middlemen

Estate agents, solicitors, building societies, insurance people, and all the rest who are trying to amass a fortune as swiftly as possible out of the housing market, have needs of their own. From your own workplace you know that you do things not only for your customers, but also to keep the organisation going and see to your own creature comforts.

Trips abroad, cameras and other valuable prizes are offered on a local and regional basis to the 'representative of the month' by agency chains. The winners are those who get the most 'instructions' (houses for sale). Competition is keen, not only within the firms, but also between agencies. Blows have been struck when a representative of one agency has gone poaching from another. Don't get caught in the crossfire. You could find yourself in court, at best as a witness, and, at worst, as a losing defendant who is refusing to pay two commissions because rival agencies are claiming to have been the effective cause of your sale.

So when you are dealing with these middlemen, recognise that much of the advice you get from them is not only what they think is best for you, but also what is best for them. For instance, they want to deal with as few people as possible for as much money as possible. Agencies plead professional ethics as a reason for not dealing with more than one potential buyer – what miserable pleaders they are. An agency may choose a buyer with a house for sale so that it can swell the number of houses on its books – that buyer is not necessarily the best for you.

CHAPTER 5
The moneylenders

Bridging loans

You may have seen a house you particularly want, but have to exchange contracts quickly before you can organise your sale, or perhaps having made an acceptable 'subject to contract' offer to buy and having accepted an acceptable 'subject to contract' offer to sell, your purchaser has withdrawn at an embarrassingly late stage in the pre-contract game.

What are the options? One is obviously to lose your intended purchase, but bridging loans offer one way forward if you can afford to pay two mortgages – that on the house you wish to sell and that on the house you wish to buy.

If you are tempted to do this, ask yourself a question and make sure you get an honest answer. How quickly will your house sell and will you really get what you want for it? If you get it wrong and you still bridge, month after anxious month can pass before you get rid of your old home. One good tip is have the house you wish to sell structurally surveyed and if you are recommended to get specialist reports on the boiler, the electricity or whatever, get them. You will soon find out if there is a 'nasty' hiding under the floorboards that might have an adverse impact on your ability to sell, or to sell at the price you want or even need.

House exchanges

If you are buying a new house from a builder, you may find the builder will offer to take your own house in part exchange. He normally insists you buy a house with a higher market value, say 25 per cent, so this doesn't work if you are thinking of retiring and moving to a smaller house to release some capital for your old age.

This has the advantage for those who want a new house of taking you out of any chain. However, it seems that under the Stamp Duty Land Tax regime entering into an exchange will not save you any tax – although the builder may be eligible for relief on the purchase of your house, you will still have to pay Stamp Duty Land Tax on the value of your old house, plus the cash paid for the new one.

The builder's lawyers will generally carry out a cursory investigation of your title and will normally ask you to submit the barest minimum of paperwork. A formal Office Copy of your title (if registered), a copy of your title deeds if not, replies to the Seller's Property Information Forms and the Fixtures, Fittings and Contents Form, plus a local search, and that is about it.

You may still need to borrow on the new house, but if not, the deal can go through very quickly. Perhaps as soon as you get a reply to your local search, which can vary from a 24-hour turnaround with some councils to several weeks with others. Five to ten working days, however, is a comfortable 'norm'.

Mortgages

Many of you will have to borrow money to aid the purchase. Time was when the only serious options were the building societies and 'mortgage famines' were not unknown. If they didn't know you, you joined a queue. Sometimes the queues were limited to first-time borrowers. In other cases, perhaps you got to jump the queue if you were an existing member. Perhaps you borrowed from them last time, or perhaps you were saving up for a deposit. Then the banks started to become involved, and then many building societies decided to convert to public company status and so on. Throughout the last housing boom, lack of money to lend was not a problem. However, although the Bank of England base rate is incredibly low at present, the recent credit crunch has led to banks being much more cautious with their money and there is talk of imposing a minimum loan to value ratio, so that 100 per cent mortgages may become a thing of the past. Be sure to investigate all of the criteria before you start to look so that you know you can afford your dream home.

Time was also when the building societies operated prudent, if inflexible, rules. A sole buyer could not borrow more than two and a half times his salary. Couples could not borrow more than three times the higher salary. Other permutations were acceptable in some cases. If the surveyor selected to value the house for the building society felt it was worth less than you were paying, that didn't always matter if you were providing a substantial contribution to the house. You are at liberty after all to lose your own money. But not theirs and so if they felt there was a risk, the answer was to insure. They took out, at your expense, a mortgagee protection policy. If the house was sold at a loss by the lender, they recouped the loss from the insurers. Unfortunately, they were their insurers not yours and so – invoking the insurance concept of 'subrogation' – the insurers would then chase the borrowers (if they had any money) for the loss.

In time, back in the 1970s, some institutions started to lend without asking for proof of ability to pay, particularly the secondary lenders. This worked well when prices were continually on the up, but when they fell they often recouped the loss by suing the surveyor or, if that failed, the solicitor. Sloppy file-keeping or inadequate procedures cost the legal profession a great deal, but at least the borrower was not chased for the loss!

In those days there were few payment options. A repayment mortgage involved the payment of interest and some capital each year. An endowment mortgage involved paying interest only. The capital came from an endowment policy that had to be paid for each month as well, but the theory was, at the end of the 20- to 25-year period, that the insurers would pay more than you needed to pay off the mortgage, and you would make a profit. Or you could rely on your pension insurance policy's lump sum to cover the capital. Unfortunately, your insurance salesman can only guess what the results are in the light of circumstances prevailing when you take out the endowment or mortgage. In the event for many borrowers, a stable economy with low rates of inflation has resulted in a lower performance for these schemes than expected and there will be borrowers with endowment and pension mortgages who will have less than they need when the money becomes available to pay off the capital.

Nowadays there are so many different types of loan on offer that the best that can be recommended is to shop around. Although there are now many different types of loan, the fact that banks are more reluctant to lend money in the current climate and that prudence is the watchword for many means that getting a mortgage, any mortgage, is no longer a given. Work out what is the best deal or type of loan for you and what you can realistically afford. Get a decision in principle on a mortgage and put this in place before you even start looking for a house and you will be in a much better position to move when your offer is accepted. Once you have found a house, the next step is for your lender to have it valued, to ensure that it wants to follow through on the decision in principle. You will be expected to meet the costs of a valuation and the lender may or may not accept your nominee surveyor. The valuation is just that. It's not a structural survey and although the law requires a person carrying out a valuation to spot some of the more glaring faults, a large hole in the roof or major cracks suggesting subsidence, for example, there are limits to what the borrower can sue for.

Some lenders use in-house surveyors. That is, surveyors on the payroll. However, the norm is for a local firm to supply a report in a more or less standard form, so ascertain what levels of report are available (simple valuation or full structural survey, or sometimes something in between) and what they will cost. Note also that surveyors frequently highlight problems for referral to others. If a major structural problem is highlighted, try a civil engineer; these can be relatively rare in any area and can be overworked folk and so don't expect them to rush around at the first sign of a cheque. Wiring, heating, rising damp, etc.: with all these problems, the surveyor is likely to recommend you hire an appropriate specialist.

If you hire someone to check on the damp course and timber, try to make sure you keep his survey and his guarantee (one without the other is useless) for when you come to sell, and try to select a contractor whose guarantee is backed by insurers. Contractors come and go and after a year or so it's not unknown for guarantees to become simply pretty sheets of paper with no legal or practical value whatsoever.

CHAPTER 6

No agents, please!

Why private vendors win

There are a lot of houses to be sold. In Great Britain there are nearly $12^{1}/_{2}$ million owner-occupied houses. On average, spread over a year, close on a million houses change hands.

How, you may ask, can I compete in such a crowded market?

You must find some ways of drawing attention to your house; of marking it out from all others; of making potential buyers curious enough to come and view it. Not to worry.

You have already taken a decision that singles your house out as something different and especially attractive to any buyer. YOU HAVE DECIDED TO JOIN THE ONE IN THREE OF ALL VENDORS WHO SELL FOR THEMSELVES.

As soon as you announce the sale, you will signal to the whole wide world (particularly the twenty odd square miles that really matter) that your property is so good it's expected to sell itself. It doesn't need the wiles of a high-powered salesman to push it onto someone who doesn't really need it, at a higher price than he wanted to pay. It's also attractive to a lot of potential buyers who want to avoid agents because:

- They know that an agent's commission is added onto the price, so in effect it's the purchaser who pays it.

- An established agency cannot have avoided making enemies along the way. *You only need one buyer*, and that buyer might be so embittered by previous experiences with estate agents that never, ever, will that person have anything more to do with agents.

- Inexperienced buyers are afraid of smooth-talking salesmen, particularly those who, to hide the fact that they have no special expertise, overlay what they have to say with an inappropriately pompous language which hermetically seals off conceptual orientational realisation, and assails the unfortunate recipient's auditory structural system as a load of bull falling from a great height.

- Experienced buyers know that they can bargain directly with a private vendor. Quite rightly, they expect to get more sense out of the butcher than the block.

- Buyers are sick of collecting particulars from agents who, by describing the property in a different way, disguise the fact that every agent in town has the same stock for sale. Luckless viewers have wasted journeys. *When they come to a private vendor it's delightfully uncomplicated, and they will not get involved as witnesses in disputed commission claims.*

A quick look at the houses for sale pages of your local newspaper could easily lead you to believe that private sales are very few and far between. But a recent survey found that only two-thirds of all house sellers used estate agents. That leaves a third who didn't. Over three hundred thousand vendors a year go it alone and win. Just keep your eyes open. Count the private adverts. Count the private For Sale boards – are they anywhere near a third of the total? Isn't that proof that a private sale doesn't have to be advertised again and again, and that a private For Sale board doesn't take root?

So, all in all, yours has the edge over the other properties with which you are in competition. You will get more viewers, and therefore sell quickly. That's another privately sold house off the market; buyers have to jump at an opportunity to buy privately or they miss out. **Private sales are prompt sales.**

Don't worry that by working on your own you will miss the one (in 20) potential buyer who comes from out of town. It is unlikely, given the internet (the private vendor's best friend), that you will miss even this buyer. In any event, such a buyer has always researched the market thoroughly. He has to; he can't afford wasted journeys. He knows what he is looking for, where it should be, and about what price it should be going for. He also knows the districts in which he is likely to hunt down his quarry, and will be cruising past your house this weekend. When you put your For Sale board up he will see it. He knows everything about every other house in the district from the agents' particulars. But there is something crucial that he doesn't know about your house just from the board: the price.

The car will have to stop. He will have to walk up your whitewashed path, stare at your dozzled-up front door, ring the bell and wait for you to come and offer to show him why yours is better than any of the rest, and if any mention is made about yours being higher priced than the others, 'Well, we can talk about that when you have looked round, can't we.'

There are two other situations which many think cannot be coped with unless an agent is brought onto the scene – they are wrong!

Just because you live alone and are fearful of having a stranger in the house doesn't mean to say you can't sell without an agent – you certainly can.

When alone, you should follow your usual precaution of having the door on the chain. If you make a telephone appointment, get the name, address and telephone number of the caller and check identity by ringing back; also check with the telephone book and/or directory enquiries and then arrange for a near neighbour, clergyman or social worker to attend. Or if the prospect comes from the board, ask him to wait while your friend can pop round. No prospective viewer will object to waiting a few moments – not if his intentions are honourable.

Even if you got an agency that promised to accompany viewers, that would not mean to say that, having given a false name and address, the conperson, whose face you now know, would not come back to wreak villainy upon you. In any case, estate agents have not been able to protect themselves or property against violence.

Selling a vacant house that is at a distance from your home is really a simple job. Don't fall for being the cat and allowing the mice to play. What you require is someone to hold the particulars and the keys, who was a friend and neighbour of the previous occupant. Get your board up with your own telephone number on and you are in business. Such a keyholder will have a friendly and true interest in getting you good money because he will wish to protect the value of his own greatest asset, which lies nearby.

CHAPTER 7
Selling

Marketing your house – what you must do first

Before 21 May 2010, sellers had to have a Home Information Pack or HIP before they put the house on the market. The use of HIPs has been suspended by the Coalition Government. It is likely that HIPs are going to be permanently scrapped, as they did not speed up the process of buying and selling homes as had been hoped, and the packs were regarded as an expensive barrier to the housing market. What is still required, however, is an Energy Performance Certificate for your home (which was a part of a HIP). This need not have been obtained before you begin marketing your home but it must have been commissioned when you first put the house on the market and must be obtained within 28 days of putting your house on the market. A number of places offer these certificates and a quick look in *Yellow Pages* or on the internet should help you to locate someone who can supply such a certificate for you.

Fixtures and fittings: what is included?

More trouble and anguish is caused by the failure of people to decide what they are selling than by any other single cause. Get it clear right at the start.

When you do move, leave more than you said you would. It doesn't need to be much to make the purchasers feel they have done better than they really expected.

As a matter of courtesy, curtain rails and all but the most expensive light fittings should be left. Don't mention them all in the particulars, or some smart alec will say he doesn't want them, so 'how much off the price' for putting you to the trouble of taking them down. Although you will have to give the information at some point, you may feel that you are in a stronger negotiating position if you don't disclose all of your hand at once.

What constitutes a fixture and a fitting, nobody seems to know. So try appealing to common sense; it's quicker and cheaper than consulting a professional.

Custom seems to say that fixtures are permanencies and semi-permanencies that one can't simply pick up and walk away with. Basically it includes things which are attached to the property. One way of looking at it is whether removal of the thing in question would damage the property. Television aerials, for example, are fixtures. You can put the lamp shade under your arm and walk away with it but the light switch is a different matter. It's the bits and pieces other than what are obvious parts of the house (such as the doors) and what are obviously not part of the house (such as a heavy plant pot in the garden that's too heavy to lift) which cause the trouble. Situations where it's not strictly breach of contract to remove an item but would be a breach of good faith to do so should be avoided. All this is not to say that you simply cannot take the doors. Of course you can – but you must make it clear to the purchaser that you so intend because anyone can reasonably assume that a door is a fixture and part of a house. So have a slow walk round every room and look at everything in it. Look, and think about things like the cooker or fixed washing machine that someone else might assume should count as a fitting and be included in the price without being detailed or argued about. In each of the rooms make a decision. Is it to be left or not?

Make a list of the things which someone might assume you are including in the price. Decide which you would sell and at what price. Mark the prices on a separate list from your list of particulars, the drawing up and printing of which will form the content of a later section. This early appraisal of what you are selling is your first step towards your valuation. Most buyers now expect to receive the Fixtures, Fittings and Contents Form published by the Law Society and available through legal stationers.

Valuations are easy: use comparisons

If you go to a rent or land valuation tribunal or arbitration, you will see and hear the professionals at it: people who can hardly squeeze through the door for the spread of letters behind their names.

'It's far too much. One on the east side of it went for much less,' says the one in the natty blue suit. 'Ah, but one on the north and another on the west side brought substantially more,' drawls the fat one.

The arbitrator listens to their comparisons and decides on something near the middle. In the end, comparisons and compromise are the only sensible way.

You can compare your own house with similar ones, and do it as well as anyone else. As a matter of fact, you have started already. Since the day you bought the house you, like other proud owners, have taken an interest in the property for sale in your district. You will, of course, have marked and remembered the ones that were offered for sale at more money than you browbeat the previous owners down to, and ignored the ones sold at a lower figure. You did right at the time; it made you feel much better and more successful. You must also remember that estate agents often don't actually have any formal qualifications in property valuation. Most, but not all, have experience of the market. There is no reason why you can't carry out a comparison yourself.

But it's down to brass tacks now; how accurate your valuation is will determine how long it will take you to sell, and whether you get what you ask, or what someone else is prepared to pay.

You need to collect information on two points: how much similar properties have *actually* fetched, and what opposition there is in the market on this very day.

Forget what you were asked to pay when you bought. If you actually paid less than the original asking price for your house, that price was the best that the vendor could get for it. If the vendor could have got more, he would have. If you were left thinking you had been done a favour, try to remember how it was done and use that bargaining skill when your prospects arrive, and do them a favour. It's only fair.

You will sell more quickly than the opposition if they have decided their price by adding up such things as: so much to pay off the mortgage, deposit for new house, new car, new washing machine and a good holiday – what the vendor wants as opposed to what his property is worth.

Don't let anyone flatter you into wishing for the moon. There are plenty of agencies who, to get a job, will raise your hopes unduly. They know the market. They also know that vendors will always come to their muttons later. In the meantime it swells the number of houses they have on their books. It makes them look big now at the expense of making you look small later on when you have to reduce your price.

Since 1 April 2000 it has become easier to find out what properties actually fetched in the neighbourhood, because it became compulsory to provide this information to the Land Registry. You don't need to do lots of searches at the Land Registry to find this information out. You can go onto www.ourproperty.co.uk and sign up for free. This site allows you to search particular streets so that you can find out what properties actually sold for – invaluable ammunition in the armoury of the private vendor, particularly if the house next door sold in the past few months.

You should then start comparing your property with others that are currently on the market by collecting details of properties of a similar age and type from your local paper's property column. If an agent to whom you apply for particulars asks for your name and address, give it. Don't play about with the 'It's for a friend' routine. The thing here, as in all house buying, selling and conveyancing procedures, is: be bold. And that is what we will call the users of this book: 'Mr & Mrs Bold'.

When you have found some properties which you think will make useful comparisons, go and do the viewing bit. Ask the vendors how they decided on their price. If the way they shape the reply is persuasive, note it for future use; if not, make a note not to say such silly things yourself when the time comes.

I know it's extremely hard, but don't look for the faults, and therefore justifications, for why your house is better and consequently worth more than theirs. Try to see those elements that are better than yours and could justify the vendor's price. For instance, if the house you are viewing is set well into the middle of a large development, give it points for not having to suffer as much early morning traffic noise as a house at the entrance and exit of the same estate. But if yours is at an entrance, don't continue comforting yourself with the vain thought, 'Oh, we soon got used to it, after a while you don't hear them. In any case, we might get someone whose job takes them out before anyone else.' Such musings, when you first moved in and discovered the disadvantage, might have made you feel better about the bargain you had made, but it's for real now.

Don't be shy about viewing other properties just for your own valuation purposes. No doubt others will do the same to you later. In any case, when you have read the section on 'Showing them round', you will realise that no viewer is an absolute waste of time.

Tradition says that purchasers always want something knocked off, so when you have worked out the going rate for a house such as yours, add about two per cent on to that figure to arrive at your asking price, thus leaving yourself a little room for negotiation. We will look at what, when, where and how to bargain later.

When you are fixing your opening price don't let anyone flatter you into asking way over the odds, with the hare-brained notion that you might catch an out-of-town buyer (more about them later too!) or someone who is desperate or doesn't know what he is doing. 'You can always come down later' is a prescription for an idiot. Of course you can always come down … and down … and down again. Making a deal when time has run out and it's you who is desperate is no time to decide on a price. So do so before you announce the sale. Make up your mind what you will take and not what you will be given.

It's silly to miss a perfectly good buyer who won't even come to view during the period you are trying for top price. By the time you come down to a realistic figure your buyer could be happily settled into another house. Your best buyers are those who come first. Don't miss them. Give them credit for having researched the market and done their comparisons too.

If you ask too much, your house will become a drag on the market even after being reduced below its real value. Don't let greed make you miss a buyer. You only need one!

Buyers know that private vendors don't have to pay agents' fees and therefore expect that fact to be reflected in the price asked. So take that into account when you decide what is the lowest price you will take. Vendors of property advertised by agents don't get the asking price. What they do get is what is left after the traditional two per cent put on to knock off has been negotiated away; less the professional creaming off; less the dreaded VAT and advertising costs. Because private vendors' houses sell more quickly than agency houses, your advertising costs should be lower than theirs; you pay no VAT or the rest of the list. So you can keep your price down and still make more money than if you let an agent mess about with it.

Now set about making the house itself look attractive.

Window dressing

This is the acquisitive society. We are all at it. But last year's luxuries give way to this year's pressing desires. And we need somewhere to store what, to us, are former favourites to which we are sentimentally attached, but to viewers will look like junk.

As soon as you decide to sell and have given notice of intention to your lender, get rid of the junk as quickly as the dustbin men will take it away. Bottles, jars, containers of all sorts that you never had time to fill with home-made preserves. Magazines and newspapers you intended to read again and never did. Offcuts of material from cotton to chipboard that you were sure would come in useful, together with the bent nails and screws which never did either. The clothes you hoped would come back into fashion. Let the lot go. Make it look as if there is bags of cupboard room. The fewer things there are on the wall-to-wall carpeting, the larger the room looks.

We all imagine that a house or garden that is neat, tidy and well kept will easily remain so. Viewers seem to think so too. A mucky house in a tatty garden has to be sold muck cheap. So tidy it up. It makes the happy home look more spacious and valuable immediately you have done so.

Modernisation

If, after looking at other properties, you feel that you have been left behind in the race to fit new kitchen units, central heating, bathroom suites and the like, think long and hard before, in a bid to compete, you decide to make such improvements yourself. You will have to add the cost to your asking price. And what if the first person to answer your advertisement would have bought, except that the style of your new bathroom suite brought out an instant attack of the dry heaves? As a matter of fact, you can, in your advertisement, use an unmodernised state to mark yours out from the rest.

'Built 40 years ago and now due for a face-lift, will suit handyman' – there's a disadvantage turned into an advantage for you!

If you have not already been tempted to become a do-it-yourself home improver, the present is not the time to experiment. A pressed-for-time reluctant handyman's botching shows.

There are plenty of enthusiastic improvers who are never so happy as when the house is in the process of transmogrification. Who are you to deny them the pleasure – at a price? Let them do it at their leisure. What is more, there are always one or two hopefuls looking for just such houses as yours, and to hear that the house has 'every modern refinement' is an immediate turn-off for them, even though in the long run such a house will cost them more than a fully modernised one.

If you have made changes to your home, do make sure that you have copies of all the necessary documentation consenting to the works of modernisation or alteration in your possession when you sell, in particular the Part P certificate for any electrical works in the kitchen.

Decorations

Viewers are a suspicious lot. Is there any wonder? So, although you are not covering up any cracks and damp patches, a full paint-and-dec job is not recommended. It would be unlikely to deceive anyone, anyway. It's a simple device and people know about it. No matter how old the decorations and fittings, the essential thing is for the house to be clean and give the impression that it could be lived in until such time as a buyer can cover up your 'vile interior decorations'. There is no harm in a bit of judicious touching-up. Odd spots where paint has been chipped off over the years can be improved with a deft stroke of coloured chalk.

Give the whole house a spring-clean. In particular:

- Clean and polish the windows.

- Shine up the furniture.

- Burnish the brasses.

- Replace or cut shorter the dirty ends of drop cords.

If you are selling an empty house where someone has died, or moved out into an institution, make sure you remove all remaining day-to-day personal effects such as engagement calendars, part-used tubes of toothpaste, and bottles of pills and potions which evidently failed.

The hall

Decide where the negotiations are to take place after viewers have looked round the rest of the house (the hall is a good choice if it is of sufficient size), and give it the full treatment, knowing the viewer will get the first and final impressions there. If you have the nerve for it, during the negotiations, you can say modestly, 'Sorry about the state of the hall. It's the only place we haven't got round to.'

Central heating

Let air out of the radiators. You don't want the diabolical bangings to start in the middle of a viewing session.

Gates, fences and paths

Take an objective look at the outsides. If the gate is hanging off, take it down to the rubbish tip or put it well out of sight so that your purchaser can discover it later, and smarty that he is, put it back securely. It won't matter what kind of lazy so-and-so he calls you then – you won't be within earshot. If a fence is dilapidated, tidy it up. A viewer might wonder if you are in dispute with a neighbour about whose responsibility it is. And if there is a sacked estate agent's board hanging around – get rid!

Tidy up the verge;; sweep the pavement and gutters. As a matter of fact, you should do this whether you are selling or not. Look after the area and it will look after you. If you have some white paint left over from doing the outside walls, or failing that some white emulsion, add plenty of thinners and give a concrete drive, path or steps the treatment. If you are not sure it will 'take' on your particular brand of concrete, experiment on a small section first. A parked caravan or boat should be moved to some other friendly haven for a while and any oil stains cleaned off. Buyers don't always have sufficient imagination to conjure up a vision of how expansive your uncluttered drive would be. But if they start eyeing it up because they too own a caravan you can come clean and inform them, going on to say, if it's true, that you have never had any complaints from council and neighbours.

Gardens

Tidy up. If the job would be too much, get some weedkiller for the beds and then give it a light forking. 'Lovely colourful garden this can be, just haven't had time this year, except to make it ready for planting.' If you can't even do that much, wait until just after Christmas; there is not much to choose between one snow-covered garden and another, but in any case, get cracking with the weedkiller on the paths; it's neither time-consuming nor costly. Lop any overhanging shrubs, which, after a shower of rain, would drench a viewer's coat sleeves as he pushes by.

The front door

If necessary, replace the front door handle, letterbox and any other adornments. In summer or autumn a colourful hanging basket can work wonders. If there happens to be a hook to hang one on, it would be cheap at the price. If the door sticks, for goodness sake have it adjusted, even if it means your family having to put up with a few draughts for a week or two. It's the first impression that counts, and your viewer's first is formed while standing staring at your front door.

Ventilation

No matter what the season and what the cost in extra heating, open doors and windows every day, making sure the house gets a complete blow-through, particularly if some chain-smoker has just been in to view.

Delightful as the roly-poly dachshund draught excluder might look at the foot of a door, send it walkies. You don't want viewers to think that you live on windy ridge.

House names

If your house has both a number and a name, take the name down. Names are a matter of taste and we all know there is no accounting for that. A Yorkshire person might find 'Beck Side' pleasantly inoffensive – but a southerner …!

What if your house is only identified by the name? It isn't everybody who knows that the name can be changed by telling the local authority (usually buildings department) of one's intention, so you are allowed to drop that into the conversation. However, if the name includes, more or less truthfully, the words 'old' or 'cottage', that is more than all right. They are sure winners at attracting viewers.

The message that you should be getting so far is: spend only what you must on making your house and its environs look attractive and free from problems. You should do the same even if you decide to use a property shop. Having done what you can, you are now ready to put a For Sale board in your neat garden, or For Sale bills in your sparkling windows.

For Sale boards

From first to last you need viewers. It's said that one picture is worth a thousand words and one demonstration is worth a thousand pictures. So, unless you have the most compelling reasons against it (they are sometimes prohibited in conservation areas – check with your local authority), you must put out a For Sale board. If not a board, then a bill in the window. You will be surprised how many people will see it, even if you live in a cul-de-sac. Postmen, milkmen, newsagents, canvassers and neighbours can all spread the word if you only let them know.

Estate agents admit that they get 30 per cent of their buyers from For Sale boards and went barmy at the government's proposals for only one small board in any garden and no 'sold' boards anywhere. But now that the law has been changed, they are having to settle for spending more of their clients' money on newspaper advertising.

If estate agents are sending hopefuls to other houses in your vicinity, they are bound to see your board or window bill, and if your outsides look OK they won't want to buy the one the agent has for sale without first hearing about and seeing yours. In fact, they might only cruise by the agent's; they know all about that one already from the particulars they collected. Curiosity killed the cat, and your board will attract the curious.

It's worth the expense of getting a professional-looking board. Window bills or For Sale boards can be hired and put up by firms found under 'signs' in the *Yellow Pages*.

How to put up your own For Sale board

You need:

- about eight feet of 3- x 1-inch wood for a post, if it's to be sunk into the ground, less if you screw it to the gate post;
- four bricks;
- a screwdriver;
- a garden spade.

Don't have anything more on your board than 'FOR SALE Apply within' and your telephone number. 'By appointment only' is rejecting, and wise birds think: 'Hello, you can only go when the bagpipe teacher next door isn't giving lessons.' 'View weekends only' tells the burglar when to call. Let viewers get out of their cars and ask for the details or, if you are not indoors, they can have a quiet look around the outside. Why not? You've nothing to be ashamed of, have you? If you have, get it attended to, now!

If you are putting the board in soil, dig a hole about 18 inches square and about 18 inches deep. Stand the board in the hole. Place two bricks at the bottom of the hole, one on either side of the post and parallel with one another, cover with about six inches of soil, then place a further two on top of and at right angles to the first two. Fill in and tamp down. You will be surprised at how firm your home-made board will be.

If you have a wooden gatepost, have the post for your board a little shorter, drill a couple of holes about 18 inches apart in it, and screw the post to the gatepost.

If people come in from a board or a window bill, you are halfway there. You haven't wasted an afternoon waiting in, when you could have been watching your favourite football team making a mess of it again. Indeed, you could have been doing something useful like drafting an advertisement to open up the market even further.

Advertising

This is a case of following the crowd. If it works for them, it will for you; hopefully, your board in the garden will have done the trick and, if not, your very first advertisement might.

Not all advertising has to be paid for; if you can come up with a story about why you are moving that looks like a news item, you could keep all the money in your pocket.

Anyone changing job, emigrating or doing anything adventurous or unusual should certainly contact the local newspaper and radio station to tell them about it. If you have children at school, is there a school magazine? Other parents might want to buy your house, believing that it's the atmosphere seeping out of your walls that makes your children so well behaved and brilliant. Do you have a parish magazine? Do you belong to any organisation to which you can give advance information of your move by sending an apology for absence, so that it goes into the minutes? You are not supposed to advertise in a radio interview, but what is more natural than, to the presenter's question 'when', you should reply 'when the house is sold, and that will be the biggest wrench because I doubt whether we'll get another with a spring of real ale gushing from the rockery and an open view over the nudist camp' … Keep the list going until you are stopped.

If you are moving away to be near your daughter, who everyone will be glad to hear has just had a baby, tell them. You've met some of the people in the area to which you are moving, and though they can't compare (who could?) with your locals, they seem a splendid bunch.

All these little strokes can be pulled for the sake of a short letter and a postage stamp or a telephone call. At the newspapers, ask for the news desk. At radio stations, ask for a presenter by name if you know one. They all need something to fill their columns and programmes and you really ought to help – where's your public spirit? Another 'free' advertisement is someone else's, so answer private 'wanted' advertisements.

Still another way of keeping your money where it rightly belongs is by putting postcards in local shop windows. At least it lets the talkative shopkeeper know.

And don't forget the internet – a number of sites allow you to advertise for free or for a fee – it's the best way of reaching the widest audience.

Advertisers who spend millions on media space know that only a proportion of it works; the trouble is they don't know which! Estate agents have a better idea because their advertising is specific and so it's easy to monitor the source of each response. They know where and when is best; follow their example and use the same papers on the same days as they do.

Don't be tempted by reductions for a series of advertisements. If your first attempt doesn't work, you might want to alter the 'copy' in some way.

The copy: composing your advertisement

There are three formats to choose from in a newspaper advert:

1. **Display:** One which will be placed among other 'boxed' adverts. The trouble with display is that it can get lost among the others, so ask if you can have a choice of borders. Borders to display adverts can be varied. Look through the paper at the different styles and choose. If you don't see anything outstanding, ask if they will accept a border drawn by you. If they will, get a sheet of Letraset transfers from an artists' shop and make your own. White print on black background,

if you fancy it, is called 'reversing out'.

It won't cost anything to ask if you can have your advert placed in one of the better positions. Although we read from left to right we only do so when we have time. Right-hand pages and top-and-bottom right-hand corners are said to be best.

If there is a property section, the first page is best and failing that, the last. Ask: if you don't ask, you don't get.

2. **Semi-display (classified):** Your advert appears in the column to which the class of thing you are offering refers – hence classified advertising; in your case the class is property. You will have noticed that a semi-displayed advertisement has lines (rules) separating it from other advertisements and you can choose where you want capital letters and where smalls, and how many spaces between the lines.

3. **Classified:** What you get for your money varies a little between newspapers, but generally it's a capital letter for the first word and the rest in smalls, apart from proper names, where good grammar demands a capital. Don't spurn the classified. Anyone who is actively in the market will be searching the whole paper. He won't miss you; neither will the nosy parkers who are usually gossips and will spread the word for you.

Advertising in national newspapers is costly. The first thing to consider is this: research shows that nine out of ten buyers move less than 10 miles, and only one in a hundred moves more than 100 miles.

For every reader of one of the nationals, there are ten for the local paper and the cost of advertising in a national is ten times that of a local, added to which, buyers don't expect to see local properties advertised nationally, unless there is something very special about them.

So stick to the locals, unless your house is special because:

*   it's in the upper bracket and has loose boxes, paddocks, fishing rights, private golf course, sound and video recording studio or other necessities for the rich;

*   it's in the area to which a large company is relocating staff from all over the globe; or

- houses in the area are being sold as weekend homes.

In any case, a local buyer is much easier to deal with than the man from Timbuktu.

The wording: what to put on; what to leave out

You need a headline. This goes for advertising on the internet as well as in a newspaper. As we know that people don't move very far and their choice is governed by district and price, these are two essential elements of your advertisement. If nothing else is read, those two items are, so make them your beginning and end. Least said, soonest mended.

Say what is for sale; give the asking price and arrangements for contacting you. Best to give the enquirers an invitation to view over the weekend. If they all come at once, so much the better; it proves what a good house it is, otherwise why are so many people interested? People always want what they think others want.

If you have an answerphone, assume that every call is a response to your advertisement, and put a message on giving viewing particulars. Just because callers are ringing about some totally unrelated subject, it doesn't mean to say that they or their friends wouldn't be delighted to buy your house now that they know it's for sale.

Don't bother unduly about the name and address of an interested party. The wicked give fake ones anyway. Estate agents dress it up as part of the confidential professional service that they are giving you, when they insist on names and addresses from enquirers. But the real reason is far more mundane: their own need to prove that they introduced the buyer – their commission claim rests on it.

From escorting a lady to view once or twice, I knew that she was insisting on a walk-in pantry. I also knew she adored wisteria; she thought it the epitome of elegance and class. I got a house for sale in exactly the right location for her and not only was there a wisteria but it was in full bloom. I telephoned and said we were giving her the first chance, even before full particulars were ready. One of our representatives was going to view in an hour's time. Could he pick her up on the way? Yes, it was a bungalow; yes, it had a garage. But for the moment that was all we knew, apart from the fact that, in an aside, the owner had said the wisteria was a picture. The lady viewed, found for herself that there was no walk-in pantry, and went on to convince herself that walk-in pantries weren't the be-all and end-all of life. But to get a wisteria like that going from scratch could take at least seven years. SOLD, to the lady who liked wisteria.

However, if you have a fine wisteria or fine anything else, don't put it into your advertisement. There are people who can't stand the sight nor smell of things creeping up the walls, but if they view and are impressed by your electronically operated garage doors, they will make light work of digging the offending plant out. On the other hand, the one buyer you want might not come if he knows about those doors; his cat might have lost a life in one.

Photographs

Sometimes there is a case for using a photo of a detached house if it's individually styled, but as builders have, in recent years, built thousands of detached houses having only minimal variations in their elevations there are few compelling reasons for using one.

As for semi-detached or terraced (mews, town, etc.) houses, I don't know how anyone interested in buying a house in this country can have avoided learning what they look like. Indeed, the mere mention of a development is sufficient to bring to mind the type of houses there. So why our eyeballs have to be rattled week after week, with page after page of silly little photos of semis and terraced houses I'll never know, and as for a tiny picture of a block of flats ... who wants to go viewing a barracks? Because that is what many agency photos make them look like.

If advertising on the internet, people will expect a photo. If you have a fabulous lounge, or a wonderful bathroom, why not photograph that instead of the front of the house to mark you out from the crowd?

Instructions to printers

Always make your instructions to printers as clear as you can. Compositors work at speed and they are not mind-readers. Instructions should always be circled and preferably in a different colour.

Words that will conjure up a picture in the reader's mind must be carefully chosen:

- **backing onto woodland:** burglars lurking

- **oak beams:** charm, cosiness

- **exceptional opportunity:** why hasn't somebody taken it, then?

- **great potential:** work

- **sea view:** peace or bank holiday chaos on the roads

- **overlooking river or lake:** damp for the old, too deep for the young

- **near golf course:** can nip over the fence for a few quick swings or collect other people's lost golf balls

- **old:** immortal, tried and trusted

- **Victorian:** solid, spacious

- **prestigious:** schoolteachers and many others know the words come from prestidigitation – which means trickery!

- **cottage or cottage style:** if you can use it, do so. It's the biggest crowd-puller there is. But the picture some people conjure up at the thought is so chocolate-boxy that you are in grave danger of disappointing them, should they come and you have no white palings, no roses round the door and it's simply an old house in a street.

So, don't overdescribe: people will drive by instead of coming in to keep an appointment. You are buying disappointment and will lose confidence.

There is a buyer for everything

If your For Sale board and your first advertisement don't work, immediately remember that the hallmark of true entrepreneurs is that they are never 'counted out'. They try and try again. So alter your advertising copy a little. Go from one section of the paper to another; if you didn't succeed in the classified, try display and so on.

Tomorrow is another day. New buyers come into the market every single day.

Don't advertise more than twice in the same paper in the same week. Be ready to change the wording.

Example particulars

PARTICULARS OF PROPERTY FOR SALE

Mr & Mrs T Bold

offer

FOR SALE PRIVATELY
(no agents)

14 Plevna Place, Blossomton

£275,000 Freehold

Registered at Her Majesty's Land Registry Title No. EDN999707

- Entrance Hall
- Lounge
- Separate Dining Room
- Kitchen
- Utility Room
- Cloaks with WC
- Good decorations
- Central heating
- Large Bedroom with en suite shower

- Second Bedroom
- Good Third Bedroom
- Second and Third Bedrooms have washbasins
- Bathroom with WC
- Well-insulated loft
- Quality fittings throughout
- Manageable gardens
- Garage and car port off wide street

Gas, electricity and mains water are connected. The Council Tax paid last year amounted to £1,079.

Vacant possession by arrangement.

There are nursery and playschools within walking distance. A sitter-in club operates in the district. The Orchard shopping centre is just around the corner, as is the regular bus service to town. Ten minutes' car journey to mainline and inter-city trains.

Plevna Place is off Orchard Road, which is directly off the A444 at Bericote Cross Road close to the local park.

Viewing at any reasonable time.

If you wish to confirm, please telephone 01234 28370

This house is in a very pleasant and respectable neighbourhood and has been very reasonably priced at £275,000 for an EARLY SALE.

No agents   Mr & Mrs Bold, 14 Plevna Place

These particulars are believed to be correct but do not constitute an offer or any part of a contract.

Your predecessor sold the house to you, your old neighbours sold to your new ones. The area isn't littered with empty houses that no one will live in. Of course you will sell your house and you will sell it yourself, keeping your money where it belongs.

Particulars

People have come to expect a set of particulars. If for no other reason, that is why you should have some, but you must not allow interested parties to use them as a substitute for viewing. At the risk of boring you, curiosity killed the cat.

Salesmen believe that one demonstration is worth a million words. It's certainly true of houses. Differences can be so subtle, only inspection can prove which is the best buy. Yet people are basically idle; it doesn't take a lot to put them off. They sit in their armchairs, leafing through a fistful of agents' particulars, and no matter how well a house has been proposed and worthily recommended, they will blackball it without actually seeing it for themselves. If they got everything they thought they needed to know from the particulars, what need is there to view? How can a house get sold if it's left to buyers to decide, on a whim, which is best for them? They need our encouragement to work at it, which translated into a few words means: view and buy ours.

Try to restrict the distribution of your particulars to those who have been shown round. Give a copy to help them remember you and yours better than all the other run-of-the-mill properties they have seen.

Estate agents can get away with the most appalling rubbish and the silliest descriptions, because people don't take a lot of notice of their 'bijou residence of great charm and delight', knowing it means 'a poky hole with old-fashioned fittings', although agents can now be prosecuted if they do misrepresent key information.

Private vendors can stick to plain language. Describe but don't overdo it. Big is as good as six-and-three-quarter metres – or is it kilowatts? Who knows? Who cares, apart from surveyors, who have to make a great performance with their tape measures in an effort to impress the gullible. If your rooms are the wrong size for other people's carpets and you have given the game away in your particulars, they won't view. If they only find out when they come, they'll be delighted to hear that one of their neighbours-to-be is a carpet fitter, who needs a bit of weekend work; he's good and he's cheap!

Photographs

If you think a picture stuck onto your particulars will help prospects to remember your house, get some self-adhesive mini-prints made. This is particularly straightforward with digital cameras and the range of prints available. Alternatively, you can go to a specialist printer.

When taking the photograph, stand on a stepladder; it helps to keep the walls in proper perspective. Wait until fog, cars, vans, police, cats and dogs and canvassers are out of the way. Shut the garage doors, draw all but decorative curtains well back and take all of the washing in.

Drafting

If you can type the particulars, so well and good, but if your handwriting is clear, that's something different. Most people will expect typewritten particulars and with home computers, this should be fairly straightforward. Failing your being a typist or a handwritist, your local duplicating agency or photocopier will do both typing and printing on A4-size paper for you. Choose a copier who has a standard border that your particulars can be laid on for copying. Just because it's cheaper for quantities, don't buy more than you need. Twenty should be plenty. In any case, you might want to make some adjustments later.

On our specimen particulars shown on page 58, we have tried to give the prospects plenty of reading. Not as much as would make them feel they knew it all without viewing, but more information than they are likely to get from an agent.

If your house is registered, this is obviously a good thing to show. Estate agents don't show it, and one can only speculate on the reason. It can't possibly be the cost – it's free! Perhaps they don't understand the matter, or if they do they want to keep the knowledge to themselves believing that a little knowledge is a dangerous thing for clients to have.

But as T.H.Huxley says, if a little knowledge is a dangerous thing, where is the man who has enough to be safe? Or as I would have it: a little knowledge in the hands of house buyers is a dangerous thing for the professionals in their search for easy pickings. But no matter who is right, estate agents and solicitors don't seem unduly disturbed at the moment. They know that no matter how many For Sale boards rot away, how many sold-subject-to-contract slips dance on and off the boards, how many mortgage applications fail, how many bridging loans have to be paid or chains collapse, most people get moved, jobs get cobbled together somehow, and if sleep is to be lost, it won't be theirs. They have seen it all before.

If, because you have a mortgage or for any other reason, you haven't got the deeds to flash under a prospect's nose, put your name and address on a Form OC1 and send it to the Land Registry with a fee currently of £8. In reply you will receive an official Land Registry certificate of search, proving the registration and the title number. You can then show it to a prospect, who might be one of the growing band of buyers who know they can buy without the aid of a solicitor. Knowing so early on in the proceedings whether the house is registered or not is valuable. In any case it's something new and different, and gives a stamp of approval to the proceedings: he'll remember *your* house all right.

Although you would not wish to print it on the particulars, another thing you could usefully do would be to call at the local council office and ask if there is anything special about to happen round your way, such as a new building, a sewage farm or road widening. It's as well to know about it now. Knowledge is power, and sometimes very profitable. Some kinds of development enhance a house's value. If so, you don't want to sell to some speculator; keep the profit for yourself.

Disclaimers

All estate agents write one at the foot of their particulars, some briefly and some at great length, such as:

Allwind & Waters state for themselves and the vendors of the property described herein that the acceptance of a copy of these particulars is made on the understanding that the applicant has read and understood the content and meaning hereof and that these particulars are intended as a general guide only and do not constitute any sort of contract or offer or part thereof and that no person of either sex in the employ full or part time of Messrs Allwind & Waters has any authority to make any representation warranty or give any guarantee whatever in relation to this property.

Why any honest, hard-working qualified and competent persons should subject people with whom they are trying to do business to such an eyesight test I don't know. If staff are incompetent, they should be moved on, and certainly not be let near the tens of thousands of pounds of 'what is most probably our most important and valuable possession'.

Private vendor's disclaimer

Having been rigorously honest and above all painstaking about the things you do put in, you can use the delightfully simple: These particulars are believed to be correct but don't constitute an offer or any part of a contract.

Showing them round

Lonely, elderly and single people fear lest having a board in the garden will attract all sorts of villains. That fear is no reason for paying a thousand pounds or more to an agency.

Though an agent might get the name and address of every enquirer, do you really expect any villain whose dearest wish is to rape, plunder, pillage and set fire to you to give a correct address? Even if an agent accompanies every enquirer, having once seen the house and ingratiated himself, the enquirer can call back unaccompanied and wreak villainy upon you.

If you don't use, or haven't yet got, a chain on your door, you must. If you don't, sooner or later you will be done over, selling a house or not, agents or no agents. You can always keep an enquirer on the other side of the door and make an appointment for a time when a friend can come round, or even when you have arranged for other viewers to come.

Ask yourself, 'Could anyone sell me a house I didn't really want?' Even if he had graduated from a top business salesmanship school, got a gold medal from the professor for it, had all the patter and ready-thought-out glib answers to all the searching questions, had manoeuvred you into saying 'yes' at every twist and turn in the conversation, including the final 'yes', so that you could get home in time to watch The Party Political Broadcast – would you really feel bound? Wouldn't you find some reason for, at least, forgetting it?

Buyers have plenty of time to forget it. The cooling-off period allowed in consumer protection legislation is but a fleeting moment compared with the time solicitors take to get contracts signed and exchanged – the point at which, and not before, neither party can back out except at the risk of severe penalties.

No matter how many books you have read on selling, no matter how many seminars, courses or lectures you have attended to be talked at, or successful role-plays you have accomplished about selling, the message with regard to selling houses is that if they have been properly prepared, they don't need super-salesmen: **they sell themselves.**

Your task is to allow someone who wants your house to know that it's for sale, and then to let him have it (the house). Put no obstacle in his path. Smooth that path. Prepare yourself, and any other members of your household who might come in contact with viewers to do just this:

1. Let him in.

2. Show him round.

3. Let him know that others are interested.

4. Bargain if you must.

5. Carry out the instructions on what to do when a buyer says 'I will'.

If people knock on the door in response to seeing the board in your garden, and you are not alone in the house, let them in. Only if the most embarrassing scene is being enacted within should you ask them to come back later. From first to last, remember that doubtless this is your most prized possession that you are trying to sell. You must be prepared to work at it and accept some inconvenience.

You only need one buyer and he may well be standing before your very eyes. It might cost you another £50 in advertising before you get another viewer, so a bird on the doorstep can be worth two in the bush.

If people ring up for an appointment to view, remember the walk-in pantry lady, and say as little as possible over the phone.

Don't worry too much about the problem of time-wasters. They might arrive at the same time as a genuine prospect, and the so-called time-waster might just jerk the prospect into action.

When the viewers come in daylight make sure the curtains are drawn well back. Have doors onto landings and passages open to let light in. It all makes a house look more airy and spacious.

For evening viewers, use only the softest of lighting and try to have lamps already switched on. Don't switch lights off as you vacate rooms.

They might think you extravagant, but if they ask to see the electricity bills, they will be convinced that they, being more careful than you, will have less to pay.

Decide beforehand who is to lead the conducted tour if there should be more than one of you at home when the viewers arrive. Leave the others seated comfortably in the lounge. They must not be smoking, arguing or drinking anything because you don't want to look unfriendly by not offering a portion to the visitors. The television, radio or CD player should only be playing if your neighbour is giving a bagpipe lesson. Otherwise, all that the loungers have to do is politely acknowledge (they must not ignore) the presence of the viewers. Children should be introduced properly.

Those who are light-fingered work to the four As: they will steal anything from anybody, anywhere, any time. So don't leave pocketable things around. Don't actually search viewers as they leave, but just have it at the back of your mind that everybody is not as honest as you are.

You should enter each room first, and then invite viewers to follow you. If the view is worth seeing, ask them to step to the window. Open cupboard and wardrobe doors to show how spacious they are. Draw attention to thermostats on radiators and situations of power plugs. Don't draw attention to things that are big enough to see such as fireplaces and tiled walls. Demonstrate water pressure at sinks, baths and WCs. Similarly, an electronically controlled garage door needs to be demonstrated, because it too is not immediately obvious to the unassisted eye.

When you've shown them round, invite their questions and answer as honestly as you can. If you don't know the answer, say so.

If a viewer says, 'Oh dear, I thought there might be a bidet', keep your witty remarks to yourself until after he's gone. And don't let it cast you down. It could be you've got a buyer here and such carping is a tactic in the strategy of bargaining, about which more later.

You can't put anyone off buying his dream home but do avoid any unintended insult. He'll only get his own back later if you give one.

Safety lies in getting as many clues about him as soon as possible. Ask the royal question, 'Have you come far?' The answer to that or subsequent get-to-know-right-by-guessing-wrong statements will help you get the picture and determine your future chat.

If you are asked how long your house has been up for sale and the truthful answer is: 'Just this week', say so. If it's a while longer, say, 'Oh, not long, houses along here never are'. If the viewer is a smarty and bowls you a guess-wrong-to-get-to-know right, such as 'A week?', it's own-up time folks, because such a questioner will treat you with utmost suspicion from then on if you don't.

Don't introduce negative thoughts by bragging about the money you have spent on eradicating woodworm and the guarantee against its recurrence that you got.

Owner-occupiers are inordinately proud of their houses and when they are conducting prospective purchasers round, it shows, so the sensitive viewer will often say anything to avoid giving offence when trying to bring the visit to a comfortable close. Team viewers, such as husband and wife, will naturally wish to discuss together the merits of the house, not in front of the vendor, but after leaving, and the real purchaser can quite easily turn out to be the one who walks round without saying a word, and succeeds in leaving you with the feeling that you have been wasting your time.

Prospects who have made appointments will turn up to view. At the gate, they may realise that yours is not for them, but for courtesy's sake will come to the door.

However, as soon as a viewer steps over the threshold, most of us get a feeling of whether what we have to offer is what he is looking for. If you sense it's not, show him round and show him out. In the cases where you feel that there is a glimmer of hope, keep him there and take your time in showing him as much as possible, with such little tricks as asking him to admire the view. But don't let the conversation stray, for long, from points about the house; keep to such things as the local shops and the price.

Nevertheless, the safest plan is to treat all viewers as buyers, but ignore what they say, or fail to say, initially about their intentions. Prefer to wait for further action to develop and until it does, keep on showing viewers round.

How to negotiate

You will have already calculated what is the very best deal you can hope for and what is barely acceptable to you; what are the optional extras you will sell and what are the extras you intend to include in your price. You can then bargain on these points if required to. Being prepared, you won't have to rely on the other party to make up your mind for you.

Don't bargain at all unless you have to. Put it off as long as possible. As you are showing the nicest part of your nature, the more time viewers have to get to know you, the less they will want to offend by offering too little. In any case, there are still a few around who find it embarrassing and ill-mannered to bargain and that is still another reason why your price must be realistic in the first place.

If, initially, you are asked, 'Will you take an offer?', answer 'Of course, come in and have a look round and we'll have a talk about it.' Then get off the subject with, 'Have you come far?'

The opening from a serious prospect

It usually goes something like: 'Will you take an offer?' Well, you are open to an offer; it all depends what he has in mind. When you are given a figure, no matter what it is, look shocked. If no figure is forthcoming, keep fencing, saying that you have stated your price and hope to get it, but for a quick decision from a good buyer you will talk. By the way, has he sold his house? Will it be cash, or will he require a mortgage; how quickly could he complete?

There is a lot of guesswork in bargaining. He who has the most facts wins, so get to know as much as you can about the other party as soon as possible. In a bargaining situation, delay is a most useful weapon so use it if you can. If he won't talk, you must ask questions; the other side then has to reveal some of his hand.

Reluctant bargainers

If you really don't feel up to all the argy-bargy, you could advertise 'no offers'. But as your first task is to draw as many viewers as possible and 'no offers' could stop some coming, prefer to wait and reply to offers with, 'I know that people expect to bargain for houses, but I have never been accustomed to it and have therefore made sure that my asking price is the most reasonable that anyone could expect to get it for.' Then hand them a copy of your particulars on which you have already written that little lot, or words to that effect.

Never accept the first offer. The deal will collapse if you do, because the prospect thinks he could have got it for less. Never say 'no', say 'maybe'. Hide this book from the gaze of prospects. Because you are selling for yourself, they think you are an amateur and they will be relaxed, an ideal bargaining atmosphere – don't lose it.

Give satisfaction. People get more satisfaction from the things they have to work for.

Bargaining points

Use things you intended to include in the purchase price as bargaining points; for example, if you had included the carpet and curtains, you can counter with 'all right, but I couldn't possibly include the carpets and curtains at that price'.

Half a loaf is better than none, particularly if your half has the butter on.

Making a benchmark

When some people receive their first offer, they are known to say, even though it's hardly true, that they have got as good an offer already, so if, just for the look of the thing, the new man will add £2,500 to his offer, that could tie things up and leave things comfortable all round.

Anglers need patience

If people don't bite first time, don't worry, they might have taken the bait.

The harder you fight in the beginning, the less you give away in the long run.

Keep reminding the bargainer of the bargain he is getting, compared with what is being offered elsewhere.

Use Stamp Duty Land Tax bands. Stamp Duty Land Tax is payable at one per cent on properties over £125,000; three per cent on properties over £250,000 and four per cent on properties over £500,000. If you really want somewhere around, but less than the figure which happens to be the point at which Stamp Duty Land Tax becomes payable, or at which the rate of Stamp Duty Land Tax changes, make your asking figure a little above it. You can then, with a long face, agree to bring your price down to save him tax. The purchaser has won, honour is satisfied, big deal! Think about whether you are dealing with a first-time buyer. If your house is worth around the £250,000 mark, remember that until 25 March 2012 first-time buyers pay no Stamp Duty Land Tax, provided that the purchase price is less than £250,000. If you know your buyer, you will have a much more successful negotiation.

Never show triumph. Always let them appear to win.

If they send an expert

He is on their side. About the dry rot, lay off the tommy rot; don't try to influence him. If you can overcome your generous instincts, don't even offer a cup of tea. Let him report – 'Hard people, they won't give anything away, don't seem to care whether they sell to you or not, maybe got a queue'.

The manipulators

This is the one who, when you think it's all agreed and you are waiting for contracts to be signed, comes back time and again for more. Remedy: ask for a final set of demands in writing. Another good reason for knowing about contracts and how solicitors work. Read on – all will be revealed.

Box yourself in

Cut off your retreat. Burn down your bridges: tell the bargainer that you are anxious to move quickly and, to get a quick sale, you set your price where you did, in spite of being told that you could get far more. As a matter of fact, agents have never stopped ringing, offering to do just that, but you know what they are – anything to get people signed up. But you have pitched your price with just the odd bit added on, to allow a modest bargain and you can't possibly go lower, what with the mortgage and all that.

Don't leave the bargaining to an agency or a solicitor but if you find he has got involved don't tell him your rock bottom deal. He wants the job out of the way; he has not got the time for lengthy bargaining sessions.

If in doubt

Say nowt.

Forget pride

Derogatory remarks about your pride and joy are intended to cost you money.

Free option

If you agree to let someone know, if and when you decide to reduce your price, make sure that you have got an offer out of him first so that when you do go back, you go with a new price that allows you some elbow room.

Problems

They don't go away – they go into corners and breed. Our ruin is often caused by not what we say, but what we fail to say and/or get into writing.

Closing an interview

'We are expecting someone else soon. Will you let me know by next Wednesday as I have half-made promises elsewhere.'

To sum up

Cups of tea, a guided tour of your holiday snaps, or a privileged look into the eggcup containing your gallstones will not sell your house. Nor will playing the super-salesman. Your job is to get the viewers. Houses sell themselves if you will only:

- let viewers look round;
- let them bargain if they must;
- let them agree to buy;
- let them pay a deposit;
- let them go home;
- be natural – be yourself;
- be a listener as well as a talker;
- be modest about the house;
- don't show off; it's the house that is on view, not you.

What to say when a buyer says 'I will'

'Who is your solicitor?' 'I am acting for myself and you can tell your people to get in touch with me. Will you please pay me a deposit now as a sign of good faith?', although this latter statement is very unlikely to get a positive response!

Of course, people have to get mortgages. Of course, many have to get their own houses sold and, of course, if they are really serious they will have done as much as they can towards sorting these problems out before they meet you. Ask them where they are at in the process and if possible check their answers. Acting for yourself you can then so easily be honest and fair to everybody – but chiefly yourself.

For instance, you can keep a buyer keened up while you are looking for reserves by being ready to say, 'I do hope you will be able to buy it, but as you know, there's many a slip twixt cup and lip, so I will have to keep the board out. But I promise you that you are top of my list. I won't sell to anyone else without getting in touch with you. That's fair, isn't it?'

Even if there are a dozen, they are all top of the list, because you don't really fancy the chances of the previous ones if someone turns up an hour later with the folding money, ready to sign a contract then and there. It can happen and it can be done – see later.

For expedition, the seller should prepare a complete set of papers ready for the buyer including the following:

- Property Information Forms
- Fixtures, Fittings and Contents Form
- Office Copy entries and a filed plan
- Copy of lease (if leasehold)
- Copy of any relevant Consents (to modernisation, etc.)

It's also advisable to get local water and environmental searches completed. You no longer need to do this by law, as the Home Information Pack has been suspended, but it will get things moving more quickly, although this is a cost that usually falls on the buyer so may be one that you may not wish to incur.

Never say die

If your home is clean, neat, tidy and properly priced, your buyer will come. See the bargain-hunter off. Keep on showing viewers round right up to the minute you get a contract signed.

CHAPTER 8

Contracts

A contract is a legally binding agreement to do something. Contracts for the sale and purchase of land must be in writing, contain all the important terms agreed by the parties and, importantly, must be signed by the parties. Either both parties may sign one document or there can be an exchange of identical documents, one signed by each party which are literally 'swapped'. This is the usual position when selling houses. Parties must be identifiable and over 18 years of age. Lunatics and some drunkards are debarred. What transforms a simple agreement into a contract is that the contract is made for 'consideration'. Consideration is a matter of inducement for something promised, so it has to be valuable, for example money.

A vendor's contract says in effect: you, Mr Rashley, have induced me to promise you vacant possession of my house by offering to pay me £275,000. And if Mr Rashley puts his signature to this agreement (upon that valuable consideration of £275,000) called a contract (that the vendor, too, has signed), and fails to keep his bargain, then he is bound and can be sued if he doesn't complete the bargain contracted for.

The Law Society and Oyez publish a property contract called an 'Agreement (incorporating the Standard Conditions of Sale (Fourth Edition))'. All the main headings required for a contract for the sale of a freehold or leasehold house situated in England and Wales are there – see example at the end of this chapter. If you are selling, have three copies ready as soon as you put the house on the market.

Solicitors will choose from either the Law Society's contract or draft their own. The conditions are set out in full on the inside of the agreement.

These conditions occupy line after line of fine print (literally as long as an arm). So stand well back and if any of it has been altered, have a closer look, and if you still don't know what is going on, ask for an explanation. Often, the standard conditions will be altered by means of 'Special Conditions', which form a page at the front of the contract.

Just remember:

Vendor: You want the money.

Purchaser: You want the house.

That's all there is to it!

Contracts for the sale of land (in our case with buildings on) usually include the following:

1. **Description of the parties:** Names and addresses of both vendor and purchaser.

2. **Description of what is being sold:** Only where just part of a registered title or unregistered land or rights of way are included in the sale should a plan of the area accompany the draft contract. In all other cases, the inclusion of a plan is unnecessary and will not usually govern the scope of the contract in any event. A plan may, however, be necessary if you are buying a new house 'off plan' and want to ensure that the house when built corresponds with what you were promised at the outset.

   If the property is unregistered, there should be, if the conveyances say so, a plan among the deeds. If there isn't a mention of such a plan, then there will be a description. Often there are both. Plans are easier to understand than descriptions, but just because a plan is included doesn't mean that this takes precedence over the description in the deed. If registered, you will receive a copy of the plan with the Office Copies (something else which you will learn about in chapter 10).

   There may be included in the description of what is being sold, a recital of any rights that are sold with the land, such as light, water, way and drainage. Usually the contract just refers to the Office Copies, where this is all noted or in the case of unregistered land, to an earlier document containing these rights. However, these rights can be mentioned here in general terms at this stage, and answered in a little more detail when requisitions (questions) on (about the) title (ownership) are received after exchange of contracts. The fourth edition of the Standard Conditions of Sale provide that the buyer is not allowed to ask questions regarding title after exchange of contracts if the vendor proves his title before exchange of contracts. He is only allowed to ask questions about things if he learned about them for the first time after contracts were exchanged. If the vendor doesn't adduce title before contracts are exchanged, the purchaser has six working days after he adduces title to ask any questions about the title that he may have. Realistically, it is best to sort out any questions about rights of way or restrictive covenants before you exchange contracts to make sure that the standard conditions do not prevent you from doing so and you are locked in to making an expensive mistake. If in doubt as to whether the house is entitled to the access that the vendor claims that it has (for which he relies on an old deed which hasn't been registered), consult a solicitor on this point.

3. **The price.**

4. **The amount of deposit (customarily ten per cent of the price, but often less),** and how it's to be paid and by whom it will be held acting as stakeholder (agent/bank manager/solicitor or vendor and purchaser, who open a joint bank account for this purpose only). If the other side has a solicitor who will agree to be stakeholder, you can agree. Otherwise, the deposit is relatively unprotected as it can be released to the seller before completion. If completion didn't happen for any reason, the deposit monies may not be very easy to recover. However, if completion fails to occur due to the fault of the buyer, the deposit will be forfeit.

It's quite normal for a seller to borrow his buyer's deposit for use as his deposit and so on up the buying chain, if there is one. This applies only by agreement, as set out in Standard Condition 2.2.2. This often means it's the poorest person at the bottom of the chain who has to stump up the deposit, then used by each person up the line.

The fourth edition of the Standard Conditions contains restrictions on how the deposit can be paid. A banker's draft is no longer acceptable. Unless the Standard Conditions are altered, the deposit must be paid either by cheque drawn on the client account of a solicitor or licensed conveyancer or by 'direct credit', i.e. CHAPS transfer. As you are doing it yourself, you will need to use a CHAPs transfer, which will incur a fee, but you probably would incur this fee through your solicitor anyway.

5. **The date for completion:** This is a matter for agreement between the parties. The purchaser should make up the difference between the deposit paid and the purchase price on the completion date, and in exchange the vendor should give full vacant possession. What, you may ask, if either side finds that he can't complete to the exact date? Don't be frightened, and, furthermore, don't despair – it isn't a legal problem yet. Whether you are doing the job for yourself or paying a Skinner, the hiccup would have occurred and it would have been yours to cure. However, it's advantageous to complete as soon as possible to prevent paying unnecessary interest. This will be prescribed by the contract and will be a few per cent over the base rate.

If your opposite number to the contract gives what sounds like a good reason for delay, then you must come to some new understanding, and if your vendor is being silly and says he wants more money, has changed his mind about the house he wanted to buy or move into, or simply changed his mind full stop, then you have to make some decisions. What are your options? If it's postponement, you can calmly accept his new date. But if you decide that the contract should be kept, then you must give the other party written notice to complete. The notice must be reasonable and take into account the circumstances of the particular case. If you are faced by this very unusual circumstance, have a look at the standard notice period in Condition 6.8 of the Standard Conditions of Sale, which gives ten working days with which completion must take place. But check the 'Special Conditions' first to see whether this has been altered in any way. If, following the expiry of a notice to complete, the purchaser fails to complete, you have a choice. You can either walk away and forfeit the deposit and sue for any additional losses or you can force the purchaser to complete the contract by suing for 'specific performance'. The purchaser can sue for damages if the vendor fails to complete.

If you had a problem with your washing machine, you would first look at the instructions and if you were stumped, you wouldn't be afraid to consult a service engineer. So if after giving notice you haven't got a sensible new arrangement, then consider going to a solicitor for advice.

The only (very rare) circumstance in which either or both of the parties to the contract can insist that the contract be completed or come to an end on the very date contracted for is where a clause has been inserted in the contract saying that 'time is the essence' of the contract. If time is not of the essence of the contract, service of a notice to complete has the effect of making time of the essence. Therefore, the other party must complete on the date that the notice to complete expires, which is the number of days (after service of the notice) which is set out in the contract. If time is or has been made of the essence and, say, a purchaser says, 'but I can't complete until the day after the date specified for completion or the expiry of the notice', the vendor is at liberty to put the contract at an end and confiscate the deposit. If it's the vendor who cannot or will not complete, and time is the essence, the purchaser can put an end to the contract, demand the deposit back, and, if he has suffered any loss, possibly sue for damages.

6. **The capacity in which the vendor sells:** You must choose between 'full' and 'limited' guarantee in the contract. Full title guarantee is for both freehold and leasehold. It implies that vendors:

(a) have the right to dispose of the property as they are purporting they have;

(b) will at their own cost do all that they can reasonably to give the purchaser the title that they purport to give, which includes doing what they reasonably can to ensure that the purchaser is entitled to be registered with at least the class of title registered before the disposition;

(c) assert that the property is free from all financial charges (e.g. mortgage) and incumbrances and all other rights exercisable by third parties that the vendor knows about and could reasonably be expected to know about, but you don't have to refer to items already on the Register or 'overriding interests' of which the purchaser has notice.

The circumstances whereby a vendor could not give full title guarantee (which in particular will not guarantee that the title is free from all financial charges) include:

(a) where a trustee disposes of property under a will, then he would not sell with full title guarantee;

(b) a mortgagee in possession, which would also not sell with full title guarantee;

(c) executors selling following the death of the former owner.

7. **Extras (or 'chattels'):** Items that are not fixtures and fittings, which can pass by delivery, and have been bargained for separately are sometimes included by reference to a separate inventory. If included in the purchase price (stated in the contract) and a separate value has been agreed for them, that price is stated in this clause, particularly if doing so will reduce the Stamp Duty Land Tax payable on the transfer or conveyance (more about this later).

8. **Covenants:** These are usually included in the contract by reference to the Office Copies for registered land. However, they may be noted in the contract and a full copy may be attached to the draft contract. This is usually only appropriate on sales of part of land where the vendor wishes to take covenants from the purchaser to restrict the use of land in the future or of unregistered land. This will be the case for new covenants. Old covenants should be apparent from the Register or the deeds or the Land Charges search.

    The seller should always mention those covenants he knows of, even if he has no idea who can enforce them, or whether they can be enforced. The buyer must decide what relevance they have. The clause in the contract will say that the purchaser, having been supplied with a copy, is deemed to have full knowledge of them and no requisitions (questions) or objections shall be raised in respect thereof. Normally this means that the vendor will answer questions about the covenants having been kept, but that he is not getting himself involved in trying to get any of them changed and the purchaser cannot back out just because something turns out to be worse than he first thought.

9. **Freehold or leasehold:** A freehold is a title with unlimited duration; a leasehold property is held on a lease, which comes with responsibilities to a landlord. Most flats are leasehold. In the latter case the lease should be referred to. Put the lease through the copier and attach to the draft contract. Again provide in the draft contract that there are to be no requisitions or objections, but be prepared to answer sensible questions if you know the answer for sure. If you are buying freehold and Skinner offers limited title guarantee or puts any fancy work on the contract that you don't easily understand, the Registrar will always give limited guarantee in cases of doubt. Do remember though that limited guarantee may be insufficient for those purchasers with a mortgage. Full title guarantee will usually be

required as this is a higher assurance as to the title. A person will usually sell with limited title guarantee if he is selling as the executor of an estate, because he will not necessarily have personal knowledge of the property.

10. **The rate of interest to be paid or contract rate** for the period between the completion date in the contract, and the date on which completion actually happens. Fix the rate at a little above your bank's minimum lending rate, or the prevailing building society rate, or just write 'Law Society rate', which is usually a rate above the base rate, currently four per cent above the base rate of Barclays Bank.

11. **Title:** A statement about how the vendor intends to prove that he is the owner. This is done by:

    (a) registered property: saying that the Office Copies will be supplied; or

    (b) unregistered property: quoting a conveyance or some other good root of title of the property which is at least 15 years old. More about (a) and (b) later.

12. **Risk:** What happens if the house is destroyed or seriously damaged between the date you exchange contracts and the date you were to complete? If the Law Society's contract is being used, the answer is simple. The buyer can withdraw from the contract and ask for his deposit back.

    Under the Standard Conditions of Sale, the risk remains with the seller until completion but solicitors do usually vary this in the contract depending on the circumstances.

    Be very wary of buying under a contract that places the risk on the buyer from date of exchange. In the absence of any contract clause to the contrary, when the parties exchange contracts, in a sense the property becomes the buyer's. It's his property subject only to paying the price and taking a transfer or conveyance. So at common law, if it's destroyed, it's his problem. It may also be the seller's if the buyer cannot raise funds to complete – which may well be the position if money is being borrowed.

    Historically, the buyer is insured from exchange but insurance is not the whole answer. The reinstatement monies are not really likely to equal the purchase price and a bridging loan to complete may not be readily available given the buyer needs the purchase price but the land and the smouldering ruins are likely to be worth considerably less. If you draft your contract using the Law Society's contract, you are unlikely to change the position, but if you are the buyer reading this to see what the vendor is up to, note that if the written contract says 'Condition 5.1 does not apply', it means the risk is yours!

So that's what a basic contract is all about. Further clauses can be added, and in the crusade against the gazumper on the one hand and the gazoffer on the other, suggestions follow in the next chapter for some additional clauses that have already saved thousands from nervous breakdown.

Completed example of Standard Conditions of Sale

CONTRACT

Incorporating the Standard Conditions of Sale (Fourth Edition)

Date	:	*12 July 2010*
Seller	:	*Mr & Mrs R Bold* *14 Plevna Place, Blossomton ED2 8JD*
Buyer	:	*Mr John Smith* *12 Quain Road, London SW10 7XX*
Property (freehold/leasehold)	:	*14 Plevna Place, Blossomton BX10 1AB*
Title number/root of title	:	*EDN999707*
Specified incumbrances	:	*N/A*
Title guarantee (full/limited)	:	*Full*
Completion date	:	*21 August 2010*
Contract rate	:	
Purchase price	:	
Deposit	:	*£275,000*
Chattels price (if separate)	:	*£27,500*
Balance	:	

The seller will sell and the buyer will buy the property for the purchase price.

WARNING	Signed
This is a formal document, designed to create legal rights and legal obligations. Take advice before using it.	*Clive Smart* *Constance Smart* *Thomas Bold* *Prudence Bold* Seller/Buyer

Reproduced for educational purposes only by kind permission of the Solicitors' Law Stationery Society Limited

Completed example of Standard Conditions of Sale (continued)

STANDARD CONDITIONS OF SALE (FOURTH EDITION)
(NATIONAL CONDITIONS OF SALE 24th EDITION, LAW SOCIETY'S CONDITIONS OF SALE 2003)

1. **GENERAL**

1.1 **Definitions**

1.1.1 In these conditions:
- (a) "accrued interest" means:
  - (i) if money has been placed on deposit or in a building society share account, the interest actually earned
  - (ii) otherwise, the interest which might reasonably have been earned by depositing the money at interest on seven days' notice of withdrawal with a clearing bank

  less, in either case, any proper charges for handling the money
- (b) "chattels price" means any separate amount payable for chattels included in the contract
- (c) "clearing bank" means a bank which is a shareholder in CHAPS Clearing Co. Limited.
- (d) "completion date" has the meaning given in condition 6.1.1
- (e) "contract rate" means the Law Society's interest rate from time to time in force
- (f) "conveyancer" means a solicitor, barrister, duly certified notary public, licensed conveyancer or recognised body under sections 9 or 23 of the Administration of Justice Act 1985
- (g) "direct credit" means a direct transfer of cleared funds to an account nominated by the seller's conveyancer and maintained by a clearing bank
- (h) "lease" includes sub-lease, tenancy and agreement for a lease or sub-lease
- (i) "notice to complete" means a notice requiring completion of the contract in accordance with condition 6
- (j) "public requirement" means any notice, order or proposal given or made (whether before or after the date of the contract) by a body acting on statutory authority
- (k) "requisition" includes objection
- (l) "transfer" includes conveyance and assignment
- (m) "working day" means any day from Monday to Friday (inclusive) which is not Christmas Day, Good Friday or a statutory Bank Holiday.

1.1.2 In these conditions the terms "absolute title" and "official copies" have the special meanings given to them by the Land Registration Act 2002.

1.1.3 A party is ready, able and willing to complete:
- (a) if he could be, but for the default of the other party, and
- (b) in the case of the seller, even though the property remains subject to a mortgage, if the amount to be paid on completion enables the property to be transferred freed of all mortgages (except any to which the sale is expressly subject).

1.1.4 These conditions apply except as varied or excluded by the contract.

1.2 **Joint parties**
If there is more than one seller or more than one buyer, the obligations which they undertake can be enforced against them all jointly or against each individually.

1.3 **Notices and documents**

1.3.1 A notice required or authorised by the contract must be in writing.

1.3.2 Giving a notice or delivering a document to a party's conveyancer has the same effect as giving or delivering it to that party.

1.3.3 Where delivery of the original document is not essential, a notice or document is validly given or sent if it is sent:
- (a) by fax, or
- (b) by e-mail to an e-mail address for the intended recipient given in the contract.

1.3.4 Subject to conditions 1.3.5 to1.3.7, a notice is given and a document is delivered when it is received.

1.3.5
- (a) A notice or document sent through a document exchange is received when it is available for collection
- (b) A notice or document which is received after 4.00pm on a working day, or on a day which is not a working day, is to be treated as having been received on the next working day
- (c) An automated response to a notice or document sent by e-mail that the intended recipient is out of the office is to be treated as proof that the notice or document was not received.

1.3.6 Condition 1.3.7 applies unless there is proof:
- (a) that a notice or document has not been received, or
- (b) of when it was received.

1.3.7 A notice or document sent by the following means is treated as having been received as follows:

(a) by first-class post:	before 4.00pm on the second working day after posting
(b) by second-class post:	before 4.00pm on the third working day after posting
(c) through a document exchange:	before 4.00pm on the first working day after the day on which it would normally be available for collection by the addressee
(d) by fax:	one hour after despatch
(e) by e-mail:	before 4.00pm on the first working day after despatch.

1.4 **VAT**

1.4.1 An obligation to pay money includes an obligation to pay any value added tax chargeable in respect of that payment.

1.4.2 All sums made payable by the contract are exclusive of value added tax.

1.5 **Assignment**
The buyer is not entitled to transfer the benefit of the contract.

2. **FORMATION**

2.1 **Date**

2.1.1 If the parties intend to make a contract by exchanging duplicate copies by post or through a document exchange, the contract is made when the last copy is posted or deposited at the document exchange.

2.1.2 If the parties' conveyancers agree to treat exchange as taking place before duplicate copies are actually exchanged, the contract is made as so agreed.

2.2 **Deposit**

2.2.1 The buyer is to pay or send a deposit of 10 per cent of the total of the purchase price and the chattels price no later than the date of the contract.

2.2.2 If a cheque tendered in payment of all or part of the deposit is dishonoured when first presented, the seller may, within seven working days of being notified that the cheque has been dishonoured, give notice to the buyer that the contract is discharged by the buyer's breach.

2.2.3 Conditions 2.2.4 to 2.2.6 do not apply on a sale by auction.

2.2.4 The deposit is to be paid by direct credit or to the seller's conveyancer by a cheque drawn on a solicitor's or licensed conveyancer's client account.

2.2.5 If before completion date the seller agrees to buy another property in England and Wales for his residence, he may use all or any part of the deposit as a deposit in that transaction to be held on terms to the same effect as this condition and condition 2.2.6.

2.2.6 Any deposit or part of a deposit not being used in accordance with condition 2.2.5 is to be held by the seller's conveyancer as stakeholder on terms that on completion it is paid to the seller with accrued interest.

2.3 **Auctions**

2.3.1 On a sale by auction the following conditions apply to the property and, if it is sold in lots, to each lot.

2.3.2 The sale is subject to a reserve price.

2.3.3 The seller, or a person on his behalf, may bid up to the reserve price.

2.3.4 The auctioneer may refuse any bid.

2.3.5 If there is a dispute about a bid, the auctioneer may resolve the dispute or restart the auction at the last undisputed bid.

2.3.6 The deposit is to be paid to the auctioneer as agent for the seller.

3. **MATTERS AFFECTING THE PROPERTY**

3.1 **Freedom from incumbrances**

3.1.1 The seller is selling the property free from incumbrances, other than those mentioned in condition 3.1.2.

3.1.2 The incumbrances subject to which the property is sold are:
- (a) those specified in the contract
- (b) those discoverable by inspection of the property before the contract
- (c) those the seller does not and could not reasonably know about
- (d) entries made before the date of the contract in any public register except those maintained by the Land Registry or its Land Charges Department or by Companies House
- (e) public requirements.

3.1.3 After the contract is made, the seller is to give the buyer written details without delay of any new public requirement and of anything in writing which he learns about concerning a matter covered by condition 3.1.2.

3.1.4 The buyer is to bear the cost of complying with any outstanding public requirement and is to indemnify the seller against any liability resulting from a public requirement.

3.2 **Physical state**

3.2.1 The buyer accepts the property in the physical state it is in at the date of the contract unless the seller is building or converting it.

3.2.2 A leasehold property is sold subject to any subsisting breach of a condition or tenant's obligation relating to the physical state of the property which renders the lease liable to forfeiture.

3.2.3 A sub-lease is granted subject to any subsisting breach of a condition or tenant's obligation relating to the physical state of the property which renders the seller's own lease liable to forfeiture.

3.3 **Leases affecting the property**

3.3.1 The following provisions apply if any part of the property is sold subject to a lease.

3.3.2
- (a) The seller having provided the buyer with full details of each lease or copies of the documents embodying the lease terms, the buyer is treated as entering into the contract knowing and fully accepting those terms.
- (b) The seller is to inform the buyer without delay if the lease ends or if the seller learns of any application by the tenant in connection with the lease; the seller is then to act as the buyer reasonably directs, and the buyer is to indemnify him against all consequent loss and expense.
- (c) Except with the buyer's consent, the seller is not to agree to any proposal to change the lease terms nor to take any step to end the lease.
- (d) The seller is to inform the buyer without delay of any change to the lease terms which may be proposed or agreed.
- (e) The buyer is to indemnify the seller against all claims arising from the lease after actual completion; this includes claims which are unenforceable against a buyer for want of registration.
- (f) The seller takes no responsibility for what rent is lawfully recoverable, nor for whether or how any legislation affects the lease.
- (g) If the let land is not wholly within the property, the seller may apportion the rent.

3.4 **Retained land**
Where after the transfer the seller will be retaining land near the property:
- (a) the buyer will have no right of light or air over the retained land, but
- (b) in other respects the seller and the buyer will each have the rights over the land of the other which they would have had if they were two separate buyers to whom the seller had made simultaneous transfers of the property and the retained land.

The transfer is to contain appropriate express terms.

4. **TITLE AND TRANSFER**

4.1 **Proof of title**

4.1.1 Without cost to the buyer, the seller is to provide the buyer with proof of the title to the property and of his ability to transfer it, or to procure its transfer.

4.1.2 Where the property has a registered title the proof is to include official copies of the items referred to in rules 134(1)(a) and (b) and 135(1)(a) of the Land Registration Rules 2003, so far as they are not to be discharged or overridden at or before completion.

4.1.3 Where the property has an unregistered title, the proof is to include:
- (a) an abstract of title or an epitome of title with photocopies of the documents, and
- (b) production of every document or an abstract, epitome or copy of it with an original marking by a conveyancer either against the original or an examined abstract or an examined copy.

4.2 **Requisitions**

4.2.1 The buyer may not raise requisitions:
- (a) on the title shown by the seller taking the steps described in condition 4.1.1 before the contract was made
- (b) in relation to the matters covered by condition 3.1.2.

4.2.2 Notwithstanding condition 4.2.1, the buyer may, within six working days of a matter coming to his attention after the contract was made, raise written requisitions on that matter. In that event, steps 3 and 4 in condition 4.3.1 apply.

4.2.3 On the expiry of the relevant time limit under condition 4.2.2 or condition 4.3.1, the buyer loses his right to raise requisitions or to make observations.

4.3 **Timetable**

4.3.1 Subject to condition 4.2 and to the extent that the seller did not take the steps described in condition 4.1.1 before the contract was made, the following are the steps for deducing and investigating the title to the property to be taken within the following time limits:

Step	Time Limit
1. The seller is to comply with condition 4.1.1	Immediately after making the contract
2. The buyer may raise written requisitions	Six working days after either the date of the contract or the date of delivery of the seller's proof of title on which the requisitions are raised, whichever is the later
3. The seller is to reply in writing to any requisitions raised	Four working days after receiving the requisitions
4. The buyer may make written observations on the seller's replies	Three working days after receiving the replies

The time limit on the buyer's right to raise requisitions applies even where the seller supplies incomplete evidence of his title, but the buyer may, within six working days from delivery of any further evidence, raise further requisitions resulting from that evidence.

4.3.2 The parties are to take the following steps to prepare and agree the transfer of the property within the following time limits:

Step	Time Limit
A. The buyer is to send the seller a draft transfer	At least twelve working days before completion date
B. The seller is to approve or revise that draft and either return it or retain it for use as the actual transfer	Four working days after delivery of the draft transfer
C. If the draft is returned the buyer is to send an engrossment to the seller	At least five working days before completion date

4.3.3 Periods of time under conditions 4.3.1 and 4.3.2 may run concurrently.

4.3.4 If the period between the date of the contract and completion date is less than 15 working days, the time limits in conditions 4.2.2, 4.3.1 and 4.3.2 are to be reduced by the same proportion as that period bears to the period of 15 working days. Fractions of a working day are to be rounded down except that the time limit to perform any step is not to be less than one working day.

4.4 **Defining the property**

4.4.1 The seller need not:
- (a) prove the exact boundaries of the property
- (b) prove who owns fences, ditches, hedges or walls
- (c) separately identify parts of the property with different titles

further than he may be able to do from information in his possession.

4.4.2 The buyer may, if it is reasonable, require the seller to make or obtain, pay for and hand over a statutory declaration about facts relevant to the matters mentioned in condition 4.4.1. The form of the declaration is to be agreed by the buyer, who must not unreasonably withhold his agreement.

4.5 **Rents and rentcharges**
The fact that a rent or rentcharge, whether payable or receivable by the owner of the property, has been, or will on completion be, informally apportioned is not to be regarded as a defect in title.

Reproduced for educational purposes only by kind permission of the Solicitors' Law Stationery Society Limited

Completed example of Standard Conditions of Sale (continued)

4.6 **Transfer**

4.6.1 The buyer does not prejudice his right to raise requisitions, or to require replies to any raised, by taking any steps in relation to preparing or agreeing the transfer.

4.6.2 Subject to condition 4.6.3, the seller is to transfer the property with full title guarantee.

4.6.3 The transfer is to have effect as if the disposition is expressly made subject to all matters covered by condition 3.1.2.

4.6.4 If after completion the seller will remain bound by any obligation affecting the property which was disclosed to the buyer before the contract was made, but the law does not imply any covenant by the buyer to indemnify the seller against liability for future breaches of it:
(a) the buyer is to covenant in the transfer to indemnify the seller against liability for any future breach of the obligation and to perform it from then on, and
(b) if required by the seller, the buyer is to execute and deliver to the seller on completion a duplicate transfer prepared by the buyer.

4.6.5 The seller is to arrange at his expense that, in relation to every document of title which the buyer does not receive on completion, the buyer is to have the benefit of:
(a) a written acknowledgement of his right to its production, and
(b) a written undertaking for its safe custody (except while it is held by a mortgagee or by someone in a fiduciary capacity).

5. **PENDING COMPLETION**

5.1 **Responsibility for property**

5.1.1 The seller will transfer the property in the same physical state as it was at the date of the contract (except for fair wear and tear), which means that the seller retains the risk until completion.

5.1.2 If at any time before completion the physical state of the property makes it unusable for its purpose at the date of the contract:
(a) the buyer may rescind the contract
(b) the seller may rescind the contract where the property has become unusable for that purpose as a result of damage against which the seller could not reasonably have insured, or which it is not legally possible for the seller to make good.

5.1.3 The seller is under no obligation to the buyer to insure the property.

5.1.4 Section 47 of the Law of Property Act 1925 does not apply.

5.2 **Occupation by buyer**

5.2.1 If the buyer is not already lawfully in the property, and the seller agrees to let him into occupation, the buyer occupies on the following terms.

5.2.2 The buyer is a licensee and not a tenant. The terms of the licence are that the buyer:
(a) cannot transfer it
(b) may permit members of his household to occupy the property
(c) is to pay or indemnify the seller against all outgoings and other expenses in respect of the property
(d) is to pay the seller a fee calculated at the contract rate on a sum equal to the purchase price and the chattels price (less any deposit paid) for the period of the licence
(e) is entitled to any rents and profits from any part of the property which he does not occupy
(f) is to keep the property in as good a state of repair as it was in when he went into occupation (except for fair wear and tear) and is not to alter it
(g) is to insure the property in a sum which is not less than the purchase price against all risks in respect of which comparable premises are normally insured
(h) is to quit the property when the licence ends.

5.2.3 On the creation of the buyer's licence, condition 5.1 ceases to apply, which means that the buyer then assumes the risk until completion.

5.2.4 The buyer is not in occupation for the purposes of this condition if he merely exercises rights of access given solely to do work agreed by the seller.

5.2.5 The buyer's licence ends on the earliest of: completion date, rescission of the contract or when five working days' notice given by one party to the other takes effect.

5.2.6 If the buyer is in occupation of the property after his licence has come to an end and the contract is subsequently completed he is to pay the seller compensation for his continued occupation calculated at the same rate as the fee mentioned in condition 5.2.2(d).

5.2.7 The buyer's right to raise requisitions is unaffected.

6. **COMPLETION**

6.1 **Date**

6.1.1 Completion date is twenty working days after the date of the contract but time is not of the essence of the contract unless a notice to complete has been served.

6.1.2 If the money due on completion is received after 2.00pm, completion is to be treated, for the purposes only of conditions 6.3 and 7.3, as taking place on the next working day as a result of the buyer's default.

6.1.3 Condition 6.1.2 does not apply and the seller is treated as in default if:
(i) the sale is with vacant possession of the property or any part of it, and
(ii) the buyer is ready, able and willing to complete but does not pay the money due on completion until after 2.00pm because the seller has not vacated the property or that part by that time.

6.2 **Arrangements and place**

6.2.1 The buyer's conveyancer and the seller's conveyancer are to co-operate in agreeing arrangements for completing the contract.

6.2.2 Completion is to take place in England and Wales, either at the seller's conveyancer's office or at some other place which the seller reasonably specifies.

6.3 **Apportionments**

6.3.1 Income and outgoings of the property are to be apportioned between the parties so far as the change of ownership on completion will affect entitlement to receive or liability to pay them.

6.3.2 If the whole property is sold with vacant possession or the seller exercises his option in condition 7.3.4, apportionment is to be made with effect from the date of actual completion; otherwise, it is to be made from completion date.

6.3.3 In apportioning any sum, it is to be assumed that the seller owns the property until the end of the day from which apportionment is made and that the sum accrues from day to day at the rate at which it is payable on that day.

6.3.4 For the purpose of apportioning income and outgoings, it is to be assumed that they accrue at an equal daily rate throughout the year.

6.3.5 When a sum to be apportioned is not known or easily ascertainable at completion, a provisional apportionment is to be made according to the best estimate available. As soon as the amount is known, a final apportionment is to be made and notified to the other party. Any resulting balance is to be paid no more than ten working days later, and if not then paid the balance is to bear interest at the contract rate from then until payment.

6.3.6 Compensation payable under condition 5.2.6 is not to be apportioned.

6.4 **Amount payable**

The amount payable by the buyer on completion is the purchase price and the chattels price (less any deposit already paid to the seller or his agent) adjusted to take account of:
(a) apportionments made under condition 6.3
(b) any compensation to be paid or allowed under condition 7.3.

6.5 **Title deeds**

6.5.1 As soon as the buyer has complied with all his obligations on completion the seller must hand over the documents of title.

6.5.2 Condition 6.5.1 does not apply to any documents of title relating to land being retained by the seller after completion.

6.6 **Rent receipts**

The buyer is to assume that whoever gave any receipt for a payment of rent or service charge which the seller produces was the person or the agent of the person then entitled to that rent or service charge.

6.7 **Means of payment**

The buyer is to pay the money due on completion by direct credit and, if appropriate, an unconditional release of a deposit held by a stakeholder.

6.8 **Notice to complete**

6.8.1 At any time on or after completion date, a party who is ready, able and willing to complete may give the other a notice to complete.

6.8.2 The parties are to complete the contract within ten working days of giving a notice to complete, excluding the day on which the notice is given. For this purpose, time is of the essence of the contract.

6.8.3 On receipt of a notice to complete:
(a) if the buyer paid no deposit, he is forthwith to pay a deposit of 10 per cent
(b) if the buyer paid a deposit of less than 10 per cent, he is forthwith to pay a further deposit equal to the balance of that 10 per cent.

7. **REMEDIES**

7.1 **Errors and omissions**

7.1.1 If any plan or statement in the contract, or in the negotiations leading to it, is or was misleading or inaccurate due to an error or omission, the remedies available are as follows.

7.1.2 When there is a material difference between the description or value of the property, or of any of the chattels included in the contract, as represented and as it is, the buyer is entitled to damages.

7.1.3 An error or omission only entitles the buyer to rescind the contract:
(a) where it results from fraud or recklessness, or
(b) where he would be obliged, to his prejudice, to accept property differing substantially (in quantity, quality or tenure) from what the error or omission had led him to expect.

7.2 **Rescission**

If either party rescinds the contract:
(a) unless the rescission is a result of the buyer's breach of contract the deposit is to be repaid to the buyer with accrued interest
(b) the buyer is to return any documents he received from the seller and is to cancel any registration of the contract.

7.3 **Late completion**

7.3.1 If there is default by either or both of the parties in performing their obligations under the contract and completion is delayed, the party whose total period of default is the greater is to pay compensation to the other party.

7.3.2 Compensation is calculated at the contract rate on an amount equal to the purchase price and the chattels price, less (where the buyer is the paying party) any deposit paid, for the period by which the paying party's default exceeds that of the receiving party, or, if shorter, the period between completion date and actual completion.

7.3.3 Any claim for loss resulting from delayed completion is to be reduced by any compensation paid under this contract.

7.3.4 Where the buyer holds the property as tenant of the seller and completion is delayed, the seller may give notice to the buyer, before the date of actual completion, that he intends to take the net income from the property until completion. If he does so, he cannot claim compensation under condition 7.3.1 as well.

7.4 **After completion**

Completion does not cancel liability to perform any outstanding obligation under this contract.

7.5 **Buyer's failure to comply with notice to complete**

7.5.1 If the buyer fails to complete in accordance with a notice to complete, the following terms apply.

7.5.2 The seller may rescind the contract, and if he does so:
(a) he may
(i) forfeit and keep any deposit and accrued interest
(ii) resell the property and any chattels included in the contract
(iii) claim damages
(b) the buyer is to return any documents he received from the seller and is to cancel any registration of the contract.

7.5.3 The seller retains his other rights and remedies.

7.6 **Seller's failure to comply with notice to complete**

7.6.1 If the seller fails to complete in accordance with a notice to complete, the following terms apply.

7.6.2 The buyer may rescind the contract, and if he does so:
(a) the deposit is to be repaid to the buyer with accrued interest
(b) the buyer is to return any documents he received from the seller and is, at the seller's expense, to cancel any registration of the contract.

7.6.3 The buyer retains his other rights and remedies.

8. **LEASEHOLD PROPERTY**

8.1 **Existing leases**

8.1.1 The following provisions apply to a sale of leasehold land.

8.1.2 The seller having provided the buyer with copies of the documents embodying the lease terms, the buyer is treated as entering into the contract knowing and fully accepting those terms.

8.1.3 The seller is to comply with any lease obligations requiring the tenant to insure the property.

8.2 **New leases**

8.2.1 The following provisions apply to a contract to grant a new lease.

8.2.2 The conditions apply so that:
"seller" means the proposed landlord
"buyer" means the proposed tenant
"purchase price" means the premium to be paid on the grant of a lease.

8.2.3 The lease is to be in the form of the draft attached to the contract.

8.2.4 If the term of the new lease will exceed seven years, the seller is to deduce a title which will enable the buyer to register the lease at the Land Registry with an absolute title.

8.2.5 The seller is to engross the lease and a counterpart of it and is to send the counterpart to the buyer at least five working days before completion date.

8.2.6 The buyer is to execute the counterpart and deliver it to the seller on completion.

8.3 **Consent**

8.3.1 (a) The following provisions apply if a consent to let, assign or sub-let is required to complete the contract
(b) In this condition "consent" means consent in the form which satisfies the requirement to obtain it.

8.3.2 (a) The seller is to apply for the consent at his expense, and to use all reasonable efforts to obtain it
(b) The buyer is to provide all information and references reasonably required.

8.3.3 Unless he is in breach of his obligation under condition 8.3.2, either party may rescind the contract by notice to the other party if three working days before completion date (or before a later date on which the parties have agreed to complete the contract):
(a) the consent has not been given, or
(b) the consent has been given subject to a condition to which a party reasonably objects.
In that case, neither party is to be treated as in breach of contract and condition 7.2 applies.

9. **COMMONHOLD LAND**

9.1 Terms used in this condition have the special meanings given to them in Part 1 of the Commonhold and Leasehold Reform Act 2002.

9.2 This condition applies to a disposition of commonhold land.

9.3 The seller having provided the buyer with copies of the current versions of the memorandum and articles of the commonhold association and of the commonhold community statement, the buyer is treated as entering into the contract knowing and fully accepting their terms.

9.4 If the contract is for the sale of property which is or includes part only of a commonhold unit:
(a) the seller is to apply for the written consent of the commonhold association at his expense and is to use all reasonable efforts to obtain it
(b) either the seller, unless he is in breach of his obligation under paragraph (a), or the buyer may rescind the contract by notice to the other party if three working days before completion date (or before a later date on which the parties have agreed to complete the contract) the consent has not been given. In that case, neither party is to be treated as in breach of contract and condition 7.2 applies.

10. **CHATTELS**

10.1 The following provisions apply to any chattels which are included in the contract, whether or not a separate price is to be paid for them.

10.2 The contract takes effect as a contract for sale of goods.

10.3 The buyer takes the chattels in the physical state they are in at the date of the contract.

10.4 Ownership of the chattels passes to the buyer on actual completion.

Reproduced for educational purposes only by kind permission of the Solicitors' Law Stationery Society Limited

Completed example of Standard Conditions of Sale (continued)

SPECIAL CONDITIONS

1. (a) This contract incorporates the Standard Conditions of Sale (Fourth Edition).

   (b) The terms used in this contract have the same meaning when used in the Conditions.

2. Subject to the terms of this contract and to the Standard Conditions of Sale, the seller is to transfer the property with either full title guarantee or limited title guarantee, as specified on the front page.

3. The chattels which are on the property and are set out on any attached list are included in the sale and the buyer is to pay the chattels price for them.

4. The property is sold with vacant possession.

(or) 4. The property is sold subject to the following leases or tenancies:

Seller's conveyancers*:

Buyer's conveyancers*:

*Adding an e-mail address authorises service by e-mail: see condition 1.3.3(b)

©2003 Oyez   The Solicitors' Law Stationery Society Ltd,
7 Spa Road, London SE16 3QQ

11.2003   F41896
5065046

© 2003

Standard Conditions of Sale   The Law Society

4th Edition

Copyright in this Form and its contents rests jointly in SLSS Limited and the Law Society

Reproduced for educational purposes only by kind permission of the Solicitors' Law Stationery Society Limited

CHAPTER 9

Gazumping and gazoffing

No buyer wants to be gazumped.

Most vendors think they should get more than they have already been offered (and accepted verbally), and fancy a bit of gazumping for themselves.

Vendors hate it when their subject to contract buyer goes off – they are gazoffed.

So this will be an even-handed chapter. In business, few people do their opposite numbers any favours. Why should you expect the housing business to be any different?

You must keep control of events and keep your wits about you, as you do when buying a car or a cardigan. You can't possibly win if you 'leave it all' to solicitors and agents. The lazy and shy buy themselves a lot of worry and aggravation by allowing themselves to be tied up with an unsatisfactory buyer or seller, about whom they don't know enough. They bring in too many cooks, who before spoiling the broth consume a lot of it.

Weak chains that leave you wide open to a gazumper or a gazoffer are created because people who wouldn't dream of going out to buy anything else without cash or credit card gaily go viewing houses and 'promising' to buy tens of thousands of pounds' worth of bricks and mortar, without a round'un in their pockets. Vendors have already promised 'to buy something from someone who has already promised' – and so on and so forth. The pressure is on from day one of the promise. Mortgages being sought (although it's wise to obtain a decision in principle before even looking to buy); solicitors making mountains out of molehill 'searches';

buyers have to be found to close one end of the chain and vendors the other. The weeks tick by with everybody making excuses to everybody.

Agencies prefer purchasers who have houses for sale, as they are a fruitful source of business. Failing that, someone who will enrich them by over £600 by buying a mortgage endowment scheme from their agency. But the slightest hiccup or attack of greed has only to rear its ugly head and it's trouble for all. Big trouble.

It's time for some novel ideas. They won't come from solicitors, estate agents or moneylenders, with whom the market is crowded, all trying to get a slice of your cake. Any time they have for inventive thinking is devoted to that one objective.

The government's conveyancing committee found that over the last 10–15 years, the period of time a sale remains subject to contract has gradually lengthened. The initiative to shorten that period with the introduction of Home Information Packs (HIPs) was not successful and the use of such packs has now been suspended by the Coalition Government, which has vowed to scrap HIPs altogether.

One would have predicted that the time taken would have become shorter. A prime reason why purchasers can't sign up is, always was and always will be that they need to be satisfied that the vendor has good title to the property. The whole of the country is now covered by the registration system. Since 2003, any transfer of land must be registered. Not much remains unregistered. Everybody in the business knows that anything to do with contracts and conveyancing is simpler, easier and swifter once property is registered than it was before.

Everybody also knows that the longer the time between a buyer saying 'I will' and a contract being signed, the greater the opportunity for gazumping, gazoffing and corruption.

So why don't the parties get signed up? What has happened to cause the delay in getting on contract?

The only coherent reasons that come from the professionals are that some local authorities take weeks and months to return the searches, and: 'We are still pursuing our enquiries on the title', which in the case of a transfer of a lease may mean that they are waiting for the landlord to respond to questions.

Less coherent to the layperson, but equally daft, is: 'We are waiting for engrossments'. 'Engross' means 'write', and engrossing a contract means entering a few lines into the blanks on a printed form.

By the time you have read a little more, you will recognise these for the threadbare excuses that they are, for not having done little jobs that could have been done in their own offices. For instance, you can see in the Appendices a copy of an actual search form; judge for yourself how long it would take to fill that in and despatch.

What is new is the proliferation and size of chains in which so-called purchasers haven't yet signed up with their own purchasers, who haven't yet signed up with theirs, even unto the third and fourth 'purchaser'. There are more and longer chains. This is what is new. Why?

How many estate agents per 100,000 houses were there in your town 15 years ago? How many are there today? Four times, five times, six times? And they are all fighting for a share of what remains of the saleable houses, after nearly a third of the vendors have chosen the best purchasers for themselves and given the agencies the cold shoulder. So when an agency gets a house that is really saleable and can choose among potential buyers, it would be daft to choose someone who had nothing to sell! Ergo, a chain is born.

Agents can be very persuasive when they are forging another link in the paper chain. They seem to have a good argument when they say it saves a lot of time and prevents breakdowns in communication if you take their total package, thus keeping the whole thing under one roof. The promise is false; it can't be kept, because, as we have seen, the people who attempt to hold chains together are solicitors, and it's a rigid rule of the Law Society (their union) that a solicitor must not act for both parties to a transaction unless both clients are previously established as such. So if there is to be a master mariner at the tiller to navigate seas littered with the twin icebergs of gazumpers and gazoffers, it can only be yourself.

The cure

Flitsville no longer suits you, and you will be a winner if you can decide to sell first. So be business-like, sit down quietly with everybody who lives in your house and whose life will be affected, and decide what you will do, where you will go, how much you can afford, how you will buy, and how you will go about selling.

If you want to move to within a few miles of where you are now, join the 90 per cent of all house buyers who move less than 10 miles. Look at the local property-for-sale columns. How many houses are advertised in the price bracket you will be able to afford? How many more are skulking in agents' files? If, at the time of your family conference, there are half-a-dozen houses for sale that would suit you (if the vendors knocked a couple of thousand off), be sure that if, when you have sold yours, all those six have been sold or withdrawn, another five or six will have taken their place. Why get yourself into chains, gazumping, gazoffing and generally wasting your time, survey and other fees and everybody else's? You can avoid all this if you sell first. And be sure that when you turn up able to produce an official contract for sale of your own house, and mortgage offer, you will be a sight for sore eyes to any vendor. If he says he can't move out in time, put it to him, 'You could move in with relatives, friends, bed and breakfast, or pay for us to go in a hotel for the interim.'

A vendor needs to find out the strength of an interested viewer's capacity to buy. In order of preference they are:

1. first-time buyers who have a note from a lender saying that, subject to valuation, more than sufficient monies to buy your house will be on offer (even try to see their bank book showing that they have the difference between the loan and the purchase price on deposit);

2. an 'own house sold' buyer (see his contract);

3. a 'need not sell my own house' buyer – again, it would be wise to see the mortgage offer;

4. a 'must sell my own house' buyer.

The excuse 'We have not completed the searches' sounds awful, doesn't it? In reality, searching at this stage consists in sending off two forms with ready-printed questions on them to the local authority, which fills in the answers and returns them. With the increase in the ability to obtain electronic searches, this is no excuse at all.

Think! Surely any vendor's Skinner should know how long the local authority is taking to return search forms in that area, so why didn't the agency which brags that it liaises with solicitors get the process started with the new property when it put Flitsville on the market? What are these searches?

How to prepare the 'legal' side of your sale

Not only purchasers need replies to the local authority searches before putting pen to contract. If there is a skeleton or a potential crock of gold in the council's cupboard, don't you think, as a vendor, that it would be a good idea if you knew these things before putting your house on the market? You can easily search to find out if your house is registered. If you don't know whether or not your house is registered, you find out by applying for an 'Index Map Search'. You fill in Form SIM including a description of the property, enclose the relevant fee (currently £5) and the Land Registry will tell you whether your house is registered, and the title number. If it's registered, all the nonsense about investigating title is a cover-up for delay and an attempt to justify high fees. So you can prove your title before you start to sell, because once anyone's ownership has been registered at HM Land Registry that title of ownership is guaranteed by the state. If the house is paid for, you should be in possession of your Land Certificate. However, since the Land Registration Act 2002 came into force in October 2003 the Land Registry considers that a Land Certificate no longer has any legal significance. The vendor proves title by obtaining an official copy of the Register. This is done by sending off Form OC1 (with the current £8 fee) and get a photocopy from the Registry. This gives up-to-date information with regard to the state of the title. You can show this copy to serious prospects; that's the investigation of title seen off.

The last place on earth to have left deeds or Land Certificates is a solicitor's office. I have seen piles of deeds on open wooden shelves, stuffed into old sideboards and, at best, 'fire resistant' metal cupboards. A solicitor likes you to leave valuable documents with him. It's his way of trying to make sure that you will go to him again and again. So well and good if this arrangement suits both parties, but it's nice to be able to change. There is power in holding the deeds – so have that power for yourself. Get them into the old homestead – safely filed under the piano lid as did the old gent, to whom I will introduce you later.

At this stage it's worth checking the Council of Mortgage Lenders' *Handbook* referred to in chapter 1 just to see if you have some problems that need to be addressed. Do you have deeds that refer to covenants but details on which are not available? Did you get married a second time and think it was a wonderful idea to transfer your houses to you and your new husband or wife? These and other situations are problem areas and although you might ignore them, your buyer is unlikely to do so. See what the *Handbook* says about indemnity insurance.

Not STC, but CST (subject to contract, contract subject to)

There will be occasions where the vendor and his purchaser very much want to secure the sale but cannot, because something is missing, for example uncertainty on a completion date, absence of a local authority search certificate, some problem in obtaining a satisfactory survey or perhaps a mortgage offer.

These are all problems that can be covered by an adequately drafted contract clause, or at least they can be if neither party has a problem with someone else they are dealing with in a chain. Perhaps the first rule to follow is don't contract to buy a new house if you have not sold your existing house. That can cause an expensive headache. Selling before buying is normally less of a gamble. You can at least park your belongings in store and yourself and your family with relatives. Perhaps this is not to be advised if property prices are moving up by the day! So if you wish to sell or buy and you can live with the uncertainty on the completion date and both sides are in this happy position, perhaps a completion date three to six months hence would give all concerned a chance to settle their affairs.

The other problems can be dealt with by making the 'contract subject to' or 'CST' to a satisfactory solution to the problem, in hand. This is usually unappealing to a buyer due to the great uncertainty of the matter. The buyer cannot ensure when or if the problem will be resolved. There could be a dispute as to whether it had been and this can make life difficult, particularly if there is a sale to tie in. However, should you agree to such a condition, the cardinal rule is to define what you need to know before you can safely go ahead; make sure the contract can be terminated if an answer is not forthcoming after two to three months (say) and decide how to link this to a completion date.

Suppose, for example, you want to exchange before you have a satisfactory search. It's fair to say that this problem cannot arise with HIPs because it ought to have been sorted out beforehand, unless the search is not a compulsory search which needs to be included in the HIP. You can make the contract subject to that, but questions need to be addressed. Is it satisfactory to whom and what would not be satisfactory? Suppose it shows the local authority is taking enforcement proceedings for the removal of an extension erected without planning permission? Would that be satisfactory? Probably not. Suppose it says the authority is widening a road 150 metres away? Would that be satisfactory? Think what questions are being asked, what the answers might be and what would not be acceptable. Generally, where these clauses are used, the parties agree a search is satisfactory if nothing is revealed that would have a material impact on the value of the house. This still leaves room for uncertainty and so if the buyer has a few bottom lines, cover them as well.

Suppose the buyer is willing to exchange if a satisfactory mortgage offer is available? Here, too, what is satisfactory? Tie this down. If you are the buyer, perhaps any offer would be satisfactory, so if the seller has a relative who is a loan shark, perhaps the seller could engineer an offer 'you cannot refuse', to quote the movies.

Final comment: when drafting, you may know what you want and may be able to express it, but half the trick with any drafting is asking what you don't want. Make sure you cover it and if in doubt take the advice of a solicitor.

CHAPTER 10

The Registers

There are two systems of land conveyancing in England and Wales: the registered system, in which case title to the land is registered at the Land Registry, and the unregistered system, where the title is not registered at all. The unregistered is an older and more complicated system, but not many years will pass before all land is registered and thus conveyancing of property made much simpler for all. By the way, all references to land include everything built on it.

So it helps if the layperson conveyancer gets an early grasp of the point that all conveyances are of *land* whether built on or not. Whether it sells for a million or one pound, the recipe is the same.

Official records of the property with which you are about to deal may be found in the three main categories of registry:

1. **The local council**, which is required to keep a register of notices affecting dangerous structures, public notices about infringements of building regulations, compulsory purchase orders, smoke control zones and other things it wants to make sure do or don't happen to the property. When we come to it, you will see that you quite easily find out about that little lot by the simple expedient of sending off a couple of forms (LLC1, CON 29R and CON 29O if appropriate) which have printed on them the questions you need to ask.

    When buying, you must always carry out a local search. In addition, an environmental search and a separate water drainage search are now required by lenders. It's important to realise that searches relate to the land you searched and no other. If the neighbours have planning permission to build something you will be offended by, the search will not tell you this, so if you are concerned, go to the council. Ask to see some staff in the planning department and ask what they have on the area that you think might be of importance. You can also now search planning applications for many councils online, so find out which borough the house you are buying is in, and have a look at its website.

2. **The Land Charges Department** at Plymouth, which keeps a register of various charges (mortgages), interests (e.g. rights of way or restrictive covenants) and notices such as second mortgages and Class F charges (right of spouse to occupy the matrimonial home) which relate to unregistered land so cannot be registered at the Land Registry. Pending writs or orders (bankruptcy) and pending actions (bankruptcy) are also kept at Plymouth, and you will need to send off a Form K16 to find out about any bankruptcy orders, writs, etc., whether you are buying registered land or not.

3. **The Land Registry** is the third place where official records of land transactions are kept. This is the one that did the trick of simplifying the act of transferring the ownership of a house from one owner to another. Where a house is on registered land, all the tiresome business of proving title and tracing back the covenants and conditions through a series of conveyances is dispensed with, because it was done once and for all when the title was registered. And not only that; when the Land Registry sends you a copy of the Register which shows that Feather owns the property, a state guarantee is incorporated in it. If the Register shows you as the owner, that ownership is guaranteed by the state.

Initially, the Land Registry Act 1862 covered only London and made registration of title compulsory for any sale which took place after 1898 in that area. No extension of the compulsory system of registration was made until 1925. Since 1925, the system of registration has been gradually extended to cover the whole country. However, just because the land registration system covers the area where the house is situated, it doesn't mean to say that the owner's title is already registered. If the owner bought before compulsory registration came in for the area, it will only be registered if it's on a biggish, newish development, or if it was voluntarily registered.

The piecemeal extension of the registration system means that if you are buying in Lambeth, you can be certain that the title will be registered, unless it has been in the same ownership, since February 1900 (or before); on the other hand, fewer properties in Plymouth will be registered because registration only became compulsory in January 1974.

Until 1966, any owner could voluntarily apply to have his ownership registered. But in 1966, registration became limited to compulsory areas, plus those cases where the Registrar can make an exception, for example where the title deeds were lost or destroyed during the War, or where there are complex building developments taking place.

If you went to the Land Registry and looked at the actual Register, what is produced on the following pages is what you would see. It's also what would be reproduced on the Land Certificate in Mr and Mrs Smart's possession, if they had no mortgage. In view of Charge no. 3 in the Charges Register, the Land Certificate would have been held at the Land Registry, and a Charge Certificate issued to and held by the building society as proof of its interest. Following the coming into force of the Land Registration Act 2002, Charge Certificates are no longer issued and the Land Registry will simply supply the lender (or new owner) with a copy of the Register. Registered owners and mortgage lenders will also be able to obtain a title information document, but this is for information only. As you will by now appreciate, what matters is the official copy of the Register.

Though we refer to the Land Registry (singular) it contains a number of Registers (plural). These are: The Property Register, Proprietorship Register and Charges Register. The references made to your property in these Registers constitute what used to be known as the 'deeds' to your property and can consist of as few as four pieces of paper having as little as two dozen lines of typing on them.

The Registrar will, at a cost of just a few pounds, supply copies ('Office Copies') of these entries. You are still the registered proprietor (i.e. shown as being the owner of the property at the Land Registry, albeit subject to the existence of the charge), even though your lender may own a significant part of the property through the mortgage. The registers at the Land Registry are no longer confidential and anyone may inspect and obtain copies of the entries. Since 1 April 2000, registered titles disclose the price the registered proprietor paid for his interest in the property. A word of warning: a Land Registry copy of the title and of any deeds noted on the

Specimen of Land Registry entry

Land Registry

Official copy of register of title

Title number EDN999707	Edition date 18. 03. 2010

— This official copy shows the entries in the register of title on 18 March 2010 at 14:27:42
— This date must be quoted as the "search from date" in any official search application based on this copy.
— The date at the beginning of an entry is the date on which the entry was made in the register.
— Issued on 18 March 2010
— Under s.67 of the Land Registration Act 2002, this copy is admissible in evidence to the same extent as the original.
— For information about the register of title see Land Registry website www.landregistry.gov.uk or Land Registry Public Guide 1 – A guide to the information we keep and how you can obtain it.
— This title is dealt with by Land Registry Edenshire office.

A: Property register
The register describes the registered estate comprised in the title.

EDENSHIRE : BLOSSOMTOWN

1. (16.03.1967) The Freehold land shown edged with red on the plan of the above title filed at Land Registry and being 14 Plevna Place, Blossomton (ED2 8JD)

2. (16.03.1967) The land has the benefit of the rights granted by but is subject to the rights reserved by the Transfer dated 6 January 1972 referred to in the Charges Register.

B: Proprietorship register
This register specifies the class of title and identifies the owner. It contains any entries that affect the right of disposal.

Title absolute

1. (16.11.1977) PROPRIETOR: CLIVE SMART and CONSTANCE SMART both of 14 Plevna Place, Blossomton, Edenshire ED2 8JD.

Specimen of Land Registry entry (continued)

Title Number EDN999707

C: Charges register
This register contains any charges and other matters that affect the registered estate.

1. (16.03.1967) A Conveyance of the land in this title dated 27 January 1967 made between (1) Thomas Dick (Vendor) and (2) Charles Harry (Purchaser) contains the following covenants:-

    "The Purchaser for the benefit of the remainder of the Vendor's land hereby covenants with the Vendor to the intent that the burden of the covenant may run with and bind the land hereby conveyed to observe and perform the stipulations and restrictions set out in the schedule hereto.

    THE SCHEDULE before referred to:

    1. No further building shall be erected on the said land without the consent of the Vendor.

    2. Not at any time to carry on or suffer to be carried on the said land any trade or business for the sale of intoxicating liquors and no building erected on the said land shall be used except as a private dwelling house.

2. (14.02.1972) A Transfer dated 31 January 1972 made between (1) Sunshine Investments Ltd and (2) Brian Feather and Pauline Feather contains restrictive covenants.

    Note: Original filed.

3. (16.11.1977) REGISTERED CHARGE dated 1 November 1977 to secure the monies including the further advances therein mentioned.

4. (16.11.1977) Proprietor: HEART OF ENGLAND BUILDING SOCIETY of Jury Street, Warwick

End of register

Specimen of Land Registry entry (continued)

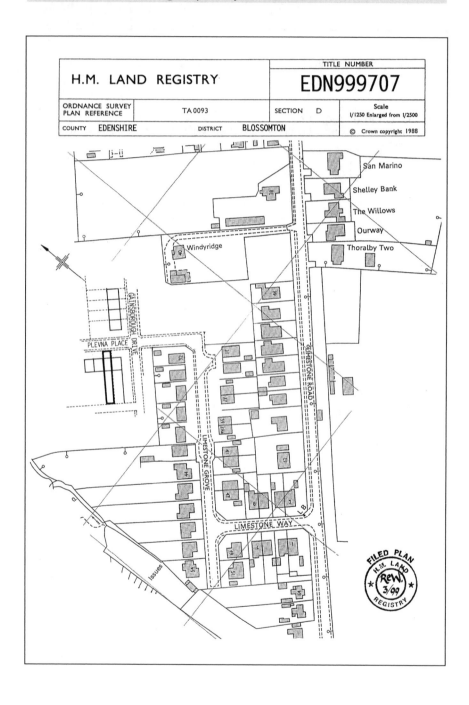

title can be produced in court as if they were original deeds; ordinary photocopies don't enjoy this statutory blessing and although this may seem a waste of time and money, a purchaser should always insist on an official Office Copy. A print-out of the title information which can be obtained from the internet will not be sufficient.

The Land Registration Act 1925 used to set out what a seller is obliged to do to give satisfactory evidence of title to a buyer. It has been repealed as from 13 October 2003. The law now leaves it up to the parties to decide what evidence of title they require, but Condition 4.1 of the Standard Conditions of Sale provides for proof of title by Office Copy entries, and you need to watch out in case this has been altered. One consequence of not complying with the requirements of the contract is that if the purchaser doesn't complete on time, no interest can be demanded for late payment and the powers available to the vendor to rescind cannot be exercised till after the breach is remedied.

The key to unlocking the files at the Land Registry is the title number, which is a reference number. Every registered property has one. The title number appears at the top of each page of the Office Copies. So that you can see how the Land Registration system works in practice (and what a pleasant surprise awaits you when the simplicity of it all is proved to you on the arrival of the Office Copies), let us take a look at a set that shows the various types of entry which could appear on Mr and Mrs Smart's title to no. 14 Plevna Place, Blossomton, Edenshire, title number EDN999707.

A swift look through our example will convince you that it's mostly self-explanatory; where it's not immediately clear, hold tight, just a little detective work and clarity is at hand. However, first of all note the number of pages and check you've got them all. Just for fun, the old-style manual Register of your property may consist of say five pages and you only get three. Don't panic; it turns out that two are blank, and somewhere on your Office Copy it will be noted 'pages 4 and 5 are blank. Not photographed'.

Section A: Property Register: Describes the land by reference to the title plan and the postal address, because that is sufficient to identify it. In the case of leasehold property, details of the lease (date, parties, term and ground rent) are given. This section may also mention any rights of way which benefit the land, such as rights to pass over a private road. In this section there is also mention of an entry in the Charges Register – its bark is worse than its bite, more about it later.

Section B: Proprietorship Register: Here we see that in our example the proprietor has Title Absolute and this is the one that you will usually come across and want the property to have if you are a buyer. It's the best class of title and applies to 99 per cent of freeholds. The Registrar only gives the description Title Absolute where he is entirely satisfied about the owner's ownership of the property. Title Absolute means that the ownership is guaranteed by the state.

A leasehold property can have Title Absolute. This is only so in cases where the Registrar can guarantee that the lease was validly granted, because the lessor (grantor of lease and original landlord) had proved that he owned the freehold or a longer lease of the land. Good leasehold title is shown in those cases where the superior title has not been investigated by the Registrar and is acceptable now to lenders only if it satisfies the CML *Handbook* (paragraph 5.4.2). Banks, building societies, etc. therefore require proof before the funds are released to the buyer.

Possessory title

This is very rare indeed. It's the weakest form of title and exists where full evidence is not supplied, perhaps because deeds were lost or because it's based on adverse possession, for example so called 'squatter's title'. Possessory title is acceptable now to lenders only if the CML *Handbook* is satisfied (paragraph 5.4.3).

The Proprietorship Register shows the present owners. Until recently, Land and Charge Certificates also showed the names of previous owners. Office Copies now issued don't show previous owners, as in our example. Likewise, the price paid was shown in some old-style manual registers; all registrations since 1 April 2000 show the price paid.

Look closely at the Office Copy. Look if a price appears on the Office Copy. If not, this is not actually anything to be alarmed about if the date next to the vendor's name in section B, the Proprietorship Register, is before 1 April 2000. There was no requirement to record a price before this date. If the date of registration is after 1 April, however, ask why no price is shown. If the property was the subject of a gift, even a partial gift where an owner transfers the house into his name jointly with that of spouse or partner, you must appreciate that if the person making the gift is later bankrupted, that gift can be annulled if it took place within five years from the date of the presentation of the bankruptcy petition.

Purchasers in good faith are protected, unless they were aware of the surrounding circumstances and 'the relevant proceedings'; and unless they can prove to the contrary, they will not be regarded as having purchased their home in good faith! They will know of the gift, of course, from the Land Registry entry and they will be at risk.

For this reason, where the buyer can tell the property was the subject of a gift within the preceding five years, it may well be unmarketable unless the seller can satisfy the buyer and his lender that no problems can arise. The purchaser can do this by applying for solvency and bankruptcy searches (see page 129) against the donor of the gift to check that he was solvent at the time of making the gift to ensure it cannot be set aside. However, it can be set aside if it was made within the last two years even if the donor was solvent at the time of making the gift. There is a further problem if the gift is between husband and wife: the husband is presumed to be insolvent at the time of the gift unless the contrary can be shown. If these assurances cannot be given – and it's difficult to see how they can be conclusively given – the seller should organise and pay for adequate indemnity insurance.

If you are borrowing to fund the purchase, you cannot ignore this. No solicitor who knows of this will sign off a certificate of title for one of the CML lenders unless insurance is taken out. For those of you with access to the internet, have a look at section 5.12 of the CML *Lenders' Handbook for England and Wales* at www.cml.org.uk.

Section C: Charges Register: This is where the elementary detective work comes in. So gather round, while I tell you the story behind the sample produced here.

On 16 March 1967, a teetotal farmer called Thomas Dick sold his smallholding together with his house and rhubarb shed to Charles Harry, on condition that Mr C. Harry wouldn't do any further building and wouldn't convert the house to a pub, or the shed to a disco. The years went by and Mr C. Harry got it into his head that he would like to build a few houses on the land, so on his accountant's advice he and his Mrs formed Sunshine Investments and tried to look up Mr T. Dick, but he couldn't even be dug up, for he had been cremated. They therefore searched out his kith and kin, and found, as is sadly the case in such matters, that kith and kin, reacting against the strong strictures of husband and father, had turned to the bottle with a vengeance once he was out of the way, and, now being on the hard times he had predicted for those who took to the drink, were easily persuaded to remove the restriction on building – for a consideration.

Sunshine Investments, alias Mr C. Harry, built the houses and sold one to Mr Feather, who subsequently sold to Mr Smart, from whom you now wish to purchase. However, before Sunshine Investments were able to do their bit towards solving Mr Feather's housing problem (their own too) the Blossomton Council planning committee had to be pacified, and they made it a condition that no one actually went to live in the new houses until the new main sewer being built from Here to There had been completed. As the condition has obviously been complied with, the entry is now of no interest to anyone.

Sunshine Investments also got themselves a solicitor, Mr Newman. He was a young solicitor, and being rather inexperienced in the business, thought that creating the legal framework was all art and no science. Like all young artists, he didn't know where to stop. He got out the volumes of Forms and Precedents, got every reference on restrictions, covenants, exceptions and reservations, and tacked them onto every transfer to every purchaser. It mattered not that there were no cesspits; he put in the rules governing cesspits, and preceded the rule with the words: 'if ever there be …'

The Registrar couldn't put all Mr Newman's blatherings into the Charge Certificate, but they existed, so 'copy in certificate' was inserted as a 'Note'. You will be sent a copy. Sometimes the copy will consist of the last conveyance which was drawn before the land became registered. In any case, it will list the restrictions on the property. And that is the copy that the vendor must attach to or refer to in the draft contract at 'Incumbrances'.

There is not a lot you can do about restrictive covenants. You either accept them or try doing what Sunshine Investments did and buy out the covenantee or, once you've bought the land, apply to the Land Tribunal to have them discharged/modified, which is both difficult and potentially costly. Anyway, have a look through them, and if you had intended putting up kennels for dog breeding purposes and find that there is a restriction on using the land for any business purpose, put your thinking cap on. If there is no other property around, you may be pretty safe, but if the house is on an estate, no doubt all the other houses have similar restrictions entered on their titles. You would only need one neighbour, one light sleeper who never seemed able to go shopping without stepping into a pile of ordure, for your life to be made a misery and your doormat fouled with summonses. That said, there is unlikely to be anything really onerous in the covenants, if indeed there are any at all. But for the general run of people, what are the covenants most likely to turn up? They fall into a pattern and the commonest are:

1. not to use the house for any trade or business;

2. to keep the fence or fences in repair either by yourself or with the assistance of your neighbour;

3. not to build another house on the plot or extend the present one without permission from the previous owner (or original owner of the plot – not likely to be the person you purchased from);

4. if you build a house on the plot it must be of at least £x in value;

5. not to do anything to cause a nuisance;

6. the dos and don'ts applicable to all owners on the estate.

So, if you find any or all of 1–6 above either in the Charge Certificate or in the copy of covenants, etc., which comes with the Charge Certificate, how do you interpret them for your own purposes? If you are sufficiently irreverent, you have no doubt cracked the code for yourself. Irreverence is the key to the door to doing your own conveyance, and a sure shield against being showered with a load of bovinus excrementus which might result in a loss of confidence, which would never do. However:

1. So what? You are buying the house to live in.

2. Probably nothing could be done, as money would have to be spent to enforce it.

3. Put it this way: if the house has a double garden and you were buying it with the idea of putting a little bungalow on it for your granny, you would ask the vendor to put you in touch with the person whose consent is required. The question of whose consent is required may be a difficult one for interpretation. Ten to one it can't be done, because he will have changed his name to Wraith, and there is but the ghost of

a chance of finding his kith and kin who either know or care about the covenant. If the consent is that of someone who has disappeared or ceases to exist, the requirement to get his consent expires. So you could go ahead and be pretty certain that you were safe. There are, of course, insurance companies who will indemnify you against the risk of someone turning up and trying to make trouble. Covenants are taken for the benefit of land so you may have to take advice as to whether any of your neighbours could enforce the restriction or whether you need consent of the person who presently owns the land which belonged to the original covenantee. The solution to this is likely to be taking out an insurance policy for a one-off premium against such problems, which protects you and future owners of the property.

4. As at 3. above. You might ask Skinner to produce evidence that the house you are buying actually cost that amount to build, but you are unlikely to receive much of a reply unless it's something in the nature of 'There is no builder's receipt in the deeds but the vendor has received no notice of breach of covenant.' In any case, inflation will no doubt have dealt with this little problem.

5. Other people might think that we cause nuisance, but we know that it's they who cause it. They are wrong and we are right, but perverse as always, they think they know best. So we can accept this covenant because first, we never cause nuisance and second, we have an ordinary common law obligation, like everybody else, not to cause nuisance anyway.

6. If we didn't like the results achieved already by this covenant, we would not want to live here anyway. There is an added bonus for the layperson conveyancer because you will know, and have a copy of, this little lot and if any of them start upsetting any of us we will know that as usual they are in the wrong.

Covenants are promises, and the only difference between a covenant and any other kind of promise is that it's contained in a deed. At some point in the history of the buying and selling of the land in question, some owner has said in effect to a buyer, 'I will only sell to you if you will promise this, that and the other, and also promise that when you sell, you will have your buyer make the same promises to you and so on ad infinitum.' Do remember, however, that lenders will require indemnity insurance to cover breach of covenants.

There are one or two important things to be said about this ruling-from-the-grave covenanting. It may be difficult to say who could enforce it anyway. One thing to remember is that covenants are taken to protect land and will only be enforceable against a 'successor in title' (that's you) if they do confer some benefit on land which was owned or retained by the person taking the benefit of the covenant at the time that it was given. In general, it's difficult, if not impossible, to enforce any covenant expressed to be in favour of a person, without reference to land he owns or owned which is affected by the covenant. It must also be remembered, however, that it's not only the original covenantee (i.e. the party who managed to extract the promise in the first place) who can enforce a restrictive covenant – if the covenant benefited land then owned by the covenantee, the present owner of that land will probably be able to enforce the covenant. You would have to read the deed creating the covenant to find out which of your future neighbours have that power. If the house is on an estate, chances are all of the houses are subject to the same restrictions so all your neighbours will be able to enforce the covenants. If you come across a 'no building or extension' covenant in the Charges Register of a property you are thinking of buying, and your inspection has shown the covenant to have been broken, what do you do about it? The first thing is to ascertain how long the extension or building has stood there. In addition to the owner's say-so, ask for some independent evidence to be produced. Although not conclusive, if reliable evidence shows the breach occurred more than 12 years earlier, the covenant is generally no longer enforceable. But the breach is still a blot on the landscape, as the CML *Handbook* (paragraph 5.7) requires indemnity insurance to be obtained if the breach is less than 20 years old. Any person who retains a solicitor to act for him whether as a purchaser or as a bank or building society will or at least should know of this requirement and should demand that the vendor fund insurance against risk; not necessarily the risk that the covenant is enforceable, but the risk that any owner who tries to sell or mortgage within the 20-year period will be faced with a demand that he meet the cost of such an insurance policy. These CML rules have to be complied with by the buyer or the funds will not be released. The questions of enforceability of covenants are notoriously tricky and it's best to take legal advice if you do plan to do something that would infringe a covenant.

If you are the vendor, you can put the potential buyer's mind at rest by offering to insure him against risk for the next ten years. If you are the buyer, you can pull a long face and say that but for your partner's silly emotional feeling for the place, you would have cried off immediately and you will now do so unless a few pounds are knocked off the price agreed before you knew about this diabolical covenant.

Vendor: Having read earlier about bargaining, you will know that emotion will overpower reason every time so if you can catch the eye of his partner for a few seconds, test the strength of the emotion – if it's genuine, you are home and dry at your original price.

However, for purchasers who can manage to pull off the reduction-for-covenant gambit, the next step is to get the insurance and that is the dead hand of the past dealt with.

Entries 3 and 4 refer to the present owner's mortgage. 'Charge' is an abbreviation of 'Legal Charge' and that is the fancy term for mortgage.

In our example, we have not been able to cover all the things that might be entered on a Charges Register. For instance, one of Smart's lenders might not like further mortgages to be entered unless they know about it, so you get 'no disposition of the property may be made without the prior consent of the proprietor of Charge no. ....'. Don't worry, the lenders will not let go without their money, so their charge (mortgage in this case) will be deleted when you come to register your new ownership.

Another really irritating one is where there is an entry that the land is subject to covenants set out in a deed dated the umpteenth of Nerth. In the remarks you then read 'deed not lodged with the Registry'. These people might never turn up to bother you. But like it or not, because of the CML *Handbook* (paragraph 5.7), the prudent purchaser will now insist that his vendor fund indemnity insurance for the reasons stated above.

You're not really reading a whodunnit, so you are allowed to see how Mr Newman's story ends when you come across the real mother and father of Rigmarole in, and referred to in, the Property Register, and it starts off about sewers and unmade roads and rights across them. Ten to one you will find that the rigmarole was inserted as a condition of planning permission being granted for the estate to be built. Once the house was completed and its drains connected to the main sewer in the road, and the council had taken over responsibility for the maintenance of the road (it had become a public highway) and the sewer, the rigmarole became of academic interest only, except in so far as all subsequent inspectors of Office Copies have, at least, to give it a quick glance. It's worth checking though to see whether the road has been adopted by the council – if not your right to access of the property over it becomes important.

It's unlikely that you will come up against a caution. Cautions are a dying breed. No more cautions can be entered on the Register since 13 October 2003 but 'old' cautions still remain. Like many other terms and phrases in the lawyers' armoury, 'caution' has an ominous ring to it, so let us cut it down to size before the few readers to whom it might apply are faced with it. Cautions were, almost without exception, hostile. That is because a caution was used where the owner of the property would not co-operate with a person who requires protection of his interests. Now a person would enter a 'unilateral notice'. If you come up against a caution, the vendor should already know about it, and as he wants his sale to you to go through, should already have made arrangements for the caution to be removed. The difference between a notice and a caution is that if the sale goes through despite the caution, the purchaser is not bound by the right unless it's an 'overriding interest'. However, if the right is protected by a notice, it will have priority over the purchaser's interest.

The most common caution you are likely to see entered nowadays is one by a wife or partner who wishes to let all who are interested in purchasing know that, though the house was not bought in joint names, it is, in fact, the matrimonial home. Registering the caution makes sure that if the person whose name the house is in tries to sell or mortgage the house, the cautioner will get to know if anything is stirring, and can then take appropriate action.

A prospective purchaser who finds a caution on the Register will quite rightly ask the vendor to have it removed by clearing up whatever problem exists between himself and the cautioner. A caution against dealing can be withdrawn at any time without fee, using Form WCT. The vendor will persuade or induce the cautioner to write to the Registrar asking for the removal of the caution (Form WCT) from the Register and the caution will be removed promptly and without involvement of fuss or feathers.

However, if the vendor knows the caution to be simply silly and vexatious, he himself can apply for its removal using Form CCD. He must do one or the other or both, and purchasers need proof that he has done so before completion. The Registrar then gives the cautioner notice of the proposed dealing, and informs him that he intends to remove the caution. The onus is then on the cautioner to take action, and if he doesn't make a serious objection within 15 business days after notification, the caution is cancelled. The caution has been 'warned off'. When he hears from the Registrar, the cautioner may, if he wishes, put his case to him. If the Registrar thinks that cause has been shown, he must order that the caution is to continue until withdrawn or otherwise disposed of under Land Registration Rules 2003. If it's not possible to dispose of the objection by agreement, the Chief Land Registrar must refer it to the Adjudicator of HM Land Registry. The Adjudicator can either deal with the matter himself or require that one party start proceedings in the High Court or the County court within a particular time. There is an appeal from the decision of the Adjudicator to the High Court.

More common than a caution now is a restriction. You will often see a restriction where a property is owned in joint names. A 'restriction' prevents a sale from being completed (or rather the registration of a conveyance from being completed) unless the conditions in the restriction have been complied with. Like a caution, a restriction doesn't give priority unless the interest protected also takes effect as an overriding interest. The most common restriction will be 'no disposition by a sole proprietor of the registered estate under which capital money arises (unless a trust corporation) is to be completed unless authorised by the court'. This is the tenant in common restriction. It's always important, if possible, to buy from two people, not one. The restrictions will give notice of various interests. Another may say that no completion can take place unless notice has been given to a third party. It's important to discuss this with the vendor to see what steps have been taken to deal with the people who are entitled to the restriction to make sure no third party holds up your purchase. A restriction can be removed or cancelled by sending off Form RX3.

Note B at the end of the Register tells you when the copy, in our example 16 March 1995, was taken from the actual Register. Office Copies come to you from the Registry by first-class post, but even so they are obviously out of date by the time you are proving to yourself how simple it all is by glancing through the entries. On 17 March the Smarts could have sold the house to Mr G.A. Zump, and he could have registered the transfer to himself on 18 March 1995 before you have time to do anything about it. Here you are with a copy of the Register which clearly shows Smarts as the owners on 16 March; how could one possibly stop the ubiquitous Mr Zump? There is a way, and again, it's a form, OS1 by number. You will meet it again later and be properly introduced.

CHAPTER 11

Introducing conveyancing for laypeople

This chapter is an introduction to conveyancing. Liken it to the picture on the lid of a jigsaw puzzle box. Having studied it, you can then start interlocking the pieces contained in the rest of this Guide.

Having read so far, you are ready to do your own conveyance. While reading what follows, if you have a flow diagram-cum-checklist, keep it by your side.

There is, of course, a lot that is slightly technical which you might have to read twice before you think that you have grasped the point. You will certainly, as with any technical instruction, find that understanding comes the quicker when, instead of just the printed page, you have the actual nuts and bolts of the job in front of you. Every time you wire an electric plug it becomes easier – it's the same with conveyancing.

In the days when a solicitor could act for both parties, even if he had never acted for them before, I met an aged gentleman who was selling a house he had lived in for over thirty years. When he was asked who his solicitor was, he said, quite simply, 'I don't need a solicitor. I own the house, the deeds are under the piano lid, and when I get my money, the buyer can have keys, house and deeds, and I'm off into a Home with the proceeds.' I gave him a receipt for the deeds and took them to Donald Turnbull, solicitor for the purchaser, who, being the wise old bird he was, made no fuss and got on with it. After all, what had he to do? He looked at the last conveyance in the pile, made sure that the purchaser therein named was the aged gentleman, and bingo, aged gent had proved title (it's even simpler and safer nowadays where we have registered title). A month later the old boy was ensconced in the Home, terrorising the Matron with his merciless logic.

So if you have got your house paid for, follow the example of the aged gent, by getting your title deeds to the property which prove you are the owner. Whether your house is paid for or not, *get the whole file of your purchase transaction* from the solicitor who acted for you years ago and pop the papers under your piano lid to be ready. However, if the property is subject to a mortgage, the deeds will be with the lender. Now title is registered and no Land Certificates are supplied, you can get Office Copy entries to prove title direct from the Land Registry – just fill out Form OC1 and pay the fee.

As you take your first, confident step, keep firmly in mind that you are out to achieve three things:

1. Save yourself a lot of money, particularly if you are buying as well.

2. Get the purchase price safely out of the buyer's pocket and into yours.

3. Make certain you are completely shot of the house and have no continuing liabilities, which you do by virtue of Clause 3 in the 'Special Conditions of Sale'.

No. 1. : to save all that lovely money, read on. No. 2. only requires that you are numerate and can count the money in banknotes or recognise a telegraphic transfer for the same sum. You may have jibbed just a tiny bit at no. 3. Don't. Just think of the hassle, worry and money you're about to save yourself. In any case, even if you pay Skinner & Deskbound, you will no doubt have to do most of the running about for yourself, and also fill in the kind of forms that solicitors send to their clients nowadays.

Selling a registered house

Whether you intend to travel 50 yards or 50 miles, your journey begins with a single step. You may not know whether you can walk 50 yards let alone 50 miles, but you have not much to lose by risking one stride, and emboldened by the success of that one stride, you will not lack confidence for the next two. So let me give you, the layperson conveyancer, the confidence to take that first stride by explaining step-by-step how to complete the simplest of all housing transactions, that of selling a second-hand, freehold, registered house in England or Wales, which is free of mortgage.

Step no. 1. is to get out your Land Certificate and copy the title number on to Land Registry Form OC1, Application for Office Copies and add your name and address. Look in Appendix 2 at the back of this Guide for details. If you don't know your title number, or you don't have a Land Certificate because you bought after 2003, don't panic. You can deal with this by writing on the top of the form 'PLEASE SUPPLY TITLE NUMBER' and fill in the rest of the details. The Land Registry will only accept applications with a request to supply the title number if a postal address is supplied, which should not prove a problem if the Office Copy relates to a house or flat. You used to be able to find out the title number for free by inserting the postal address in the property enquiry form at www.landregistry.gov.uk. However, this now costs £4, you are required to be a registered user and this does not give you an official copy – you may as well fill out the form and obtain an official copy by post.

If the search reveals more than five title numbers, the Land Registry will reject the application and will require you to carry out an Index Map Search by filling out Form SIM, which will tell you whether or not the land is registered. A few days later, you will then receive an official copy of the Register. This may refer to other documents, such as documents containing covenants or rights of way. These documents will be referred to in the copy of the Register, often with the words 'copy in certificate'. These documents will be required by your buyer and can be obtained by sending off Form OC2.

While waiting for the Office Copies to come from the Land Registry, spend a few minutes making up three copies of the contract. Keep one copy for your file and put the other two, with the Office Copies, when you receive them, into an envelope, addressed to the purchaser or his Skinner, with a covering letter saying that you are acting for yourself in the sale of your house. Stund, of Skinner & Stund, will probably shudder with horror, but will write back acknowledging receipt, and, as though such a thing had never been heard of before, will ask you to confirm that you are indeed acting for yourself. In return for your confirmation, he will send you a letter giving the game away that he knew all the time that people are doing their own conveyancing nowadays. He will then say he must make it clear that he will 'take no responsibility for you in law or otherwise'.

There is no kind of business in the land that isn't regulated by general and particular laws which protect those with whom they deal. All that is being made clear is that he owes you no duty of care and that you won't have any redress if you rely on his advice as to how you should conduct your transaction. Nobody can write themselves out of the law, and nobody should know that better than Stund. What 'or otherwise' means I just don't know – you try asking. I've never managed to get a sensible excuse, let alone an explanation. Though you might feel like writing in retaliation, don't bother; it's best to take no notice. You have already landed a left and a right where it hurts most, in the pride and in the pocket.

You may now receive from Skinner printed 'Enquiries before Contract' or 'Pre-contract Enquiries' or even his own endless list of typed questions; they are all known colloquially in the trade as 'preliminary enquiries' and they may be referred to as such by Skinner, whatever they are actually called. They comprise questions for you to answer! Or you may be asked for the 'Seller's Property Information Form'; the idea is the same: to supply routine information to the buyer, but here the seller has to obtain the form and volunteer the answers. I recommend that the seller should complete the 'Standard Property Information Forms' as they are simpler and easier to fill in. These can be obtained online from legal stationers. Part I is to be completed by the seller and Part II by the seller's solicitor if one is being used. If the purchaser has any other queries arising out of the standard form, you will have to answer these as fully as possible.

It's up to each solicitor to decide whether to send you enquiries or ask for you to volunteer answers by means of the 'Seller's Property Information Form'. However, these are different from an examination paper, because you only have to answer the questions to which you are absolutely certain you know the answers. If you don't know the answers, or are not certain about them, you calmly ask the examiner to check up for himself by replying 'Not as far as I am aware, but please make own enquiries', or simply put 'I don't know'. At first reading, the form may appear quite fearsome. But really it's quite straightforward, if you keep it firmly fixed in your head that you don't intend giving any hostages to fortune, and you intend cleaving to the old established precept of *caveat emptor*, which is Latin for let the buyer beware. Buyers please take note. This doesn't mean you can write 'I don't know' for every question; if you do know the answer you must say so. If you think that the answer is given elsewhere in information he already has, cross-refer to this information and attach a photocopy so that there can be no excuses. One question that you should always expect is 'Are there any disputes?'. This must be answered honestly. If at all possible, avoid disputes with neighbours if you intend to sell, because it will be off-putting for a buyer.

In the parcel under the piano lid, you might find the form your solicitor received from your vendor's solicitor when you bought. From that, you will see how little a solicitor is satisfied with, when he is protecting his paying customers in the parlous procedures entailed in the biggest business operation of his client's life. 'To the best of my knowledge, no, but please rely on your own searches.' 'I don't know.' 'There may be, but never brought to my attention.' These are the kind of woolly replies to give and expect to woolly questions. Remember also that if you answer any question 'To the best of my knowledge' or, more cryptically, 'Not to my knowledge', the law expects you to have made a reasonable stab at finding out the answer. If you cannot be bothered and use these phrases to avoid the trouble of checking out the answer, don't be surprised if you get a claim form for any loss your buyer thinks he suffered because of your insouciant indifference to his question.

Remember, conveyancing is an administrative business transaction, and only becomes contentious when such things as fraud raise their ugly heads, e.g. if someone had recently given the property to you as seller to remove it from the clutches of his creditors or if you have negligently or deliberately answered these questions incorrectly. Irreverence may be the key to doing your own conveyancing, but that doesn't mean that you can be slapdash and fail to take the most straightforward precautions.

However, Skinner could pick on some answer you have given and ask you to be more specific. If so, and you honestly don't know the answer, just stick at it, saying you have nothing to add. If he seems to be giving you the run-around, consider the possibility that he knows the proposed purchaser has gone off. If you do suspect this, check up with the purchaser direct. **Though solicitors consider it unethical for one solicitor to speak with another solicitor's client, there is no law, rule or ethic on earth that prevents the two principals (in this case vendor and purchaser) discussing matters between themselves.**

When your replies to the 'Enquiries before Contract' or 'Seller's Property Information Form' have been accepted and your contract approved, it will be signed by Feather and sent back to you. You now collect the deposit and in exchange, hand over your copy of the contract, which you now sign. Don't be surprised if the solicitor tells his client you should not be paid the deposit, in case you pinch it. The solicitor may suggest he be allowed to act as 'stakeholder' rather than you. All this expression means is that whoever has the money must hand it to the seller if the sale completes. If it doesn't, it stays in limbo unless the contract is repudiated (i.e. cancelled by either party because of a breach by the other). In this case the seller gets it if the buyer is in default, but it's returned to the buyer if the seller is in default. If you have this problem, you will have to deal with it as best you can, but remember if you are buying a house at the same time and are using the Standard Conditions of Sale, you can still require your buyer to allow the money to be released to the solicitor who is acting for the person selling your new property to you. Remind your buyer's solicitor of this; that might persuade him to review the position. He, after all, will know that if you are paid money without quibble and do pinch it his insurers will probably have to refund it.

If you have arranged for someone else to act as stakeholder, repair to his office and exchange the contract you have signed for the one signed by the purchaser, and see to it that the balance of the deposit is handed to the stakeholder. Contracts have now been exchanged. Your sale is now tied up. If the buyer backs out, you have to decide whether to be merciful or merciless. That is to say, you give him back all, part or none of his deposit, depending on the circumstances. If he backs out because he says you misrepresented something to him, this may end up in litigation. If this happens, you should consult a solicitor.

After exchange of contracts, Skinner may send a questionnaire entitled 'Requisitions on Title'. Treat it with Olympian calm. Requisition means question. Title means ownership. So he is asking you questions to find out if you are the owner, when all the time you know and he knows you are the owner, because it says so on the Land Registry Proprietorship Register, and your title (ownership) is thus guaranteed by the state. In reality it's very unlikely you will be asked much about the title. If you have proved title before contract under the fourth edition of the Standard Conditions of Sale, there can be no further questions. They keep changing the form, so you may get questions raising problems which have already been solved, like 'Where will completion take place?' and 'Have you got receipts for Council Tax and suchlike bills paid?'. In the main, the questions are to do with practicalities: what's the position on Council Tax and utilities bills, do you have the deeds, how do we get the keys, where do we send the money and so on. I know it's difficult, but try to be courteous, remembering all the while that even if you were paying a solicitor, all these problems would still be yours to solve, because he would only be acting as a postbox.

There is an example of the 'Requisitions on Title' in Appendix 7. This has not been filled out because there are myriad answers to the questions that it poses. However, chapter 12 contains some guidance on how to fill out the form.

Skinner, on behalf of your purchaser Feather, now sends you a Land Registry Form TR1, in draft state, for your approval. This is the form which authorises the Land Registry to transfer the house out of your ownership into Feather's. The draft only calls for names and addresses to be filled in, the money, the property and the class of title, i.e. full or limited. If the draft is in order, accept it and write acknowledging the fact. Sign the Form TR1 at the first signed 'as a deed line' in the presence of a witness, who also signs, and then hold onto it (see Appendix 8 for details). Don't date this form. The transfer should not be dated until completion. There is nothing to do now, but while away the time before completion date by dreaming about what you will spend the money on.

If your buyer is supposed to sign the TR1 because it contains an indemnity covenant (i.e. he promises to indemnify you if it turns out he breaches any covenants imposed on the property), make sure the buyer signs it before you do. Indemnity covenants? Go back to chapter 10, 'Section C: Charges Register' for a refresher.

The law on covenants is a bit of a tangle. If you sign a transfer that contains them, the person who sold you the house (or others depending on the circumstances) can sue you if your buyer breaks any of the covenants. Covenants on land are an area (law not geography) where lawyers in Victorian days got themselves into a bit of a tangle. First, they decided positive covenants involve spending money: to keep a fence in good order or to contribute to maintaining a fence, drains or a road. They decided negative or 'restrictive' covenants don't involve spending money: covenants not to run a bawdy house, for example. Then they decided that if X makes covenants with Y to do something (i.e. only to use the property for residential purposes) that don't involve spending money, anyone who can prove they have or acquired the right to enforce restrictive covenants can sue Y's successors. This is not the case with positive covenants, which cannot be enforced against successors.

So you need your buyer to promise to indemnify you if he breaks them and you are sued. You may also need an indemnity covenant if you were the person who made the agreement, which comprises a restrictive covenant in the first place, i.e. you were the first purchaser of a brand new house. The only remedy your vendor may have in these cases is to sue you, if he can find you. If you can get the money back from your buyer, fine. If not, tough! The Standard Conditions of Sale require your buyer to add an indemnity clause to the transfer, but don't be surprised if the point is overlooked and it never appears in your transfer. As the person at risk, it's for you to make sure it's not left out when you are sent the draft transfer for approval.

If your house has a leasehold title, the landlord can continue to pester you for the rent and service charge if your buyer doesn't pay it, unless the lease was granted after 1 January 1996 or you are not the first person to whom the lease was granted and you didn't enter into a direct covenant with the landlord. You don't need an indemnity covenant in this instance since the law implies one.

Remember also the covenants you give in the transfer. Your promise to sell with full title guarantee, for example, places certain duties on you. If the house has a leasehold title, you promise that you have complied with all the covenants (referred to in section 4 of the Law of Property (Miscellaneous Provisions) Act 1994 – see www.opsi.gov.uk). The sales of leasehold property are deemed to include this covenant unless expressly excluded. Solicitors normally make a point of adding a clause to the effect that these covenants should not be construed as your promise that the premises have been repaired and decorated in strict conformity with the lease.

Sometimes purchasers will ask you to let them have the keys before completion. If Feather needs to get the money from the sale of his own house to Dither, in order to buy yours, it can be difficult for him. But if Dither gets knocked down by a bus on his way to complete, and you have let Feather into possession of your house, it will be a great deal more difficult for you.

Sellers of a vacant property will no doubt be asked to accept an undertaking from Feather that if you let him have the key solely for the purpose of decorating and repair, he will not go into possession. Now it might seem a bit dog-in-the-manger to refuse, and Skinner might try to assure you that it's the usual thing, and the undertaking he has drafted for Feather to sign gives you ample protection. If you feel under pressure, write to Skinner and ask for his personal indemnity underwriting the

Feathers' undertaking. You never know, he might give it. But if he can't trust his own client, how can you?

Letting a purchaser into possession before completion can also have implications for Stamp Duty Land Tax. This is the tax which has replaced Stamp Duty on sale of land. Stamp Duty was a charge on documents – so the tax wasn't payable until the transaction completed and the transfer signed. Stamp Duty Land Tax is a charge on transactions and is payable within 30 days of the 'effective date'. In general the 'effective date' is completion – so all well and good unless the transaction is 'substantially performed' before this date. Allowing a purchaser into possession before completion amounts to 'substantial performance'. This won't make too much difference if you allow the purchaser in one or two days before, but it might cause problems if you let him in two or three weeks before completion is due to take place.

A CHAPS payment is the layperson conveyancer's best friend, but a solicitor is unlikely to make such a payment and trust you to hand over the deeds. A personal completion utilising a bank draft is more likely, but note that the fourth edition of the Standard Conditions of Sale excludes the possibility of paying the money due on completion by banker's draft, so unless this has been altered, payment must be made by 'direct credit', i.e. CHAPS transfer.

If the buyer is all tied up at his end and cannot attend the completion personally, leave the keys with a neighbour you can trust. A further qualification to being trustworthy that the neighbour requires is to be on the telephone, because the keys must not be handed over until you have rung up saying all is well. On completion day toddle along to the appointed venue. You will have with you the completed Form TR1, the lease if a leasehold property, any other title documents you hold and the keys (if not with the neighbour). If the deposit is being held by a stakeholder, Skinner will, in addition to handing you the balance of the purchase price, give you a letter authorising the release of the deposit. You give Skinner the Land Certificate, Form TR1 and the keys. And that is your sale completed. That is conveyancing in a nutshell. Now to the detail. However, in addition, because you are unrepresented you will have to provide a certificate of identity and prove your identity to the Land Registry – otherwise it will not register the purchase. This is something that you have to be prepared for and is dealt with in chapter 12 below.

CHAPTER 12

Conveyancing: the sale and purchase of a registered house

The previous chapter on selling a registered house confined itself to the work a vendor of such a house is faced with. The reason for limiting its scope was so that you could judge for yourself the simplicity of the operation. Aanyone who is good at making a précis will have already noted that a very simple transaction indeed could be carried out, and it goes like this:

A purchaser goes to a house that is for sale and says, 'I will give you £175,000 for it if you can prove to me that you are the owner.' The vendor says, 'Come back in a couple of hours with the money.' The purchaser returns with the money and confirms that the vendor is ready to leave and the house is vacant. The vendor has an office copy and a signed Form of Transfer in one hand and the keys in the other. The purchaser swaps his £175,000, for those three items. The deal is done.

The purchaser sends the Land Certificate and the Transfer to the Land Registry along with Form AP1 – Application to Change the Register, the Land Transaction Return SDLT1 – see page 156, Form DI, in which you should insert any 'disclosable overriding interests' such as legal rights of way or leases of which you are aware, and the registration fee. He is now the registered proprietor (subject to the verification of identity of any unrepresented parties). This is to prevent fraud.

Because people tend not to take other people's word for things nowadays, it takes a bit longer than this, but basically what appears above is the beginning and end of a sale and purchase of registered land. It contains everything that has to be done to transfer ownership.

The instructions that follow are for the purchase and sale of a freehold dwelling in England or Wales which is already registered.

The procedures for buying from a council are completely different; leases and gifts are special cases. Transferring a leasehold property is similar in many ways. However, if you require a lease drafted from scratch, this is likely to be more complicated. If you are buying from a developer, you are not likely to have much choice in the matter. If you are buying from a council, you may, in fact, require legal advice.

The instructions should also be read with reference to chapter 8, regarding contracts. For the purpose of illustration, we will assume that you are a first-time buyer and need to take a mortgage, or that you are the vendor of a £175,000 house. There is some repetition of what has gone earlier – unfortunately, it cannot be avoided so please look on it as part of the teaching and learning process.

One general rule of thumb, which is obvious and hardly needs mentioning, is that if you send something to the other party to the transaction, **always keep a copy for yourself**. This will avoid disputes and means that you can save time if the other party loses the things that you have sent to him.

Vendor: As soon as you seriously put your house up for sale, send off an Application for Office Copies Form OC1 (see Appendix 2) and Form OC2 if necessary. Fill in your name and address and title number, which you have got from your lender or the solicitor who acted for you when you bought (he cannot charge you for this service, by rights he should have performed it earlier) (or alternatively write 'Please Supply Title Number' on the top of the form), and – with a cheque for £8 for each copy required – send it to the appropriate Land Registry, the address of which you will find in Appendix 12 or online at www.landregistry.gov.uk (it's not always obvious which is the appropriate Land Registry). A copy of the title plan is currently also £8. Notify your lender/s that you will be redeeming your mortgage/s. You will also have to obtain an Energy Performance Certificate in respect of the house. Copies of documents referred to in the Register are currently £12 and to obtain a copy of any lease from the Land Registry is £24 on an application made by post.

Purchaser: Until you are sure you can find the money for the purchase, sign nothing, apart from the lender's application form. Any letters you send to anyone must have written somewhere about them 'subject to contract' and it's safest to keep on doing that right up to the point where you do sign the contract.

I take it for granted that you will keep your wits about you, and have at some time completed a licence or passport application form, and have, therefore, clerical expertise. That little caution given, I will not labour the points that are usually made ad infinitum and ad nauseam elsewhere about how careful one must be. It would be all right if such labourings genuinely helped people either towards a better understanding, or to being able to cope for themselves and ease their worries, but when, after scaring the living daylights out of you, the only advice given is: go to a professional to deal with a contract for you, survey for you, buy for you, sell for you, it's just a waste of reading time. You can always leave things to others – at a price.

One cardinal rule, and it goes for all business transactions, is: never let go of both ends. Have the house, or have the money. The cynic would say, preferably have both, but never be in the position where you have neither.

Before committing yourself to anything, reread the chapter on contracts because the vendor whose heart you warmed with those magic words 'I would like to buy your house' has been on the phone to Skinner and gleefully said that he has found a buyer and Skinner says, 'Leave it all to me.' What, at this point, Feather has left to him is the sending of a draft contract and that is what in the fullness of time you can expect to receive, but he might also write to you as he did to our vendor in the previous chapter, saying that he won't be responsible for you in law or otherwise. If he does, join in the fun by ringing up Feather and ask what Skinner is covering up – what is wrong with the house, is it down for road widening, is there a deed missing, has he got the scrolls or hasn't he? – plus any further nonsense you can think up. Then forget about it.

Vendor: Send off to the purchaser's solicitor two copies of your draft contract, the Property Information Forms and the Office Copies, which you should have received by now. You should also include the Fixtures, Fittings and Contents Form, which should be completed on all residential sales. This should list those items which are to remain in the property and those which may be taken by the seller.

Purchaser: Receive draft contract and possibly Office Copies. If you don't get a Land Registry Office Copy and file plan, demand it. The Standard Conditions of Sale make it the duty of the seller to prove his title in this way, admittedly only after the contract, but it's customary for the seller to supply these before contracts are exchanged. Don't be fobbed off with a photocopy made in the office of your seller's solicitors. This may be useful as a starter, but don't leave the matter there. The Land Registry frequently updates the format of these so why be fobbed off with something that might well be out of date?

Peruse the Office Copies in the light of the knowledge you gained from chapter 10, 'The Registers'.

Put the draft contract on one side for a while. Content yourself with asking the vendor's solicitors if they are sending you the Seller's Property Information Forms and if not, send them two copies of the Enquiries before Contract or preliminary enquiries. Before you do, have a quick look at these, and if the questions they contain don't cover everything you would like to ask about, and hopefully get a sensible answer to, put those extra questions in writing. For instance, buyers of new houses should ask: 'Is the design, construction and layout of the sewers such as will meet the criteria required for their adoption by the water and any other authority?'

Even if you have already seen a form filled out by the vendor regarding fixtures and fittings and details of the items he intends to leave and those he intends to take, it's worth asking whether or not anything has changed. Also, one question which should always be asked is, 'Are there any disputes with the neighbours?' and in relation to a leasehold property, any dispute with the landlord or breaches of covenant. Look carefully at the Property Information Forms and ask the questions that you want answered but are not covered.

Vendors now have to deal with preliminary enquiries (see page 112), if you have not sent the Seller's Property Information Forms already and purchasers can look over their shoulders. Indeed, anyone who has not coped with these enquiries before will do well to have his seconds ready in his corner, for this form will be the one that will (at first) make you wish you had never bothered, that is, until you have really started pencilling in some replies in the copy which is intended for you to keep. As you read on and pencil away, the colour will come back to your cheeks, and you will realise how childish it was to be frightened.

Most of the questions are easy, daft or both, but we will have a quick run down Enquiries before Contract, first noting that in some of the forms the column headed 'Replies' already has displayed in bold type at the beginning or end 'These replies on behalf of the vendor are believed to be correct but the accuracy is not guaranteed and they don't obviate the need to make appropriate searches, enquiries and inspections.'

The law assumes you have made all proper enquiries, so don't place too much reliance on this disclaimer. Also, the law on misrepresentation still applies, as should the good old British principle 'my word is my bond'. The following are common questions which appear in one form or another.

- One relating to boundaries and whether you know of any disputes about them. If you know the answers, give them; if you are not sure, use the formula 'I know of none' and give the same answer to the question on notices, particularly in so far as it refers to your predecessors in the house.

- One asking for copies of any Housebuilding Council guarantee, insurance policies covering defective title, or road maintenance agreements. If you have any, comply; if not, you can't, so just reply 'none in my possession'.

- Questions about whether services such as gas, electricity, water and drains are connected, and if any of them come to you through someone else's property: the first part is easy, the second is easier when you know how. Answer: 'Please rely on your own survey.' Deal with the question about access and roads in a similar fashion. About rights of way: if you know of any say so; if not, say 'I'm not aware'.

- There will normally be a question that could frighten you out of your wits and send you scurrying off for legal help. Don't let either happen. It asks: 'Please give full details of all overriding interests affecting the property as defined by the Land Registration Act 2002 Schedule 3.' This question refers to other people's rights over the property which are not recorded on the Register, such as the rights of people who live in the property who are not joint owners or those people, such as neighbours, who have rights of way over the property. If you don't know of any, answer 'I am not aware of any, but the property is sold subject to any that there may be that are not overreached.' Having answered that question, you've broken its back. This means that the property will be sold subject to any rights of way, etc., but if a person has an interest in the property, it will not bind the purchaser if the money is paid to two people, rather than one.

It's downhill all the way now and you can answer the remaining questions with variations on our old friend 'I don't know of any, but please rely on your own survey.' Even with the question about Council Tax band, though you have the latest Council Tax bill sitting in front of you, it's safest and perfectly acceptable to reply 'I think £x, but please check with local authority.'

Even though you have specified the fitted wardrobes, shelving and such like in a final clause of your contract, this doesn't stop the question cropping up again. You will find this kind of duplicate questioning all the time. You just have to put up with it and give it the short shrift it deserves. You are asked how long will it be after the exchange of contracts, before the vendor (he means you) is able to give vacant possession. The usual period is one month, but of course you may make it longer, shorter or tag onto whatever date you give 'or before'. So give a date which you think is suitable to the purchaser and also make it clear where and how you insist on having the money: 'Vacant possession will be given on completion which will take place at (state venue) on the umpteenth of Nerth. A CHAPS payment will be required for the balance of the purchase price.' A cheque or a banker's draft could bounce.

You will also be asked when possession of the property will be given. You answer, 'When I receive the balance of the money by CHAPS payment on completion'. No solicitor would agree to completion not taking place in his office; he would be negligent if he sent off his client to an alternative venue, and the mortgage money by CHAPS, without having the deeds. If you are also buying a house, you may wish to add a suggested completion date to tie in with your purchase, but see later for more on this subject.

When the preliminary enquiries have been completed to your satisfaction, send them off. They may come back with supplementary questions, and some of them may appear to be intended to annoy you. Don't let annoyance creep in, just press on, courteously pointing out that you can only sell what you have got, but you are not a qualified surveyor, and if he wants to be absolutely certain where such things as the drains run, he is welcome to have a sniff around provided he does no damage.

It takes some believing, but this is the right way to deal with the Property Information Forms, and Skinner's acceptance of your answers will be your proof.

Purchaser: Receive the Property Information Forms form, duly completed, and glean from them what you can. Though we made fun of the question about overriding interests on behalf of our vendor, do be careful that as a purchaser the laugh is not on you, because one of the overriding interests protected by Schedule 3 of the Land Registration Act 2002 is the rights of a person in 'actual occupation' of the land. This means that it's possible for someone, apart from the registered proprietor, to claim rights of occupation (and the courts will not shift him), even though he has not registered that right anywhere. It's wise to ask if there is anyone over the age of 17 living with the seller who is not also an owner of the house. If the answer is 'yes', it's wise to get him to sign the contract to provide a written assurance on his part that he claims no interest in the house and will vacate on or before the date the sale is to be completed. If you don't do this, he may still be there when you move in and with a better claim to the house than you! Another way to protect yourself is to make sure that the property is registered in two names and that you get a receipt signed by both registered owners. This latter precaution will not assist you if the person in occupation has a lease. In matrimonial situations, the spouse's right of occupation is registrable for both registered and unregistered titles and doesn't take effect without registration. Overriding interests are not confined to rights to occupy or the rights (whatever they may be) of the persons in occupation such as a lease; they include third party rights such as legal easements (like rights of way, rights of light), so someone may have a right of way over the property although you could not see it on the Register.

So at the risk of repetition: throughout this Guide you will find endless warnings about making sure, before you sign a contract, that the vendor can give you vacant possession on completion, and *never ever* complete the purchase of a house before you have seen with your own eyes that the house is completely vacated, and that if there has been any kind of dispute about ownership and/or occupation, that the locks have been changed. If you think you may gain further enlightenment by asking supplementary questions, ask them, but remember they were stock questions, so you can't expect better than stock answers. Best of all is to make a trip to the property and, using the form as a checklist, go through the items with the vendor.

And it's at points like this that layperson conveyancers like us come out on top because we leave our desks and look at the problems – not the papers about them!

Have a look at boundaries, walls and fences with your own eyes. The general run of houses in town and suburban areas have clearly defined garden walls, hedges and fences, but in rural areas it isn't always so. However, first check what is within the boundaries against the plan in the Office Copies. A 'T' mark against a boundary indicates that the owner of the land on which the 'T' is situated is responsible for the upkeep of that boundary, wall or fence. Otherwise, strong (but not conclusive) evidence is that the owner of the land on which the fence posts are situated (which hold up the fence) is responsible for that fence. If there is more within the fences than the plan shows, it's possible that your vendor has pinched it. Ask him about it. Ask the neighbour. If there is a problem, it isn't much trouble to move a fence, but what about a garage? Always check that a garage is within the boundary shown on your plan. Indications that there may be a dispute about boundaries, or whose responsibility it is to maintain a particular fence, could be evidenced by its broken-down appearance. If you have any reason to suspect that there is any kind of dispute, go hotfoot to the neighbour and ask his point of view on the matter particularly if it's about a shared drive.

Disputes between owner-occupiers of suburban properties about who owns what and who can go where are the most frustrating, intractable, time-consuming and above all ruinously costly to resolve at law. If you come across a hint of such a dispute, my advice is, run a mile. Hard lines on the vendor who hasn't had the courage or foresight to come to terms with his neighbour; his best hope is that his prospective purchaser has not read this book and the business is being conducted at arm's length by Skinner, Write & Reams, so that Feather is blocked from the knowledge by a heap of paper and only finds the pig after moving into the poke.

If, in order to get to the house or garage, you have to traverse an unmade road, or anything which looks as if it may not be a public right of way (the council will tell you if it is, in reply to your enquiry form – see later), there should be a note on the Office Copy, saying you have a right of way over the track or common drive or whatever. On the other hand, does anyone else have a right of way over the land which is shown, on the plan, to be that which you are contemplating buying, and if so, who will be responsible for the shared access way's upkeep? If you have seen other people walking over the land, ask how long they have been doing this for and whether they have permission to do so.

If the copy of the deed plan which came as part of the Register has produced no satisfactory answer about the approach to the property, ask the vendor or the solicitor what is proposed. Usually, it will be that the vendor makes a statutory declaration that he has used the way for 20 years or more and this is usually thought to be acceptable. It's evidence that the access has been in use for so long and the law will adopt a convenient fiction to the effect that a right of way does actually exist. This also applies if the land is common land or a right can be acquired over common land under the Countryside and Rights of Way Act 2002. If the vendor has driven over the common land for 20 years, it's likely that a right of way by prescription has arisen, but get the vendor's solicitor to confirm this. If he cannot, insist on insurance. However, if it really is the house of your dreams, you really should consider taking legal advice.

It would be a surprise if you found a house that had electricity which was not connected to the mains. The owner would probably be so proud of his generator and his independence of 'those wicked power workers' that he would show it off without being asked. If the gas supply was bottled, you could hardly miss the evidence. Nevertheless, check both.

If you have any doubt about the water supply, see the replies to your water drainage search, i.e. to discover if it's metered and connected to the mains. Do have a swift look for the lid of the cast-iron box which houses the stop-tap and is usually to be found just outside the boundary to the front garden. If you are buying out in the sticks and think that the water supply may be coming to you across someone else's land, write to the local water authority and ask it. If the answer you receive is in the affirmative, then you have a further point to investigate: 'What will happen if the water supply is stopped, for any reason, by this neighbour?' If the vendor or his solicitor had anything about these matters, there should be such a letter in existence from a previous purchase. Even if there is, it will still be worth while writing and quoting the letter and asking if things remain the same.

Drains can be a bit of a stinker. All your life you have simply pulled the string or pushed the plug, and what has to go has gone, and you never had to give a second thought as to where it was going or how it could possibly get there. The thought that it would answer back and refuse to go was too awful to contemplate. Buyers in built-up areas can be pretty sure it goes into the main drain; where it goes after that we don't worry our heads.

A house which is not connected with the main sewer will almost certainly drain into a cesspit/cesspool or a septic tank. In the case of the latter, the owner will need to have it emptied every four or five years, depending on the size of the family (the former don't have to be emptied). This is no problem. Everything functions as if there were a mains drainage, but when the tank is cleared by hydraulics into a tanker, there is a bill to pay. When the water companies started to send their bills separately from the Council Tax accounts, they divided the bill between water and sewerage charges, at which the septic tank owners said, 'Oh, no!' to the sewerage charge, and won their point. All of which little excursion into recent history is to tip you off that the water company's bill, unless it shows a specific charge for sewerage, will tell you that you don't have connection to the main sewer.

More difficult to establish is whether you drain through anyone else's land, or vice versa. The cases where this is likely is where a house has been built in the garden of another house. It could become really important if you wanted to build an extension or garage.

So have a look round at the manholes; you might learn something, but as manholes have sometimes been covered over, this inspection may not be sufficient. If you intend spending a lot of money on your extension or garage, get your builder in to have a poke around – if there is bad news he will delight in giving it to you. If necessary, look in the *Yellow Pages* for a firm that specialises in sniffing around the drains and get a quote.

You are told that no building requiring planning permission has been carried out in the past four years. Does that square with what you find on inspection? For our purposes, just about everything needs planning permission, but often the permission comes from the law: the Town and Country Planning (General Permitted Development) Order 1995. Telephone the planning department where the house is located to see what it can send you regarding these provisions. It's worth the effort. Houses can be enlarged without permission subject to certain conditions, unless permitted development rights have been removed when planning permission was first granted for the estate – something which is quite common in gated developments. Roofs can be added or enlarged. Porches can be added. Sheds, garages and swimming pools can be added. Parking spaces can be laid. Satellite antennae can be installed. In all these cases, if the works come within the very detailed limitations laid down by the law, no further planning permission is required. Overstep the mark, and it is! But they still have to get, and be built in accordance with, building regulation approval, which is a different thing from planning approval. If your vendor gives a categorical answer 'no', or even (if he has lived in the house for less than four years) the time honoured 'not as far as I am aware', you may think that sufficient. A solicitor would, unless someone like his client, have alerted him otherwise.

Vendor: Receive any supplementary questions and answer them as best you can.

Purchaser: Receive answers to supplementary questions and decide whether to settle for what you are being offered. If you are satisfied, you can now involve yourself in the expense of sending off a few forms with their appropriate fees.

If you are borrowing money, carry out a Land Charges Department bankruptcy search using Form K16, which is sent to the Land Charges Department at Plymouth. The search is against you and your partner if buying in joint names. All you do is write in your names as required in the form and pay £2 per name. It's required by your lender, so first ask if it plans to do its own. If so, you will be charged, so save your money. Otherwise, do it about eight working days before the date for completion. Your lender will wish to see the answer.

Enquiries of Local Authority CON 29, together with Search of Local Land Charges LLC1, can be posted to the local council, just as Skinner & Deskbound would do. Ask about the fee; it varies. There are a number of different CON 29 forms. CON 29R includes the questions which apply in every case. CON 29O includes optional questions which only apply in certain circumstances and include the ability to make a commons search (to find out whether or not land is common land and the rights of access that entails). Have a look at CON 29O and see whether or not you think those might be applicable or if you want, for your own peace of mind, to know the answers. The local authority searches will be valid for approximately six months so it's unlikely (unless you have been incredibly unlucky) that you will need to carry out fresh searches.

However, I suggest that you take them to the council offices, and do a real search around for yourself while you are there. Ask if you can have a look at the development map and the planning applications approved and pending. Don't attempt to use the jargon. Keep it simple. You will get two surprises. First, how much help you get if you start the service by smiling, and saying to the official, 'I wonder if you can help me?' and second, the amount of information you can so easily pick up that you won't if you simply rely on the forms. Care is needed, though. Some local authorities give less information on a personal search than they would in reply to a professional one (in some cases, it's the really important information, such as planning records, that is withheld).

The town development map is divided up and each division is coloured. Some are even coloured and hatched. How a division is categorised tells you what the council intends for it. If the area is coloured, say a dirty brown with black dots, it could mean that the area is intended for obnoxious industries. If anyone owns a house in that area and he wants planning permission to convert it to a bone and bladder boiling factory, he might get it. A nicely coloured pink area might mean an area primarily intended for residential use, and if you send off your forms of local search, those are the kind of answers you will receive. That is to say, you would learn it's an area intended for, say, obnoxious industries, green belt, inner ring road or residential – and that is all.

If you want to know if anyone is even thinking about doing something nasty at the bottom of the garden, ask. Particularly if you are buying property bordered by a peaceful plot of land containing succulent fruit and veg; even better, where beyond the prospective patch there are open fields. What a lovely view! What a set-up for anger and frustration, if you simply send off the forms in the usual manner and wait for what the gods send.

In a few months you could be looking at a brick wall and someone else's line full of washing where you thought you had a view over the undulating countryside. As soon as you saw the builders coming, you would be off to your legal advisers asking what you could do about it and why you had not been told what to expect. You will now find that in addition to facing a brick wall, you are banging your head on one and paying legal fees for the privilege of doing it. That's when it will be borne in on you that in spite of all your GCSEs, 'A' levels, degrees and diplomas, you are a twit. You bought land (with a house on it) in an area designated residential and you are now surprised when a house builder gets busy with the bricks and mortar creating residences in the area. My dear reader, this isn't a question for a lawyer, it's plain common sense and a problem of understanding the English language!

What can you do to save yourself from twittery? When you go to the local council offices, ask to see the list of planning permissions granted in the area over the last ten years or so (the spread of years is important; people often sit on development permission for years, but councils give the permission subject to time limits which vary – ask). Then be really cute and ask for the list of planning applications pending! In many cases you will now be able to obtain information on planning permissions granted and planning permissions pending from the local council's website.

When you leave the forms, the official will tell you when to expect the LLC1 and CON 29 to be returned to you, bearing the council's stamp, which gives a warranty against negligent replies on its part. When forms do arrive, have a look through for anything unusual. So unusual is it for anything unusual to appear, the authorities have duplicated replies ready. Even so, duplicated or not, you want the job doing properly, otherwise you wouldn't be doing it yourself, so you will scrutinise each answer. If you find anything you don't understand, call the local official and ask.

If, in spite of all the form-filling and chatting up of the officials, you still suspect there might be something nasty in the pipeline, have a chat with the Citizens Advice Bureau and the local newspaper to see if they know anything to the area's advantage or disadvantage.

There is very little to fill in on the two forms you take or send to the council offices. There are two CON 29 forms: CON 29R and CON 29O. You will need CON 29R answering and it will cost you a fee to have that done for you. Local authority fees tend to vary from council to council and may change frequently, so you need to ring the office.

You will learn from the replies you receive about such things as whether the road fronting the property is maintained at the public expense, whether the council is about to grab any land within 200 metres of your boundary in order to lay new roads, and whether it or the appropriate Secretary of State intends constructing a road, underpass, overpass, forward pass, flyover or elevated road within 200 metres of the property. The form doesn't ask about 201 metres plus; that is why layperson conveyancers come off best, because they have a chat with the officials. They don't have sleepless nights every time they read in the newspapers about some poor soul waking up to find the council ready with some diabolical scheme that will either knock the house down or tens of thousands of pounds off its value.

CON 29O consists of optional questions. Have a look down the Part II questions and see if you think any of them might have a bearing on the house you are interested in buying. It will cost you extra for each of the questions in Part II that you tick, as an indication to the officials that you require that particular question answering. The kind of things you can learn from ticking a question range from 'Has the council authorised the service of a building preservation notice?' to 'Has the council or the Secretary of State authorised the making of an order for the compulsory acquisition of the property?'.

The requisition for a search of the local Land Charges Register Form LLC1 is even easier to complete. It has to be sent in duplicate and it comes to you with a copy; all you have to do is insert a carbon, tick that you require all the Register searching, put the address of your intended purchase and your own name and address in, enclose the fee and that is it.

There are further searches you should carry out using a letter or appropriate forms. First, telephone the local water company, ask who to speak to about water and drainage enquiries and then talk to him to see what a search costs. Then write with a cheque. The water company will answer the questions and send along a plan showing what is connected and what can be found in the area, so if your house is not connected to its sewers, you will be able to see if there are sewers in the area and you will be able to ask the cost of connection.

Environmental issues are now all the rage. The CON 29R may give meaningful answers to environmental questions, but many solicitors now carry out online environmental searches or 'envirosearches'. For a fee, these will tell you what is happening in your area – if it appears – in any of a wide variety of paper records. Is your house in a flood plane? Was it built on infill land? What is the risk of subsidence? Have there been environmentally unfriendly activities in the area, etc.?

Two specialist searches that may be necessary are coal mining searches and commons searches. You now get coal mining information on your envirosearch (so far as it exists) and commons searches should be made only where it seems relevant to do so. If you are buying a house in an inner London borough, there is probably no need for this, but if you are buying in the country there probably is. Even if the area seems to have been residential for some time, open land nearby could be common land and there have been cases of houses being registered (incorrectly) as common land so it can be worth checking. This is particularly so if you are buying an idyllic house with a private access across 'Greenfield Common', or similar.

You **the purchaser** can now turn your attention to the draft contract. It has to be read through and a decision made as to whether the terms are acceptable or not. It's not a take-it-or-leave-it situation; that is why it's a draft contract. If there is anything about which you are not clear, speak to the vendor, his solicitor or both, and get one or the other to explain (not explain away with excuses such as 'it's usual') until you understand. If there is anything with which you cannot agree, strike it out. Here are nine points you should watch out for when perusing the draft contract:

1. Compare the information given in the preliminary enquiries with what the solicitor has written concerning the items, referred to as 'chattels' in the agreement, which the vendor said he was including in the price agreed. You will need to ask the vendor to confirm what he actually intends to leave. There should be a list of contents that are included, attached to the contract.

2. Is the amount of deposit stated correctly? If you are using the Standard Conditions of Sale, you can use the deposit from your sale as the whole or part of a deposit for your purchase. If you aren't using the Standard Conditions of Sale, put a clause in the contract allowing you to use your purchase deposit.

3. Check to whom and under what conditions the deposit is to be paid. You should insist that whosoever receives the deposit does so as stakeholder, because a stakeholder cannot part with the money unless he has been satisfied that completion has taken place. You may have paid a holding deposit to an estate agent, or even the whole amount of the deposit; if so, the clause about the deposit should take care of that situation.

4. There should be a clause stating the capacity in which the vendor sells, called 'title guarantee full/limited'. If such a clause doesn't appear in the draft contract, ask for one to be inserted. If the vendor owns in his own right, insist he sells with full title guarantee. If he doesn't, as executor of an estate, for example, he will wish to sell with limited title guarantee. Be especially careful if the vendor is not going to sign but has appointed an agent under a power of attorney to sign. If he sells by power of attorney, you are entitled to a copy of the power; if as

executor or administrator, probate or letters of administration with Will annexed out of the Principal Registry or district Probate Registry is sufficient proof of a person's death and of the executors' title to the property. In the case of a lender selling after a borrower's default, you will be pleased to hear that you don't concern yourself with whether the 'mortgagee (one who lent) in possession' is properly exercising his rights under the mortgage. You just need to know whether the power of sale has arisen by looking at whether the redemption date has passed. Ninety-nine per cent of vendors are giving full title guarantee and if yours isn't, ask his solicitor to give you the real evidence that he might have the right to sell.

It's not unusual, however, for a vendor to place some limit on his responsibilities. His solicitor will generally name the bits he doesn't want his client to subscribe to. You will have no idea what this means unless you look at the legislation, which is The Law of Property (Miscellaneous Provisions) Act 1994. A decent local library should hold *Halsbury's Statutes of England* and you can look it up there. However, if you are on the internet or have a friend who is willing to do this for you, print off a copy from www.opsi.gov.uk and click on the link to 'legislation' on the left-hand side.

5. Here is a nice easy one for you. Check that the address and/or description of the property to be sold is correct. If the property being sold is part of an existing registered title, then you should also be provided with a plan, for more detailed description.

6. If you were told that you are buying a freehold, check that it says so in the description.

7. If your vendor agreed to include items such as carpets in the sale price, they should be in the contract, but if the price you are paying is just over the level at which Stamp Duty Land Tax becomes payable, fix a price for the item (£x) and ask that the clause has added to it 'and £x of the purchase price shall be apportioned to these items'. On the other hand, take account of how this will affect your mortgage. Building societies don't lend on furnishings. So, say their maximum advance is 90 per cent and you are buying at £50,000, your top mortgage is £45,000; there is £2,000 worth of carpets, etc., included in the purchase price, the highest the building society surveyor can value the house at is £48,000 and the maximum advance is £43,200, so your deposit now

becomes £6,800 instead of the number you first thought of. Bear in mind, however, that it's highly unlikely that a solicitor, acting for a vendor, would allow unrealistic apportionments to be made, since this would be a fraud on the Revenue. The Stamp Duty Land Tax return requires you to fill in the amount which is paid for chattels. This return is signed by you. The Revenue will enquire as to whether the apportionment is reasonable and may investigate if it doesn't think that it is. Therefore, I leave to your honesty and ingenuity the rest of the sums on which your decision rests.

8.   Look at the rate of interest (contract rate) in the contract. This is usually four per cent above base rate. If it specifies the Law Society's rate, that is 4 per cent over base rate of Barclays Bank. You will be expected to pay interest at that rate if you delay completion beyond the date which eventually gets inserted in the contract. The most likely reason for your getting caught with having to pay this type of interest will be if your purchase money is dependent on the sale money from your present house, and you can't make your purchaser complete simultaneously. If the rate is the same as in your sale contract, and you have your purchaser tied to four per cent above base rate also, then you have a source from which to collect any penalty money. Unfortunately, the period for which this interest is payable is limited. After the time allowed in each contract, the deposit is forfeited by the seller.

9.   Covenants clause: with the draft contract, Skinner should send you a copy of all the covenants. There is not much you can do about them, but you certainly want to know everything there is to know, because you buy property warts and all, and once you are the owner, you will be responsible for seeing that the covenants (if any) are adhered to.

You can also ask to be assured that the previous owners have kept to the covenants. For instance, if there is a covenant that only a certain type of house should be built on the plot, and plans should have been approved and agreed by some previous owner, ask to see the approvals. If there is anything in the contract you feel should be amended, mark it in red ink and send it back to the vendor.

Remember, if there is a suspicion that there has been a breach of covenant within the last 20 years, no Council of Mortgage Lenders (CML) member will lend money on the house unless someone pays for restrictive covenant indemnity insurance and since it's your vendor's blemish, not yours, make sure it's a term of the agreement that he pays and get an offer before you contract.

Purchaser: When agreement has been reached on the draft contract, you can put it to one side and give your attention to the replies you will have received to your enquiries of the district council.

The Enquiries of Local Authority form usually comes back with a printed list of answers. In 999 cases out of 1,000, it will confirm that the road is made up, taken over and maintained at public expense; that there are no road widening proposals, and no proposals to build a new road within 200 metres of the property. If you had been afraid lest the council had an army of workmen at the ready, itching to get on with demolishing a garage or extension which had previously been built infringing building regulations and planning permission, the replies will either confirm your suspicions or put your mind at rest.

If it turns out that the road is about to be made up, you will want to know what the cost is likely to be and how much the vendor is prepared to knock off the price to meet it. If the property is about to be pulled down for slum clearance or the infringement of building regulations, your course of action is obvious.

Having called at the council office, you will have put flesh on the bones of the more-or-less standard answers on the form. You will have found out if there is to be a motorway within 201 metres or whether there is any development scheme in the offing that could affect the property, being either a whole shopping precinct, or an application to convert the quaint little antique shop on the corner to a fish and chip shop. In the unlikely event of your getting a reply that you don't understand, either call in on the council or give it a ring.

Form LLC1 will drop through your letterbox at the same time. The council will certify that either 'The search requested reveals no subsisting registrations' or 'The search reveals the registrations described in the schedules hereto …'. If there are any schedules attached, they are likely to refer to smoke control and planning controls that have long since been dealt with. The search might show that an improvement grant was agreed. That doesn't mean to say the grant was taken up, but you will want to know from the vendor if it was, and if so, whether any part of it has to be repaid on a sale taking place. If there is any verbiage that you don't understand in the replies to your searches and you think it could affect you, ring up the council and ask – council officials are invariably helpful to the learner conveyancer.

You are now almost in a position to send off your signed part of the contract, either in the form it was originally drafted or as amended by agreement.

It's about this time you should be thinking of insurance and so reread the information on 'risk' at page 79. The first question is should the insurance come into force when you exchange or when you complete? Then how much do you insure for? It should be for the reinstatement value of the house and all necessary expenses and it should be inflation-linked. This sum may well be less than the price you are paying, but then the land is not going anywhere, is it? Only the buildings are at risk. If you are borrowing, the lender's valuer will probably have stated the minimum level of required insurance. Otherwise you are on your own!

In its offer of a mortgage, the lender may nominate an insurance company. Unless you have some root and branch objections to the nominees, get your insurance with them then write and let the lender know. Check that the offer of a mortgage which you have received is a firm one. In addition, if your purchase is dependent on receiving the money from your own sale, you will realise that ideally the contracts should be signed simultaneously, but this is difficult to imagine because it entails getting all the parties together at the same time in the same place, and if everyone is taking the same precaution then all would need to be ambidextrous. The only sensible solution, therefore, if your purchase is dependent on your own sale, is to make absolutely certain that you have received your sale contract signed by your purchaser and that any conditional clauses can and will be met, before you sign up to buy, and that if necessary you can find overnight accommodation.

So here is your checklist on the eve of exchange of contracts:

- Draft contract has been agreed and one of your copies has been returned unsigned to vendor.

- Satisfactory replies have been received in the Seller's Property Information Forms or Enquiries before Contract.

- You are satisfied with the replies you received to the forms you sent to the council, what you learned on your fact-finding tour and to your water company and envirosearch.

- If the Office Copies revealed anything such as a caution or a Matrimonial Home charge, check that the vendor has obtained cancellation of the registration of such a charge or notice. If there is a restriction, you need some confirmation that the condition in the restriction will be complied with. This could be as simple as making sure that there are two people registered as owners of the property. If there is a notice registered on the title (which will bind you after you complete), you need to find out what this right relates to. If it is, for example, a right for the neighbour to use the shared drive, all well and good, but be alert to such entries as they will not be removed when you become the registered proprietor.

- You have got a firm offer of a mortgage.

- If it applies, you have your own sale tied up. If a deposit cheque bounces, the contract is automatically washed out.

- You have checked that everyone over the age of 18 who lives in the house is prepared to move, whether their names appear on the Register or not, by getting them to sign a statement to this effect in the contract.

- There are no problems with the survey of the property.

So here goes! Insert the agreed date for completion into the contract. This is usually one month hence, so if you feel there is still a lot of reading left in this chapter also remember there is one month to do it in. There is no reason why it shouldn't be earlier than the usual month if it will save either party paying money on bridging loans. Sign the contract and send it off to Skinner, together with the balance of the agreed deposit, which will need to be sent early enough to clear – the usual period is four working days, although if you wish to pay by personal cheque a special condition to this effect will have had to have been inserted in the contract. Alternatively, you can send it in the form of a bank draft or electronic transfer. For money laundering reasons the solicitor would probably be happier with CHAPS transfer. Finally, don't forget to put the date of signing at the top of the contract.

Two words of warning. Skinner needs to know whether he can exchange with you or whether you have other plans; for example, you are waiting for something like a search certificate, amended mortgage offer, or for your own buyer to reach the stage where he can exchange with you, so unless Skinner has your carte blanche to exchange on receipt tell him to hold it to your order till you are ready to release contract – that is, allow him to exchange with you. Also, if there is a chain with you in the middle, you may well find you cannot exchange at all since no one will trust you to honour your word. You can show them your tattoo 'Death before Dishonour', but it will cut no ice. What happens, for example, is the buyer at the bottom of the chain tells the next one up that he is ready and that contracts can be exchanged before, say, 4.30 that day. If the recipient is ready, he tells the next person up the line and so on. The system works because the authority given is irrevocable and is backed by the professional ethics that solicitors adhere to, all of whom should also be insured against error. You don't enjoy this sainted status and will be seen as the 'Weakest Link'. The answer is get Skinner to act as your agent, so it's his word people act on, not yours. What he does for you is purely a private matter between the two of you.

Vendor: We have not forgotten you! The astute reader will have realised by now how little a vendor has to know or do in order to be his own conveyancer. However, you must rouse yourself, at this point, to receive the signed contract from the purchaser. Check that the contract he has signed is identical to the one you have signed, otherwise the contract will be void. At this point have a word with the stakeholder to make sure the deposit will be paid.

Even if your purchaser is getting a 100 per cent mortgage, I think you should still insist on a deposit. After all, if he is such a good risk that the lender doesn't require him to have a stake in the house, he should have no difficulty in raising a bank loan for five per cent of the purchase price. If you don't get a deposit, your contract is shaky. There is a difference between having rights and asserting them. You cannot get blood out of a stone. It's much more costly to sue for damages than to simply hold onto the deposit if he backs out of the deal. Sign your copy of the contract and send it to the purchaser.

Contracts are now said to be exchanged. The deal is now binding and neither side can back out without penalty. If you have a mortgage on the property, write to your lender saying that contracts have been exchanged. Ask how much will be required to pay off your mortgage on the completion date. Also ask for the daily rate that will be charged in the unlikely event of completion being delayed.

Purchaser: Receive vendor's part of the contract and check details. Pay particular attention that both parties have signed if the house is owned jointly or even if it's not owned jointly, that all people in occupation have signed or at least given a signed release of their rights. While all this has been going on, you have been dealing with the solicitor for the lender. Every mortgage lender has a list of solicitors who act for it in the completion of mortgage advances – no others will be used by the lender. If there is a mortgage, everything bar agreeing to the contract will be done by the lender's solicitors.

Most solicitors are on the rolls of most mortgage lenders, although CML members are suspicious of sole practitioners. So when a purchaser gets a mortgage, what do you know, the solicitor acting for him in his purchase may also get instructions to act for the lender. It makes sense by saving too many solicitors trailing round too many other solicitors' offices to complete a sale.

The solicitor acting for the lender will write, asking you to produce a number of documents. As the information contained in the papers he requests could in the future be quite useful to the layperson conveyancer, photocopy them, because lenders usually keep the lot.

This is what they require:

- Enquiries before Contract and vendor's solicitors' replies or completed Seller's Property Information Forms;

- local authority search forms and replies;

- vendor's part of the original contract;

- Land Registry Office Copies;

- copy of transfer;

- replies to Requisitions on Title;

- copies of any other documents of title, e.g. deeds of covenants, licences for alterations, licences to assign.

You will have noticed one new item in the above list. It need not cause you any trouble. It's the transfer, the very form which does the trick of getting your vendor's name off the Land Register and putting yours on. The transfer form is TR1, and you will remember meeting it on the very first page of this chapter, and now you come face to face with it, you will find that, though of supreme importance, it's the easiest of the lot (example provided in Appendices 8).

Buyers on new estates will require Form TP1 instead of Form TR1. The draft is usually provided by the developer, because he wants to put in a swathe of conditions that were not in the conveyance of the land to him. TP1 (Transfer of Part) is also the form that is used when buying from someone who is only selling part of his registered title.

After exchange of contracts, you are expected to send a draft of the transfer form to the vendor's solicitor. Fill in the title number, which by now you will almost have memorised, the address of the property you are buying, leave a blank for the completion date, put in the price you have dragged the vendor down to, exclusive of cost of any extras, then put in the name and present address of the vendor and finish the labour by inserting your own name and new address.

If you are married or buying jointly with someone else, you will need to decide what is to happen when one of you dies. This is dealt with by section 10 on the form. The Land Registry needs to know whether you are buying as 'joint tenants' or as 'tenants in common'. There are two ways of owning property jointly: joint tenants or tenants in common. Joint tenants means that when one of you dies that person's share automatically passes to the other owner by survivorship; tenants in common means that the share of the person who dies does not pass to the other owner automatically but rather passes in accordance with his Will. The only way that property can be owned in unequal shares is if it is held as tenants in common. The reason that the Land Registry needs to know is so that it can put a restriction on the title if you hold as tenants in common. This restriction will prevent the survivor from selling the property on your death unless he ensures that there are two registered proprietors. If you want the ownership to be in joint names, simply put the two names on the form. Section 10 of TR1 requires you to tick whether you want the property held as 'joint tenants', 'tenants in common in equal shares' or on some other basis. If you do not want to hold in equal shares, you need to set out on the form the shares that each of you will have. You will have to sign the transfer if you are buying jointly. If you want your partner to have all of your interest in the house on your death, tick the first box 'joint tenants'. If you want to share the property equally but you want to choose who receives your interest in the property on death through your Will, tick the second box ('tenants in common in equal shares'). If you want to hold the property on some other basis, the final box will be appropriate and you can either refer to a separate trust deed or write the percentages which each person is to own, but it's important that you tell the Land Registry in these circumstances that you will be holding the property as 'tenants in common' and then set out the percentages. This may be necessary if you and your partner are putting in different amounts of money. If you want to hold the property on a more complicated basis, with provisions as to what will happen if you fall out and conditions as to buying one another out in those circumstances, consider asking a solicitor to draw up a trust deed.

Finally, complete the certificate of value, which the Revenue man requires – he doesn't trust the property-owning classes. If you can manage to buy a house for £125,000 or less, you have no Stamp Duty Land Tax to pay. Agree to pay the vendor an extra £1 if he will leave the cat-flap and with a purchase price of £125,001 you will have to pay Stamp Duty Land Tax at a rate of one per cent of the whole purchase price (£1,200). Being a freeborn Englishman the Revenue man expects you to get up to every trick in the book in order to side-skip paying your money over to him. Unless you sign otherwise, he suspects you of trying to buy the house in bits: £5,000 for the billiard room, £5,000 each for each of the bathrooms and £2,000 each for each of the bedrooms and so on, all done in separate transactions. So the Revenue insists that you certify that the 'transfer hereby effected doesn't form part of a larger transaction or series of transactions in respect of which the amount or value or aggregate amount or value of the consideration exceeds £…'. If the purchase price is £125,000 or less, that is the figure you put in. You enter the next higher figure, either at which tax starts to be payable (£125,001) or at which Stamp Duty increases – at £250,001 it increases to three per cent and over £500,001 it increases to four per cent. You will have to file a Land Transaction Return, which contains a similar certificate. If you are a first-time buyer, there is no Stamp Duty Land Tax to pay on properties bought for less than £250,000 until March 2012.

Vendor: Receive the draft transfer and check it. Also check the amount being paid and the spelling of all names.

Purchaser: Your conveyancing doesn't have to be done overnight. If, from reading the instructions so far, it seems to you that there are a lot of fiddling little things to do, bear in mind three things.

In the first place they are mainly practical and not legal. Second, even after contracts are exchanged, you should have approximately one month to do it all in. Lastly, but fruitiest of the lot, a number of people's hopes are riding on your buying the house and it's surprising how helpful others can be when they need to be.

During the next few pages references to yourself, your lender's solicitor, the vendor's solicitor, his lender's solicitor and where you are selling at the same time, your purchaser's solicitor and his lender's solicitor, not to mention the lender's solicitor for your own sale if you are changing lenders, could lead you to think that for completion day you might have to put up a marquee (light refreshments to be served) in the garden or, if wet, book St Pancras Town Hall. *Not so.* Solicitors are capable of wearing many hats at the same time and you'll no doubt finish up with only one if you're a first-time buyer without a mortgage, or two if you are involved in a chain.

Send off two Requisitions on Title forms. This form asks questions about the date for completion and what money will be required: a completion statement. It also asks the vendor to produce receipts for outgoings and is mainly referring to rates, i.e. payments due under the lease such as the service charge or ground rent.

If the Seller's Property Information Form or Enquiries before Contract were completed again now, it asks, would the replies be as they were hitherto? A question concerns mortgages. It starts strongly with 'all subsisting mortgages must be discharged on or before completion' but then weakens and goes on to ask what form of undertaking to hand over receipts is proposed. So if on the Charges Register of the Office Copies you received there was a charge (mortgage) to a finance company, write in the space provided for additional questions: 'Please advise whether Form DS1 will be supplied on completion or whether the charge will be discharged by Electronic Discharge and provide the appropriate undertaking.'

The vendor or his solicitor must twiddle his thumbs till the mortgagee either provides the DS1 or uses the Electronic Discharge Service (EDS) or files an e-DS1. Many banks and building societies now use EDS. This is a communication from the bank's computer transmitted direct to the Land Registry confirming that the charge has been paid off and has the effect of cancelling the charge (after some checks are made by the Land Registry) and all entries on the Register relating to the charge. There is no need for a further application to remove reference to the vendor's charge from the Register.

The best a purchaser will get is a solicitor's undertaking to pay off the mortgage and send DS1 on as soon as he has it or alternatively to notify the purchaser when the charge has been discharged by Electronic Discharge and provide a copy of the bank's letter confirming this. The undertaking from the person acting as the vendor will not be acceptable to the buyer's solicitor regarding the production of the DS1 and it has to be given by a solicitor redeeming the mortgage. If the vendor is acting for himself, no purchaser should accept such an undertaking since it's not backed by the Law Society, but probably in this case the lender has its own solicitor to act on the redemption of the mortgage, so the purchaser can simply ask for information on what is due and then pay it himself out of the purchase price asking the lender's solicitor to supply the undertaking.

He can even do this if the lender is not paying anyone to represent its interest, but trying to get anyone in its offices these days who can be relied on for anything more than reading out blurb on a computer over the telephone can be a bit difficult. The whole point about big money-lending institutions is that ideally everyone else does the work for them and without charging; in recent years the dumbest kid on the block, who will still happily do this, and pay insurers to pick up the tab if anything goes wrong, is the less-than-streetwise solicitor. He rests secure in the vanity that he is a professional, and a person of note in the community, while everyone else gets on with reality.

A note of warning here to purchasers acting for themselves: most mortgage lenders are CML members and they invariably require their borrowers to get legal advice on their responsibilities and liabilities as a borrower. Before you contract to buy the house, make sure the people you are borrowing from are not going to insist you get advice or need to sign before a solicitor even as a mute witness. The trouble with borrowing other people's money is that they can lay down rules like this. After all, they don't lend money for your convenience, whatever their marketing department might say.

The vendor's solicitor should provide any information and documents you will require in order to register your ownership, but he might, just for fun, retain papers or information you are going to need. But not to worry, because in sending you the Standard Conditions of Sale, he has bound himself to provide all the documents you will need.

Also, use the space at the end of the form into which you can feed any additional questions that your lender may ask in response to the documents you will have sent it. Its response will also almost certainly include:

- The printed mortgage form for you to sign in front of a witness. Have a scan through the mortgage form (legal charge) but don't invite a headache. It's a take-it-or-leave-it situation – no variations are allowed. Before you sign, do make sure that you understand the basics of the payments that you will have to make so that you do not get any nasty surprises further down the line. Nowadays, most lenders require that mortgage documents are executed in front of a solicitor. They will also insist on the solicitor registering their charge (i.e. solicitors' costs and the registration fee) at the Land Registry and will expect the buyer to pay for this. As you are not planning to use a solicitor, arrange one of two things with such a lender, either to sign on completion in front of its solicitor or for the lender to waive the point. It isn't a legal requirement, being neither oath nor statutory declaration.

- An account made up of the fees you have to pay its solicitor, Land Registry fees, pre-completion search fees, Stamp Duty Land Tax (although this would probably go direct to the Revenue as a mortgage does not attract Stamp Duty Land Tax), etc. The total will be deducted from the money produced on completion day. This amount would probably be not much less than if the buyer used a solicitor of his own who would act on the lender's behalf for free.

- A sheet of requisitions (questions) about your purchase. Lenders don't have a standard form. You will find that the questions are similar to those you asked the vendor's solicitor in your Enquiries before Contract.

  Copy off the answers you were given and if there are any you haven't already got the answers to, get on to the vendor's solicitor right away and get the answers back to the lender as quickly as possible, in case they raise supplementaries, as you can do without being harassed by their questions right up to completion day.

  This form will also ask you if you intend to live in the house and to confirm that the whole of the difference between the mortgage advance and the purchase money is being found out of your own resources and without recourse to any other form of borrowing. The lender might also enclose a list of any further documents it requires on completion. If it doesn't, ask it to let you have such a list as soon as possible.

- If applicable, NHBC Form 12 and the NHBC agreement itself.

Vendor: Receive Requisitions on Title – post-exchange questions on title asking about redeeming the mortgage, the completion statement, the payment and purchase monies, etc.

There is a sample of the form of Requisitions on Title in Appendix 7. You will note that that form has not been filled out because there are myriad answers that can be given to these questions, which depend on the circumstances. The guide that follows should be read together with the blank form in the Appendix. This is the information that the requisitions are looking for:

Question 1

Simply answer yes or no. If there have been changes since filling out the Seller's Property Information Form, then this is the place to say so.

Question 2

This is about handing over the keys and if the property is tenanted, confirmation that notice of the sale will be given to the tenant so that he will pay the rent to the new owner.

Question 3

3.1 is only really relevant if the property is unregistered and so the title deeds are the proof of the title of the vendor. If the property is registered, title is guaranteed by the state.

3.2 relates to the documents that may be referred to such as the original deeds, which contain restrictive covenants or rent charges, etc., or original leases.

Question 4

The Law Society's Code of Completion by Post can be found at www.lawsociety.org.uk/productsandservices/goodpractice/conveyancing/

annex25e.page. The buyer's solicitor may not wish to adopt this code where dealing with a non-solicitor.

Question 5

5.1 requires the preparation of a completion statement. The requisitions refer to an apportionment. This is generally relevant where you are selling a leasehold property and there is a service charge. If the service charge has already been paid for the period from 1 January to 1 July and the sale is completing in June, you may want the purchaser to refund you 1/6 of what you have already paid. This may have been dealt with in the contract.

5.2 is self explanatory. This should be the account where the vendor wants the money to be paid.

Question 6

6.1: the mortgages that are going to be paid off on completion of the sale should be listed here. As referred to above, any purchaser will usually require that any mortgages/charges over the property are redeemed on completion, otherwise he will have difficulties in registering the purchase and the charge will remain on the property. The reference to the Housing Act charge relates to 'right to buy' properties. If a right to buy property is sold within a certain period of the right to buy being exercised, the discount has to be repaid. This is a charge on the property which is registered on the Register. The purchaser simply wishes to ensure that this sum will be repaid prior to completion.

6.2 requires a promise that the charges will be redeemed and the necessary documentation will be sent over to the solicitor for the purchaser once the charge has been redeemed. This will allow the purchase to be registered. As referred to above, many banks now use Electronic Discharges. If there is a mortgage on the property, this is something to raise with the solicitor acting for the mortgagee.

6.3: this confirmation can only be given if the mortgagee with a charge on the property has confirmed that the vendor is authorised to receive the money to redeem its charge on its behalf. If the mortgagee has solicitors acting, it may be that the mortgage company will want its solicitors to receive this part of the purchase price. This will depend on the arrangements with the mortgagee and so the mortgagee and its solicitor should be contacted.

Prepare a completion statement, as requested, by showing the purchase price minus deposit paid. Don't worry about the Council Tax because it's levied on the occupier; simply let the local authority know the date you are moving out and if you have managed to overpay tax it will reimburse you. The purchaser cannot be made to pay for water if you have paid in advance; so ask your water company for an apportioned rebate up to completion date.

Purchaser: Receive replies to Requisitions on Title form and completion statement. Double-check that all of the charges that appear on the Office Copy Entry are mentioned in the requisitions. If you are buying without a mortgage, you can skip the next bit until we come to Form OS1. About this time you should be in possession of the list of documents your lender will require on completion. It will always require a minimum of:

1. Vendor's Land Certificate (or Charge Certificate if the house is mortgaged). Now Land Certificates and Charge Certificates are no longer produced, an Office Copy Entry should suffice.

2. Vendor's lender's solicitors' undertaking to send you a Land Registry Form DS1 discharging vendor's mortgage.

3. Transfer Form TR1 signed by the vendor. Form TP1 if buying from a builder or part of a registered title (i.e. a new title being carved out of an existing larger title), TR2 for a repossession.

    These three forms you will, of course, receive from Skinner on completion. The rest of the documents your lender will ask you to produce are:

4. Mortgage form (Legal Charge) signed by you.

5. It will probably ask you for a copy of the Land Transaction Return, SDLT 1, which is to be provided to the Revenue together with payment of any SDLT which may be due

    Much of the information on the SDLT 1 is provided by means of codes. These codes are to be found in the guidance notes (which are fairly self-explanatory). You need to ask for SDLT 6, which are the guidance notes. Alternatively, the guidance notes may be found on the Stamp Office website: www.hmrc.gov.uk/so.

6. The reply you received to the Form K16, the bankruptcy form (see page 129).

7. It will require the certificate issued in response to Form OS1, Application by Purchaser for official search. This is a very important form which is, again, a name-and-address job, plus enter the title number and in box 8, 'search from date', the date of issue of Office Copy. If you are borrowing money, give the name of the lender and tell the Land Registry it is for a mortgage, so complete box C on the form. If you are not, search in your name and tell the Land Registry you are purchasing and fill in box P. If you search in your own name as the purchaser, your lender cannot rely on the reply and will not accept it. An important form this, which was mentioned in chapter 10, 'The Registers', so we won't labour it again. Suffice to say that you are enquiring of the Registry whether anyone has registered any dealings in the land since the date the Office Copies were made for you.

    There is a fee for this service, currently £4. Don't send this form off until about 10 days before the date agreed for completion, for, as you will see it gives you protection (priority expires box) for 30 working days, 6 weeks, in other words, from the date the application was received in which to complete and register your deal. Though this is a lender's requirement, you should use this form even if you are not taking a mortgage. If you are buying from a landlord who has other properties registered under the same title number or a builder who is developing an area of land, use Form OS2, Search of Part. The Registry needs to know which part, and it's up to the vendor to provide you with sufficient identification (plans, plot no., etc.) to satisfy the Registrar. If you register within the priority period, you will not take the land subject to any interest which was registered in the meantime.

8. Form AP1 Application to Change the Register.

9. Form DS1. This is the form that tells the Land Registry to cancel the registration of the vendor's lender's mortgage. Only the vendor can supply this and then not for a week or more after completion. Or not at all if Electronic Notification applies. What the lender will actually want is a cast-iron guarantee that the mortgage will be paid off. Normally, a vendor's solicitors' undertaking will suffice. This will state that the vendor's solicitors will pay off the mortgage from the purchase monies and will forward Form DS1 to the buyer's solicitors when sealed by the lender as evidence that payment has been received.

If the discharge is accompanied by other transactions, the form will be lodged under cover of Form AP1. If stand alone, it's to be accompanied by Form DS2. You will not have a DS1 if the vendor's lender is using the Electronic Discharge system at the Land Registry.

The solicitor for the building society will expect you to pay his fees.

You might not be absolutely certain exactly which forms and documents will be 'lodged with this form' as Panel 3 (DS2) requires. Don't worry, you can safely rely on the lender and Skinner to help you out on completion day, because you are not the only party to this deal and matters have gone so far by now, that in 999 cases out of 1,000 your vendor is just as anxious to see the colour of your money as you are to see that of the person who is buying your present abode. So you have them. And as US President Richard Nixon once said, 'When you have them by the balls, their hearts and minds are sure to follow'!

Vendor: Sign the transfer form and get your partner to sign beside you if the house is in joint names. You will need to sign this in front of an independent, adult witness who should afterwards add his name, address and occupation in the spaces provided. If you have no mortgage to pay off, choose your spot for completion. If you have a mortgage, then as the Charge Certificate (if there is one) and the rest of the papers will have to be sent to your lender's solicitor (if it has one) you will have to use his office. If the lender doesn't have a solicitor, you are going to have to ask your lender to send the deeds to a solicitor on its panel to act in this capacity, and it might be willing to conduct a completion meeting on site but don't bank on it. It would rather have the money by CHAPS transfer. The lender's solicitor doesn't have much to do, but nevertheless charges the lenders and they in turn charge you by adding the fees onto the outstanding balance of your account with them. His job is to collect and give a receipt for the money and hand over the Charge Certificate to you.

Let your purchaser know the venue and exact time. Also inform him that you will require the balance of the purchase price in the form of a CHAPS payment, which has the advantage over a cheque in that it cannot be stopped and it will not bounce.

In case you are wondering how you would cope with paying off your mortgage in order to lay your hands on the deeds for handing over on completion of a sale, this is how it's done:

Get to know the exact amount of money required on the due date (called a redemption figure). At the same time ask if your lender will give you and the purchaser's solicitor 'the usual' undertaking to send the deeds on to your purchaser's solicitor after completion and confirmation that the mortgage has been discharged, in return for a CHAPS payment made payable to your lender, which you will have arranged to be made as part of the purchase money on completion of your sale, to pay off your mortgage with. You are released from the mortgage, and hey presto, the deeds (or Land Certificate if there is one) are sent on to your purchaser's solicitor in a short time. The purchaser's solicitor can also give you the balance of the purchase price in the form of a second CHAPS payment; don't be surprised if a fee for this second payment is debited from the sale price, because the purchaser's solicitor may tell his client that since you have no solicitor who could accept one payment and distribute it, why should his client pay for two? Don't give them the keys of your property until you see the colour of their money.

In practice, don't be too surprised to find no one trusts you or wishes to meet with you at completion, or can say at what time he can complete. So for a more likely scenario, see 'Planning for completion' below.

Purchaser: Receive the completion statement and the request about how the money is to be split. If you don't receive them seven days before completion, gee the other side up – you will soon have plenty of problems coping with crockery and curtain runners, without having uninvited last-minute jobs to do on the financial side.

You have no doubt bought and sold motor cars in the past. Collecting the money on one, paying out on another; paying off the HP on one and obtaining HP on another, are all very fiddly; all on the surface very complicated. Housing transactions are much the same, the big difference being that when the money from the sale of one car is being used to purchase another, both cars can be at the scene of completion. Unless you are moving next door or across the street, this is not possible with housing transactions. So look at the purchase at this stage as being of the title deeds (the Land or Charge Certificate and the transfer form), which represent the house. Anyway, approach the financial side of completion of your purchase as you did swapping cars and you won't go far wrong.

Planning for completion

You now have an interesting dilemma. How to complete? Since you are not a solicitor and since a solicitor will represent everyone or nearly everyone else in the chain, you have a problem. There was a time when you demanded your buyer to come to your property to complete, or if you had a mortgage you would go to the offices of the lender or its solicitors. Here you would swap deeds, cash (or its equivalent) and the keys. This was common 30 years ago, but not now.

The idea that you ask a solicitor to come to your house to complete will cause great merriment. The likelihood is that the solicitor will retell the story at dinner parties to the amusement of all and in time the story will no longer be recognisable. You will have become an urban legend, but for all that, you will receive no visitors at completion. What with electronic cash transfers (often the slowest and most annoying part of the whole process), computerised access to Land Registry records, the ability to search using a computer or the telephone, movement of letters and draft documents by post, fax and email attachments, people don't expect to pay a solicitor to wander around the countryside for completions and so none will. Not that it was ever practicable if there is a long chain that stretched around the country but, here and there, localised completion meetings were once commonplace.

Every case is different, so try to cobble together a completion plan, but the more people there are in the chain the less likely it is that you will be a welcome visitor to the offices of your lender's or your buyer's solicitor, so be prepared to have to pay someone to complete for you. If you are able to make this call, don't be surprised to find out that no one will be able to tell you exactly when he can complete. It can take a long time for money to wander around the country from bank to bank.

Also take your passport with you, in case an objection is raised to handing you a bank draft. In fact, all the solicitors you deal with will insist that you identify yourself, as a safeguard against fraud and as they are required to obtain evidence of identity to comply with their obligations under the money laundering legislation. Your lender's solicitor is given guidance on what to ask for. For those of you on the internet, have a look in section 3 of the CML *Lenders' Handbook for England and Wales* on www.cml.org.uk.

Vendor: What are the possibilities?

You are not buying and have no mortgage to pay off. Lucky you. Your buyer's solicitor is not going to call on you and you will not be given any cash until he has all that he thinks he needs. Your best solution is to ask if he will accept from you the signed transfer to be held to your order until you are paid. He will not be handing you a box of bank notes or a bank draft and will want to send the money to you by CHAPS transfer to an account nominated by you. You should ask that he undertakes not to part with the transfer until his bank has irrevocable instructions to send the money to you.

You are not buying but have a mortgage to pay off, so ask your lender to nominate a solicitor to represent its interests and ask him to do the same for you as explained in the previous paragraph.

Life becomes fun if you are selling and buying. Your old house is in Devon, the new house is in Essex, your old lender is in Kent and the new lender is in Leeds, and the solicitor who represents your seller is in none of these places. Much the same can be said of your seller and your buyer. Also there are roadworks on the M4 and cones (but no sign of work or workman) on the M25 so flying visits are out. Clearly you are going to have to find a solicitor in the chain to act as your agent.

Don't ask your original lender's solicitors. They have absolutely no interest whatsoever in seeing the matter is completed on the day of your choosing. Next week is as good as this week. Your lender will not be that fussed whether the deal goes through on the day or a week late. After all, the longer it takes the more interest you pay it. Try to persuade someone more closely connected with the transaction, such as the solicitor who represents the people you are borrowing money from, for the new house. They do have an interest in completing the loan since that is what their clients do for a living. Lend money. Or try the solicitor who represents the person buying your house or the solicitor who represents the person you are buying from. He too has clients who will expect 'their man' or 'their woman' to get the job done. Again, you will need your chosen solicitor to act as your agent and to hold documents/money to your order until he receives instructions that everything is in place.

Assuming you come up with a workable plan, what next?

You are wearing two hats. You are a vendor and also a purchaser, and the solicitor who is going to do the deed for you will need the relevant documents, search certificates and so forth. The best thing to do is to ask what he wants. Then if he misses something, it becomes his primary problem. It will also be his task to ensure the correct money comes and goes, to supply any undertakings required and to see you get the residue (if any) due to you.

As the vendor, all you will normally be asked for is the Transfer Form TR1 of your house. Your purchaser's solicitors will have typed it, and chances are they will have told you how to sign it.

If there are deeds, you may not have them. The bank or building society that has the mortgage over your house has these, and they will have been passed to its solicitors. The solicitors who will be carrying the sale through for you will supply the undertaking the purchaser's solicitors will demand, namely that the mortgage will be paid off and that Form DS1 (the Land Registry's formal release) will be sent on to the purchaser's solicitors when received or alternatively notification that the charge has been discharged under the Land Registry's Electronic Discharge system or by an e-DS1.

Purchaser: The likely problems and the possibilities are much the same. However, first things first. Arrange with the vendor or his agent for the keys to be available to you or your representative (you can't be in two places at once), for a swift inspection to make sure that everything that was to be left behind is still there, and everyone who was to move out has gone. Make sure you are truly getting vacant possession on completion and if anyone is still there, don't complete, no matter what fanciful explanations or excuses are tried on you. Such a case is one in a million but who wants to be a statistic? This final inspection is made to avoid the greatest calamity of all that can possibly befall a purchaser of a house intended for his own immediate occupation. So whether employing a solicitor or doing your own conveyancing, make sure that no person is left in the house, and also make sure the fixtures and fittings and any extras you are paying for have not been taken.

Now for the possibilities:

You are paying cash and don't need a mortgage. Your seller's solicitor can say where completion is to take place and may just be willing to have you call at his office to complete.

Make sure you have all the identification the solicitor is obliged to see under the money laundering legislation. Ask him beforehand what he wants you to bring and ask how he wishes to receive the money. Don't be surprised if a bank draft is not welcome, but if that is how you wish to pay, insist on this if the contract allows it. However, the fourth edition of the Standard Conditions provides that the balance may only be paid by 'direct credit' – again, to guard against money laundering – so unless you altered it you will have to pay by CHAPS.

When you get to the meeting, check the papers. Remember, the Office Copy is the proof of title. Make sure the transfer has been properly signed by the vendor and witnessed, and make sure anything else you need (which depends on circumstances) is available, for example undertakings to pay off an existing mortgage on the house and to send you Form DS1 or the notification that the charge has been discharged under the Electronic Discharge scheme when this has arrived in his office.

When all of this is in order, hand over the bank draft in exchange. On the other hand, perhaps you were properly required to pay by CHAPS transfer and so the money may be sitting in his bank account while you are sitting in his chair! Anyway, take up what you want and ask him to telephone the estate agents to release the keys. Then leave!

You are buying and do need a mortgage. In this case, the people you are borrowing money from will have their own solicitor (although you pay normally) and it may be that he has agreed to complete for you (and his own clients). In this case, he will want from you the various papers listed at pages 148-50 as relevant to the transaction.

The probability is that they will have asked you for all these papers before the day of completion and it's extremely unlikely that they will wish to see you at completion, except to the extent necessary to carry out their money laundering checks. In this case, they will be taking up the deeds, checking the transfer and demanding the necessary undertakings for paying off any existing mortgage on the house. They will probably leave it to you to worry about ensuring the keys are released, but you never know. They might just telephone when the transaction was completed.

Whichever option applied, the job is done. You've got yourself a new house!

Cash buyers

For you, there is still work to do. You will need a certificate that you have paid the Stamp Duty Land Tax and the transfer will need to be registered. If you are borrowing on the house, the lender's solicitor may well insist on attending to these formalities, although the Stamp Duty Land Tax Return must be signed by the purchaser. Otherwise, it's down to you. There are two deadlines you should comply with:

Stamp Duty Land Tax

Stamp Duty Land Tax is payable if the cash price stated in the transfer is above £120,000. In the unlikely event that the purchase price was below £120,000, you must still notify the Revenue of the transaction. You get 30 days from the effective date (which is either completion or, if earlier, the date when you were let into possession of the land) to submit the Land Transaction Return, failing which you will be fined £100. HM Revenue & Customs claims it pockets this money in the interests of fairness, but it would say that, wouldn't it? The form you need to fill in is the SDLT 1. It looks quite formidable at first but it isn't. Rather than supplying a box to fill in that you have purchased the property, you have to fill in 'codes'. These are found in the guidance notes Form SDLT 6. Each SDLT1 has a unique number and photocopies are not acceptable. They can be ordered from the orderline on 0845 302 1472 or alternatively you can fill it in online – www.hmrc.gov.uk/so – then click 'Complete your returns using the online service'. You must send a cheque with the Return, but you must not send any other documents other than SDLT 2, 3 or 4, which apply when the transaction is more complicated than the purchase of one house. Not just any office, mind. All Land Transaction Returns must be sent to HMRC SDLT, Netherton, Merseyside, L30 4RN.

Under no circumstances whatsoever should you post the Return to your local tax office! This will confuse them considerably. If you have sent the Return correctly filled in with the right amount of tax, the Revenue will send you a Land Transaction Return Certificate to show you have paid the duty. You will need this when you come to register the purchase.

Registration

A transaction is void if it's not registered within a month. In any event, you should aim to see that your application is with the Land Registry the day before the last day of the priority period noted in your search. You are not the legal owner of your house until you are registered. Double-check your search certificate received from the Land Registry to find that date. The reason for getting your application in before 'the search expires' is to make sure you get there before anyone else – a creditor waiting in the wings, for example. Searches can no longer be extended, but they can be renewed. However, renewal doesn't afford the same protection, so try to get it right first time. If you slip up, generally it doesn't matter, but it might, and if it does it could prove to be an expensive mistake because others may register and will then have priority over your interest.

Your application is usually made using Form AP1. Complete the form and send along the Transfer Form TR1, the Land or Charge Certificate, a cheque for the fees, Land Transaction Return Certificate and if your vendor had a mortgage you will also send along Form DS1. The DS1 might not be available for days, if not weeks after completion, so if necessary just send it along later. It may even be that there is no DS1 if your vendor's lender is using the Electronic Discharge scheme. If this applies, it tells the Land Registry its mortgage can be cleared from the record rather than issue a DS1 that an applicant can send along. The registration fees change from time to time, so telephone the relevant Land Registry, ask for enquiries and ask for the figure.

As you are unrepresented in the transaction, you will need to provide proof of your identity to the Land Registry and fill out Form ID1, which must be sent with your TR1. A separate ID1 must be filled out for each party who is not legally represented. So if you are buying jointly, you will both need to fill out ID1. The purpose of this is to prevent fraud. If you are legally represented, the solicitor acting for you is required to carry out money laundering checks to confirm your identity. Obviously, you won't have done this if you are acting for yourself. The form requires you to prove your identity either by going to a solicitor and taking along the ID specified on the form together with a passport photograph and Form ID1 (the solicitor may charge a fee for verifying your identity) or alternatively you can go along to a Land Registry Customer Information Centre with your

ID and a passport-size photograph so that the Land Registry staff can verify your identity. If you do this, take your application with you and ring for an appointment first and check that the Land Registry will accept the ID that you want to bring. Do note that if more than one person needs his identity to be verified at a Customer Information Centre, each person has to attend at the same time. Further practical information on this can be found in Land Registry Public Guide 20, available at www.landregistry.gov.uk. If your vendor is not represented either, he too will need to prove his ID and fill out a Form ID1 to be submitted with the application, and if all parties want their identity verified at a Land Registry Customer Information Centre, they must all attend at the same time.

A final word on registration: it's very important that you send your Land Transaction Return Certificate (or self certificate if the transaction was exempt from SDLT) together with your AP1 and TR1. If the Land Transaction Return Certificate is not enclosed, the Land Registry will reject your application. The only exception to this is where the Revenue has held onto your Land Transaction Return for 20 days. So check and double-check before sealing the envelope to send off to register your interest!

Builders

If you bought from a builder, the preceding observations are essentially correct, save that the builder's solicitors will have supplied the transfer and plan using Transfer Form TP1 and the Land Registry application form is called FR1 for 'First Registration'. Plus, the documents you send along with the application are listed by you, using Form DL and you will also need to tell the Land Registry what the builder's deposit number is (if there is one).

His Land Certificate (if he has one) will be placed on deposit with the Land Registry and it will issue a filing number called a Deposit Number. Your builder vendor will tell you what that number is. Have a look at the standard forms sent to you when you first received the legal papers. It should be there somewhere. If you don't have it, telephone the relevant Land Registry two to three days before completion and ask enquiries if the Land Certificate is on deposit. Tell them the title number and they will tell you the answer. If it's not on deposit, don't worry; since 13 October 2003 the Land Registry has not accepted Land Certificates on deposit, so it's not required for your registration as owner of your new house.

In this chapter and those covering contracts, mortgages and registered land I have covered the typical and some not very typical situations that can arise. The same situations can and do arise with unregistered properties, so they will be covered again in the next chapter. If necessary, refer to that. If you come across anything else that doesn't yield to common sense, telephone the Land Registry enquiries department. From a buyer saying 'I will', to completion taking place, occupies one or two calendar months, so you need not feel rushed.

Delays

Delay may occur in many transactions for a variety of reasons – it may be someone's fault, it may be no one's fault. The standard terms and conditions provide for payment of interest if there is a delay – who is liable to pay that interest depends on who is at fault. If the other party to the transaction demands interest from you, look at the contract. Know the contract inside out. Work out the cause of the delay. If you do not think that you are liable to pay interest under the contract, say so and say why.

Pundits never tire of telling us that buying our first house is the biggest investment of our lives. If you are young, and have a lifetime of buying and selling in front of you, your biggest investment has been in the time spent reading and putting into practice these few pages. Tell everybody!

CHAPTER 13

Conveyancing: the sale and purchase of an unregistered house

In chapter 12, I described all that has to be done to transfer ownership of registered property in England and Wales. Even if you have an unregistered house, some of the information in that chapter will be relevant to you, so it is best to read that first before you start.

What about unregistered? It's supposed to be more difficult, or so we are told. Judge for yourself.

This is a brief summary to start you off, but do read the whole chapter!

Overview

First, look at your deeds and extract all the conveyances you can find. Find one which is at least 15 years old and that is your 'root of title'. All this means is you contract to prove you and your predecessors have owned the house for at least 15 years. Perhaps you bought more than 15 years ago? If so, your conveyance is your root of title. If not, go back in strict date order and pick the one that is at least 15 years old. Copy all of these to your buyer. Your buyer or his solicitor may ask for certified copies. This means that you will need to go to a solicitor so that he can sign to confirm that these deeds are true copies of the original. This will cost a small fee.

A specimen conveyance

Specimen Conveyance

This Conveyance is made the   day of   20

BETWEEN the Vendors Xavier Lax and Susan Lax his wife both of 14 Plevna Place, Blossomton and the Purchasers Bernard Strong and Ivy Strong his wife both of 127 Lowfield Road, Blossomton.

WHEREAS the Vendors is the estate owner in fee simple in possession of the property hereby conveyed free from encumbrances except as hereinafter mentioned and has agreed with the Purchasers for the sale to them of the property for the sum of £20,000 (twenty thousand pounds)

THIS DEED WITNESSETH

1. That in consideration of the sum of twenty thousand pounds now paid by the Purchasers to the Vendors (the receipt of which the Vendors hereby acknowledges) the Vendors with full title guarantee hereby conveys to the Purchasers ALL THAT land and property known as 14 Plevna Place, Blossomton as shown and outlined in red on the plan attached to a conveyance between Henry Feather and the Vendors and dated the first of April 1971 and subject to the covenants therein contained TO HOLD the same unto the Purchasers in fee simple as joint tenants in law and equity/tenants in common (decide)

2. With the object of giving the Vendors a full and sufficient indemnity but not further the Purchasers hereby covenant with the Vendors to observe, fulfil and perform the above-mentioned covenants and indemnify the Vendors against all actions and claims in respect thereof

3. IT IS HEREBY CERTIFIED that the transaction hereby effected does not form part of a larger transaction or series of transactions in respect of which the amount or value or aggregate amount or value of the consideration exceeds £60,000

IN WITNESS OF WHEREOF the parties have hereunto set their hands and seals the day and year first above written

SIGNED AND DELIVERED as a deed by (Vendors)
in the presence of   (witness)

SIGNED AND DELIVERED as a deed by (Purchasers)
in the presence of   (witness)

Also send along any Land Charges Department name searches you find with the deeds and look at the conveyance to you to see if there is any reference to covenants in an earlier document. If there is, find your copy of that deed and make sure your buyer gets a copy, even if it dates from before the conveyance you select as your 'root of title'. You may have the original deed, or you may find you have a copy as part of an 'abstract of title'. This is a typewritten summary of the material contents of the deeds that made up the title at the time the abstract was typed.

The conveyance or transfer to the buyer is, by custom, typed up by the buyer and it's normally dealt with after exchange of contracts. The buyer can type up another conveyance with the new names and sale price (see the specimen opposite) or he can use a Land Registry Form TR1, provided the property is adequately described. Look, for example, at the description in the specimen conveyance.

This is the main difference between buying and selling registered land and buying and selling unregistered land. The title searches are a little different but see below. As for Stamp Duty Land Tax and registration everything said in the previous chapter applies. On the sale of an unregistered house it must be registered, but in this case the Land Registry application form is called FR1 not AP1 and it must be accompanied by a list of the documents you are submitting called Land Registry Form DL.

Looking more closely at the deeds

Conveyances and transfers are deeds and a deed is an instrument in writing, signed, sealed and delivered; such an instrument of transfer of property, from one person to another, is called a conveyance. If you were the cautious buyer of a second-hand lawnmower, and asked the seller to prove it was his to sell, he would produce the receipt. It's the same with an unregistered house. The first part of any conveyance shows this clearly as you can see from our specimen conveyance opposite.

Like the lawnmower buyer, the purchaser of a house needs to be convinced that what the vendor is offering is his to sell. This is usually done by producing a copy of the conveyance which the vendor obtained when he bought. It will be something like our specimen. A copy of the conveyance referred to will come with the draft contract. If the date on the conveyance, showing the present vendor as the purchaser, is more than 15 years old, he has proved title, because when X Lax moved, his solicitor proved to Strong's solicitor that everything was in order.

It seems to be assumed that if, within 15 years of a person taking possession of a property, no one comes along kicking up a fuss about the ownership, then everything must be in order. But what if the house has changed hands 11 times during the past 15 years? Simple enough, if every transaction was a straightforward sale and purchase; you need to see 11 conveyances, linked in the progression A to B; B to C; C to D; ... K to Lax. When you are purchasing an unregistered property that has changed hands a number of times in the past 15 years, apart from wondering why it was so unloved, comfort yourself with this thought about the title: all the purchasers in the chain are likely to have employed highly trained solicitors either to check the title or to supervise their clerks' checking of it. No doubt lenders' solicitors will have satisfied themselves about it too. If you are taking a mortgage, the lender's solicitor will be giving things the once-over at your expense (plus VAT) and you might feel justified in relying on him. If you have any queries, please ask him. Ask nicely; you can only be refused.

It's interesting to play detective with a pile of conveyances, but the important ones are the last one and the one before that which is more than 15 years old. Add a clause to the draft contract saying that copies will be provided which cover the previous 15 years, and ask for them to be forwarded as soon as possible.

I have never met anyone who paid for a house and was subsequently in trouble because one of William the Conqueror's hangers-on hadn't the right to sell. It's the last conveyance that counts and you've met the vendor. You need to check that the person named in the last link of the chain as the purchaser is the same as the one named in your contract; that the address of the house you are buying corresponds; that the plan is the same as the one sent with the draft contract, and that after the words TO HOLD it says 'in fee simple' because these two words define the property as freehold, as opposed to leasehold; if it were leasehold, it would refer to the lease in the section beginning ALL THAT. If, for example, the vendor is a personal representative of someone who has died, the person named in the contract will not be the person named in the last conveyance. If this situation applies to you, ask to see the grant of probate or letters of administration. The vendor cannot make good title without this.

If your vendor hasn't owned the property for 15 years or more, you will have to apply all the above checks to the conveyances which take you back over the period required.

As we have said, a conveyance forms what is known as 'good root of title'. It's the most usual because it indicates that an investigation of the title was carried out at the time of its making, and in 99 cases out of a 100 proof of ownership of the average house will be by production of a conveyance, or a series of linked conveyances.

Sometimes, another document is required to forge a link. Obviously, a deceased person cannot pass on ownership by making a conveyance. In such a case a devise (see Glossary) is a good root and the document which forms the link between the deceased owner and the next is a copy of the grant of probate, or letters of administration, issued by the High Court out of either the Principal Probate Registry or a District Probate Registry, which shows who was appointed to administer the deceased's estate. This is often followed by an assent by the personal representatives into the name of a beneficiary. If the personal representatives sell in the course of the administration, they will be named as vendors, but it's still necessary to check that they had a grant of probate (executors) or letters of administration (administrators).

When the personal representatives ('executors' if there is a Will, 'administrators' if not) have finished administering the deceased's estate (i.e. paying the debts and the legacies), they will wish to transfer the property to a beneficiary. They do this by means of a document called an Assent. It's necessary to appreciate that since 1 April 2000, the beneficiary must register his title and so if you are offered a title with an Assent granted after this date, insist the property be registered before you contract to buy it.

A purchaser need not worry overmuch lest a solicitor fails to tie up all these documents, because in sending you the Law Society's Standard Conditions of Sale contract, he has bound himself to do so. A vendor will expect to find all title documents in his deeds parcel, for the same reason.

If the above last four paragraphs apply to your case (and they normally do), please read them again. After all, you didn't fully grasp that two plus two equalled four the first time you heard about it. At the moment, you are dealing with a hypothetical case. Once you have a set of forms and documents on the table before you, it will be that much easier to shuffle them about with the aid of these paragraphs.

In case of difficulty, and if the vendor's solicitor hasn't already sent one, ask for an 'epitome of title', which is a list of the deeds that take you back to the root of title or the deed which created the covenants, or both.

In the rest of this chapter, the information will be divided between that for a purchaser and that for a vendor. But don't eschew the other side's information; it's good to know what the other chap is up to, and in any case, you may well be changing roles in a few years' time.

Vendor: Your first step is to get hold of the deeds. If your house is paid for and you haven't already got the deeds at home, go to wherever they are and get them. If the property is still mortgaged, write to the head office of your lender and ask if it will send the title deeds to its branch office nearest your home, as you are selling the property, acting for yourself, and will need to make copies of the relevant documents. Bear in mind that the title deeds are yours. They are only deposited with the lender as security for the money it has lent you.

The bundle, though referred to as 'the deeds', is made up of all sorts of papers that are and are not deeds. There will be copies of old Land Charges Department search certificates, receipted mortgages and, of course, conveyances, and it's the last with which you concern yourself at this stage. They are typed on stout paper, folded and marked on the outside front:

DATED 8 June 1920

Mr V. A. CATER

to

Mr N. SCONCE

Conveyance

of all that messuage or dwelling house known as
and situated at

14 Plevna Place, in the County of Eden

Skinner, Standing & Still Solicitors
Blossomton

When you look at your deeds, bear in mind the three things your purchaser needs to know about the property at this point:

1. that you own it;

2. what, if anything, goes with it – rights of way, etc.; and

3. what can and cannot be done with it.

If you bought 15 years or more ago, your luck is in. Photocopy the conveyance to yourself, make a copy of the plan if there is one, and copy out the covenants and conditions if they are not 'recited' in your conveyance. But if, during the past 15 years, the house has changed hands a few times, you will need to copy each of the conveyances covering the period that takes you back to the root of title, as given at paragraph 4.2.2 of your agreement.

But what if the house is built on a plot of land sold off from a larger area of land? In that case, you can only expect to find a written summary of previous deeds on which the builder's solicitor (clerk) will have endorsed something like 'examined against originals at the offices of Messrs Skinner & Stonehart solicitors of that parish'. Copy it.

You will also have to photocopy more than the conveyance to yourself (even if you've been the owner for more than 15 years), if the mention of restrictive covenants in your conveyance confines itself to saying that the benefits, easements and covenants are those 'contained, mentioned or referred to in a conveyance dated … between So and So and Thingummy'. You root out the conveyance to Thingummy and hopefully the list is set out there of what you HOLD/SUBJECT NEVERTHELESS to. This is the set of capital letters which usually heralds the covenants, restrictions, etc. in a conveyance. Photocopy the whole conveyance. Sometimes it will be easy: a straightforward conveyance to you without a covenant in sight. Sometimes you have to beaver away at the pile.

Hopefully, you will get all that is required at the first go. Even if you only think you have, *that is what matters at this stage,* because you send the lot on to your purchaser's solicitor. And if what you have sent is accepted, you move to the next step. On the other hand, if you have made some mistakes or omissions, Skinner will let you know that you've missed a link in the chain, so off you go to the originals again, this time knowing precisely what you are looking for.

If you are not sure of your purchaser and think the sale might go off, either take two copies of everything (because a solicitor might be on holiday when you request a return) or take one copy and, at this stage: 1. rely on paragraph 4.2.2 of your contract or 2. if there is an epitome of title, copy that and add on short notes regarding transactions since the last one mentioned on it. In your covering letter to Skinner itemise what you are sending, as a reminder for yourself and to avoid disputes later. As a general rule, always keep a copy of the things that you have sent to the other party. This will save time later, as well as avoid disputes.

But for the present, concern yourself with preparing your draft contract. From the conveyance to you, get the date to answer the question beginning 'root of title/title no.'. If the conveyance to you is less than 15 years old, you have to rummage around to find one that is more, and put the parties and date of that in. Completion date is usually left blank at this stage, but there is nothing to stop you putting a date in if you wish – the purchaser can always ask for an amendment. If you are using the Standard Conditions of Sale, fourth edition, and you wish to include anything in the purchase price that you think needs specifying, there is provision for the cost of chattels and a list of itemised chattels on a separate pre-printed form.

Send two unsigned contracts to Skinner, send along the Fixtures, Fittings and Contents Form and ask Skinner if he will accept a completed Property Information Form or whether he prefers to send you his own preliminary enquiries (see page 112) and send along your epitome of title. This is a form that lists the documents of title. Copies must also be sent along. The list is in columns and contains certain information: date, document name, type, whether you are sending a copy or the original, whether a copy or an original will be handed over on completion, etc. It's not just a list; it's an explanation. Years ago, before the days of photocopies, the practice was for the vendor's solicitors to type out a résumé or abstract of the more important clauses in all the required documents. These are called 'abstracts of title'. No solicitor is going to do this now, but if the property has not changed hands for years or if a very old document is referred to and has to be produced to the purchaser's solicitors, you might be shown an abstract for the relevant title or copy.

If your house is mortgaged, you will have to obtain copy documents from your lender or its solicitors. Ask for a copy of all deeds, all searches, all planning permissions and any other consents.

When you have Skinner's answers on enquiries versus the Property Information Form, act accordingly. As for your answers on either, he will no doubt be fully satisfied with your information, but if he isn't, he will write for more information. In that case, reply as best you can.

Don't part with any original deeds at this stage.

Purchaser: You have viewed the house a couple of times and if you need a mortgage, you have got at least half a promise of one. You have bargained the price down with Feather, told him you are acting for yourself and given him your name and address. Receive the draft contract from your vendor's solicitor, who may well not be as helpful as the vendor (above) and you may only receive the draft contract with a copy. Don't worry, he will give evidence of title later on. If you don't like the look of anything in the contract, give the vendor's solicitor a ring and agree the alterations you require and write them into the draft. The kind of things you are looking for are basically the same as for the purchaser of registered property.

The covenants are included in a conveyance, not necessarily the one to your vendor. His may only give the date and the parties to the conveyance in which the covenants were set out in full. Skinner must either set them out in full in the contract, or supply you with a copy of them and refer to the conveyance from which they came, and if he doesn't, insist, because if you are a surgeon and there is a restrictive covenant against surging in or around the premises, you will not wish to waste further time and money on surveys and such like.

Land Registry: Send off Search Form SIM. Give the address and either cut a piece out of a local street map or sketch a little plan of the surrounding streets (it needn't be to scale) to help with identification, if you think the postal address might not be sufficient. When you get the form back it will reveal if there is a caution against first registration, and whether the land is registered or not (don't take the vendor's word on this – he might not know what he is talking about). If it's registered, you will be given the title number, and your task is much simpler from now on – you take your instructions from the previous chapter, after you first find out why your vendor didn't know this! If in reply to Form SIM they give you anything you don't understand, ring the enquiries department.

Land Charges Form K15 Application for an Official Search: search against the names of all owners to find the root of title. If you cannot extract this information from the copy deeds you have been sent, ask your vendor for a list. He may not have it but ask just in case. When searching for land charges you can only search against names, not against the address of the property, so the list of names is important. If you know the names of the owners of the property before the root of title, search against their names too. If a restrictive covenant is registered against a previous owner, you will be bound by the covenant even if that person owned and sold the property more than 15 years ago. The 'priority period' of an official search is 15 working days from the date of the certificate and is given in the certificate. You will not be bound by any entry made in the Charges Register during the priority period, provided that the purchase completes during the priority period. Practically speaking, you will need to have found out about any land charges before you exchange contracts, so you are likely to have to carry out two K15 searches, one before exchange and one afterwards in readiness for completion.

Your lender will need to know if you have been bankrupt. So together with your Search Form K15 you can send an application for an Official Search (Bankruptcy Only) K16, provided that completion is not more than a fortnight ahead – lenders need up-to-date information. Put in the name/s of the intending borrower/s, enclose a cheque to the tune of £2 for each of the names to be searched on the K15 and K16 forms, and send them off to the address at Plymouth given on the back of the forms.

It's not strictly necessary to search between the dates they acquired the property and sold it (or died) since you can always search from 1926 to the year of your search. It's a good idea to include the name of the vendor at this time on your Form K15, just in case a nasty turns up, but remember you do need a clear certificate that covers the vendor's name on the date you are actually completing the purchase. The priority period, i.e. when the search expires, will appear on the reply.

For instance, your vendors may not be as lovey-dovey as they appeared when they showed you round 'Shangri-La', and if the house was bought in one name, the partner might have registered a Class F charge to protect matrimonial interests. You need to know about any Class F charge as soon as possible, and certainly before you get too involved. If they have come to some arrangement about sharing the proceeds of the sale, so well and good. However, as soon as you receive your protection period certificate from Plymouth get the cautioner to sign an application to cancel the charge. See chapter 14, 'Matrimonial homes'. A lender's solicitor will expect you to produce the certificate on completion.

Couples do some barmy things when love turns, at best to indifference, at worst to hate. They often do all they can to make things difficult for the other side. If you had been buying a registered title, the Office Copies would have wised you up on this problem. It's so that you don't get caught in the crossfire that I say: K15 to Land Charges Department as soon as possible and certainly before you sign the contract.

Other things that may turn up following your search are records of various third party rights against the property – these can be anything from second mortgages, to options to purchase, to restrictive covenants. If they are registered, they are binding against you as a purchaser. This applies to interests registered both before and after the root of title. The fact that you didn't know about it will cut no ice. If it's registered, you will be bound.

It's all very well having a contract that is enforceable, but who wants the bother and expense of enforcement? And what if you came up against someone who thought that he and his case was something special, and it would be unjust for the law to be applied to him? Such a situation has all the makings of a Supreme Court case. *Having rights and asserting them are two vastly different things.* In a word you should take a practical approach and make sure there are not nasty surprises waiting around the corner just after you've signed the contract. Possession really is nine points of the law! And another thing – always change the locks when you move in, particularly if the house has been standing vacant for any length of time.

'Enquiries of Local Authority Form CON 29R' if you think necessary together with 'Search of Local Land Charges LLC1'; councils require you to provide two copies of each.

Take them to the council as recommended earlier. CON 29R is the form you should fill out in every case, only fill out CON 29O if you think it may apply to you. The kind of questions in CON 29O are such as relate to public footpaths, existing and contemplated, building preservation orders and so on, also questions about registration of houses in multiple occupation. If you tick any of them, look up the fee given on the form and add it to the standard fee.

The LLC1 form is printed in duplicate, one copy for the council to retain, and one to be returned to you with the answers. Use a carbon to complete. The local Land Charges Register is divided into 12 parts, and the first question which faces you on the form is which parts you require searching. Strike out 'Part(s) … of' and you will get the lot. It's much simpler, and costs very little more than picking and choosing. Like a lot of things the prices keep moving up, but mercifully the charges are, in this instance, printed on the back of the form. The reference in the fees section of the form to 'each parcel' means plots, so it doesn't concern the buyer of a single house.

'Seller's Property Information Form': two copies will normally be volunteered by the vendor's solicitor. If your vendor is a company (has 'Ltd' or 'PLC' after the name) you need to be extremely careful that the company is not in the process of being wound up. If you are buying such a house that is not registered, you should make a company search at Companies House, Crown Way, Cardiff CF4 3UZ, tel. 029 2038 0950, www.companieshouse.gov.uk/info/ (check fee), either by calling there, or, if it's too far away, by asking your CAB to give you the address of a land agent or credit reference agency who might help. The trouble here (and a solicitor is just as subject to it as you are) is that it takes time for a note of a winding-up petition to be put on a company's file. Nevertheless, any sale made after winding-up proceedings have commenced is only a purported sale and is null and void unless validated. If this looks like it might be the case, you need to get advice.

As the case where you are likely to come across a company as a vendor is with a newly built house, and it will be on an estate where the Registrar has already agreed to register the property, the chance of your having to cope with this problem is extremely remote. It could occur in the case of a shop and house, because many small shopkeepers have been persuaded to trade as limited liability companies in the last few decades. In such cases, caution is the order of the day.

Vendor: Cope with any amendments to the contract, but don't be bullied into giving undertakings, or adding anything to the contract you don't fully understand. Keep asking for explanations and never be fobbed off with 'It doesn't really mean what it says.' or 'It's usual, but doesn't apply in this case.' If it doesn't mean what it says or doesn't apply, it may as well be struck out. On the other hand, if you are asked to take something out and you are told, 'Oh! you don't need that.', you can riposte, 'Well, if you know it's doing no harm, you won't object to it remaining.'

Purchaser: Receive the Seller's Property Information Form from Skinner and glean from his answers what you can. Remember that the vendor might not want to buy these forms and send you the answers, in which case it's for you to buy some forms called Enquiries before Contract (or similar) (see page 112). It doesn't really matter what they are called, since they generally cover about the same issues. If you are not satisfied, or suspect that he knows more than he is telling you, send him a few supplementaries in the form of a letter, but remember he was answering stock questions first time round, so it should occasion little surprise that all you got in return were stock answers. There is a time limit on post-contract requisitions – Condition 4.1.1 of the Standard Conditions – so it's vital to get the title approved before contacts are exchanged, by the solicitor acting for your lender. On the other hand, no one will thank the vendor's solicitor if he refuses to answer sensible questions that might lead to a satisfactory completion. Also, check, in particular, whether there are any disputes.

Using the Seller's Property Information Form as a guide, carry out your inspection of the property and its environs, paying particular attention to the area of land within the fences, any facilities such as drives that are shared, and the neighbours' attitudes towards them.

If, on inspection, it turns out that the road leading to the house is badly potholed, it could be an indication that it's not maintained by the council which has not adopted it, so pay attention to Enquiries of Local Council. If it's a private road, after the description of the property in the contract it should say 'together with a right of way over the road coloured sky blue pink on the said plan'. On the other hand, it might say the words 'and the road has been taken over'. Not to worry: of such redundancies are roots of title made up.

CON 29R and CON 29O and LLC1 will come back from the council with its printed answers. Check them through. If replies on either form cause any head-scratching, ask the person who wrote the replies what he means. Council officials will always explain meanings; what they are not empowered to do is advise what should be done about them. But you never know. A remark such as 'My goodness, I wonder what other people do in such a circumstance...' might just elicit a useful hint of how to deal with a problem that is not simply of a technical nature.

Remember also to carry out your water and drainage searches and check out environmental issues. Consider also whether you need to carry out a commons search. See chapter 12 for details of what needs to be done and why.

By now, the Land Registry should also have returned your search of Index Map Form SIM, showing the house to be unregistered, but if there is any kind of entry, it's your vendor's problem. Let him know, or to be more accurate, remind him, because he will almost certainly already be aware of the entry.

The reply to your K15 will come to you in the form of a Certificate of Result of Search. Whereas the Land Registry keeps a Register of land and the name(s) of the owner(s) of each registered parcel of land, the Land Charges Department keeps a Register of interests, which third persons can have in an unregistered house, and which can be registered against the names of **people**. So if your vendor is called Tom Jones, the computer will throw up all the Tom Joneses known to it and you will have to decide which entries belong to your vendor. Luckily, it also gives the addresses where the ubiquitous Joneses lived when the various charges were registered against them. If none of the entries applies to your vendor, he or his solicitor must write on the Certificate of Result of Search words to the effect that it's certified that none of the entries applies to him.

You should, however, search against the name not only of your vendor but also of everyone who has ever owned the land, whose name you know, not just down to the root of title. This is because you will be bound by any Land Charge that is registered, and if you didn't search against a particular name you may live to regret it.

Obviously, a bankruptcy charge would alert you to the fact that all is not well. More likely than not your reply will show 'no entries'. If there is one, it's likely to be one of the following: C (i) is a second (puisne) mortgage. D (ii) is a splatter of covenants which no doubt you already know of. F is a matrimonial home entry. One of the spouses, not being a joint owner, is protecting rights.

What do you do with any of these in the event of one or all showing up? In the case of C (i) second mortgage, as the reply you get will say no more than that the entry exists, you write, quoting the date and reference number, to the Land Charges Registry, asking for a copy of the details. You will have to take appropriate steps to ensure it will be paid off on completion. Get an undertaking from the vendor's solicitor, or if the vendor is acting for himself, you may be at your lender's solicitors' office at completion. Get the vendor to authorise him to pay off the second charge. He will take up sufficient funds on completion to pay off both debts. Matrimonial Homes Class F we have already dealt with.

You will no doubt already know the contents of a D (ii) entry. The vendor or his solicitor should have put a copy with the draft contract. If he hasn't, ask him to bring the job to the top of the pile of 'things to be done today'.

By now, you have sufficient knowledge to give you confidence to go forward, or back out of the deal.

So let us have a little recap of what a purchaser of an unregistered freehold house in England or Wales will have done up to this point.

He will have:

1. received the draft contract in duplicate with map;

2. called at the local council and deposited LLC1 for information about the council's interests in the property;

3. sent or taken Form CON 29R and CON 29O (if applicable) to the council asking questions about roads, drains and restrictions on use;

4. sent Form SIM to the Land Registry to find out if registered, and if not, any cautions against first registration;

5. received Seller's Property Information Form from vendor's solicitor, with what he knows about any boundary disputes, rights of way, planning consents and such like, or sent his own questions, the Enquiries before Contract, to the vendor's solicitor;

6. carried out a Land Charge search using Form K15 against the name of the vendor and all known owners since 1926;

7. dealt with drainage and environmental issues.

It looks a pretty big list of forms, but you should be able to cope, particularly as nowadays solicitors seem to think nothing of taking two calendar months to get to the stage you are now at – I've seen houses built quicker. If you can deal with this increasingly bureaucratic world, and are in a position mentally and financially to buy a house, the forms should not cause you any difficulty, which with the application of a little logic and common sense, you can't solve for yourself.

Having received satisfactory replies, or your vendor being able to satisfy you on any points raised, you are now ready to exchange contracts, provided you have received a satisfactory mortgage offer from your lender.

Our vendor, doing his own conveyance, has been told to send off copies of the previous conveyances with his draft contract. This seems a sensible way to do things as the buyer's solicitors can then check through all of the documents of title, saving the seller from having to work this out.

Note that in the contract, the covenants will be either set out in full or reference made to their first appearance in the deeds and you should expect a copy of them (written out in full) before you sign the contract. And remember that if the covenants predate your vendor's ownership, there is nothing you can do about them.

However, by now, all things having gone well, you can agree a completion date with the vendor. Enter it into the final copy (engrossed) contract, sign but don't date it, and send to the vendor's solicitor, together with the smallest deposit you have been able to get away with. Also it is sensible to keep a copy for yourself.

For the purchaser, this is also the time to decide if the house needs to be insured before contracts are exchanged or whether insurance can be left to between contract and completion. That is after you have exchanged but before you complete. See further at page 79.

Vendor: Receive the contract signed by the purchaser, and check that the deposit is with a stakeholder or in a joint bank account. Enter the completion date on your copy, sign it, enter the date of your signing and send it off to the purchaser. You have got his part of the contract and he has got yours. Contracts are now said to be 'exchanged'.

If you have not already sent copies of the deeds and documents which prove your title, let Skinner have them now.

If you bought less than 15 years ago, the only link in the title chain before the conveyance to you might be an abstract, and a solicitor will have endorsed it 'Examined against the originals at the office'. This type of endorsed abstract is intended to be used as if it were a set of deeds when you come to sell, and any solicitor would accept it from a brother solicitor.

If in response Skinner sends some obscure requisitions (questions), answer fully, but be ready with the masterpieces:

Question: Who now holds the 1876 indenture?

Answer: I don't know.

Question: Was the plot conveyed in 1975 part of the one conveyed in 1920?

Answer: I suppose so, but form your own view.

If he persists in asking what this or that means, give him 'it means what it says'. Eventually, they give up what they should never have started.

Purchaser: Receive vendor's signed and dated part of the contract. Contracts are now said to be 'exchanged' and the property is at the buyer's risk if the standard conditions of contract have been altered. The standard conditions are frequently deleted or amended so do check that the contract is in the same terms as the one you signed, and if you have not already done so, immediately arrange for the property to be fully insured with the same company as your lender will eventually use.

If you didn't receive copies of the deeds (conveyances, etc.), you should expect them now. Check the conveyances, watching for the points at page 164.

An abstract should show, in summary, an unbroken chain of ownership leading to your vendor. It might compress onto three or four pages the meat of a dozen conveyances, mortgage deeds, deeds of gift, probates and Wills. In an abstract, the full names and addresses of parties are not repeated over and over again. When an identical description of a property appeared in a subsequent deed it's referred to as 'all the before abstracted premises'. Exceptions and reservations (e.g. where a vendor had two properties and reserved a right of way over land sold) are similarly treated, and Wills are not set out in full, but only the date of the Will and names of the executors are put in.

Abstracts of title are written in lawyer's speed hand, which consists of abbreviations which are based on omitting vowels. However, Absd doesn't mean absurd but abstracted. Here are a few more abominations to be going on with:

thereabouts:thrbts, vendor:vndr, property:ppty, hereditaments:hrdmts, indenture:indr, solicitors:slrs, mortgage:mtge.

You soon get a grsp of it, but be crfl not to let it creep into your gnrl vcblry or it might be thought you need new dntrs.

Requisitions on Title form should now be dispatched.

Vendor: Receive the Purchaser's Requisitions on Title. You only have to prove title going back to the conveyance you agreed to deduce title from, your 'root of title'. Remember that when you and previous owners bought, highly trained solicitors checked out the title so there can't be much if anything wrong with it. That is the theory! However, do your best and give the answers required in relation to providing a completion statement. This is an account showing the precise amount you will require to be paid when you hand the keys over and sign the conveyance. It's sufficient to let your local authority know the date when you are moving out and it will split the Council Tax and anything you have paid in advance will come back to you. Water companies are not always so obliging, so check with them and, if necessary, show in your completion statement how much you need in order to reimburse you for the water rate paid in advance. So make up the bill and send it off with your replies. The approach to the requisitions is the same as in the case of registered land (see page 146 above).

Purchaser: In reply to your Requisitions on Title, you receive a list of the documents that will be handed over to you (or your lender) on completion and you are informed who will give a statutory acknowledgement and undertaking for the production and safe custody of any document of title not handed over. The form also asks for receipts for last payments of outgoings. If the previous owner does a moonlight flit leaving the Council Tax unpaid, there is no need to worry because Council Taxes are a personal debt on the occupier, so if they are outstanding for a period before you became the occupier, that debt doesn't belong to you – the council must look to your predecessor for payment. There is a space for further questions.

If you have raised some questions on the title and feel you haven't altogether got satisfactory answers, bear in mind two things. First, if the conveyance to your vendor looks all right and the person described in there as the purchaser is now your vendor, then it should be all right because a wizard of the law checked out that his predecessors were all that they had cracked themselves up to be. Second, if you are taking a mortgage, the lender's solicitor will make sure that you are getting good title, and will keep on asking questions which you pass on to Skinner until the lender is satisfied. After all, if you default in your payments and it has to sell the house to settle your account, it will only have as good a title (proof of ownership) as you got at this point.

You now prepare a draft of the 'instrument of transfer' you intend to use. As your purchase is subject to compulsory registration use TR1 (TR2 for repossession). If you are buying in joint names and you wish survivor to take all, put 'x' in the first box at 10. In layperson's language, the clause now reads: 'If between now and the next time the house is sold, one of us dies, the remaining partner/spouse is entitled to the whole of the sale price, on the strength of the survivor's signature alone.' The printed form gives three options: the first two involving you having equal shares and the final one allowing you to choose the shares in which you hold the property. It's important that you think about and understand the difference between joint tenants and tenants in common. Refer to chapter 12 for more information. If you want complicated provisions, it may be worth consulting a solicitor to draw up a trust deed for you to govern how the shares in the property should be held. For consideration put 'x' in the first box and the agreed price. The space for title number you leave blank, because one has not yet been allocated by the Registry.

If you are buying a new house on a development, the builder's solicitor should provide the 'instrument' Form TP1, because only part of the vendor's land is being transferred.

Vendor: Receive and check the draft. Look for any deductions or additions that have been made to the one you got when you bought. If there are any with which you disagree, amend in red ink and bounce it back. Heed previous warnings about 'Oh, it's usual.' and 'It doesn't mean what it says.' Make sure that indemnity covenants have been correctly entered. If needed, see page 115. When you are satisfied send it back marked 'approved'. But don't sign it. You do that when you get the money.

Purchaser: When your draft instrument of transfer comes back, look for the red ink. It's extremely rare to find any, but if you do and you understand and accept, so well and good. If you don't accept, argue about it. If you don't understand, ask for an explanation, as you are perfectly entitled to one. When you are satisfied send it to Skinner so that he can have the vendor sign it ready for completion day. (You only need to sign it and have your signature witnessed if you are giving a covenant.)

From now on, your job is basically the same as that handed out to the purchaser of a registered house. What differences there are only arise if you are taking a mortgage, and in relation to what your lender's solicitor will want you to produce just before or on completion.

The lender's solicitor will, no doubt, have written to you asking for the following (even if he hasn't written, get them off to him as soon as you can and ask him if there is anything further required because of the time limit there might be for asking questions on title):

- local authority search forms and replies;

- the results of your enquiries concerning water drainage and environmental issues;

- the Seller's Property Information Forms or your own Enquiries before Contract;

- the contract;

- copy title deeds and the replies to your Requisitions on Title received from vendor's solicitor;

- Transfer Form TR1 to yourself (one of your copies);

- replies to your Land Charges searches in Form K15 plus copies of any specific entries you ordered from the Land Charges Registry;

- reply to your bankruptcy search (against you) in Form K16;

- letter from the water company regarding sewers and water mains;

- any indemnity policies, old or new. That is, policies copied to you by the vendor and any policy you have taken out;

- any indemnity insurance obtained by you, etc.;

- he may ask for a copy of the SDLT1 (Land Transaction Return), but this cannot be completed until the date of substantial performance is known and must be signed by you;

- Form FR1 – application to the Land Registry for first registration of a property (below).

As most lenders don't return these documents, it's useful to keep copies for your use in future transactions.

The lender's solicitor will respond by sending you the mortgage deed, an account of fees and Stamp Duties, a sheet of Requisitions on Title and a list of the documents required to be handed over on completion. Deal with them as the purchaser of a registered property was instructed on pages 148-50.

SDLT 1 is the Land Transaction Return, which you have to submit to the Revenue when you pay the Stamp Duty Land Tax. It requires filling in by means of codes – these are found in the Guidance Notes, which are in Form SDLT6 available from the Stamp Office or online at www.hmrc.gov.uk/so.

Vendor: Receive the supplementary Requisitions on Title, and root about in the conveyances for answers, not forgetting the time honoured 'I cannot say', 'I presume so', and other such masterpieces. If you have paid for the house, all you are waiting for now is the money and you will have notified your purchaser of a suitable place for him to pay it over. If you still have a mortgage, completion will take place at your lender's solicitors' office whither the actual deeds will have been sent. On your Form of Requisition you told him to whom you wanted the CHAPS payment sending to. If you need the completion money splitting between yourself, mortgage redemption money, or even between you, the redemption money and the vendor of the house you are now buying, say so.

You will also be asked when possession of the property will be given. You answer, 'When I receive the balance of the money by CHAPS payment transfer on completion.' A solicitor acting for a purchaser would be negligent if he sent his client's money off by CHAPS to a private individual without having the title deeds; expect completion at Skinner's office. Alternatively, you can send the deeds to the purchaser's solicitor and extract from him an undertaking that he will hold them to your order. If you are also buying a house, you may wish to add a suggested completion date to tie in with your purchase.

Purchaser: Pass on the vendor's replies to your lender.

You are now geared up for completion. The problems and pitfalls and the completion procedures are essentially the same as those applicable to buying and selling registered land and reference should be made to chapter 12.

Form FR1: First Registration Application. This form is fairly self-explanatory. You must disclose any 'disclosable overriding interests'. These are listed in Schedule 1 of the Land Registration Act 2002, and paragraphs 7–13 of Schedule 12 found at www.uk-legislation.hmso.gov.uk/acts.htm. They include things like legal rights of way and legal leases. You should also send along any Land Charges searches together with your FR1.

A registration fee is normally payable for registering a Legal Charge (mortgage), but when it's done at the same time as a first registration or a transfer for monetary consideration, an abatement of fees applies, i.e. there is no fee to pay for registering the charge. Make sure that no one charges you both for registering your purchase (dealing for value) and for registering a legal charge.

A cash buyer will no longer receive a Land Certificate. However, he may obtain a title information document from the Land Registry. Make sure you put a note of the title number in one or two safe places and put the document under the piano lid ready for the next time.

When you come to register, you will need to prove your identity and fill out Form ID1, having your identity certified either by a licensed conveyancer or solicitor or by a Land Registry employee at a Land Registry Customer Information Centre. A separate ID1 must be filled out for each party who is not legally represented. So if you are buying jointly, you will both need to fill out ID1. The purpose of this is to prevent fraud. If you are legally represented, the solicitor is required to carry out money laundering checks to check your identity. Obviously, you won't have done this if you are acting for yourself. The form requires you to prove your identity either by going to a solicitor and taking along the ID specified on the form together with a passport photograph and Form ID1 (the solicitor may charge a fee for verifying your identity) or alternatively you can go along to a Land Registry Customer Information Centre with your ID and a passport-size photograph so that the Land Registry staff can verify your identity. If you do this, take your application with you and ring for an appointment first and check that the Land Registry will accept the ID that you want to bring. Do note, however, that if more than one person needs their identity to be verified at a Customer Information Centre they all need to attend at the same time. Further practical information on this can be found in Land Registry Public Guide 20, available at www.landregistry.gov.uk. If your vendor is not represented either, he too will need to prove his ID and fill out a Form ID1 to be submitted with the application. If all parties want their identity verified at a Land Registry Customer Information Centre, they must all attend at the same time.

I do hope you will have noticed that throughout this book the few dire warnings given have been about parting with your money for nothing, or making untested assumptions about what other people who are involved in your house buying and selling will do, won't do, will charge and won't charge.

So maybe a final caution will be acceptable. Your goal is to get the job done – your means are the best and easiest you can find. Your goal is not to do as 'good a job' as solicitors do by aping their style and means. No matter how expert you try to make yourself look, no solicitor I have ever met will recommend you for an honorary law degree. Neither should any layperson conveyancer go lording it over those poor souls who do employ solicitors.

They are, no doubt, already smarting from being smacked in the face by the solicitors' final account.

There are those who are capable but haven't, as yet, tried, and you will get more respect if you tell them what, at the end of the transaction, you honestly feel about it as I did years ago, saying, 'I don't know what all the fuss was about, it will be a cakewalk next time!'

CHAPTER 14
Matrimonial homes

Hitherto, care has been taken not to offend half the population by giving the impression that only the male sex is capable of understanding and coping with a property deal. Hence the use of the all-purpose 'person', or 'spouse', and sometimes leaving the reader to decide whether Skinner is Mr, Mrs, Miss or Ms. But in this chapter taking the risk of giving unintended offence, such general terms will be abandoned. It will be assumed that we are dealing with property where the ownership is vested solely in the husband's name, and a claim to have the house treated as the matrimonial home is being made by the wife. This is done for two reasons: first, because clarity demands it, and second, because it corresponds to the situation in the real world. However, any husband who needs to protect his interests in a house that was 'put in the wife's name' will not find it too difficult to transpose the term 'husband' for 'wife', and vice versa as necessary.

A wife might not be certain whether the house was in fact purchased jointly by her and her husband. If there is a mortgage, it's easy – ask the building society. In other cases, ask the solicitor who acted. If you suspect that the solicitor might be afraid of breaching confidence (or is biased in favour of your husband), make the enquiry in writing, because if it's in joint names then as you paid half the solicitors' costs, you have a right to any information in his file. For him to refuse you the information is naughty and he knows it. A wife who knows or learns that the house was bought in joint names is fully protected. In theory, the house cannot be sold or mortgaged without her consent, nor can she be evicted without a court order – such a wife need read no further except out of curiosity and academic interest.

186 | House Buying, Selling and Conveyancing

Reference here to 'the Act' will be to the Family Law Act 1996. The purpose of the Act (and earlier legislation) was to protect the right of a spouse (normally a wife) to occupy the matrimonial home if owned by the other spouse. Once a wife registers her right in the appropriate Register, all intending purchasers and lenders of money on mortgage will have notice of her rights and they continue negotiations at their peril, until they have the written assurance in the correct form that the wife will agree to withdraw her charge from the Register.

But before sending off forms in all directions, the wife needs to establish whether her husband is the freeholder or holds the property on lease. 'Lease', by the way, includes tenancy. In the case of a leaseholder, if the lease was granted before 13 October 2003 it will not be registered unless the lease was for more than 21 years, or has been transferred since 13 October 2003 and had not less than seven years left to run. Any lease for a term of less than seven years cannot be registered. Even so, a wife cannot be evicted without a court order.

Another simple point, but worth making, just in case, is that before a wife can protect her interest in and right to occupy the house, her husband must have a right of occupation. Wives' rights of occupation arise on the latest of the following events:

- the date when the husband acquired the house;

- the date of the marriage; or

- 1 January 1968.

So how does one go about registering a wife's right to occupy? As you have already suspected, it's a matter of form-filling again. It's something you can do, easily and cheaply, for yourself. Where you don't know whether the house is registered or not, send off Form SIM to the Land Registry for your area with 'This search is being made solely for the purposes of the Family Law Act 1996.' written across the top, and no charge will be made.

You will get a reply within a day or two telling you whether it's registered or not; if it's registered you will be given the title number. You then send off Form MH1. There is no fee. The Registrar will inform your husband of the registration.

In the case of an unregistered house, the required form is K2, which is sent to the Land Charges Department, Plumer House, Tailyour Road, Crownhill, Plymouth, PL6 5HY, no matter where the house is situated. The fee in this case is £2 and you will be informed within a day or two that a Class F Land Charge has been registered in your name. Your husband will not know unless you tell him.

Where you suspect that dealings are imminent, and the time taken in to-ing and fro-ing outlined above might be too long for safety, I suggest you assume both that it is, and that it isn't registered. Send a Form SIM (no fee) as recommended above, and pin it to a Form MH1. In the box for the title number write 'Please supply title number for purpose of Matrimonial Homes Act 1983. URGENT'. At the same time send off a Form K2 with its current £2 fee to Plymouth. That's belt and braces for you!

Once you've got a charge on a Register (or both as in the previous paragraph), basically it stays there until death or divorce you do part, and it's known as a charge. Following the abolition of cautions against dealing, the charge is protected as an agreed notice, which will give the wife priority over a purchaser. Even if you do divorce, a judge can make what is known as a 'continuation order' of the wife's right of occupation, which can now continue even though the marriage is at an end. But note: though the judge has said so, it doesn't mean that the whole world has notice. The charge did die with the marriage, so get a copy of the judge's order from the court office quickly and attach it to a Form MH2 in the case of a registered house, or K8 if the house is unregistered. There is no charge for a Form MH2, but the K8 requires a £1 fee and goes to Plymouth. If for any reason you hadn't got a charge onto one of the Registers before the court hearing, then you must get a Form MH1 or K2 off as swiftly as possible, as explained before.

Judges don't always make continuation orders; the reverse may happen – they may order that the right of occupation is at an end. In this case, the husband should send off a copy of the order with a Form MH4 and this is sufficient if the property is registered. No fee is required to have the charge removed at the appropriate Land Registry.

In the case of unregistered land, you need to send the evidence, a covering letter, and a Form K13 together with a fee of £1 to the Land Charges Department, Plymouth, to have the Class F Charge removed from the Register.

A wife may apply to have the registration removed at any time, by sending Form MH4 to the Land Registry, or in the case of an unregistered house, Form K13 to the Land Charges Department.

Once a wife's right of occupation is registered, it does no more than ensure that the house is not sold or mortgaged except with her consent or a court order. When a wife is in occupation she can achieve the same end for some time, by simply refusing to show viewers or building society and finance company surveyors round the property. No lender will want to lend, and no purchaser will want to negotiate for a property that has such an unco-operative person living in it.

A wife can only protect her right of occupation in respect of one house; if her husband owns more than one, she will register her right for the one she prefers.

A registration of right to occupy says nothing about how the proceeds will be divided if and when the house is sold. It's essential that the parties try to find a solution between themselves on this point. Recourse to the courts should be the very last resort. Costs can be ruinous, and you might eventually have to pay them yourself, even though you were granted legal aid. A person who lodges a caution without reasonable cause is liable in damages to anyone injured as a result.

Earlier in this book, purchasers were advised to treat these entries with grave suspicion, so you will realise that the sooner cautions are removed the better. When an armistice is being arranged, consider putting in a condition that the house be put in joint names (transfer of ownership by way of gift), a little job that you can easily do for yourself.

For a more detailed account, readers with access to the internet should access the Land Registry's homepage, www.landregistry.gov.uk, where two explanatory leaflets can be found – Explanatory Leaflet 4 for members of the public and Practice Leaflet 10 for legal practitioners. All the Land Registry forms mentioned in this article can also be printed off and completed before printing. This doesn't apply to the Land Charges Department's K forms but these can be purchased from The Stationery Office, as can the Land Registry MH forms. Readers who don't have access to a computer can obtain the two leaflets from the Citizens Advice Bureau.

CHAPTER 15

Flats

Thus far, this book has concentrated on the sale of houses, which principally have freehold titles. However, a significant number of people, particularly first- or last-time buyers, will probably find that they will be buying flats. This is increasingly the case in areas where space is at a premium and developers, keen to make the most money possible, cram in as many units on their land as they can.

If you do buy a flat, chances are it will be leasehold. The reason for this is that, as we saw in chapter 11, it's almost impossible to enforce positive covenants (i.e. ones that require spending money) against subsequent owners of freehold land. This causes problems in a block of flats where it's necessary to deal with rights/obligations to repair the exterior/common parts, rights of support and so on. The way that this is solved is by giving the flat owners long leases. This not only means that there can be mutual obligations and a consistent regime for enforcing obligations but it also means that the freeholder retains a measure of control over the development. The problem with this is that, no matter how long the lease was at the beginning, leases are wasting assets and do limit, depending on the terms of the lease, the way in which the owner can deal with the property.

The principles of registration searches, etc. are basically the same for leasehold titles as for freehold. For the detail of the conveyancing process, refer to those chapters. However, there are a number of other things that a purchaser of a flat should look out for when deciding whether or not to sign on the dotted line.

What are the terms of the lease?

The terms of leases vary considerably. The lease governs the relationship between you and the freeholder, and often with other people in the block. It's obviously of great importance. If you buy the flat, whatever is written in the lease will be binding on you. There is no real question of varying the obligations. It's therefore important to study it carefully to check you won't be prevented from holding your brass band rehearsals at the property if that's what you intend to do. It's particularly important to take note of covenants against parting with possession or subletting if you intend to use this flat as the start of your buy-to-let empire. Failure to comply with the lease could lead to the landlord being in a position to bring the lease to an end, which will mean all of your money will have been wasted. You should never purchase a flat, or any other leasehold property, without reading the lease. As always, if you don't understand something, ask!

The basic structure of all leases is similar. It will start off with the name of the parties, the length of the term and the level of ground rent. It will then proceed to detail the obligations of the tenant and then the obligations of the landlord. Usually it will provide that the landlord is to maintain the exterior of the property and the common parts and that the tenant is to pay a proportion (either a fixed percentage or a 'reasonable' proportion) of the costs of such maintenance, repair, etc. as a service charge, usually on a quarterly basis. Often it will provide that service charges are paid in advance so that the freeholder can meet expenses as they arise. Other things that you need to look out for in a lease are any rent review provisions (which mean that the rent can be increased) and the 'provisos'. This is a clause which may be called 'right of re-entry' which sets out the circumstances in which the landlord can bring the lease to an end – usually on the failure of the tenant to comply with the covenants in a lease. It is called a 'proviso' because the clause begins 'PROVIDED THAT…'.

Service charges

When purchasing a flat, you should ask the vendor about the level of service charges. This is an ongoing liability that must be budgeted for. If the sum appears very high for the services that the freeholder seems to provide, ask why. It may be that the building is inefficiently managed, which might herald problems later on. You should also ask for copies of the service charge accounts over the last few years, to give you some indication of the consistency and level of charges. Vendors should dig out the service charge accounts over the past few years and have copies ready to give to the purchaser or his solicitor in response to the inevitable question! It's important to check the terms of the lease to see when the service charge is payable. The lease may provide for a regular payment, with a top-up payment once a year. It's important to budget for this and to see how much this is likely to be over a year. As well as works which will be carried out within the current year, most leases allow the landlord to charge a sum 'on account of future expenditure' or to set up, what is called, a 'sinking fund'. The purpose of this is to ensure that the flat owners are not stung with a big bill if an item of major expenditure is undertaken, such as the replacement of the lifts or external redecoration.

There is extensive protection of long leaseholders of flats to prevent a landlord from charging an excessive service charge for shoddy or unnecessary work. The detail of the protection afforded to leaseholders in respect of service charges is beyond the scope of this book. However, it's obviously best to avoid potential problems. As stated above, you may be able to spot a badly managed block not only by the standard of maintenance, but also by the level of charges. A service charge in a residential block is only payable if it's reasonable. It's vital to ask the vendor whether or not there are any disputes with the landlord regarding the services provided or the level of service charges, as you don't want to walk into a potentially costly and stressful legal battle.

Purchaser: Ask the vendor and his landlord whether there are any proposed 'qualifying works'. These are works on a building or any other premises which will cause one or more leaseholder to pay more than £250 in respect of that item. The landlord must notify the leaseholders of these proposed works before they can be carried out if they want to recover the costs of doing the works, although there is a provision for the landlord to ask for the statutory requirements to be dispensed with. The landlord must follow consultation requirements in order to charge more than £250 to each leaseholder for any particular item of expenditure. It's best to ask this question before you buy so that you don't find yourself landed with a hefty bill for new windows and all the disruption that will inevitably be involved in the work shortly after you move in. The vendor may also be able to give you some idea about how often the freeholder carries out major decorating work (unless it's prescribed in the lease), so you should be able to work out how often you will be faced with bills for external redecoration and all the paraphernalia which goes with it.

Vendor: It may be that some of the questions that you are asked by your purchaser are not within your knowledge but are known only to the landlord. You must send off any such questions to the landlord as soon as possible to get the necessary information so that the landlord doesn't delay the transaction. Copies of Seller's Property Information Forms for leasehold properties are available from legal stationers.

Consents to assignment/subletting

Leases often contain restrictions on assignment (sale) and/or on subletting. Usually the leaseholder is not permitted to assign or sublet without the landlord's consent, such consent not to be unreasonably withheld. There may also be a requirement that a modest registration fee is paid to the landlord when he records the fact that you, Mr Bold, have taken an assignment from Mr Feather. If you intend to let out your new purchase, it's important to be aware of such a restriction and what the landlord will require to be satisfied that he should consent to a subletting.

In the case of any purchase of a lease where the landlord's consent to an assignment is required, this must be obtained before there can be completion. Vendors should make sure that landlords are not allowed to drag their feet and cause the purchase to go off.

Breaches of covenant

It's also important to check whether there have been any breaches of covenant. This is a more immediate problem in the case of a lease than where a purchaser discovers that his vendor has breached a freehold restrictive covenant. The reason for this is that in the case of a lease, the chances are that any breach of covenant renders the lease liable to forfeiture. This means that the landlord can bring the lease to an end and retake possession of the property (albeit with a court order). It's all very well that your vendor promised you that there were no such breaches, but this may not get you too far if you want to live in the flat rather than have to pursue the vendor for damages. It's better to deal with the potential problem before it even arises. A favourite covenant is a covenant against alterations. If it appears that there have been alterations, it's important to ask to see copies of any consents to such alterations and make sure that any conditions have been complied with. If there was no consent or conditions were not complied with, tell your vendor to apply for retrospective consent. In addition, get the landlord to confirm that there have been no breaches of covenant and, in particular, that all the rent and service charge is paid up to date.

'Share of freehold'

Many flats are advertised as having a 'share of freehold'. This doesn't generally mean that the flat itself has freehold title; there will still be a lease and the covenants contained in it will have to be adhered to. What it will probably mean is that the freehold on which the block stands is owned by a limited company and the shareholders of that limited company are the owners of the flats in the block. If this is the case, and it's fairly common, the purchaser must ensure that the vendor transfers his share in the limited company to the purchaser on completion of the sale of the property, or if the company is limited by guarantee rather than shares, that he is registered as a member of the new company. If you are buying a flat which involves becoming a member of a freehold company, you should ask to see the company documentation as well as the other documents regarding the title to the property. As a vendor, this is available from Companies House for a small fee. It's wise to do a search at Companies House with regard to the freehold owning company to make sure that it has not been struck off for failure to file a return or accounts (which is also fairly common). If you find that it has been, let the vendor know and tell him he should make arrangements to restore the company to the register of companies. It is possible to do this using an administrative procedure (depending on the circumstances) or by making an application to the court for an order restoring the company to the register. Further information can be found on the Companies House website at www.companieshouse.gov.uk in the 'Frequently Asked Questions' section.

Leaseholders who own the freehold of the block through the means of a limited company have more freedom to deal with the flat because if they don't like the lease, they can theoretically change it. Usually the leases are longer in blocks with share of freehold. However, even if the flat you are thinking of buying does come with share of freehold, changing the lease might not be so easy, as you are not able to act alone and agreement with your new neighbours (or at the very least, a majority of them) would still be required. Dealing with questions of lease extension or purchase of the freehold by the tenants in the block is beyond the scope of this book. In order to ensure that the extension of a lease is properly dealt with, as well as any notices which require the landlord to grant a lease extension or sell the freehold to the tenants for the benefit of a purchaser, advice of a specialist solicitor will be required.

CHAPTER 16

Commonhold

It's a fact that people prefer freehold interests to leasehold interests because a lease, which is limited in duration, is a wasting asset. Freehold interests are seen as more marketable. Therefore in 2002 the government passed the Commonhold and Leasehold Reform Act 2002, which provided for a new form of freehold ownership, called commonhold, designed to deal with properties (principally flats) which shared common parts and maintenance obligations. These interests are freehold interests, i.e. of unlimited duration. The common parts are owned by a commonhold association. The nature of the commonhold will be determined by the commonhold association's memorandum. The relationship between the association and the unit holders will be regulated by the articles of association. The relationship between the unit holders will be regulated by the commonhold community statement.

Don't be surprised if you hear this term being bandied around by estate agents and the like. Don't let it put you off. It's simply another way of holding land.

It has been possible to create commonholds since 2004. Although it is possible to convert existing blocks of flats (held on a traditional freehold/leasehold basis with a residents' company owning the freehold) into commonhold, in general commonhold will probably be used principally for new developments. Until one of the units is sold, the common parts will continue to be owned by the developer as was formerly the case. As soon as one of the units has been sold, the common parts will be transferred to a body known as a 'commonhold association' in which each of the unit holders in the development (i.e. the owners of the flats or houses) will have a share. The model is similar, although not identical, to the model of the 'shared freehold' mentioned in the previous chapter. However, only one of the unit holders can be a member of the commonhold association and if you are buying jointly, you will need to nominate one of you to be the member of your association for your unit.

You will need to carry out a search not only in relation to the unit itself but also relating to the common parts and the property held by the commonhold association. A search of the Index Map (using Form SIM) in relation to a commonhold unit will tell you not only the title number of the unit itself but also the title number of the common parts. This will be important and will allow you to obtain the documents relating to the commonhold association which will detail the rights and restrictions in relation to the development. An Office Copy entry in relation to the title to the common parts is obtained by filling in Form OC1 in the usual way. You should also obtain copies of the commonhold community statement and the articles of the commonhold association which you will need to apply for on Form OC2. More details can be found in Practice Guide 12 from the Land Registry at www.landregistry.gov.uk.

Instead of the rights and restrictions of the unit holders being contained in a lease, they are contained in a commonhold community statement. This will let you know what you are getting yourself into, to what your obligations are to your new neighbours and their obligations to you and what limits there are on your rights. This will usually require you to make contributions to maintenance on the estate or the development. Have a look at chapter 15 on flats and leaseholds to give you some ideas about the questions you should ask. The main difference between a leasehold and a commonhold interest is that whereas a lease is a wasting asset, a commonhold is a type of freehold and is indefinite in duration. When you buy a commonhold unit, however, you will be bound by the terms of the community statement and the articles of association. It's therefore very important that you ask for copies of these when making enquiries before you sign on the dotted line.

CHAPTER 17

Tricks of the trade for layperson conveyancing

Having read this book, you can assume you know at least as much about conveyancing, particularly your own, as any solicitor or clerk who might be acting for the other side. Because most Skinners are gentlefolk, they will, in the hope of future non-conveyancing business from you, be helpful and treat you kindly. However, if they seek to put you in the wrong, refer back to the book, thank them for their interest and tell them you are working out of the Bradshaw, for sadly, there are people who having heard that conveyancing is only a form-filling job, get a few forms and have a go, and building society managers and solicitors do right to give them short shrift.

Conveyancing is not like fitting a bath panel. You just can't get a pack of forms and hope to 'figure it out on the job'. So please, when recommending layperson conveyancing, make sure the aspirant conveyancer has a guide to work from. Reading someone else's guide and then trying to muddle through will get you wound up into Skinner's wringer.

- If you bought a property before the date when compulsory registration was extended to the area you live in, you are under no obligation to register it now. It will have to be registered by whoever purchases it from you.

- A leaseholder paying an annual rent for the privilege of standing on someone else's land with a lease which has a long time to run can ask the freeholder to sell the freehold interest to the lessees of the building under the Leasehold Reform (Housing and Urban Development) Act 1993, as amended. There are, however, complicated rules which must be got right to trigger these rights. Also, there are rules as to how to pass the right to buy the freehold on to a purchaser. A solicitor should be consulted. Even if you are selling and there is a move afoot by your neighbours to purchase the freehold, don't dismiss this out of hand. You want to be involved. Your flat will be more valuable and it's more difficult to join in later on. You will also be in a better position than your neighbour who is also selling but decided he didn't want to join in.

- You must be careful not to get into disputes with your neighbour, particularly about a few inches of a boundary. If your neighbour insists on making trouble, let it be he who traipses off to a solicitor. Let it be he whom the solicitor warns about high costs in such a case. But at least Skinner can get something out of it by sending you one of his bullying letters threatening you with virtual destruction and certain damnation if you don't let Mr & Mrs Angel have all their own way. Treat the letter with a pinch of salt, unless you happen to know that your neighbour is extremely rich. In such a case telephone your CAB for advice.

- While there are no registers from which you can learn who owns vacant land or derelict property, you can ask around. Local parsons and old established doctors are likely sources of information. Alternatively, you could complete an Index Map Search, Form SIM, to find out if the property is a registered title. If it is, you can then find out further details by applying for Office Copies, using Form OC1.

- Quarter days are 25 March, 24 June, 29 September and 25 December. A lease may select some other date such as 1 April, July, October and January.

- You will have fewer questions from Skinner & Probe when you do your sale conveyance if you have already bought out the owner of any 'rent charge' there might be on your property. These are annual charges on freehold land and occur in certain parts of the country. You are entitled to redeem a rent charge (sometimes called 'chief rent' or 'ground rent', depending on the area) for approximately ten times the amount of the annual charge. Get yourself an application form from Rentcharges Unit, Government Office for the North West, City Tower, Piccadilly Plaza, Manchester M1 4BE. Alternatively, it may turn out that a rent charge is necessary because you live in a gated development. If this is the case, it's better to leave well alone.

- Some conveyances don't contain a plan showing the boundaries and rely only on words. Sometimes you get both words and plans and sometimes one clashes with the other. Words are the stronger unless the conveyance says otherwise.

- A survey of estate agents' services boldly suggested that you have a go at selling for yourself for a couple of weeks. If at the end of that time you have had no joy, you should give it to an agent, they say. Surely, if what agents say is true, and they have national link-ups and buyers hanging on the back of the door, the best way is to let them have a go for a fortnight, and if their computers, books and door-hooks are bare, then settle down to the board and advertising routine for yourself.

- Most solicitors will provide your purchase file. Don't fret if they won't. Content yourself by asking them what they have to hide, but if you think there is something in it that is really necessary for you to have, an alternative source could be your lender's records. Keep in mind: the house is yours. The deeds are yours, and those deeds are only deposited with the lender as security for the loan.

- Vendors, don't get too involved with a prospective purchaser's solicitor until a mortgage offer has been issued. Deposits subject to contract are paid today and back tomorrow. £100 paid as a survey fee is lost forever, and therefore more binding.

- Mortgage offer – if the purchase is to be funded by a loan not only never exchange till you have seen and accepted it, but read it very carefully to make sure you can comply with any conditions that appear in the offer. They come in all shapes and sizes and are often long-winded, turgid and badly worded. Also make sure the lender's solicitor is happy with the title, searches and other papers. If you exchange and find you cannot meet a requirement, or he doesn't like the look of your papers, you will have a serious problem. Remember also the role of the lender's solicitor is to act as the lender's insurer. If the money is advanced and it all goes wrong, he compensates his client. On the one hand, he will know that. On the other, he is probably being paid peanuts to deal with the job, so don't be too surprised that he is not going to take any risks or waste too much time helping you out.

- You are in a chain. Your vendor can't complete to contracted date. Write a nice letter to your purchaser, giving the new date. If in reply you receive a snotty letter, use it as a model for a similar one to your vendor, but add a covering note saying where you got the idea from.

- Solicitors sometimes refer to a Land Registry Cover. To be precise, they mean a form for dealing, such as an AP1.

- If a conveyancing clerk asks you for a 'fully attested, certified, adjusted engrossed memorandum free of scrotage, together with vesting and singlet assent to reversion of entailed combination by teazle', ask him for a draft of the wording that would satisfy.

- When you pay your last payment to your lender, write asking for:

  - Registered property: the Charge Certificate and sealed Form DS1 or DS3 or confirmation it has discharged the charge using the Electronic Discharge Service. You can send it all to the Land Registry (no other form required) and in return you will receive your Land Certificate. No need for a solicitor. The Land Registry makes no charge, and neither should your erstwhile lender.

  - Unregistered property: ask for your deeds and check that the legal charge has something like, 'received all the money intended to be secured herein' signed and sealed on it. Check that the conveyance to you is in the parcel and that it has been stamped by HM Revenue & Customs.

- Master controlled inactivity: just because you get a letter with an official heading, be it from Town Hall or Skinner & Hall, it doesn't mean that you have to answer it immediately, if at all.

- If you are told that there is a delay with the searches, phone the council and find out how long it is taking nowadays to deal with them.

Buying at auction

When the gavel falls, a binding contract between the last bidder and the vendor is made. Don't worry about having a bout of involuntary head nodding. The auctioneer knows the difference between a bidder and a nutter.

Follow the drill outlined below. Attend some auctions no matter what the property for sale. If it's obvious that the property is worth £50,000 and the bidding opens at £25,000, make a bid. It's exciting, it's free and you have had a dress rehearsal and prepared yourself for the real thing later.

You prepare by doing what any house buyer should do, or have done for him, before signing a contract:

1. See and approve the contract.

2. Have Enquiries before Contract form answered.

3. Have local authority forms completed and answered.

4. Send search forms to Land Registry/Legal Charges Dept.

A vendor's solicitor should have prepared a set of the above and the agent will have a supply. If all the replies on the forms meet with your approval, so well and good. If not, ask questions until you are satisfied or lose interest. So far you haven't spent a penny … and that is how it should be. If you need a mortgage, leave your enquiries about it as late as possible; others could be in the same position and some anxious soul might already have paid a survey fee to one of the local lenders who can then give you an idea of what could be borrowed. Give them all a chance of not wasting a survey fee for you.

Follow the instructions given earlier about actually visiting the local council offices and gleaning information that other bidders might not hear about, because their hired helps have relied only on the paperwork. You might find out from the officials that 50 years ago there was a proposal to do something nasty in the vicinity. Ask the auctioneer if there is any likelihood of the plan being revived. He will only be able to give a vague reply. You react with a long face for all to see because you will have positioned yourself at the end of the front row where, by sitting sideways-on, you can keep an eye on the whole assembly and know whether the auctioneer is getting genuine bids or taking them off the chandeliers.

Layperson conveyancers should not waste their time trying to find the solicitor Skinner. When I first quarried the person, there was no lawyer by the name of Skinner in a practice that had the name of Skinner in its business name, and even if there were, then or now, we are not referring to him or any person by the name of Skinner who has or has ever had a certificate to practise law.

Postscript

A word about electronic conveyancing

You will have seen the odd reference, as you have been reading this book, to the fact that the law on land registration was altered as from 13 October 2003, when the Land Registration Act 2002 came into force. This Act basically overhauled the law to ensure that the Register was a more accurate reflection of the position on the ground, by reducing the number of overriding interests and requiring registration of those that the vendor (or purchaser) is aware of. The idea is to make the purchaser of a registered house even more secure than he is at the moment.

However, the other main reason for the new Act was, in an increasingly technological age, to pave the way for electronic conveyancing. Once electronic conveyancing is possible there can be simultaneous completion and registration; so the headache of ensuring that you get your AP1 to the Land Registry before your priority period expires will disappear (unless, of course, in the unlikely event that you have the patience of a saint and your vendor has managed to drag his feet so much that completion doesn't take place until your priority period has expired).

Electronic conveyancing (e-conveyancing) will require a number of trials, regulations and consultations before it can come into effect. A consultation paper has been submitted to the government. It's anticipated that e-conveyancing will be introduced in phases. There is already automatic registration of charges and now banks and building societies can discharge charges electronically too. An increasing amount of the information held at the Land Registry is available on the internet, although much of this is only available to professionals. E-conveyancing will eventually come in over a substantial period of time. Although at the date of the last edition of this book it was anticipated that the e-conveyancing provisions would be fully in force by summer 2009, we are now past the summer of 2010 and it is still not a reality. The current plan is for electronic transfers (e-transfers) to come into force in late 2010/early 2011. Further details can be found on the Land Registry website at www.landregistry.gov.uk under the link e-conveyancing.

E-conveyancing is unlikely to mean that the layperson conveyancer will be able to register himself as legal owner from the comfort of his own home – although his computer probably should have been packed and in the removal van before time for completion came round! Although the Land Registry has not been persuaded to use the introduction of e-conveyancing as an excuse to deprive laypeople of the right to do their own conveyancing, it seems likely that the layperson conveyancer would have to attend a Registry office or nominated terminal to carry out the conveyancing, but the details have not yet been finalised. When it does come along it will hopefully make the whole process a lot simpler and more painless. However, it's unlikely that paper conveyancing will be phased out completely and wholly replaced by the electronic system. This only affects registration of title and doesn't affect the carrying out of other searches and obtaining environmental reports, so pen and paper will not be wholly redundant. All that can be said for the moment is watch this space!

Glossary

Absolute title	Highest and most unquestionable title.
Abstract of title	A summary of documents proving title.
Administrator	Person entitled to administer an estate where a person dies intestate. His title to do so is proven by 'letters of administration' issued by the Principal Probate Registry or a District Probate Registry.
Assent	The title of a legatee or devisee is not complete until the deceased's executor/personal representative has completed an assent which then becomes a good root of title. If there is an assent after 13 October 2003, the person mentioned as the legatee or devisee in the assent ought to have been registered and the assent should have been on Form AS1.
Assignment	Transfer of benefit of lease.
Attested	Witnessed.
Beneficial owner	Person/s owning land for own benefit.
Beneficiary	One who has the beneficial interest, i.e. receives the rent or is the occupier. A beneficiary may be, but is not necessarily, a registered owner.
Caution against dealing	Means of protecting a right by requiring notice of dealing in land to be given to cautioner; no new cautions can be entered since 13 October 2003.
Caution against first registration	Means of protecting a right against unregistered land so that the cautioner can be notified when someone applies to register the land.

CHAPS transfer	Clearing House Automated Payment System, a form of payment which will result in funds being transferred on the same day that they have been sent. This is required under the standard terms and conditions and will be arranged by the bank for a fee.
Charge/legal charge	Mortgage.
Commonhold	Type of freehold ownership that principally applies to flats which came into force in 2004.
Conveyance	A written instrument of transfer of real property used when the land is not registered at HM Land Registry.
Counterpart	Lease signed by tenant – the counterpart is signed by landlord.
Covenant	Promise written in deed.
Deed	Is 'signed and delivered'; all transfers of freehold and leasehold property must be by deed. A signature on a deed must be witnessed.
Demise	Part of property let to a lessee/tenant under a lease.
Devise	A gift by Will of land or other real estate. A bequest is a gift by Will of personal estate.
Easement	Right over someone else's land such as a right of one landowner to use another's land for right of way, water, drains, etc.
Equity	(On redemption) the money owing to you after the loan has been paid off.
Escrow	A deed delivered conditionally; it doesn't become effective until the condition is satisfied, e.g. other party signs his part.
Estate	(a) real: ownership of freehold/leasehold; (b) personal: ownership of effects other than land.
Execute	Sign.
Executor	Person appointed in Will of deceased person to carry out provisions of Will; probate proves entitlement to do so and title to land (and other property) in the deceased's estate.

Fee simple	Largest estate in land – often equivalent to freehold.
Filed plan	The plan from which Land Registry identifies land.
Flying freehold	(So called) applies to (a) upper parts of buildings where party has an interest unlimited by time; the soil is owned by another; very rarely (b) foreshores; and (c) interest in part of area of meadows allocated by annual drawing of lots.
Freehold	Absolute ownership unlimited by time, as opposed to leasehold.
Incumbrance	A mortgage upon either real or personal estate.
Indenture	Deed made by more than one party; conveyance used to be called an indenture.
Intestate	Leaving no valid Will.
Joint and several liability	Two or more parties who render themselves liable to a joint action against all, as well as to a separate action against each in case the agreement or bond is not kept.
Joint tenants	Co-owners of land with or without buildings on it; survivor takes all (see also Tenants in common).
Land	General real estate term, refers to land and all buildings that stand on it.
Notice	Means of protecting a third party interest in registered land.
Office Copy	An official copy of the registers of title held at the Land Registry showing the registrable interests in and owners of a piece of registered land. It will not show overriding interests.
Overriding interest	The rights of persons other than owners to occupy property; also rights of third parties, e.g. to walk over the land or rights under short leases; these rights don't have to be registered at the Land Registry to be effective.
Parcels	The pieces a hitherto single plot has been split into.
Private treaty	Sale not by auction.

Repudiation	Serious breach of contract entitling the other party to treat the contract as at an end ('accept the repudiation'), e.g. failure to complete following service of notice to complete.
Rescission	Unwinding a contract – backing out because you were induced to enter the contract by reason of a misrepresentation.
Restrictive covenant	Promise in a deed restricting use of land.
Root of title	Document from which good title of ownership is proved – at least 15 years old (will become archaic when all land registered); to give good title, there has to be an uninterrupted claim in title from the root to the seller.
Scrotage	A Bradshavian neologism.
Seisen/seised	Possessed of land as freeholders.
Service charge	Money payable to the freeholder (or management company) of a flat to pay for the general upkeep of the block and other services provided to the leaseholders of the flats.
Sitting tenant	Tenant of house or flat; usually, this term means a tenant who has acquired security of tenure and whose tenancy cannot be ended by the landlord giving notice.
Specific performance	Forcing completion of contract by an action.
Stakeholder	Holder of deposit which he doesn't pass to vendor without authority of buyer, or return to buyer without permission of vendor.
Stamp Duty	Payable on some deeds and documents which cannot be used as evidence or registered at the Land Registry unless properly stamped with duty paid, or 'adjudicated' or 'particulars delivered'; now abolished for land transactions.

Stamp Duty Land Tax	Replacement for Stamp Duty. Charged on transactions not documents; no need to submit transfer to the Revenue – simply fill in a Land Transaction Return. Land Registry will refuse to register property without certificate from the Revenue or self certificate.
Tenant for life	Person entitled to benefit of real estate for term of his life, after which it will pass to others as determined by an existing Will or trust.
Tenants in common	The property is owned in shares and each owner can bequeath his part to whom he wishes. Shares don't necessarily have to be equal.
Tenure	The mode of holding or occupying lands. No person except the Sovereign can be the absolute owner of land in England, so the rest of us hold immediately of the Crown (freehold) or mediated by a freeholder (leasehold). How far a tenure extends is called the tenant's estate, hence estate in fee simple, etc. Most titles of freehold land are registered with absolute title.
Testimonium	Formal introduction to the attestation clause in a deed.
Title	Evidence which signifies a person's right to enjoyment of land.
Trust	Created when property transferred to a person (trustee) to apply for benefit of another.
Trustees	Where two or more people are entitled to the legal estate they hold the legal title as trustees. Purchasers need receipt for purchase monies on conveyance or Form TR1 (standard Land Registry transfer form) signed by at least two of them unless there are two joint tenants and only one survives; the survivor can then deal with the estate.
Vacating receipt	Receipt written and signed on the Legal Charge showing all monies intended to be secured by the deed to have been paid off.

Appendices

Some of the main forms mentioned in this book are listed below, and completed examples included for guidance on following pages. Appendix 7, Completion Information and Requisitions on Title, has been left blank intentionally – see chapter 12 for guidance on its completion.

You can obtain your forms from: HM Land Registry, at its website www.landreg.gov.uk; the Law Society at www.lawsocietyshop.org.uk; and legal stationers such as Oyez at www.oyez.co.uk.

1. **Form OS1**   Application by Purchaser for Official Search
2. **Form OC1**   Application for Office Copies of Register
3. **Form K15**   Application for an Official Search
4. **Form LLCI**   Requisition for Search of Local Land Charges
5. **Form CON 29R**   Enquiries of Local Authority
6. **Form CON 29O**   Optional Enquiries of Local Authority
7. **Form TA13**   Completion Information and Requisitions on Title
8. **Form TR1**   Transfer of Whole of Registered Title(s)
9. **Form AP1**   Application to Change the Register
10. **Form ID1**   Certificate of Identity for a Private Individual
11. **Form FR1**   First Registration Application
12. **District Land Registries**

Appendix 1: Completed Example Form OS1 – Application by Purchaser for Official Search

Land Registry
Application by purchaser for official
search with priority of the whole of the
land in a registered title or a pending first
registration application

OS1

Use one form per title.

If you need more room than is provided for in a panel, and your software allows, you can expand any panel in the form. Alternatively use continuation sheet CS and attach it to this form.

Land Registry is unable to give legal advice but our website www1.landregistry.gov.uk provides guidance on Land Registry applications. This includes public guides and practice guides (aimed at conveyancers) that can also be obtained from any Land Registry office.

See www1.landregistry.gov.uk/regional if you are unsure which Land Registry office to send this application to.

'Conveyancer' is a term used in this form. It is defined in rule 217(1) of the Land Registration Rules 2003 and includes, among others, solicitor, licensed conveyancer and fellow of the Institute of Legal Executives.

LAND REGISTRY USE ONLY
Record of fees paid
Particulars of under/over payments
Reference number
Fees debited £

Where there is more than one local authority serving an area, enter the one to which council tax or business rates are normally paid.	1	Local authority serving the property: **Edenshire County Council**
Enter the title number of the registered estate or that allotted to the pending first registration.	2	Title number of the property: **EDN999707**
Insert address including postcode (if any) or other description of the property, for example 'land adjoining 2 Acacia Avenue'.	3	Property: **14 Plevna Place, Blossomton, Edenshire, ED2 8JD**
Enter the full names. If there are more than two persons, enter the first two only.	4	Registered proprietor/Applicant for first registration SURNAME/COMPANY NAME: **Bold** FORENAME(S): **Thomas** SURNAME/COMPANY NAME: **Bold** FORENAME(S): **Prudence**

5	Application and fee	
	Application	Fee paid (£)
	Official search of whole with priority	£8

See fees calculator at www1.landregistry.gov.uk/fees

Fee payment method

Place 'X' in the appropriate box.

The fee will be charged to the account specified in panel 6.

X   cheque made payable to 'Land Registry'

☐   Land Registry credit account

☐   direct debit, under an agreement with Land Registry

Appendix 1: Completed Example Form OS1 – Application by Purchaser for Official Search (continued)

If you are paying by credit account or direct debit, this will be the account charged.	**6** This application is sent to Land Registry by	

Key number (if applicable):

Name: **Thomas and Prudence Bold**
Address or UK DX box number:
1 Prospect Avenue
Blossomton
Edenshire
ED2 2NW

Email address: **tb@email.uk**
Reference:

Phone no:	Fax no:

Place 'X' in one box only.

For a search of a registered title enter a date falling within the definition of 'search from date' in rule 131 of the Land Registration Rules 2003. If the date entered is not such a date the application may be rejected.

7 Application and search from date

X I apply for a search of the individual register of a registered title to ascertain whether any adverse entry has been made in the register or day list since **18 MARCH 2010** *

☐ I apply for a search in relation to a pending application for first registration to ascertain whether any adverse entry has been made in the day list since the date of the pending first registration application.

Provide the full name(s) of each purchaser or lessee or chargee.

8 The applicant:
Thomas Bold
Prudence Bold

9 Reason for application

I certify that the applicant intends to

Place 'X' in the appropriate box.

X **P**urchase

☐ take a **L**ease

☐ take a registered **C**harge

If a conveyancer is acting for the applicant, that conveyancer must sign. If no conveyancer is acting, the applicant (if more than one person then each) must sign.

10

Signature of applicant or their conveyancer: *Thomas Bold*
PRUDENCE BOLD

Date: **12 July 2010**

WARNING
If you dishonestly enter information or make a statement that you know is, or might be, untrue or misleading, and intend by doing so to make a gain for yourself or another person, or to cause loss or the risk of loss to another person, you may commit the offence of fraud under section 1 of the Fraud Act 2006, the maximum penalty for which is 10 years' imprisonment or an unlimited fine, or both.

Failure to complete this form with proper care may result in a loss of protection under the Land Registration Act 2002 if, as a result, a mistake is made in the register.

Under section 66 of the Land Registration Act 2002 most documents (including this form) kept by the registrar relating to an application to the registrar or referred to in the register are open to public inspection and copying. If you believe a document contains prejudicial information, you may apply for that part of the document to be made exempt using Form EX1, under rule 136 of the Land Registration Rules 2003.

© Crown copyright (ref: LR/HO) 07/08

* This should be the date which is shown at the top of the Official Copy of Register Entries in relation to the property and is described as the 'search from' date in the Official Copy.

Appendix 2: Completed Example Form OC1 – Application for Office Copies of Register *

Land Registry
Application for official copies of register/ plan or certificate in Form CI

OC1

Use one form per title.

If you need more room than is provided for in a panel, and your software allows, you can expand any panel in the form. Alternatively use continuation sheet CS and attach it to this form.

Land Registry is unable to give legal advice but our website www1.landregistry.gov.uk provides guidance on Land Registry applications. This includes public guides and practice guides (aimed at conveyancers) that can also be obtained from any Land Registry office.

See www1.landregistry.gov.uk/regional if you are unsure which Land Registry office to send this application to.

LAND REGISTRY USE ONLY
Record of fees paid

Particulars of under/over payments

Reference number
Fees debited £

Where there is more than one local authority serving an area, enter the one to which council tax or business rates are normally paid.

Use a separate form for each registered title.

Place 'X' in the appropriate box.

1   Local authority serving the property:

     Edenshire District Council

2   Details of estate

     (a) Title number if known: **EDN999707**

     (b) (Where the title number is unknown) this application relates to

☐ freehold	☐ leasehold	☐ manor
☐ franchise	☐ caution against first registration	
☐ rentcharge	☐ profit a prendre in gross	

3   Property

     Flat/unit number:

     Postal number or description:

     Name of road:

     Name of locality:

     Town:

     Postcode:

*Applications can also be made in person at Land Registry Offices

Appendix 2: Completed Example Form OC1 – Application for Office Copies of Register (continued)

4	Application and fee		

Application	Total number of all copies or certificates requested in panel 7	Fee paid (£)
Official copy of register /plan or certificate of inspection of title plan		**16**

See fees calculator at www1.landregistry.gov.uk/fees

Fee payment method

Place 'X' in the appropriate box.

The fee will be charged to the account specified in panel 5.

X   cheque made payable to 'Land Registry'

☐   Land Registry credit account

☐   direct debit, under an agreement with Land Registry

5	This application is sent to Land Registry by

If you are paying by credit account or direct debit, this will be the account charged.

Key number (if applicable):

Name: **Clive Smart and Constance Smart**
Address or UK DX box number:
14 Plevna Place
Blossomton
Edenshire
ED2 8JD

Email address: **smart@email.uk**
Reference:

Phone no: **01234 778 998**   Fax no:

Please note that the facility of issuing copies electronically is not available at present. When it is, a direction will appear on our website and details will be given in Public Guide 1 and Practice Guide 11. Until there is a direction, you do not need to complete this panel to obtain an official copy in paper format.

Official copies issued electronically are in 'Portable Document Format' (PDF) which replicates the appearance of the hard copy version. You will need Adobe Acrobat Reader (which you can install free from www.adobe.com) to open the document.

Place 'X' in the box if applicable.

6	Issue of official copies in paper format where an email address has been supplied

If you have supplied an email address in panel 5, then, unless you complete the box below, any official copy will be issued electronically to that address, if there is a direction under section 100(4) of the Land Registration Act 2002 by the registrar covering such issuing.

X   I have supplied an email address but require the official copy(ies) to be issued in paper format instead of being issued electronically

7	I apply for

Indicate how many copies of each are required.

  2   official copy(ies) of the register of the above mentioned property

  ___   official copy(ies) of the title plan or caution plan of the above mentioned property

  ___   certificate(s) of inspection of title plan, in which case either

Place 'X' in the appropriate box.

     i. ☐   an estate plan has been approved and the plot number is:

     or

State reference, for example 'edged red'.

     ii. ☐   no estate plan has been approved and a certificate is to be issued in respect of the land shown on the attached plan and copy

Appendix 2: Completed Example Form OC1 – Application for Office Copies of Register (continued)

Place 'X' in the appropriate box.	8	If an application for registration is pending against the title
	☐	I require an official copy back-dated prior to the receipt of the application
	X	I require an official copy on completion of that application

9

Signature of applicant: *Clive Smart*

CONSTANCE SMART

Date: **12 March 2010**

WARNING

If you dishonestly enter information or make a statement that you know is, or might be, untrue or misleading, and intend by doing so to make a gain for yourself or another person, or to cause loss or the risk of loss to another person, you may commit the offence of fraud under section 1 of the Fraud Act 2006, the maximum penalty for which is 10 years' imprisonment or an unlimited fine, or both.

Failure to complete this form with proper care may result in a loss of protection under the Land Registration Act 2002 if, as a result, a mistake is made in the register.

Under section 66 of the Land Registration Act 2002 most documents (including this form) kept by the registrar relating to an application to the registrar or referred to in the register are open to public inspection and copying. If you believe a document contains prejudicial information, you may apply for that part of the document to be made exempt using Form EX1, under rule 136 of the Land Registration Rules 2003.

© Crown copyright (ref: LR/HO) 07/08

Appendix 3: Completed Example Form K15 – Application for an Official Search (Unregistered Land)

Form K15   Land Charges Act 1972

APPLICATION FOR AN OFFICIAL SEARCH
NOT APPLICABLE TO REGISTERED LAND

Application is hereby made for an official search in the index to the registers kept pursuant to the Land Charges Act 1972 for any subsisting entries in respect of the undermentioned particulars.

Fee panel

Place "X" in the appropriate box. See Note 1 overleaf.

X A cheque or postal order for the correct fee accompanies this application.

☐ Please debit our Credit Account with the appropriate fee payable.

☐ Please debit our Direct Debit under an authorised agreement with Land Registry.

IMPORTANT: Please read the notes overleaf before completing this form

For Official Use Only				PERIOD OF YEARS *(see Note 5 overleaf)*	
STX			**NAMES TO BE SEARCHED** *(Please use BLOCK LETTERS and see Note 4 overleaf)*	From	To
		Forename(s)	**CLIVE**	1980	2010
		SURNAME	**SMART**		
		Forename(s)	**CONSTANCE**	1980	2010
		SURNAME	**SMART**		
		Forename(s)			
		SURNAME			
		Forename(s)			
		SURNAME			
		Forename(s)			
		SURNAME			
		Forename(s)			
		SURNAME			

COUNTY *(see Note 6 overleaf)*   **EDENSHIRE**

FORMER COUNTY

DESCRIPTION OF LAND

(see Note 7 overleaf)

FORMER DESCRIPTION

Particulars of Applicant *(See Notes 8, 9 and 10 overleaf)*		Name and address (including postcode) for despatch of certificate
KEY NUMBER	Name and address (including postcode)	(Leave blank if certificate is to be returned to applicant's address)
THOMAS BOLD **1 PROSPECT AVENUE** **ORCHARD VALE** **EDENSHIRE** **ED5 7AB**		

Applicant's reference	Date	FOR OFFICIAL USE ONLY
	15 APRIL 2010	

Appendix 3: Completed Example Form K15 – Application for an Official Search (Unregistered Land) (continued)

NOTES FOR GUIDANCE OF APPLICANTS

The following notes are supplied for assistance in making the application overleaf. Detailed information for the making of all kinds of applications to the Land Charges Department is contained in Practice Guide 63 – *Land Charges – Applications for registration, official search, office copy and cancellation*, which is obtainable on application at the address shown below.

1. **Effect of search.** The official certificate of the result of this search will have no statutory effect in relation to registered land (see Land Registration Act 1925, s.59 and Land Charges Act 1972, s.14).

2. **Bankruptcy only searches.** Form K16 should be used for Bankruptcy only searches.

3. **Fees.** Fees must be paid by credit account, by Direct Debit under an authorised agreement with Land Registry or by cheque or postal order made payable to "Land Registry" (see the Practice Guide referred to above).

4. **Names to be searched.** The forename(s) and surname of each individual must be entered on the appropriate line of the form. The name of a company or other body should commence on the forename line and may continue on the surname line (the words "Forename(s)" and "Surname" should be crossed through). If you are searching more than 6 names, use a second form.

5. **Period of years to be searched.** The inclusive period to be covered by a search should be entered in complete years, e.g. 1968-1975.

6. **County names.** This must be the appropriate name as set out in Appendix C to the Practice Guide referred to above. Searches affecting land within the Greater London area should state "GREATER LONDON" as the county name. ANY RELEVANT FORMER COUNTY SHOULD ALWAYS BE STATED. Appendix C as referenced above provides relevant guidance.

7. **Land description.** It is not essential to provide a land description but, if one is given, any relevant former description should also be given (see the guide referred to above).

8. **Key Number.** If you have been allocated a key number, please take care to enter this in the space provided overleaf, whether or not you are paying fees through your credit account or by Direct Debit.

9. **Applicant's name and address.** This need not be supplied if the applicant's key number is correctly entered in the space provided overleaf.

10. **Applicant's reference.** Any reference must be limited to 25 characters, including any oblique strokes and punctuation.

11. **Despatch of this form.** When completed, send this application to the address shown below, which is printed in a position so as to fit within a standard window envelope.

The Superintendent
Land Charges Department
Search Section
Plumer House, Tailyour Road,
Crownhill, PLYMOUTH PL6 5HY
DX 8249 PLYMOUTH (3)

Crown copyright (ref: LR/HO) 2/07

Appendix 4: Completed Example Form LLC1 – Requisition for Search of Local Land Charges

Form LLC1. *(Local Land Charges Rules 1977 Schedule 1, Form C)*

The duplicate of this form must also be completed:
a carbon copy will suffice

For directions, notes and fees see overleaf.

Insert name and address of registering authority in space below

⌐ EDENSHIRE COUNTY COUNCIL ⌐
HIGH STREET
BLOSSOMTON
ED4 9IJ
⌐⎯⎯⎯⎯⎯⎯⎯⎯⎯⎯⎯⎯⌐

Official Number ⎯⎯⎯⎯⎯⎯⎯⎯
(To be completed by the registering authority)

Register of local land charges

Requisition for search
and official certificate
of search

Requisition for search
(A separate requisition must be made in respect of each parcel of land except as explained overleaf)

fold

An official search is required in *Part(s)* **1-12** ⎯⎯⎯⎯ *of* ¹
the register of local land charges kept by the above-named
registering authority for subsisting registrations against the land
[defined in the attached plan and]² described below.

Description of land sufficient to enable it to be identified

14 PLEVNA PLACE
BLOSSOMTON
EDENSHIRE ED2 8JD

Name and address to which certificate is to be sent

⌐ THOMAS BOLD ⌐
1 PROSPECT AVENUE
ORCHARD VALE
EDENSHIRE ED5 7AB
⌐⎯⎯⎯⎯⎯⎯⎯⎯⎯⎯⎯⎯⌐

Signature of applicant *(or his solicitor)*

Thomas Bold

Date
2 APRIL 2010

Telephone number
(01234) 567 890

Reference

Enclosure
Cheque/Money Order/Postal Order/Giro

Official certificate of search

To be completed by
authorised officer

It is hereby certified that the search requested above reveals
no subsisting registrations³

or the ⎯⎯⎯⎯⎯⎯ registrations described in the Schedule
hereto³ up to and including the date of this certificate.

Signed ....

On behalf of ....⁴

Date

1 Delete if inappropriate. Otherwise insert Part(s) in which
  search is required.

2 Delete if inappropriate. (A plan should be furnished in
  duplicate if it is desired that a copy should be returned.)

3 Delete inapplicable words. (The Parts of the Schedule should
  be securely attached to the certificate and the number of
  registrations disclosed should be inserted in the space provided.
  Only Parts which disclose subsisting registrations should be sent.)

4 Insert name of registering authority.

Reproduced for illustrative purposes only by kind permission of Oyez Professional Services Limited and the Law Society of England and Wales

Appendix 4: Completed Example Form LLCI – Requisition for Search of Local Land Charges (continued)

Directions and notes

1   This form and the duplicate should be completed and sent by post to or left at the office of the registering authority.

2   A separate requisition for search should be made in respect of each parcel of land in respect of which a search is required except where, for the purpose of a single transaction, a certificate is required in respect of two or more parcels of land which have a common boundary or are separated only by a road, railway, river, stream or canal.

3   'Parcel of land' means land (including a building or part of a building) which is separately occupied or separately rated or, if not occupied or rated, in separate ownership. For the purpose of this definition an owner is the person who (in his own right or as trustee for any other person) is entitled to receive the rack rent of land, or, where the land is not let at a rack rent, would be so entitled if it were so let.

4   The certificate of the result of an official search of the register refers to any subsisting registrations, recorded against the land defined in the application for search, in the Parts of the register in respect of which the search is requested. The Parts of the register record:

Part 1	General financial charges.
Part 2	Specific financial charges.
Part 3	Planning charges.
Part 4	Miscellaneous charges.
Part 5	Fenland ways maintenance charges.
Part 6	Land compensation charges.
Part 7	New towns charges.
Part 8	Civil aviation charges.
Part 9	Opencast coal charges.
Part 10	Listed buildings charges.
Part 11	Light obstruction notices.
Part 12	Drainage scheme charges.

5   An office copy of any entry in the register can be obtained on written request and on payment of the prescribed fee.

Fees

In England, fees payable to registering authorities for local land charge services under the Local Land Charges Act 1975 (other than the fee for a personal search of the local land charges register) are set by individual registering authorities and the fee for a personal search of the local land charges register is set by the Lord Chancellor. In Wales, these fees are set by the National Assembly for Wales.

Information about the fees should be obtained from the relevant registering authority.

Oyez   7 Spa Road, London SE16 3QQ

2007 Edition
3.2007   F7315
5063019

LLC1

Reproduced for illustrative purposes only by kind permission of Oyez Professional Services Limited and the Law Society of England and Wales

Appendix 5: Completed Example Form CON 29R – Enquiries of Local Authority

CON 29R Enquiries of local authority (2007)

A duplicate plan is required for all searches submitted directly to a local authority.
If submitted manually, this form must be submitted in duplicate. Please type or use BLOCK LETTERS.

The Law Society

A.

Local authority name and address	
EDENSHIRE COUNTY COUNCIL HIGH STREET BLOSSOMTON ED4 9IJ	Search No: .... Signed: .... On behalf of: .... Local authority/private search company/ member of the public (indicate as applicable) Dated: ....

B.

Address of the land/property

UPRN(s): **14 PLEVNA PLACE**

Secondary name/number:

Primary name/number:

Street:

Locality/village: **BLOSSOMTON**

Town: **EDENSHIRE**

Postcode: **ED2 8JD**

C.

Other roadways, footways and footpaths in respect of which a reply to enquiry 2 is required

N/A

D.

Fees
£ **100** _____ is enclosed/is paid by NLIS transfer (delete as applicable)

Signed: **THOMAS BOLD**

Dated: **12 APRIL 2010**

Reference: **PLEVNA**

Telephone No: **(01234) 567890**

Fax No:

E-mail:

E. (For HIPs regulations compliance only)

Names of those involved in the sale (this box is only completed when the replies to these enquiries are to be included in a Home Information Pack)

Name of vendor:

Name of estate agents:

Name of HIP provider:

Name of solicitor/conveyancer:

Your personal data – name and address – will be handled strictly in accordance with the requirements of the Data Protection Act. It is required to pass on to the relevant authority(ies) in order to carry out the necessary searches.

Notes

A. Enter name and address of appropriate Council. If the property is near a local authority boundary, consider raising certain enquiries (e.g. road schemes) with the adjoining Council.

B. Enter address and description of the property. Please give the UPRN(s) (Unique Property Reference Number) where known. A duplicate plan is required for all searches submitted directly to a local authority. The search may be returned if land/property cannot easily be identified.

C. Enter name and/or mark on plan any other roadways, footways and footpaths abutting the property (in addition to those entered in Box B) to which a reply to enquiry 2 is required.

D. Details of fees can be obtained from the Council, your chosen NLIS channel or search provider.

E. Box E is only to be completed when the replies to these enquiries are to be included in a Home Information Pack. Enter the name of the individual(s) and firms involved in the sale of the property.

F. Enter the name and address/DX address of the person or company lodging or conducting this enquiry.

F.

Reply to

THOMAS BOLD
1 PROSPECT AVENUE
ORCHARD VALE, BLOSSOMTON,
EDENSHIRE ED5 7AB

DX address:

Oyez 7 Spa Road, London SE16 3QQ

© Law Society 2007   4.2007 F7616

5033382

Conveyancing 29R (Enquiries)

Reproduced for illustrative purposes only by kind permission of Oyez Professional Services Limited

Appendix 5: Completed Example Form CON 29R – Enquiries of Local Authority (continued)

CON 29R Enquiries of local authority (2007)

PLANNING AND BUILDING REGULATIONS

1.1. Planning and building decisions and pending applications
Which of the following relating to the property have been granted, issued or refused or (where applicable) are the subject of pending applications?
(a) a planning permission
(b) a listed building consent
(c) a conservation area consent
(d) a certificate of lawfulness of existing use or development
(e) a certificate of lawfulness of proposed use or development
(f) building regulations approval
(g) a building regulation completion certificate and
(h) any building regulations certificate or notice issued in respect of work carried out under a competent person self-certification scheme

1.2. Planning designations and proposals
What designations of land use for the property or the area, and what specific proposals for the property, are contained in any existing or proposed development plan?

ROADS

2. Roadways, footways and footpaths
Which of the roads, footways and footpaths named in the application for this search (via boxes B and C) are:

(a) highways maintainable at public expense
(b) subject to adoption and, supported by a bond or bond waiver
(c) to be made up by a local authority who will reclaim the cost from the frontagers
(d) to be adopted by a local authority without reclaiming the cost from the frontagers

OTHER MATTERS

3.1. Land required for public purposes
Is the property included in land required for public purposes?

3.2. Land to be acquired for road works
Is the property included in land to be acquired for road works?

3.3. Drainage agreements and consents
Do either of the following exist in relation to the property?
(a) an agreement to drain buildings in combination into an existing sewer by means of a private sewer
(b) an agreement or consent for (i) a building, or (ii) extension to a building on the property, to be built over, or in the vicinity of a drain, sewer or disposal main

3.4. Nearby road schemes
Is the property (or will it be) within 200 metres of any of the following?
(a) the centre line of a new trunk road or special road specified in any order, draft order or scheme
(b) the centre line of a proposed alteration or improvement to an existing road involving construction of a subway, underpass, flyover, footbridge, elevated road or dual carriageway
(c) the outer limits of construction works for a proposed alteration or improvement to an existing road involving (i) construction of a roundabout (other than a mini roundabout), or (ii) widening by construction of one or more additional traffic lanes;
(d) the outer limits of (i) construction of a new road to be built by a local authority, (ii) an approved alteration or improvement to an existing road involving construction of a subway, underpass, flyover, footbridge, elevated road or dual carriageway, (iii) construction of a roundabout (other than a mini roundabout) or widening by construction of one or more additional traffic lanes
(e) the centre line of the proposed route of a new road under proposals published for public consultation
(f) the outer limits of (i) construction of a proposed alteration or improvement to an existing road involving construction of a subway, underpass, flyover, footbridge, elevated road or dual carriageway, (ii) construction of a roundabout (other than a mini roundabout), (iii) widening by construction of one or more additional traffic lanes, under proposals published for public consultation

3.5. Nearby railway schemes
Is the property (or will it be) within 200 metres of the centre line of a proposed railway, tramway, light railway or monorail?

3.6. Traffic schemes
Has a local authority approved but not yet implemented any of the following for the roads, footways and footpaths (named in Box B) which abut the boundaries of the property?
(a) permanent stopping up or diversion
(b) waiting or loading restrictions
(c) one way driving
(d) prohibition of driving
(e) pedestrianisation
(f) vehicle width or weight restriction
(g) traffic calming works including road humps
(h) residents parking controls
(i) minor road widening or improvement
(j) pedestrian crossings
(k) cycle tracks
(l) bridge building

3.7. Outstanding notices
Do any statutory notices which relate to the following matters subsist in relation to the property other than those revealed in a response to any other enquiry in this form?
(a) building works
(b) environment
(c) health and safety
(d) housing
(e) highways
(f) public health

3.8. Contravention of building regulations
Has a local authority authorised in relation to the property any proceedings for the contravention of any provision contained in Building Regulations?

3.9. Notices, orders, directions and proceedings under Planning Acts
Do any of the following relate in relation to the property, or has a local authority decided to issue, serve, make or commence any of the following?
(a) an enforcement notice
(b) a stop notice
(c) a listed building enforcement notice
(d) a breach of condition notice
(e) a planning contravention notice
(f) another notice relating to breach of planning control
(g) a listed building repairs notice
(h) in the case of a listed building deliberately allowed to fall into disrepair, a compulsory purchase order with a direction for minimum compensation
(i) a building preservation notice
(j) a direction restricting permitted development
(k) an order revoking or modifying planning permission
(l) an order requiring discontinuance of use or alteration or removal of building or works
(m) a tree preservation order
(n) proceedings to enforce a planning agreement or planning contribution

3.10. Conservation area
Do the following apply in relation to the property?
(a) the making of the area a conservation area before 31st August 1974
(b) an unimplemented resolution to designate the area a conservation area

3.11. Compulsory purchase
Has any enforceable order or decision been made to compulsorily purchase or acquire the property?

3.12. Contaminated land
Do any of the following apply (including any relating to the land adjacent to or adjoining the property which has been identified as contaminated land because it is in such a condition that harm or pollution of controlled waters might be caused on the property)?
(a) a contaminated land notice
(b) in relation to a register maintained under section 78R of the Environmental Protection Act 1990
  (i) a decision to make an entry
  (ii) an entry
(c) consultation with the owner or occupier of the property conducted under section 78G(3) of the Environmental Protection Act 1990 before the service of a remediation notice

3.13. Radon gas
Do records indicate that the property is in a 'Radon Affected Area' as identified by the Health Protection Agency?

NOTES:
(1) References to the provisions of particular Acts of Parliament or Regulations include any provisions which they have replaced and also include existing or future amendments or re-enactments.
(2) The replies will be given in the belief that they are in accordance with information presently available to the officers of the replying Council, but none of the Councils or their officers accept legal responsibility for an incorrect reply, except for negligence. Any liability for negligence will extend to the person who raised the enquiries and the person on whose behalf they were raised. It will also extend to any other person who has knowledge (personally or through an agent) of the replies before the time when he purchases, takes a tenancy of, or lends money on the security of the property or (if earlier) the time when he becomes contractually bound to do so.

(3) This Form should be read in conjunction with the guidance notes available separately.
(4) Area means any area in which the property is located.
(5) References to the Council include any predecessor Council and also any council committee, sub-committee or other body or person exercising powers delegated by the Council and their approval includes their decision to proceed. The replies given to certain enquiries cover knowledge and actions of both the District Council and County Council.
(6) Where relevant, the source department for copy documents should be provided.

Reproduced for illustrative purposes only by kind permission of Oyez Professional Services Limited

Appendix 6: Completed Example Form CON 290 – Optional Enquiries of Local Authority

CON 290 Optional enquiries of local authority (2007)

A duplicate plan is required for all searches submitted directly to a local authority.
If submitted manually, this form must be submitted in duplicate. Please type or use BLOCK LETTERS

The Law Society

A.

Local authority name and address	Search No:...............................
EDENSHIRE COUNTY COUNCIL	Signed:.................................
HIGH STREET	On behalf of:
BLOSSOMTON	Local authority/private search company/ member of the public
EDENSHIRE ED4 9IJ	(indicate as applicable)
	Dated:.................................

B.

Address of the land/property

UPRN(s): **14 PLEVNA PLACE**

Secondary name/number:

Primary name/number:

Street:

Locality/village: **BLOSSOMTON**

Town: **EDENSHIRE**

Postcode: **ED2 8JD**

C.

Optional enquiries (please tick as required)

- [ ] 4. Road proposals by private bodies
- [ ] 5. Public paths or byways
- [x] 6. Advertisements
- [ ] 7. Completion notices
- [ ] 8. Parks and countryside
- [ ] 9. Pipelines
- [ ] 10. Houses in multiple occupation
- [ ] 11. Noise abatement
- [x] 12. Urban development areas
- [ ] 13. Enterprise zones
- [ ] 14. Inner urban improvement areas
- [ ] 15. Simplified planning zones
- [ ] 16. Land maintenance notices
- [ ] 17. Mineral consultation areas
- [ ] 18. Hazardous substance consents
- [ ] 19. Environmental and pollution notices
- [ ] 20. Food safety notices
- [ ] 21. Hedgerow notices
- [ ] 22. Common land, town and village greens

D.

Fees

£ **100** is enclosed/~~is paid by NLIS transfer~~ (delete as applicable)

Signed: *Thomas Bold*

Dated: **12 APRIL 2010**

Reference: **PLEVNA**

Telephone No: **(01234) 567890**

Fax No:

E-mail:

Notes

A. Enter name and address of appropriate Council. If the property is near a local authority boundary, consider raising certain enquiries (e.g. road schemes) with the adjoining Council.

B. Enter address and description of the property. Please give the UPRN(s) (Unique Property Reference Number) where known. **A duplicate plan is required for all searches submitted directly to a local authority.** The search may be returned if land/property cannot easily be identified.

C. Questions 1-3 appear on CON 290 Enquiries of local authority (2007).

D. Details of fees can be obtained from the Council, your chosen NLIS channel or search provider.

E. Enter the name and address/DX address of the person or company lodging or conducting this enquiry.

E.

Reply to

THOMAS BOLD
1 PROSPECT AVENUE
ORCHARD VALE, BLOSSOMTON
EDENSHIRE ED5 7AB

DX address:

Oyez 7 Spa Road, London SE16 3QQ © Law Society 2007 4.2007 F7619

5033384

Conveyancing 290 (Optional Enquiries)

Reproduced for illustrative purposes only by kind permission of Oyez Professional Services Limited

Appendix 6: Completed Example Form CON 29O – Optional Enquiries of Local Authority (continued)

CON 29O Optional enquiries of local authority (2007)

ROAD PROPOSALS BY PRIVATE BODIES

4. What proposals by others, still capable of being implemented, have the Council approved for any of the following, the limits of construction of which are within 200 metres of the property?
   (a) the construction of a new road
   (b) the alteration or improvement of an existing road, involving the construction, whether or not within existing highway limits, of a subway, underpass, flyover, footbridge, elevated road, dual carriageway, the construction of a roundabout (other than a mini roundabout) or the widening of an existing road by the construction of one or more additional traffic lanes

   This enquiry refers to proposals by bodies or companies (such as private developers) other than the Council (and where appropriate the County Council) or the Secretary of State. A mini roundabout is a roundabout having a one-way circulatory carriageway around a flush or slightly raised circular marking less than 4 metres in diameter and with or without flared approaches.

PUBLIC PATHS OR BYWAYS

5.1. Is any footpath, bridleway, restricted byway or byway open to all traffic which abuts on, or crosses the property, shown in a definitive map or revised definitive map prepared under Part IV of the National Parks and Access to the Countryside Act 1949 or Part III of the Wildlife and Countryside Act 1981?
5.2. If so, please mark its approximate route on the attached plan.

ADVERTISEMENTS

Entries in the register
6.1. Please list any entries in the register of applications, directions and decisions relating to consent for the display of advertisements.
6.2. If there are any entries, where can that register be inspected?

Notices, proceedings and orders
6.3. Except as shown in the official certificate of search:
   (a) has any notice been given by the Secretary of State or served in respect of a direction or proposed direction restricting deemed consent for any class of advertisement
   (b) have the Council resolved to serve a notice requiring the display of any advertisement to be discontinued
   (c) if a discontinuance notice has been served, has it been complied with to the satisfaction of the Council
   (d) have the Council resolved to serve any other notice or proceedings relating to a contravention of the control of advertisements
   (e) have the Council resolved to make an order for the special control of advertisements for the area

COMPLETION NOTICES

7. Which of the planning permissions in force have the Council resolved to terminate by means of a completion notice under s.94 of the Town and Country Planning Act 1990?

PARKS AND COUNTRYSIDE

Areas of outstanding natural beauty
8.1. Has any order under s.82 of the Countryside and Rights of Way Act 2000 been made?

National Parks
8.2. Is the property within a National Park designated under s.7. of the National Parks and Access to the Countryside Act 1949?

PIPELINES

9. Has a map been deposited under s.35 of the Pipelines Act 1962, or Schedule 7 of the Gas Act 1986, showing a pipeline laid through, or within 100 feet (30.48 metres) of the property?

HOUSES IN MULTIPLE OCCUPATION

10. Is the property a house in multiple occupation,or is it designated or proposed to be designated for selective licensing of residential accommodation in accordance with the Housing Act 2004?

NOISE ABATEMENT

Noise abatement zone
11.1. Have the Council made, or resolved to make, any noise abatement zone order under s.63 of the Control of Pollution Act 1974 for the area?

Entries in register
11.2. Has any entry been recorded in the noise level register kept pursuant to s.64 of the Control of Pollution Act 1974?
11.3. If there is any entry, how can copies be obtained and where can that register be inspected?

URBAN DEVELOPMENT AREAS

12.1. Is the area an urban development area designated under Part XVI of the Local Government, Planning and Land Act 1980?
12.2. If so, please state the name of the urban development corporation and the address of its principal office.

ENTERPRISE ZONES

13. Is the area an enterprise zone designated under Part XVIII of the Local Government, Planning and Land Act 1980?

INNER URBAN IMPROVEMENT AREAS

14. Have the Council resolved to define the area as an improvement area under s.4 of the Inner Urban Areas Act 1978?

SIMPLIFIED PLANNING ZONES

15.1. Is the area a simplified planning zone adopted or approved pursuant to s.83 of the Town and Country Planning Act 1990?
15.2. Have the Council approved any proposal for designating the area as a simplified planning zone?

LAND MAINTENANCE NOTICES

16. Have the Council authorised the service of a maintenance notice under s.215 of the Town and Country Planning Act 1990?

MINERAL CONSULTATION AREAS

17. Is the area a mineral consultation area notified by the county planning authority under Schedule 1 para 7 of the Town and Country Planning Act 1990?

HAZARDOUS SUBSTANCE CONSENTS

18.1. Please list any entries in the register kept pursuant to s.28 of the Planning (Hazardous Substances) Act 1990.
18.2. If there are any entries:
   (a) how can copies of the entries be obtained
   (b) where can the register be inspected

ENVIRONMENTAL AND POLLUTION NOTICES

19. What outstanding statutory or informal notices have been issued by the Council under the Environmental Protection Act 1990 or the Control of Pollution Act 1974? (This enquiry does not cover notices under Part IIA or Part III of the EPA, to which enquiries 3.12 or 3.7 apply).

FOOD SAFETY NOTICES

20. What outstanding statutory notices or informal notices have been issued by the Council under the Food Safety Act 1990 or the Food Hygiene Regulations 2006?

HEDGEROW NOTICES

21.1. Please list any entries in the record maintained under regulation 10 of the Hedgerows Regulations 1997.
21.2. If there are any entries:
   (a) how can copies of the matters entered be obtained
   (b) where can the record be inspected

COMMON LAND, TOWN AND VILLAGE GREENS

22.1. Is the property, or any land which abuts the property, registered common land or town or village green under the Commons Registration Act 1965 or the Commons Act 2006?
22.2. If there are any entries, how can copies of the matters registered be obtained and where can the register be inspected?

NOTES:
(1) References to the provisions of particular Acts of Parliament or Regulations include any provisions which they have replaced and also include existing or future amendments or re-enactments.
(2) The replies will be given in the belief that they are in accordance with information presently available to the officers of the replying Council, but none of the Councils or their officers accept legal responsibility for an incorrect reply, except for negligence. Any liability for negligence will extend to the person who raised the enquiries and the person on whose behalf they were raised. It will also extend to any other person who has knowledge (personally or through an agent) of the replies before the time when he purchases, takes a tenancy of, or lends money on the security of the property or (if earlier) the time when he becomes contractually bound to do so.
(3) This form should be read in conjunction with the guidance notes available separately.
(4) Area means any area in which the property is located.
(5) References to the Council include any predecessor Council and also any council committee, sub-committee or other body or person exercising powers delegated by the Council and their approval includes their decision to proceed. The replies given to certain enquiries cover knowledge and actions of both the District Council and County Council.
(6) Where relevant, the source department for copy documents should be provided.

Reproduced for illustrative purposes only by kind permission of Oyez Professional Services Limited

Appendix 7: Form TA13 –
Completion Information and Requisitions on Title *

Completion information and requisitions on title

WARNING: Replies to Requisitions 4.2 and 6.2 are treated as a solicitor's undertaking.

Address of the property

Postcode ☐☐☐☐☐☐☐

Seller

Buyer

This form should be completed and read in conjunction with the explanatory notes available separately

1 Property information

Is the seller aware of any change in the written information given by and on behalf of the seller prior to exchange of contracts or have you become aware of any changes? (This includes any information in the TransAction forms, the Home Information Pack, replies to other pre-contract enquiries, correspondence between us and, if appropriate, replies to any requisitions on title already raised).

☐ Yes ☐ No ☐ Enclosed
☐ Given below

If Yes, please give details:

The Law Society

1 of 6

www.hips.lawsociety.org.uk

TA13

© Law Society 2007

© The Law Society

*This example is blank intentionally; see chapter for 12 guidance.

Appendix 7: Form TA13 –
Completion Information and Requisitions on Title (continued)

2 Vacant possession

2.1 If vacant possession (of whole or part) is to be given on completion:

(a) What arrangements will be made to hand over the keys?

☐ will be left with agents

☐ will be left with seller's solicitors

☐ other (please give details)

(b) By what time will the seller have vacated the property on the completion date?

☐ already vacant

☐ by time in contract

☐ other (please give details)

2.2 If vacant possession (of whole or part) is not being given, please confirm that an authority to the tenant to pay the rent to the buyer will be handed over or be included with the documents to be remitted to the buyer's solicitors on completion.

☐ Confirmed

3 Deeds and documents

3.1 If the title is unregistered, do you hold all of the title deeds?

☐ Yes ☐ No

If No, please give details:

3.2 Please supply a list of the deeds and documents to be handed over or remitted to the buyer's solicitors on completion.

☐ Enclosed

© The Law Society

Appendix 7: Form TA13 –
Completion Information and Requisitions on Title (continued)

4 Completion

4.1 Will completion take place at your office? ☐ Yes ☐ No

If No, where or how will it take place?

WARNING: A reply to requisition 4.2 is treated as an undertaking. Great care must be taken when answering this requisition.

4.2 If we wish to complete through the post, please confirm that:

(a) You undertake to adopt the Law Society's Code for Completion by Post; and ☐ Confirmed

(b) The mortgages and charges listed in reply to 6.1 are those specified for the purpose of paragraph 3 of the Code. ☐ Confirmed

5 Money

5.1 Please state the exact amount payable on completion. £

If it is not just the balance purchase money, please provide copy receipts for any rent or service charge or other payments being apportioned. ☐ Enclosed ☐ Not applicable

5.2 Please provide details of your bank and the account to which completion monies are to be sent:

Name of bank

Address of bank

Branch sort code
☐☐ ☐☐ ☐☐

Client account name

Client account number

© The Law Society

Appendix 7: Form TA13 –
Completion Information and Requisitions on Title (continued)

6 Mortgages and charges

6.1 Please list the mortgages or charges secured on the
property which you undertake to redeem or discharge
to the extent that they relate to the property on or before
completion (this includes repayment of any discount
under the Housing Acts).

**WARNING: A reply to requisition 6.2 is treated as an undertaking. Great care must be taken
when answering this requisition.**

6.2 Do you undertake to redeem or discharge the
mortgages and charges listed in reply to 6.1 on
completion and to send to us Form DS1, DS3,
the receipted charge(s) or confirmation that notice
of release or discharge in electronic form has
been given to the Land Registry as soon as you
receive them?

☐ Yes ☐ No

6.3 If you agree to adopt the current Law Society's Code
for Completion by Post, please confirm that you are
the duly authorised agent of the proprietor of every
mortgage or charge on the property which you have
undertaken, in reply to 6.2, to redeem or discharge.

☐ Confirmed

7 Additional requisitions

Additional requisitions not raised prior to exchange
are attached:

☐ Yes ☐ No

**WARNING: These replies should be signed only by a person with authority to give
undertakings on behalf of the firm.**

Buyer's solicitor

Date ☐ D / M M / Y Y

Seller's solicitor

Date ☐ D / M M / Y Y

TA13 *Completion information and requisitions on title*   www.hips.lawsociety.org.uk

© The Law Society

Appendix 7: Form TA13 –
Completion Information and Requisitions on Title (continued)

Additional requisitions not raised prior to exchange

Completion information and requisitions on title **TA13**

© The Law Society

Appendix 7: Completed Example Form TA13 – Completion Information and Requisitions on Title (continued)

The Law Society

This form is part of the Law Society's TransAction scheme.
The Law Society is the representative body for solicitors in England and Wales.

© Law Society 2007

Appendix 8: Completed Example Form TR1 – Transfer of Whole of Registered Title(s)

Land Registry
Transfer of whole of registered title(s)

If you need more room than is provided for in a panel, and your software allows, you can expand any panel in the form. Alternatively use continuation sheet CS and attach it to this form.

Leave blank if not yet registered.	1 Title number(s) of the property: **EDN999707**
Insert address including postcode (if any) or other description of the property, for example 'land adjoining 2 Acacia Avenue'.	2 Property: **14 Plevna Place** **Blossomton, Edenshire ED2 8JD**
	3 Date: **20th July 2010**
Give full name(s).	4 Transferor: **Clive Smart and Constance Smart**
Complete as appropriate where the transferor is a company.	For UK incorporated companies/LLPs Registered number of company or limited liability partnership including any prefix: For overseas companies (a) Territory of incorporation: (b) Registered number in the United Kingdom including any prefix:
Give full name(s).	5 Transferee for entry in the register: **Thomas Bold and Prudence Bold**
Complete as appropriate where the transferee is a company. Also, for an overseas company, unless an arrangement with Land Registry exists, lodge either a certificate in Form 7 in Schedule 3 to the Land Registration Rules 2003 or a certified copy of the constitution in English or Welsh, or other evidence permitted by rule 183 of the Land Registration Rules 2003.	For UK incorporated companies/LLPs Registered number of company or limited liability partnership including any prefix: For overseas companies (a) Territory of incorporation: (b) Registered number in the United Kingdom including any prefix:
Each transferee may give up to three addresses for service, one of which must be a postal address whether or not in the UK (including the postcode, if any). The others can be any combination of a postal address, a UK DX box number or an electronic address.	6 Transferee's intended address(es) for service for entry in the register: **14 Plevna Place, Blossomton, Edenshire ED2 8JD**
	7 The transferor transfers the property to the transferee

Appendix 8: Completed Example Form TR1 – Transfer of Whole of Registered Title(s) (continued)

Place 'X' in the appropriate box. State the currency unit if other than sterling. If none of the boxes apply, insert an appropriate memorandum in panel 11.

8 Consideration

  X The transferor has received from the transferee for the property the following sum (in words and figures):

  Two Hundred and Seventy Five Thousand Pounds (£275,000)

  ☐ The transfer is not for money or anything that has a monetary value

  ☐ Insert other receipt as appropriate:

Place 'X' in any box that applies.

Add any modifications.

9 The transferor transfers with

  X full title guarantee

  ☐ limited title guarantee

Where the transferee is more than one person, place 'X' in the appropriate box.

10 Declaration of trust. The transferee is more than one person and

  ☐ they are to hold the property on trust for themselves as joint tenants

  X they are to hold the property on trust for themselves as tenants in common in equal shares

Complete as necessary.

  ☐ they are to hold the property on trust:

Insert here any required or permitted statement, certificate or application and any agreed covenants, declarations and so on.

11 Additional provisions

Appendix 8: Completed Example Form TR1 – Transfer of Whole of Registered Title(s) (continued)

The transferor must execute this transfer as a deed using the space opposite. If there is more than one transferor, all must execute. Forms of execution are given in Schedule 9 to the Land Registration Rules 2003. If the transfer contains transferee's covenants or declarations or contains an application by the transferee (such as for a restriction), it must also be executed by the transferee.

12 Execution

Signed and Delivered
as a Deed by   **Clive Smart**   *Clive Smart*

In the presence of
Signature of Witness   *George Ross*
Name of Witness   **George Ross**
Address of Witness   **6 The Willows**
                                Blossomton
                                Edenshire EH78 1ZA
Occupation   **Teacher**

                                Constance Smart
Signed and Delivered
as a Deed by   **Constance Smart**

In the presence of

Signature of Witness   *George Ross*
Name of Witness   **George Ross**
Address of Witness   **6 The Willows**
                                Blossomton
                                Edenshire EH78 1ZA

Occupation   **Teacher**

WARNING
If you dishonestly enter information or make a statement that you know is, or might be, untrue or misleading, and intend by doing so to make a gain for yourself or another person, or to cause loss or the risk of loss to another person, you may commit the offence of fraud under section 1 of the Fraud Act 2006, the maximum penalty for which is 10 years' imprisonment or an unlimited fine, or both.

Failure to complete this form with proper care may result in a loss of protection under the Land Registration Act 2002 if, as a result, a mistake is made in the register.

Under section 66 of the Land Registration Act 2002 most documents (including this form) kept by the registrar relating to an application to the registrar or referred to in the register are open to public inspection and copying. If you believe a document contains prejudicial information, you may apply for that part of the document to be made exempt using Form EX1, under rule 136 of the Land Registration Rules 2003.

© Crown copyright (ref: LR/HO) 07/09

Appendix 9: Completed Example Form AP1 – Application to Change the Register

Land Registry
Application to change the register

AP1

If you need more room than is provided for in a panel, and your software allows, you can expand any panel in the form. Alternatively use continuation sheet CS and attach it to this form.

Land Registry is unable to give legal advice but our website www1.landregistry.gov.uk provides guidance on Land Registry applications. This includes public guides and practice guides (aimed at conveyancers) that can also be obtained from any Land Registry office.

See www1.landregistry.gov.uk/regional if you are unsure which Land Registry office to send this application to.

'Conveyancer' is a term used in this form. It is defined in rule 217(1) of the Land Registration Rules 2003 and includes, among others, solicitor, licensed conveyancer and fellow of the Institute of Legal Executives.

LAND REGISTRY USE ONLY
Record of fees paid
Particulars of under/over payments
Reference number
Fees debited £

Where there is more than one local authority serving an area, enter the one to which council tax or business rates are normally paid.

1   Local authority serving the property:
Edenshire District Council
Full postcode of property (if any): **ED2 8JD**

Enter the title number of each title that requires an entry to be made in that register.

2   Title number(s) of the property:
EDN999707

Place 'X' in the appropriate box.

Give a brief description of the part affected, for example 'edged red on the plan to the transfer dated ....'.

3   The application affects

   X   the whole of the title(s)

   ☐   part of the title(s) as shown:

See fees calculator at www1.landregistry.gov.uk/fees

4   Application, priority and fees

Applications in priority order	Price paid/Value (£)	Fees paid (£)
Transfer	275,000	280
Total fees (£)		280

Fee payment method

Place 'X' in the appropriate box.

X   cheque made payable to 'Land Registry'

The fee will be charged to the account specified in panel 7.

☐   direct debit, under an agreement with Land Registry

Appendix 9: Completed Example Form AP1 – Application to Change the Register (continued)

List the documents lodged with this form. Copy documents should be listed separately. If you supply a certified copy of an original document we will return the original; if a certified copy is not supplied, we may retain the original document and it may be destroyed.

5 Documents lodged with this form:

Form TR1

Form ID1 for Thomas Bold
Form ID1 for Prudence Bold

Land Transaction Return Certificate

Provide the full name(s) of the person(s) applying to change the register. Where a conveyancer lodges the application, this must be the name(s) of the client(s), not the conveyancer.

6 The applicant:

Thomas Bold and Prudence Bold

Complete as appropriate where the applicant is a company. Also, for an overseas company, unless an arrangement with Land Registry exists, lodge either a certificate in Form 7 in Schedule 3 to the Land Registration Rules 2003 or a certified copy of the constitution in English or Welsh, or other evidence permitted by rule 183 of the Land Registration Rules 2003.

For UK incorporated companies/LLPs
Registered number of company or limited liability partnership including any prefix:

For overseas companies
(a) Territory of incorporation:

(b) Registered number in the United Kingdom including any prefix:

7 This application is sent to Land Registry by

If you are paying by direct debit, this will be the account charged.

Key number (if applicable):

Name: **Thomas Bold and Prudence Bold**
Address or UK DX box number:

This is the address to which we will normally send requisitions and return documents. However if you insert an email address, we will use this whenever possible.

14 Plevna Place
Blossomton
Edenshire
ED2 8JD

Email address: **tb@email.uk**
Reference:

Phone no: **01234 74577**	Fax no:

Complete this panel if you want us to notify someone else that we have completed this application.

8 Third party notification
Name:
Address or UK DX box number:

Email address:
Reference:

9 The address(es) for service for each proprietor of the registered estate(s) to be entered in the register is

Place 'X' in the appropriate box.

In this and panel 10, each proprietor may give up to three addresses for service, one of which must be a postal address whether or not in the UK (including the postcode, if any). The others can be any combination of a postal address, a UK DX box number or an electronic address.

X the address of the property (where this is a single postal address)

☐ the address(es) for service from the transfer/assent

☐ (for existing proprietors who are remaining in the register) the current address(es) for service in the register

☐ the following address(es):

Appendix 9: Completed Example Form AP1 – Application to Change the Register (continued)

Where a charge has an MD reference we will ignore an address given in this panel unless the charge is in favour of a United Kingdom bank and neither the charge form nor any agreement we have with the lender specifies an address for service.

For permitted addresses see note to panel 9.

Complete as appropriate where the lender is a company. Also, for an overseas company, unless an arrangement with Land Registry exists, lodge either a certificate in Form 7 in Schedule 3 to the Land Registration Rules 2003 or a certified copy of the constitution in English or Welsh, or other evidence permitted by rule 183 of the Land Registration Rules 2003.

10 Name and address(es) for service of the proprietor of any new charge to be entered in the register:

For UK incorporated companies/LLPs
Registered number of company or limited liability partnership including any prefix:

For overseas companies
(a) Territory of incorporation:

(b) Registered number in the United Kingdom including any prefix:

If this statement applies (i) place 'X' in the box and (ii) enclose Form DI.

Section 27 of the Land Registration Act 2002 lists the registrable dispositions.

Rule 57 of the Land Registration Rules 2003 sets out the disclosable overriding interests that you must tell us about.

11 Disclosable overriding interests

☐ This application relates to a registrable disposition and disclosable overriding interests affect the registered estate.

12 Confirmation of identity

When registering transfers, charges, leases and other dispositions of land, or giving effect to a discharge or release of a registered charge, Land Registry relies on the steps that conveyancers take, where appropriate, to verify the identity of their clients. These checks reduce the risk of property fraud.

Full details of the evidence of identity that is required can be found in Practice Guide 67 and in Public Guide 20.

Where a person was not represented by a conveyancer, Land Registry requires 'evidence of identity' in respect of that person, except where the first alternative in panel 13(2) applies.

'Evidence of identity' is evidence provided in accordance with any current direction made by the Chief Land Registrar under section 100(4) of the Land Registration Act 2002 for the purpose of confirming a person's identity.

If this application is to register a transfer, lease or charge, or to give effect to a discharge in Form DS1 or a release in Form DS3 complete one of the following

Place 'X' in the appropriate box.

Conveyancer is defined in rule 217(1) of the Land Registration Rules 2003 and includes, among others, solicitor, licensed conveyancer and fellow of the Institute of Legal Executives.

☐ I am a conveyancer, and I have completed panel 13

X I am not a conveyancer, and I have completed panel 14

Appendix 9: Completed Example Form AP1 – Application to Change the Register (continued)

13 Where the application is sent to Land Registry by a conveyancer

(1) Details of conveyancer acting

If you are sending an application to register a transfer, lease or charge, for each party to each disposition that is to be registered state in the table below the details of the conveyancer (if any) who represented them.

Where a party is not represented by a conveyancer you must also complete (2) below.

Place 'X' in the box in the second column if the person or firm who is sending the application to Land Registry represented that party in the transaction. Otherwise complete the details in the third column. If the party is not represented insert 'none' in the third column.

Name of transferor, landlord, transferee, tenant, borrower or lender	Conveyancer's name, address and reference
	☐ Reference:
	☐ Reference:
	☐ Reference:

If you are sending an application to give effect to a discharge in Form DS1 or release in Form DS3 for each lender, state in the table below the details of the conveyancer (if any) who represented them.

Where a lender is not represented by a conveyancer you must also complete (2) below.

Place 'X' in the box in the second column if the person or firm who is sending the application to Land Registry represented that party in the transaction. Otherwise complete the details in the third column. If the party is not represented insert 'none' in the third column.

Name of lender	Conveyancer's name, address and reference
	☐ Reference:
	☐ Reference:

Appendix 9: Completed Example Form AP1 – Application to Change the Register (continued)

(2) Evidence of identity

Where any transferor, landlord, transferee, tenant, borrower or lender listed in (1) was not represented by a conveyancer

Place 'X' in the appropriate box(es).

Insert the name of each unrepresented transferor, landlord, transferee, tenant, borrower or lender for whom you give this confirmation.

☐ I confirm that I am satisfied that sufficient steps have been taken to verify the identity of

_____

_____

and that they are the registered proprietor or have the right to be registered as the registered proprietor

Evidence of identity is defined in panel 12. Full details of the evidence of identity that is required can be found in Practice Guide 67.

☐ I enclose evidence of identity in respect of each unrepresented transferor, landlord, transferee, tenant, borrower or lender for whom I have not provided the confirmation above

14 Where the application is sent to Land Registry by someone who is not a conveyancer

(1) Details of conveyancer acting

If you are sending an application to register a transfer, lease or charge (ie a mortgage), for each party to each disposition that is to be registered, state in the table below the details of the conveyancer (if any) who represented them.

You must also complete (2) below.

If the party is not represented insert 'none' in the second column.

Name of transferor, landlord, transferee, tenant, borrower or lender	Conveyancer's name, address and reference
Clive Smart and Constance Smart (Transferor)	**Stephen Skinner Skinner & Co 1 Blossomton Road Blossomton BL1 1NN** Reference: **SS.Smart.1**
Thomas Bold and Prudence Bold (Transferees)	**None** Reference:
	None Reference:

Appendix 9: Completed Example Form AP1 – Application to Change the Register (continued)

If you are sending an application to give effect to a discharge in Form DS1 or release in Form DS3, for each lender state in the table below the details of the conveyancer (if any) who represented them.

You must also complete (2) below.

If the party is not represented insert 'none' in the second column.

Name of lender	Conveyancer's name, address and reference
	Reference:
	Reference:

(2) Evidence of identity

Place 'X' in the appropriate box(es).

Evidence of identity is defined in panel 12. Full details of the evidence of identity that is required can be found in Public Guide 20.

[] for each applicant named in panel 6 is enclosed

X for each unrepresented transferor, landlord, transferee, tenant, borrower or lender listed in (1) is enclosed

If a conveyancer is acting for the applicant, that conveyancer must sign.

15

Signature of conveyancer: _____

Date:

OR

If no conveyancer is acting, the applicant (and if the applicant is more than one person then each of them) must sign.

Signature of applicant: *Thomas Bold*

Date: **22 July 2010**   *PRUDENCE BOLD*

WARNING
If you dishonestly enter information or make a statement that you know is, or might be, untrue or misleading, and intend by doing so to make a gain for yourself or another person, or to cause loss or the risk of loss to another person, you may commit the offence of fraud under section 1 of the Fraud Act 2006, the maximum penalty for which is 10 years' imprisonment or an unlimited fine, or both.

Failure to complete this form with proper care may result in a loss of protection under the Land Registration Act 2002 if, as a result, a mistake is made in the register.

Under section 66 of the Land Registration Act 2002 most documents (including this form) kept by the registrar relating to an application to the registrar or referred to in the register are open to public inspection and copying. If you believe a document contains prejudicial information, you may apply for that part of the document to be made exempt using Form EX1, under rule 136 of the Land Registration Rules 2003.

© Crown copyright (ref: LR/HO) 07/09

Appendix 10: Completed Example Form ID1 – Certificate of Identity for a Private Individual

Land Registry
Certificate of identity for a
private individual

ID1

WARNING

If you dishonestly enter information or make a statement that you know is, or might be, untrue or misleading, and intend by doing so to make a gain for yourself or another person, or to cause loss or the risk of loss to another person, you may commit the offence of fraud under section 1 of the Fraud Act 2006, the maximum penalty for which is 10 years' imprisonment or an unlimited fine, or both.

Who needs to complete this form?

- Any person who is not a conveyancer, or who is not a UK bank or building society, who is lodging one of the following applications with Land Registry.
  - Transfers (whether or not for value).
  - Transfers and deeds relating to the appointment or retirement of trustees.
  - Leases (whether or not for value) that are being registered.
  - Charges (mortgages) that are being registered.
  - Discharge of a charge in form DS1.
  - Release of a charge in form DS3.
  - Surrenders of leases.
  - Most voluntary and compulsory applications for first registration where the title deeds have been lost or destroyed.
  - All other applications for compulsory first registration completed on and after 10 November 2008.
- Any person who is a party to one of the above transactions who is not represented by a conveyancer where the application is being lodged by someone who is also not a conveyancer.
- Any person who is a party to one of the above transactions who is not represented by a conveyancer, and although the application is being lodged by a conveyancer, that conveyancer is not able to confirm that they are satisfied that sufficient steps have been taken to verify the person's identity.

Please note that where the application is being lodged by more than one person, or a party to a transaction comprises more than one person, each one must complete a separate form and produce evidence of their identity.

This form can also be used to provide evidence of identity for:

- a person who has changed their name and the change is confirmed by deed poll, statutory declaration or statement of truth.
- an attorney in the circumstances described in Land Registry's Practice Guide 67 and Public Guide 20 (see below).

NOTE: This form does not have to be completed for voluntary first registrations unless the title deeds are lost or have been destroyed, or for charges or leases which are merely being noted. This form is also not required where the true value of the land to which the transaction relates is not more than £5,000, or if Land Registry has issued a facility letter in respect of an individual's identity.

For exceptions to our requirement for evidence of identity for first registrations where the deeds have been lost or destroyed, please see Practice Guide 2 – *First registration of title where deeds have been lost or destroyed.*

Why do I have to complete this form?

Appendix 10: Completed Example Form ID1 – Certificate of Identity for a Private Individual (continued)

We are asking for this information to guard against registration fraud. It is important that where an applicant, or parties to a transaction are not represented by a conveyancer or where title deeds have been lost or destroyed, that evidence of identity is produced to enable registration to proceed.

How do I complete this form?

You must complete section A. You must then get your identity verified by a conveyancer or by personally attending one of our customer information centres. You will need to take evidence of your identity with you including a recent passport-size photograph in which your face is clearly visible. Please see sections B3 and B4 for the types of evidence which will be needed.

The conveyancer or a member of Land Registry will complete section B of this form. Please note that a conveyancer may charge a fee to verify your identity.

Both section A and section B of this form lodged in support of an application must be completed, dated and signed no more than three months before the time of lodgement. Information about completing this form can be found in:

- Public Guide 20 – Evidence of identity – non-conveyancers, if you are not a conveyancer, or

- Practice Guide 67 – Evidence of identity – conveyancers, if you are a conveyancer.

Both guides and all our forms are available on our website www.landregistry.gov.uk and from any Land Registry office, free of charge.

We strongly advise that you use these guides. In addition to providing information about this form they also explain who is a conveyancer and how you should complete certain panels of the application form(s) you will also have to lodge.

Please note that if your application is not in order, including if the wrong forms are used, the application might not be accepted for registration.

What should I do if I want Land Registry to verify my identity?

If you plan to visit a Land Registry customer information centre, we strongly advise that you telephone first to check that the evidence you intend to produce is sufficient and to make an appointment.

Our customer information centres are open between 8.30am and 6pm on Mondays to Fridays. You must always make an appointment to ensure that the matter is dealt with promptly, giving us at least 24 hours' notice. To make an appointment telephone Customer Support on 0844 892 1111 or complete the form on our website www.landregistry.gov.uk.

Please note that we will not verify your identity in advance of you making your application and if we are unable to confirm your identity your application will be rejected. Please note also, that all individuals for whom verification of identity is required must attend at the same time.

If you can't go to a conveyancer and are not able to attend one of our customer information centres to have your identity verified, you should contact Customer Support to discuss whether alternative arrangements are possible. You can contact Customer Support at customersupport@landregistry.gsi.gov.uk or by telephoning 0844 892 1111 from Monday to Friday between 8am and 6pm.

Is this form open to public inspection?

No. This form, and any supporting evidence produced to Land Registry where we are verifying your identity, is automatically excepted under rule 133 of the Land Registration Rules 2003 (as amended) from the public right of inspection

Data Protection: Please note though that Land Registry may share data provided in or in connection with this application form for anti-fraud purposes and may carry out checks concerning the information provided.

Appendix 10: Completed Example Form ID1 – Certificate of Identity for a Private Individual (continued)

Section A

A separate form must be completed by each individual person for whom evidence of identity is required.

1. Title (e.g. Mr, Mrs, Miss, Dr., etc.,)   Mr
2. First name(s) *(Provide full name(s))*   Thomas
3. Surname   Bold
4. Date of birth   14.01.1960
5. Current address   1 Prospect Avenue, Orchard Vale, Edenshire ED5 7AB
6. How long have you lived at this address?   15 years
7. List any other address you have lived at within the last five years
8. Home telephone number   01234 678 901
9. Work telephone number *(if any)*   01234 596 909
10. Mobile telephone number *(if any)*   07715 321 456
Details of the application
11. Type of application *(e.g. transfer, mortgage, discharge etc)*   Transfer
12. Title number(s) *(if known/applicable)*   EDN999707
13. Address of property *(including postcode, if any)*   14 Plevna Place, Blossomton, Edenshire ED2 8JD
14. Certificate   I certify that the information that I have provided in this form is correct to the best of my knowledge and belief. I authorise the Land Registry to make such additional searches and checks as necessary to confirm my identity.   Signed _____ *Thomas Bold* _____ Date 22 July 2010   *Please note that your identity must be verified by a conveyancer or by a member of Land Registry who must complete section B of this form.*

Appendix 10: Completed Example Form ID1 – Certificate of Identity for a Private Individual (continued)

Section B (for completion by a conveyancer or Land Registry)
Complete all parts of this section.

1.
Place 'X' in the appropriate box.

☐ I have known the person named in section A for at least two years

☐ I have **not** known the person named in section A for at least two years

2.

Certificate

I *(name of certifier or member of Land Registry)* _____

of *(name of firm or Land Registry office certifying identity)* _____

Status

☐ solicitor   ☐ licensed conveyancer   ☐ legal executive   ☐ notary public

☐ barrister   ☐ registered European lawyer   ☐ Land Registry member

I certify that *(name of individual whose identity is being verified)* _____

has produced to me the original(s) of the evidence of identity indicated in panel 3 below and which I have inspected. I confirm that the photograph attached in panel 4, and which I have signed, is a true likeness of the person who has provided this evidence.

Signature of solicitor, licensed conveyancer, legal executive, notary public, barrister, registered European lawyer or Land Registry member

_____

Date_____

Note: Land Registry may contact conveyancers to check that a form completed in their name is genuine. Conveyancers are advised to keep a record of persons for whom they have verified identity.

Appendix 10: Completed Example Form ID1 – Certificate of Identity for a Private Individual (continued)

3. Evidence of identity inspected (enter a cross against the item(s) checked)
You must inspect either:

One of the following **(List A):**

☐ Current valid full passport - State the country of issue and number of the passport:

_____

☐ Current United Kingdom, EU, Isle of Man, Channel Islands photocard driving licence (not a provisional licence) – State the number of the licence _____

☐ Current identity card issued by the UK Identity and Passport Service to a non-UK national resident in the UK – State the number of the card _____

OR

Two of the following **(List B)** but no more than one of each type:

☐ Cheque guarantee card or credit card bearing the Mastercard or Visa logo, an American Express or Diners Club card, or a debit or multi-function card bearing the Maestro or Delta logo which was issued in the United Kingdom and is supported by an original account statement less than three months old*

☐ Utility bill less than three months old*

☐ Council tax bill for the current year

☐ Council rent book showing the rent paid for the last three months

☐ Mortgage statement for the mortgage accounting year just ended*

☐ Current firearm or shotgun certificate

* These must be postal statements; they must not be statements sent electronically.

4. Photograph of person named in section A

Staple or loosely attach the recent passport-size photograph here

Please sign your name on the back of the photograph and add the date.

Please staple or otherwise loosely attach the photograph to the form. Please do not glue the photograph to the form.

© Crown copyright (ref: LR/HO) 09/10

Appendix 11: Completed Example Form FR1 – First Registration Application

Land Registry
Application for first registration

FR1

You must lodge the documents of title with this application; these must be listed on Form DL.

If you need more room than is provided for in a panel, and your software allows, you can expand any panel in the form. Alternatively use continuation sheet CS and attach it to this form.

Land Registry is unable to give legal advice but our website www1.landregistry.gov.uk provides guidance on Land Registry applications. This includes public guides and practice guides (aimed at conveyancers) that can also be obtained from any Land Registry office.

See www1.landregistry.gov.uk/regional if you are unsure which Land Registry office to send this application to.

'Conveyancer' is a term used in this form. It is defined in rule 217(1) of the Land Registration Rules 2003 and includes, among others, solicitor, licensed conveyancer and fellow of the Institute of Legal Executives.

LAND REGISTRY USE ONLY
Record of fees paid
Particulars of under/over payments
Reference number
Fees debited £

Where there is more than one local authority serving an area, enter the one to which council tax or business rates are normally paid.

1   Local authority serving the property:

Edenshire District Council

Insert address including postcode (if any) or other description of the property, for example 'land adjoining 2 Acacia Avenue'.

On registering a rentcharge, profit a prendre in gross or franchise, insert a description, for example 'Rentcharge (or as appropriate) over 2 Acacia Avenue'.

2   Property:

14 Plevna Place
Blossomton
Edenshire
ED2 8JD

Place 'X' in the appropriate box. Only use the third option where the property has an address and is fenced on the ground.

Enter reference, for example 'edged red'.

Enter nature and date of document.

3   The extent of the land to be registered can be clearly identified on the current edition of the Ordnance Survey map from

   X   the attached plan and shown: **edged in red**

   ☐   the plan attached to the:

   ☐   the address shown in panel 2

Place 'X' in the appropriate box.

4   The class of title applied for is

   ☐ absolute leasehold
   X absolute freehold   ☐ good leasehold
   ☐ possessory freehold   ☐ possessory leasehold

5   Application, priority and fees

See fees calculator at www1.landregistry.gov.uk/fees

Applications in priority order	Price paid/Value (£)	Fees paid (£)
First registration of the freehold/leasehold estate	£275,000	280
Total fees (£)		280

Fee payment method

Place 'X' in the appropriate box.

The fee will be charged to the account specified in panel 7.

   X   cheque made payable to 'Land Registry'

   ☐   direct debit, under an agreement with Land Registry

Appendix 11: Completed Example Form FR1 – First Registration Application (continued)

Provide the full name(s) of the person(s) applying for first registration. Where a conveyancer lodges the application, this must be the name(s) of the client(s), not the conveyancer.	6	The applicant: **Thomas Bold and Prudence Bold**
Complete as appropriate where the applicant is a company. Also, for an overseas company, unless an arrangement with Land Registry exists, lodge either a certificate in Form 7 in Schedule 3 to the Land Registration Rules 2003 or a certified copy of the constitution in English or Welsh, or other evidence permitted by rule 183 of the Land Registration Rules 2003.		<u>For UK incorporated companies/LLPs</u> Registered number of company or limited liability partnership including any prefix: <u>For overseas companies</u> (a) Territory of incorporation: (b) Registered number in the United Kingdom including any prefix:

If you are paying by direct debit, this will be the account charged.	7	This application is sent to Land Registry by Key number (if applicable):
This is the address to which we will normally send requisitions and return documents. However if you insert an email address, we will use this whenever possible.		Name: **Thomas Bold** Address or UK DX box number: **14 Plevna Place** **Blossomton** **Edenshire** **ED2 8JD** Email address: **tb@email.uk** Reference:
		Phone no: **01234 74747** · Fax no:

Place 'X' in the appropriate box.	8	The address(es) for service for each proprietor of the estate to be entered in the register is
In this and panel 10, each proprietor may give up to three addresses for service, one of which must be a postal address whether or not in the UK (including the postcode, if any). The others can be any combination of a postal address, a UK DX box number or an electronic address.		**X** the address of the property (where this is a single postal address) ☐ the following address(es):
Where the applicant is more than one person, place 'X' in the appropriate box.	9	Where the applicant is more than one person
		☐ they hold the property on trust for themselves as joint tenants
		X they hold the property on trust for themselves as tenants in common in equal shares
Complete as necessary.		☐ they hold the property on trust:

Where a charge has an MD reference we will ignore an address given in this panel unless the charge is in favour of a United Kingdom bank and neither the charge form nor any agreement we have with the lender specifies an address for service.	10	Name and address(es) for service for the proprietor of any charge to be entered in the register:
For permitted addresses see note to panel 8.		
Complete as appropriate where the proprietor of the charge is a company. Also, for an overseas company, unless an arrangement with Land Registry exists, lodge either a certificate in Form 7 in Schedule 3 to the Land Registration Rules 2003 or a certified copy of the constitution in English or Welsh, or other evidence permitted by rule 183 of the Land Registration Rules 2003.		<u>For UK incorporated companies/LLPs</u> Registered number of company or limited liability partnership including any prefix: <u>For overseas companies</u> (a) Territory of incorporation: (b) Registered number in the United Kingdom including any prefix:

Appendix 11: Completed Example Form FR1 – First Registration Application (continued)

11 Disclosable overriding interests

If this statement applies (i) place 'X' in the box and (ii) enclose Form DI.

☐ Disclosable overriding interests affect the estate.

Rule 28 of the Land Registration Rules 2003 sets out the disclosable overriding interests that you must tell us about.

12 Certificate

The title is based on the title documents listed in Form DL which are all those under the control of the applicant.

Details of rights, interests and claims affecting the estate (other than non-disclosable interests falling within rule 28(2) of the Land Registration Rules 2003) known to the applicant are, where applicable, disclosed in the title documents and Form DI if accompanying this application.

Place 'X' in the appropriate box.

X The applicant knows of no other such rights, interests and claims. Only the applicant is in actual possession of the property or in receipt of the rent and profits from the property.

If applicable complete the second statement with details of the interest(s); for interests disclosed only by searches do not include those shown on local land charge searches. Certify any interests disclosed by searches that do not affect the estate being registered.

☐ The applicant knows only of the following additional such rights, interests and claims, including those of any person (other than the applicant) in actual possession of the property or in receipt of the rent and profits from the property:

If you do not place 'X' in the box we will assume that you have examined the applicant's title or are satisfied that it has been examined in the usual way.

13 Examination of title

☐ I/we have not fully examined the applicant's title to the estate, including any appurtenant rights, or satisfied myself/ourselves that it has been fully examined by a conveyancer in the usual way prior to this application.

Appendix 11: Completed Example Form FR1 – First Registration Application (continued)

14 Confirmation of identity

When registering transfers, charges, leases and other dispositions of land, Land Registry relies on the steps that conveyancers take, where appropriate, to verify the identity of their clients. These checks reduce the risk of property fraud.

Full details of the evidence of identity that is required can be found in Practice Guide 67 and in Public Guide 20.

Where a person was not represented by a conveyancer, Land Registry requires 'evidence of identity' in respect of that person, except where the first alternative in panel 15(2) applies.

'Evidence of identity' is evidence provided in accordance with any current direction made by the Chief Land Registrar under section 100(4) of the Land Registration Act 2002 for the purpose of confirming a person's identity.

The requirement of registration is contained in section 4, Land Registration Act 2002. Further guidance is contained in Practice Guide 1.

If this application is to register a transfer, lease or charge, dated on or after 10 November 2008 **and** the requirement of registration applies, complete one of the following

Place 'X' in the appropriate box.

☐ I am a conveyancer, and I have completed panel 15

Conveyancer is defined in rule 217(1) of the Land Registration Rules 2003 and includes, among others, solicitor, licensed conveyancer and fellow of the Institute of Legal Executives.

X I am not a conveyancer, and I have completed panel 16

15 Where the application is sent to Land Registry by a conveyancer

(1) Details of conveyancer acting

If you are sending an application to register a transfer, lease or charge, for each party to each disposition that is to be registered, state in the table below the details of the conveyancer (if any) who represented them.

Where a party is not represented by a conveyancer you must also complete (2) below.

Place 'X' in the box in the second column if the person or firm who is sending the application to Land Registry represented that party in the transaction. Otherwise complete the details in the third column. If the party is not represented insert 'none' in the third column.

Name of transferor, landlord, transferee, tenant, borrower or lender		Conveyancer's name, address and reference
Clive Smart and Constance Smart	☐	**Stephen Skinner Skinner & Co 1 Blossomton Road Blossomton BL1 1NN** Reference: **SS.Smart.1**
Thomas Bold and Prudence Bold	X	**None** Reference:
	☐	Reference:

Appendix 11: Completed Example Form FR1 – First Registration Application (continued)

(2) Evidence of identity

Where any transferor, landlord, transferee, tenant, borrower or lender listed in (1) was not represented by a conveyancer

Place 'X' in the appropriate box(es).

Insert the name of each unrepresented transferor, landlord, transferee, tenant, borrower or lender for whom you give this confirmation.

☐ I confirm that I am satisfied that sufficient steps have been taken to verify the identity of

_____

_____

and that they are the transferor, landlord, transferee, tenant, borrower or lender listed in (1) (as appropriate)

Evidence of identity is defined in panel 14. Full details of the evidence of identity that is required can be found in Practice Guide 67.

☐ I enclose evidence of identity in respect of each unrepresented transferor, landlord, transferee, tenant, borrower or lender for whom I have not provided the confirmation above

16 Where the application is sent to Land Registry by someone who is not a conveyancer

(1) Details of conveyancer acting

If you are sending an application to register a transfer, lease or charge (ie a mortgage), for each party to each disposition that is to be registered, state in the table below the details of the conveyancer (if any) who represented them.

You must also complete (2) below.

If the party is not represented insert 'none' in the second column.

Name of transferor, landlord, transferee, tenant, borrower or lender	Conveyancer's name, address and reference
Thomas Bold and Prudence Bold	**None** Reference:
	Reference:
	Reference:

(2) Evidence of identity

Place 'X' in the appropriate box(es).

Evidence of identity is defined in panel 14. Full details of the evidence of identity that is required can be found in Public Guide 20.

X   for each applicant named in panel 6 is enclosed

X   for each unrepresented transferor, landlord, transferee, tenant, borrower or lender listed in (1) is enclosed

Appendix 11: Completed Example Form FR1 – First Registration Application (continued)

	17
If a conveyancer is acting for the applicant, that conveyancer must sign.	Signature of conveyancer: _____
	Date:
	OR
If no conveyancer is acting, the applicant (and if the applicant is more than one person then each of them) must sign.	Signature of applicant: *Thomas Bold* _____
	Date: **22 July 2010** *PRUDENCE BOLD*

WARNING
If you dishonestly enter information or make a statement that you know is, or might be, untrue or misleading, and intend by doing so to make a gain for yourself or another person, or to cause loss or the risk of loss to another person, you may commit the offence of fraud under section 1 of the Fraud Act 2006, the maximum penalty for which is 10 years' imprisonment or an unlimited fine, or both.

Failure to complete this form with proper care may result in a loss of protection under the Land Registration Act 2002 if, as a result, a mistake is made in the register.

Under section 66 of the Land Registration Act 2002 most documents (including this form) kept by the registrar relating to an application to the registrar or referred to in the register are open to public inspection and copying. If you believe a document contains prejudicial information, you may apply for that part of the document to be made exempt using Form EX1, under rule 136 of the Land Registration Rules 2003.

© Crown copyright (ref: LR/HO) 07/09

Appendix 12: District Land Registries

Areas served

Administrative area	Land Registry Office
England	
Barnsley	Nottingham
Bath & North East Somerset	Plymouth
Bedford	Peterborough
Birmingham	Coventry
Blackburn with Darwen	Fylde
Blackpool	Fylde
Bolton	Fylde
Bournemouth	Weymouth
Bracknell Forest	Gloucester
Bradford	Nottingham
Brighton & Hove (City of)	Coventry
Bristol (City of)	Gloucester
Buckinghamshire	Leicester
Bury	Fylde
Calderdale	Nottingham
Cambridgeshire	Peterborough
Central Bedfordshire	Peterborough
Cheshire East	Birkenhead
Cheshire West and Chester	Birkenhead
Cornwall	Plymouth
County Durham	Durham
Coventry	Coventry
Cumbria	Durham
Darlington	Durham
Derby (City of)	Nottingham
Derbyshire	Nottingham
Devon	Plymouth
Doncaster	Nottingham
Dorset	Weymouth
Dudley	Coventry
East Riding of Yorkshire	Kingston upon Hull
East Sussex	Coventry

Appendix 12: District Land Registries (continued)

Administrative area	Land Registry Office
Essex	Peterborough
Gateshead	Durham
Gloucestershire	Gloucester
Halton	Birkenhead
Hampshire	Weymouth
Hartlepool	Durham
Herefordshire (County of)	Telford
Hertfordshire	Leicester
Isle of Wight	Weymouth
Isles of Scilly	Plymouth
Kent	Nottingham
Kingston upon Hull (City of)	Kingston upon Hull
Kirklees	Nottingham
Knowsley	Birkenhead
Lancashire	Fylde
Leeds	Nottingham
Leicester	Leicester
Leicestershire	Leicester
Lincolnshire	Kingston upon Hull
Liverpool	Birkenhead
Luton	Peterborough
Manchester	Fylde
Medway	Nottingham
Middlesbrough	Durham
Milton Keynes	Leicester
Newcastle upon Tyne	Durham
Norfolk	Kingston upon Hull
North East Lincolnshire	Kingston upon Hull
North Lincolnshire	Kingston upon Hull
North Somerset	Plymouth
North Tyneside	Durham
North Yorkshire	Durham
Northamptonshire	Leicester
Northumberland	Durham
Nottingham (City of)	Nottingham

Appendix 12: District Land Registries (continued)

Administrative area	Land Registry Office
Nottinghamshire	Nottingham
Oldham	Fylde
Oxfordshire	Gloucester
Peterborough (City of)	Peterborough
Plymouth (City of)	Plymouth
Poole	Weymouth
Portsmouth	Weymouth
Reading	Gloucester
Redcar and Cleveland	Durham
Rochdale	Fylde
Rotherham	Nottingham
Rutland	Leicester
St Helens	Birkenhead
Salford	Fylde
Sandwell	Coventry
Sefton	Birkenhead
Sheffield	Nottingham
Shropshire	Telford
Slough	Gloucester
Solihull	Coventry
Somerset	Weymouth
Somerset	Plymouth
South Gloucestershire	Gloucester
South Tyneside	Durham
Southampton	Weymouth
Southend-on-Sea	Peterborough
Staffordshire	Birkenhead
Stockport	Fylde
Stockton-on-Tees	Durham
Stoke-on-Trent (City of)	Birkenhead
Suffolk	Kingston upon Hull
Sunderland	Durham
Surrey	Durham
Swindon	Weymouth
Tameside	Fylde

Appendix 12: District Land Registries (continued)

Administrative area	Land Registry Office
Thurrock	Peterborough
Torbay	Plymouth
Trafford	Fylde
Wakefield	Nottingham
Walsall	Coventry
Warrington	Birkenhead
Warwickshire	Gloucester
West Berkshire	Gloucester
West Sussex	Durham
Wigan	Fylde
Wiltshire	Weymouth
Windsor and Maidenhead	Gloucester
Wirral	Birkenhead
Wokingham	Gloucester
Wolverhampton (City of)	Coventry
Worcestershire	Coventry
Wrekin (County of the) (otherwise known as The Wrekin)	Telford
York	Durham

LONDON AUTHORITIES

Barking and Dagenham	Telford
Barnet	Wales
Bexley	Croydon
Brent	Wales
Bromley	Croydon
Camden	Croydon
City and County of the City of London	Wales
City of Westminster	Croydon
Croydon	Croydon
Ealing	Wales
Enfield	Wales
Greenwich	Telford
Hackney	Wales
Hammersmith and Fulham	Birkenhead

Appendix 12: District Land Registries (continued)

Administrative area	Land Registry Office
Haringey	Wales
Harrow	Wales
Havering	Birkenhead
Hillingdon	Wales
Hounslow	Wales
The Inner Temple and The Middle Temple	Wales
Islington	Wales
Kensington and Chelsea	Birkenhead
Kingston upon Thames	Croydon
Lambeth	Telford
Lewisham	Telford
Merton	Croydon
Newham	Telford
Redbridge	Birkenhead
Richmond upon Thames	Telford
Southwark	Telford
Sutton	Croydon
Tower Hamlets	Wales
Waltham Forest	Wales
Wandsworth	Telford

Wales/Cymru

All Areas	Wales/Cymru

Addresses of Land Registry Offices

England

**HM Land Registry
Headquarters**
32 Lincoln's Inn Fields
London WC2A 3PH
Tel: 020 7917 8888
Website: www.landreg.gov.uk

Birkenhead

Land Registry
Birkenhead Office
Rosebrae Court
Woodside Ferry Approach
Birkenhead
Merseyside CH41 6DU
Tel: 0151 472 6666

Coventry

Land Registry
Coventry Office
Leigh Court
Torrington Avenue
Tile Hill
Coventry CV4 9XZ
Tel: 024 7686 0860

Croydon

Land Registry
Croydon Office
TrafalgarHouse
1 Bedford Park
Croydon CRO 2AQ
Tel: 020 8781 9100

Durham

Land Registry
Durham Office
Southfield House
Southfield Way
Durham DH1 5TR
Tel: 0191 301 3500

Fylde

Land Registry
Fylde Office
Wrea Brook Court, Lytham Road
Warton
Preston PR4 1TE
Tel: 01772 836700

Gloucester

Land Registry
Gloucester Office
Twyver House, Bruton Way
Gloucester GL1 1DQ
Tel: 01452 511111

Kingston upon Hull

Land Registry
Kingston upon Hull Office
Earle House, Colonial Street
Hull HU2 8JN
Tel: 01482 223244

Appendix 12: District Land Registries (continued)

Leicester

Land Registry
Leicester Office
Westbridge Place
Leicester LE3 5DR
Tel: 0116 265 4000

Nottingham

Land Registry
Nottingham Office
Chalfont Drive
Nottingham NG8 3RN
Tel: 0115 935 1166

Peterborough

Land Registry
Peterborough Office
Touthill Close, City Road
Peterborough PE1 1XN
Tel: 01733 288288

Plymouth

Land Registry
Plymouth Office
Plumer House, Tailyour Road
Crownhill
Plymouth PL6 5HY
Tel: 01752 636000

Portsmouth

Land Registry
Portsmouth Office
St Andrew's Court
St Michael's Road
Portsmouth PO1 2JH
Tel: 023 9276 8888

Stevenage

Land Registry
Stevenage Office
Brickdale House
Swingate
Stevenage SG1 1XG
Tel: 01438 788 889

Telford

Land Registry
Telford Office
Parkside Court
Hall Park Way
Telford TF3 4LR
Tel: 01952 290355

Tunbridge Wells

Land Registry
Tunbridge Wells Office
Forest Court, Forest Road
Tunbridge Wells
Kent TN2 5AQ
Tel: 01892 510015

Weymouth

Land Registry
Weymouth Office
Melcombe Court
1 Cumberland Drive
Weymouth
Dorset DT4 9TT
Tel: 01305 363636

Appendix 12: District Land Registries (continued)

Wales/Cymru

Land Registry
Wales Office
Ty Cwm Tawe
Phoenix Way
Llansamlet
Swansea SA7 9FQ
Tel: 01792 355000

Index

This index covers all chapters. An 'i.' after a page number indicates an illustration.

A

abstracts of title 168, 177
access 126-7
administrators 165
advertising
    estate agents on 29-31
    For Sale boards 26, 38, 39, 50-2
    free 52-3
    as misleading 30-1
    particulars 58i., 59-62
    photographs 56, 60
    in press 29
        small ads 53-5
    scope 53, 57, 59
    wording 55-6, 57
Agreements (incorporating Standard Conditions of Sale)
  75, 81-4i., 114, 144, 165
    items 74-80
    scope 73-4
alterations 16-17, 46-7, 191-2, 193
answering machines 55
AP1 forms 157
apportionments 134-5, 142, 147

Assents 165
assignment 192
auctions 200-1

B
bankruptcies 94, 100-1, 129, 170, 172, 174
borrowing 144, 153
   loans
      bridging loans 33
      mortgages *see* mortgages
   part exchanges 23, 34
boundaries 123
   fences 48, 126
   plans 126, 199
bridging loans 33
builders 130
   Deposit Numbers 158
   documentation 158
   limitations 5
   for new property 20-1
   NHBC 12, 13
   part exchanges 23, 34
building regulations 136

C
CABs (Citizens Advice Bureaux) 22
cash buyers 156-8, 182
cautions 188
   removal 107-8
   restrictions from 107, 138
caveat emptor (let the buyer beware) 112
cavity walls 5
CCD forms 107
central heating 10, 48
certificates of value 142
chains
   avoiding 87-8

lengthening 86-7

weaknesses 85-6, 139, 200

CHAPS payments 75, 117, 124, 150, 151, 155, 181

Charges Register 95, 96-7i., 101-8

chattels 78, 133, 134-5

chief rent 198-9

Citizens Advice Bureaux (CABs) 22

cleaning 47-8, 49

CML (Council of Mortgage Lenders) 13, 15-16, 90, 100, 101, 105

coal mining 132

commonhold community statements 196

Commonhold and Leasehold Reform Act 2002 195

commonholds

scope 195-6

searches 196

commons land 127, 132-3

communication 59

answering machines 55

deferral 200

dialogue, buyer-seller 113

legalese and 177, 199, 200

networking, estate agents 29

companies

bankruptcies 172

freeholds 193-4

water 71, 132, 178

completion 20-1, 146-7, 158, 174, 181-2

cash transactions 156-8, 182

dates 76-7, 138, 157, 176, 198, 200

documentation 148-50 *see also individual documents*

interest rates 79

locations for 124, 150, 152, 154-5, 181

moving in before 116-17

mortgages and 13

other parties 117, 150, 152

payment 150-1, 155

CHAPS 117, 124, 150, 151, 155, 181

in person 117
plans for 152-5
proof of identity 152, 157-8
scope 117
on vacancy 125, 154
CON 29 forms 129, 131-2, 171, 173
confidence 110, 122
considerations 73
continuation orders 187
contract subject to (CST), subject to contract (STC) and 90-1
contracts 20, 111, 159, 172
  breaches 114
  CST and STC 90-1
  delays 86-7
  drafts 121, 122, 133-6, 168, 169
  exchanging 79-80, 114, 137-40, 176, 177
    titles and 74-5
  at fall of gavel 200
  information in agreements 73-84i., 114
  interest rates 135
  scope 73
conveyances 162i. *see also individual terms*
cooling-off periods 63
costs 22
  commission, estate agents 2, 31
  fees 45-6, 145, 151, 181-2
  loans
    bridging loans 33
    mortgages *see* mortgages
  part exchanges 23, 34
Council of Mortgage Lenders (CML) 13, 15-16, 90, 100, 101, 105
Council Tax 124, 178
councils 93-4, 129-30, 131-2, 136-7, 171, 173, 201
Countryside and Rights of Way Act 2002 127
courtesy, at viewing 63, 64
covenants
  mortgages for 106

positive 115, 189

restrictive 78, 101-5, 115-16, 135-6, 138, 167, 169, 170, 176

    breaches and indemnity 104-6, 115-16, 135-6, 192-3

D

damage to property 3-4, 79-80

damp 3-5

    damp courses 5-6

        guarantees 36

    sources 5, 6-9

    types 7-8

deceased owners 48, 133-4, 141-2, 165, 179 *see also* covenants

decoration 3-4, 6-7, 9, 47, 191-2

deeds 161

    mortgage surrender for 150-1

    Office Copies 95, 99, 110

    possession 89, 166

    scope 163-82

delays 86-7, 88-9, 159, 200

deposits 21, 75, 113-14, 133, 134-5, 138, 139

    Deposit Numbers 158

dialogue, buyer-seller 113

dimensions 3

distances, relocation 38-9, 54

DIY 6-7, 46-7

DL forms 158, 163

doors, front 49

drains 10, 127-8

driveways 4

    garages 126

    tidying up 49

dry rot 7-8

DS forms 143, 144, 149-50, 154, 157

E

electricity

    independent sources 127

system 9
electronic transactions 143-4, 147, 203-4
endowment mortgages 35-6
Energy Performance Certificates 28, 41
engineers, structural 36
engrossment 87
Enquiries before Contract 112, 122-5, 173 *see also* Seller's Property
  Information Forms
Enquiries of Local Authority forms 136
environmental issues 132
epitomes of title 166, 168
estate agents
  on chains 86, 87
  commission 2, 31
  competing 32
  on contact details 55
  For Sale boards 26, 51
  HIPs 28
  mistrust of 27-32, 37-8, 43, 59
  particulars 38
  safety and 39
  trial runs from 199
  ubiquity 27, 87
executors 133-4, 165
expertise 121, 183, 197
extensions, buildings 136

F
family 3, 26, 64, 87-8, 101-2
  matrimonial homes 94, 107, 170-1, 185-8
Family Law Act 1996 186
fees 45-6, 145, 151, 181-2
fences 48, 126
financial services, estate agents 30
fire damage 3-4
first-time buyers 21, 88
first transactions 25-6

fixtures and fittings 41-2, 121
   movability 42
Fixtures, Fittings and Contents Forms 42, 121
flats
   leases 189, 190-4
   scope 189
floors 7, 8-9
For Sale boards 50-1
   estate agents 26, 51
   private 26, 38, 39
      making 51-2
FR1 forms 181
fraud 113
freeholds 100
   commonholds 195-6
   leaseholds and 78-9, 164, 186, 189, 197-8
      as share of freeholds 193-4
   rent charges 198-9
front doors 49

G
garages 126
gardens 3, 49, 126, 130
gas
   independent sources 127
   system 10
gates 48
gazoffing and gazumping 85
gifts 100-1
grants, improvement 136
ground rent 198-9
guarantees 6
   full and limited title 77, 78-9, 116, 133-4
   limitations 36
   warranties and 11-14, 19

H

halls 48
HBF (House Builders' Federation) 13
heating 10, 48
HIPs (Home Information Packs) 28, 41, 86, 91
HM Revenue & Customs 135, 143, 156
Home Information Packs (HIPs) 28, 41, 86, 91
homes
    matrimonial 94, 170-1, 185-8
    restrictions 2-3, 22-3
honesty 59, 112-13
    limitations 3, 27-32, 37-8, 43, 59, 64
House Builders' Federation (HBF) 13
husbands, occupation rights 185

I

ID1 forms 157-8, 182
improvement grants 136
Index Map Searches 89, 174, 196
Inland Revenue (HM Revenue & Customs) 135, 143, 156
instruments of transfer 179
insurance 137, 176
    for covenants 104, 105, 115-16, 135-6
    for gifts 101
    for mortgages 35, 137, 199
interest rates
    on completion 79
    in contracts 135
internet 1, 29 *see also individual terms*
investments 17

J

joint tenants, tenants in common and 141, 179

K

K2 forms 187
K13 forms 187-8

K15 forms 169-70, 174-5
K16 forms 94, 129, 170
keys
    early surrender 116-17
    keyholders 39-40, 117

L
Land Certificates 89
Land Charges Department 94, 188
Land Registration Acts 89, 95, 99, 125, 181, 203
Land Registration Rules 2003 108
Land Registry 44, 61, 89, 94, 95, 108, 111, 120, 157-8, 169-72, 182, 188, 203-4 *see also* registered property; unregistered property
Land Registry Acts 94
Land Transaction Returns 143, 156, 158
last-time buyers 21-3
Law of Property (Miscellaneous Provisions) Act 1994 116, 134
Law Society of England and Wales 13
Leasehold Reform Act 1993 198
leaseholds
    freeholds and 78-9, 164, 186, 189, 197-8
        as share of freeholds 193-4
    restrictions from 23, 116, 189, 192-3
    scope 190
    service charges 147, 190-2
    Title Absolute in 100
legalese 177, 199, 200
let the buyer beware (*caveat emptor*) 112
lighting 64
LLC1 forms 131, 132, 136-7, 171-2, 173
loans
    bridging loans 33
    mortgages *see* mortgages
locations
    for completion 124, 150, 152, 154-5, 181
    distances 38-9, 54
    for negotiation 48

restrictions on 17

M

magazines 52
  estate agents 29
major works 17, 130-1, 136, 191-2
markets, buyers and sellers 25-6, 88
matrimonial homes 94, 170-1, 185-8
  cautions from 107
MH forms 187
modernisation 46-7
mortgages 15-16, 91, 106, 139, 140, 143, 144, 145-6, 147, 150, 155, 174
  auction properties 201
  DS forms 143, 144, 149-50, 154, 157
  electronic transactions 143-4, 147
  endowment mortgages 35-6
  insurance 35, 137, 199
  limitations 34-5
  minimum documentation 148-50
  moving before completion and 13
  scope 36, 134-6, 180
  second 174
  surrender for deeds 150-1

N

names
  of buyers 55
  of owners 115, 140-1, 164, 170, 174, 179
  of property 50
National House Building Council (NHBC) 11-14, 15, 19
negotiation 23, 29, 30, 45, 66-70
  agreements from 70-1
  locations for 48
neighbours
  disputes 112, 126, 198
  troublesome 2-3, 104
networking, estate agents 29

new property
  attractions 19-20
  completion 20-1
  contracts 20
  NHBC cover 11-14, 15, 19
  payments 21
  unfinished 20-1
newspaper advertisements
  estate agents 29
  small ads 53-5
NHBC (National House Building Council) 11-14, 15, 19
noise 2-3
numbers
  Deposit Numbers 158
  title numbers 99, 111, 187, 196
nuisance 104

O
OC forms 61, 89, 111, 120, 196
Office Copies 95, 99, 108, 110, 111, 122
OS1 forms 108, 149
overriding interests 123-4, 125, 181

P
part exchanges 23, 34
particulars 38, 58i.
  disclaimers 61-2
  drafting 60-1
  limitations 59
  photographs 60
  scope 59-60
  viewing and 59-60
paths 4, 49
payments 150-1
  CHAPS 75, 117, 124, 150, 151, 155, 181
  documentation after 200
  staged 21 *see also* apportionments; deposits

photographs 56, 60
planning permission 106-7, 128-9, 131-2, 136
plans 74
    for completion 152-5
    development plans 98i., 130
    verification, wording and 126, 199
possessory titles 100-1
preliminary enquiries 112, 122-5, 173 *see also* Seller's Property
    Information Forms
Premier Guarantee 13
prices 21, 25-6, 37, 39, 42, 100, 106
    valuations 36, 43-6
    see also deposits; negotiation
printers 56
private sales
    For Sale boards 26, 38, 39
        making 51-2
    out-of-town buyers for 38-9, 54
    particulars 58i., 59-62
    scope 37-8
    vacancy 39-40
Property Register 95, 96i., 99
property shops, estate agents 29-30
Proprietorship Register 95, 96i., 100
provisos 190
purchase files 199

Q
qualifying work 191
questions 16-17, 22, 145, 176-7 *see also* individual terms

R
radio interviews 52-3
registered property 86, 157-9, 197, 198, 200
    boundaries in 123, 126
    Charges Register 95, 96-7i., 101-8
    electronic transactions 143-4, 147, 203-4

extensions, buildings 136
garages 126
land as 93
matrimonial homes 186
in particulars 60
planning permission 128-9, 131-2, 136
plans 74, 98i.
Property Register 95, 96i., 99
Proprietorship Register 95, 96i., 100
records 120
rights 74-5, 123-4, 125, 126-7, 138
scope 94-5, 119-20
simplicity 119
as unregistered property 169
utilities, independent sources 127-8
see also individual documents; completion; searches; titles
rent charges 198-9
Requisitions on Title 114-15, 143, 146-8, 177-8
rewiring 9
right-to-buy property 147
rights 74-5, 123-4, 125, 126-7, 138, 171 *see also individual terms*
rights of way 126-7
risk 23, 79-80, 137 *see also* covenants; insurance
roads 106-7, 131, 136, 173
roofs 6, 7
roots of title 161, 165, 167, 169-70, 178

S
safety 39, 62
SDLT (Stamp Duty Land Tax) 34, 68, 117, 134, 135, 143, 156, 181
SDLT forms 148, 156, 181
searches 71, 89, 91, 129-30, 132, 149, 157, 169-70, 171-2, 173-4, 196
coal mining 132
commons land 132-3
delays 86-7, 88-9
environmental 132
scope 93-4

of water companies 71, 132
see also individual documents
seasonal factors 26
Seller's Property Information Forms 112-13, 122, 125, 143, 172-3
senior citizens 3, 21-3
service charges 147, 190-2
sheltered accommodation 22-3
shop windows, estate agents 29-30
SIM forms 89, 111, 169, 186, 196
sinking funds 191
solicitors 30, 76, 153, 164, 181, 197, 199
    as agents 150, 153-5
    on chains 86, 87, 139
    on documentation 89 *see also individual documents*
    on duty of care 111-12
    on keys surrender 116
    limitations 144
    on marital homes 185
    multi-tasking 140, 143
    on private conveyancing 111, 113-14
    on restrictive covenants 102
    on searches 88-9
    see also mortgages
stakeholders, for deposits 113-14, 133
Stamp Duty Land Tax (SDLT) 34, 68, 117, 134, 135, 143, 156, 181
Standard Conditions of Sale 75, 81-4i., 114, 144, 165
    items 74-80
    scope 73-4
subject to contract (STC), contract subject to (CST) and 90-1
subletting 192
subsidence 4, 14, 19
substantial performance 116-17
surveyors 36
    disclosures 11
    liabilities 14
    suing 14-15
surveys 28-9, 201

disclosures 11
full structural 14-15
limitations 14
NHBC 11-14
specialist 36

T
tax
    Council Tax 124, 178
    SDLT 34, 68, 117, 134, 135, 143, 156, 181
tenants in common
    joint tenants and 141, 179
    restrictions on 108
tidying up 46, 48-9
timbers 7-8
Title Absolute 100
titles 34, 74-5
    abstracts of title 168, 177
    epitomes of title 166, 168
    full and limited 77, 78-9, 116, 133-4
    possessory titles 100-1
    proof of 74-5, 79, 86, 89, 99, 100, 109-10, 114, 122, 178
    Requisitions on Title 114-15, 143, 146-8, 177-8
    roots of title 161, 165, 167, 169-70, 178
    Title Absolute 100
    title numbers 99, 111, 187, 196
Town and Country Planning (General Permitted Development)
    Order 1995 128
TP1 forms 141-2, 179
TR forms 115, 140-2, 154, 179
TV reception 4

U
unregistered property 93, 94, 198, 200
    abstracts of title 168, 177
    bankruptcies 170, 174
    cash transactions 182

death and 165
epitomes of title 166, 168
insurance 176
interests in 174, 187
   matrimonial homes 170-1, 187
multiple conveyances 164
plans 74
registered property as 169
restrictive covenants 167, 169, 170, 176
rights 74-5, 171
roots of title 161, 165, 167, 169-70, 178
scope 161, 163, 175, 179-80
see also individual documents; completion; searches
utilities 123
   electricity 9, 127
   gas 10, 127
   water 10, 71, 127-8, 132, 178

V
vacancy 39-40, 138
   completion on 125, 154
   dates 124
valuations 36, 43-6
ventilation 50
viewing 31
   by appointment 2-3
   first 3
   follow-up 3-4
   negotiation, locations for 48
   note-taking in 1-2
   particulars and 59-60
   perception in 11
   safety 39, 62
   scope 1, 47-50
   strategy 62-6
   structural inspections 3, 4-11
   for valuations 44-5

W

walls 5

warranties, guarantees and 11-14, 19

water

    companies 178

      searches 71, 132

    drains 10, 127-8

    independent sources 127

      from wells 10

    pressure 10

    see also damp

WCT forms 107

wells 10

wet rot 8

wives, occupation rights 185, 186-8

woodworm 8

Y

young people 3